The End of
THE ANCIENT WORLD
and
the Beginnings of
THE MIDDLE AGES

*the text of this book is printed
on 100% recycled paper*

PLATE I

Rome   Constantinople

THE TWO CAPITALS

Ivory in the Vienna Museum

The End of
THE ANCIENT WORLD

and

the Beginnings of
THE MIDDLE AGES

by

FERDINAND LOT

HARPER TORCHBOOKS / The Academy Library
HARPER & ROW, PUBLISHERS

New York

CONTENTS

CONTENTS

LIST OF ILLUSTRATIONS

INTRODUCTION TO
THE TORCHBOOK EDITION

By Glanville Downey

*Professor of Byzantine Literature, The Dumbarton Oaks
Research Library and Collection, Harvard University*

"THIS tragedy of the ancient world refusing to die, is one of the most poignant spectacles which can present themselves to the eyes of the historian or sociologist." This is the spectacle unfolded for us in Ferdinand Lot's book. All students of antiquity and the Middle Ages are grateful for the distinguished gifts which enabled one of the most respected French historians of his generation to produce this study; and when he wrote the words quoted (p. 236, below), he was speaking from such intimate command of the sources and such insight into their significance that the book has maintained itself as a classic since its publication, in French in 1927 and in English translation in 1931.

The two-fold topic—the nature of the decline of the ancient world, and the evolution by which this world became the world of the Middle Ages—has indeed remained one of the most fascinating studies for historians, both those whose principal concern is for antiquity and those whose interests are primarily in the Middle Ages. This is an inquiry that affects our understanding of a major part of the origin of our own civilization and of the way in which our culture was transmitted to us. If our own civilization is based primarily on the Judaeo-Christian and the Graeco-Roman heritages, what was it in the Graeco-Roman world that rendered the western half of the Roman Empire incapable of dealing with its problems, while the eastern half succeeded in maintaining its traditions? Was it a defect of the Empire or was it a natural process which it was impossible for the Empire to resist?

In addition to its significance for the subsequent history of Europe, the spectacle in itself is one of uncommon interest for the student of the problems and phenomena of history. What were the processes by which these changes came about, and what can we learn from them? Do they suggest that our own civilization is fated to decline? The sources are often scanty, sometimes contradictory. On some points which would be of major importance we have little reliable information, or even none at all. All the resources of the historian's skill and judgment are needed if we are to come to any fruitful understanding of this long and involved historical evolution. It is no wonder that one of the historians of the generation that succeeded Lot's has repeated that "there are few questions in history that have aroused more sustained controversy than the causes of the fall of the Roman Empire."[1]*

Ferdinand Lot was born in 1866 and died in 1952. As he himself tells us in his Introduction (p. 3, below), he began to write this book in 1913, when he was forty-seven years old, and completed it (after a long interruption) in 1921, when he was fifty-five. Thus the book represents some of the best years of Lot's mature powers as a scholar, and it has come to be regarded as one of the masterworks of historical writing of its day and—at least in the opinion of some—Lot's most important work.[2]

Within the framework of the famous series of historical studies, *L'Évolution de l'humanité*, edited by Henri Berr, Lot set himself to provide a new survey, comprehensive and at the same time carefully focussed, of a problem whose importance was compelling the attention of contemporary historians. When does antiquity end and when do the Middle Ages begin? What forced the change? The year before Lot began to write, the Austrian scholar Alfons Dopsch (1868-1953) published the first volume of his well-known *Wirtschaftliche und soziale Grundlagen der Europäischen Kulturgeschichte, aus der Zeit von Caesar bis auf Karl dem Grosse*,[3] and it was just about this time that Henri Pirenne (1862-1935) began to formulate the famous theory that was finally worked out in his posthumous *Mahomet et Charlemagne*.[4]

Of course the problem was by no means newly discovered. In one of the best-known passages in historical literature Edward Gibbon (1737-1794) tells how in Rome, on the 15th of October, 1764, he first conceived the idea of writing the decline and fall of the city. It has been well said, by a modern student

---

* The Notes to the Introduction may be found on p. xix ff.

of the decline of Rome, that "the answers to this problem themselves form a commentary upon the ages that proposed them,"[5]
and Gibbon's work, first published between 1776 and 1788, has
never ceased to draw readers, both as a distinguished achievement of historical writing, and (for later generations) as an
instructive specimen of eighteenth-century historical thought.[6]

The complexity of the question, and the difficulties it offers,
have only had the effect of heightening the challenge it presents
to historians.[7] In Lot's own day, scholars were not content with
the answers offered by their colleagues and predecessors, and
new studies continued to appear all the time while he was writing his book. Vladimir G. Simkhovitch's theory (1916) that
the collapse of the Empire was due to the exhaustion of the
soil is famous not only in its own right but because, after its
original publication, it was incorporated in the author's work
entitled *Towards the Understanding of Jesus.*[8]   The explanation
of Ellsworth Huntington (1917), that the decline was caused by
climatic change, was a bold approach to the problem, but it has
not met with acceptance.[9]   Another well known theory which
has not won followers is that of the distinguished German historian Otto Seeck, who saw the collapse as stemming from what
he called *"Die Ausrottung der Besten"*—the persistent extermination, by the emperors of the third century, of the most capable
of the men who served the empire.[10]

At about the same time, Tenney Frank concluded (1916) that
some of the radical developments in the evolution of the Empire
reflected the results of a racial change. An influx into the West
of Greek and Oriental slaves took place, and when these newcomers or their descendants were emancipated, the whole character of the Roman people was altered.[11] A related view of the
problem was reached by Martin P. Nilsson in his book *Imperial
Rome.* According to Nilsson, the Romans ought to have dominated the barbarians by intermarrying with them. Instead,
the birthrate of the Romans was declining at the time when they
encountered the barbarians, and so they were unable to impose
their culture on the newcomers by intermarriage. Instead, the
Roman blood became progressively diluted and a "mongrel"
race resulted.[12]   M. I. Rostovtzeff, as a Russian émigré, laid
stress upon the social revolution which brought about "a gradual
absorption of the higher classes by the lower, accompanied by a
gradual levelling down of standards."[13]

K. J. Beloch traced the decay of Rome to the earlier decline of the Greek city-states and the formation of the Roman Empire as a world-state; this prevented the full development of Greek civilization, and the Roman culture was incapable of withstanding the difficulties of all kinds which it eventually encountered.[14] Another view is that of W. E. Heitland, who concluded that the decay of the ancient world was caused by the fact that that world was so constructed that it was never possible to give the masses of the ordinary people an effective share in the government.[15]

From the side of economic history, several scholars advanced the hypothesis that the decline of the ancient world was due to its failure to develop adequate methods and organization for its industry.[16]

But not all scholars have been satisfied that the problem has been thoroughly understood; new aspects of it have been interrogated and new theories advanced. A. E. R. Boak has recently emphasized the effects of the decline in population and of the manpower shortage; the answer to the problem he finds in "a deficiency in the personnel necessary to maintain the economic and political structure of the Western Roman Empire."[17] Another contribution has been offered by George R. Monks, who believes that the corruption of the bureaucracy (which was of course a part of the general corruption of the public) became a definite factor in the imperial collapse, both because it undermined public morale and because it made it difficult for the government to collect the revenues upon which it depended.[18]

To compare the modern answers to the problem with Gibbon's conviction—that the "decline and fall" represented "the triumph of barbarism and religion"—is to measure the changes which have taken place in the thinking of historians. For scholars today, "the idea of the 'ruin of the ancient world' is antiquated."[19]

Ferdinand Lot would have followed these investigations with keen interest, though to be sure there may be some of them he might not have accepted. Although we have learned so much—or because we have learned so much—scholars will not cease to try to find the answer to the problem, or to try to find the terms on which different answers might be viewed in relation to one another. When the student realizes the complexity of the story, and the significance that the understanding of it may have, he will appreciate the nature of the task Lot had before him. To trace all the changes that were in progress; to keep together all the threads of the evolution; to show the interaction of the diverse elements within the vast Empire, was a formidable undertaking. Lot was more concerned with "seeing life steadily and seeing it whole" than with arguing a thesis. To him, it was clear that "the Empire died of an internal malady" (p. 236, below). Lot might well have agreed with a point of view formulated by Rostovtzeff,[20] namely that "none of the existing theories fully explains the problem of the decay of ancient civilization . . . Each of them, however, has contributed to the clearing of the ground . . ." Each theory may have in it a certain amount of the truth, and the reader may feel that the problem is often a question of determining how much emphasis is to be placed on the various factors involved. We may view the whole evolution, in the words of A. H. M. Jones, as "the result of a complex of interacting causes which the historian disentangles at his peril."[21]

But have we, indeed, seen the problem in its true light? Which is more important, to understand the decay of antiquity, or to appreciate what grew out of the decay? It would have been interesting indeed to have Ferdinand Lot's reaction to the fresh approach of W. C. Bark, who argues that the decline of the ancient world was a salutary thing in that it produced a new medieval world which had so many features to commend it. "Medieval men, happily for them and for us, found a way to keep much of the best of the classical past while discarding the worst of it."[22] Here is a question for the historian as he views our contemporary civilization in the light of its sources. It is the long and intricate historical process at the base of these problems that Lot places before us.

* * * *

Ferdinand Lot the scholar and teacher would have rejoiced to see the advances in research on many of the topics on which he had written in his book. It is our good fortune that when a revised edition of his work was published in the year before his death (1951) he was able to add forty-two pages of *notes additionelles*. In these Lot called attention to new work which had been published since the appearance of the first edition (1927), and took the occasion to extend—and in some cases modify—his original views. In the present edition these additional notes are reproduced below (usually in condensed form) in the order in which they correspond to the pages of the English translation. In addition, the editor of the present edition, so far as has been practicable, has supplied references to work which has been published since 1951, or escaped Lot's attention when he was compiling his additional notes.

Before turning to these addenda we must notice three important areas in which especially significant changes in scholarship have taken place since the time when Ferdinand Lot made his original studies.

The first is the problem of the conversion of Constantine the Great and the formulation of the new theory of the political basis of the role of the Christian Roman emperor. As Lot declared (p. 39, below), "Constantine's conversion is the most important fact in the history of the Mediterranean world between the establishment of the hegemony of Rome and the setting up of Islam . . . Since the adoption of Christianity we have been living on a different plane." When Lot took up the question of Constantine's conversion, the emperor had been badly treated by modern historians and some writers had even denied that the emperor was a sincere Christian. Even if, as Lot himself believed, Constantine was a religious man, there was still a question whether his conversion might not (as Lot thought) have represented a "sudden impulse" (see below, pp. 29-32).

Since Lot's day an important amount of study has been devoted to Constantine's conversion and its motives, and today many scholars are convinced that Constantine became a genuine Christian, as a result of a true religious experience, and that his motives in the toleration and then support of Christianity were sincere and did not represent the cynical political considerations which some earlier writers saw in them.[23] Constantine's conversion made necessary the formulation of a new theory of the political basis of the Christian Roman Empire and a new statement of the emperor's role and of his relations with God and with his subjects.[24] All this has come about since Lot published his first edition. As a consequence, not only our knowledge of Constantine's own reign, but our whole understanding of the subsequent relations of the church and the government, and of the role of the church in the new Christian society, has been placed on a new basis.

In the present book as well as in his other work, Lot's concern was primarily with the West, and the plan of his book did not include any extensive description of the Later Roman Empire in the East and the Byzantine state which succeeded it. Lot understood very well that the historical development in the East was different from that in the West, and that the difference reflected the fact that in the East, "the Orthodox Church, Greek civilization and the State came to be so well fused" (p. 184, below). No city in the West, in the later empire and the Middle Ages, could match Constantinople. But it did not fall within Lot's sphere to investigate the question that has concerned historians more and more in recent years, namely, why did the Empire in the East survive so long, and maintain its cultural tradition so successfully, while at the same time the western part of the Empire went through a process of decay and transformation? The terms of this question have become more and more plain as interest in Byzantium has increased, and students have come to recognize that the peculiar strength of the Empire in the East was drawn from that fusion of Christianity and classical culture, and that integration of church, society and state which Lot pointed out but did not have occasion to present in detail.[25] Life in the East became totally unlike that in the West. The reader of Lot's book who is curious to compare the two worlds may find the other part of the image in Louis Bréhier's work *Le Monde byzantin* (1947-1950), which followed Lot's volume in the series.

Another subject that has had a marked development in recent years is the history of education, as scholars have begun to study the effect of educational theories and practices on the development of the state and on the course of history. Concerned with the evils of "pseudo-humanistic education" (p. 163, below) and the stereotyping effect of rhetoric, which is such a well-known feature of the literature of the day, Lot perhaps did not fully realize the strength which was found in the appeal to classical literary standards, particularly in the East, and did not understand the recognized value which the traditional curriculum had for the formation of character.[26]

These are areas in which Ferdinand Lot would have welcomed the results of the new research. In one topic, the development of Christian art, Lot himself came to feel that he had made a mistake in emphasis. When he originally wrote, Lot saw Christian art only as one aspect of the general process of decline which he was tracing. Viewed in comparison with the best periods of classical art, Christian art was indeed, as Lot presented it, disappointing and decadent. Yet it is a characteristic and revealing expression of the new Christian society and the new Christian civilization, and when he wrote his addenda in 1950 Lot confessed that he regretted having neglected this side of his theme. The resources of photography and printing have advanced so much in recent years that the means now at our disposal for the appreciation of this art are much finer than they were in Lot's time.[27]

If Lot had been able to rewrite his book in 1950, these are the topics in which he would have made important changes. He could have introduced many small improvements here and there—as the new notes which follow will show. Yet it seems fairly clear that he would have wished to leave the plan of the book on the whole unaltered. Of course the book is one man's view, and a specialist reading the book today might feel that he would write this or that page differently; but no one has undertaken to write a new book, and this is a tribute to the learning and skill in Ferdinand Lot.

*   *   *   *

Ferdinand Lot's whole life (1866-1952) was passed in and near Paris. Born at Plessis-Picquet, this "prince of medieval studies" lived for more than fifty years in the same peaceful house at Fontenay-aux-Roses. After study at the École des chartes, he began his teaching career in 1900 at the École pratique des Hautes-Études. From 1909 until 1936, when he retired at the age of seventy, he was professor at the Sorbonne. He had early made his place as a remarkable teacher, and he was one of the last of the great scholars whose publications range over a wide variety of subjects. The first part of a bibliography of his writings, in which 229 items are listed, was published in the *Mélanges d'histoire du Moyen Âge offerts à M. Ferdinand Lot par ses amis et ses élèves* (1925), but his publications continued to appear during the remainder of his life, and indeed after his death.[28] In addition to *La fin du monde antique et le début du Moyen Âge*, some of his best known books are: *L'impôt foncier et la capitation personelle sous le Bas-Empire* (1928); *Les destinées de l'Empire en Occident, de*

395 à 388 (in collaboration with C. Pfister and F. L. Ganshoff, in the *Histoire générale* edited by G. Glotz, 1931-1933); *L'art militaire et les armées au Moyen Âge en Europe et dans le Proche Orient* (1946); *Nouvelles recherches sur l'impôt foncier et la capitation personelle sous le Bas-Empire* (1955); and the unfinished work *Recherches sur la population et la superficie des cités remontant à la période gallo-romaine* (1945-1950). In his latter years he wrote several works intended for the non-specialist reader, such as *Les invasions germaniques* (1935) and *Les invasions barbares et le peuplement de l'Europe* (1937). His wife, Myrrha Lot-Borodine (1882-1957), was herself a scholar and wrote on Byzantine church history and Orthodox spirituality.

Dumbarton Oaks
Washington, D. C.
January, 1961

NOTES

1. A. H. M. Jones, "The Decline and Fall of the Roman Empire," a public lecture which offers valuable insights into the problem, printed in *History,* October, 1955, pp. 209-226.
2. See for example the judgment of F. Vercauteren, one of Lot's pupils who became a distinguished historian, in the memoir which follows this introduction.
3. Vienna, 1912-1913; second edition, Vienna, 1923-1924. The English version, *Economic and Social Foundations of European Civilization* (2d ed., London, 1953), is condensed from the second German edition.
4. Brussels, 1937. The English translation, *Mohammed and Charlemagne,* was published (New York) in 1939. See G. C. Boyce, "The Legacy of Henri Pirenne," *Byzantion,* XV, 1940-1941, pp. 459-463.
5. F. W. Walbank, *The Decline of the Roman Empire in the West* (London, 1946), p. 1.
6. In fact today it may be drawing more readers than ever. The edition of *The History of the Decline and Fall of the Roman Empire* edited with additional notes by J. B. Bury (London, 1897-1902, and reprinted), was long a standard work of reference. More recently there have been new editions and abridgements. Two reprints of portions of Gibbon's work have been published by Harper and Brothers: *The End of the Roman Empire in the West* (Harper Torchbooks, 1958), and *The Triumph of Christendom in the Roman Empire* (Harper Torchbooks, 1958). There has also been a new edition of the complete work edited by C. Dawson (Everyman's Library, 1954). Volumes of selections have appeared, edited by D. A. Saunders (New

York, 1952), and by S. Harcourt-Smith (London, 1954), and there has recently been a one-volume abridgement by D. M. Low (London, 1960).

7. A valuable survey of some of the efforts to show the reasons for the decline of the ancient world is provided by M. I. Rostovtzeff, *The Social and Economic History of the Roman Empire,* 2d ed., revised by P. M. Fraser (Oxford, 1957), pp. 535-541. Rostovtzeff's presentation suffers from too great an emphasis on social and economic factors. Another useful summary and criticism of some of the views may be found in N. H. Baynes, "The Decline of the Roman Power in Western Europe; Some Modern Explanations," *Journal of Roman Studies,* XXXIII, 1943, pp. 29-35, reprinted in his *Byzantine Studies and Other Essays* (London, 1955), pp. 83-96. Another valuable review of the question is that of A. Piganiol, *L'Empire chrétien, 325-395* (Paris, 1947), pp. 411-422. See also the recent study of W. C. Bark, *Origins of the Medieval World* (Stanford, 1958; Anchor paperback, 1960), p. 2. with notes on pp. 113-114. The lecture of A. H. M. Jones, cited above (note 1) offers a judicious assessment. For the non-specialist reader, R. M. Haywood (*The Myth of Rome's Fall,* New York, 1958), has provided an excellent picture of the last years of the Empire in the West, with a summary of the principal theories about its decline.

8. Originally published in *Political Science Quarterly,* XXXI, 1916, pp. 201-243, this study was included in the author's book *Towards the Understanding of Jesus* (New York, 1937), pp. 84-139. This investigation, published originally in wartime, appears to have escaped Lot's notice.

9. "Climatic Change and Agricultural Exhaustion as Elements in the Fall of Rome," *Quarterly Journal of Economics,* XXXI, 1917, pp. 173-208. For an acute criticism, see Baynes, *Byzantine Studies* (cited above, n. 7), pp. 86-88. Huntington was handicapped by his unfamiliarity with the ancient sources. This study, written during the war, seems not to have come to Lot's attention either.

10. *Geschichte des Untergangs der antiken Welt,* vol. I, ed. 4 (Berlin, 1921), pp. 269-307.

11. "Race Mixture in the Roman Empire," *American Historical Review,* XXI, 1916, pp. 689-708. See also his *An Economic History of Ancient Rome* (Baltimore, 1927), pp. 207-218. Frank's theory is criticized by Baynes, *Byzantine Studies* (cited above, n. 7), pp. 89-91.

12. *Imperial Rome* (London, 1926), pp. 317-367. For some pithy comments, see Baynes, *Byzantine Studies* (cited above, n. 7), pp. 91-92.

13. Rostovtzeff, *Op. cit.* (above, n. 7), p. 534.

14. "Der Verfall der antiken Kultur," *Historische Zeitschrift,* LXXXIV, 1900, pp. 1 ff. A similar view is held by A. J. Toynbee, *A Study of History,* IV (New York, 1939), pp. 61-62.

15. *The Roman Fate, an Essay in Interpretation* (Cambridge, England, 1922); *Iterum; or a Further Discussion of the Roman Fate* (Cambridge, England, 1925); *Last Words on the Roman Municipalities* (Cambridge, England, 1928).

16. See the discussion of this theory by Rostovtzeff, *op. cit.,* (above, n. 7), pp. 348 ff., 537-538, with notes on pp. 693, 751.

17. *Manpower Shortage and the Fall of the Roman Empire in the West* (Ann Arbor, 1955). See the discussion of Boak's arguments by M. I. Finley, *Journal of Roman Studies,* XLVIII, 1958, pp. 156-164.

18. "The Administration of the Privy Purse; An Inquiry into Official

Corruption and the Fall of the Roman Empire," *Speculum*, XXXII, 1957, pp. 748-779.

19. Rostovtzeff, *op. cit.* (above, n. 7), p. 748, n. 1.
20. *Ibid.*, (above, n. 7), p. 541.
21. These are the concluding words of his lecture cited above (note 1). Like Lot and Jones, J. B. Bury saw the decline of the Roman Empire in the West as stemming from a variety of causes, some being "contingent." See *Selected Essays of J. B. Bury*, ed. by H. Temperley (Cambridge, England, 1930), pp. xxv-xxvii.
22. *Op. cit.*, p. 112.
23. Of the extensive literature, only a selection of the especially significant items can be listed here. Fundamental are: N. H. Baynes, *Constantine the Great and the Christian Church* (Proceedings of the British Academy, XV; London, 1930); K. F. Stroheker, "Das konstantinische Jahrhundert im Lichte der Neuerscheinungen, 1940-1951," *Saeculum*, III, 1952, pp. 654-680; H. Doerries, "Das Selbsterzeugnis Kaiser Konstantins," *Abhandlungen der Akademie der Wissenschaften zu Göttingen, Phil.-histor. Klasse*, 1954; A. H. M. Jones "Notes on the Genuineness of the Constantinian Documents in Eusebius' Life of Constantine," *Journal of Ecclesiastical History*, V, 1954, pp. 196-200. Other important studies are: A. Alföldi, *The Conversion of Constantine and Pagan Rome*, transl. by H. Mattingly (Oxford, 1948); K. Aland, "Eine Wende in der Konstantin-Forschung," *Forschungen und Fortschritte*, XXVIII, 1954, pp. 213-217; H. Doerries, *Constantine and Religious Liberty*, transl. by R. H. Bainton (New Haven, 1960); G. Downey, "The Builder of the Original Church of the Apostles at Constantinople: A Contribution to the Criticism of the *Vita Constantini* Attributed to Eusebius," *Dumbarton Oaks Papers*, VI, 1951, pp. 53-80; A. H. M. Jones, *Constantine and the Conversion of Europe* (London, 1948); H. Koch, "Constantin le Grand," *Byzantion*, XXV-XXVI-XXVII, 1955-1957, pp. 457-472; H. Kraft, *Kaiser Konstantins religiöse Entwicklung* (Tübingen, 1955); L. Voelkl, *Der Kaiser Konstantin; Annalen einer Zeitwende, 306-337* (Munich, 1958); J. Vogt, *Constantin der Grosse und sein Jahrhundert* (Munich, 1949); J. Vogt and W. Seston, "Die Constantinische Frage," *Relazioni del X Congresso Internazionale di Scienze Storiche (Roma, 1955)*, vol. II (*Storia dell Antichità*) pp. 377-443. J. Burckhardt's book on Constantine is still read (e.g., *The Age of Constantine the Great*, transl. by M. Hadas, New York, 1949, and Anchor paperback, 1955), but it is now of more significance as an example of the distinctive point of view of the historiography of the nineteenth century than as an objective study of Constantine.
24. In this study the lead was taken by N. H. Baynes, whose exposition is of fundamental importance: "Eusebius and the Christian Empire," *Annuaire de l'Institut de philologie et d'histoire orientales*, II, 1933-1934, pp. 13-18, reprinted in his *Byzantine Studies* (cited above, n. 7), pp. 168-172. See also W. Ensslin, "Der Kaiser in der Spätantike," *Historische Zeitschrift*, CLXXVII, 1954, pp. 449-468; H. Berkhof, *Kirche und Kaiser; Eine Untersuchung der byzantinischen und der theokratischen Staatsauffassung im vierten Jahrhundert* (Zurich, 1947); K. M. Setton, *Christian Attitude Towards the Emperor in the Fourth Century, Especially as Shown in Addresses to the Emperor* (New York, 1941); F. E. Cranz, "Kingdom and Polity in Eusebius of Caesarea," *Harvard Theological Review*, XLV, 1952, pp. 47-66; G.

Downey, *"Philanthropia* in Religion and Statecraft in the Fourth Century after Christ," *Historia,* IV, 1955, pp. 199-208.

25. Here again one must turn first to the four studies of N. H. Baynes, reprinted in *Byzantine Studies* (cited above, n. 7), pp. 1-82. Reference may also be made to J. B. Bury, "Causes of the Survival of the Roman Empire in the East," *Selected Essays of J. B. Bury* (cited above, n. 21), pp. 231-242; G. Downey, *Constantinople in the Age of Justinian* (Norman, Okla., 1960). A review of the more important bibliography concerning the Byzantine Empire—which has had a marked growth since Lot's time—has been contributed by Peter Charanis to the English translation of C. Diehl, *Byzantium: Greatness and Decline* (New Brunswick, 1957).

26. H.-I. Marrou's comprehensive history of education in antiquity appeared in its second French edition (1950) as Lot was writing his additional notes. We now have the English translation, *A History of Education in Antiquity,* transl. by George Lamb (New York, 1956). Of even greater importance for the period treated by Lot is H. O. Taylor, *The Emergence of Christian Culture in the West: The Classical Heritage of the Middle Ages* (Harper Torchbook edition, 1958) with foreword and bibliography by K. M. Setton. One must also consult R. R. Bolgar, *The Classical Heritage and its Beneficiaries* (Cambridge England, 1954 and forthcoming Harper Torchbook). On the relation between education and public life, see three articles by G. Downey, "Education and Public Problems as seen by Themistius," *Transactions of the American Philological Association,* LXXXVI, 1955, pp. 291-307; "Justinian's View of Christianity and the Greek Classics," *Anglican Theological Review,* XL, 1958, pp. 13-22; "Julian and Justinian and the Unity of Faith and Culture," *Church History,* XXVIII, 1959, pp. 339-349. Other studies of contemporary education by G. Downey are "Education in the Christian Roman Empire: Christian and Pagan Theories under Constantine and his Successors," *Speculum,* XXXII, 1957, pp. 48-61; "The Christian Schools of Palestine," *Harvard Library Bulletin,* XII, 1958, pp. 297-319.

27. Outstanding as an introduction and as a collection of material is W. F. Volbach, *Early Christian Art* (New York, 1960). The photographic record of a notable exhibition is preserved in *Early Christian and Byzantine Art: An Exhibition Held at the Baltimore Museum of Art, 1947, Organized by the Walters Art Gallery* (Baltimore, Walters Art Gallery, 1947). The best monograph on the subject is C. R. Morey, *Early Christian Art: an Outline of the Evolution of Style and Iconography in Sculpture and Painting from Antiquity to the Eighth Century* (2d ed., Princeton, 1953). Other studies (cited by Lot in his "additional notes") are: J. Strzygowski, *L'ancien art chrétien de Syrie* (Paris, 1936); J. Lassus, *Sanctuaires chrétiens de Syrie* (Paris, 1947); A. Grabar, *Martyrium* (Paris, 1943-1946); J. Ebersolt, *La miniature byzantine* (Paris 1928); L. Bréhier, *La Sculpture et les arts mineurs byzantins* (Paris, 1936); R. Delbrück, *Spätantike Kaiserporträts* (Berlin, 1933); H. L'Orange, *Studien zur Geschichte des spätantiken Porträts* (Oslo and Cambridge, Mass., 1933); R. Paribeni, *Il ritratto nell'arte antica* (Milan, 1934); A. Grabar, *L'empereur dans l'art byzantin* (Paris, 1936); J. Babelon, *Le portrait dans l'antiquité* (Paris, 1942). Some more recent works are: J. G. Davies, *The Origin and Development of Early Christian Church Architecture* (New York, 1952); W. Lowrie, *Art in the Early Church*

(New York, 1947, and forthcoming Harper Torchbook); D. Talbot Rice, *The Beginnings of Christian Art* (Nashville, 1957); E. H. Swift, *Roman Sources of Christian Art* (New York, 1951). It must be remembered that Lot's unfavorable comments on mosaic work (below, p. 145) were written before the discovery of the large and important corpus of mosaics found in the excavations at Antioch in Syria; see D. Levi, *Antioch Mosaic Pavements* (Princeton, 1947).

28. For an appreciation of his work, and a list of his principal writings, see the biographical notices by F. Vercauteren, *Le Moyen Âge* LVIII, 1952, pp. 461-472; R. Bossuat, *ibid.*, pp. 472-480; C. Brunel, *Bibliothèque de l'École des Chartes*, CXI, 1954, pp. 334-339; F. L. Ganshof, *Revue Belge de Philologie et d'Histoire*, XXX, 1952, pp. 1269-1281.

AN APPRECIATION OF FERDINAND LOT

by Fernand Vercauteren[1]

IN 1909 M. Lot obtained the chair in the Sorbonne which he was to occupy with singular luster until 1936. The same year he had published, in collaboration with one of his pupils, the late Louis Halphen, his book on *Le Règne de Charles le Chauve. Première partie: 840-851.* In it may be found, amplified to perhaps its ultimate development, the critical and analytical method which had characterized almost all of his previous works. These are, in the most complete sense of the word, "annals," indispensable labors preparatory to a history of this important reign, and it is surely to be regretted that the continuation of such a peculiarly learned work was never published.

He did not give up the history of the Carolingian period and of the first years of the Capetians—in 1908 he had issued, likewise with the collaboration of Louis Halphen, an important publication of texts, the *Recueil des actes de Lothaire et de Louis V rois de France (954-987)*—and while he continued to study, with remarkable critical delicacy, a series of sources, we can see that from this point on Ferdinand Lot transfers his attention to earlier periods, to the very origins of the Frankish state, the history of the great Germanic invasions, and likewise that of the Later Roman Empire. The fruit of these new interests was to be a book published in 1927, *La fin du Monde Antique et le début du Moyen Âge.* It is highly characteristic to see that at the very moment when Ferdinand Lot was guiding his researches in these new directions, two other great historians, Henri Pirenne and Alfons Dopsch, commenced, in their turn, and quite without any mutual understanding, to investigate the same period and to ask themselves the same questions: When does antiquity end and the Middle Ages begin?[2] How is the transition from the one epoch to the other to be explained? What events, essentially, determine this transition?

As is well known, all three scholars provide different solutions for these problems. For Alfons Dopsch there is no break either between the Roman world and the Merovingian world, or between the latter and Carolingian society. It seems to him that there is an evident continuity which characterizes the historical evolution from Caesar to Charlemagne and, for the Austrian historian, there is no division during these eight centuries. Henri Pirenne, on the contrary, while emphasizing that the situation of the Roman and Mediterranean world continues the same after the invasions (which do not seem to him to affect society essentially), insists on the importance of Islam, which inaugurates a new period in history and brings on the disappearance of the Roman and Mediterranean influences which characterized the kingdoms born of the German invasion.

Ferdinand Lot makes it plain that in principle he is sceptical with regard to these theories. Faithful to his critical method and to his respect for facts as such, and to his concrete vision of history, he considers the essential characteristics of Roman-Germanic society from the third to the eighth century to be decadence and attrition. He vigorously opposes the view of André Piganiol, who felt himself justified in writing that "Roman civilization was assassinated [by the barbarians]."[3] Lot strongly emphasizes that, when the new forces which are developing on the fringes of this aged and decrepit world—the papacy, Islam, vassalage—make themselves felt effectively, the ancient world will have lived its life and the Middle Ages will really commence.

This book is one of the masterpieces of contemporary historical literature and, in our opinion, the most important work, and the richest in substance, of all those written by Ferdinand Lot. The documentation which he employed in these pages is enormous, but it never prevents the author from rising to a comprehensive view of the events and making them live again with dramatic solidity.

Having arrived at the full maturity of his learning and his talent, Ferdinand Lot did not abandon his monographic researches on the Carolingian epoch and did not relinquish the works of pure learning which characterized the first period of his scholarly activity; but from this time on he was to direct his attention more and more willingly to the history of the Later Roman Empire and to the history of the centuries which saw the foundation of the Germanic kingdoms in Western Europe. We note, in this connection, his important memoir on *L'Impôt foncier et la capitation personelle sous le Bas-Empire*, in which he makes clear the Roman origins of these medieval taxes and, perhaps, of the *taille*. Of even greater scope was the voluminous work which he published in collaboration with Christian Pfister and François-Louis Ganshof in the *Histoire générale* edited by Gustave Glotz: *Les destinées de l'Empire en Occident de 395 à 888*. In this work, a masterly summation of the history of the early Middle Ages, he not only treats his subject with an impressive documentary and critical apparatus, but he also puts forward highly original new views on certain debatable problems, such as the origins of the system of vassalage and the benefice.

Ferdinand Lot had a concrete and precise vision of history; eager to understand before everything else the why and the how of things, he would gladly have made his own the famous words of Ranke: *wie es eigentlich gewesen ist*. He detested nothing so much as hazy theories (and this is the origin of his irritation with racial doctrines) and hasty generalities. False ideas, however seemingly brilliant, he took pleasure in deflating with a sarcastic phrase, carefully sharpened with dry scepticism. This turn of mind made him anxious to replace the hollow formulas (for determining a population figure, or the proceeds of a tax) with which people had been so long content, by calculations which were founded, not on statistics—which are lacking—but on approximations which, handled critically and with common sense, ought to make it possible to establish categories of reasonable size.

He made preparations for these investigations by a series of monographs which tend to show that the large domains of the Carolingian period generally have an extent which varies between 2,000 and 4,000 hectares,[4] and that often they correspond to a village of the present time. For the rest, he was profoundly convinced that, from the third to the ninth century, the population was very sparse and that the urban population in particular was surprisingly small, a city at this period having generally only a few thousand—or even only a few hundred—people. On this latter question he had assembled an enormous collection of precious information which he brought together in his *Recherches sur la population et sur la superficie des cités remontant à la période gallo-romaine*. This work, which deals only with the cities of the south of France, was not finished. We must hope that so far as the documentation left by this great scholar may permit, it may be brought to completion, for it throws new light on an aspect of urban history which is still too much neglected.

This care for numerical analysis Ferdinand Lot applied also to the estimating of military forces, and he showed brilliantly that the sources almost always exaggerated in an excessive fashion the numerical size of medieval armies. In the course of his investigations he saw that there did not exist in French a study on the history of armies in the Middle Ages comparable to the works of Sir Charles Oman or of Hans Delbrück. He conceived the ambition of writing this book and had the joy of bringing it to completion; *L'Art militaire et les armées au Moyen Âge en Europe et dans le Proche Orient* appeared in 1946. It is a book of capital significance on a subject of capital importance, and one can only admire the intellectual power and the strength as a worker which Ferdinand Lot demonstrated once more when he had reached eighty years. What must be emphasized equally is the prodigious faculty this eminent scholar possessed of renewing his interests and at this time taking up a subject new to him and treating it in a profoundly original and practically definitive way.

This desire to renew himself, to keep abreast of new tendencies in historiography and to make use of new methods and new auxiliary sciences, can be seen again in the interest which Ferdinand Lot took in investigations of place names and personal names. He was, indeed, particularly well prepared for these studies since he had a very solid philological training and was, in addition, one of the most eminent historians of medieval literature and philology.

One is staggered by the prodigious activity that Ferdinand Lot displayed after he had arrived at the threshold of old age. To his many learned works he added a series of books intended for a wider public. These have a clarity of exposition and a delicacy of touch which betoken the scholar familiar for many years with his subject, expressing himself with that luminous simplicity which only prolonged association with the sources gives. All these qualities may be found in *Les invasions germaniques* (1935), *Les invasions barbares et le peuplement de l'Europe* (1937), *La France des origines à la guerre de Cent Ans* (1939), *La Gaule* (1947), *Naissance de la France* (1948), books in which, in terms of the best kind of popularization, he distilled his inexhaustible knowledge of ten centuries of history.

Ferdinand Lot was a modest man who sought neither official honors nor the applause of the public. The *Académie des Inscriptions et Belles Lettres* did itself the honor to enroll him among its members and on several occasions awarded prizes to his works, notably the Grand Prix Gobert. The rank of member of the *Académie* was, in his eyes, only an empty title of self-esteem, and he consecrated to the *Institut* a notable portion of his activity, and published a number of important works under its auspices. He was attached above all to his family, to his studies, and to his teaching; when at the end of the day he had finished his courses at the Sorbonne, he made his way quietly along the Boulevard Saint-Michel, was swallowed into the train —or the subway—at the Gare de Sceaux and returned among the crowd of commuters to his peaceful house at Fontenay-aux-Roses. There he worked, wrote and meditated among the joys, trials and sorrows that a long life inevitably brings with it.

If he enjoyed the high esteem of his peers, the respectful admiration of his pupils, and the most flattering reputation among the medievalists of Europe and America, he carefully abstained from putting himself or his work on display. And perhaps the University and the public did not sufficiently realize that among the historians of the last hundred years Ferdinand Lot can with good reason be counted as one of the greatest.

NOTES

1. A translation of the closing pages of the "Necrology" of Lot by his pupil and friend Fernand Vercauteren, published in *Le Moyen Âge*, LVIII, 1952, pp. 461-472. The translation begins at p. 465. The earlier pages of the "Necrology," not reproduced here, have to do with Lot's training as a graduate student and the beginning of his teaching career. This picture of Ferdinand Lot by one of his students who became a distinguished historian himself is offered here because it gives a sympathetic estimate of Lot both as a historian and as a person, based on intimate acquaintance. M. Vercauteren's footnotes, which are mostly concerned with specialized bibliography, are not reproduced here. An exception is made in the case of one footnote (below n. 3) which is of special interest as it gives Lot's view of a theory of André Piganiol's.

2. [While French-speaking scholars are able to write of *le Moyen Age*, English usage restricts us to "the Middle Ages." "Middle age" has come to have an altogether different application which might make it difficult to use it about the historical, as well as the human, epoch. The problem may appear distressing to some English-speaking scholars, but it seems difficult to find a solution. G. D.]

3. A. Piganiol, *L'Empire chrétien*, p. 422. Concerning this book Ferdinand Lot wrote as follows: "All in all, his book [i.e. that of Piganiol], so richly documented, is the antithesis of the present work. And that is why the reading of it cannot be too strongly recommended to those who wish to form a personal opinion" (*La fin du Monde Antique et le début de Moyen Âge*, edition of 1951, additional notes, p. 534).

4. [One hectare = 2.471 acres. G. D.]

ADDITIONAL NOTES
TO THE TEXT

Page 10: On Sassanian history, see A. Christensen, *L'Iran sous les Sassanides*, 2d ed., Copenhagen, 1944.

Pages 13 ff.: On collegiality and the division of the Empire, see J.-R. Palanque, "Collegialité et partage dans L'Empire romain au IV⁰ et V⁰ siècles," *Revue des études anciennes*, XLVI, 1944, pp. 47-64, 283-298. On the plan of the Tetrarchy and Diocletian's administration, consult W. Seston, *Dioclétien et la tétrarchie*, I: *Guerres et réformes, 284-300*, Paris, 1946. On the theory of the divine descent of the emperor, see Lily Ross Taylor, *The Divinity of the Roman Emperor*, Middletown, Conn., 1931, and W. Ensslin in *Cambridge Ancient History*, XII, 1939, pp. 352 ff. The army is studied by D. Van Berchem, *L'armée de Dioclétien et la réforme constantinienne*, Paris, 1952. On the court ceremonial which Diocletian imitated from the East, consult A. Alföldi, "Die Ausgestaltung des monarchischen Zeremoniells am römischen Kaiserhofe," *Mitteilungen des Deutschen Archäol. Instituts, Röm. Abteilung*, XLIX, 1934. On the reckoning of regnal years, beginning in 293, see H. Stern, "Natalis imperii," *Annuaire de l'Institut de philologie et d'histoire orientales et slaves*, IX, 1949, pp. 551-559 (*Mélanges H. Grégoire*, I).

Pages 17-18: On *iugatio* and *capitatio* see the studies of Lot cited above (p. xviii-xix), and A. Déléage, *La capitation du Bas-Empire*, Mâcon, 1945. Aerial photography has revealed the ancient boundaries of fields in a region in North Africa: A. Julien, *Histoire de l'Afrique du Nord*, Paris, 1931, p. 115.

Page 19: On Diocletian's edict of maximum prices, see L. C. West, "The Coinage of Diocletian and the Edict of Prices," *Studies in Roman Economic and Social History in Honor of A. C. Johnson*, Princeton, 1951, pp. 290-302.

Pages 23-25: On Diocletian and Christianity, see the suggestive study of H. Mattingly, "Jovius and Herculius," *Harvard Theological Review*, LXV, 1952, pp. 131-134. For the persecutions, see B. J. Kidd, *A History of the Church to A.D. 461*, Oxford, 1922, and H. von Schoenebeck, *Beiträge zur Religionspolitik des Maxentius u. Constantin*, Leipzig, 1939.

Pages 28 ff.: Concerning Constantine's conversion and his religious policy, see the Foreword, p. xvi. On the history of the church in the fourth century, see Kidd *op. cit.*, and the *Histoire de l'église*, edited by A. Fliche and V. Martin, vols. II-V, also J. Zeiller, *L'Empire romain et l'église*, Paris, 1938, and J.-R. Palanque, *Saint Ambroise et l'Empire romain*, Paris, 1933.

Page 33: On the use of Christian symbols by Constantine, see A. Alföldi, "The Initials of Christ on the Helmet of Constantine," *Studies in Roman Economic and Social History in Honor of A. C. Johnson*, Princeton, 1951, pp. 303-311.

Page 35: For studies of the foundation of Constantinople, see A. Frolow, "La dédicace de Constantinople," *Revue de l'histoire des religions*, CXXVII, 1944, pp. 61-127; E. Gren, "Zu den Legenden von der Gründung Konstantinopels," *Eranos*, XLV, 1947, pp. 153-164; A Alföldi, "On the Foundation of Constantinople: A Few Notes," *Journal of Roman Studies*, XXXVII, 1947, pp. 10-16.

Page 40: Lot mentions the pagan reaction of Julian only very briefly; see also J. Bidez, *La vie de l'empereur Julien*, Paris, 1930; G. Ricciotti, *L'imperatore Giuliano l'Apostata secondo i documenti*, Milan, 1956; R. Andreotti, *Il regno dell'imperatore Giuliano*, Bologna, 1936; G. Downey, "The Economic Crisis at Antioch under Julian the Apostate," *Studies in Roman Economic and Social History in Honor of A. C. Johnson*, Princeton, 1951, pp. 312-321; idem, "The Emperor Julian and the Schools," *Classical Journal*, LIII, 1957, pp. 97-103. On the pagan element in the Empire, and particularly in the aristocracy, see A. Alföldi, "Die Kontorniaten," *Festschrift der Ungarischen Numismatischen Gesellschaft zur Feier ihres vierzigjährigen Bestehens*, (Budapest, 1943); H. Bloch, "A New Document of the Last Pagan Revival in the West, A.D. 393-394," *Harvard Theological Review*, XXXVIII, 1945, pp. 199-204; G. Downey, "Themistius and the Defense of Hellenism in the Fourth Century," *ibid.*, L, 1957, pp. 259-274.

Page 46: On the religious policies of Theodosius the Great we now have the studies of W. Ensslin, "La politica ecclesiastica dell'imperatore Teodosio agli inizi del suo governo," *Nuovo Didaskaleion*, II, 1948, pp. 5-35; "Die Religionspolitik des Kaisers Theododius d. Gr.," *Sitzungsberichte der Bayerischen Akad. d. Wissenschaften, philosoph.-histor. Klasse*, 1953, No. 2.

Page 53 (cf. p. 297): The term Caesaropapism, a recent invention, has sometimes been incorrectly employed, and the whole subject of the relations between church and state, in both East and West, has recently attracted intensive study, as a result of which our understanding of the relationship has been greatly clarified. See *Byzantium: An Introduction to East Roman Civilization*, ed. by N. H. Baynes and H. St. L. B. Moss (Oxford, 1948), pp. xxviii-xxix, 86, 129-132, 274-280; also W. Ensslin, "Staat und Kirche von Konstantin d. Gr. bis Theodosius d. Gr. Ein Beitrag zur Frage nach dem 'Cäsaropapismus,'" *Hellenika*, Parartema 9 (1955), pp. 404-415, and F. Dvornik, "Pope Gelasius and Emperor Anastasius I," *Byzantinische Zeitschrift*, XLIV, 1951, pp. 111-116.

Pages 55 ff.: On the monetary and economic crises see G. Mickwitz, *Geld und Wirtschaft im römischen Reich des 4. Jh. n. Chr.* (Helsingfors, 1932); idem, *Die Systeme des römischen Silbergeldes im IV. Jh. n. Chr.* (Helsingfors, 1933); idem, "Le problème de l'or dans le monde antique," *Annales d'histoire économique et sociale*, VI, 1934, pp. 235-247; A. Segrè, "Inflation and its Implication in Early Byzantine Times," *Byzantion*, XV, 1940-1941, pp. 249-279; idem, *Circolazione monetaria e prezzi nel mondo antico* (Rome, 1922); *The Cambridge Economic History of Europe from the Decline of the Roman Empire*, vols. I-II (1941-1952); J. Toutain, *The Economic Life of the Ancient World* (New York, 1930); F. Heichelheim, *Wirtschaftsgeschichte des Altertums* (Leiden, 1938; an English translation of volume I, with revisions, has been published, *An Ancient Economic History*, Leiden, 1958). On the annona (p. 57) see D. van Berchem, *L'annone militaire dans l'Empire romain au IIIᵉ siècle* (Mémoires de la Société nationale des Antiquaires de France, 1936, pp. 117-202).

Pages 63 ff.: On ancient technology, see R. J. Forbes, *Metallurgy in Antiquity* (Leiden, 1950); idem, *Studies in Ancient Technology*, 6 vols. (Leiden, 1955-1958); E. A. Thompson, *A Roman Reformer and Inventor, Being a New Text of the Treatise De Rebus Bellicis with a Translation and Introduction* (Oxford, 1952).

Pages 65-67, 71: On the population of Rome and of the Empire, see

L. Homo, *Rome impériale et l'urbanisme dans l'antiquité* (Paris, 1951);
S. Mazzarino, *Aspetti sociali del quarto secolo* (Rome, 1951), pp. 217-269;
F. G. Meyer, "Römische Bevölkerungsgeschichte und Inschriftenstatistik,"
Historia, II, 1954, pp. 318-351.

Pages 75 ff.: In his revised edition, Lot added notes on methods of
communication and the transportation of travellers, citing R. Lefebvre des
Noëttes, *L'attelage; le cheval de selle à travers les âges* (2d ed., Paris,
1931); D. Gorce, *Les voyages, l'hospitalité et le port des lettres dans le
monde chrétien aux IVe et Ve siècles* (Paris, 1925); E. Vaillé, *Histoire
générale des postes françaises*, I: *Des origines à la fin du Moyen Age*
(Paris, 1947). See also Reincke, "Nachrichtenwesen," Pauly-Wissowa,
Realencyclopädie der klassischen Altertumswissenschaft, XVI (1935), cols.
1496-1541.

Page 78: On agriculture, see M. Bloch, *Caractères originaux de l'histoire
rurale française* (Paris, 1931).

Pages 86 ff.: On the Constantinian monarchy, see now A. Piganiol,
L'Empire chrétien, 325-395 (Paris, 1947).

Page 90: On the army see W. Seston, *Dioclétien et la Tétrarchie*, I (Paris,
1946), pp. 295-351, and H. Nesselhauf, "Die spätrömische Verwaltung der
gallisch-germanischen Länder," *Abhandlungen der Akademie der Wissenschaften zu Berlin, Phil.-histor. Klasse*, 1939. On recruitment, see Seston,
op. cit., pp. 301-302, 367-372. Lot made an estimate of the military forces
of the Empire in A.D. 400 in his article "La Notitia Dignitatum utriusque
imperii, ses tares, sa date de composition, sa valeur," *Revue des Études
Anciennes*, XXXVIII, 1936, pp. 335-338. In his edition of 1951 (pp. 520-
521) Lot observed that he had come to be less certain concerning "the
preponderance of the barbarian element in the Imperial armies" (p. 91
infra).

Page 91: On the defense of the frontiers, see now R. Mouterde and
A. Poidebard, *Le limes de Chalcis, organisation de la steppe en Haute-
Syrie* (Paris, 1945); J. Vannerus, "Le limes et les fortifications gallo-
romaines de Belgique," *Mémoires de l'Académie royale de Belgique, classe
des lettres*, ser. 2, vol. XI, pt. 2 (1943); J. Baradez, *Vue-aerienne de
l'organisation romaine dans le Sud-Algérien: Fossatum Africae* (Paris,
1949).

Pages 97 ff.: On Constantine's legislative reforms, see now J. Declareuil,
Rome et l'organisation du droit (Paris, 1924), pp. 349-419; M. Sargenti,
Il diritto privato nella legislazione di Costantino (Milan, 1938); Mme C.
Dupont, *Les constitutions de Constantin et le droit privé au début du IVe
siècle: les personnes* (Lille, 1937). The Code of Theodosius, containing
some of the legislation of Constantine, is now available in English translation: *The Theodosian Code and Novels, and the Sirmondian Constitutions*,
transl. by Clyde Pharr (Princeton, 1952).

. Pages 100 ff.: Further study has shown that the introduction of the caste
system, and the imposition of the controls of a corporative state, represent
primarily an effort on the part of the government to preserve the state,
ensure economic production, and forestall any recurrence of the crisis of
the third century. See, among others, F. Oertel, "The Economic Life of
the Empire," *Cambridge Ancient History*, XII (1939), pp. 268-281.

Pages 107 ff.: On the colonate, see F.-L. Ganshof, "Le statut personnel
du colon au Bas-Empire," *L'Antiquité classique*, XIV, 1945, pp. 261-277;
P. Collinet, *Le colonat dans L'Empire romain* (Brussels, 1937); F. Lot,
L'impôt foncier et la capitation personelle sous le Bas-Empire (Paris, 1928),
pp. 61-70.

Pages 114 ff.: For the cities and the curiales, we now have F. F. Abbott and A. C. Johnson, *Municipal Administration in the Roman Empire* (Princeton, 1926) and the two monographs of A. H. M. Jones, *The Cities of the Eastern Roman Provinces* (Oxford, 1937) and *The Greek City from Alexander to Justinian* (Oxford, 1940), as well as the instructive study of P. Petit, *Libanius et la vie municipale à Antioche au IVe siècle après J.-C.* (Paris, 1955). The famine at Antioch in the reign of Julian provides an illuminating example of the problems involved in the management of the food supply; see the note on p. 40, *supra*.

Pages 128 ff.: A recent study of the patronage system has given us fresh information: *Libanius, Discours sur les patronages; Texte traduit, annoté et commenté par L. Harmand* (Paris, 1955).

Pages 135 ff.: Lot came to believe that his treatment of the decay and end of ancient art had not been adequate; see the Foreword, pp. xvii-xviii, *supra*.

Pages 151 ff.: Since Lot wrote, our knowledge of the literature of the late imperial period, both pagan and Christian, has been enriched by a number of studies and handbooks. Two of these are H. O. Taylor, *The Emergence of Christian Culture in the West*, reprinted in the Harper Torchbook series (1958) with a foreword by Kenneth M. Setton, and E. Hatch, *The Influence of Greek Ideas on Christianity*, reprinted in the Torchbook series (1957) with a foreword by F. C. Grant. Both of these contain valuable bibliographies. In addition, consult N. K. Chadwick, *Poetry and Letters in Early Christian Gaul* (London, 1955); E. M. Pickman, *The Mind of Latin Christendom* (New York, 1937); E. K. Rand, *Founders of the Middle Ages* (Cambridge, Mass., 1928; reprinted, New York, 1957); C. N. Cochrane, *Christianity and Classical Culture: A Study of Thought and Action from Augustus to Augustine* (New York, 1944; reprinted 1957); H.-I. Marrou, *Saint Augustin et la fin de la culture antique* (Paris, 1938-1949); P. Courcelle, *Les lettres grecques en Occident de Macrobe à Cassiodore* (2d ed., Paris, 1948); F. J. E. Raby, *A History of Secular Latin Poetry in the Middle Ages* (Oxford, 1934); idem, *A History of Christian-Latin Poetry from the Beginnings to the Close of the Middle Ages* (2d ed., Oxford, 1953); R. R. Bolgar, *The Classical Heritage and its Beneficiaries* (Cambridge, Eng., 1954). For the history of Christian literature we now have J. Quasten, *Patrology* (Westminster, Md., 1950—in progress), and B. Altaner, *Patrology*, transl. by Hilda C. Graef (Freiburg and Edinburgh, 1960).

Page 167: Justinian's closing of the schools of philosophy at Athens is now better understood. These schools were the last in which pagan philosophy was still being taught by pagans; elsewhere, at Constantinople, Gaza and Alexandria, classical philosophy was being taught by Christian professors. See G. Downey, "Julian and Justinian and the Unity of Faith and Culture," *Church History*, XXVIII, 1959, pp. 339-349.

Page 171: On the corruption of public spirit, see A. Bayet, *Histoire de la morale en France*, II: *La morale païenne à l'époque gallo-romaine* (Paris, 1931), and George R. Monks, "The Administration of the Privy Purse; an Inquiry into Official Corruption and the Fall of the Roman Empire," *Speculum*, XXXII, 1957, pp. 748-749.

Pages 187 ff.: On the barbarian invasions, see now P. Courcelle, *Histoire littéraire des grandes invasions germaniques* (Paris, 1948); E. A. Thompson, *A History of Attila and the Huns* (Oxford, 1948); C. D. Gordon, *The Age of Attila* (Ann Arbor, 1960); F. Lot, *Les invasions germaniques; la pénétration mutuelle du monde barbare et du monde romain* (Paris, 1945); L. Schmidt, *Geschichte der deutschen Stämme* (2d ed., Munich, 1934); R.

Latouche, *Les grandes invasions et la crise de l'Occident au Ve siècle* (Paris, 1947).

Page 196: Doubt has been cast on the authenticity of the story of St. Ambrose forbidding the Emperor Theodosius to enter the church; see F. H. Dudden, *The Life and Times of St. Ambrose* (Oxford, 1935), II, pp. 387-388.

Page 198: On the estimate of Theodosius' reign see the studies of W. Ensslin cited above in the comment on p. 46.

Pages 201 ff.: On the settlement of the barbarians, see G. Des Marez, "Le problème de la colonisation franque et du régime agraire dans la Basse-Belgique," *Mémoires publiées par la classe des lettres et des sciences morales et politiques de l'Académie royale de Belgique*, 2d ser., vol. IX, 1926; K. Schumacher, *Siedlungs- und Kulturgeschichte der Rheinlande von der Urzeit bis an das Mittelalter* (Mainz, 1925); L. Halphen, *Les barbares, des grandes invasions aux conquêtes turques du XIe siècle* (5th ed., Paris, 1948). On the history of the years A. D. 395-410 we now have the valuable monograph of E. Demougeot, *De l'unité à la division de l'Empire romain, 395-410* (Paris, 1950).

Page 203: The descriptions of the crossing of the Rhine in A.D. 406 have been studied by F. Vercauteren, "Note sur la ruine des villes de la Gaule d'après quelques auteurs contemporains des invasions germaniques," *Annuaire de l'Institut de philologie et d'histoire orientales*, II, 1934, pp. 955-963 (*Mél. Bidez*, II).

Page 209: On the unity of the Empire, see J.-R. Palanque's study cited above in the comment on pp. 13 ff. The loss of Pannonia is described by A. Alföldi, *Der Untergang der Römerherrschaft in Pannonien* (Berlin, 1924-1926).

Page 210: The date of the end of Roman rule in Britain has been disputed; see F. S. Salisbury, *Journal of Roman Studies*, XXIII, 1933, pp. 217-220, and F. Lot, *Revue des Études Anciennes*, XXXVIII, 1936, pp. 315-318. On the establishment of the Angles and Saxons in Britain, see R. G. Collingwood and J. N. L. Myres, *Roman Britain and the English Settlements* (2d ed., Oxford, 1937; Oxford History of England, I), and F. M. Stenton, *Anglo-Saxon England* (Oxford, 1943). On the loss of Africa to the Empire, and its occupation by the Vandals, see now C. A. Julien, *Histoire de l'Afrique du Nord* (2d ed., Paris, 1951-1952) and C. Courtois, *Les Vandales et l'Afrique* (Paris, 1955).

Page 219: On the political significance for Syria and Egypt of the monophysite heresy, see E. R. Hardy, *Christian Egypt: Church and People: Christianity and Nationality in the Patriarchate of Alexandria* (New York, 1952); G. Downey, "Coptic Culture in the Byzantine World: Nationalism and Religious Independence," *Greek and Byzantine Studies*, I, 1958, pp. 119-135; A. H. M. Jones, "Were Ancient Heresies National or Social Movements in Disguise?" *Journal of Theological Studies*, N. S. X, 1959, pp. 280-298.

Page 238: On "hospitality" and the settlement of the barbarians on Roman soil, see F. Lot, "Du régime de l'hospitalité," *Revue Belge de Philologie et d'Histoire*, VII, 1928, pp. 975-1011.

Page 251: Concerning the problem of the disappearance of the Western Empire, see also H. Fischer, "The Belief in the Continuity of the Roman Empire among the Franks of the Fifth and Sixth Centuries," *Catholic Historical Review*, N.S. IV, 1924-1925, pp. 536-553.

Pages 255 ff.; For the reigns of Justin and Justinian, we now have the monographs of A. A. Vasiliev, *Justin the First* (Cambridge, Mass., 1950) and of B. Rubin, *Das Zeitalter Iustinians* (Berlin, 1960—in progress). For an interpretation of some aspects of Justinian's policies and achievements, see G. Downey, *Constantinople in the Age of Justinian* (Norman, Okla., 1960). On the Roman army in the time of Justinian, see the first volume of Lot's *L'art militaire et les armées au Moyen Age en Europe et dans le Proche Orient* (Paris, 1946).

Pages 267 ff.: In his edition of 1951, Lot noted that this chapter should be compared with L. Halphen, *Les barbares* (5th ed., Paris, 1948), chapter VIII, "Retour offensif des barbares et la lutte pour la sauvegarde de l'Empire en Orient," pp. 108-120. On the city of Rome at this period (pp. 268-269) we now have the monograph of L. Homo, *Rome médiévale, 476-1420* (Paris, 1934). On the Persians (pp. 269-270) see the study of Christensen, cited above, comment on p. 10.

Page 272: On Latin as the language of the army, see Lot, "La langue de commandement dans les armées romaines," *Mélanges dédiés à la mémoire de Félix Grat* (Paris, 1946), I, pp. 203-209.

Page 280: On law, see E. Levy, *West Roman Vulgar Law: The Law of Property* (Philadelphia, 1951; Memoirs of the American Philosophical Society, XXIX).

Page 297: With the older views concerning Justinian's supposed Caesaropapism, represented by Lot, should be contrasted the more recent studies cited above, comment on p. 53.

Page 317: The dates of Clovis' victory over the Alemans and of his baptism have been disputed; see the review of the question by A. Van de Vyver, *Le Moyen Âge*, LIII, 1947, pp. 177-196. Lot did not agree with all of Van de Vyver's conclusions.

Pages 326 ff.: On the expeditions of the Franks into Italy, see Lot, *L'art militaire et les armées au Moyen Âge en Europe et dans le Proche Orient* (Paris, 1946), I, pp. 83-90.

Pages 349 ff.: On the administration see Lot, *L'impôt foncier et la capitation personelle sous le Bas-Empire et à l'époque franque* (Paris, 1928). On the Counts of the Cities, see F.-L. Ganshof, "Saint Martin et le comte Avitianus," *Analecta Bollandiana*, LXVII, 1949, pp. 203-223 (Mél. P. Peeters, I).

Page 363: The problem of the origin of the place-names in Burgundy and Franche-Comté has been discussed by E. Gamillscheg, *Romania Germanica; Sprach- und Siedlungsgeschichte der Germanen auf dem Boden des alten Römerreiche* (Berlin, 1934).

Pages 365 ff.: On the occupation of the land in the Rhine regions, see K. Schumacher, *op. cit.* (comment on pp. 201 ff.), also R. Forrer, *L'Alsace romaine, études d'archéologie et d'histoire* (Paris, 1935) and R. Latouche, *Les grandes invasions et la crise de l'Occident au Ve siècle* (Paris, 1946), pp. 254 ff., 319 ff. Lot refutes Pirenne's theory of a rupture in economic life in the fifth and sixth centuries (Lot, *Les destinées de l'Empire en Occident*, Paris, 1940-1941, pp. 347-365).

Pages 371 ff.: On intellectual and artistic life, see now R. H. Bezzola, *La tradition impériale de la fin de l'antiquité au XIe siècle* (Paris, 1944); H.-I. Marrou, *History of Education in Antiquity* (New York, 1956); L. Bréhier, *L'art en France des invasions barbares à l'époque romane* (Paris, 1930); J. Hubert, *L'art préroman* (Paris, 1938); E. Mâle, *La fin du paganisme en Gaule et les plus anciennes basiliques chrétiennes* (Paris, 1950).

Pages 385 ff.: On religious life, see the *Histoire de l'Église*, ed. by A. Fliche and V. Martin, volume IV, *De la mort de Théodose à l'élection de*

Grégoire le Grand (1937) and volume V, *Grégoire le Grand; les états barbares et la conquête arabe* (1938). On the power of the bishops (p. 388), see C. de Clercq, *La législation religieuse franque, de Clovis à Charlemagne* (Louvain, 1936). On the rural parishes (p. 390), cf. W. Seston in *Revue d'Histoire et de Philosophie Religieuses,* XV, 1935, pp. 243-254. Lot observes (edition of 1951, p. 544) that he does not agree with all of Seston's conclusions.

    Pages 394 ff.: On lay society, see Samuel Dill, *Roman Society in Gaul in the Merovingian Age* (London, 1926).

PREFACE
By Henri Berr

Antiquity and the Middle Ages

*T*HE *present volume is intended to establish the link between the first and second sections of the "Evolution of Humanity."*[1] *It introduces the Middle Ages. To what extent it is justifiable to use this traditional term for the period into which we are entering is a question which will be dealt with at the end of the Preface.*

In the first section, the progress of human organization and the effort of human co-operation were seen to result in empires— the Empires of the East, Alexander's Empire and the Hellenistic monarchies, the Roman Empire, which inherited a thousand-year-old experience and definitely founded the State, while at the same time it absorbed into itself the essence of a civilization in which Hellas and the East were blended.

But this mighty Mediterranean Empire, instead of developing along continuous lines, was destined to decline fairly soon and to go under, after violent and unavailing struggles. The "tragedy" of its obstinate conflict with implacable Destiny is "one of the most thrilling spectacles that could present themselves to the historian and the sociologist" and the fall of the ancient world is "perhaps the most important and most interesting problem of universal history."[2]

In several earlier volumes, P. Jouguet, L. Homo, A. Grenier, V. Chapot and J. Toutain have pointed out the various causes of political ruin and of intellectual and moral decadence: in the present volume, F. Lot gathers together all this material in a masterly synthesis, and shows us, in a world that is coming to an end, the elements of a new world.

Although external circumstances aggravated the situation of the Roman Empire, it was above all an internal disease that undermined it: it is impossible to give a better explanation than F. Lot's of "the dissolution of all its vital forces," that condemned it to death.[3]

---

[1] A series edited by Henri Berr, in which this book originally appeared.
[2] Lot, p. 172.
[3] p. 84. Cf. Chapot, vol. xxii, p. 474.

The trouble was primarily political in origin : the insufficient organization of the Imperial power. It is a known fact that no inviolable law of succession ever ensured the nomination of the Emperor against the whims, caprices and deeds of violence of the legions.[1] *The first Emperors reigned through the army ; in the end it was the army that reigned through the Emperors. The army crowned and uncrowned them, acclaimed and killed them, for base or futile motives ; and the Eastern pomp that surrounded them served scarcely any other purpose than to mask their weakness.*

Doubtless there were remarkable men among them, " supermen " who delayed the breakdown, and without whom the world would have been plunged in darkness as early as the third century : a Septimius Severus, a Probus, an Aurelian, a Diocletian, a Constantine, a Valentinian I, a Theodosius.[2] *But the burden was heavy, even for " lucid intelligences " and " wills of iron ".*[3] *No " collective consciousness ",*[4] *no Roman nation*[5] *had come into being : since inner unity was lacking, it was in order to unify the Empire from without and from above that an absolute monarchy appeared necessary. Yet the Emperor, however valuable he may have been, was not in a position to decide and carry out everything by himself in the vast orbis romanus. An administration, a bureaucracy came into existence which rendered incontestable service, and gave a model—valuable, albeit incomplete—to future states, but which, by gradually encroaching on the Emperor's power, finally paralyzed it.*[6] *How could this machinery, which was " too vast, too scientific, too complicated " and could not take the place of a national spirit, have prevented the Empire from dividing into two and being dismembered—or the West from being " shivered in pieces " ?*[7]

The mechanization, or rather the " rigidity and lifelessness "[8] *of this Empire, from which life was gradually retreating, manifested itself also by the establishment of a " caste system ". There no longer existed amongst individuals any public spirit,*

---

[1] pp. 8, 12.   Cf. Honto, vol. xviii, p. 452.
[2] pp. 10, 173, 183.   Cf. Chapot, vol. xxii, pp. 78-80.
[3] Homo, vol. xviii, p. 452.
[4] Lot, p. 225.
[5] Homo, vol. xviii.   Avant-propos, p. xv.   Cf. Chapot, *Les causes de décadence du monde antique* in the·*Rev. de Synth. hist*, vol. xlii (Dec., 1926), p. 88.
[6] Homo, vol. xviii, p. 452.
[7] Lot, p. 186.
[8] p. 100.

*any care for the common interest : what remedy was to be found
for the panicky flight from duties and obligations ? How was
complete anarchy to be avoided ? Each man should be fixed in
his status,* ordo, *" chained to his post ". Henceforth a man's
status would be hereditary, in perpetuity, whether he were soldier
(this had become the lowest rank),* tradesman, colonus *or official.*

*The colonate, in particular, was becoming consolidated. And
here we see the converging of the political and economic phenomena
of Roman decadence. The part played by the towns and that of
the country districts gradually interchanged. The importance of
the Roman City, second only to that of the Greek, is well known.*[1]
*In Latium, and throughout the whole of Italy, the city had absorbed
the rural population. Now it was perishing, and the country
was soon to attract the nobility themselves, after enslaving the poor.*

*F. Lot gives an illuminating account of this evolution. On the
economic life of the period he has some pages that are admirable
in their precision and their vigour. The Empire had not been
sufficiently creative of wealth : it had soon reached the state when
it was consuming more than it produced. It has been said that
Rome was an " octopus " ; one can say of the ancient town in
general that it was " tentacular "*[2]. *It had no genuine industrial
activity, in consequence no productive class, a decreasing and
rapidly impoverished population*[3], *and side by side with idle
poverty, insolent and sterile wealth. The latter came from
conquest and plunder ; it neither involved industry nor succeeded
in stimulating it. Men's needs were relatively modest, their
tastes stable ; Lot points out " the monotonous and boring
character of Roman civilization "*[4]. *Technical invention ceased
early here, and slavery was not able to supply the deficiency of
machinery.*[5] *Commerce, which was much despised and very
limited, served principally to bring back to the East the gold
drained from it by the West. Roman capital, instead of being
invested in industry, commerce and agriculture, instead of
rendering enterprize fruitful, was preferably employed in usury,
which is the opposite of credit. Banking organization was
incomplete ; and there came a moment when, specie becoming*

[1] See vol. x, xv and xviii.
[2] Lot, p. 75.
[3] See p. 66. Cf. on the difficulties of statistics applied to demography
the discussions of the *Centre int. de Synthèse* (Bulletin 4, not yet published).
[4] p. 73.
[5] See vol. ii and xx, Avant-Propos.

scarce, a retrograde step was taken towards a more primitive economy, that of the payment of services in kind.[1]

Thus Rome exploited her Empire to the pitch of exhaustion. There was one source of wealth, however, which was inexhaustible—the land. And that is why the land—particularly after the upheaval of the third century—became for all, rich or poor, an object of care, and almost of love. The poor man, the colonus, is attached to the soil in the interests of agriculture, the breast that suckles everyone, not without some benefit for himself.[2] *The rich man, for his part, flees from the cities, which are losing all attraction and are becoming fortresses, stifling men in their narrow confinement, and establishes himself with deliberate intent in the country districts. For nearly fifteen centuries the nobles continue to live there. At the end of the Empire the great estates have their autonomous life. The landed aristocracy is the power—or rather a dustheap of powers—in the decline of the City and of the State.*[3]

In addition to all these elements of decay there was the " malady of religion ".[4] *We know to what extent Christianity, from the political point of view, contributed to the dissolution of the Empire. That it was persecuted is due to the fact that it did not allow itself to be assimilated into paganism, and rejected the cult of the Emperor. For a long time ancient society was rent by the conflict. Constantine, on the subject of whose enterprizes F. Lot makes some profound reflexions, merely reversed the rôles. Did he proclaim tolerance ? In actual fact he installed Christianity and made paganism face persecution—an act of madness or of genius fraught with good as well as evil consequences. In any case the immediate result was that Christianity, supported by the authorities, involved the State in theological quarrels, in defence of an orthodox creed. The crisis within the Empire was aggravated by the triumph of Christianity, as it had already been by its earlier development.*[5] *Even without the Barbarians, the vitality of the Empire had been deeply affected. But the Barbarians came, and their action was decisive—they provoked the débâcle.*

Volume XXII showed us, all round Romania, *a belt of various*

---

[1] LOT, pp. 59, 83-84.
[2] pp. 113-114.
[3] pp. 125, 182. Cf. CHAPOT, p. 477.
[4] pp. 23, 183.
[5] p. 42. See vols. xxviii to xxx.

*peoples—Vandals, Goths, Alemans, Franks, Saxons, Burgun-
dians, Heruls, Alans, Scots, Picts, Sarmatians, Quadi, Moors,
Nubians—at different stages of civilization, who finally brought
the march of conquest to a standstill, and constituted a danger that
it was possible for a long while to avert, although it exercised a
disquieting influence on the* limes[1]—*this was the* Barbaricum.[2]

Certain of these " Barbarians "[3] *forced their services on the
Empire preparatory to dictating to it, and filtered into it long
before invading it. In the east, Rome came to pay tribute to
barbarians in order to go on being feared by other barbarians.*[4]
*In the west it was the barbarians who gradually filled the army.
The defence of the* limes, *which was too extensive, became impossible ; the towns of the interior were more or less protected by their
walls ; the frontier was rather badly watched by soldier-labourers
who were being demilitarized by the land. The fighting army,
unlike the ancient legion, was composed of horsemen borrowed
from Germany. In the middle of the fourth century, soldier or
miles was the synonym of* barbarus . . . *A Roman army,
in the fourth and fifth centuries, meant simply an army in the
service of Rome.*[5]

*In this period the onward thrust became more and more violent,
being due partially to migrations caused by new arrivals in the
history of the west. On this racial upheaval, on the character of
the Nomad empires which destroyed the agricultural empires and
on the part played by the chieftain of these empires F. Lot has
some important pages*[6] *; he draws a striking picture of this tidal*

---

[1] CHAPOT, pp. 76-78.

[2] AMMIANUS MARCELLINUS, in JORGA, *Essai de Synthèse de l'Histoire de
l'Humanité*, vol. ii, p. 17.

[3] This word calls for a note. For the ancients βάρβαρος (*barbarus*)
meant everyone who was not Greek or Latin : in Cornelius Nepos *Barbarus*
is the King of Persia, but the word having by a natural tendency acquired a
derogatory meaning, it served even in antiquity to denote uncivilized peoples
(the Barbarian is not the " primitive man ") and rude, even brutish customs.
L. HALPHEN in *Les Barbares* without defining the word contrasts (p. 87) the
" authentic barbarians " with the Persians, wrongly called barbarians and
(p. 27) considers the Huns as " Asiatic barbarians more uncivilized than all
the others." For us on the whole the Empires of the East and of the Far
East are not included among barbarian lands. It would be better to do away
with this very vague term if it were not in common use for the period which
is here in question : Gregory of Tours already speaks of the " barbarism which
was let loose at the beginning of the sixth century."

[4] CHAPOT, p. 284. According to the very striking verse of Rutilius
Namatianus Rome was a captive before she was taken : *et captiva priusquam
caperetur erat.*

[5] LOT, pp. 262-3.

[6] pp. 188ff.

wave of warriors which caused the German peoples to flow back. The Goths by means of victories and treaties established themselves in the east, while the Franks penetrated into the west in increasing numbers. A period of intrigue, disorder, and extreme confusion began, in which barbarians who were Federates fought against other barbarians who asked only to be allowed to become Federates themselves,[1] in which the power passed over to the Patricians who were masters of the army while the Emperor became effaced as a preliminary to the disappearance of the Western Empire (476).

It no longer needs to be proved that the " great invasion " was not the devastating torrent that people had for so long imagined it to be. Nevertheless the arrival of these successive waves, the more or less definite settlement, with some degree of force, of these rapacious and migratory bands,[2] these inconvenient " guests ", supported by the owners of the land through prudence, cowardice or Christian resignation, was bound not merely to complete the political dissolution and to aggravate the economic retrogression but also to compromize Græco-Roman civilization. At first the barbarians had become Romanized, but in the end Romania became " barbarized ". Besides the disruption of the Western Empire, its intellectual decadence was the inevitable result of the invasions.

We have seen that the Romans, who were eminently gifted for action and were wonderful organizers, had developed literary qualities and artistic tastes but slowly and under the influence of Greece and the East, and that their aptitude for speculation had always been very weak, æsthetic enjoyment and disinterested research not really being their forte, and their government never really troubling itself about education.[3] It goes without saying that during the long process of political and economic disintegration of which we have just spoken, the intellectual standard could only deteriorate, especially in the west.[4] The last spasmodic efforts of Latin literature coincided with the periods in which there was a strong government ; with the ensuing anarchy and

---

[1] On the contract of *Federation* and on the requisitions of land, see L. HALPHEN, *Les Barbares*, p. 24.

[2] To obtain a vivid picture of this disorganizing and reorganizing work, see an essay by MARK BLOCH, *Observations sur la conquête de la Gaule Romaine par les rois francs*, in the *Rev. Hist.*, March-April, 1927, Note, p. 178. Cf. JORGA, in *op. cit.*, vol. ii, ch. 4, and L. HALPHEN, *op. cit.*, ch. 2.

[3] See vol. xvii. and xxii. Avant-Propos.

[4] For the East, see vol. xxxii.

impoverishment, on the other hand, ignorance and indifference to intellectual and artistic interests increased.

In principle and in origin, there was a contradiction between Christianity and the search after literary or plastic beauty. Literature was doubtless fundamentally renewed by the inspiration of Christianity ; but the antiquated form was forced upon the new inspiration, and, with the exception of some works in which genius bursts through in spite of all, rhetoric in prose and the superstitious imitation of great models in verse mark a decline which nothing can any longer arrest. Yet this phraseology of the schools and this conventional poetic diction are still remnants, though the sole remnants, of the intellectual acquisition of past centuries ; whereas philosophy, which at Rome had never been either original or very highly esteemed, and science, which in antiquity had always been too speculative and had busied itself too little with matter,[1] were submerged by the " torrent of religiosity coming from the east "[2]. Revelation annihilated the effort of Greek reason.[3]

The intellectual twilight preceding the " deep night " of the Merovingian period, and the moral corruption of this decadent world, Lot has powerfully depicted. If certain souls, touched by the teaching of Christ, became mellow with gentleness and human kindness, others—among the officials and the courtiers—tended towards harshness and every kind of vice ; and the masses in the towns became more and more degraded, more and more atrophied by games, obscene spectacles, and the encouragements offered to idleness. Life retreated from the city ; the land, to repeat the statement once again, attracted to it " all the life that was left in society ".[4] In the last part of this closely-written volume we see as though reacting and seething in a crucible the diverse elements contained within the East—Roman survivals, provincial tendencies, the spirit of Christianity, Germanic manners and customs.

This Roman Empire, whose prestige had fascinated the Barbarians, persists as an ideal framework, and only disappears in 1806 with the last Roman Emperor of German nationality. But Justinian's attempt to reconstitute a real unity around the Mediterranean lake was a vain and to a certain extent a disastrous

---

[1] See the Introduction to Vol. xiii, p. xviii, 1.
[2] LOT, p. 170.
[3] See ROBIN, vol. xiii, p. 439.
[4] LOT, p. 183.

*one. Byzantium, moreover, was no longer a Roman state, and
the West was obliged to split off from it. Under barbarian
dynasties—while central Europe is a nameless chaos and England
is being torn between the Saxons and the Celts—Romano-Germanic
States are being formed ; Vandal in Africa, Ostrogothic and later
Lombard in Italy ; Visigothic in Spain ; Frankish in Gaul.
Lot reveals the particular features resulting both from the character
of the invaded areas and from the character and the number of the
invading Barbarians ; thus Italy remains a " country of towns "
while urban life elsewhere declines, a country where the authority
of the kings, which everywhere else is to become sovereign, is
limited by that of the dukes.[1] It would have been possible, from
that moment, for nations to be born, had not various circumstances—the ambitions of Justinian, the Musulman invasion,
the Germanic advance—plunged everything once more into
disorder.*

*This complicated history, the details of which are little known,
is summed up with restraint and clearness in Lot's pages, from
which certain powerful personalities stand forth half-revealed
amid the mist which envelops them. He lays emphasis on the
Frankish kingdom, the one that acquired the greatest coherence
and extent, and for which " the highest destiny was in store after
the disintegration of the ancient world ".[2] Among the Germanic
tribes which dispute over Gaul, the Franks are victorious, thanks
to one man who was both gifted with political commonsense and
devoid of scruples. Clovis by his baptism united the force of the
barbarians with that of Christianity, and thus forged a new
" historic force ". A force, but not a nation. At most Austrasia,
Neustria, Burgundy were to represent rough attempts at " nationalities ". The France of the Merovingians was a sort of amorphous
protoplasm from which portions were cut off and divided at
pleasure ; there was land there without definite boundaries and
human material without a pronounced character.*

*The king, an absolute monarch, soon to be invested with divine
right when the " alliance of throne and altar "[3] begins, deals as
he chooses with his kingdom, which is his personal property.
No more " respublica " ; no more public services ; but by the
side of the king an aristocracy which is to have its own leader,*

---

[1] pp. 287, 293. For Spain, where the fusion of races is more prompt than
elsewhere, see pp. 279, 280, 293.

[2] p. 312.

[3] See LAVISSE, *Histoire de France*, vol. ii, p. 274.

the Mayor of the Palace, " sole minister in this absolute monarchy,"
and which is not slow to create a new régime.[1] The era of the
barbarian dynasties is for Lot an " accursed period of history ".
The ancient world was not " regenerated " by them, as some have
maintained. The economic retrogression went on and became
more marked. The land, which was the wealth of the rich and
the sole resource of the coloni, gradually became the basis not
merely of the economic system but also of the organization of
society. In the decayed towns, industry was practically non-
existent, while commerce declined to an extraordinary extent.
Coinages multiplied, and later money disappeared. In this
world of restricted bounds a return was made to natural economy.

For the mind this was the onset of night. Intellectual interests
died out one after another. Simultaneously with the knowledge
of Greek all philosophy disappeared ; even theology became
barren for several centuries. Some practical discoveries are not
incompatible with this intellectual decline, because they are not
the results of science ; we know that just as animals have their
" organs ", so homo faber creates tools.[2]

But in this decadence which he describes in a striking fashion
Lot discerns the instrument of a future recovery. Catholicism
preserved and fostered two precious elements, a principle of
administration represented by the secular clergy and especially
the bishop, and a preoccupation with morality concentrated in
the monasteries—the spirit of Rome and the Spirit of Christ.[3]

No doubt, in the very act of expanding, the Catholic religion
became contaminated by many pagan survivals and associated
with the lowest and most cruel passions. Nevertheless a current
of faith and mysticism had flowed from the East into the West,
and the barbarians who came from their Nordic forests, with
what were in effect new understandings, had brought with them
a living spontaneity and resources of zest and enthusiasm.

In a profound and interesting parallel, which invites discussion,
Lot sets up a contrast between the classical and romantic literature,
art and psychology. He does not merely decry a traditionalism
which " gives us the impression of a crushing uniformity "[4] in
the art of the time of the Empire, but he also arraigns the classical

[1] Lot, pp. 354ff.
[2] See Preface of vol. ii.
[3] See also Cournot, Traité de l'enchaînement des idées fondamentales,
pp. 675, 678.
[4] p. 148.

spirit *as " an obstacle to the renewal both of form and substance "
which " wished to stereotype language by placing before men the
imitation of unsurpassable models "*[1]. *But when he speaks of
the " blighting influence of the masterpieces, especially in ' classical ' works, which are not like the products of the romantic
periods refreshed and inexhaustibly quickened by subjectivism "*[2],
is he not projecting into the whole of Antiquity the narrow ideal
of French classicism ?

" As for the substance," he says, " classicism is interested in
the universal only. It rejects everything which is particular or
' singular '. If the truth be told, it lives on commonplaces.
Inevitably it became, and that very soon, monotonous, poor and
barren. Death lies in wait for all ' objective ' classical literature."[3]
" Not only the literatures of Antiquity, but modern letters also
nearly perished, one hundred and fifty years ago, through desiccation. Rousseau and the Romantics, by introducing subjectivism
into modern literature, saved it from death."[4]

*Doubtless Græco-Roman literature became exhausted, but only
through the exhaustion of men's minds. In the period of the
Renaissance and even in André Chénier's time, it recovered,
along with its prestige, a fructifying power. It is only because
it was misunderstood in the seventeenth century and interpreted
through the medium of the then prevailing rationalism that it
seemed but rarely able to inspire masterpieces and to doom to
monotony a classicism devoid of matter and stifled by rules.*

" It is only since yesterday, since the eighteenth century ",
Lot says again, " that man has dared to show his fellows that he is
not ashamed of displaying his personal joys and griefs. Since
the triumph of subjectivism, literature stands assured of an
infinite future ".[5] *But romantic subjectivism also has its
dangers, excesses and monotony. It was not long in calling forth
the reaction to objective realism. Is not the store of impressions
received by the mind from reality as rich as that of personal
emotions ? Is the object more quickly exhausted than the subject ?
Has not romanticism, in the last resort, worked on behalf of
realism by vivifying the reproductive imagination which is closely
connected with feeling and by elaborating for it a whole technique
of colours and sounds ?*

[1] p. 165.
[2] p. 157.
[3] pp. 165, 166.

[4] p. 225.
[5] p. 166.

However that may be, in the course of the centuries with which we are dealing, it was through the development of sensibility and the imagination that, in the intellectual impoverishment of the times, a renewal was prepared. Christian art, completely impregnated with mysticism, was destined to blossom late. But an evolution was accomplished in which " colour dethrones plastic art "[1] : stained-glass windows, tapestry, mosaic, hollowed and pierced stone played on and penetrated by the light, sparkling gems, jewelled and cloisonné goldsmith's work, forms of art whose dazzling richness could at one and the same time stimulate the taste of the decadents and satisfy that of the barbarians, came from the East and spread via Byzantium and Ravenna, but also via Southern Russia and through the agency of the Goths.[2] In art as in religion, from the fourth century onward, " a new soul takes the place of the ancient soul "[3].

And herein lies F. Lot's supreme merit : he goes to the heart of his subject, he interiorizes history. A scrupulous medievalist— one of the masters who have given to French erudition its perfect sureness of method and its rigorous precision—he has penetrated a mass of material which is enormous, although he declares it to be " poor, fragmentary and uncertain "[4]. Not limiting himself to facts, he plumbs the very depths of psychology, both collective and individual.[5] This volume, rich in scholarship, will hold the reader's interest by analyses and reflections in which the brilliance of style and the force of expression often equal the power of the thoughts ; it is in our opinion one of the finest books written by a historian.

There emerges from it this essential idea : that the ruin of the Empire, the barbarian invasions, the expansion of Christianity resulted in " a complete transformation of human psychology "[6], or rather in a new mentality. The exterior world is different,

---

[1] p. 149.
[2] pp. 136ff.
[3] p. 150.
[4] p. 2.
[5] Psychology of certain ethnic groups (Romans, Greeks, p. 77). Psychology of the church (pp. 48, 52). Psychology of certain barbarian emperors and chiefs (Constantine, pp. 38, 44. Clovis, pp. 317, 318 ; Charles Martel, pp. 342, 343). If he throws individuals into relief, he also shows the limits of their activity and—among other causes—the part played by chance. There is often a contradiction between men's plans and actual events. Constantine's enterprises are a striking example.
[6] p. 2.

*but " above all a renovation has taken place in the world within ".
There is a kind of break in psychological continuity.*[1] *" Between
the men of the new and those of the ancient times there will no
longer be a thought in common ".*[2] *Oriental mysticism brings
about a veritable " transvaluation of values ".*[3] *" This transformation is as phenomenal as if a sleeper on waking should see
other stars shining above his head."*[4]

*Of " ancient man " Lot has a conception as to which we should
be inclined—as we were in the case of his reflections on ancient
art—to make certain reservations. In the first place, was there
not a considerable difference between the Spartan, the Athenian,
the Alexandrian, the Roman of the Republic and the Roman of
the Empire ? " The triumph of Christianity," says Lot, " by
transforming human psychology, has dug an abyss between us
and antiquity."*[5] *But in certain respects are not some of these
ancient men nearer to us than the men of the Middle Ages ?*[6]
*Moreover, on the subject of allegory, which for the men of this
period was a " science ", does not Lot declare that " the difference
between these minds and our own may be said to be not merely
quantitative, but qualitative " ?*[7]

*There is therefore a mentality peculiar to the Middle Ages as
distinct from the modern as from the ancient mentality.*

*At this point we are ready and prepared to treat this question
of the " Middle Ages " and the divisions of history, in general.*

*The expression " Middle Ages " is known to date from the
seventeenth century ; the first time it was used was in 1688*[8], *by
Christopher Kellner—Cellarius—a professor of history at the
University of Halle who died in 1707. It has had a brilliant
career, owing to the fact that it fulfilled a practical need and
pedagogic requirements : it was useful, for the exposition of
facts, and especially for the arranging of scholastic courses, that
there should be, in addition to divisions by countries, reigns,*

---

[1] p. 2.
[2] p. 2 ; cf. p. 171.
[3] On this Oriental mysticism see vols. xi, xiii, xv.
[4] p. 186 ; cf. LAVISSE, *Histoire de France*, vol. ii, i, p. 81.
[5] p. 39.
[6] " The introduction of Western rationalism with Pythagoras and Socrates
was a sort of false beginning twenty centuries in advance of the era of
our civilization." (L. BRUNSCHVICG, *Les progrès de la conscience dans la
philosophie occidentale*, vol. i, p. 75.)
[7] p. 376.
[8] *Historia antiqua* (1685) ; *H. medii aevi* (1688) ; *H. nova* (1696).

institutional periods or great events proper to such and such a country (Royalty, Republic, Empire ; the Peloponnesian War, the Hundred Years War), large slices of general history. But is there anything more in this than a convention—and a questionable one at that ? Does this intermediate period between antiquity and modern times correspond to an objective reality, and to a reality which is not unique ? Is it possible to deduce from various times and circumstances, or even from the evolution of peoples, a concept of the Middle Ages which should represent one phase of it ?[1]

This problem has been clearly defined and amply treated in recent times. In the course of discussion it seems that a certain number of points have been fixed, and that over and above the terminological question, the happy result has been a deepening of historical research.

First and foremost, all sharp divisions in history are obviously artificial. Nothing ends and nothing begins absolutely. There is something absurd in setting hard and fast limits to a period by dates. Whether it be a revolution or a death, no event breaks all the threads connecting it with the past or the future.

Moreover, the web of history is complex—made up of the most diverse elements, political, economic, religious, intellectual, moral. Evolution does not proceed at the same rate with all of them. A revolution does not produce its effects all at once and in every sphere. Can we assume that the political element is preponderant ? This is a theory which agrees with current practice, and which still has energetic supporters in Germany,[2] but it seems more and more open to discussion, both in itself and by reason of the uncertainty of the landmarks it provides. Do the Middle Ages begin in 395 with the partitioning of the Empire ? Or in 406 with the onslaught of the Huns and the Germanic reflux ? Or in 476, with the death of Romulus Augustulus ? Or between 630 and 730, with the Moslem invasions ? And when do they end ? In 1453, with the fall of the Eastern Empire ? Yet some people give as their limit the invention of printing (1440?) or the discovery of America (1492). Can the mind be satisfied by a division of " general " history that opens with a political event

---

[1] See KURT BREYSIG, *Der Stutenbau und die Gesetze der Weltgeschichte ; Kulturgeschichte der Neuzeit*, vol. ii, *Altertum und Mittelalter als Vorstufen der Neuzeit*.

[2] See A. CARTELLIERI, *Weltgeschichte als Machtgeschichte* ; L. HALPHEN in the *Revue historique*, vol. clv, p. 170.

and closes with circumstances of an intellectual or geographical order ?

As for particular histories, not only do they tend, as we have indicated above, to adopt other dates than general history, dates which vary from one to the other, but they themselves hesitate as to their own divisions.

Certain economists hold that the real Middle Ages begin in the tenth century, after a transition period which lasts from the invasions to the Capetians and culminates in self-contained economy ; it coincides with the feudal period, and from the end of the thirteenth century the development of towns and the great commercial currents are preparing the way for modern economics.[1]

" It is usual ", says a recent historian, " to call by the name of medieval philosophies the philosophic doctrines which developed from the ninth to the fourteenth centuries of our era " ; but " this delimitation according to time is certainly of a rather artificial nature " : the attitude which characterizes the philosophy of modern times begins to take shape as early as the thirteenth century and is definitely constituted from the fourteenth century ; " as a self-contained historic period, the Middle Ages do not exist ".[2]

In literary history, Gaston Paris was inclined to reserve the name of Middle Ages for the period from 842 (the Strasburg Oaths) to 1328 (accession of the Valois) : others prolong it until 1515 (accession of François I) or even 1548 (suppression of the Guilds). In art, says André Michel, there was first, in Merovingian and Carolingian times, a period of " reciprocal penetration, complex influences, experiments and amalgamations " ; then comes the " Romance " period when the world begins to adorn itself with the " white robe of the churches " ; then the Gothic period, from the middle of the twelfth to the fifteenth centuries, when the æsthetic expression of Christianity was produced in all its originality ; but with the fourteenth century, " a new art was being conceived within the bosom of Gothic art ". The art of the Middle Ages may therefore be said to cover fourteen centuries, " between the glorious period of antiquity and the time when humanity returned to the works and the lessons of that period as though beauty were to be found there alone ", or about three

---

[1] See G. MARTIN, *Histoire économique et financière de la France,* in HANOTAUX, *Hist. de la Nation Française,* vol. x.

[2] GILSON, *Philosophy in the Middle Ages,* vol. i, p. 3.

*centuries when it definitely " entered into the service of Chris-
tianity* "[1]. *And these very variable dates that we have just
mentioned concern France more especially. How greatly would
the diversity be increased if we were to consider merely the whole
of Western Europe !*

*How is a solution to be arrived at in the midst of these diffi-
culties ? Most decidedly it can only be by starting from a centre,
and from within. We must start from a centre, that is from a
collection of historic manifestations which present clearly defined
characteristics, and try to discover how far this differentiation
extends, in time and in space, allowing for intermediate zones,
for fringes of transition. And we must start from within, which
means that we shall work back from these diverse manifestations
of human activity which do not all develop at the same time or in
the same degree, to man the agent, and that in the psychology of
an individual we shall find the deep-lying, unquestionable
characteristics of a historical period. This has been fully
realized by Ferdinand Lot. It is true that he concludes his book
with the statement that in the eighth century, with the rise of new
" forces "—Islam, the Papacy, Vassalage—" the Middle Ages
really begin " ; and it may appear at first sight that this statement
is not consistent with the opening thesis—that it was above all the
" interior world " which was renewed. Nevertheless, if we look
more closely, what are these historic " forces " but the expression
in institutions of certain phases of the inner life ? The Papacy,
like Islam, is the final stage of a religious revolution by which
oriental mysticism exerted an ever-widening influence and
achieved exceptional intensity. Vassalage is the translation of
that fidelity between man and man which was the basis of Germanic
society, and which, general circumstances being favourable, was
to substitute political partitioning for the unifying process of
Rome.*

*The " contemporary of King Dagobert " is indeed a new man :
he escapes from the moral sway of Greece and Rome, from the
sovereignty of reason, both speculative and practical ; his earthly
field of vision is strangely restricted : it is towards the beyond that
his gaze is directed and it is there that he fixes the " object of his
desires* "[2]. *A new man, yet one whose mentality has been*

---

[1] *History of Art*, vol. i, ii, pp. 925ff ; ii, 1, p. vii ; iii, 1, p. i.
[2] See PRÉVOST-PARADOL, *Essai sur l'Hist. universelle*, vol. i, pp. 426, 429
(a somewhat neglected work which still has its value).

*prepared by preceding centuries[1] and has its roots in the Far East.
We must not exaggerate the opposition between East and West[2] ;
yet we must recognize it, understanding by the word " West " the
essentials of the Græco-Roman heritage.[3] Moreover this heritage
is never entirely lost[4], as is proved by the organizing activities of a
Charlemagne, of the Catholic Church, and of the Papacy. And
when, between the tenth and the thirteenth centuries, the principles
which distinguish the new age in religion, art and social life
develop, at the same time there reappears the tradition of antiquity :
mysticism, romanticism, feudalism coincide with scholasticism—
that is to say, with the renewal of Greek speculative thought—with
the development of the communes, with a strengthening of the
central power, with an improvement of economic conditions in the
West. The Renaissance is seen to dawn early, especially in
Italy : it assumes a clear and definite character long before the
date usually assigned to its beginning.*

*In short, there is not, as has been justly said, one, but several
" Middle Ages ".[5] Between the rational and unifying development of Græco-Roman civilization and the later renewal, in the
West, of the same development, several fairly differentiated
periods succeeded one another. There was the period of dissolution and invasions ; the period in which, after Charlemagne's
brilliant attempt at a Christian empire, vassalage became organized*

[1] It would seem that "from the beginning of our era the faculty of
judgment . . . is everywhere warped. . . . The sole aim of human
life is to bring man closer to God, to identify him with Him, to see God, to
hear Him, to speak to Him, to communicate with him in a thousand ways,
is the unappeased longing which burns in every heart." BOUCHÉ-LECLERCQ,
Hist. de la divination dans l'antiquité, in BRUNSCHVICG, *op. cit.*, p. 77.

[2] Certain people, particularly in Germany nowadays set up the East,
Asia, "*Asiaticism*," against the West, against "*Romanity*," without taking
into account all that the West, ancient, medieval, modern, has either
assimilated or consciously rejected, of oriental elements. See H. MASSIS,
Défense de l'Occident, and A. CHAUMEIX, *Les jeunes et l'exotisme*, in the *Rev.
des deux Mondes*, 1st June, 1927, p. 699.

[3] See BRUNSCHVICG, *op. cit.*, p. xiv ; CAULLERY, *Hist. des Sciences
biologiques*, in HANOTAUX, *op. cit.*, vol. xv, p. 18 (" Under the influence of the
East, superstition and the love of the supernatural spread on all sides. . . .
The development of Christianity takes place at the expense of ancient culture ;
Greek science is supplanted by the cosmogony of the Bible "). COURNOT,
op. cit., p. 631.

[4] Cf. F. SCHNEIDER, *Rom unde Romgedanke im Mittelalter*, in *Historische
Zeitschrift*, vol. cxxxv, p. 261.

[5] The division into " high " and " low " *Middle Ages* is current, but
unsatisfactory and too general. In Germany the *Historische Zeitschrift*
makes sharp divisions that are very absolute and questionable : *römisch-
germanische Zeit* (Cf. the *Spätantike* of GELZER. H. Ž., vol. cxxxv, p. 173)
und frühes Mittelalter bis 1250 ; *späteres Mittelalter*, 1250-1500.

and government disorganized ; the period when the new ideal manifested itself most consciously and most brilliantly, while at the same time a provisional framework took shape : feudalism, the Papacy, the Holy Empire ; and finally a period when elements of the past—which are elements of the future—intervene, when authority is born anew, and a Europe comes into being. The unity of this whole phase is in the predominance of feeling over reason. It may be said that at this time, the " man of feeling " is king.[1]

It will be understood why in this volume we have not rejected the term " Middle Ages ", but have on the other hand taken care not to give it too precise a definition.

Our second section opens with a series on the origins of Christianity, its development, and the moral crisis in the ancient world. There follows a second series, of which the present volume is the first, in which we show how, while Byzantium with its many-sided civilization survives, the West crumbles, and later takes shape again on a new basis. In a third and fourth series we demonstrate the part played by religious imperialism and reveal the characteristics of an art and a civilization inspired by faith. Finally, in the series concluding we consider Europe as a whole whose parts gradually become unified, and trace an evolution which takes place in institutions and in men's minds and foreshadows the Renaissance.

In every case we lay emphasis on the social and intellectual life and on the logic which is therein manifested. For in this, according to our hypothesis, lies the very heart of history.[2]

It goes without saying, for anyone who adopts the scientific attitude, that the Middle Ages are neither to be glorified nor depreciated. Considered objectively, there is neither progress nor retrogression en bloc. They are a period of incubation. A

[1] For details and bibliographical information on this question of the " Middle Ages " and of periods in general, we recommend the debates of the *Centre international de Synthèse*, Bulletin No. 1 (appendix to the *Revue de Synthèse historique*, vol. xli. June, 1926), paper by O. DE HALECKI and R. EISLER on the *Division of History into Periods*, pp. 16 and 21 ; discussions, Bulletin No. 2 (R.S.H., vol. xlii, Dec., 1926), DE HALECKI, plans for articles on *Divisions* and *Middle Ages* for the *Vocabulaire historique du Centre*, pp. 11, 16 ; discussion ; observations by L. FEBVRE. Cf. in the *R.S.H.*, vol. xlii, p. 61, H. SÉE, *La Division de l'Histoire en periodes*, concerning Troeltsch, and vol. xliii (June, 1927), p. 3, O. DE HALECKI, *Moyen Age et Temps Modernes*, concerning Von Below.

[2] See our General Introduction, vol. i, pp. xiii-xv.

cataclysm took place which was the result of a multiplicity of contingencies. But the ancient world " was growing old " and the barbarian " migrations " not only invigorated the peoples of the earth but brought them " that youthful ardour, that bold confidence, that aptitude for change and progress the gift of which has been lost to advanced civilizations, and of which barbarism is merely the uncultured and fleeting form ".[1]

HENRI BERR.

[1] Prévost-Paradol, *op. cit.*, vol. i, p. 451.

THE END OF THE ANCIENT WORLD
AND THE BEGINNING OF THE MIDDLE AGES

INTRODUCTION

THE fact that the Middle Ages did not follow abruptly on " antiquity " is, *a priori*, self-evident. Even the idea of an intermediate period between ancient and modern times arose only with difficulty. The seventeenth century may have caught a glimpse of it, but it has only recently been accepted by science.

For a long time historians unfolded their narratives without troubling to punctuate them chronologically and without feeling the need of any major pause. When, only a century ago, the concept of medievalism had secured attention, the doctrine of evolution, of the slow, continuous transformation of nature and humanity, made men overlook the fact of discontinuity. So much was this the case that the fundamental differences between the period to which the term " antiquity " should properly be confined and subsequent times would no doubt have continued to be disregarded had it not been for the necessity of making divisions in historical narrative for pedagogic purposes. Unfortunately these chronological divisions, made for the benefit of schools, were so clumsily and sometimes so ludicrously carried out, that as a result every attempt to discriminate between antiquity and the Middle Ages has been discredited.

Nevertheless this separation corresponds to a reality and it would be dangerous to refuse to make it. If it is true that the river of time glides on continuously, it is also true that the rate of its progress is not even. Sometimes it becomes so slow that its movement is scarcely noticeable and it seems possible to give an account of several centuries in a few pages only. At other times it rises and overflows in a sudden spate and the historian, crushed by the confused throng of abundant facts, spends a whole lifetime in re-tracing a few revolutionary days.

In the history of humanity there are periods when men no longer understand their ancestors, their fathers, themselves even. It is as though a break had occurred in psychological continuity. A contemporary of Septimius Severus or even of Diocletian might have been able to recognize himself in an ancestor of the time of Augustus. Their taste, language, art, world-outlook and passions had undergone only modifications of the kind which alter contours without concealing fundamental resemblances. But what is there in common between a contemporary of Diocletian and a contemporary of King Dagobert? The world contemplated by the men of the seventh century is entirely different from that which presented itself to the eyes of the men of the third or of the fourth century. The Roman Empire, except in the East and in a form which is no longer Latin, has ceased to be. New nations have invaded it and are themselves threatened by other peoples still more fierce and strange. New languages, laws and customs have been established. Above all a renovation has taken place in the world within. Men have turned away with indifference or distaste from things which were dear to their nearest ancestors. They no longer understand ancient literature, because they no longer love it; even the form and language in which it is transmitted elude them. The magic of the plastic arts no longer charms their eyes. The gods are dead, killed by the one God whose commandments impose a rule of life so new that henceforth this world will assume a secondary rôle; the sage imbued with "the new philosophy" will place the object of his desires in the sphere of the world beyond. Between the men of the new and those of the ancient times there will no longer be a thought in common.

To follow up properly so complete a transformation of human psychology would require the help of fine, accurate and copious evidence. Unfortunately our documents are poor, fragmentary and uncertain. Faced with "the most difficult problem of history" the historian feels cruelly inadequate for his task. In order not to abandon it and to soothe his uneasy or tortured conscience, he will have to remember always the greatness of the end he has before him and also the fact that excessive humility should not prevent us from serving at the altar.

A work such as is here presented to the public can only be of the nature of a compilation. No one can be so vain as to imagine himself a specialist in all the branches of so vast a subject. At every step we have to lean on the work of our predecessors and our contemporaries. The author claims as his own merely the plan and perhaps a few ideas.

This book, begun in 1913, was finished after a long interruption in October, 1921. Nevertheless the bibliography has been brought up to date till the middle of the year 1926. It will therefore not cause surprise if the theory set forth in the text is not always found in agreement with the works referred to in the notes.

FERDINAND LOT.

August, 1926.

PART I

THE CRISIS OF THE THIRD CENTURY AND THE RESTORATION OF THE EMPIRE

CHAPTER I

THE POLITICAL CRISIS OF THE THIRD CENTURY

THE power of the Roman Emperor, among the most absolute which the world has ever known, was nevertheless not monarchical in essence.[1] The Princeps is all-powerful, not because he is considered as descended from the gods, like the monarchs of the East and the kings of certain Germanic peoples ; but rather because he embodies in his person the *Respublica*, the authority of the Roman people, which is absolute. Accordingly his power is not a personal power, still less is it hereditary ; it is *delegated*. His power depends first and foremost on armed force. The Emperor is he who possesses, by delegation, the command of the army, which like all real command is absolute. This command is called the *imperium*. During the republican period many persons held the *imperium*. These were the commanders-in-chief, the *proconsuls*. They were *imperatores*, but only for the duration of the campaign. On the day after the triumph, this absolute power expired. The establishment of the Empire consisted in limiting the number of those on whom the *imperium* was conferred to one man, and in conferring upon him this office for life.

In its essence, the Empire remains none the less a *magistracy*. The idea of the sovereignty of the State continues in theory to be associated with the Emperor, who is the embodiment of the *Respublica*. If he receives the title of Augustus, that is *holy* and *sacred*, he does so no doubt because he is the living symbol of the *Dea Roma*. At his death, it is decided

---

[1] **CCCXLIV**, 26, 42, 111 ; **CCLIV**, vol. iv., 224-231 : **CCLX**, vol. i., §62 ; **CXLIX**, 147 ; **CDXLI**, 92-99 ; **CCCLVII**, 284.

whether he should be deified, or canonized as we should say, whether his *numen* or genius shall receive divine honours.

Does the proconsular imperium contain only this military side ? Has it not also a civil side, one of jurisdiction ? It is a disputed question.[1] It seems obvious that the *imperium*, although it forms the strong and stable element of the power of the Princeps, is not sufficient to give his authority plenary jurisdiction, for the reason that the proconsular power could be exercised only outside Rome (until Septimius Severus' time) and Italy. The Emperor also causes the *tribunicia potestas* to be assigned to him for life, and this confers on him the right of " *intercessio* " or general protection of the Roman people and renders his person sacred and inviolable. But he only assumes this power after the former, which is obviously fundamental.[2]

Other functions were able to gather round this nucleus : the Emperor is *pontifex maximus*, censor, *princeps Senatus ;* from time to time he takes the consulship, but these titles do not procure him any important increase of his power. Possibly from the time of Vespasian, the whole collection of rights constituting the imperial power was handed over *en bloc* by a *senatus-consultum*, which was likewise a law (the *lex regia*) acclaimed on the Campus Martius. This law confers the *imperium*, but not the *tribunicia potestas*.

The imperial magistracy does not aim at substituting monarchy for the republic. In the beginning the Empire appears as a measure of expediency.[3] A permanent dictatorship, for the remedying of the social and political upheavals which threaten the existence of the Roman Republic, is entrusted to the first citizen of the state : that is the meaning of " *princeps*". But the legal organs of the state, the Senate and the *comitia*, persist at the beginning of the Empire. Legislative power is not the exclusive function of the Emperor ; he can initiate laws, but only in the same way as any other magistrate, and when his " constitutions " or *acta* come to have the force of law, they will probably be legally based on the *tribunicia potestas* with which he is invested.

[1] **CCCXLIV,** vol. v., 42 ; **CXXXIV,** vol. v., 135 ; **CLXI,** vol. iii., 275 ; **CXLIX,** 155, 197 ; **CCCLVII,** 284 ; **CCCXXXII,** vol. i., p. 235 ; **CCLXVI,** vol. iii., 209, 404, 406 ; **CCLIV,** vol. iv., 224.

[2] **CCCXXXII,** vol. i., 241, 370, 375 ; **LIII,** 148.

[3] **CCCLVII,** 283.

Nor, at the beginning of the principate, has the Emperor any real functionaries at the centre of Empire ; up to the time of Hadrian he draws from amongst the circle of his "friends" the members of a council such as every head of State must have.

But the old machinery continues. The *comitia* having died of old age, the administration and the treasury as well as legislation are gathered in the hands of the Senate.[1]

Had the whole of the territory continued to be governed by the latter, the Empire would have been an aristocracy with a military dictator at its head. But this was by no means the case. The Emperor's position went on growing at the expense of the Senate's. In actual fact, the Emperor not only commanded the army and made war and peace, but also took into his hands the power of the whole State and set up an administration of his own. This was because from the beginning the Princeps and the Senate partitioned the provinces amongst themselves. To administer those which he kept for himself, the Emperor had perforce to have his governors and his treasury (his *fiscus*, opposed to the *aerarium*); and as the army was at his disposal, he made continual encroachments on all the spheres of activity left to the Senate.[2]

We need not retrace the slow but continuous evolution whereby the principate was transformed into a monarchy or quasi-monarchy.[3] In the third century this evolution was still far from complete. Under the principate of quite a young man Alexander Severus (March 12th, 222—February-March, 235) it seemed as though the Senate were going to recover its supremacy in the Roman State. It provided the Regency Council and helped the mother-Empress Mammæa. After reaching his majority, Alexander did nothing without the advice of the Senate ; he handed over to it the election of his principal functionaries, the Prætorian and Urban Prefects and the governors for the proconsular provinces ; often he asked it for candidates for all the other provinces. In Rome he assigned to the Prefect a committee of fourteen consulars whose task it was to help him in trying cases and to supervise each a "*regio*" of the town. He gave the Prætorian

---

[1] See L. HOMO, vol. xviii., and V. CHAPOT, vol. xxii.
[2] CCCXLIV, vol. iii., 274; vol. v., 158, 190, 236, 397; LIII, 182; CCXXVII.
[3] See sketch in CCCLVII, 349.

Prefects senatorial rank, so that a Roman Senator might be tried by none but his peers. He sent out no rescript, issued no Constitution without taking the advice of his council in which Senators predominated. He nominated the Consuls himself, but had them designated by the Senate. He diminished the authority of the imperial procurators and submitted their election to popular approval; he restored the *aerarium* by the side of the *fiscus*. Nothing disturbed the concord of the two powers reunited in this new form of government, which Herodian calls aristocracy (VI, 1.) The idea of the senatorial Empire was almost realized; some even dreamed of restoring the Republic, and these hopes are to be found even in the speeches which Dio Cassius attributes to Mæcenas and Augustus.[1]

It is precisely at the end of this reign that, with the assassination of Alexander Severus and of his mother, there broke out the formidable crisis which nearly shattered the Roman world to fragments and brought its civilization, still so brilliant at the beginning of the third century, to an end.

Here we see in full light and without any concealment the fundamental vice of the Empire. The Roman Empire, despite appearances, has no constitution. It rests on force only, a brute force let loose by the lowest appetites.[2]

Who confers this absolute power of the first citizen which gathers up in itself the *majestas* of the Roman people? It rests on no solid legal basis. Who designates the military dictator, or the *imperator*? The Senate, above all the army, the warrior force of the Roman people, at the dictation of circumstances, for the common good. But after the separation between the army and the Roman people, the former continues to play a preponderating rôle in the choice of the Ruler of the State. It seems that the Emperor's power has full legality only when the Princeps has obtained the support of both the army and the Senate. But to which of these two powers does the lawful initiative belong? No one knows.[3] Designation by the Senate might be more reassuring but it is not more legitimate. In actual fact, it is the army which

---

[1] See L. Homo, vol. xviii.; **CCLXXXVI, 3**.

[2] **CC, 37**.

[3] **CCCXLIV**, vol. v., 152; **CCCXXXII**, vol. i., 236, 244, 369; **CXVI**, vol. i., 1, 649; **CXXXIV**, vol. v., 135-144.

designates the Emperor, because force is in its hands. It sometimes happened that it begged the Senate to make the choice, but this request always concealed a command or a trap.

During the ancient period of the history of Rome, the army was a small concentrated force : it could spontaneously designate the man to whom it looked for salvation. But since the first century B.C., since the first institution of a permanent paid force, there is no longer one army but several armies. The Emperor is the chief who leads them and to whom they look for victory and booty. When there is one chief only, the Emperor, the army is scattered, the legions (the 24th, 30th, 32nd, etc.) are encamped on the frontiers of the Empire, on the Rhine, the Danube, the Euphrates. This removal from Rome and Italy at first leaves the imperial guard, consisting of the nine, afterwards ten, Prætorian cohorts encamped outside Rome, in a privileged position. Nevertheless from the second half of the first century we see the frontier legions taking part in the election of the Emperor ; from the end of the second century this even becomes the rule, the power of the Prætorian soldiers having been broken by Septimius Severus (193-211).

The motives which induced the army, or rather the armies, to intervene were not of a very high order; the Emperor is made or unmade for money or from caprice. Sometimes the legions raise to imperial rank a man with no military ability, if he happens to be rich, e.g., Didius Julianus. Then they weary of him and kill him. They also kill the Emperor if he is too strict in the matter of discipline. They kill him from caprice or for the pleasure of killing, sometimes even from some plausible motive, as when the man appointed is incapable of conquering the barbarians. Naturally these armies fought with each other, each claiming to impose on the rest the man of its choice. In the third century these armies do not always even need to be roused by ambitious individuals. Their rising appears spontaneous; suddenly an army will offer supreme power to men who tremble to accept it. To be elected Emperor, during the half-century which follows Alexander Severus, is a tragic fate. Those elected, such as Gordian, Decius, Saturninus Tetricus, accept the principate as a decree of death. The disease which has continually afflicted the Roman world during the first two centuries of the Empire and even from the time of Marius and Sulla rises to fever pitch. There is no longer a Roman people. The Senate is only a shadow ; the representative of the *Respublica*, the head of the State, all-powerful and formidable despot though he be, is the humble slave of a hundred-headed monster, of a Caliban without ideals, faith or law, of the so-called Roman army. And the history of the Empire is and will be only a series of *pronunciamentos*.

The man who for half-a-century delayed the catastrophe, Septimius Severus, laid aside all hypocrisy ; he would have no play-acting like his predecessors. His precept to his sons, on his death-bed in Britain, was, we are told, "make the soldiers rich and don't trouble about the rest". Caracalla acted in conformity with this cynical advice.[1]

It would not be possible here to retrace the history of the so-called period of the Thirty Tyrants. The following is merely a picture of the Empire as it was at the moment when a few rude soldiers succeeded in stemming the tide of anarchy.

The licentiousness of the armies coincided with a renewal of activity by the barbarians on the Rhine and the Danube. In Mœsia the Goths crossed the Danube. The Emperor Decius was beaten and slain (November, 251) ; even his body could not be found. In the East the danger was still more serious. The old Parthian monarchy, so long deadly to the Greeks and Romans, had just fallen. A new Persian Empire was set up in 226-227 by Ardashir. The Arsacids had kept some tinge of Hellenism ; in religion they were indifferent. With the Persians one religion triumphed, Mazdaism, upheld and propagated by a powerful priestly organization, that of the Magi.

The Persians were fanatics. In the countries which they reduced they razed the temples to the ground and imposed the Mazdean religion ; thus they acted in Armenia when Sapor (Shapûr) got possession of it. Parseeism was incompatible with Græco-Hellenistic culture. They were two civilizations which challenged each other. The clash between them was very violent, and disastrous to the Romans. The Emperor Valerian was made prisoner (260) by the Persian King Sapor, who is said to have inflicted the most humiliating treatment

---

[1] Probable interpretation of **CXXVIII**, vol. vi., 128, 244-245.

on him, using him as his footstool for mounting his horse.
A gigantic bas-relief at Nakeh-Rousten near Persepolis shows
Valerian kneeling before the Persian King, who is on horseback. Legend has it, that at the prisoner's death his skin,
after being tanned, dyed red and stuffed, hung for several
centuries in a Persian temple.[1]

Gallienus, Valerian's son and successor, was incapable of
ransoming or of delivering his father. All that he could do
was to entrust the military forces and give the title of *dux*,
later of *imperator* (but not of Augustus) to Septimius Odænathus,
who was of Arab origin and all-powerful in the oasis of
Palmyra, half-way between Syria and the Euphrates. Odænathus succeeded in curbing the enemy with Syrian and Arab
troops, armed in the Roman fashion.[2]

This Gallienus, under whom thirty tyrants—in reality
eighteen candidates for the purple—tore the Empire asunder,
has a very evil reputation. But we must not forget that we
only know of him from a late and hostile source, the so-
called Trebonius Pollio. It is a fact that under his principate
the revolt broke out which split the Empire into twenty
fragments. As these revolts were simultaneous, Gallienus
succeeded in keeping Italy only. Pannonia elected successively Ingenuus, Regalianus, and Aureolus ; Egypt, Macrianus
and Æmilianus ; Greece, Valens ; Thessaly, Piso ; Isauria,
Trebellianus ; Africa ; Celsus. The Gauls for nearly twenty
years (257-274) obeyed Emperors of their own, Posthumus,
Victorinus, Tetricus.

We see here signs of a particularism which was, if not
national, at least provincial. None of these Emperors really
had the intention of breaking away from Rome and setting up
a separate State. Except in Palmyra under Zenobia there
was no separatism. All or nearly all fought the barbarians,
as for example Posthumus, who after beating the Franks,
struck coins with the inscription " *salus provinciarum* ".
But had this position continued long, the Empire would have
broken up into six, eight or ten parts. At the head of each
province or group of provinces an Emperor would have ruled
who would have been too weak to triumph over the others.
In the long run, provincial particularism would have created

[1] **CXXVIII,** 419 ; **CCXXXIX,** 150.
[2] **CCXXXIII,** 48, 49, 200.

nationalities. The position in the second half of the third
century would have been that of the fifth and sixth centuries.
Only, instead of the Romano-Germanic Kingdoms of the
Ostrogoths in Italy, the Visigoths in Spain, the Franks and
the Burgundians in Gaul, and the Vandals in Africa, there
would have been states with a Roman civilization, which
might have been very interesting provided that these fragments
of Empire had been strong enough to withstand the thrust
of the barbarian hordes. The pressure of the latter is from
the third century onwards so mighty that the losses of
Romania to the advantage of Germanism would have been
still more serious. However that may be, it is to a series
of Illyrian Emperors that we owe the restoration of the
unity of the Empire[1] with Aurelian in 274, the expulsion of the
barbarians and the stamping out of the particularist tendencies in the East, Gaul and elsewhere, and the final overthrow
of the Senate's power.

Unfortunately this restoration of the unity of the Empire,
though almost in the nature of a miracle, brought about no
change whatsoever as regards the fundamental vice of the
Empire. On the contrary the frenzy of the army became
more acute. All the Emperors fell under the blows of their
own soldiers. Gallienus, who in spite of all had successfully
defended Italy against the Alamans, after defeating several
usurpers and reconquering Pannonia, was slain as being too
effeminate (268). Tacitus, an old Senator whom the army
had accepted because he was rich, perished at the end of six
months on the ground of his weakness. In reality, as he had
nothing left after distributing all his wealth among the
soldiers, they put him out of the way (275). Men of the
most outstanding character, soldiers who had risen from the
ranks, Aurelian and Probus, were assassinated by their
comrades-in-arms on the pretext that they were too exacting
disciplinarians. The greatest services to the State and even
to the army counted for nothing. It might be that on the day
after the crime the soldiers regretted their madness, but they
began again at the first possible opportunity. They must
always have something new.

---

[1] Claudius II, " The Goth " fights the Goths at Naïssus (Nish) in 269 ;
Aurelian triumphs over Tetricus and Zenobia.

CHAPTER II

THE RESTORATION OF THE ROMAN WORLD

I. DIOCLETIAN AND THE RESTORATION OF THE EMPIRE

THE great merit of the soldiers' new Emperor, the Dalmatian Diocletius, who changed his name, which revealed a very humble origin, into Diocletianus, was that he did away with all fictions.[1] The Roman people had for several centuries been a phantom only. But the Senate kept something of its ancient prestige. The semblance of a Roman Republic directed by it had been given new life in the third century. But the history of the favourite Emperors of the Senate, Alexander Severus, the Gordians, and Tacitus, had shown up glaringly all the impotence of this decrepit body. Diocletian deliberately ignored it: even for the making of laws and administrative regulations it was no longer consulted. On whom was he to lean? On the very day following his victory over Carinus (284) Diocletian realized that he would be no more successful than his predecessors had been for half a century in keeping the reins of government entirely in his own hands; it was only too evident that in future the Empire could no longer be directed by a single ruler. Wisdom demanded that he should meet the inevitable half-way and provide himself with a colleague, choosing such a one as would not threaten to become a rival and an enemy. Diocletian's glance fell upon a comrade-in-arms, Maximian, to whom he was bound by a tie of friendship. The latter, albeit unlettered and rude, had at least military gifts, which seem

---

[1] The man is not even known to us. His biography, supposed to have been written by a secretary, has not come down to us. The chapters in which Ammianus Marcellinus (c. 400) and Zosimus (c. 500) dealt with his reign in their Roman histories have disappeared. The only person who tells us a little about him is Lactantius, a Christian rhetorician who loathed him. We are ignorant even of his outward appearance. There is no authentic bust and the coins only show a conventional type (see J. J. BERNOUILLI, **XXXII**, vol. iii., 1894, p. 193-5). But numismatics come to our aid, and also abundant legal sources.

to have been lacking in the Emperor, and he respected
Diocletian for his superior ability; he consented to
be the hand that served the brain. The titles
Jovius and Herculius adopted officially by the two friends
openly proclaimed this conception. The choice was a happy
one: Hercules never betrayed Jupiter. Maximian was given
the title of Cæsar, and very soon after (from 286) of
"Augustus", and was truly Diocletian's right-hand man.

Even this measure was insufficient. The attacks of the
Persians in Asia, of the Germans in Europe, risings and
rebellions in Britain, Egypt, and Mauretania, were too much
for the two "Augusti". In 293 Diocletian went a step
further towards the division of power. Each of the two
Emperors took a lieutenant who received the *imperium*,
the *tribunicia potestas*, the diadem, and hence the actual
sovereignty, but with the title of "Cæsar" only, which left
him in a subordinate position in relation to his "Augustus".
Diocletian took for his collaborator Galerius, who though
an uneducated Dacian was a good soldier; Maximian chose
Constantius Chlorus, an Illyrian of high birth and a pleasing
personality. Each of the Cæsars thus brought to his
"Augustus" those qualities which the latter lacked. Family
alliances strengthened the political ties: the two Cæsars,
Galerius and Constantius, who were already married, were
obliged to divorce their wives and marry, the one Diocletian's
daughter, the other Maximian's daughter-in-law. Finally
these sons-in-law became the fictitious sons of their fathers-
in-law, by "adoption". Diocletian reserved the East for
himself, leaving to Galerius the supervision of the Danube
provinces; the other Cæsar had under his control Gaul and
Britain. The supreme power was divided, but there was no
dismemberment of the Empire; each "Augustus" had the
right to pass through the territory entrusted to his "Cæsar".
Legislative and administrative unity remained theoretically
in the hands of the two "Augusti", but actually it was
exercised undivided by Diocletian who remained the mainspring of the mechanism.

From the year 293 probably, Diocletian fixed the period at
the end of which he would consider his task accomplished
and resign his power voluntarily. In order to prevent all
future conflict he demanded of Maximian an oath, taken in

the temple of Jupiter Capitolinus, that he would abdicate at the same time as himself.[1]

From being a magistracy, the " empire " had become, by force of circumstances, a monarchy. The attempt was made to invest it with a fictitious prestige.

Diocletian, who had risen from the ranks like all his fore-runners (after Gallienus), thought he could throw dust in people's eyes by surrounding the person of the Emperor with a ceremonial borrowed from the East. He re-introduced the wearing of the mystic diadem, the symbol of eternity, which Aurelian had borrowed from the Sassanids. He allowed himself to be styled " master " (dominus), but this was not an official title. Under his principate, court offices continue to rank as inferior to public offices. Not until the second half of the fourth century do the former rise in the scale to the detriment of the latter, in proportion as the idea of public service fades.

The organization of the army, the sinew of power, was certainly the object of the Emperor's special attention. Unfortunately, however, the history of the Roman army for this period is an extremely obscure subject.[2] The facts which appear approximately true may be given as follows :

The prætorian soldiers, who had been so dangerous in the preceding century, saw their prerogatives more and more diminished. Already Septimius Severus had expelled from their ten cohorts the Italians, who were unruly and presumed upon with their origin, to replace them by those soldiers from the provincial legions who had most distinguished themselves. Diocletian drew to the cohorts especially his rude and devoted compatriots from Illyria. Under his successor Constantine even the name " prætorian ", so detested, was to disappear. The number of the " urban cohorts " under the command of the Urban Prefect was reduced.

---

[1] Diocletian's " system ", already sketched by GIBBON in 1778 (**CLXVI,** vol. ii., 1812, p. 385) has been expounded by Jakob BURCKHARD (**XLV,** 1854, 2nd ed., 1880) with a mechanical rigidity which gives it the false appear-ance of a theorist's invention. Aug. Wilh. HUNZINGER (**CCXLIV**) protested with reason ; but he is strangely deluded in thinking that criticism consists in accepting the account of Lactantius, a bitter and unintelligent enemy. " The constitutional reforms of Diocletian are not the results of a priori speculations ; he does not appear as a political theorist of the family of the Siéyès " says GOYAU very truly in his work on the tetrarchy, **CLXXVII.**

[2] See **CLXXX** and **CLXXXI.**

The head of the prætorian guard, the Prætorian Prefect, who has been compared with the Grand Vizier of the Moslem States, had been formidable in the second and third centuries. On more than one occasion he had had the Emperor assassinated in order to take his place. The splitting of the prefecture into two was destined to diminish the geographical area of his power. Later, before the end of Constantine's reign, the Empire was to be divided into four prefectures. The most effective measure was the reduction of the Prætorian Prefect to almost exclusively civil functions by entrusting the real command to " the masters of the militia ", a change destined to be achieved by Constantine. Legions drawn from the provinces to Italy and entitled " Palatine " made up a second guard, a rival and counterpoise to the first.

A serious measure, the breaking up of the legion into six detachments equal in number to the tribunes, begun probably before Diocletian, must have been carried out under his reign. Each of these detachments led an independent life and was garrisoned no longer on the frontiers merely, but in the towns which from about the years 260-270 had become fortresses.

The distinction between " legions " and " auxiliaries " tended to be obscured. The cavalry, indispensable for the struggle against the Goths, the Persians, etc., assumed an increasing importance, especially in the Imperial guard, the *Schola.*

For the command, Diocletian continued a previously established practice. Gallienus (†268) had removed the Senatorial order from the command of the legions in 261, a step dictated no doubt by jealousy or fear, but also by necessity. For men of this class the army was not a career, but a preparatory stage for civil offices. These ways were no longer compatible with the times. The six young nobles at the head of each legion could not but be amateurs ; as for the young men belonging to the often humble order of provincial Senates, the *decuriones,* they lacked prestige and experience. Diocletian debarred these also from the army. The times were hard. For the struggle against the barbarians and the Persians, professionals were needed. It was not so much an act due to a tyrant's whim as one of imperious necessity which gave the high command to officers drawn from the equestrian order or, worse still, risen from the ranks. All the Emperors after Gallienus belong to the latter class: they rose step by step, starting from the bottom, up to the Imperial throne, which appears as the natural goal of a military career.

The tendency was to entrust high commands on the frontier and even in the interior to courtiers who add to their new title of *duces* that of *comites*, that is to say, friends of the Emperor. Later the *comitatus*, for a long time merely a mark of distinction, will denote a function. Although men of high birth and those of the middle station were excluded from the army, a thing destined to bring about serious consequences, nevertheless, under Diocletian at least, it does not appear that the command was given over to recently naturalized barbarians, as was soon to become the custom.

It would be rash to try and fix exactly the scope of the changes introduced in weapons and tactics. An Eastern Iranian influence is, however, undeniable. Having to fight against cavalry, the infantry is more lightly armed. The archer, an Asiatic soldier, assumes an importance which has not hitherto been his in the Roman world. One part of the cavalry, the number of which had been considerably increased, consisted of cuirassiers, clad in coats of mail from head to foot: the medieval " knight " makes his appearance from the end of the third century. As for the really important factor, the morale of the army, that seems still to have been excellent. The Empire not only ran no serious danger but its ties seemed actually to be tightened ; the barbarians in Europe and Africa were checked and the frontiers of Persia were moved back ; the latter had to yield five provinces in the upper valley of the Tigris, and to suffer the restoration of the Kingdom of Armenia under the suzerainty of Rome (297). These successes are a by no means negligible sign of social recovery. " The Army", Victor Duruy[1] observes, " in many respects sums up in itself a people's civilization."

After the army comes the source of its maintenance, taxation. The Emperor caused the latter to be rigorously enforced. He needed money for the upkeep of Imperial pomp which he maintained from motives of policy, to dazzle the populations, rather than from personal taste. To this reign is attributed a famous fiscal innovation, the assessment

[1] CXXVIII, vol. vi., 370.

of the land-tax on the basis of the *caput* or *jugum*. After each land-survey (it was in principle revised every fifteen years), the taxable resources of each financial district were assessed as a definite number of *capita*. This *caput* or *jugum* was not a real or geometric unit but a fiscal unit established by rather rough approximate methods of calculation ; each *caput* consisted of five *jugera* (rather more than three acres) of vineyard, or in other cases of twenty *jugera* of good agricultural land, forty of land of medium quality, or sixty of bad land ; or again of 225 full-bearing olive trees or of 450 olive trees of the second class. Elsewhere the *jugum* appears to be the amount of " plough-land " which will maintain a peasant household.

The tax was then apportioned by "cities", and in each city by estates; each land-owner was liable for a certain number of *capita* or fractions of a *caput* according to the importance of his landed property. This reform had manifold advantages. For a long time the provinces had paid the " tribute " either in money, or in kind, or in both ways, in virtue of old agreements, advantageous to some parts of the Empire which were lightly taxed, but burdensome to others. Henceforth each district paid in proportion to its landed wealth. Even Italy was from now on subject to the land-tax.

Surcharges and reductions became easy. There seems to have been a really stable commutation rate for each *caput*. Seven gold solidi, or roughly one hundred francs in intrinsic value, seems in the main to have been the rule in the fourth and fifth centuries. The taxpayers in the *civitates*, knowing the number of the *jugera* of their small state, and the taxation figure at which it was assessed by the regulations, found in this system a comparative safeguard, while the government, having a very accurate knowledge of the extent of its revenues, was in a better position to draw up its budget.[1]

As an addition to these fiscal measures, we should notice an attempt to remedy the great economic crisis from which the Roman world was suffering. Diocletian succeeded where Aurelian had failed. In 296 he restored a sound currency. He brought back into circulation the true silver denarius, equal to $\frac{1}{96}$ of a pound, weighing 3.41 grammes as under

---

[1] Cf. *Revue historique de droit*, 1925, p. 38.

Nero, under the name of *argenteus minutulus* or *argenteolus*; the *Antoninianus*, which had been debased in the extreme, disappeared or survived only as a copper coin. The gold piece, the *aureus*, was made $\frac{1}{60}$ of a pound and consequently weighed 5.45 grammes.[1] In 301, with a view to bringing down prices, the Emperor conceived the idea of creating a nominal money of silver-washed bronze, the *denarius communis*, representing $\frac{1}{50,000}$ of the gold pound, giving the gold pound of 327 grammes a value of 240,000 grammes of bronze.[2]

In the same year, in order to put an end to the ruinous speculations brought about by the monetary confusion, the Emperor, in an *Edictum de pretiis rerum venalium*, took steps to fix, not indeed the prices of commodities, clothes, objects of everyday use, salaries, fees, etc., but the maximum which could be charged. The edict seems to have aimed especially at the *Pars Orientis*. Its failure was complete; tradesmen concealed their commodities, prices mounted and there were riots. The edict had afterwards to be withdrawn.

We may usefully notice the fact that the number of the *provinces* was increased to a hundred. A double advantage accrued from this measure; being less extensive (the size of some of them was excessive) the provinces were better administered and the Emperor had less to fear from governors whose sphere had been diminished. Diocletian's innovations in this department have however been exaggerated; he increased the number of the provinces by fourteen only, twelve of which were in the East. What was of infinitely greater importance was the fact that the Senate was deprived of the adminstration of those provinces which for several centuries had been reserved for it. All the provinces were henceforth at the disposal of the Emperor.

A new grouping appears—the *diocese*, which includes several provinces. At the head of each of them (there were twelve dioceses) there was a *vicarius*, intermediary between the *præses* or governor of the province, and the Prætorian Prefect. By this measure, the authority of the latter was further circumscribed.

---

[1] **XIII**, vol. i., 531; **CCCXXII**, vol. i.

[2] 288,000 grammes according to Dattari (*Revue belge de numismatique* 1914; cf. the answer of Maurice in the *Revue numismatique*, 1920.

At the centre, Diocletian did not so much innovate as carry out the changes begun before him. From the commencement of the third century the freedmen had been debarred from office. Even the subordinate services of the administration had been militarized ; the civil servants, called *officiales*, bear titles which remind us of the ranks in the army ; centurions, *cornicularii*, *optiones*, etc. They became the auxiliaries of the superior officials. Thus the *Cæsarians* had to carry out the decisions of the fiscal procurators. The civil service is entitled " militia ".

The body which inspired policy and the administration was the Council of the Princeps, the *Consistory*. The slow evolution was thus completed which in three centuries transformed the circle of friends of the princeps into an organ of government, a " Council of State". The Emperor demanded much work from it.

The legislative activity of Diocletian was indeed considerable. No other Emperor has left us so great a number of rescripts or of edicts : one thousand two hundred. Their spirit is most praiseworthy. The ruler undertakes to put down fraud and to protect the weak, the slave, women, the debtor, the poor free man, against the rich ; the labourer against his " dominus ", the father against the ingratitude of his children.

The reform of legal procedure was completed. In civil suits, the double proceedings, *in jure* before the Prætor and *in judicio* before the jury appointed by the Prætor, were simplified : the magistrate took cognizance of the facts and gave judgment. It is true that the magistrate was now only a functionary, but the complexity of the old system had its own inconveniences. In criminal cases the *cognitio extraordinaria* replaced the formulary procedure ; the magistrate and not the accuser now took in hand the *inquisitio*. The Emperor discouraged the use of torture. He mistrusted the militarized police and dismissed the " *frumentarii* ", spies and *agents provocateurs* who infested the capital and the provinces.

But we must not be deceived by appearances. This plentiful legislation, full of good intentions, is devoid of originality. The council which speaks in the name of the Princeps repeats old decisions. It is not without reason that a hostile contemporary, Lactantius, declares that the knowledge of law no longer existed under this reign. According to a good judge,[1] from the simplicity of the questions on which the Emperor is consulted it would seem as though there were no longer any Bar or magistracy existing at all. Such is the prevailing ignorance that the Emperor had to intervene at every instant to indicate the legal rulings to be applied by the governors of provinces. At least we must allow this son of a Dalmatian slave the credit of having encouraged the study of law (notably at Beirut) and of having felt the need of a great body, the Council of the Princeps, in which should be concentrated the feeble legal lights of the times.

Further we must say in defence of the magistrates of this time[2] that their ignorance was sometimes excusable and their task less easy than in the past. They had to apply Roman laws to peoples who up to that time had more or less completely preserved their autonomy. We have seen that Diocletian's predecessors worked at the Romanization of the Empire from the point of view of legislation. There still remained much to do, and Diocletian was one of those who made the most effective contribution by making the use of Roman law general. Assuredly, legislative unity did not yet exist. Diocletian allowed municipal regulations and local customs to be invoked, but only in cases of slight importance. It is under the reign of Diocletian that we begin to find the expressions, *jus Romanum, leges Romanæ*, instead of *jus civile Romanorum, jus nostrum, jus gentium*. Up to that time, Roman law had in a certain measure kept the character of municipal law. It had been created for the needs of a town, and at least in cases which presented a religious aspect, men had not been able to give it the necessary suppleness to turn it into national law.

In truth, the ancient city state was too narrow a crucible in which to remould the world. Devoid of all life, material or spiritual, Rome had become an obstacle to the expansion of *Romania*. While Aurelian had enlarged its precincts and surrounded it with new walls, as though he saw in it the

---

[1] Ed. Cuq, **XCVIII**, 1884, p. 499.

[2] The governors of provinces. The Romans, Cuq justly remarks (*Instit. judiciaires*, 964) never made a clear separation between jurisdiction and administration. A. de Broglie (**LX**, vol. ii., 195) had already drawn attention to the fact that the principle of the division of the two powers was foreign to their ideas. See also J. Declareuil, vol. xix.

palladium of the Empire and wished to give it new life, Diocletian immediately and deliberately abandoned it. From 284 Rome ceases to be in any real sense the capital of the Empire and becomes a sanctuary where certain rites are performed, the *vicennalia* and the " triumphs " (the latter will become exceedingly rare)—a unique museum, a dead city. The Emperor resides in the East, preferably at Nicomedia, on the borders of Europe and Asia. His colleague settles at Milan, the better to watch the barbarians who are threatening the Alps. His lieutenants, the "Cæsars", encamp at Treves and Sirmium on the look-out for the attacks of the Germans and the Iranians of Europe (the Sarmatians, Roxolani, and Iazyges). Henceforth the Princeps is destined to come to Rome on rare occasions and for a few days only. He feels a provincial, out of his element there, and moreover the business of the Empire very soon calls him away. The contrast is striking between the life of the emperors at the end of the third and fourth centuries and that of their predecessors who never left the " city " and frittered away there their health, intellect and life in mad or senseless orgies.

On the whole, the work of Diocletian, as far as we can form any judgment of it in view of the poverty of our sources, seems considerable and fruitful. He succeeded in bringing back at least a semblance of prosperity to the Empire. His success is attested by an enemy and a Christian, Lactantius. Monuments also bear witness to it : famous baths, the palace at Salona (Spalato) in Dalmatia, basilicas, porticos, and a number of buildings for civil or military purposes at Rome, Milan, Antioch and Edessa.[1] Without being exactly a lettered man, the Emperor encouraged learning ; he created the school of Nicomedia and Constantius Chlorus revived the schools at Autun. Letters and the arts thus had their share in this re-making of the Roman world.

Twenty years had passed from the death of Carus, the happiest years which the Roman world had known since the time of Severus Alexander. After having gone to celebrate at Rome his " vicennalia ", and " triumphed " with his colleague (November 304) Diocletian decided that the moment had come to make room for the young. His work appeared to him firmly established, and he felt the approach of old age (he was nearly

[1] **CXLVII.**

sixty) and the attacks of disease. He solemnly abdicated near Nicomedia, in front of the temple of Jupiter, on May 1st, 305. On the same day in the West, Herculius, bound by his oath, resigned the purple, raging. Doubtless the system of the *Tetrarchy* was destined to break down on the day after this double ceremony. But it was not so much a system as a measure of expediency. Cure for the disease of the Empire there was none. It was a great thing to have thought of an empirical remedy which should allow the patient to recover his strength and to meet the future onslaughts of fate.

II. DIOCLETIAN AND CHRISTIANITY

The end of the reign of Diocletian is marked by a measure which has left an indelible stain on the memory of the great statesman, the resumption of the persecution of the Christians. It is well to pause awhile and consider this question.

The Empire had been suffering for two centuries and a half from an internal malady, Christianity. The antagonism between the Roman State and the New Dispensation, allayed after being dormant for longer or shorter periods, began again at intervals with a bitter fury. The government undertook to exterminate the sect while the Christians resisted with the force of inertia alone, which was nevertheless invincible.

From a distance we must make an effort to understand the motives for the violence of this antagonism or even its cause.[1] Rome's toleration for foreign religions is a well-known fact. The only religion which, along with Christianity, was persecuted, namely Judaism, owed this to the folly and the fanatical aggressiveness of its followers. Still, after the destruction of Jerusalem, a *modus vivendi* was found which left the Jews complete liberty of conscience and even of religious practices, although the latter, such as circumcision, were forbidden to the other inhabitants of the Empire.

It is a noteworthy fact that the persecutions recommenced

---

[1] In A. LINSENMAYER, CCC, will be found an account of the theories of Allard, Leblanc, Boissier, Guérin, L. Duchesne, Mommsen, K. J. Neumann, A. Kneller, J.-E. Weiss, Hardy, Ramsay, Harnack and Callewaert. BOUCHÉ-LECLERCQ's fine book, LI, marked by so personal a way of thinking and such an exquisite style, does not in fact go beyond the end of the third century ; the end is not dealt with. We may supplement it with the works of ALLARD, III-VI, and of P. BATTIFOL, XXII, written in quite a different spirit. See also LINSENMAYER, CCC.

at critical moments in the history of the Empire, such as the tragic reigns of Decius and Valerius, at moments when public opinion in its anxiety looks for the cause of the common misfortunes. The Christians, who had the reputation of bad citizens and enemies of the gods whose wrath they drew down, were the " traitors " specially marked out to serve as scape-goats.

But nothing of the kind can be discovered at the end of Diocletian's principate, which on the contrary was crowned by prosperity. The Emperor decided to recommence persecution only after a long hesitation which lasted for several years (from 299 to 303). The reason which finally determined him to adopt a policy of repression remains a mystery. It has been suggested that regrettable incidents may have occurred in the army. The Christians were considered as not very good soldiers. Certain sects, the Montanists for example, declared military service to be incompatible with Christianity. But Montanism had been condemned and the " Catholic " Church was less strict. Gradually Christianity had won converts even in the army. Did breaches of discipline arise through soldiers refusing to obey the order to sacrifice ? It may have been so ; but these are mere suppositions.

It is worth while pointing out that Diocletian was at this period of his life under the influence of Galerius, whose mother was a devout pagan and had transmitted to her son her hatred of Christianity. The truth is that even in the periods of calm, there never existed between the Christian Church and the State anything more than a tacit and precarious truce which was at the mercy of the slightest incident. The immediate occasion of the rupture seems to have been the burning of the palace at Nicomedia. This was Diocletian's favourite town. In a few years he had turned it into the finest city of the East after Antioch and Alexandria.

Thus the last persecution, like the first under Nero, was started by the belief in the mania of the Christians for incendiarism.

This last persecution was the longest, lasting no less than eight years (303-311)[1]. In spite of tradition, it is not certain that it was the most cruel, at least as long as Diocletian ruled.

[1] **V; CCLXXXIV,** vol. iii.

Its objects were things rather than persons. The churches were shut or overthrown, and the sacred books were destroyed. The number of victims does not seem to have been very high. The magistrates showed that rather weary bored good-nature which was habitual to them in matters of this kind.

Diocletian's Christian opponent, Lactantius himself, in ridiculing their precautions, their long hesitations and the ease with which they were satisfied by feigned recantations, bears witness to the comparative moderation of their repressive measures.

Nevertheless the Christians bowed under the shock and there was nothing to foretell their long resistance, still less their ultimate success.

It was in the very year which followed the commencement of the persecution that Diocletian decided the moment had arrived to abdicate, considering his work to have been brought to a successful conclusion. In the sumptuous retreat which he had long before prepared for himself on the shores of his native country at Salona, we may be certain he was not troubled by any scruple as to the legitimacy of his edict or by any anxiety as to its efficacy. The abolition of Christianity was the crowning act of his restoration of the Empire which had so long been torn asunder. Henceforth there would be a single flock under a many-headed shepherd.

III. THE SUCCESSION OF DIOCLETIAN

Had Diocletian fixed the details of the system of what has been called the *Tetrarchy* ? Perhaps not, but it does not matter. This system had its inner logic. It was his desire that the " Cæsars " should succeed the " Augusti " and should adopt " Cæsars " in their turn. It was part of the tradition that one of the " Augusti " should have a kind of precedence over the other. Galerius thus followed the lines laid down by his predecessor in appointing the two new Cæsars, Severus and Maximin Daïa. It is true that the sons of Maximian and of Constantius, Maxentius and Constantine, were debarred from the throne ; but this also was in conformity with the spirit of the tetrarchy in which the choice of the ruler and fictitious parentage counted for more than the claims of blood. Only here they came up against the force of circumstances. The

evicted princes rose up in revolt and chaos began once again.
After seven years' fighting, supreme power in the West fell
into the hands of Constantine, who defeated Maxentius at the
Milvian Bridge, near Rome (October 28th, 312).   Another
twelve years were needed for the son of Constantius Chlorus
(died in 306) to succeed in making himself master of the whole
of the Empire.   At first an attempt was made to continue
Diocletian's system.   Constantine gave his sister in marriage
to Licinius, the successor of Galerius ; having conquered his
colleague several times, he spared him and left him the East
(315).   It was only in 323 that Constantine decided to take
the government of the whole Empire into his own hands
and to suppress his rival.   The tetrarchy like the dyarchy
had had its day.   When he makes his will (337) Constantine
will divide the Empire between his sons and nephews as he
would have disposed of private property.   We have here
already a partition in the Merovingian or Carolingian style,
based solely on the rights of blood.

He had three sons remaining who were all successively
proclaimed Cæsars.   The Empire was divided into three parts.
Constantine had the West (Gaul, Britain and Spain), Constantius the East with Egypt, Constans Italy with Illyricum and
Africa.   The nephews were not forgotten.   One of them,
Delmatius, was to have as his portion Thrace, Macedon
and Achæa ; another, Hannibalian, a part of Armenia and
of Pontus with the Eastern title " King of Kings ".

The unity of the Empire was restored to the advantage of
Constantius by the suppression of the nephews, who were
massacred by the army (337), by the victory of Constans at
Aquileia over his brother Constantine II who was slain (340),
and by the murder of the conqueror who fell a victim to the
" magister militum " Magnus Magnentius (350).   Succession
by descent had in fact not put an end to the revolts of com-
manders and their attempts to usurp the Empire.   Nevertheless
we must admit the fact that from the time of Diocletian they
were rarer and did not succeed.   In 353 Constantius, having
defeated and slain Magnentius, found himself master of the
whole of the Empire.   But, from 361, he saw rising up against
him his cousin Julian (son of Julius Constantius the brother
of Constantine the Great) whom he had made Cæsar with
the task of defending Gaul against the barbarians.   After the

short reigns of Julian (died June 26th, 363) and of Jovian (died February 17th, 364), a new dynasty is established on the throne in the person of the valiant and cruel soldier Valentinian. But on the very day of his election by the army assembled on the plain of Dadastania, February 26th, 364, the soldiers in acclaiming him insisted on his taking to to himself a colleague. Valentinian chose his brother Flavius Valens and entrusted to him the East with the Balkan Peninsula. The division of the Empire into two large parts had become an imperious necessity.[1] From this period these two halves were never re-united, except for an insignificant space of time under Theodosius (three months, from the end of September, 394, to January, 395).

---

[1] In 365 the Court Offices are duplicated : there are as many in the East as in the West, and the Senate of Constantinople ranks equal to that of Rome.

CHAPTER III

The Roman Empire and the Church in the Fourth Century[1]

I. CONSTANTINE AND THE EDICT OF MILAN

HAVING vanquished Maxentius under the walls of Rome, at the Milvian Bridge, Constantine promulgated soon afterwards, in February, 313, the very famous *Edict of Milan*, which marks the decisive turning point in the history of the relations between the Church and the State.[2]

Are we to say that Christianity triumphed all at once, and that because the Emperor was converted, as his Christian panegyrists affirm, at the moment when he staked his all against Maxentius ?

Let us note, first of all, that the edict of toleration does not issue from Constantine alone. In the same year (June 13th) Licinius also issues one in the East, at Nicomedia, and Licinius is not and never will be a Christian. Constantine and Licinius had been preceded in this course by Galerius, the bitter enemy of Christianity. On April 30th, 311, when seriously ill, he had published at Nicomedia a proclamation whereby he forswore persecutions. " In return for our indulgence, they (the Christians) shall pray to their God for our salva tion, for the State, and for themselves in order that the Common-wealth may enjoy perfect prosperity and that they may live in their homes in security." Another persecutor, Maximin Daïa, followed this example when he felt himself threatened by fate (May-June, 313).

The edict of Milan is therefore no innovation. It is not a measure with special reference to the Christians. It begins as follows : " Having come to Milan under happy auspices and seeking with care all that can be useful to the public good and peace, amongst other things that can serve the

---

[1] **LX ; XXII, and XXIII ; CXXVI,** vol. ii. and iii. ; **CCCXIII, CCCXVIII.**

[2] The text of the beginning of 313 has not reached us. We use the confirmation of June.

majority of men, we have thought that it was necessary above all to regulate all that concerns the worship due to Deity, in order to give both to Christians and to all the free power to follow the religion of their choice. May, therefore, the Deity, in his celestial habitation, show his satisfaction, and his favours both to us and to the peoples who live under our authority."

Thus the edict of Milan proclaims the freedom of worship, " a unique moment in history, when that State religion ... which had become a useless and hateful tool seems finally to expire. But it was only a lightning flash of good sense which shot across the political sky. From the year 325 State religion will re-appear and with it its inevitable accompaniment, intolerance ".[1]

The Edict therefore is no proof at all that Constantine passed over to Christianity. Was he even ever a Christian ?

This has been denied. Apart from Christian apologists, historians[2] agree in seeing the founder of the Christian Empire as a shrewd statesman, at bottom a religious sceptic, or at most a deist. They bring together all the points which show that up to his final victory over Licinius, Constantine kept the balance between Paganism and Christianity. The Christian symbols to which Christian apologetics appeal they match with others which are definitely pagan.

If the coins, from a certain date onwards, bear the Christian monogram, we read on the reverse "*soli invicto comiti*", an invocation to the Sun-god, the god of the Emperors and of the army since Claudius II and Aurelian (the son of a priest of the Sun), the god also of Constantine himself in his youth. If the Emperor grants privileges to the Christian Churches, he does the same for the temples. He does not give up his purely pagan title of *pontifex maximus*. He entrusts the public offices to pagans as well as to Christians. At Court, he is surrounded by philosophers and rhetoricians who naturally were pagans. He closed down the temples, it will be objected ; but two or three only, that of Æsculapius at Ægae and of Aphrodite at Heliopolis, which had become houses of ill fame. He prohibited sacrifices, even in the home ; but that was because

---

[1] **CXXVIII**, vol. vii., p. 61.
[2] In France, Duruy, Bouché-Leclercq and Albert Réville ; in Germany, Niebuhr, Burckhardt, H. Schiller, O.Seeck, Ed. Schwartz, etc.

he wished to bring everything into the light and under his control. Even after 324, after he had became a Christian " as far as he could be " he was still careful in his attitude to paganism. At most he defended Christianity and became a Christian at the end of his life, because he felt in this religion a " force which he did not wish to leave outside the grasp of his government ". He seized the already fully established power of the episcopate. He realized what unique function-aries he would gain for his service, by attracting to himself the bishops. Constantine resembles Bonaparte signing the Concordat to reconcile the Revolution and the Church and to turn the bishops into more submissive prefects. " Supreme pagan pontiff by right, he would easily be the real head of Christendom and would thus rule over men's souls as well as over their bodies ".[1]

These interpretations of Constantine's thought are ingeni-ous and probable. But they may also be entirely erroneous. There is a mania for crediting great men of the past with deep laid political schemes the idea of which perhaps never occurred to them.[2] We forget that they may have been visionaries[3], and in that case the motives which they obeyed are of so special a kind that every psychological reconstruction based on political sense is bound to come to grief. In the first place, to think of Constantine as a disillusioned sceptic is more than arbitrary. There were no free-thinkers at this time. All men from the lowest to the highest social stratum were religious or at least superstitious, even Diocletian, even Marcus Aurelius. Constantine when pagan was necessarily religious, Constantine when Christian was most certainly so. We see him concerned as to the problems of Christ's essential nature and his relation to the Father. He endeavoured to restore unity to the Church. Had he been indifferent, he would calmly have suffered the followers of Athanasius and of Arius to excommunicate each other and to set church against church, confining himself to maintaining the public peace and preventing the disciples of Jesus from killing each other. Doubtless he would have done better to adopt this attitude. But he intervened ; and if he did so, it was because he

---

[1] Here are summed up the views of **XV, CXXVIII, CCCCVI, CCCCLV.**
[2] Cf. **XLIX,** vol. i., 30.
[3] The figures of Constantine are conventional and give no real idea of him. See **XXXII,** vol. iii., 218 ; **DXII,** 259-268.

believed in Truth, in the Absolute. In his adherence to Christianity sincerity played a part, and that part must have been great.

If we hold that he adhered to Christianity from policy we must believe that he had some interest in doing so. But what was this interest ?

A sovereign like Henry IV, absolutely unable to bring over to his own faith subjects the majority of whom profess a doctrine different from his, may think it necessary to abandon his individual sentiments in order to bring about that unity of belief he deems indispensable for the good functioning of society. In that case Constantine, even if he had been Christian at heart, would' have been obliged to turn pagan. In spite of its marvellous power of expansion during the first three centuries of its existence, Christianity was far from having conquered the majority of the inhabitants of the Roman world. The only lands in which, at the beginning of the fourth century, it could claim approximately half the population, are Asia Minor, part of Thrace, Cyprus and Edessa. It exercised a considerable influence on the ruling classes at Antioch, in Coele-Syria, at Alexandria (including Egypt and the Thebaid), at Rome, where there were 30,000 Christians, or one-twentieth of the population, in Lower Italy and some parts of Upper Italy, in Proconsular Africa and Numidia, in some parts of Thessaly, of Macedon and of the Southern coasts of Gaul. It was very little spread in Palestine, where Judaism had regained the upper hand, in Phœnicia and Roman Arabia, in the interior of Achæa, Macedon, Thessaly, Epirus, Dardania, Dalmatia, Mœsia, Pannonia, in North Italy, Mauretania, and Tripolitana. It was almost non-existent on the coasts of the Black Sea, in the Western part of Upper Italy, in middle and Northern Gaul, in Belgica, Germany, Rhætia and Britain.

Thus the country in which Constantine was born, and which had been ruled by his father and until 312 by himself, counts amongst the least Christian in the Empire. It is a paradox that the Emperor Constantine, a Westerner, should have imposed a religion which was widespread only in the *Pars Orientis* of the Empire. If there was any emperor to whose interest it was to embrace Christianity, it was Galerius and Maximinus Daïa ; but these on the contrary were its

worst enemies. To go over to Christianity was, for a sovereign
who reigned in the West, an act of sheer folly politically.
It was even dangerous, for the army, the only real force of
the State, was wholly pagan, addicted above all to the worship
of the Sun, and was destined for a long time to remain so.

It being proved that Constantine had everything to lose
and apparently nothing to gain by embracing Christianity,
there is only one possible conclusion, namely that he yielded
to a sudden impulse, which we may call one of a pathological
or supernatural order as we prefer.[1] He staked his fortune
on the God of the Christians. Men's minds were troubled by
the tragic fate of all those who had persecuted the Christians.
Galerius himself, their fiercest adversary, had just done public
penance and was asking his victims to pray for his salvation.
At Rome, Maxentius, who had the more numerous army,
had invoked by incantations all the powers of the pagan
world, infernal and supernal, and his magic practices disturbed men's imaginations. For Constantine there was left
the possibility of trying his luck by making an appeal to the new
god, the God of the Christians. His conversion was an act
of superstition.

But was he really converted ? This brings us back to the
question already raised. If by conversion is understood
an inner moral reformation, the answer will no doubt be in
the negative. But that is not the point at issue. The point
is whether the Emperor, after his victory over Maxentius,
gave any external official signs of his adherence to the new
Faith.

These signs are indisputable.

At the moment of engaging in battle with his rival Maxentius, Constantine was not content with a mental prayer to the
God of the Christians, but had the symbol Ἰησοῦς Χριστὸς
engraved on his soldiers' shields. But to make use of this
talisman was to enter on an irrevocable compact with the
Deity who granted victory. After that it was impossible to
draw back without risking the wrath of heaven. On the day
after the victory, when Constantine made his entry into Rome
on October 29th, 312, he allowed the wholly pagan Senate to

---

[1] The apparition of the cross in the sky in the West, with the words ἐν
τούτῳ νίκα (by this conquer). The apparition of Christ to the Emperor
the following night.

offer him a statue as a symbol of his divinity, but he had a cross put in its hand. The imperial standard, the *labarum*, was the old *vexillum*, that is to say a banner affixed to a staff surmounted by a crown ; but into this crown was introduced the monogram which changed the standard into a Christian image. The labarum dates if not from the year 312, as Constantine himself claimed through a confusion of memory, from 317. On March 1st, at Sardica, he raised to the rank of Cæsars his sons Crispus and Constantine II whom he had had by Minervina and Fausta respectively. The portraits of the two young princes figured on the banner. This was proclaiming in striking fashion the adherence of the ruler and his children to Christianity.

The study of Constantinian numismatics brings the strongest proofs.[1] In 314 the Emperor issued coins commemorating Claudius II, Constantius Chlorus, and Maximian Herculius as whose heir he posed. On these he allowed no representation of any rite connected with the pagan consecration of the *divi*. Maxentius, who had set up the same claim to succeed them, acted differently. In the same year, the mint at Tarragona made use of the cross as a monetary device. Further, in a series of coins struck at Scissia (Sissek, at the confluence of the Save and the Kulpa), the mint of Upper Pannonia, from 317 to 320, two Christian monograms are seen on the Emperor's helmet. This is the indisputable sign of the Emperor's public profession of faith in Christianity. Indeed, if the selection of images, legends, and symbols on the reverse is left to the free choice of the officers of the Mint, the representation of the Emperor on the obverse has an official and sacred character. To introduce even a slight change in the devices without the ruler's knowledge, would be punishable by the penalty incurred by the crime of *læsa majestas*. The officer of the mint probably drew his inspiration from the devices painted on the shields in October, 312 ; the second of these monograms is in fact unknown before Constantine's reign.

Once won over to Christianity with a full and perfect adherence, Constantine could from prudence use diplomacy

---

[1] The numismatics and even the history of Constantine have been given a new interpretation by the works of M. Jules MAURICE. See **CCCXXII, CCCXXIII.** Cf. O. VOETTER, **CCCCXCIX,** p. 68, and plate ii., fig. 74, 75.

towards paganism. But this was only for a short time. It was impossible for so despotic a character with unlimited power at his disposal not to wish to impose his faith on all. The toleration—which lasted about ten years—for non-Christians quickly became precarious. The Emperor's official impartiality was hypocritical. Even during this period (313-323) the Christians were constantly favoured.

The Jews were forbidden under pain of burning to stone those of their co-religionists who passed over to Christianity. Pagan municipalities were forbidden to force Christians to perform the sacrifices. Clerics received exemption from the " munera ". Manumission in church was permitted. Wills were allowed to be made in favour of the Church. Sunday was made an obligatory day of rest.[1] The penalties directed against celibacy were abolished. Civil jurisdiction was for a short time granted to the bishops.[2]

But it is especially after his final victory over Licinius in 324[3] that Constantine gives free rein to his zeal. The god of the Christians, who has once more favoured him and given him the Empire in its entirety, is indeed the true God. The *labarum* is engraved on coins. In the effigies struck at this date the Emperor and the figures round him appear in the attitude of prayer with their eyes upraised to heaven.[4] On the other hand he will not allow his images to be kept in pagan temples. He is entitled in the East Νικητὴς Κωνσταντῖνος and no longer Ἀνίκητος (*invictus*), a term which recalls too much the *Sol invictus*, the god of his family and of his youth. He builds temples in the East, at Antioch, Nicomedia and in the Holy Land. (In 325 the celebrated basilica at Jerusalem was consecrated.)

He constantly intervenes in the affairs of the Church ; for example in the quarrel between the Catholics and the Donatists in Africa on the very day after his triumph over Maxentius. He calls together the Council of Nicæa (July -25th, 325) the holding of which coincides with his *vicennalia*. Only twenty

---

[1] The administration which had remained pagan pretended it was a question of honouring the Sun.
[2] This privilege is according to Duruy (vol. vii., p. 80) only a pious fraud. The law is authentic. See CHÉNON, **LXXXI**, 1904, p. 264.
[3] Not 323. See JOUGUET, **CCLII**, 1906, p. 231.
[4] Julian does away with these effigies. They must therefore have a Christian meaning.

years separate this ceremony from Diocletian's triumph at Rome, and yet an abyss yawns between these two dates.

He undertakes propaganda. He invites his subjects to become converted to Christianity ; he distributes presents of gold and silver pieces, with Christian designs. He will write to his Persian rival Sapor to beg him to protect the Christians and to induce him to become a Christian himself.

He becomes aggressive. He condemns the worship of Apollo whose oracle had let loose the persecution of Diocletian. In 326, in the repetition at Rome of the ceremony of his *vicennalia*, he upbraids his soldiers for sacrificing to Jupiter Capitolinus and brings upon himself the scorn of the Senate and the Roman people who had in large majority remained pagan. He forbids (after 330) functionaries to offer sacrifices to the gods in official ceremonies ; in general they must abstain from all public participation in pagan worship. Private sacrifices had already been forbidden for several years[1] ; in the repair of public buildings, the temples are excluded.

It is true that he kept to the end his title of *pontifex maximus*, but he refrained from carrying out the functions of the office which were left to a *promagister*. The Christians realized the great advantages they stood to gain from the sovereign's remaining at the heart of paganism in order the more surely to destroy it.

It is true also that he received baptism only on his death-bed (May 22nd, 337). But in the fourth century it was far from unusual not to ask for baptism until reaching adult age. Performed *in extremis*, it was considered a sure means to eternal salvation.[2]

But the most striking manifestation of the Emperor's sentiments is the foundation of Constantinople.

The foundation of Constantinople is from every point of view a very important historical event. It resulted in displacing the axis of the Roman world and, in a short time, in substituting Greek for Latin civilization in the East. But why did he set up a competitor with Rome ? Why did he build a second Rome ?

---

[1] It would not be safe to say that it was possible to apply these laws. But that does not matter : the intention which dictated them loses nothing of its significance.

[2] See Franz Jos. DOELGER, **CCX**, p. 387-477.

It would be vain to try and find personal motives for this act. It is fantastic to imagine that the republican memories of Rome could have annoyed the Emperor. At Rome the Senate was powerless. It might be unpleasant to come into contact with the jeering and insolent populace, in the circus for example ; but this plebs was too debased to be formidable. Residence at Rome was on the contrary very agreeable. Its palaces, its baths, its circuses and theatres, its large and beautiful gardens, made it the finest town in the world. It would take Constantinople a long time to supplant Rome or even to equal it in its attractions.

Were there any military reasons ? What were they ? In 324 the Goths ceased to be threatening and Persia was torn by faction. The danger was on the Danube and above all on the Rhine. The place for a war-lord such as Constantine was in the West.

Were the provinces of the East richer than the West ? At this time we cannot be certain that they were. The Goths in the third century had caused as much havoc in the Balkan Peninsula and in Asia Minor as the Franks and Alemans had in Gaul and Italy. Besides, how can such a circumstance matter to a great statesman who resides wherever his presence is necessary ?

As for asserting that Constantine could foresee the mighty consequences of his work, that would be to imagine that he was gifted with so penetrating a vision of the future that no man has been able to equal him. Had this power of foresight been given him, he would have perceived things so strange and so contrary to all that he could desire, that he would have drawn back. The foundation of Constantinople is a sheer enigma. It is not the culmination of a process of evolution. If, as a matter of fact, Rome ceased to be the capital from the year 284, and men's minds became accustomed no longer to associate with Rome the Emperor's customary residence, this was due to the force of circumstances and not to any premeditation. Never had the idea of doing away with Rome as a capital occurred to an Emperor. Even the Syrian madman Elagabalus did not attempt to place the capital in the East. The Illyrian Aurelian, who had no cause to be pleased with the Senate and the people (we may remember the revolt of the officials of the Mint), enlarged the area of Rome and surrounded it with a solid rampart. We cannot really attribute to Diocletian the intention of removing the capital from Rome. If he resided in the East, preferably at Nicomedia, the reason was that being less of a soldier than a statesman he left his right hand " Herculius " at headquarters in the West. If Herculius and his Cæsar were more often at Milan, Aquileia and Treves than at Rome, it was in consequence of an imperious necessity and not from any deliberate purpose.

The idea of setting up a rival to Rome is Constantine's very own. The foundation of Constantinople was the result of a startling decision.[1] On September 18th, 324, when the last battle against Licinius began (not far from Chalcedon) Constantine could not be certain that he would not be beaten back to the West. On November 8th, the creation of the new capital has already been decided. What transpired in Constantine's soul in this brief interval ? We are reduced to conjectures. What stands out in Eusebius' account is that the Emperor at the moment of engaging in the final struggle against his rival was in a state of mind altogether similar to that of October 28th, 312. Licinius, in spite of the edict of toleration, had not taken the leap and become a Christian. Far from having done so, he spent his time consulting magicians.

Constantine, shut in a sort of tabernacle in which he had placed the cross, never ceased praying ; he talked with God, " like Moses ". Having triumphed in a battle in which his rival put himself into his hands, Constantine owed the God of victories a striking sign of his gratitude. He showed the latter by transporting his capital from that Rome which was infected with an incurable paganism to a new city which was wholly Christian. The choice of Byzantium must certainly have come into his mind in the course of the battles fought close to the old town where he pressed hard upon Licinius a few weeks before. He was struck by its strategic advantages. But without an acute psychological crisis, how could he have transported to the East the capital of the Empire, at the very moment when the disappearance of his rival restored unity to the Roman world ? All that modern writers tell of the superior vitality of the East in

---

[1] We will here only refer to **CCCXXIII.** L. BREHIER, **LV,** criticises brilliantly the time-honoured theory which attributes to Constantine deep political designs divorced from all religious ideas.

comparison with that of the West, is, as far as this date is concerned, a pure hypothesis invented for the requirements of the theory.

The decision once taken, the work went on with extra-ordinary rapidity. The ancient town of Byzantium had till then played only a very secondary rôle, in spite of the theory which attributes to fine geographical sites a so-called inevitable value. Constantine allowed it to remain only as the nucleus of the new capital.[1] The new additions increased its area four or five fold. Begun in November, 324, it received the name of *Constantinopolis* from 326 at least. The inauguration took place on May 11th, 330.

The pagan temples which were boldly ransacked (their bronze doors, gilded roofs and statues were taken from them) served to adorn the New Rome. The administration, which had remained pagan, set up the statue of Tyché or Fortune, but in the old town, and, as soon as the Emperor was installed, he tolerated no manifestation of paganism in it. Constantine was so pleased with his capital that, except for some rare interruptions, he never left it till his dying day (May 22nd, 337).

Constantinople was born of the whim of a despot who was prey to intense religious exaltation. Nevertheless few con-certed measures of statesmanship have had more important and more lasting results. During a long series of centuries the destinies of a great State were bound up with this city. Over and over again Constantinople rebuilt the Empire. Greek civilization, both ancient and medieval, was saved from total destruction because it found on the Bosphorus an impregnable refuge. Nothing of all this would have been, without Constantine's will. But was this the object of his will ? It seems not.

The New Rome, according to his idea, was to be entirely Roman. He transported to it a part of the Senate and built palaces for the old families which he attracted there.[2] The laws were wholly Roman. The language of the Court and of the officers was Latin. The new Rome was to be the instru-ment of the Faith's triumph, and the capital of Christianity.

---

[1] For the plan see **CCCCLI**, vol. i. ; cf. OBERHAMMER in *Geograph. Jahr-buch*, vol. xxxiv.

[2] **CCLXXXVI, CCCXXIII**, vol. i., 186.

What actually happened was that Constantinople became once more a Greek city. Two centuries after its foundation, the descendants of the Romans who had been transplanted into the *pars Orientis* had forgotten the language of their fathers, no longer knew anything of Latin literature and looked upon Italy and the West as half-barbarous lands. By changing their language they had changed their soul. Constantine thought he was regenerating the Roman Empire, but without suspecting it he founded the Empire which is so justly called " Byzantine ". The unique services rendered to Hellenism had a disastrous counterpart in their effect on Latin civilization. Now that Rome is no longer a capital, the West is neglected and the *pars Orientis* will not hesitate to save itself by turning the blows of the Germans and the Huns against the Latin West, which they will shatter to fragments. This was not what was foreseen by Constantine, a Latin who knew little or no Greek.

By an unexpected turn, Rome ceases to be the stronghold of paganism and becomes the head of Christianity. The bishop's power rose, overcoming all resistance, and we see him taking in the West the place of the Emperor, when the throne is vacant. Between the old and the new Rome a conflict of religious authority arises, latent at first but afterwards becoming acute and ending in a radical rupture. Constantinople severs all ties and creates schism. That too was not the wish of Constantine, who passionately desired for the unity of faith.

Hence in spite of appearances, Constantine failed in his purpose.[1] But do great men accomplish exactly what they intend ? It is perhaps better that they should be powerless to dominate the latent forces which they have called to life and let loose upon the world without knowing precisely why.

Constantine's conversion is the most important fact in the history of the Mediterranean world between the establishment of the hegemony of Rome and the setting up of Islam. To it is due the triumph of Christianity, which by transforming human psychology, has dug an abyss between us and antiquity. Since the adoption of Christianity we have been living on a different plane.

---

[1] Broglie already realised the futility of his work.

Constantine made it triumph because his was a violent and despotic nature with strong convictions ; also, and above all, because he was able to employ in the service of his religious policy the tremendous forces which the Roman State entrusted to its head.

We must now draw up the balance sheet of gains and losses resulting to the State and the Church, from their marriage.

II. THE CONSEQUENCES FOR THE STATE

The gain, at the first glance, is not easy to discover.   One gain to the State was to disarm the hostility of a section of the subjects of the Empire. But this section, taken as a whole, formed but a minority and a submissive minority at that. The persecutions had never raised any serious revolts or even riots. Abasement before the authority of the Emperor was a tradition with the Christians. From the second century, in the time of Marcus Aurelius, the nascent episcopate makes advances to the government.[1] The open hostility of such people was not very formidable. Their passive resistance however was more to be feared. The Christian was by nature a bad citizen, refusing to take any interest in the things of this world. He was a sorry soldier or even shirked military service.

The attitude of Christians to the world was, it is true, bound to alter, as soon as the State embraced Christianity ; but doubtless the most eminent Christians did not consent in a single day to give up the best of their powers to the political and administrative life of the Roman State. For a long time " civil society had only the outcasts of the society of souls ".[2] Yet in order to rally to itself these poor and lukewarm citizens the Roman State displeased and afterwards persecuted the innumerable pagan sects.

We have just said that in the last years of his life, Constantine had abandoned toleration and begun to emphasize his hostility to paganism. His children imitated him. Constantius renewed the interdict against sacrifices and spared only those temples which were situated outside towns.

The pagan reaction of Julian was only a flash in the pan. At the end of the century, persecution began once more.

[1] CCCCV, 286, 384, 615.
[2] RENAN, CCCCV, 499.

Theodosius renewed (380) the interdict against sacrificing animals, but still tolerated incense. In 392 he forbade any rite whatsoever. Moreover, bishops and monks roused the people to pull down the temples and the government shut its eyes. Gratian (about 382) confiscated the revenues of the temples and of the priests. The last temples were destined to be closed by Justinian.

All the favours of the sovereign went as a matter of course to those who became Christians—that is to say Christians conforming to the theological opinions of the Emperor. The pagans were tolerated in the army, even at the head of the army when they were indispensable. Yet Honorius was careful to remove non-Catholic soldiers from service within the palace.

These violent measures, the insults to the gods of the State, the desertion of the Capitol, the suppression of the altar of Victory which adorned the Senate-house, exasperated or threw into consternation every class of the population, the highest or Senatorial class as well as the lowest. The polemics (at the end of the fourth and in the fifth century) between pagans and Christians show that these measures had shattered the confidence in the stability and future of the Roman State of a considerable, indeed the most considerable part of the population.[1]

Let us imagine a king of France anxious to be converted to Protestantism, the religion of a small section of his subjects, and animated by a pious zeal against " idolatry ", destroying or letting fall into ruins the most venerated sanctuaries of his kingdom, the abbey of Saint-Denis, the Cathedral of Rheims in which the most august acts of his reign take place, consigning to the flames the oriflamme and the crown of thorns which sanctifies the Sainte-Chapelle, and we shall have but a slight idea of the madness which seized the Roman Emperors in the fourth century.

This political folly succeeded because paganism had no unity of doctrine and no homogeneity. Being an aggregate of cults of every kind of origin, without any holy books, sometimes without even a regular clergy, it could offer no concerted resistance. Thus all the cults were exterminated one

---

[1] **XLIX,** vol. i., 94-99 ; vol. ii., 271, 301, 302, 341 ; **CXXVI,** vol. ii., 630 ; **XV,** 252 ; **CCLXXXVI, 146.**

by one while the panic-stricken populations were unable to offer any effective resistance to the Vandalism of the Christians. The Emperors thus succeeded without encountering any revolt.   But, from the point of view of statesmanship, the destruction of the old religion of the Roman city-state was unmitigated folly.

In the course of the fifth century, the pagans, who had been in a majority, become a minority ; in the sixth century their disappearance is complete. At the same time, the Christians were reconciled to earthly life and became attached, even very strongly attached, to the goods of this world. Would Christian society pour some of its strength into the State with which it was henceforth to live on good terms ? Yes, if the Church was united.

But it is rent at its heart and drags the State along in the career of its internal quarrels. It was an unhappy coincidence that the period of their union fell together with that of the great theological controversies about the essential nature of Christ and his relations to God the Father. Four centuries were needed for the establishment of Christology (325-680) from the first Ecumenical Council of Nicæa to the sixth Ecumenical Council of Constantinople. It brought about an unprecedented ferment in men's minds, troubled their conscience and embittered their feelings.

" Orthodoxy " had to be imposed by authority through a long series of acts of force. The inevitable result was that individuals and countries which refused to adopt this or that creed were bound to resist not merely the spiritual authority of a particular bishop or Council, but the Emperor who made the creed his own, and desired to impose it on all. Political rebellion was the inevitable consequence of religious opposition.

The controversy between Athanasians and Arians at once weakened the effect of Constantine's conversion. The State found itself immediately dragged into the vortex of theological disputes. Constantine was in ill luck. At the moment when, throwing all caution to the winds, he proclaimed his Christian faith and started proselytizing, the most passionate controversy which ever troubled the Christian world began to rage, concerning the nature of the tie which unites Christ to God the Father.[1]

---

[1] Apart from " Donatism " in Africa. See **CCCXVII, CCCXLV,** vol. iii.

The Arian controversy began about 318 at Alexandria.[1] Arius, a priest of the Church of Baucalis, noticed, or thought he noticed, " Sabellianism " in the views of his bishop concerning the Trinity, and retorted in emphatic terms by denying the eternity of the Son. The agitation was by no means calmed down when Alexander succeeded in getting Arius excommunicated by a council and forcing him to leave Egypt. On the contrary, from Palestine and Nicomedia Arius sent forth letters in which he formulated his doctrine more precisely. Being a very learned theologian and very competent in the handling of Aristotelian logic, he quickly won adherents.[1]

The chief concern of Arius was to avoid Ditheism without however falling into Sabellianism. One way only lay open for him, to subordinate the Logos to God the Father. But so far there was nothing new, since all teachers who had busied themselves with the same matters had, like him, made the Son subordinate. The originality of Arius lay not so much in his doctrine as in the uncompromising strictness of his reasoning.

It is not easy for one who is not a believer, to say wherein Arius' doctrine could be heretical. The doctrine of subordination had been the weapon which had enabled illustrious doctors of the Church to fend off Ditheism and Modalism. As for *homoousia*, it had been condemned by the Council of Antioch in 270. His opponents Alexander and above all the deacon Athanasius were obliged to formulate the contrary doctrine which till then had been vague. The " shattering clarity " of Arius no longer allowed men to rest satisfied with such vagueness. The Son is not of the nature of things made and created; therefore he has always existed, and the Father has always had the Son with him. They are inseparable. The Son, in principle, is perfect and infallible. Nevertheless Father and Son are two distinct persons, the Father alone being unbegotten.

The value of Arius' opponents lay not in their reasoning and dialectic, in which they were definitely inferior to him, but in the depth of their Christian feeling. Athanasius grasped at once that what was essential to Christianity, ever since the time of St. Paul, was the redemption. The latter

[1] **CXXVI**, vol. ii., 128; **CCIV**, 177; **CCCCVI**, 74; **CCCCLXXXIII**, vol. ii., 22, 30.

is possible only if God "enters into humanity". Consequently the Christ-Logos is God, fully God. Otherwise he would not be the Saviour, but only a hero after the ancient model, a man who had become a god. We see that as far as regards the relations of the Persons, Athanasius gets out of the difficulty as best he can. If there is any danger of being accused of Modalism, that is unfortunate, but "the interests of religion must come before everything".

Everyone, Catholics, Protestants and free-thinkers,[1] agrees that Athanasius defeated Arius in the struggle, because he was carried along by the rising wave of popular feeling which instinctively adopts every theory which exalts Christ, without troubling about the difficulties or even the contradictions bound to arise from his assimilation to God. This is the explanation of the final victory of the Athanasian Creed. But we must admit that to timid, conservative minds, opposed to all definition because to define means to innovate, Athanasius was as unbearable as Arius. Also we must not be surprised that the majority of bishops showed themselves irresolute, going from one side to the other according to circumstances.

Arianism at once received a crushing blow. Constantine, whom this commotion, of which he understood very little, took by surprise, was scandalized. His slumbers, he comically complains, were troubled. He implores his new brothers to have pity on him and not to draw down the wrath of Heaven. Resolved to put an end to this disturbance, the august policeman convoked a Council at Nicæa in June, 325. There issued from it the famous formula called the Nicene Creed.[2]

Arius and two bishops (Eusebius of Nicomedia and Theognis of Nicæa) were exiled. The triumph of those who later will be called the "orthodox" party is surprising. *Homoousia* was enforced rather than accepted. It seems certain that the Emperor exercised his influence on the Council.[3] If he sided with the party of the Bishop of Alexandria, it goes without saying that this was not from any theological conviction—he was too ignorant of the things of the spirit—but to

---

[1] So **XCI**, 235; **CXXVIII**, vol. vii., 103, 109, 114; **CXCVII**; **CCIV**, 183; **CCCCVI**, 77, 88-92, etc.

[2] Greek text in **CCCCLXXXIII**, vol. ii., 34; **CXXV**, vol. ii., 149.

[3] **CXXV**, vol. ii., 154; **XLIX**, vol. i., 72-75; **CCCCLVII**, vol. iii., 410, 553.

being acted on by personal influence, probably that of Hosius of Cordova. *A priori* he could not but be ill disposed towards Arius. An authoritarian like the Emperor always looks with disfavour on a subordinate disputing the opinion of his superiors. Arius' greatest error in the eyes of Constantine was, no doubt, that he was only a priest whereas Alexander was a bishop. The uncompromising nature of the condemnation in the creed, which is determined to allow no ambiguity to remain, is something unusual; it reveals a strong and dominating will, the will of the sovereign. It is a significant and disquieting fact that the first great Council held by the Church should have deliberated and voted under the pressure of a man who so short a while before had been a pagan.

The orthodox triumph was too swift and complete. Minds were not prepared for it.[1] The exiles were recalled. Constantine was circumvented by the Arians or the Semi-Arians, and it was from one of the exiles, Eusebius of Nicomedia, that he received baptism on his death-bed (May 22nd, 337).

In the period which followed, men of the middle, conservative party spent their efforts in the search for a formula of conciliation. Some thought they found it in the formula of ὁμοιουσία : the nature of Christ is similar (ὁμοιουσία) to that of the Father, but not identical with it (ὁμοουσία). The Semi-Arians were very numerous in the East, and the East has always been the brain of Christianity. They had on their side many bishops and the Emperor Constantius ; hence Athanasian orthodoxy was "completely routed" (Duchesne) in the middle of the fourth century. Imperial pressure caused Athanasius to be condemned (at Arles 353, and Milan 355). What is more, in 355, at Sirmium a declaration of submission is extorted from the old Hosius by an Arian. The Emperor abandoned the Nicene formula from 357 to 361.

Orthodoxy was saved by the accession of Julian, who with scornful disdain recalled Athanasius from exile. It could breathe again and draw up its ranks once more. The reign of Valens (364-378), a determined Arian, however, nearly brought about the ruin of orthodoxy. Under this reign the majority of the bishops in the *pars Orientis* were Anti-Nicene.

---

[1] "The Nicene formula had no tradition in its favour in the East, for even Alexander of Alexandria had spoken of three *hypostases* in the sense of *ousiai*." (Harnack, 195) ; **XCI**, 249.

Orthodoxy was saved this time by the West. In the course of the fourth century the number of Christians there had increased enormously, and these Christians suffered passively the influence of the only great episcopal see, that of Rome. The Bishop of Rome, no great theologian and more amenable to the inspiration of popular piety than the Eastern bishops, was Nicene, save for one defection, that of Pope Liberius.[1]

The Emperor Valentinian (364-375) was indifferent or impartial. Gratian (375-383) was under the influence of the Bishop of Rome, Damasus, and of the Bishop of Milan, Ambrose, both ardent Nicenes. At the death of Valens (378), Gratian took to himself as colleague in the East the Spaniard Theodosius, a Western Nicene. Theodosius in 381 convoked at Constantinople a Council,[2] which took up again the Nicene Creed, omitting ἐκ τῆς οὐσίας τοῦ πατρός. The Emperor restored (July 30th, 381) the Nicene bishops who had been deposed or exiled. Nevertheless it took long for the effects of this Council to make themselves felt. It was Ecumenical in name only (there were only 150 bishops, all of them Eastern). The Emperor had no doubt acted wisely in not convoking the Western bishops who were too stubborn and were in deadly conflict with the Eastern bishops. By a series of clever measures, Theodosius succeeded in slowly calming over-excited minds, so much so that Arianism died out in the East towards the beginning of the fifth century. In the West, it is true, Gratian, who was assassinated (383), was replaced by his brother Valentinian II, whose mother, Justina, was an Arian. But Valentinian could only keep his position by the help of Theodosius. As for the pagan reaction under the pseudo-Emperor Eugenius (394), it was immediately stifled. The day of Arianism was over; but in order to get rid of it, Catholicism had to have recourse to the coercion of the secular power.

In the course of this long controversy, there was a good deal of intellectual fuming and bitterness of feeling. The Emperor had sided now with one, now with the other doctrine, and had time after time set the whole of his subjects against

---

[1] P. BATIFFOL denies the defection of Liberius in XXII. Personally we have not been convinced by him.

[2] BATIFFOL, XXIII, 112-146.

him. To crown misfortune, chance would have it that Christianity should reach the barbarians, the Goths, Vandals and Burgundians, by way of Arian bishops (Ulfilas, Bishop in 341).

Now, since 376 the Visigoths had passed the barrier of the Danube and were encamped on Imperial territory in Mœsia, nominally as subjects of the Empire. The powers of absorption of *Romania*, already weakened, declined still more in consequence of doctrinal differences. The Arian Goths might doubtless have been assimilated by the Arian East, but this became impossible after the East had by order become Nicene.

III. THE CONSEQUENCES FOR THE CHURCH

The gains and losses of the Christian Church from its union with the State are far easier to determine.

The gains.—These are striking. From a persecuted minority the Christian Church suddenly becomes all-powerful. From Constantine onwards, it is the first institution in the State.

The assertion is repeatedly made that the triumph of Christianity was inevitable ; sooner or later it was bound to come. It is easy to say this. We forget that Christianity was not the only religious power to appeal to the masses. It had competitors, four or five of them formidable ones. It is certain that the ancient Roman religion had for a long time been completely outworn. The faded old Latin cults had from the time of the Republic been assimilated for better or worse to the Greek Pantheon. But if this syncretism had given Roman religion more variety, poetry and colour, it had yet been unable to produce a philosophy and morality for it.[1] The first Emperors realized so well that the ancient cults were no longer anything but an empty husk that they applied themselves to establishing the worship of Rome and of Augustus as a prop for the national sentiment of the greater Rome. It has been said that this worship was neither so artificial nor so degrading as has been thought. Still the fact remains that it was a political rather than a religious rite, and it was bound to perish as soon as the party chiefly interested, the Emperor, should cease to uphold it.

For food to appease their hunger for mysticism, and for an answer to the anxious questions as to man's fate after death,

[1] **XLIX, LI, CCCCLII—III, DVI, CCLXX.**

Greeks and Romans alike went to Oriental religions.[1] Whatever the superiority of the Christian religion over its rivals
may have been, propaganda alone would not have been
sufficient to ensure its triumph, or even numerical superiority.[2]
For this it had to capture the all-powerful forces at the disposal
of the Emperor.

We may think that in default of Constantine, some other
Emperor might have become converted. In the first place,
this is not in the least certain. In the second place, would the
moment have been equally favourable ? It is quite certain
that Constantine's conversion came at a critical and decisive
moment. Let us imagine the Emperor taking no interest
in theological controversies. The Arian crisis would have
come all the same. Who would then have enforced unity of
doctrine ? The Emperor himself, as we have seen, only succeeded in doing so after sixty years of struggles—and the
movements which followed (Nestorianism, Monophysism,
etc.) instead of being separated by an interval of time would
have started at once. How can we believe that this Christianity, torn asunder by such deep cleavages, would have preserved its power of expansion and have offered any great
attraction to a pagan Emperor ?

Church historians agree in recognizing the fact that the
fourth century controversies, in spite of appearances, had a
more serious importance than the sects of the second and
third centuries, which were maladies from which the fresh
and robust organism of the Christian Church recovered by
itself. Constantine's conversion is thus a " miracle ".[3]
It saved the Church. And the Church has felt the truth of
this so strongly that it has forgiven him everything, his
crimes and even his baptism, performed by a bishop more than
suspect of Arianism.

Straightway the Church—through its representatives, the
bishops—attached itself passionately to the State and made
many concessions to it. The episcopate was " bewitched "

---

[1] **XCV—CCCCVII—CCCCLXXXIV.** On the mysteries proper : P. FOUCART,
Des Associations religieuses chez les Grecs (1873) and *Mystères d'Éleusis* (1904).
REITZENSTEIN, *Die hellenistischen Mysterien, ihre Grundlage und Wirkung*
(1910).

[2] We should not be misled in this matter by the comparative ease with
which the Emperors imposed Christianity. There are other examples of a
despotic power enforcing the ruler's views on his subjects.

[3] HARNACK, **CCIV,** 135, 138, 141.

by Constantine. The heads of the men who but the day before had been persecuted and were now the ruler's intimate councillors, were turned. "Authority loves authority. Men as conservative as the bishops must have felt an overpowering temptation to become reconciled with the public power whose action they recognized as working most often for good. The hatred between Christianity and the Empire is the hatred of those who some day must love each other ".[1]

At bottom, the Church felt the need of the secular arm. As it went on organizing itself, it felt more and more the Catholic need for unity and realized the impossibility of triumphing over dissenters without the help of force. The excommunicated heretic could set up chapel against chapel. It was impossible to exterminate him without having recourse to public authority. Very significant is the affair of Paul of Samosata. To rid themselves of their excommunicated colleague, the Fathers of the Council of Antioch appealed to the Emperor Aurelian, a devotee of the worship of the Sun, who was soon afterward to issue an edict against the Christians. No shame was felt in asking the pagan to exile the Christian bishop whose opinions did not conform to those of his colleagues (about 270).

The Christian Church was not organized for civil and political life.[2] In its expectation of the "Kingdom" it had for a long time dwelt in a provisional abode. When it felt itself becoming a majority and a power in the State, and became reconciled to the idea of living the life of this world, it became aware that it had omitted to work out a code of private and public law which alone makes normal existence possible. Such a law existed, Roman law, the most perfect ever known. The Church adopted it and fitted itself into the framework of the ancient legal institutions. In consequence, it had to submit and to submit completely to the organism which maintained these institutions. The only precaution which it took, a very wise one, was to get its clergy exempted from the ordinary jurisdiction.[3]

---

[1] RENAN, CCCCV, 615, 618 ; cf. CLXXXV; CCCCVI, 73 ; CCCCLV, 82.
[2] CCCCXXVIII, vol. ii., 469-509.
[3] But these privileges lasted only for a time and were withdrawn, for the most part, by the great Emperor's successors. The *privilegium fori* in criminal matters seems to have been granted only between 412 and 452. See further XXVII, 67 ; CCLXXVIII—CCCCLXXXVII.

Much more did Christianity lack the military organization which would one day be indispensable in the struggle against a dread rival, Islam. More than ever it will have need of the strong arm of the layman to defend itself, and this need will prevent it from absorbing everything, and with or against its will, it will bend it to the powers of the world.[1]

The losses.—These are above all ethical.

Leaning on the State and disposing of the State, the Church will very quickly become intolerant and persecuting. From Theodosius onwards the pagans are hunted down. Relapses to paganism or to Judaism are punished by Gratian and Theodosius in May, 381 and 383 (Cod. Theodos., xvi., 7, 1 and 3) and Roman orthodoxy is imposed " on all the peoples which our clemency rules ", February 28th, 380. Heresy is treated as a crime and so is schism under Honorius. Exile will not suffice : torture and punishment will be used even against Christian dissenters.

In short, the Christian Church will fight against every independent opinion. It will wish to kill all free thought, and it is almost incomprehensible that it did not succeed.

For the help of the State, the Church must pay by sub-mitting to the State.[2] From the Council of Arles (August, 314) onwards, it offers to excommunicate those who refuse to do military service.[3] From this to the approval of the faults and crimes of the state is but a step, too easily taken.

The Church becomes accustomed to employing the secular arm for conversions. It grows impaired and loses its powers of assimilation. Personal propaganda will cease from about the fifth century. Henceforth Christianity will try and obtain recruits only by angling for the confidence of barbarian kings and their courts. Once the ruler has been won over, he is used for imposing the faith on his subjects by gentle or violent pressure.

Further, the victory was too swift and complete. These herds of Roman and later of barbarian pagans, thrust by consent or force into the bosom of the Church, debased and changed Christian feeling. These multitudes surreptitiously

---

[1] ESMEIN considers that the Church is not so much absorbed in as by the State (*Droit constitutionnel*, 6th ed., p. 1179). Jean CRUET looks upon it as a " disaffected State " (*La vie du droit*, p. 220).

[2] CCLXVII, vol. iii., 228 ; CCCCLV.

[3] CCVII, 87 ; CDLXXXIX, 2nd series, 158.

re-introduced into Christianity the superstitions and polytheism which were abhorrent to it. It is not that the worship of the saints is the worship of the gods, disguised under a new name. The examples brought forward in support of this are few and of no great import; the substitutions must have gone on without the knowledge of the clergy who had a keen scent for pagan mildew of every kind.[1] But these too rapidly converted masses brought to the Church insufficiently purged hearts in which the seeds of paganism, not entirely dead, throve once more. Paganism is the weed which continually shoots up anew in Catholicism.[2]

Having become the majority, Christian society saw the level of its morality fall. The Church, vastly enlarged, could no longer remain the society of the pure and saintly, who in fear and trembling await with mortifications the end of the world. Now that it was identified or nearly identified with the " World ", the Church was profoundly under the degrading influence of life, and this was fatal, the world being evil.[3] There was only one way of escape : to live artificially outside the world by seeking the desert or solitude, shutting oneself up alone as a recluse or collectively in a monastery. It is no accident that hermit, and later, monkish asceticism first appears in the East at the very moment of the Church's triumph.[4]

Unwelcome in the West, asceticism yet imposes itself irresistibly in the fifth and sixth centuries. The monastery appears as the only means of realizing Christian life, the world being no longer fit for it ; the convent is the only possible Kingdom of God on this earth.[5] Henceforth " to take up a religious life " will mean renouncing the life of this world. A dualism and even an opposition is established between the religious and the social life.

By an inevitable rebound, the world will feel itself incurably depraved and powerless against the forces of evil. It will leave the task of interceding for it before God to the solitaries

---

[1] The theories of Gelzer, Usener, Saintyves, etc., have been submitted to a penetrating criticism by P. DELAHAYE, **CIX.**

[2] **CCCCLXXXV.**

[3] " To be able to live, every Church must compromise with the Devil " says Élie HALÉVY (*Hist. du peuple anglais au xix*ᵉ *s.*, vol. i., 268.)

[4] **XIV, XVI, XXXV, XXXVI, CCVI—CCVIII, CCCCLXX,** 47 ; **DXXI.**

[5] **CCCCV,** 167, 208, 241, 627, HARNACK (*Essence du christianisme*, p. 102-112) protests against the idea that the Gospel is ascetic and monkish.

and saints, who replace the martyrs now that persecution has ceased. Trusting in them, the world will put off the burden of virtue and quickly resign itself to living a poor, a very poor Christian life. Its demands for strictness will be confined wholly to the saints (monks and bishops). As regards them, men's veneration is exacting and suspicious. The more depraved men are, the more strict guardians are they of the virtue of their pastors. The reason is that this virtue is the sinner's safeguard. It alone stops the sluices of God's wrath perpetually suspended over a wicked world. Hence Renan's pessimistic aphorism that " Christianity foundered in its victory " is not wholly false.[1]

Our conclusion is then that if the State made a bad bargain, the Church on its side, while realizing a gross material profit, suffered terrible spiritual losses.

What then was the point of this union ? Is it not possible to imagine that it would have been better for this ill-assorted pair never to have united ?

The State might have given up persecution and remained impartial and neutral without letting itself be dragged into the vortex of controversy. It might have confined itself to its task of policing and to preventing people from killing each other.

The Church, relying only on its moral strength and on supernatural intervention, might have refrained from forcing the pagans to desert the temple for the basilica, and from persecuting dissenters. It would have remained a minority and have become a majority only through free proselytism. This would have taken it a few centuries more, but would not this have been preferable to the risks incurred by being invaded by the semi-pagan or semi-orthodox ? Besides, was it right for it to spend its best forces in the attempt to achieve strict dogma, at the risk of neglecting the deeper sources of religious life, fed by feelings and not by metaphysical formulæ ? Such a view is fanciful because it is entirely modern.

Every Church is militant by nature, because it believes itself to be in possession of absolute truth. The Christian Church could not allow " the light to lie hid under a bushel ". Proselytism is a vital necessity, while proselytism by force is a pitfall, but an inevitable one, the attraction of which no

[1] CCCCV, 634.

dogma can escape. Respect for the convictions of opponents and modern tolerance are the fruit, found only in a few people, of the development of conscience or of a conviction that belief in absolute truth is an intellectual disease. With most men they are the result of a great weariness. With recuperation of strength, we may notice that intolerance immediately recovers its virulence.

In every union one of the pair dominates over the other. The result in this respect has been different in the East from what it was in the West.

In the East, the Church from the first gave the Emperor such an important rôle, that afterwards it found it impossible to put him back in his proper place. In the sixth, seventh and eighth centuries, the Emperor plays a predominating part not merely in the external but also in the internal, doctrinal history of the Church, which relies on him to crush dissenters. In the Greek Christian Church and in its daughter Churches, the Bulgarian, Russian, etc., the clergy will always be dominated by the supreme lay power. In this respect, the institution of Cæsaro-Papism, which was the scourge of Eastern Christianity, must recognize for its founder Constantine himself.[1]

In the West, things nearly turned out differently, because after 476 there was no longer an Emperor. It has been said : " The Empire was destroyed in appearance only ; its secrets were kept alive by the higher Roman Church officials ".[2] It is also claimed that " The Roman Church crept insidiously into the place of the Roman Empire. Indeed, the latter was continued in the former. The Pope, the *Pontifex maximus*, succeeded Cæsar. The Pope is the Emperor ".[3]

These views are only partially right. At the moment when the Pope becomes identified in Italy with the *Respublica Romanorum* (the middle of the eighth century) it is far too late to replace the Emperor. The Church in Italy also had borne the yoke of the Emperor of the West, then that of the Gothic King and finally (from 557) the far heavier one of the Byzantine Emperor. Subsequently in order to fight against the

---

[1] GELZER, **CLVIII**; HAHN, **CC**, ch. 5, 6; STREHL, **CCCCLXX**, 545; HARNACK, *Essence*, 270.

[2] RENAN, **CCCCV**, 624.

[3] HARNACK, **CCVI**, 300, and *Essence*, 294, 301.

Lombard domination, it had been obliged to call in the Franks. The latter were protectors rather than masters. But, in 800, the papacy committed the great mistake of raising up a phantom of the Western Empire, powerless to bring back the Roman Empire but quite capable of oppressing the Church.

In spite of all its efforts, the Church was never destined to succeed in dominating the State. The real reason for this was, as we have seen, that the Christian Church had not been constituted for the life of this world. It brought to society no new legal or social idea. Consequently it accepted without any opposition and without any real distaste the institutions of the Roman State. The latter was able to preserve its framework and continued its life. Still more did this apply to the barbarian States, which had been only superficially Christianized.

The medieval and modern State, which is partly the heir of the Roman State, has therefore not been able to be absorbed by the Church. All imbued as it is with Christianity it has yet preserved the consciousness of being a thing apart from the Church. If the State had not been deeply rooted in the Roman past, the medieval State would have dissolved in the Church, and the Church in the State, and it is impossible to see how the modern conception of the separation between the religious consciousness and the State could have developed or even have been born.

Therein lies the secret of the profound difference, far more profound than is recognized, between Christian and Moslem States. Islam brings with it not only a religion but also a system of laws and a political theory the equivalent of which it would be vain to look for in the Gospel. But even this way of speaking is not quite accurate : laws, customs, usages even are all indistinguishable in religion. And as its law, polity, and usages are elementary, made for an undeveloped society, it is a superhuman task to adapt a Moslem society to modern life. Here religion will not be content with its proper share. It is useless to try and put it in its place, for its place is everywhere or nowhere.[1]

---

[1] Renan, *L'Islamisme et la Science*, lecture at the Sorbonne, March 29th, 1883 ; Goldziher, **CLXXV** ; cf. two remarkable anonymous articles in the *Revue de Paris*, Jan. 15th and Sept. 1st, 1916.

CHAPTER IV

Economic Retrogression of the Roman World

I. THE MONETARY AND ECONOMIC CRISES

IT is an established fact that the Roman world underwent a most serious economic upheaval, from the third century and even from the second half of the second century onwards. It is equally certain that this fact involved political and social consequences of the first importance. These we may express by saying that " the Empire from the third century onwards is a preparation for the Middle Ages ".

The most evident signs of this economic upheaval are presented to us by the debasement of the coinage and the chaos of prices. At the end of the Roman Republic monetary economy had, from a period dating far back, succeeded what is called " natural " or domestic economy, in which exchange values exist hardly or not at all. Each estate, large or small, furnishes all that is necessary for the subsistence of the family, and the products in kind are consumed on the spot or at the most are exchanged for other products in kind, e.g., wine for oil if the estate does not produce enough olives, etc.

But the Mediterranean world had long since left this stage behind,[1] the Greek countries before the fifth century B.C., Latin Italy about the third century. Monetary economy was even far enough advanced for Julius Cæsar to be able to make one of the precious metals, gold, the standard of value ; he had adopted the gold standard as we should say. Cæsar struck the *aureus* in the proportion of forty to the pound, or 8.180 grammes, i.e., of the intrinsic value of about 27.71 francs.[2] The gold and silver issues were plentiful, the value of gold being approximately twelve times that of silver. In the first century under Nero we notice a slight deterioration in the coinage. The *aureus* weighs 7.4 grammes or 7.6 grammes (value of about 25 francs). As for the silver

---

[1] **CDXXX, CLXIX, CCCXXVIII.**
[2] Pre-war value, i.e., over £1 (Translator's note).

coinage, whereas the practice was to strike only 84 denarii
to the Roman pound of 327 grammes, which made each denarius 3.90 grammes in weight (value in modern money 0.86 francs),
Nero struck 96, reducing the weight of the denarius to
3.41 grammes (value in modern money 0.75 francs). Under
the Antonines the deterioration becomes more marked. It
becomes worse under Septimius Severus. The gold piece
has from 50 to 60 per cent. base metal ; the issue diminishes, a
proof that the metal has become rare.[1]

As for silver coins, base metal was present in the proportion
of from 50 to 60 per cent., and the real value of the denarius
fell to 0.40 or 0.30 francs, while the legal tender remained
the same, the Emperor's effigy on the coin giving it a forced
circulation.

As the third century advances, the fall becomes more and
more rapid. The only money in circulation is the *antoninianus* struck by Caracalla. Its weight is irregular and the
make abominable. The proportion of base metal rises to 90,
95, 98.5 per cent. under the reigns of Gallienus and of
Claudius II, when the *antoninianus* is only a piece of copper
or of lead with a thin covering of silver. As Mommsen says, it
is nothing more than a " metal assignat ". In spite of Imperial
commands, prices suffered from corresponding upheavals.
Never had the world seen such an economic disorder. Aurelian's efforts to remedy this state of things were fruitless.
Diocletian succeeded in the difficult task of restoring a sound
coinage. In 296 he resumed the issue of silver coins on the
basis of 96 to the Roman pound. Constantine continued
and completed the reform. Gold coins reappeared, though
doubtless they were much rarer.[2]

Diocletian's attempt to fix a maximum price for provisions,
salaries, and articles of common use (301) met with a very
different fate, resulting in complete failure and in Constantine's revoking the edict.[3] In spite of these measures, the
distress of the Roman world continued.[4] Unmistakable signs
make it clear that society was in a state of economic retrogression, monetary economy yielding more and more to

[1] Cf. above, pp. 18-19.
[2] XIII, CCCXXII.
[3] XLVI ; D.
[4] CCLXVII, vol. iii., 226.

natural or domestic economy. More than one step backward
was taken.

The State received the land-tax very often, indeed most
often, in kind, although in theory it reserved to itself the right
of demanding payment in money or in kind according to its
needs.[1] It devolved on the governors to inform the Urban
Prefect (entrusted with the provisioning of Rome) of the
state of prices of provisions in their province. Constantine
regulated in the most minute detail the collection of tributes
in kind and their transportation to the public stores. In 363
Julian had to order that the collection in Campania should
be in money.

In addition, the tax-payers were liable to requisitions of
foodstuffs (*cellaria*) according to the nature and the products
of their country ; bread, wine, oil, vinegar, lard, bacon,
fodder for cattle, wood, equipment, cloth, vessels, beasts of
burden (horses, mules). In Thrace 20 *capita*, in Scythia
and Mœsia 30, in the East and in Egypt 33 *juga* had to con-
tribute a *vestis*. These dues also could be commuted into
money, if the administration in view of the price-level thought
this commutation profitable.

The *annonariæ species* and the *annonariæ functiones* (dues)
were bound to entail all kinds of cartage and forced labour,
seeing that it was necessary to transport the products delivered
as taxes or requisitions to the State granaries and stores.
Such a system is detrimental to the tax-payer whose time and
work it wastes. It is also detrimental to the State because of
the inevitable losses in the provisions in the stores from
theft and embezzlement of all kinds. It has been calculated
that under the system of taxation in kind two-thirds of the
revenue are lost on the way. On their side the tax-payers,
who paid in kind the land tax on which the State subsisted,
were paid in kind by their *coloni*. Valentinian I forbade
landowners to exact dues in money, except in districts where
such payment was the established custom.[2]

To these receipts in kind corresponded salaries in kind.
The Imperial annona and manufactures fed and clothed the
Court. Magistrates (governors), counts, all the upper civil

[1] **LX,** vol. ii., 240 ; **XLII,** 282, 294 ; **CCCXLIV,** vol. x., 279, 291 ; **CCXLII,**
vol. i., 375 ; **DIII,** vol. ii., 92 ; **CDXL,** vol. ii., 71.
[2] **CCCCXXX,** 213, 253 ; O. Seeck in **CCCXCVII,** vol. iv, 508.

service staff were entitled to requisitions by way of salary, Some of them abused this right to the point of crushing the peoples. Doctors, architects and professors lived on annonæ.[1] What is far more serious, the army's pay tended more and more to be in kind. Under the Early Empire, the soldiers' pay was 225 denarii (since Domitian 300) for the legionaries, 375 for the urban cohorts, and 750 for the Prætorians. The soldier paid for his food, clothes, weapons and camping outfit, the cost of all these being taken out of his pay.

Under the Republic, only the allies had provisions in kind instead of pay. In addition to the pay there were extraordinary largesses, *donativa*, distributed in money on solemn occasions (like the accession of the Emperor, etc.); half was paid into a fund where it formed a *peculium* (the *castrense peculium*) under the guardianship of the standard-bearer of the legion.

On leaving the army, the veteran received a pension of 12,000 sesterces (3,000 denarii) in the case of a legionary and 20,000 (5,000 denarii) in the case of a Prætorian.[2]

The army being the real master of the State, it will not be surprising to find the practice of pay continuing for a long time. We know that Septimius Severus left behind him the precept " Make the soldiers rich and do not trouble about the rest ". Caracalla increased the pay by 70,000,000 drachmæ (denarii). His father had raised the legionary's pay to 500 denarii, on condition that he kept himself and his family. Severus Alexander was wont to say : " The soldier must have a full purse ".[3] Maximian (235-238) gorged the army with gold. These Emperors and their successors distributed extravagant largesses which far from appeasing the armies' greed only served to rouse it. The Senator Tacitus (275-276) was raised to the throne because of his vast fortune, but six months of distributing to the troops were enough to scatter it.

It would be rash to assert that the change from pay in money to pay in kind took place from the middle or from the second half of the third century.[4] It would even be inaccurate to say that in the following century pay in money disappeared entirely. No general measure was taken with regard to this,

---

[1] DI, vol. iii., 227.
[2] LIII, 223, 286 ; CCCXXXII, 263 ; CCCLI, 112 ; especially CXXII, 218-241.
[3] XV, 233.
[4] CCCLI, vol. ii. 185, 317.

and here and there an allusion shows that pay in money continued in the middle of the fourth century. It continued, but in a diminished form, reduced to insignificance. It seems probable that after Constantine the soldier received money only on special occasions such as the elevation of a new Emperor, etc.; what continues is the *donativum* rather than the regular pay. Under Julian, in the middle of the fourth century, every common soldier received an annona, that is, a contribution in kind; even the *protectores*, the successors of the centurions, received six annonæ.

The pension also is no longer paid in specie. Officers and veterans receive lands, on the products of which they must keep themselves and their families; for since the time of Septimius Severus they are married. These lands (*fundi limitrophi*) are chosen from land on the frontiers, and, in the fourth century, the property passes to the son if he consents to serve in the army.

The absence of specie, entailing the disappearance of pay, was destined to lead, by way of economy, in place of the too costly Roman armies, to the preference for barbarian troops using their own weapons, fighting under their own chiefs, and receiving lands as pay for their services. This evolution has been well perceived by Montesquieu, who says in his *Considérations :* "The inability to meet these expenses (pay and largesses to the army) led to the taking on of a less expensive military organization. Treaties were made with barbarian nations who had neither the luxury of Roman soldiers, nor the same spirit, nor the same pretentions."[1]

The inevitable consequences of a system which allows services rendered to be rewarded only by means of salaries in kind, or distributions of land, are easily seen. They lead to the so-called feudal system or to an analogous system. In all the States in which this system has appeared, it is seen to co-exist with natural economy and to disappear or fade with economic changes.

We are now faced with a problem of the highest importance. How can we explain the fact that the Roman world, economically prosperous at the end of the Republic and during the first two centuries of the Empire, was irreparably ruined ? The

---

[1] 1734 edition, chap. xviii. Cf. DUREAU DE LA MALLE, **CXXVII**, vol. ii., 439 ; MARQUARDT, **CCCXLIV**, vol. x., 291, n.7.

storm of the third century was terrible in its political consequences, and the monetary system suffered serious upheavals. But Aurelian, Diocletian and Constantine set the Roman world on its feet once more, refounded the administration, improved the financial system, and the currency again became nearly as good as in the first century. Nevertheless, nothing could stop the downfall, which only became more marked in the course of the fourth and the fifth centuries.

This is a very surprising phenomenon to us, who are accustomed to an ever-growing prosperity.[1] A commercial crisis or a war may interrupt this prosperity but we are convinced that after a more or less long period of arrest, business will recover and that the production of wealth will never stop. Why do we have this conviction ? Because we live under the capitalist system, under which all the forces of society are bent on the production of values which are sold in wider and wider markets.

Was it the same with Antiquity ? In other words, had Antiquity any knowledge of a real capitalist system ?

This question the majority of the historians of this period do not hesitate to answer in the affirmative. They point to the system of monetary economy tending to replace the system of domestic economy in a far-distant past, twenty to thirty centuries before our era, in the valleys of the Tigris and the Euphrates.

Even Egypt, feudal for a long time, was to learn the monetary system from the time of the new Empire onwards, beginning with the sixteenth century before our era. The Persian Empire of the Achæmenids, ever since its re-organization under Darius, shows an interesting combination of natural and monetary economy, at least in the Western Provinces.

Coming now to Greece, the Mycenæan age bears witness to a wholesale Oriental influence, which cannot be explained without a developed commercial intercourse. Then comes a period of retrogression, the Greek " Middle Ages ", the heroic age in which a military aristocracy lives on the fruits of agriculture and especially on its flocks. The Iliad depicts the end of this period. Economy is entirely domestic ; everything is made in the home. The working of metal is the only or practically the only profession of specialists, χάλκεις

---

[1] [Written in 1914.]

(cf. the Bible), but life does not pass beyond the limits of the village.

Hesiod still depicts society sunk in agricultural and natural economy. Nevertheless he knows trade by sea, which however he fears. The Odyssey, considerably later than the Iliad, also has knowledge of the trader.

In the eighth and seventh centuries, the Greeks traversed the Mediterranean as pirates and later as merchants. What did they carry from one end to the other of this inland sea ? Some products of their soil or of their sea (oil from Attica, wine from Chios and Lesbos, purple from Cythera, copper from Cyprus and Eubœa, silver from the mines of Laurium in Attica), and above all, manufactured articles ; cloth, carpets, clothes, arms, metal wares, pottery, etc.[1]

These articles pre-suppose an advanced technique, crafts practised by skilled workmen, and consequently workshops. All this goes far beyond the natural, domestic economy stage. What is more, the style of these articles (the vases, for example) shows that certain places specialize in particular manufactures ; the beautiful vases in Italy and Sicily come from Corinth and Chalcis. From the beginning of the sixth century, one of these cities, Athens, gains commercial pre-eminence over all the rest. Attica, whose soil is so poor, being over-populated, this pre-eminence cannot be explained without the existence of an industry feeding a wholesale export trade.

Free hands not sufficing any longer, instruments of labour are procured by the purchase of slaves. It is only from the fifth and fourth centuries and up to the first that the number of slaves increases enormously in the Mediterranean world ; the commercial significance of slavery is shown clearly by the fact that the towns in which there is the biggest traffic in slaves are the most important commercial centres : Miletus in Asia, and in Greece Chalcis, Corinth and lastly Ægina, the small rocky and barren island which in the sixth century is the market of the Greek world. At the same time, the population of each πόλις is concentrated in the town, which begins to lord it over the country. Finally, the use of metal coinage (originating in Lydia) spreads very rapidly. The development of slavery, and even the political revolutions, cannot be conceived from the sixth century onwards without rich

[1] **CLXXXIX, CXCI, CCCXXVIII, CLXIX.**

and populoustowns. Wholesale trade ('Εμπορική) becomes differentiated from retail trade (Καπηλική) and the big merchant ('Εμπορος) is opposed to the tradesman (Κάπηλος).

We need not hesitate to compare the economic development of the Greek world in the seventh and sixth centuries B.C. with that of the fourteenth and fifteenth centuries A.D., and the fifth century B.C. with the sixteenth century A.D.

In the chief town, which became the centre of the life of each πόλις, the political system underwent profound modifications. At Corinth, at Ægina, and later at Rhodes (cf. Carthage), the power was usurped by the aristocracy of the rich merchants. Elsewhere (at Argos, Syracuse, Tarentum, above all at Athens) revolutions which were generally sanguinary, secured the elimination of the urban middle class, which was by no means idle, as has been asserted, but a hard-working class consisting of small artisans.

New commercial centres arose : Rhodes, later Delos and especially Alexandria in Hellenistic Egypt. The economics of the Hellenistic world (third and second centuries) are thus comparable if not to those of the nineteenth, at any rate to those of the seventeenth and eighteenth centuries.

The comparison may be pursued further. The downfall of Greece after Alexander's conquests presents striking analogies with modern facts. Its abandoned agriculture and dwindling population recall the agricultural crisis of nineteenth century England. The cause is analogous. The Oriental world, capable of infinitely richer economic returns than the poor territory of Greece, was opened to the activity of the Greeks, just as the discovery of the New World opened up new fields for the activity of Englishmen and Spaniards.

Rome too, which had been immersed for many centuries in natural economy, rapidly freed itself from it. The competition of Sicilian, Egyptian and African agriculture caused an agrarian crisis, while its conquests meant a great influx of metals and objects of value kept in the hands of the aristocracy. The latter monopolized the land, lent money to foreign states and to their fellow-citizens, and went in for speculations of every kind. The first century B.C. saw the apogee of slavery ; armies of slaves were employed not only in the performance of domestic tasks, but in industrial manufacture. There was thus a Roman capitalism and this capitalism succeeded in stifling and crushing all the other classes of society.

" Consequently, Antiquity . . . cannot present any difference from modern times from the economic point of view. It is only a crude popular belief which has given credit to the myth that the historical development of the Mediterranean peoples has proceeded continuously in an ascending line. This belief finds support in the tripartite division of history into *Antiquity*, *The Middle Ages*, and *Modern Times*. As very primitive conditions of life are found in the Middle Ages, people imagine they can reason from them to still more primitive conditions in Antiquity. On the contrary, Antiquity was far more advanced than the Middle Ages."[1]

Let us see whether at Rome capital was " invested ", as is asserted, in industry and commerce, in which case the existence of capitalism could not be called in question.

II. CAPITAL AND INDUSTRY. POPULATION

From a very early period of Roman history, the crafts became freed from the household, or from domestic economy, to be at the service of the public. Specialization in the crafts and the division of labour were far advanced from the third and second centuries B.C. onwards.[2] Crafts and trades, sometimes organized into " colleges ", tending to gather in particular streets. The town dweller could find bakers from whom to purchase bread, shops where fried fish was sold, inns, barbers' and clothiers' shops.[3] But even this does not imply any industrial capitalist production. To-day Persian carpets and china pottery, manufactured to be sent to the furthest corners of the world, are still turned out in family workshops, and do not pre-suppose real capitalist economics. Only certain articles of luxury (vases, wrought iron articles, textiles, jewels, etc.), bear witness to a real division of labour. They alone are manufactured to be sold in an often distant market.

---

[1] Résumé by SALVIOLI, **CDXXX**, p. 13-14, whose own views are directly opposed to the existence of real capitalism in Antiquity.

[2] BLUEMNER, **XLIII, XLIV** ; GUMMEURS, **CXCV**.

[3] Lists of trades connected with the clothing industry in MARQUARDT, **CCCXLIV**, *Vie privée*, French trans., vol. ii., p. 227. Mommsen's reconstruction of Diocletian's edict of maximum prices may also be read. On technique, see GROTHE, **CLXXXII**, YATES, **DXIV**, and the work of Hugo BLUEMNER, **XLV**.

But in fact capital, which was so plentiful at the end of the Republic and the beginning of the Empire, was not applied or was applied only to a small extent to industry. This already constitutes a profound and essential difference between Roman and modern or contemporary economics.

Why was no attempt made to invest money in industry ?

In the first place because of the obstacle of domestic economy. The latter was deeply rooted in the prevailing habits. Every great *villa* possessed not merely its hand-mills, bake-houses, workshops for agricultural requirements (a forge, a carpenter's shop), but also workshops for weaving and clothes, entrusted to the women and slaves. The aristocracy kept embroiderers, gilders, chasers, goldsmiths, painters, architects, sculptors, hairdressers, who were either slaves or freedmen. " Rich families felt a kind of vainglory in being able to say that all the needs of the house could be satisfied by the work within the house itself ; thus everything was manufactured in the house, even articles of luxury." To buy things outside was considered a kind of disgrace.[1]

On the other hand, modern capitalism has succeeded, at least in Western Europe, in entirely breaking down domestic industry, by making use of progress in technique. Now it is a significant fact that the technique of the crafts does not seem to have made any appreciable progress amongst the Romans.

We have here a very important special case of the phenomenon of the paralysis of invention which shows itself in all the spheres of human activity, art, literature, science and philosophy, in Greece as early as the second century B.C., in Rome in the second century A.D.

In the absence of technical improvement, capital was not required for investment in industry, while the inventive spirit, in its turn, was not stimulated by the prospect of the profits to be brought to it by capital from applying itself to

---

[1] FRIEDLAENDER, French trans., vol. iii., suppl., p. 6. Cf. Russia even in the middle of the nineteenth century : *Autour d'une vie* by Prince Peter KROPOTKINE, 1902, p. 35. At the beginning of the winter, 25 sledge-loads of peasants or serfs bring from a very great distance, from the large estates, the provisions for the winter (oats, wheat, rye, frozen poultry) ; the list of the articles to be brought by each village, drawn up by the lord himself, fills several pages. Every large family of the high aristocracy boasts of possessing coachmen, footmen, chefs, pastry-cooks, tailors, embroiderers, shoe-makers, barbers, goldsmiths, musicians (p. 26) ; there are about 150 servants in the house.

the improvement of industrial technique. These reciprocal actions and reactions of the inventive spirit and of capitalism, so marked in Europe as early as the eighteenth century and even before, did not exist in the Roman world.

But in the absence of machines and improved tools, could not the employment of human hands at a low or at a minimum price, the employment of slaves, attract capital ? Only for a moment. There have been some important enterprises started with slaves.[1]

At Rome also some attempts were made. Contractors and capitalists thought they would do good business by making profits by the work of slaves trained to practise crafts. But the profits soon showed themselves very slender. In the first place money had to be spent on buying the slave, or else, if he was already in the house, on training him, teaching him his craft. If a crisis arises, the slave has still to be kept, however inadequately.

Above all, his working capacity and his yield are very inferior to those of the free man,[2] the margin being so small that the master's profits may vanish altogether. If people kept gangs of slaves (and they did this only up to about the second century) it was from vanity and for show, rather than for any very tangible advantages. Finally, as the master wishes to use his slaves for everything, for labours of the field as well as for town crafts, he cannot carry the division of labour very far.

Thus the economics of slavery are proved to be essentially anti-capitalist. One of the conditions for the setting up of a flourishing industry is the opening up of plentiful outlets with a constant market. This means that the density of the population must be fairly high. Was this the case with the Roman Empire ?

Learned men and classical scholars of the sixteenth and

---

[1] BÜCHSENSCHUTZ, **LXIII,** 192, 335.

[2] Hence free labour did not suffer very seriously from slave labour, although GUIRAUD, **CLXXXIX,** p. 69, 70, maintains the contrary. Thus, the plebs never asked for the expulsion of slaves. " The free workman complained not of the lack of work, but of being obliged to work, of not being as rich as the ruling classes, of not being a landed proprietor." " The social question of Antiquity was not the struggle between free and slave labour, but the struggle between the landed proprietors and those who possessed no land." SALVIOLI, **CCCCXXX,** p. 146, 296 ; cf. SCHMOLLER, French trans., vol. v., p. 107. See also **LXXXIV.**

seventeenth centuries (J. Lipsius, Isaac Vossius) had a fantastic idea of the wealth and the population of the Roman Empire. Montesquieu again makes truly absurd statements,[1] such as that the world in the eighteenth century did not contain a tenth of the population of the Roman Empire. The English (Hume and Gibbon), and in the nineteenth century, Dureau de la Malle[2] and Moreau de Jonnès[3] began a reaction against these senseless ideas. Yet Gibbon reached the approximate figure of 120,000,000, which Wietersheim[4] reduced to 90,000,000. But none of these calculations had been made according to any very strict method. The enquiry was taken up once more by Julius Beloch and resulted in the book [5] which still remains the classical work on the subject. Making use of the very rare and fragmentary census rolls of the citizens of the ancient world, of the numbers of the armed contingents, of the numbers for the grain distributions at Rome, always having regard to the relation between these data and the area of the regions, and profiting from the discoveries of modern statistical science about the numerical relations between the sexes, children, adults and old men in any given State, Beloch reaches very different results. The Roman world at the death of Augustus (the only subsequent increase was the addition of Britain and for a short time of Dacia), numbered about 50,000,000 inhabitants which for a total area of 3,339,500 square kilometres (deducting the deserts of Africa), gives only sixteen inhabitants per square kilometre (France has 74 ; Spain 40 ; Germany 120 ; Great Britain 144 ; Austria-Hungary 76 ; Belgium 254 ; European Russia 24).

Needless to say, these figures, or rather assertions, have been disputed on all sides. Perhaps the most interesting and disturbing observations are those made by Hans Delbrück[6] who has proved that the figures relating to the military contingents, as they have been handed down to us by the historians of Antiquity, are not in the least reliable. To found assertions on them is to build on sand. He himself

---

[1] *Lettres persanes*, 112.
[2] **CXXVII**, 1840.
[3] **CCCXLVIII**, 1851.
[4] **DVIII**, vol. i., p. 169-268.
[5] **XXIX**, 1886. See also **LXXVI**.
[6] **CLXXXVIII**. See also Ed. Meyer, **CCCXXVI**.

gives only a very approximate estimate, of 60,000,000 or 65,000,000 inhabitants.

Even this large figure, which is quite uncertain, still leaves only a very poor average density and a population so thinly scattered would not be able to maintain industry on a large scale. It is true that this figure is only a minimum. But it is probable that the lowest estimates are the most likely. We know that large portions of the Empire were poorly populated. In ancient Greece, the fall of the population had begun in the fourth century B.C., in Sparta and even at Athens.[1] Polybius (died 124 B.C.) tells us : " We have not had to suffer either epidemics or prolonged wars and yet the towns are deserted and the lands barren. We lack men because we lack children. People are too fond of money and comfort and not enough of work. Consequently they are no longer willing to marry, or if they marry, they try to have no more than one or two children, in order to bring them up in luxury and to leave them a finer inheritance ". In the first century, Strabo writes : " Thebes is only a village and the other cities of Bœotia have suffered from the same decay ". Messenia was largely deserted, and " Laconia is nothing in comparison with what it was in the past ". In Arcadia the towns had become empty and the countryside deserted. About 214, the territory of Larissa in Thessaly was fallow. The island of Eubœa was two-thirds uncultivated and right up to the gates of the towns it looked like a desert.

In the second century A.D., the position was no better. Plutarch (died in 140) declares the Greece of his time to be incapable of arming more than 3,000 men.

The population and prosperity of Greece had emigrated into Egypt. The same was more than probably the case with Macedon.

The half-barbarous Danubian provinces (Mœsia, and further West, Illyria, Pannonia, Noricum, Rhætia) could never have had anything but a thinly scattered pastoral population.

In the West, if Southern Spain (Bætica) and the coast (Tarraconensis) were rich and populous, the interior and the West (Lusitania) were still barbarous and waste. Gallia Narbonensis was populous, and doubtless also Aquitania ; Celtica and especially Belgica were no doubt less so.

[1] GUIRAUD, **CLXXXIX**, p. 156. Cf. Ed. MEYER, **CCCXXVII**, p. 164-168.

The acquisition of Britain in the first and second centuries was unimportant. Covered as it was with forests and prairies, it had but a small population.[1]

In Africa, only Proconsularis and Byzacena, corresponding to French Tunisia, were fertile and very populous, at which fact we cannot fail to be astonished, since of its 130,000 square kilometres, two-thirds are steppes.

Of Numidia and Mauretania Cæsariensis, that is to say roughly Algeria, the Romans occupied only the Tell, the area of which is not large. Mauretania Tingitana is represented by the Spanish portion of modern Morocco, prolonged to Meknes, which means that its area and population were not very considerable.

Even Italy could not have been very populous.[2] Latium and Southern Etruria were waste land ; so was the Arno Valley, the river flowing from Florence to Pisa in the midst of marshy plains. The ridge of the Apennines has always been pastoral and hence thinly populated country. Picenum alone was populous.

Rich and fertile Campania was the most populous district of Italy, but its area was insignificant (1,000 square kilometres). In the South, the country of the Samnites, Bruttium and Lucania, and on the coasts, Magna Græcia, had enjoyed an extraordinary prosperity in the sixth and seventh centuries, according to traditions in which legend no doubt plays a large part. In the first century they were only districts of *latifundia*, populated by goats and sheep. Apulia, Cicero says, is the most deserted part of Italy.

Sicily was the granary of Rome. Yet its interior was given over to shepherds,[3] and there were forests which today have disappeared.

In our days, in fact ever since the Middle Ages, the most populous part of the Peninsula is the plain of the Po, where the density of the population reaches very high averages. But having been long inhabited by the Gauls, Gallia Cisalpina had known only a very backward agriculture. Under Augustus, the plains of the Po were still encumbered with

---

[1] Medieval England was still a sparsely populated country.

[2] BELOCH (**XXX**, vol. iii., 1903, p. 471-490) maintains that peninsular Italy had at the most only from seven to eight million inhabitants under Augustus, or half the figure put forward by H. NISSEN, **CCCLVIII**.

[3] PINDAR : πολύμαλος Σικελία.

marshes and forests ; the marshes of Parma began to be drained only in 109 B.C. ; in the middle of the first century, they still stretched from Modena to Bologna, and the *Via Aemilia* was built as a causeway. At the mouths of the river and of its tributaries, from Ravenna to Adria, it was all marshland.

Roman colonies had been established in Cisalpina. Nevertheless in the register of the towns of Italy, drawn up under Augustus, the Central and Southern districts (first to seventh centuries) included 350 communities, while the Northern districts had only 82. There were no large towns, only Padua being of any importance. Clearing and draining were however carried out during the Empire, but it was only at the end of the third or fourth century that Milan, insignificant under Augustus, became the second town of Italy.

The Eastern part of the Empire was more favoured. Diodorus Siculus and Josephus agree in estimating the population of Egypt at 7,000,000 or 7,500,000 inhabitants, not including Alexandria. This is the figure which Egypt reached a quarter of a century ago. For 30,000 square kilometres (the Nile Valley, the Fayum and the Delta), subtracting the deserts, this gives more than 200 inhabitants to the square kilometre.

The Ancients knew very well that no country in the world contained so dense a population, and Egypt was for them a country quite apart, from every point of view.

Syria and Palestine were only a narrow fringe along the Mediterranean ; the rest up to the Euphrates was only a desert. The whole could never have exceeded the present figure of 3,000,000 inhabitants (14 to the square kilometre).

Asia Minor, on the other hand, was prosperous and populous, at least in the West (Proconsular Asia, Bithynia, etc.) ; for, the centre (Galatia and Cappadocia) could never have had more than a sparse population. Estimated in our day (1910) at 11,000,000 inhabitants, or 17 to the square kilometre, this country may have reached a higher figure in ancient times.

Of the towns the most important was Rome. The estimates proposed by the scholars of the sixteenth and seventeenth centuries are simply absurd. It is difficult to believe that even in the period of her greatest extension the number of the inhabitants of Rome can have exceeded half a million. J. Lipsius attributed to her 4,000,000 inhabitants and Isaac

Vossius 14,000,000 (*sic*). Other estimates range from 1,000,000 to 2,000,000. Beloch brings these figures down to 800,000 and Ed. Meyer to 700,000. These are still too high. Dureau de la Malle has shown[1] that the only certain basis must be sought in the relation between the known area and the unknown population. The Rome of Aurelian, extending over 1,230 hectares, and including many empty spaces, cannot have been more populous than modern Rome (population 538,000 in 1901), which covers a larger space (1,411 hectares). E. Cuq has proved [2] that the *insulae* (46,602 in number) enumerated by a document of the period of Constantine, beside 1,790 *domus* (palaces), were storeys with a juridical individuality and not houses, still less "blocks". However, the conclusions of this scholar cannot be accepted; for he imagines that the poor lived elsewhere, not merely not in the *domus* but not even in the *insulæ!* Reckoning four or five persons per apartment, we get for Rome the figure of from 200,000 to 250,000 inhabitants which is quite close to that which Dureau de la Malle obtained (261,000) by supposing ancient Rome to have had the same population density as the Paris of his time. It would not be possible to increase this figure by the suburbs; for in the modern sense they did not exist, the *suburbium* being waste land.

Was Rome a market ? In a certain sense it was, and even a world market as we should say, all the products of nature and of art flowing there.[3] But Rome sold nothing in return, since practically nothing was produced there. The populace, kept in semi-idleness by the distributions of provisions and the super-abundance of shows,[4] yielded very little in return. "Rome, which made the provinces send her everything, never re-imbursed them except with the money from the taxes, that is to say, with the very sums with which these provinces had provided her. Her so-called commerce was thus only indirect robbery.[5] The capital, being an unproductive city, was truly an "octopus "[6].

[1] **CXXVII,** i., 340-408.
[2] **CII,** vol. xl., 1916.
[3] Friedlaender, **CXLV,** 5th ed., vol. i., p. 15 ; cf. on the other hand, **LXXII** ; Marquardt, **CCCXLIV,** French trans., vol. xv., p. 13.
[4] See R. Cagnat, **LXIX.**
[5] **LX,** vol. ii., p. 234.
[6] **CXXVIII,** vol. vi., p. 71 ; Salvioli, **CCCCXXX,** p. 159 ; Landry, *Manuel,* p. 29.

The new capital, Constantinople, partly deserves the reproaches applied to the old.[1] But only partly ; for it was to become the emporium of the Eastern Mediterranean and of the Black Sea. But its commercial rise would need time, as would the increase of its population.[2]

What much more than Rome resembled a great modern city was Alexandria, and to a certain extent Antioch. Extending 5 kilometres by 2, covering an area of 920 hectares, and populated by 300,000 inhabitants,[3] Alexandria remained for a long time " the world's greatest mart ".[4] This will not astonish us, if we remember that its hinterland was Egypt, the country with the densest population in Antiquity ; it reached 7,500,000 inhabitants.[5]

Speaking generally, the towns were very sparsely populated.[6] Even in the time of the Empire's greatest prosperity, the largest towns in Gaul, Nîmes, Toulouse, Autun and Treves, can never have numbered more than 50,000 inhabitants, since they did not have an area of more than from 200 to 300 hectares. Famous towns like Marseilles, Milan, Verona, Aquileia and Naples had at all times been small. Still more was this the case when, in consequence of the disasters of the third century and of the resulting depopulation, the towns had to contract, occupying now only a quarter, a tenth or sometimes even a twentieth part of their former area : (Autun for example, covered 10 hectares instead of 200). From Aurelian's reign onward, during the Latin Empire and the Early Middle Ages, a city was a fortified redoubt, rarely possessing an area of more than from 20 to 25 hectares and often even less. Thus, Bordeaux, one of the important

---

[1] Its plebs was provisioned by Egypt as that of Rome was by Sicily and Africa.

[2] The town of Constantine was not so large as Rome. Even after its enlargement under Theodosius II., its area did not reach two-thirds of that of the old capital. It is rash to allow it a million inhabitants, as is done by Victor SCHULZE, CCCCLI, vol. i., 1913, p. 185. Even a quarter of this figure is doubtless excessive. St. John CHRYSOSTOM (*Act.*, xi., 3) reckons 100,000 Christians in it. It is probable that under Constantine it did not possess even half this population.

[3] BELOCH, p. 259 ; JOUGUET, p. 7 ; SALVIOLI, p. 274. Here also we must allow for exaggeration in the ancient and modern estimates. Ancient Alexandria certainly did not possess a population superior, or even equal to that of modern Alexandria (330,000 inhabitants).

[4] Μέγιστον ἐμπορεῖον τῆς οἰκουμένης (Strabo, xvii.).

[5] See above, p. 69.

[6] The estimates found even in MARQUARDT (French trans., vol. x., p. 151) are flagrantly exaggerated. Cf. CCCXCI.

towns in Gaul under the Later Empire, had a circuit of only
2,340 metres and an area of 23 hectares. Nantes, Rouen
and Troyes had only 16 hectares. At Beauvais, Tours and
Rennes we come down to 10 hectares and at Senlis to 6 or 7.
Paris had a circuit of only 1,620 metres. In Italy, the
circuit of Verona was 900 metres, Pavia was a very small town,
while Milan and Turin covered an inconsiderable area. It
was the same everywhere.[1]

Such diminutive towns could contain only small populations.
The largest, possessing the area of a Roman camp, which
varied from 21 to 25 hectares (Lambæsis, Neuss, and Bonn)
could scarcely have had a population superior to the effective
force of a legion, say a maximum of 6,000 men.

A comparison with the small French towns of modern times
is instructive. The " city " of Limoges had in 1789 preserved
the area it had in Roman times, from 11 to 12 hectares ;
it numbered 3,000 inhabitants.[2] Modern Autun, with
70 hectares, covers a third of the area of *Augustodunum* of
the Early Empire and possesses 15,000 inhabitants, or 200 to
the hectare. Saint-Malo, where the population is crowded
in houses built in very narrow streets, in 1901 contained
7,262 inhabitants for the 26 hectares of the commune, *intra
muros*, or less than 300 inhabitants per hectare. It seems
impossible that any town of Gaul or even Italy could have
exceeded or even reached this figure.

Not only was the population not dense, but its buying
capacity was poor. The men of Antiquity, if they did not
live in opulence, had few needs. Their food was simple and
frugal, as is still that of the men of the South in our days.
The lower classes lived on wheaten bread and paste (the
other cereals being despised) and on vegetables. The use of
meat was not common, except pork and kid, whence our
word " butcher ", which means one who sells kid's flesh.
Butter was a barbarian article of food and oil was preferred
to it. Wine was drunk but little ; even the army which
was so carefully looked after, had it only every other day.[3]
Under these conditions, the trades in food-stuffs could not be
thriving.

[1] See Adrien BLANCHET, **XL** (1907), p. 284 ; for Italy, see NISSEN
CCCLIX.

[2] P. GRENIER, *La cité de Limoges* (1907), pp. 12 and 16.

[3] MARQUARDT, vol. xv., p. 35 ; E. MEYER, **CCCXXVII**, p. 153.

It was the same with clothing. Clothes were simple and rarely renewed. There was no real linen.[1] Thus there was no development in the clothing industry.[2] It did not succeed in going beyond the stage of production in private workshops, until the extension of the wool trade and the drapery industry, when the shirt of German origin ceased to be an outer garment and came to be made of real linen; this means that these changes took place only at an advanced stage of the history of the Middle Ages. Living, heating and lighting arrangements thus remained stationary.

The population of the large towns was crowded into rented houses divided into mutually independent stories (*insulæ*).[3] They were gloomy dwellings with insufficient or no heating, even in winter, except by means of *braseros*. For lighting a primitive oil lamp was used, a mere wick floating in oil. The furniture was very perfunctory, consisting of a bed (a tressel with cushions thrown on it), chests, tables and chairs. The citizen lived as little as possible inside his gloomy dwelling ; when his work was over, if he worked, he walked in the streets, under the porticos, in the forum, or frequented the circuses, the theatre and the baths where he was forced to bathe frequently, owing to the lack of linen. Speaking generally, the psychology of the man of Antiquity differed appreciably from ours. He had few wants and his tastes were very stable. Fashion scarcely existed, and it exercised its influence only on the upper classes and not on the whole of society, as it does in our day. Moreover it changed very slowly. Dress, dwelling houses, furniture, objects of art, all tended to become stereotyped into almost unchangeable forms. Whence the monotonous and boring character of Roman civilization.

This simplicity of life and absence of needs and of comfort are most unfavourable to the development of industry. The *aurea mediocritas*, so dear to the Romans and the French, is a conception incompatible with a materially advanced civilization.

It is true that in the Roman world were to be found dazzling

---

[1] A passage of St. Augustine (*Sermons*, 7, 6) quoted several times, by no means implies the existence of real linen.

[2] **CCCXLIV**, vol. xv., pp. 105-153 ; **CDXXX**, p. 128 ; **CLXXXII**.

[3] See above, p. 70.

and colossal fortunes—in comparison with the Middle Ages or the dawn of modern times.[1] But in the ordinary routine of their life, the rich, even in the town, lived on the products of their country estates and bought almost nothing. An exception must be made for articles of luxury which were imported from the four corners of the globe. But modern economics have taught us that the commerce in luxuries, which concerns only a small number of rich men, is absolutely inadequate to produce, stimulate and maintain a thriving industry : " When wealth is concentrated at one pole, luxury breaks up the equilibrium of production by diminishing the manufacture of articles of use and increasing that of articles of luxury ".[2] Industry prospers in societies in which wealth is distributed over a great number of persons and descends from the richest to the poorest by graded stages : " the more wealth is divided, the more consumption and consequently production increase."

Unfortunately, except in a very small number of towns in the East, no such gradation is found in the Roman Empire. There was little or no middle class. Between extreme luxury and resigned or snarling poverty, there was nothing. At Rome, the richest and most splendid of all the towns, over against the 1,800 *domus* (palaces) there were 46,600 apartments swarming with a starving population. People of good birth, without any means, lived on *sportulæ*. Rome was a town of beggars and remained so almost up to contemporary times.

Further, there was a profound difference between ancient and modern urban life.[3] The modern town lives above all on industry and commerce, wherein lies its peculiar function.

It was not necessarily the same with the ancient town, above all when it was the capital of the State. People of good birth there lived on the produce of their land. Industry and commerce might thrive in addition, but they did not constitute the primary function of the town. The latter did not radiate over the neighbouring territory to fertilize, enrich and civilize it, but sucked in its means of

---

[1] A just remark of FRIEDLAENDER, **CXLV** (vol. iii., p. 11) on this subject.
[2] **CDXXX**, pp. 157-160.
[3] **CCLXXIII.**

subsistence ; it was " tentacular ", to use a contemporary expression.[1]

Hence, the towns were not centres of industry connected with each other through interest or even competition. Thus there was no real industrial bourgeoisie in Antiquity, because, strictly speaking, there was no large or middle-scale industry.[2] We will not call by the name of "large-scale industry" the enterprises started under the control of the State, for the provisioning of the capitals and the army.[3] The general stores at Ostia, the two hundred and fifty enormous bakeries at Rome, and the Imperial factories of arms and textiles, certainly necessitated much money, manual labour and a numerous staff. But this was not large-scale industry ; these establishments were confined to the warehousing of commodities for the Roman people,[4] or to producing articles intended for the Emperor and his Court and not for the public. They were kept up only by dint of privileges, exemptions and compulsion. In every period and under very unequal civilizations, there have been large royal factories working in the service of the sovereign. This was the case in Egypt even in the period when monetary economy did not exist. These large Roman stores no more represent large-scale industry than do the "manufactories" of carpets, furniture and porcelain of Louis XIV and Louis XV, which worked without competition, essentially for their master the king and not for a paying public.[5]

III. COMMERCE

Commerce held an infinitely more important place than industry in the estimation of the men of Antiquity and of the Middle Ages.

[1] Cf. De BROGLIE, ii., 234-235. " While our great modern capitals, if they draw their sustenance from the provinces surrounding them, pay for it with the products of skilled industry, Rome, which imported everything from the provinces, never re-imbursed them except with the money from the taxes. Following her example, the citizens of every town wanted to live at the expense of the surrounding country." Cf. SALVIOLI (against E. Meyer, 273).

[2] " The Romans kept to the end their antipathy for industrial work." WALTZING, ii., 262-263 to 483. Cf. LAVISSE-RAMBAUD, i., 153 ; DURUY, vii., 543.

[3] For some restrictions see MARQUARDT, xv., 320-321, 323-4 ; SALVIOLI, pp. 158-159, 163.

[4] CCCLXXVI.

[5] P. MANTOUX, La révolution industrielle (against Germain-Martin), pp. 6-7.

In modern times, even the richest countries, which are at the head of the capitalist system, began by being commercial countries. The Dutch in the seventeenth, and the English in the eighteenth century, were above all middlemen and their ports were marts. The wares carried by their fleets were at first not at all, or only to a very small extent, products of Dutch or English industry. But it is equally certain that this commercial expansion preceded and determined the development of a national industry.[1]

The unification of the Greek world under Alexander and that of the Mediterranean world under Rome, did without any doubt influence to a very great extent the expansion of Mediterranean commerce. It was an inestimable boon for commerce to be able to send wares from the Pillars of Hercules to the Euphrates, and from Britain to Africa, in safety.[2]

Nevertheless, though commerce was regarded more favourably than industry, it never reached any very great volume. Producing little, the Roman world carried little and sold little. It came up against deserts in the South, the barbarians in the North, and the economically backward Persian civilization in the East, while its relations with India and China were exceedingly rare.[3] Hence, in the absence of industry in the Roman world, commerce could not convey the products of a foreign industry. Commerce on a large scale could only concern itself with objects of luxury, the high price of which makes it possible to recover the expenses of transport. But about luxury trade we may repeat the observations concerning luxury industry. It is at bottom unproductive.[4] Further, articles of luxury and of art came chiefly from the East, and large-scale commerce is fed only by articles having a large consumption and not by articles of luxury, the sale of which is capricious and may even stop completely, bringing about serious disturbances. Navigation could not thrive on the transport of purple and commodities even from the Far East (silks from China, aromatics, spices, etc.).

[1] P. Mantoux, pp. 74-75.
[2] The bringing together again under the same rule of the basin of the Southern and Eastern Mediterranean, in the time of the Califate of Bagdad, similarly determined the renascence of commerce, which, starting in the East in the ninth century, reached Italy, then France, Germany and the Netherlands about the eleventh and twelfth centuries.
[3] LXXX, CCCLIX, CCCXCVI.
[4] Schmoller, vol. v., p. 228ff.

Lastly, in this traffic, the balance was unfavourable for Rome and the West, which paid in money and sold nothing or practically nothing by way of merchandise. Gold and silver were thus drained towards the East and Far East.[1]

The deep underlying cause of this languid life of business is to be sought in the psychology of the Romans. Unlike the Greeks of the Athenian and of the Hellenistic period, they were not deeply or for a long time interested in trade ; they showed " little commercial jealousy "[2] and in spite of what has been asserted, Rome never had a commercial policy.[3] The " Italian " merchants, found to some extent everywhere from Gaul to the East, at the end of the Roman Republic and at the beginning of the Empire, were not inhabitants of Rome, but people from Southern Italy. A number of them were only traffickers who swooped down like the traders in new colonies today to make their fortune quickly by any possible means, and then were off. This class of people disappeared and were absorbed in the Hellenistic world. Trade became the monopoly of the Orientals, especially of Syrians and Jews, as early as the reign of Tiberius and it was still so after the disappearance of the Empire, in Merovingian times.[4] In navigation, the Romans played no part ; the crews were Greek, Illyrian or Egyptian.

The upper classes of society (the senatorial and equestrian classes) were turned away from commerce by prejudice and even by law. These classes, which were yet so grasping, did not possess the capitalist spirit of enterprise.[5] Large business did not get from them the help of capital which they alone

---

[1] A number of historians and economists (E. MEYER, **CCCXXVII**, p. 158, vol. i. ; BLUMNER, **XLIV**, 1911, p. 620 ; MARQUARDT, vol. ii. ; NISSEN in *Bonner Jahrbücher*, 1894 ; GRUPP, **CLXXXIV**, vol. ii., pp. 221, 230 ; STREHL, **CCCCLXX**, p. 497 ; DELBRUCK, **CLXXXVIII**, vol. ii., p. 211 ; SALVIOLI, **CCCCXXX**, p. 228, 280, etc.) have seen in this fact an explanation of the scarcity of money which began to be felt from the second century onward, and have claimed to find in this quarter an explanation of the economic crisis of the third century. This is a gross exaggeration. The trade with the Far East was not considerable enough to cause such tremendous results.

[2] MONTESQUIEU (*Esprit des lois*, **XXI**, 14). Cf. NAUDET, **CCCLI**, vol. i., p. 247 : " The Romans prided themselves on their contempt for trade ; retail trade ranked amongst infamous occupations ". L. GOLDSCHMIDT, **CLXXIII**, p. 59, also observes that amongst the Romans, industry and commerce were not considered " respectable " occupations.

[3] See J. HATZFELD, **CCXII.**

[4] *Id.*, V. PARVAN, **CCCLXXI.**

[5] SALVIOLI, **CCCCXXX**, p. 237, 247 (against Goldschmidt).

possessed and the class of real business men, with experience and enterprise, useful and respected, without which there is no real capitalist system, was not formed. But on this matter misconceptions have been possible.

Roman commercial law is complete. In imitation of the East and of Egypt, there were partnerships and joint stock companies, marine insurance, credit purchasing, negotiable instruments, perhaps also a kind of bill of exchange (*permutatio*). Banks played an important part. But it should be noted that they were deposit and current account banks ; it is not certain that they went in for discounting, and the higher forms of modern credit were unknown to them. There is an abyss between the Roman *argentarius*, who was only a money-changer or a jeweller, and the modern business banker whose credit supplies life to modern industry and commerce.

With these reservations—and they are serious—we see that the Romans of the Empire knew what is called *fiduciary* economy.[1] But this does not mean that they had reached the stage of real capitalist economics. Karl Marx[2] already showed long ago that fiduciary economy is an adjunct of monetary economy and that the latter, although a necessary antecedent of capitalist economy, is none the less fundamentally and organically distinct from it.

IV. AGRICULTURE

In default of industry and commerce, could not capital be employed in agriculture ? Whether capital is applied to industry or agriculture, it has been said, is a secondary consideration.[3]

The historians who entertain these opinions have especially in view the *latifundia* worked by means of slaves on what are maintained to be capitalist lines.

It is certain that at the end of the Republic and under the Empire, sustained efforts were made to apply to agriculture the plentiful capital which was at the disposal of the upper

---

[1] RODBERTUS and BUCHER have wrongly denied this. "Fiduciary economy exists when exchange is largely by credit and when credit notes serve as a substitute for money " (SALVIOLI, pp. 5 and 264).

[2] CCCXX, vol. iii., p. 107.

[3] E. MEYER, CCCXXVII, 154-155 ; cf. MOMMSEN and FERRERO.

classes.[1] For a man of low birth, who had made his wealth by commerce, the only means of making people forget this stain was to buy land. Small business was " sordid " ; but the merchant who retired and employed his fortune in agriculture was worthy of praise.[2]

Custom, legislation, Imperial favour, and fashion even, encouraged men to invest money in the purchase and working of large landed estates.

But the results were not proportionate to these efforts. The capitalist exploitation of the soil ended in complete failure.

The reason is that exploitation by means of slaves not only ties up large capital sums, but requires at least two other conditions in order to be remunerative, a rich soil and densely populated areas in the neighbourhood. But the most fertile parts of Italy, Gaul, etc., remained for a long time fallow ; in the absence of scientific knowledge, which is of very recent growth, and also in the absence of large cattle, the greater part of the soil was soon exhausted, especially under the system of biennial rotation.[3] The towns were very poor markets. The majority were, as we have seen, small, sparsely populated, and what was worse, far from each other,[4] conditions which militated against their being profitable markets. There remained Rome ; but being provisioned by the " annona " from Africa,[5] Sicily, etc., the capital was economically like a foreign city in relation to Italy.

Let us remember that the consuming power of the population of the towns was very limited, neither meat nor wine being in demand. The transport of wine, oil, etc. (by means of earthenware vases or wine-skins) was moreover inconvenient, and that of fruits more difficult still.[6]

Hence the large slave-worked estates knew only extensive exploitation, chiefly pasturing. They produced not so much

---

[1] GUMMERUS, CXCIV ; HEITLAND, CCXXII ; WEBER, DIV ; WESTER-MANN, DVII.

[2] CICERO, De officiis, ii., 42 ; CDXXX, p. 231 ; CCCXLIV, vol. xv.

[3] CCXXXVIII, p. 153 ; CDXXX, pp. 182-208.

[4] Thünen's studies have shown that, beyond a certain distance, the expenses of transport swallow up the profits and even more. See Ch. ANDLER, Origine du Socialisme d'État en Allemagne, p. 251.

[5] LXIX.

[6] To this should be added the fact that many kinds of fruits and vegetables were still uncommon or unknown. See CCCXCLIV, vol. xv., p. 49.

for the market as for the upkeep of the owner, his family and clients. The *latifundia*[1] come under domestic economy. They herald and prepare the way for feudal economy, it may be, but not at all for the capitalist system.

Thus, wherever this was possible, the landowner came to divide his estates into plots assigned to *coloni*.

Were these *coloni* farmers in the modern sense, that is to say small capitalist owners of cattle, agricultural implements and movable stock? Certainly not.[2] The free *colonus* had only his hands and his family to help him, but no capital ; and this no doubt explains the ease with which he became bound to the soil under the Latin Empire. But this parcelling of the estate into plots assigned to free or serf *coloni* is utterly opposed to the capitalist system of exploitation ; for—it seems scarcely necessary to point this out—large property is not at all synonymous with exploitation on a large scale.[3]

Thus, capitalism, when applied to agriculture, was unable to change its character of natural economy and nothing is less like capitalist economy than the agriculture of the Roman Empire.

Are we, at the end of this review, to conclude that at Rome there was neither any spirit of enterprise nor any effort to utilize the large sums accumulated at Rome through the conquest of Asia and Greece ? Such a conclusion would be contrary not merely to all verisimilitude, but also to all our texts. The end of the Republican period saw the rise of new men, business men and *publicani*, keen on making money and endowed with an eager spirit of enterprise. The old senatorial and equestrian classes were inspired by a frenzy of enjoyment and of spending and also by a mania for speculating. Certain typical business men are famous. The character of an Atticus or a Rabirius has been painted in a strong light, as that of men on the look out for paying investments in every part of the Roman world.[4]

---

[1] Their bad effects have been monstrously exaggerated. It is notably false that they caused the disappearance of small and medium properties ; the latter maintained themselves wherever the natural conditions permitted it. See **CDXXX,** pp. 98-120, 166, 217.

[2] There was an intermediate class of *conductores* between the landowner and the tenants. They may be compared with the French " farmers general " of Nièvre and Allier.

[3] A strange mistake of E. MEYER'S on this point, **CCCXXVIII** (p. 155).

[4] G. BOISSIER, P. GUIRAUD, DE LOUME.

There were commercial companies, even joint stock companies. Commercial law, as we have said, was by no means embryonic.[1] Nevertheless, on looking close, we see that commercial activity concentrated on three kinds of business : (1) the farming of taxes owed by the provincials, Rome's subjects ; (2) landed investments (lands, villas and their fixtures) ; (3) lending on interest. It is only too obvious that the *publicani* who squeezed the provinces were the ancestors of the "farmers general" and not at all of our modern business men.

Of the landed investments we have already spoken. They were scarcely, if at all, productive. Their aim was social and snobbish and they were of small economic value. First and foremost usury flourished.[2] " Personal capital took only the form of usury. Usury was the Italians' large scale speculation in the first century B.C. and during the Empire. Usury was practised in all its forms, both in that of the loan, pure and simple, the *versatura* (a kind of contract which is obscure but was very onerous) and of the bottomry loan practised by the big banks and also by the petty moneylenders who lent by the week or the day and were a swarm of locusts capable of impoverishing the richest countries, even real Eldorados like Asia ".[3]

The *Italici qui negotiantur*, who spread in thousands everywhere in the wake of the soldiers in Gaul and in Asia, were first and foremost usurers. Only lending by the week was looked askance upon, as ignoble. But usury on a large scale was approved of and it was not considered shameful to engage in it. And what usury ! Knights and Senators lent money to Kings in the East, then to towns, corporations and private individuals, at incredible rates of interest. The rule was 4 per cent. per month ; some lent only at 75 per cent. or 100 per cent.; Atticus, for example, who was looked upon by his contemporaries as the King of the Knights. As he was a patron of men of letters, he has, in spite of this, left behind him the reputation of a gentleman. Brutus lent at 48 per cent. " All the great names in Roman history are connected with transactions of usury."[4] So much for the provinces.

In Italy, even in settled times the rate of 12 per cent. was

[1] **CDXXX**, 40 ; **CCCXLIV**, vol. xii., 15 ; **CLXXIII** ; **CDLVIII.**
[2] **CDXXX**, 40 ; **CCCXLIV**, vol. xii., 15 ; **CLXXIII** ; **CDLVIII.**
[3] **CDXXX**, 52, 58.
[4] **CDXXX**, 215, 229 ; **CCLXXXVI**, 96. Cf. **CXI** and **CXII.**

legal. " Rome's great industry was usury."[1]   Money went
neither to the land, nor to commerce, nor to industry.   The
capital of the Roman world did not feed enterprise.
Being applied to usury, capital even dried up the spirit of
enterprise, and by attacking the sources of wealth, it discouraged production.   " Usury was at Rome, as it will always
be in countries in which there is little commercial industry,
an exorbitant tax exacted from the poor and needy by
capitalists, a cause of ruin for the people.   The less trade
there is, the more excessive is usury."[2]   There is nothing
more barren or harmful than usury.   It only thrives in
countries and times in which real credit does not exist,[3] in
other words, when the mind has not yet risen to the capitalistic conception of business.

This usurious, idle, and by no means capitalistic aristocracy
was in addition horribly spendthrift.   The luxury of the
higher classes may have been exaggerated ;[4]   but it remains
nevertheless certain that at the end of the Roman Republic
and the beginning of the Empire, senseless acts of prodigality,
involving a wholesale destruction of wealth, were indulged in.
This wealth had been created not by Rome but by the Hellenistic world.[5]   Rome's industry in the second and first centuries B.C. had been war and the spoliation of the vanquished.
Drained at Rome, without being fed by a real spirit of enterprise, capital, the product of long centuries of work of the
Mediterranean world, soon dried up.   " The fruits of conquest
were dissipated in a century."[6]   The time of the greatest
luxury extends from the middle of the first century B.C.
to the death of Nero.[7]   Already under Vespasian, the senatorial and equestrian order had almost been annihilated in consequence of the political persecutions, but also because of the
dissipation of their fortunes.   Vespasian was obliged to found

---

[1] **CXXVIII,** vol. vii., 542.
[2] **CCCLI,** vol. i., 198 ; cf. 34.
[3] **CL,** 193-194. Cf. **LX,** vol. ii. 234 : " The two sure symptoms of a real
increase of wealth were always lacking at Rome, namely the lowering of the
rate of interest on money and the increase of the population."
[4] **CXLIII,** French trans., vol. iii., 145 and Preface ; **CDXXX,** 37, 51, 90.
[5] **CLXIX.**
[6] **CXXVIII,** vol. v., 597 ; **CCCLI,** vol. ii., 209.   " The Romans, though so
resourceful in politics, never conceived of any other financial law or system
than the right of the strongest and the spoliation of the vanquished.   They
knew how to command rather than to rule ; they could conquer but not
preserve."
[7] **CLXXXIX.**

a new nobility with provincial families. From this time onward, no fortune lasted for more than three or four generations.[1]

Finally, it should be observed that the Ancients had no sound conception of the nature of productive capital.[2] They confused it with loans in kind or with specie, which is only a symbol of exchange value. We know that " the accumulation of moneyed capital is not a sign of the accumulation of capital, that is to say of reproduction ; it does not represent real wealth ". Only we have not known this for long. When the scarcity of specie began to be felt—and this was as early as the second century—in consequence of the dissipation of former riches and of the exhaustion of the gold and silver mines,[3] there resulted a disturbance of exceptional seriousness.[4]

Then began the debasing of coinage, fairly slow at first, but after the reign of Septimius Severus very rapid and culminating in a real crisis of prices. It needed but a long period (235-284) of political troubles to supervene, with its train of poverty, intestine wars, confiscations and barbarian invasions, for money which had become scarce and debased to be concealed, for commerce to become practically annihilated and the ancient prosperity to be wrecked. The fact is that the activity of the first centuries before and after our era had been only a fleeting effervescence. Roman " capitalism " had been but a thin layer swept away by the breath of the storm, and the underlying rock of natural economy very quickly came to the surface.[5]

---

[1] **DIII,** vol. ii., p. 260.

[2] **CDXXX,** 254, 263 ; **CCCLVI.**

[3] **XIII,** vol. i., col. 806 ; **CXXVII,** vol. vi., 378-384, 583-585 ; vol. vii., 543 ; **CCXXIX,** 72-91 ; **CDLVII,** vol. ii., 201 ; **CXXXVIII,** *The mining industry, as revealed by the Theodosian code, is a dead industry* (**DIII,** vol. ii., 237). Cf. **XXXIV.**

[4] Some economists will have it that moneyed stock does not matter for general prosperity. They may be right logically, but not psychologically. " Since monetary economy represents the outward manifestation of economic life, it is clear that the amount of money serving as capital in circulation forms the chief element of a country's prosperity. When this amount is reduced to the strictest minimum, it is not possible to accumulate or to form new capital or to replace riches which have been consumed " (**CDXXX,** 308). See further **XXXIV** and **CX.**

[5] **CDXXX,** 319. Cf. MARSHALL who (in *Principles*, 8th ed., 1922 Appendix A §4) : " The resemblance (between the Roman period and ours) is superficial and illusory. It extends only to forms and not to the living spirit of national life ". In a work which appeared some years after the writing of this chapter, we see WERNER SOMBART (*Der moderne Kapitalismus,* vol. ii., 107) throwing doubt on the existence of any real capitalism during antiquity.

This return to natural economy, after the arrest of monetary economy, already marks the economic Middle Ages. Politically and socially, it is the introduction to the Middle Ages.

With the material prosperity and stage of civilization reached by Ancient Society was bound up the stability of the Imperial régime. The economic system being in process of marked retrogression, the expenses ought to have been reduced. But to this men could not resign themselves. The Roman State, from the end of the third century, was like a ruined landlord who wants to keep up the same establishment as in the days of his prosperity. These attempts were all in vain. The army was badly recruited ; the decurion fled from the *curia*, the peasant from the land and the artisan from his *collegium*. The State saw only one way of salvation ; to bind every man by force to his occupation, to chain him and his descendants to the same post, and it established a real caste system. The reforms of Diocletian, Constantine and their successors betray the desperate struggle of an organism refusing to die, with natural economic forces which will not allow society to maintain with very reduced means a large and complex State.

Usually, it is only the mean, pettifogging, despotic and unpractical side of this legislation that is seen. Its tragic and impressive side is not grasped. The Emperors of the fourth and fifth centuries are arraigned for not having succeeded in galvanizing the Empire into life. They are overwhelmed with reproaches and loaded with abuse. Albert de Broglie is almost or quite alone in considering the matter fairly and justly.

" In truth, if the Empire in the fourth century, instead of giving its laws and customs to the foreign nations, let itself be overrun and vanquished by them, it is neither Constantine's pacific policy nor the military institutions which were but its natural sequel, that we should blame for this. The evil came from much further back ; its source lay deep down in a quarter which man-made laws can scarcely reach. The Empire was destined to perish through its internal sores and through the dissolution of all its vital forces and not through the fault of any military organization. Ten centuries of corruption and three of despotism had brought the old society to a state of moral and material destitution, and, *if we may use a too modern expression, to an economic condition* which made all laws powerless. To sum up everything in a word, Rome had been ruining herself constantly for four centuries and in her pecuniary ruin were dragged down all her political resources. When a society cannot supply its own wants, neither can it for any length of time provide for its own defence. In the fourth century, Rome could neither feed her citizens, provide for the upkeep of her administration, nor pay her troops ; every year her peoples were becoming impoverished, and her burdens heavier, while at the same time her forces were becoming less. This growing distress, to the causes of which Constantine could not penetrate any more than any one else of his times, and to which he brought only remedies which were impotent and sometimes worse than the disease, disappointed all his efforts, frustrated all the calculations of his policy, delivered the Empire an easy prey to its enemies, and did not allow the old Roman nations time to reinvigorate their exhausted strength in the waters of the inspiration of a new faith. It remains to examine the fate and consequences of Constantine's institutions, under this aspect and *from this point of view of social economics,* which is yet connected with high political and moral considerations ".[1] If the Roman Emperors of the Later Empire wanted the State to continue to keep up an establishment the maintenance of which the economic situation no longer allowed, the reason was that the very existence of the State was bound up with this establishment. To reproach them for the measures they took is unjust and even childish ; as well might they be arraigned for having wanted the Roman Empire to continue to exist. They only succeeded in prolonging its agony in the West. But without them the patient would have expired two centuries sooner in a crisis of burning fever. In the East, moreover, they managed, strangely enough, to maintain its existence.

[1] **LX**, vol. ii., 228.

CHAPTER V

The Constantinian Monarchy
Its Nature. Reforms and Services

I. THE EMPEROR, THE SENATE AND THE SUPERIOR OFFICIALS

THE work of transforming the " Empire " from a magistracy to a monarchy, projected by Aurelian and undertaken by Diocletian, was carried on and completed under Constantine and his successors.[1]

Having become a Christian, the Emperor no longer suffered himself to be worshipped as a god. Nevertheless he meant to remain above humanity. The etiquette was not changed, the symbolism hardly at all. The Emperor ceased to be represented as the incarnation of the sun-god, but the "nimbus" of the saint was later to encircle his head. Some day he was to be entitled ἰσαπόστολος, " equal to the apostles ".

The Palace and the Court became the centre of the " State " and " the Empire was wholly contained therein " (Duruy). The " functionaries ", civil and military, are more honoured, the nearer they are to the sacred person of the Emperor. The State services share in this " sacred " character and the title of sacred is given to them. The Imperial Council is the " sacred consistory ", and the ministry of finance is called that of the " sacred largesses ".

The old organs of sovereignty are no more than a shadow. The Senate, stripped of its prerogatives, is a mere ruin. There are no more *senatus consulta*, or financial functions. It has no initiative nor even any well defined function. The Senate is a mere deliberative assembly and sometimes a kind of high court of justice. Its purely honorary privileges have as their counterpart very heavy burdens.

Also the Roman Senate's rank declines more and more. Nevertheless, in the East, the senators keep a rank of the first order, as a social class, if not as a political body.

---

[1] The best account is still that of WALLON, **DI**, vol. iii., 125. See also **CC, CCLXVII.**

At Constantinople the Senate, from a mere municipal *curia*, became a body equal to and the rival of the Senate of Rome, from 359, when Constantine set up an " Urban Prefect ", especially from 365, when, after the partition effected between Valentinian and Valens, all the Court services were duplicated.[1] At Constantinople it is the very core of the new aristocracy of officials which was the power of the Byzantine State. It also encroaches upon the domain of the church.

The equestrian order has disappeared, or rather it has become so radically transformed that it is difficult to recognize it in the order of the *perfectissimi*, the new hierarchy which we are going to discuss.

The old magistracies which gave access to the Senate, the consulship, prætorship and quæstorship, deprived of every serious function, are only very heavy burdens (entailing the exhibition of games to the city plebs, etc.). The annual consulship is still considered the first office of the State but is merely a kind of costly honour.

The new hierarchy[2] was only completed under Constantius and Valentinus. The real divisions of society were then constituted by the hierarchy of the Imperial functionaries. To each office of the State was attached a title which was sometimes hereditary. There were :

1. The *Illustres* : the Prætorian Prefects, the Prefects of the two capitals, the *magistri militum*, the Grand Chamberlain, the Master of the Offices[3] (who was minister of the Emperor's Household and also of the police), the Quæstor of the Palace, the two ministers of finance (the *comes* or Count of the Sacred Largesses and the Count of the Privy Purse), the two Counts of the Guard (since 400).

2. The *Spectabiles* : the First Chamberlain (*primicerius sacri cubiculi*), the Primicerius of the notaries (a kind of secretary of State), the Marshal of the Palace (*castrensis palatii*), the presidents of the four great bureaux (the *magistri scriniorum*), the governors of certain provinces called pro-consular, the Vicarii of the Dioceses, the military counts and *duces* or dukes.

---

[1] CCLXXXVI, 8, 219, 231.
[2] CCCLI, vol. ii., 75, 257 ; CCCXXXII, vol. i., 315, 338 ; CCXXVII, and CCXXVIII.
[3] XLVII.

3. The *Clarissimi* : This title, at first reserved for Senators, that is to say, for personages who were not functionaries, was given to the governors of provinces, at least in the East, to the *præfectus annonæ* and to the *præfectus vigilum*.

4. The *Perfectissimi* : This was in the third century merely a title of the functionaries belonging to the equestrian order, but under Constantine it came to denote an order. Amongst the *perfectissimi* there were at first the dukes and counts, then after Constantine, the dukes passed into the rank of *spectabiles* and certain counts, those of the first class, rose to the title of *illustres ;* similarly also certain governors of provinces. In the fourth century this title is the apanage of the *magistri census*, of the primicerii of the bureaux, and of physicians. Under Justinian it was to sink into insignificance.

At the top are the *Nobilissimi*, members of the Imperial family, and the *Patricii* without any definite function ; they are important personages, called " fathers of the Emperor ".

This hierarchy exercised its power of attraction even on the *Senators* of the provincial " civitates "[1] who were not and never would be official functionaries. The " perfectissimate " became the reward of the career of a decurion. Some provincial " Senators " crept into the clarissimate whence they were soon expelled. Constantius thrust back into the *curiæ* the *curiales* whom Constantine had allowed to leave their condition. Even the heads of industrial and commercial corporations cherished the ambition of attaining the " perfectissimate ".

If it was impossible to hold any office giving the right to a title, the honorary position without any office was sought after. Thus the whole of society was brought into the Imperial hierarchy. Even the Senate became part of the " cursus ", access to it being given by the favour of the princeps to those who had held certain offices at Court or elsewhere.

It is to be noticed that the personages attached to the personal service of the ruler rose continually in dignity. The Grand Chamberlain, since 424, took precedence over the ministers of Finance and even over the minister of the Emperor's household and head of the bureaux (the *magister officiorum*). The quæstor, a new officer who owed his origin

---

[1] **CCLXXXVI**, 26, 39, 50.

to Constantine (he was the Emperor's mouthpiece, the head of the consistory, and editor of laws and rescripts) was placed above the proconsuls, between 372 and 416, and glorified with the title of " illustris ".

The Comitiva[1].—The magistrate gave way to the Courtier (*amicus, comes*).

The Imperial clientship had been, since the beginning of the Empire, the most sought after of all. The number of the friends of the Princeps rose so high that Tiberius had been obliged to divide the " friends " into three classes. They are the friends from whom, since the time of Hadrian, the Council of the Princeps is drawn and who replace the Senate in the direction of the business of State.

It was reserved for Constantine to change this *comitiva* with its three ranks into an imperial office. The personal friends of the Emperor continued to be called *amici, comites*. The title is even conferred as an honour by way of reward, on the completion of an administrative, military, municipal or collegiate career, very much like the titles of aulic and privy councillors in modern monarchies.

Constantine's innovation consisted in establishing by regulation a connection between the title of *comes* and certain offices of especial importance and thus turning the *comitiva* into an official status. To this title he attached certain definite functions.

The Council consisted of *comites primi ordinis*, having the standing of *spectabiles*. The Council was re-organized about 335 ; the young *clarissimi* of the Senate were admitted into it, and by this means the Senate, or rather some of its members, entered into the Council of the Princeps, but only by becoming his clients.

The two Ministers of Finance are, one the *comes sacrarum largitionum*, and the other the *comes rerum privatarum*. They have the rank of "illustres", and this title belongs also to their subordinates, the *comes largitionum, per Illyricum*, the *comes largitionum per Africam*, the *comes et rationalis summarum Ægypti*, the *comes commerciorum per Illyricum*, the *comes metallorum per Illyricum*, etc. Naturally it belongs also to the persons attached to the private service of the princeps, the *comes sacræ vestis, comes domorum, comes stabuli* (the latter

[1] **CCCLI**, vol. ii., 81, 230, 318 ; **CDLVII**, vol. ii., 75 ; **CVII**, 5, 78.

having the rank of *clarissimus* and later of *spectabilis*) ; also
to the chiefs of the Guard, the *comes domesticorum equitum
et peditum* since 409, and the *comites scholarum* ; they have
the rank of *illustres*.

II. THE ARMY[1]

The different corps enjoy higher esteem the nearer they are
to the ruler's person.

The Guard.—The last of the prætorians were disbanded in
312. In their place we find henceforth :

(1) *Domestici et protectores.* Recruited before Diocletian's
time from retired non-commissioned officers, these gradually
gave way to young members of good families, who in order
to be near the princeps, obtained, even by payment of money,
the favour of entering this corps. But they lowered its
military value, reducing it to the level of parade troops. They
were divided (from 409) into two bodies, infantry and cavalry,
the latter having the greater prestige.

(2) *Scholares.* These were the guards of the palace, which
explains the fact that their head was the master of the offices.
They too formed an infantry and a cavalry body ; in imitation
of Persia, the cavalry (*clibanarii*) are both cuirassiers and
archers.

The legions.—The hierarchy of the legions is wholly changed.
Hadrian had adopted local recruitment at a time when it
seemed that the Empire no longer had any serious enemy
to fear. This mode of recruitment, though simple and
economical, was attended by serious inconveniences in the
long run. Being for an indefinite period settled in the same
district and being also since the principate of Septimius
Severus allowed to marry, the soldiers borrowed the customs
and even the language of the country in which they lived
generation after generation. They were less armies of Rome
than provincial armies. Constantine did not do away with
the old and famous legions which had been encamped for
centuries on the frontiers, but he divided them into detachments along the frontier rivers, the Rhine, the Danube and
the Euphrates, garrisoned in small forts (*castella*, *burgi*).
The old name of " legion " continued to be given to the old

[1] **XV, CXXI, CLXXXVIII,** vol. ii. ; **CLXXX** and **CLXXXI, CCCXLI.**

cohort whose effective force could vary between 900 and 1,000 men ; it was commanded by a *præfectus*, while the other cohorts (from 450 to 545 men) were commanded by a *tribunus*.

Carrying on the measures inaugurated by Diocletian and Maximian, who gave precedence to the legions responsible for the Emperor's personal protection, the Jovians and Herculians, Constantine placed at the head of the army the " palatine " legions, and later the *auxilia palatina*. Next came the legions " in the suite " (*comitatenses*), then the *pseudo-comitatenses*. The re-modelling went on and became so complete, that about the year 400, out of 172 legions scarcely a quarter (29 in the East, and 11 in the West) went back further than the reign of Constantine. Very few of the old legions were judged worthy of holding a high rank in the new hierarchy ; only two, the VIII *Augusta* and the XI *Claudia* were " palatine " while ten were placed "in the suite ". All the rest were relegated to the frontiers as *pseudo-comitatenses*, or even without any title.

The corps held in esteem were brought back into the interior and garrisoned in the towns. Discussing this, Zosimus accuses the Emperor of having enervated the soldier by this town life while at the same time leaving the frontiers open. But the pagan historian detests Constantine as the first Christian Emperor, and writing a century and a half after him, he may interpret falsely the measures taken by the Emperor. The system of the linear frontier had shown itself ineffectual in the third century ; these slight cordons had never been able to prevent the invasion of the barbarians who had spread throughout the Empire, destroying defenceless towns. From the time of Gallienus and of Aurelian these towns, after being greatly reduced in extent, were all fortified and formed real strongholds (*castra, castella*) guarded by the best troops. The frontier was simply watched by a screen of farmer-soldiers. The preponderance of the barbarian element in the Imperial armies from the middle of the fourth century, makes it more than probable that Constantine had already set the example of incorporating Germans not merely in the *auxilia*, but also in the legions themselves.[1]

[1] **XVIII, CVIII,** vol. ii.

At the head of the " dioceses " Constantine placed *comites provinciarum*, who were at first temporary and afterwards permanent inspectors. Nevertheless this title could not prevail over that of *vicarii*, except for the *comes Orientis* and the *comes Ponticæ*.

The military offices, being of a specially delicate nature, were entrusted to the friends or " counts " of the Princeps. The two ministers of war and generalissimos, created by Diocletian or Constantine, the *magistri militum*, are *comites primi ordinis* with the rank of "illustres". As they resided at Court, whence their title of *præsentales*, it became necessary (under Theodosius) to give them as colleagues generals, in the countries exposed to war : *comes et magistri militum per Gallias* in the West ; *comes per Orientem, per Thraciam, per Illyrium*, in the East ; these too had the standing of "illustres". At least from Diocletian onwards, beside the commands in the large districts (Italy, Gaul, Spain, Mauretania, Britain), we find, on the threatened frontiers and territories, important military commands entrusted to dukes. About 400 there are thirteen of them in the East and twelve in the West with the rank of *spectabiles*.

Side by side with them are *comites rei militaris* (two in the East, and six in the West) also entitled *spectabiles*, the real lieutenants of the *magistri militum præsentales*. Moreover the title of *comes* is conferred on several *duces*, whence the title *comes et dux*.

The Imperial army of the interior was entrusted in each of the large natural divisions of the Empire to *comites* having the rank of *spectabiles*, as in Illyria, Spain, Mauretania, Tingitana, Africa, Britain. In Gaul, the *comes* was even *magister equitum* and " *illustris* " ; he resided at Trèves. In Italy, the whole of the forces were no doubt under the direct command of the *magistri militum*.

What was serious for the future was that the *comitiva* tended to substitute personal for State service. It was not so much the *Respublica* that was served as the Princeps. The *comitiva* heralded, from afar it is true, vassalage, that is to say a system in which all idea of State service having disappeared, only the relations between man and man are considered.

III. GOVERNMENT AND FINANCE

Government.—This was a Court government with all its pettinesses. The pronunciamentos of the prætorians and the revolts of the provincial legions were replaced by palace intrigues conducted by the eunuchs and the delators. Spies (*agentes in rebus*) multiplied. Arrests were made on the flimsiest pretexts (a dream or a jest) and they were too often followed by abominable tortures. All subjects, the lowest as well as the highest, were suspect in the eyes of the ruler, for every free man could aspire to the Empire. One of Constantine's successors, his son Constantius, already appeared as a kind of Abd-ul-Hamid.

Finance.[1]—It cannot be asserted either that the imposts were excessive or that expenditure was extravagant.

Can it be said that the land tax was exceptionally heavy under Constantine ?

Lactantius (*De mortibus persecutorum*, 23) writes : " The revenue officers are everywhere : every clod of a field is measured, the number of feet in a vineyard, the number of trees is counted, a written inventory is made of every kind of animal, men are counted by heads ". He expresses indignation at this, but the fiscal agents were only doing their duty. They were right, particularly in proceeding with care in their work of land-surveying, and of counting the number of feet of vine-land. It was only by means of this detailed return that it was possible to determine rightly the fiscal unit (the *jugum* or *caput*) the establishment of which went back as far as the reign of Diocletian.

Constantine created or developed class imposts. The members of the order of *clarissimi* paid the *follis*, also called the *aurum glebale, glebalis collatio*, in proportion to their property : two, four or eight gold pounds yearly. As the pound was equal to 72 gold solidi, this tax was heavy ; it lasted till 450, when it was suppressed by Valentinian III and Marcian. It is true that people of this class, that of " Senators ", formed an immensely rich aristocracy which held the major part of the land and was exempt from the *munera*. The reproaches of Zosimus against Constantine's memory therefore appear exaggerated.

---

[1] **CDXXXVII ; CCCXXXII ; CCCXLIV**, vol. **x.**, ; **CCLX**, vol. **i.** ; **CCXLII.**

Below them, the class of the curiales paid (from 364 onwards) the *aurum coronarium* in proportion to their landed property.[1] The *aurum coronarium* was not of a permanent nature ; having for a long time been a voluntary contribution (a crown offered to the Emperor) it kept the characteristic of not being chargeable every year, but only in exceptional circumstances. It was not this that could bring about the ruin of the curiæ.

The class of the *negotiatores*, including not merely the wholesale merchants and traders, but also the artisans and free workmen, paid the *chrysargyron* or *lustralis collatio*. In spite of this name it was chargeable every four years. Established by Constantine, this impost was suppressed by Anastasius in 501.[2]

Thus for the merchant class and for the class of the lesser landowners, the class imposts were vexatious because they were irregular rather than because they were heavy.

As regards that ill defined and little-known class called the *plebeians*, the Emperors adopted benevolent measures towards it. In the course of the fourth century, the urban population, at least in the East, was relieved of the *personal capitation*. But the latter was maintained in the country. It hit hard the small, non-curial landowner and above all the " colonus " who was still free in theory. The capitation was handed on to the Middle Ages.

Indirect taxes.[3]—The Romans combined under the name of *portorium* or *teloneum* three things which by us are distinguished : customs, town-dues, and tolls in the interior established at definite thoroughfares (*stationes*). These imposts were farmed out. From Hadrian's reign onwards, the tax-farmers properly so-called ceased to belong to the class of " knights " and were freedmen supervised by equestrian *procuratores*. The " Later Empire " introduced no change into the machinery of this institution except that it reduced the duration of the lease from five to three years, insisted on the adjudication

---

[1] We do not, however, admit that this class, any more than the senatorial class, was, in consideration of the establishment of a class impost, relieved of the land tax, as is maintained by a recent theory (CCCV).

[2] The *aurum coronarium* and the *chrysargyron* were already established in the Egypt of the Lagidæ, under the names of στέφανος and χειρωνάξιον. See BOUCHÉ-LECLERCQ, *Hist. des Lagides*, vol. iii., 305 and 335.

[3] René CAGNAT, *Étude historique sur les impôts chez les Romains*, 1882.

taking place in the presence of the Prætorian Prefect or of the vicarii, and finally placed the whole of the administration under the supreme authority of the *comes sacrarum largitionum*. It is not known what became of the *procuratores*. The comparatively moderate rate (from 4 to 5 per cent. according to the districts) rose in the fifth century to the considerable figure of one eighth.

It is to be noted that Constantine exempted agricultural implements from the payment of the tax and granted immunity to veterans and their children. On the other hand, from Theodosius onwards, the State seized the dues of the " free " municipalities, compelling them to accept a division in which it took the lion's share, two-thirds.

Duties on Transfer, etc.—The existence of the 5 per cent. tax imposed by Augustus (*vicesima hereditatum*), is no longer attested after the middle of the fourth century. It must have disappeared at the time of Diocletian's financial reforms. The same applies also to the *vicesima libertatis* on the manumission of slaves. On the other hand, the 1 per cent. tax on goods sold by auction (*centesima rerum venalium*) continued.

There is no proof of the existence of State monopolies, even in the case of salt.

On the whole, there was no increase in the number of imposts or aggravation in their oppressiveness either under Constantine or after him, at least as regards the lower classes of the population.

Expenditure.—Was this excessive ? It is certain that Constantine was fond of display.[1] He further developed Court pomp and wanted his high officials to imitate him. The Emperor was generous to the point of prodigality ; in the last ten years of his life, he was unable to refuse anything to those around him and his courtiers took large sums from him, currying favour for themselves by an outward show of hypocritical piety. Constantine built and built much ; like Diocletian he had a mania for building.

All this is true. But there is nothing under his reign which surpasses or even comes up to the lavish expenditure of his predecessors of the first, second and even third centuries.

State expenditure.—The most important or more correctly the only important source of expenditure, was the army.

[1] **CXXVIII,** 172.

But its numbers were not increased.   On the contrary, from the fourth century onwards, the Roman armies in the field include only an insignificant number of combatants, 15,000 or 20,000.   We may doubt whether the Empire was ever capable of raising more than 30,000 men for an expeditionary force.   Moreover, as we have seen, payment in money became rare.   The army was more and more paid in kind.   The same applied to "functionaries".

The distributions of provisions[1] (corn, afterwards bread, oil) were increased; for the system of feeding a half-idle plebs was extended to the new Rome.   Nevertheless there were few public expenses—expenses in connection with important buildings and amusements were borne by rich private individuals.

Besides the army, the only real public service was that of the post, reserved for the Emperor and his functionaries.   This was a heavy burden, but it fell only on the towns and villages along the route.

On the whole nothing allows us to conclude that expenditure was higher than in the preceding period.

The monetary system.[2]—We have seen that Diocletian had succeeded in bringing to an end the frightful monetary chaos of the third century.   It was reserved for Constantine to complete his work and to restore the Roman monetary system on a basis which would remain unshaken, at least in the East, for long centuries.   About 312, Constantine issued the *solidus aureus*, the gold piece of 72 to the pound (4.55 grammes), the intrinsic value of which is 15.61 francs.   At the same time, he instituted a silver piece, also struck on the basis of 72 to the pound (the pound = 72.75 francs).   It was called *miliarense*.   It was in fact equal to a thousandth part of the gold pound, given that the ratio of the value of gold to silver is about 14 : 1 (more exactly, 13.71 : the pound of 327 grammes of gold, divided by 1000 = 0.327 grammes, and multiplied by 13.71 = 4.55 grammes, the same weight as the gold solidus).   Its intrinsic value was a little above one franc (of the year 1913).

It must however be stated that this money did not have a wide circulation.   It was a luxury coinage distributed, for example, by the Consuls in their public largesses.

The current silver coins were the *siliqua* and half-siliqua. In the Roman weight system, the siliqua was a weight equal to $\frac{2}{3}$ of the obol, $\frac{1}{6}$ of the scriptulum, $\frac{1}{24}$ of the gold solidus, $\frac{1}{1728}$ of the pound. The gold siliqua was thus equal to 0.189 grammes. But as it was impossible to strike so small a coin, it was made *in silver*. Given the relation of gold to silver as 13.71 : 1, there was a silver coin weighing 2.60 grammes for the siliqua and 1.30 grammes for the half siliqua. The *miliarense* (4.55 grammes) therefore equalled $1\frac{3}{4}$ siliquæ.

V. LEGISLATIVE REFORMS AND THE PROTECTION OF SOCIETY

Constantine's legislation partly carried on that of Diocletian. The abuses of appeals to the Emperor which had the disadvantage of taking the parties away from their natural judges were checked. Nevertheless widows and orphans could accuse governors suspected of partiality. Judges were made answerable with their private fortunes for damages incurred through their neglect or bad faith. Attempts were made to take precautionary measures concerning oral or written evidence. It was forbidden to detain in prison indefinitely persons accused in civil cases. In criminal cases, every accusation had to rest on written evidence. In penal legislation the punishment of the cross (replaced by the gibbet) was abolished, as was also the branding of the forehead, " the human face being made in the image of God ". In civil legislation, the rigour of the law which allowed unlimited power to the paterfamilias was softened ; the son could, during his father's life-time, inherit a third of his mother's estate and the mother was entitled to one-third of her children's estate. Finally the Emperor resumed the charitable policy of the Antonines towards poor children.

As regards *slavery*, the Emperor, re-enforcing perhaps a law of Hadrian, treated the murder of a slave as that of a free man. Manumission was facilitated ; it could be effected in the Emperor's Council, in Church, before the Consuls and the Prætors, before the tribunal of the governors, before the municipal magistrates. As regards the *coloni*, when estates were divided, it was forbidden to part children from their parents, and brothers from brothers ; landlords were forbidden to increase their dues. The *curiales*, from 361 onwards,

no longer paid the impost in place of defaulting Senators ;
from 383 they no longer had the burdensome and dangerous
task of collecting the taxes (*exactio*) on the lands of powerful
owners.   To *traders and artisans*, Constantine granted privileges (to thirty-seven free corporations) to encourage them
and their children to improve themselves in their trade or
craft.   The Christian *clergy* was specially favoured ;   its
lands were exempted from imposts (until 360) ;   clerics were
relieved of the *munera*, forced labour, and the *aurum coronarium*.   In addition they obtained considerable legal privileges.

The checking of the abuses of the system of " patronage ".[1]—
The small country landowners were a prey to the high landed
aristocracy which had wholly passed into the " senatorial "
class of the *clarissimi*.   The latter used innumerable ways to
rob the poor of their independence and of their property under
the pretext of patronage.   The Emperors tried to protect
these poor people against their own weakness.   A law of 370
forbade *agricolæ* the *patrocinium*, under pain of confiscation of
their property.   The patron who accepted was to incur the
fine of 25 gold pieces for each estate, which fine was raised to
40 pounds in 399.   In 395, the rich were forbidden to take
under their patronage free villages (*vici, metrocomiæ*).

Nevertheless the penal legislation has been accused of being
" harsh " by V. Duruy :   " He (the Emperor) multiplied the
number of punishments by the stake ;   he condemned thereto
the Jew who cast stones at the Christian Jew ;   the tax-
collector who abused his office ;   the scribe who wrongly placed
a name on the list of those granted immunity ;   the haruspex
who entered a private house ;   the slave who mated with a
free woman ;   the accomplices in rape ;   the forger ;   those who
held communications with the barbarians ;   the creditor who
seized for debt the oxen and agricultural implements of the
debtor, etc.   He caused molten lead to be poured into the
mouth of the maid servant who helped in the abduction of a
girl ;   the workmen, called *baphii* or *gynæcii*, who spoiled a
fabric could be put to death, etc." [2]

All this is true.   But it must be observed that these
terrible penalties show a ruler who is desirous of fighting
against the corruption of society at any cost.

[1] DLXXXIII, 102, 242 ; CCCXLVI.
[2] CXXVIII, vol. vii., 206.

" It was offences against chastity that roused his most inexorable and most terrible wrath ; he seemed more enraged by outrages to morality and religion than careful to preserve the order and rights of civil society. His edicts against adultery and rape breathe the hatred of an avenger rather than the prudence of the head of an Empire. Troubling himself very little about finding a remedy for the evil provided, he inflicted on the guilty a punishment proportioned to the crime, he violated all the old laws as well as his own in order to satisfy this pious but too violent indignation ".[1]

Constantine and his successors thus did all that could be done, in the way of legislation at least, to bring about the moral regeneration of the Society of their day.

---

[1] **CCCLI,** vol. ii., 141-142.

CHAPTER VI

THE CASTE SYSTEM

IN spite of the efforts of the Emperors, we can see that ancient society became rigid and lifeless. That there was no longer any political life goes without saying, but there was scarcely any municipal life left either. Art was utterly retrograde, science stereotyped and literature insignificant. The Roman world had lost all power of conquest and was losing even its capacity for assimilating the barbarians. The peoples brought into the territory of the Empire remained the subjects of Rome, but seemed no longer to acquire a taste for Roman customs and the Latin language. The religious sphere alone was the field of a violent turmoil, because it attracted with a passionate force every faculty of heart and mind.

Everyone was ill at ease in his station in life and tried to escape from it. The peasant left the country, the workman abandoned his trade, and the decurion fled the municipal Senate. For these evils the government found but one remedy : to tie everyone down to his condition and stop up every outlet through which an escape was possible.

The watch-word was " everyone at his post " or Roman civilization would perish. It was a state of siege, for life or perpetuity. A man's station in society, his profession, came to be made hereditary. We are watching the setting up of a real caste system, a phenomenon which in this case is not primitive or spontaneous, but an experiment imposed as a measure of policy from above.

Let us review the different classes which had to submit to it.

I. " OFFICIALES."   " COLLEGIATI "

The *Officiales*.—The functionaries, or rather the servants (*officiales*) and apparitors (*susceptores*), had been militarized since the reign of Septimius Severus. The services were divided into " cohorts " whence the name of *cohortales* for the governors' servants. The servant had the privilege of the military testament. Also, service whether in the central administration (the *palace*), or in the provincial administrations, was entitled *militia* (*palatina, officialis*) the former being, as goes without saying, far higher.

These servants had various privileges.[1] They could not be arbitrarily dismissed. They enjoyed exemption from imposts and various burdens ; they received honorary titles at the end of their career. But these privileges were counterbalanced by a real slavery. The *officiales* are said to be enmeshed in the snare of their condition ; *conditionum laqueis inretiti* (l. 28, C. Th., viii., iv., *De Cohortalibus*). There was no hesitation in prolonging their services beyond the proper age, until their strength was exhausted. About the person of every governor, and every head of a department, these *cohortales* swarmed. They could not be removed, but at the same time they were subject to the caprices of the Administration which made use of them as if they were cattle. Finally, their duties were hereditary. Only for the classes of servants in the *palatium* and in the Guard was the use of coercion found unnecessary, for a reason which need not be explained.

The *Collegiati*.—The caste system was imposed in the first place on the direct servants of the State, as may easily be understood. Specie became rare and the mines were considered State property. Work in the mines was consequently bound to be compulsory and even hereditary ; for who would have consented to accept willingly a life so horrible as was that of the ancient miner ? That was the reason why public slaves and condemned criminals were employed in them. The same applied to quarries and salt mines.

On the other hand, the workmen in the mints were generally free. But it was a peculiar kind of freedom. The craft was for life and hereditary ; the artisans had to marry daughters of workmen in the same craft, and they could be pursued as runaways.

The same applied to the *fabricenses*, the armourers and smiths of the Imperial factories. They were militarized and bore a mark on their arms. They had to die *exhausti laboribus*. This treatment was also extended to the *bastagarii* employed

[1] **DI,** vol. iii., 126, 149-160.

in the transport connected with the fiscus and in supplying the requirements of the troops, to the muleteers (*muliones*), grooms (*hippocomi*), cartwrights (*carpentarii*), veterinary surgeons (*mulomedici*), servants of the public post, men engaged in gathering purple, or weaving clothes in the State factories (*gynœcea*, or *textina* to the number of seventeen in the West), either for the Emperor and the Court or for the army.

All were organized in " colleges " and subject to military regulations and discipline. Moreover, from the time of Hadrian, the " bastagarii " were grouped in " cohorts."[1]

The provisioning of Rome, and later of Constantinople, formed an indispensable public service. These towns were markets in which were sold the products of the whole Mediterranean world ; but they themselves, especially the former, produced little. Industry and commerce and private charity would have been powerless to keep alive the hungry population which gathered there. The payments in kind from the provinces were indispensable, all the more as, with the slow retrogression of the economic system, the money impost more and more yielded to that in kind. Since the companies of publicani which used to farm these services had been suppressed in consequence of their monstrous abuses, and since private individuals owing to lack of sufficient capital could not be relied on to carry them out, the State was forced to entrust the transport of provisions to an official corporation endowed with privileges, the *navicularii*. These were official ship-owners, compulsorily grouped into a corporation. The Maritime commerce between the ports of Rome (Ostia, Porto) and Africa or Egypt was even (under Maxentius) to become an hereditary duty.[2]

The provisions thus brought over had then to be prepared for consumption ; for since the time of Aurelian, bread and no longer flour merely was distributed to the people. Whence the necessity not only of large general stores at Ostia and Porto, but of vast bakeries (258) at Rome also, where corn was ground, and the bread kneaded and baked, and finally of numerous slaves. The *corpus pistorum* (millers and bakers in one) up to the time when the water-mill came into use

[1] **DIII**, vol. ii., 224-238, 243.
[2] **DIII**, vol. ii., 20, 34, 103 ; **DI**, vol. iii., 261 ; **CCCXLIV**, vol. x., 149.

(in the fourth century) remained powerful and indispensable. We must add the distributions of oil, bacon and wine at low prices or gratuitously. The corporations became official and compulsory. " The sustenance of Rome depends on the corporations " writes the Prefect Symmachus to Valentinian II (*Ep.* x., 27).

After alimentation comes the upkeep of public buildings. Quarry owners were obliged to furnish lime for Rome while corporations of lime-burners (*calcis coctores* or *calcarienses*) and of carriers (*vectores* and *vecturarii*) were charged with the transport. The large *collegium fabrum* or *fabrorum tignariorum*, included all the workmen connected with building ; it was intimately connected with the State to which it owed a certain number of days' work.

Wood, both for heating purposes and for military and naval constructions, was provided by the *dendrophori*. The bath and daily douche had in fact, become a necessity to the populace. There were 956 baths at Rome. The *navicularii lignarii* brought from Africa the wood needed for heating these. The keepers of the aqueducts which fed the baths (*hydrophylaces aquarii*) had their hands marked *felici nomine pietatis nostræ*.

The games had become an organic need ; 175 days in the year in the fourth century (135 under Marcus Aurelius) were given up to circus or theatre games. These comic or tragic representations and gladiatorial or wild beast combats demanded expenses and a staff which were very burdensome. The expenses were borne by the Emperor, that is to say by the tax-payers of the provinces and by rich private individuals. The games were a charge of the prætorship. If the Prætor died in the course of the festivals, his heirs were obliged to sustain the costs until their termination.

The service of the games was one of the important cares of the government. At the theatre, in the amphitheatre and the circus, the populace gave free vent to its turbulence.[1] Christianity tried in vain to check the passion for the games which was as violent as and no less disastrous than alcoholism in modern times.

The Emperors yielded to the will of the people : gladiators, mimes, men and women musicians, actors and actresses,

[1] DI, vol. iii., 369, 375.

charioteers were hereditarily chained to their profession which was yet branded as infamous ; they were obliged to be, in the words of the Imperial constitutions, the " slaves of the people's pleasures ". In the end the right of pursuing them as runaways came to be applied to them. Players and charioteers were forbidden to leave the city and became subject to the obligation of fixed residence.

These services were repeated on a small scale in the capitals of *civitates*. The rivers there conveyed provisions and raw materials through colleges of *nautæ* for the service of the towns, at least in part. We find in the provinces *collegia fabrum, dendrophori*, etc.

The festivals and games were held at the expense of the *duoviri*. The towns of Trèves, Cologne, Mainz, Carthage and Antioch, were no less eager for shows than Rome or Constantinople.[1]

Never have towns better deserved the epithet " tentacular " than under the Roman Empire.

II. THE MILITARY CASTE[2]

The *militia* par excellence, the army (*militia militaris*) also became a caste, in the first place by the method of its recruitment. Roman citizens had long since ceased to do military service. On the other hand, foreigners gained the standing of citizens either on their entering the army (the *legionaries*), or on their leaving it (the *auxiliaries*) after a long service (from sixteen to twenty-five years). After Caracalla's edict (212) granting citizenship to all free subjects of the Empire these measures lost some of their interest. The Later Empire, however imposed the caste system here by closing the army, below to slaves who were still excluded from military service, and above to Senators excluded since the time of Gallienus, to decurions and their children, to the *subjecti curiæ* who had to devote themselves entirely to the service of their " cities " and the raising of the imposts, and to *negotiatores*.

Soldiers could therefore be drawn only from the lowest part of the population of the towns and *vici* and by way of voluntary enlistment. The hardship and length of service, and the poor pay (replaced more and more by payments in

[1] CCLXX, vol. i., 46 ; LXII, 343 ; CVII.
[2] Cf. above, p. 89.

kind) kept away from the army even the dregs of the population. Add to this the fact that the ravages of the fourth century depopulated the countries South of the Danube, whence the best elements of the Roman army had been drawn since the middle of the third century.

There remained conscription. It became a task imposed on the large landlords and those of average means. Recruiting being local since Hadrian's reign, when circumstances demanded it, compulsory enlistment was resorted to. Every large landowner had to provide one or more recruits from amongst the so-called free men living on his estates. Like the requisition of horses, this was a due imposed on them. The Imperial constitutions speak quite crudely of *tironum sive equorum productio, equorum tironum præstatio.*

" It was one of the varieties of the collection in kind and not even amongst the more highly esteemed of these. Of the two duties at first of equal rank amongst civil obligations, that of levying soldiers and that of levying pigs " (*porcinæ species*), one became a ' sordid ' function, and it was that of levying soldiers."[1] Sometimes the State preferred to levy them itself and then exacted payment, *aurum temonarium* or *aurum tironicum* (25, 30, 36 gold solidi for each recruit). There even arose a business of providing substitutes, and a class of traders in human beings. Naturally, the *senatores* and the *honorati* gave up to the recruiting officers (curiales were charged with this *turmaria functio*) only the refuse of the population.

Once enlisted, these recruits took the oath and were marked on their arms. Their condition was unalterable and they were bound to serve until their strength was exhausted, twenty, twenty-five years or more. It is true that these soldiers could contract legal marriages, which was impossible under the Early Empire ; but the children born of these unions belonged by right to the army.[2] If they tried to escape from it, the law pursued them everywhere. Constantine was the first to impose this obligation on the sons of soldiers and of veterans. Thus service in the army also fell to the level of strict servitude.

---

[1] **DI,** vol. iii., 155 ; **CVIII,** 229.
[2] MISPOULET (*Revue épigraphique*, 1913) has however shown that there is no trace of a hereditary status before the fourth century.

We may imagine the value of an army recruited in this fashion. The *militia* became a real mark of disgrace. Its military achievement was poor and the Empire would doubtless have succumbed if it had not developed the practice of filling its armies with barbarians. We may say that from the middle of the fourth century at least, a " Roman " army had military value in proportion as it included more barbarians and fewer Romans.[1]

The barbarians entered into the service of Rome by several ways :

(1) By voluntary enlistment of individuals. In this case these became Romanized and subject to the same obligations and practices as Roman recruits.

(2) As *fœderati* ; to these we shall return.

(3) As *lœti* (a German word applied to the half-free).

These were cantoned in the country on " lætic " lands of which they enjoyed the hereditary use, on condition that their children were subject to military service like the parents.

The *lœti* were under twelve *prœfecti lœtorum* responsible to the *magister peditum prœsentalis*. They even had a corporate organization ; a Novel of Severus (465) calls them *corpora publicis obsequiis deputata*. It seems that their national law was left to them ; in order to bind them completely to their caste, a constitution (of Valentinian and Valens) in 365 prohibited marriage between *lœti* and Roman citizens and even between *lœti* and *coloni*. Thus the necessity to assimilate foreign populations settled on the territory of the Empire was sacrificed to the mania for pigeon-holing. The *lœti* are peculiar to Gaul. They are only met with in this country, especially in the north-east ; they appear to be of Frankish or Frisian origin.

The *Gentiles* on the other hand are found not only in Gaul, but also and especially in Italy. By this term are denoted the Danubian peoples, Sarmatian or Germanic, transplanted on to the territory of the Empire in conditions akin to that of the *lœti*. There are four *prœfecturœ gentilium* in Gaul, and nineteen in Upper Italy. These people were brought in probably by Constantine or rather by Constantius, whereas the introduction of the *lœti* is older. We know the names of some of these colonies of the *Gentiles*.

[1] **CVIII,** vol. ii.

The general term has left its imprint in *Gentiliacum*, Gentilly. These " Gentiles " were chiefly Iranians, that is to say Sarmatians. From these *Sarmatiæ* have come the names of Sermaise and Saumaise (Marne, Oise, Seine-et-Oise, Loiret, Niève, Yonne, Aisne, etc.) ; of Sermizelles (Yonne). The Taifali, of Gothic origin perhaps, have given their name to Tiffauges (Vendée). Thus some Germans from the Danube are met with amongst them. The Marcomanni have given their name to Marmagne (Côte-d'Or, Allier, Mayenne, Saône-et-Loire, Cher) ; the Alamans to Allemans (Aisne, Marne, Dordogne, Lot-et-Garonne), and to Allemagne (Calvados, Ain in Basses Alpes).[1]

On the frontiers the soldiers, Roman at first and later barbarian, obtained allotments (*terræ limitaneæ, fundi limitrophi*) ; but they were not obliged to cultivate and still less to clear them themselves ; they farmed them by means of slaves or coloni. These lands did not pay the land-tax ; they could not become the private property of a third party but passed to the children. But the latter were attached to the defence of the *castella* or *burgi* on the frontier, whence their name of *castellani, burgarii*. This institution, attributed to Alexander Severus by the *Historia Augusta*, is probably not earlier than Constantine.[2]

The upkeep of the army required provisioning and transport services, stores, billets, armouries, arsenals, and ambulances. All these services, as we have seen, were organized into corporations.

III. THE COLONATE[3]

The name of Constantine is attached to the first legal document which we possess on the famous institution of the Colonate (October, 332) : " He with whom shall be found a colonus belonging to another shall have not merely to restore him to the estate on which this colonus was born, but shall be obliged also to pay the capitation for the time (passed with him). . . As for the coloni who attempt to run away, it shall be allowed to load them with chains, in the manner of slaves " (*Cod. Theod.*, v., 9, 1).

---

[1] **CCCIV**, 127-137.
[2] Mispoulet, in the *Revue épigraphique*, 1913.
[3] **CLII, XXVIII, C, CCCXXXIV, CDXXII,** Seeck in **CCCXCVII**, under *Colonus*.

What is a colonus ?

" The colonus . . . is a perpetual and hereditary but non-voluntary farmer for life, for whom attachment to the soil is both a right and an obligation ; he cannot be given public duties which will take him away from it, nor ordained as a cleric, unless it be on the land which he cultivates and on condition that he remains on it. If he runs away, he is re-claimed like a slave, and once re-captured, he is vigorously punished, as is also the receiver. But the landlord cannot sell the estate without the coloni, nor the coloni without the estate, nor shift them from one estate to another, unless the former has too much land and the second too little. The fiscus itself cannot break the tie which attaches him to the land and the Imperial constitutions forbid the fiscal agents to evict the colonus unable to pay the tax ".[1]

This land, of which the colonus is the serf and which keeps him bound to its soil, he on his part possesses from father to son, and it does not return to the owner unless the colonus leaves no heir. The landlord has not the right to increase the dues or to alter the tenant's duties : the latter are fixed by a *lex* (or *mos loci*) which is considered perpetual. In civil law the colonus is a free man. He can contract a marriage, make a will, and even bring an action, at least with regard to disputes about his tenure. He is only indirectly the servant of the owner, his lord (*patronus, dominus*), through the land on which he lives and which he cultivates.

This social system is not an innovation of the Later Empire. The ancient monarchies of Asia and of Egypt, ancient Greece, and independent Gaul, very probably knew from time immemorial a serfdom of the soil which presents striking analogies to what is properly called the " colonate ".

Nevertheless, the latter, on the soil of the West at least, seems to be the result of an evolution of the Roman method of working the land. Since the end of the Republic, the small country proprietor had disappeared. Under the Empire there remained the large and average landlords who had at their disposal two methods of cultivating the land :(1) to exploit it directly by entrusting it to bailiffs and working it by means of chained slaves divided into "*decuriæ*" ; (2) by farming it out.

[1] **CLIII,** 15.

The first had gradually to be abandoned because of the considerable diminution in the number of slaves. The period of conquest once over, it was no longer possible to throw on the market herds of captives as in the second and first century B.C. Importation by purchase yielded but a small supply. On the other hand the rearing of slaves was expensive : up to the age of thirteen at the least, a slave involves cost and makes no return ; he is quickly used up and dies young. Finally agrarian slave economy needs large capital and rich lands, in view of the meagre productiveness of non-free work. But since the second century A.D. capital had disappeared, the rich lands were exhausted and slave agricultural labour became a ruinous speculation.

The class of free small farmers (*coloni, conductores*) who rented the land on a short lease (generally five years) and for money, disappeared or became extremely rare after Trajan's reign.

The land-owners had no remedy but to make a division of their estates. They divided them into two parts. One of these, the lord's demesne (*indominicatum*) included the dwelling-house (the *villa*, the future " castle ") with a small portion of the arable lands and a few meadows, the smallest part (a third or quarter of the whole), but the whole of the forests, pastures, and moors. The other part, the major portion of the arable lands, vineyards, and meadows, was apportioned into " tenures " (called *mansi* in the Frankish period) given to farmers called free (*coloni*) and also, but much more rarely, to slave " cottagers " (*casati*). The tenure called *mansus ingenuilis* or *colonica* when worked by a colonus, and *mansus servilis* when worked by a slave, is an economic unit. It is not one continuous farm, but consists of arable plots distributed in the different cantons or portions of the estate, some acres of the vineyard or meadows, and lastly of the rights of user of the lord's (*dominus*) pastures and woods in proportion to the number of head of cattle owned by the farmer. The *mansus* is in principle the amount of fields, meadows and vineyards, necessary for the upkeep of a peasant and his family ; nevertheless if the tenure is large, he has the right to take on a partner (*socius*), sometimes even two.

These tenants got off with the payment of a very small sum of money and mostly, in view of the decay of the monetary

system, with contributions of the produce (*agrarium*) ;
they appear to have paid a tenth.   Lastly and chiefly, they
gave up to the seigniorial demesne a large part of their time
and labour ;   They did gratis the tilling, sowing, harrowing,
reaping, mowing, hay-making, fencing, repairing.   The serf
cottagers had to devote to these labours (*corvadœ, manoperœ*)
half of their time, the free-born *coloni* considerably less, but
all the same a large part of their time.   The anxious problem
of manual labour was thus solved for the landowner.
" Fundamentally, the colonate is nothing else but the substitution of the system of small tenures in place of that of
mass cultivation by slave-labour ".[1]

This practice had its roots in the past ;   Cicero's friend
Atticus, a shrewd business man, had already begun to divide
his estates amongst small coloni paying their rent in produce.
It underwent a considerable development subsequently in
the second and fourth centuries, though unfortunately we
cannot follow the stages of this evolution.   If the legislation
of the Later Empire shows us, suddenly as it were, the colonate
which transformed ancient society in the West, the reason
is that the state was led by its interests to look closely into
this institution and to bring to bear upon it the forcible influence of its authority.

At the beginning its intervention was chiefly fiscal.   The
pivot of this husbandry by allotments was the colonus.   If
he deserted his farm, the estate lost in value in proportion to
the number of tenants leaving it.   The Treasury knew this
so well that in its assessment of lands, vines, meadows, etc.,
and of the cattle of the estate, it added a census of the coloni
and serfs who worked it.   By reason of the de-population or
sparseness of the population of the Roman Empire, the land,
which was almost the sole form of wealth since the retrogression
of industry and commerce, had value only through the hands
which cultivated it.   If the coloni left, it was likely that the
landowner would not find others ;   he would be ruined and
would not be able to pay the tax ;   moreover the runaway
colonus would not pay his capitation.

Well knowing that on workmen without a fixed abode the
fiscus would have no hold, the Roman State resolved that the
colonus should be inscribed on the register of the estate of

[1] **CLIII**, 144.

which he cultivated his portion ; he was *adscriptitius*, *quâ* liable to the *capitatio plebeia*, and his landlord, the *dominus*, was responsible for him.

By abandoning his tenure, then, the colonus cheated both the landlord and the State. The Emperor judged it necessary to intervene. But, at first, he had no intention of attaching the colonus to a corner of the soil in perpetuity ; he only attached him to the tax register of the estate on which he lived : it was the land much more than the man which was " ascribed to the census ". The proof of this is that if the landlord had too many coloni on one estate and not enough on another, the surplus coloni could be transferred to the latter (provided it was in the same fiscal district). Moreover, the *coloni* were not all *adscriptitii* or *tributarii* or *censiti*, or *obnoxii censibus*, or ἐναπόγραφοι. If they possessed any landed property of their own, however small, they were not placed on the estate register of the rich landlord whose estate they ordinarily cultivated, but on the registers of the free village (*vicus*, *metrocomia*) which they inhabited and their payment was collected by the fiscal agents.

At the end of the fourth century the coloni still fully had the feeling that they were attached to the tax register of the estate, but not to the estate itself ; they did not feel themselves serfs of the soil. A law having done away with the capitation throughout the diocese of Thrace (between 393 and 395), the Emperor Theodosius foresaw that the coloni would draw from this decision the conclusion that they could go wherever it pleased them. He hastened to rid them of this illusion (*Cod. Just.*, XI, 52).

The fact is that, soon passing beyond the strictly fiscal point of view, the Roman State had come to look upon the colonate, which was at first for life, then hereditary, or the serfdom of the soil, to use a modern expression,[1] as a vital necessity for society. In 371, Valentinian I writes " We do not deem that coloni have liberty to leave the land to which their condition and birth attach them. If they go away from it, and pass to another owner, let them be brought back, put into chains and punished ". It seems that the people concerned were descendants of coloni rather than coloni whose condition was recent. But new and strict measures

[1] MARC BLOCH in the *Revue historique*, vol. CXXXVI, 1921.

made exceptions for no one. Introducing the colonate into
Palestine, Theodosius describes it as follows : " Henceforth
the colonus will not be able to please himself by going where-
ever he likes with a perfect right, but after the example of
what happens in the other provinces, he shall be attached to
the owner of the estate, and no one shall be able to receive him
without incurring a fine ; further, the owner has full power
to bring the runaway back. The Emperor reminds his subjects that in all the province it is a rule established by a kind
of eternal right that the coloni must not go away from the
soil the fruits of which are their sustenance, or desert the land
which they have once undertaken to work " (*Cod. Just.*, XI, 51).
Lastly, the end of the decree abolishing the capitation in
Thrace is conceived in the following terms :   " Let the coloni
be kept by right of birth, and though they be of free estate,
let them nevertheless be reckoned as serfs of the land on
which they are born ; let them not have permission to go
wherever they wish, to remove to another place, but let the
owner legally exercise both the care of a protector and the
authority of a master ".

The colonate has become an *estate*, a *conditio*, an *ordo*, intermediate between freedom and slavery. Legislation hesitated
a long time, with a more and more emphatic tendency to
reduce to the inferior status a husband or wife and children,
in cases of marriage between colonus and non-colonus.

In the colonate were placed barbarians, undesirables and
even free cultivators ; Anastasius bound to the soil the free
born man who had worked thirty years for another, and
Justinian extends this ordinance to the children. The law,
when it speaks of the *coloni*, is inflexibly severe. There is no
leniency, no pity : " Everyone must submit to his fate ".
(*Cod. Just.*, XI, 69, 4). The only thing for whom a tone of
tenderness is discernible, is the land : " What inhumanity
to mutilate the land ", the land, the kindly mother whose
destruction is risked by her wicked children through their
desertion of her.

Society rested on agriculture. The latter was the " first of
the public services ". If the free play of private enterprise
and interests did not suffice to secure it, public authority
had to provide for it by compulsory measures. " The processes furnished by private law having proved insufficient to

secure it, Imperial constitutions provided for it by legal compulsion. The tillers were attached to the soil by measures analogous to our military conscription and naval enlistment."[1]

What is surprising is that a condition which in our view is so terrible, could have presented substantial advantages to counterbalance burdens which we consider onerous and degrading. If the land held the colonus, he also held the land. Eviction, for him and his descendants, was forbidden. What was practically indefinite possession amounted to a kind of ownership, in fact if not in law. In return for these essential benefits, the obligations in the way of dues were light ; the rent in money was of the smallest, while the portion of the produce (a tenth, it seems) was comparatively moderate. The socage services, as they were later to be called, (grinding the corn at the lord's mill, making wine in his wine-press, etc.), could be inconvenient and costly, but they too had their advantages. The only really heavy burden was the forced labour and manual toil on the lord's preserve, which used up the tenant's time and strength. But it seems not to have been really crushing (half the week) except for the "cottager" serfs ; the *coloni* proper owed appreciably less, according to the custom of the estate ; sometimes one or two days a week, but sometimes only a dozen or half-a-dozen days in the year.

There remain two servile conditions which appear degrading : the prohibition to leave the estate (the right to follow), and the prohibition to take a wife from outside. We may rest assured that very rarely did they seem hard to the *agricolæ* of the Roman world. From all time the peasant has been a stay-at-home; what he wanted then, as now, was not to wander here and there, but to cling to the soil which he loves like an animal, instinctively. As for marriage, the peasant takes a wife most often from his own neighbourhood. We may doubt whether the prohibition as to marriage, which in practice reduced itself to having to buy a licence, was more annoying than the senseless formalities with which certain modern laws have hedged about the nuptial act.

On the whole, the peasant asked for a minimum of security, stability and assurance against arbitrariness. The colonate fulfilled all these *desiderata*. We are not surprised that in the

---

[1] G. DEMANTE, *Etude historique sur les mainmortables*, p. 57.

West it survived the Roman Empire a considerable number
of centuries.

IV. THE FREE PEASANTS

Besides the *coloni* and country serfs, " cottagers " or not,
there existed here and there free peasants grouped in independent villages, called *vici* in the West, and *metrocomiœ* in
the East. The hand of the State bound these also to the soil.
These free men, like the *coloni* and the serf cottagers, were
forbidden to leave their fields ; they were serfs of their village.
They were *ascribed* to the *vicus* just as the *coloni* were to the
country estate. The village community system was enforced
on them ; they were forbidden (in Egypt) to alienate their
own property to anyone other than a fellow-villager (Anthemius
in 468). When they wished to acquire an estate (*possessio*,
massa), the *convicani* were subjected by Theodosius II (in
425) to the ἐπιβολή or *adjectio*, that is to say they were
obliged to take the fields which had been deserted as unfertile,
as well as the cultivated land.

V. THE CURIALES

The city and the large estate.—Unless we are to understand
nothing about the system imposed upon the town and its
inhabitants in the Later Empire, we must remember that
profound differences separated the ancient city from the town
of the middle ages and of modern times, from a double point
of view, that of politics and that of economics.

In the Mediterranean world, Greek and Roman, the town
had become, many centuries before the Christian era, the
point of concentration and converging focus of the political
and social forces of the people or tribe, Greek, Latin, Samnite,
Sicel, Etruscan, etc. ; the rest of the territory, the country
as contrasted with the town, had sunk into dependence on
the urban centre.[1] To cite two examples only, Attica ended
by being summed up in Athens, and Latium in Rome. So
much so, that the *Urbs*, the πόλις, gave its name to the
small State which it guided and ruled, and the *civitas*, the " city ",
was both the urban centre and the territory, often extensive,

---

[1] **LIII,** 171 ; **CDXXX,** 258 ; **CCCXLIV,** vol. viii., 20.

of which it was the head. There remained, it is true, traces of an earlier state of things, but these were survivals without any future or power.[1]

This system the Romans and even the Greeks before them, extended wherever they succeeded in imposing their dominion. The Greek and Roman colonies were cities founded after the image of the mother-city which the daughters endeavoured to resemble.

Another characteristic of which we must not lose sight, consists in the fact that the economic functions of the ancient colony have only very remote relations with modern foundations. In our days we do not found a city of set purpose, or else we invite failure ; the new town arises, so to speak, spontaneously, when the favourable economic conditions for commercial intercourse or the erection of industries are met with at some special point of the land.

Leaving aside the Greek world, which would take us too far back, in the Roman world it was otherwise. In the time of Republican Rome, the colony was a detachment of Roman citizens settled in a recently conquered country, in order to watch, to keep in check, and to Romanize it. It was a garrison, but a permanent garrison.[2] The *coloni* brought wives with them and founded families. From the period of the Gracchi, the character of the colony became modified ; the purpose of the colony was chiefly social. It was intended to relieve Rome and Latium of its superfluous plebeian population. Lastly, in the first century B.C., the colony was a means of getting rid of soldiers, when, after civil war, it became necessary to disband the armies. Sulla, Cæsar and Augustus in this way established colonies which kept the names of their founders. After Tiberius, there were scarcely any more real colonies ; this name, with the privileges which it carried, was given to towns founded quite differently, as we shall see.

Whatever the motive of its foundation, the colony had to live. On what was it going to live ? Naturally, not on commerce or industry ; the soldiers or the proletarians who formed its population had neither the taste nor the aptitude for such an occupation ; moreover only political and strategic,

---

[1] CCCXXVII, 111, 143.
[2] CCXXXVIII, 40 ; CCLXXII and CCLXXIII ; CCCLXVIII.

not economic considerations had inspired the choice of the
site for the colony.   The colony would live chiefly by working
the land and the very name *colonia* is related to *colere*, to
" cultivate ".

These *coloni* are soldiers, but farmer-soldiers ; we must
understand that each of them was to cultivate, with the help
of servants, his plot drawn by lot (whence *sors*).   The town
was thus simply the collection of the dwellings of these farmer-
soldiers surrounded by a protecting rampart ; round about
it extended the arable fields.   The part of the soil which had
not been allocated (*loca relicta subseciva*) remained *ager publicus*
or was granted to the colony as common land.   The natives
of the country district were attached to the colony by ill
defined bonds of subjection.[1]

To sum up, the colony was a fortified village, which explains
why a colony could be founded wherever one wished, provided
there was good soil.   Even today, in the South of Italy,
many towns are only big villages.   The country population,
instead of scattering in small villages or hamlets, or even,
as in France, in groups of one or two families, clings together,
dispersing over the countryside only at the times of sowing,
ploughing and reaping.

This artificial character of the Roman colonies also explains
the rectilinear plan of certain towns ;   their appearance is
that of a camp.[2]   Naturally, if circumstances lent themselves
to it, the colony, thus constituted, might become a commercial
centre, and actually it was in this case only that it subsequently
assumed a real importance, and became a town in the modern
sense.   But, originally, nothing of the sort was aimed at and
the colony might perfectly well keep its strategic character
and purely rural economy.

Daughters of Rome, these colonies had their constitution
modelled on that of the mother-city ; they had a Senate and
magistrates, endowed with functions similar or analogous to
those of Rome.   We may pass over the differences between
colonies with Roman and those with Latin rights ; at the time
with which we are dealing these had only an antiquarian
interest.   The towns of Italy had either been possessed of the
rights of citizenship without the vote (*municipia*), or had been

[1] **CCCXXXII**, vol. ii., 32, 36.
[2] **CCCXLII.**

placed under the jurisdiction of the Urban Prætor (whence the name of *præfecturæ*). The Julian (90) and Plautian Papirian (89) laws made them enter en bloc into the category of Roman cities. These towns, called *municipia*, enjoyed Latin rights.[1] To the subject cities of the Hellenic world federate or allied, Rome, in principle, left their old laws.

So much was this the case, that in the first and second centuries A.D. the Roman Empire still seemed a federation of States or of cities which merely acknowledged the hegemony of the most illustrious amongst them, *Urbs Roma*.

In fact, all these constitutions were modelled on that of Rome and her " colonies ".[2] These constitutions were old and decayed ; whence the necessity of having recourse to the Emperor on many occasions. Under Marcus Aurelius, Marseilles of its own accord gave up its old constitution. Under Septimius Severus the municipal system of Alexandria and of Egypt was altered.[3]

The Roman government made it its business to introduce the system of the city state into those countries in which it was unknown or not widely spread, in Gaul, for example. In the part conquered by Julius Cæsar, the *Tres Galliæ*, there lived sixty Celtic, Belgic and Iberian peoples, sub-divided into three hundred *pagi*. With practically few exceptions (Bourges for example) they had no knowledge of urban life. The town was the *oppidum*, the place of assembly in case of war, and at the same time the market (of this kind are Gergovie and le Mont-Beuvray). People met there periodically but lived there either not at all or very little. The Gauls lived in the country in large villages or scattered dwellings.

Rome founded colonies in the Three Gauls, as she had done in Gallia Narbonensis, where she had founded six Roman and thirteen Latin colonies, Lyons and Basle were founded in 43 B.C., then Nyon on the Lake of Geneva. Claudius created a fourth, Cologne on the Rhine, in 40 A.D. Under Vespasian arose Avenches among the Helveti, *Nemetes* (Spire) on the Rhine, Feurs among the Segusiavi and perhaps Trèves. Trajan founded the two " Ulpian " colonies, one at Nymegen and the other on the Lower Rhine. Of uncertain date are Besançon, Langres, Eauze in Novempopulania. In the centre their

---

[1] **LIII,** 175 ; **CCCXXXII,** vol. ii., 59 ; **XLII,** 204.
[2] **CVII,** 14.　　　　　　　　　　　　　　[3] **CCLI.**

number is not very high and several towns are only colonies
by name ; they are " honorary colonies".[1]

Above all, Rome pushed on with the development of urban
life in the so-called " free" States. The old Gaulish *oppida*
became capitals of the *civitas* and every *pagus* had at least a
vicus. The Gaulish aristocracy quickly developed a taste for
urban life, that is to say, for Roman civilization. From
Strabo's time (IV, 1, 11), the Allobrogian nobility had concentrated at Vienne. The Celtic institutions were at first
able to survive ; thus Autun went on being governed by the
vergobret of the *Aedui*, and Nîmes by the *prætor* of the
Volcæ. But Rome's power of assimilation was so irresistible
that, in the third century, there is no longer any trace of
these ancient institutions. At the same time the territory of
every Gaulish tribe became incorporated into the capital, and
that to such an extent that often the former gave the town
its name : *Lutetia* became Paris (*ad Parisios*), *Agednicum*
became Sens (*ad Senones*), *Cæsaromagus* became Beauvais
(*ad Bellovacos*), etc.

In the course of the third century, the unification of the
urban constitutions was completed throughout the Roman
world, with the exception of some districts in Africa, in which
the inhabitants of the *pagus* lived under the tribal system
with an organization distinct from that of the *civitas*.
Accordingly we may describe, at least in its main features,
what is called the municipal system[2] and was in reality the
system of the small States the aggregate of which constituted
the Roman Empire.

The *City* (*civitas*, πόλις) included the citizens (*cives*)
and also the aliens (*incolæ*), the latter having the duties without
sharing in the rights of citizens. The people (*plebs*) had in
the course of the second century lost the right to elect the
magistrates ; its *comitia* had ceased to assemble, except
perhaps in some towns of Africa.[3] The magistrates,
appointed for a year by the municipal Senate, or recruited
by co-option, were :

(1) The two consuls (*duoviri*) with the same insignia as
at Rome. They exercised jurisdiction as a collegium and were

---

[1] XLII, 210, 221 ; CXIII, CCLXVIII.
[2] CVII, CCXXXVIII, CCLXXII, CCXCVI.
[3] XCVII, CCLXVI, CDXVIII.

responsible for the adminstration of the town ; they had the supreme control of its finances and of the urban police.

(2) Two ædiles whose administration was also collegiate. They had under their supervision the markets, roads, buildings, the common sewer, the games and the corn-doles. Sometimes *duovirs* or *œdiles* were replaced by a college of *quatuorviri*.

(3) Below were the quæstors set over the treasury. These were not always included amongst the magistrates.

(4) Immediately after, came the pontiffs, augurs, flamens, and above all, the augustales ; they were to disappear with the triumph of Christianity in the course of the fourth century.

The Senate, wrongly termed " municipal ", an imitation on a smaller scale of that of Rome, formed the real government of the small State ; for *pagi* and *vici* had no curia. It was entitled *curia, ordo, ordo amplissimus, honestissimus, splendidissimus*, sometimes even *senatus*. Its members were called *decuriones*. The curia constituted a person, a *universitas*, whose authority extended over the whole territory of the State. The curia consisted of a hundred ordinary members, without counting the honorary patrons. In theory, every five years the duovirs in office, called this year "quinquennales", drew up the list or *album*, conforming to certain strict regulations, in which account was taken of a man's wealth, social position and respectability. In actual fact, as magistrates and ex-magistrates belonged to it by right, the *ordo* very quickly came to be recruited from a small circle of families whose members fulfilled the duties of magistrates in rotation.

The legislative and executive powers of the curia and of the magistrates were very much curtailed since the fourth century and even before ; the jurisdiction of the duovirs was confined to the police court in criminal cases and to voluntary jurisdiction (appointing a guardian, etc.) in civil cases. The curia did not legislate any longer, but formed a kind of court of appeal from the magistrates' decisions. It supervised, and like all oligarchies supervised badly, the State finances.

The honour of pursuing the " senatorial " career or the career of office (*honores*) in a small State (the successive stages were those of quæstor, ædile, duovir, quinquennalis and honorary member) was very costly. Public opinion required the candidate to show gratitude for the " honour "

paid to him by spending his money lavishly. He was obliged
to take under his charge the festivals and games given in the
chief town, and these were a terrible expense, as was the corn-
dole, at least in the big towns. He built baths, aqueducts,
theatres and amphitheatres. His generosity must not stop
at the town but had to extend to the *vici* and *pagi*. As long
as the Empire enjoyed prosperity, the *honours* were sought
after and the local aristocracy took a joy in contributing
to the embellishment and adornment of their small native
district and its capital.

But ruin came. It came at first slowly and insidiously.
Heralded first from the end of the second century, its onset
was rapid in the third century. The old families became
impoverished and then died out. The rising of the nouveaux
riches was quite insufficient to repair the losses. The curiæ
were emptied and the *cursus honorum* tempted men less and
less as its burdens (the *munera*), apportioned amongst an
ever diminishing number of persons, became heavier and
heavier. Further, it was not merely onerous but became
dangerous ; for the ædiles and duovirs, made responsible for
the financial position of the city, could be and were prose-
cuted for maladministration.

The financial position of the cities became so deplorable
that the Emperors had to appoint financial inspectors under
the name of *curators*. This institution became universal in
the time of Diocletian. It seems that at this time the curator
assumed the substance of all the financial powers, leaving only
their shadow to the magistrates of the cities. And since
about the same time the governor took away from them the
little judicial and administrative authority which was left
to them, we may ask ourselves what real functions the curiæ
could still have.

Nevertheless the Roman State was firmly resolved that
the curiæ should continue. Their existence was more than
ever necessary to it. We must not forget that the Roman
Government for a long time was acquainted only with the
system of the City State. The Empire, we must repeat,
was a federation of cities acknowledging the hegemony of the
greatest, fairest and most powerful amongst them, Rome.
The Empire would become weakened in proportion as its
component members became enfeebled.

For the maintenance of these small States, revenues were needed. What were the sources from which they came ? These in actual fact consisted merely in the produce of the estates of the cities, and in the fines imposed for offences. But the produce of the estates (farms and houses let on five years' leases) was very insufficient. Besides, these estates themselves were disposed of by the Emperors practically as of their *res privata*. Gifts and confiscations exhausted them. In fact, the city could only subsist on the constant flow of largesses from the " magistrates ".

By a kind of paradox of fate, at the moment when these magistrates ceased to exercise any real functions in their *civitas* (the curators took these over) they became more and more agents of the State.[1] Up to Diocletian's reign each *civitas* owed Rome the land tax, in kind or in metal specie, in accordance with old regulations determining the relations between the small State (*civitas*), or the *provincia* in which it was included, and the sovereign State. After Diocletian's financial reforms, the responsibilities of the curiæ grew. The decurions had to apportion between the *possessores* the total of the *juga* or the *capita* demanded from the *civitas*, carry out the levy of the land tax, and supervise the returns, and they were responsible for it, since Constantine, with their private means. The same applied to the levy of the *Chrysargyron*. They also carried out the service of the " Annona ", the collection and conveyance to the State stores of the provisions necessary for the army and for the officials ; the billeting of the military, etc. They carried out further the levy of conscripts (*præbitio tironum*).

The civil service, the public service of the notariate (bureau for the registering of members for the curia) also devolved upon them. They were the auxiliaries of the governor (*præses*) for the administration of justice : the arrest and detention of criminals, etc.

The burden of all these duties together having become crushing, no one was found since the beginning of the fourth century, to take up lightly the provincial " senatorial " career. The Roman State then took an unheard of step ; it enforced the career rigorously. Nor could it do otherwise if it did not wish the State and civilization to crumble to pieces. The

[1] **CVII**, 264, 307, 358, 370, 383 ; **CCCXXVII**, 149.

decurions could not be replaced. The State did not possess functionaries to put in their place.

In the first place, the conception of " functionaries " in the modern sense, did not exist or scarcely existed. There were " magistrates " and later personal friends of the Emperor on a temporary mission. These were the Counts, originally real aulic councillors sent on a tour of inspection. Far below them were the *officiales*, mere servants whose condition was degraded by bureaucratic serfdom.

Even if it had had the idea and the possibility of creating real functionaries, the State would have made a bad bargain. It would have had to spend vast sums in order to pay an enormous staff whose loyalty, work and honesty would certainly have left much to be desired in so corrupt a society. The State on the contrary needed citizens devoting their time, labour and wealth to their small fatherland, the city, and to the great fatherland Rome. What surprises us, is that the Emperors should have been able to think they had the right to impose such exorbitant duties and should have succeeded in getting them accepted willingly or by force.

But the ancient ideas about the citizen's rights and duties were not yet completely obliterated. The ancients had no conception of the liberty of the individual in the absolute and anarchical sense of the moderns. Liberty, for them, was the enjoyment of political rights. The citizen owed the whole of himself, body and soul, to the State. He owed to it his time, his property and even his life.

The Emperors did not think they were transgressing the limits of the rights of the State, and the free and wealthy citizens submitted. The opposition never assumed the character of more than a passive resistance. It became general only when the burden was beyond the economic forces of society.

To prevent the emptying of the curiæ, it was necessary to fill them *ex officio* or automatically, and for this purpose to find a class of persons who should regularly be obliged to bear the burdens of the curia, to be *obnoxii curiæ*, or *curiales*. This last term, which is not, as is asserted, identical with *decurio*, is only found from the third century onwards. In the third and even at the beginning of the fourth century, the *curiales* did not yet form a closed hereditary college.[1]

[1] CVII, 195-198.

A certain competency, consisting chiefly but not necessarily in landed property joined to residence, sufficed to make of a free man an eventual candidate, and to incorporate him in the curia, obliging him to undertake its duties and burdens from the moment when he was enrolled in it; he could no longer escape. The curiales formed a *consortium* responsible collectively not merely for the administration of the City, but also for the most important State services such as the levy of the tax. In consequence, the property of the *curiales* was treated as the guarantee of his *functio* : it constituted a pledge to the State and to his own colleagues ; it became *substancia curialis*.

By an inevitable logic the class of the *curiales* became a *caste*. It was impossible for the son to inherit the property without the duties. A man was thus a *curialis* by heredity, in the same way as he became a *colonus*, because the patrimony was ascribed to the curia just as the tenure of the colonus was to the country estate. The person of the *curialis* became the serf of the curia, just as that of the peasant became the serf of the soil.

If the curialis had no direct descendants, ingenious arrangements saw to it that the heirs or purchasers of his property indemnified the curia in case they were unable to fulfil the duties of curiales. The curiales were also grouped in a *consortium* as rural landowners. The lack of hands encouraged men to concentrate their labourers and resources on the most fertile portions of their estates, and to abandon the rest. The principles of a sound rural economy dictated the same policy since the working of a bad or mediocre piece of land requires more labour than that of a good one and makes a small return or none at all. The example for this procedure was set by the large farmers of the estates of the *fiscus* and of the *patrimonium*. These contractors had even conceived the idea of reassigning the good land to the " powerful " (*potentiores*), keeping for themselves only the waste lands, for which they subsequently claimed reductions of taxes or declared themselves insolvent. To put an end to these tactics, and to prevent the escape of the taxable material, Constantine decreed that every Imperial estate should form an indivisible whole as far as concerned the payment of the "*canon*" (rent for the farm and dues) and of the public taxes (land tax, *annona*) ;

the lots are jointly and severally liable, whence the name of *prædia conserva* (ὁμόδουλα) given to this class of landed property. This measure was subsequently extended to all the large estates, each of which, henceforth, formed a fiscal unit.

With the same intention, the Emperor ordained that in the territory of each *civitas*, the *prædia deserta*, and in general the *prædia* the owners of which could not be found, should be adjudicated to the *curiales*. If these compulsorily appointed *curiales* were insolvent, the ownership of the waste lands was apportioned amongst all the *possessores* of the *civitas*, doubtless in proportion to the land tax for which they were liable. These Draconian measures were supplemented by a series of others which tended towards the same end. In 371, heirs were forbidden to accept only the fertile portions of the inheritable property ; they must take all or nothing ; in 383 a law was passed concerning grants of municipal lands and the estates accruing from the confiscations of the property of pagan temples ; the *sterilia* were compulsorily assigned to the farmer general (*conductor*) under pain of revoking the grant.

Unfortunately, at the same time as the *ordo decurionum* was being shaped into a caste, other " orders " were undergoing a parallel evolution of an analogous nature. Below, trades were, as we have seen, enrolled in corporations in the service of the State or of the Cities, their members being too humble, despised and poor to suggest the idea of forcing them to enter the *curiæ*. The persons engaged in urban commerce and industry or in what little of these remained, were forcibly gathered together in the colleges of *negotiatores*, into which were indiscriminately cast both the humble retailer at a stall and the shipper or the wholesale dealer in corn, oil, wine, etc. The *curiæ* might and should have been recruited from amongst the wealthier members of this class, and in fact it did happen that the richest merchants of a commercial city had to be hustled into the curia. But this was an exceptional measure adopted unwillingly. The aristocratic prejudices of the time precluded people who lived on commerce from *honores*. The only man held in estimation was he who lived on the product of his landed property or real estate. At the most the banker was tolerated. Thus the arrangement of society into " orders " or closed classes brought almost to a complete standstill the upward movement from class to class which quickens modern societies and keeps them from becoming rigid.

The *curiæ* were being emptied from above, the wealthiest landowners and magistrates of the provinces entering the *amplissimus ordo*, the Senate of Rome, yet being exempted from attendance at its meetings from the third century onwards.[1] The laws which obliged them to be domiciled and even to buy landed property in Italy, were abolished under Diocletian and after him, so that in the fifth century the Senatorial order was subdivided into two classes, one of the " illustres " and " spectabiles " on whom real residence was obligatory, the other of the " clarissimi " living in the provinces and no longer having admission to the meetings of the Senate. Spread throughout the Empire, the *clarissimi* formed a real social class, an upper provincial aristocracy, into which entered all the people of wealth and position to be found in the provinces.

From the second half of the third century, these provincial senators who ceased de jure and de facto to belong to the small local Senate, except as patrons, resided less and less in the chief town. We have seen that, after the storm which marked the middle of the third century, urban topography underwent a complete change. The spacious and gay towns of the Early Empire which generally stretched out without meeting the obstacle of a rampart, were reduced in area and turned into fortresses. Space was strictly economized. In these dark little towns, life was assuredly as dull as could be. The aristocracy, in the West at least, abandoned these prisons and went to the country to lead a freer life. The wealthiest there inhabited real palaces built in imitation of the Italian villas. These had winter and summer apartments, baths, flower-gardens and pleasure-grounds.[2] The upper classes recuperated in an open air life, passionately devoting themselves to hunting and physical exercise, without losing as yet their taste for letters. Visits between neighbours and friends and journeys to the capital broke the monotony of life. At this time began country life, destined to become the normal existence of the nobleman for nearly fifteen centuries.

[1] CCLXXXVI, 63-66.
[2] CDXXI, CLI.

At the same time the large estate and the City tended to live separate lives. The *clarissimi* exempted from municipal *honores* and *munera*, refused the curiales entry to their estates, even for the purpose of enabling the functions involved by the assessment and the levy of the land tax to be carried out there. In 383, it was necessary to pass a decree that on the land of the *potentiores* the *exactio* should be entrusted to the governor of the province who was to carry it out by means of his *officium*.

Thus invested with a real fiscal independence, the large estate acquired by usurpation juridical authority over the men, free or not, who lived on it. Even the free villages (*vici*, *comæ*) tried to attach themselves to it. At the same time, when the aristocracy became Christianized, it began to build private churches, *capellæ*, for its own religious needs and those of the men on the estate; the bonds connecting the estate with the mother church (cathedral) of the city, tended to become slack. At the end of the Empire, the large estate, which formed an economic, fiscal, juridical and even religious unit lived an independent life apart from the City.[1]

Reduced to a chief town which was now merely a fortress and inhabited by the poorer country landowners, bankers, and lawyers who henceforth constituted the *curia*, and by *collegiati* who discharged the lower *munera*, the City in the fourth century entered upon a process of incurable decay. The curiales would have liked to flee from it and withdraw into the country like the nobles. But the law intervened to keep them back in the town which had become their prison. In 396, Arcadius forbade " the impious exodus to the country ". The estate which they preferred to the town was to be confiscated and they were to be deprived of the fields for the sake of which they showed themselves so impious as to desert their native place. The *curialis*, in the doubtless rare case when he possessed wealth, was forbidden to pass into the order of the *clarissimi*. He was forbidden (in 320) to become a cleric. The constitutions stopped up every avenue through which the curiales might essay to escape from the municipal bagnio. Nevertheless they left the town thrice every year, at the beginning of September, January and May, to carry out the levy of the land tax in the country, and these

[1] **XXVIII,** 151-178.

were not expeditions undertaken for pleasure. " The cities have lost their splendour ", the fifth century Emperors admit. The impoverished towns drained of their life blood were no longer able to feed a brilliant civilization. The decay of urban life betrays in an unmistakable manner the retrogression of society.

Thus, though the caste system enforced upon the Roman world was able to retard its decomposition, it proved itself incapable of restoring to it youth and strength.

CHAPTER VII

THE LARGE ESTATE VERSUS THE STATE AND THE WEAK

THE PATRONAGE SYSTEM

FROM the Early Empire onwards, we see the development of large landed property. Every large estate kept its boundaries, individuality and name. In France, many villages (Juilly, Vitry, Savigny, Lézigny) preserve today names of ancient Gallo-Roman landlords (Julius, Victor, Sabinus, Licinius). In Africa and Asia they are even more common than in Gaul and Italy.

The decay of industry and commerce, since the third century, contributed further to raise the exceptional position of the large landed proprietors. Henceforth landed property was the only source of wealth. The monetary chaos, which from this time onwards exhausted the Roman world, affected comparatively little the large landowners who went from estate to estate, consuming the product of their land on the spot. The wealthiest belonged to the Senate which was feared and hated by the Emperors of the third century.

We have seen that from the middle of the same century this social class was debarred from the command of the army. There remained to it the functions of civil life. Lastly and chiefly there remained its economic power, which tended more and more to become unlimited.[1]

I.   THE LARGE LANDOWNER VERSUS THE STATE

His estate was administratively outside the City territory. His autonomy was marked by boundary stones on the land.[2]

I.   The large landowner turned an estate into an *asylum*. He received in it : (1) Runaway slaves. An *oratio* of Marcus Aurelius was required to oblige the *potentior* to allow his estate to be visited and searched. (2) The curiales who

---

[1] CCLXXXVI.
[2] XXVIII, 15, 151.

wanted to escape from the burdens of the *fiscus*: these, having taken refuge on the land of the *vir potens*, were protected from the laws.[1] The constitutions of Julian and Majorian against these abuses remained useless. (3) The traders who refused to pay the *collatio*, or licence as we should say. (Theodosius, 386.)

II. He defrauded the *fiscus*. This he did in several ways : (1) by engaging in commercial transactions and refusing to pay the licence (364, Valens and Valentinian). In 408–9 Honorius and Theodosius II were forced to adopt a radical measure : the *potentiores* were forbidden *mercimonium exercere*. (2) They or their agents impudently refused to pay the land tax, knowing that the Cities would not dare to prosecute them. Hence, in 383, Theodosius adopted a series of measures : the task of recovering the capitation was to be entrusted to the *officiales* (servants) of the governor of the province. Similarly, it was the governor who was to have a survey made of these large estates (*massæ*, *fundi*, *potestates*). Thus, in every *civitas*, while the decurion had the task of levying the tribute from the *curiales*, and the *defensor civitatis* from the *minores personæ*, it was upon the *rector* of the province that fell the difficult task of making the *clarissimi* pay. But the position of some landowners was such that the governor himself could do nothing, the rich taxpayer refusing to appear before him. Already in 328, Constantine admitted that certain personages were in fact amenable only to the Prætorian Prefect and the Emperor.

III. By force or fraud he got assigned to himself *fundi limitrophi* which served to maintain the frontier armies (Constitution of Valentinian, Theodosius, and Arcadius, in 385).

II. THE LARGE LANDOWNERS VERSUS THE WEAK

THE PATRONAGE SYSTEM

The landed proprietor was " the true monarch of the countryside ".[3] It has just been said that his estate was invested with individual rights which withdrew it from the

---

[1] CCCXLVI, 80.
[2] CVII, 291, 3, 5.
[3] CCCXLVI, 82.

authority of the magistrates of the *Civitas* and sometimes
even from that of the governors.   The large landowner commanded not only his slaves and *coloni*, but also the free men
who worked on his estate and even in the neighbourhood.
From the fifth century at the least, he came to claim the right
of trying their cases.[1]

He kept men at arms.   He had private prisons.   Leo and
Anthemius in 458 forbade private individuals to keep
buccellarii, Isaurians, armed slaves.   Constitutions of 388
(Theodosius and Arcadius), 486 (Zeno), and 529 (Justinian)
forbade detention in private prisons.   The very renewal of
these constitutions proves their ineffectiveness.

He took the law into his own hands.   If he was a creditor,
he went with an armed band to seize his debtor.   In 389,
Valentinian, Theodosius and Arcadius tried to stop this
practice—in vain of course.

He interviewed in third party cases, and took the place of
one of the parties in lawsuits.   Claudius II (268–270),
Diocletian and Maximian (286) prohibited *cessio in potentiorem*
by humble persons or *tenuiores*.   One of the most serious
special cases of this practice was the transfer to the *potentior*
of a real but sometimes even of a fictitious claim to money due.

He allowed himself fraudulently to affix his *tituli* to the
disputed property.   He forced the unfortunate litigants to
agree to settlements from which he alone derived profit.

If he had influence with the *curia*, the powerful intercessor
(*suffragator*) made the candidate pay him for his intervention
in obtaining a place for him.   The Emperors, being unable
to check it, sanctioned this abuse.   Their constitutions,
such as those of Constantine and his sons, or that of Theodosius
(394 : *de usu suffragiorum ad honores obtinendos*), reveal to
us acts of downright swindling ; the *suffragatores* got their
pay in advance, often in landed property, and then did nothing
for it.

The powerful man wronged the middle and lower classes
in still further ways.   Sometimes, if he was still a member
of the municipal Senate, he made an arrangement by force
or consent with the municipal *tabularii*, to throw the burdens

---

[1] Esmein in *Mélanges de l'École française de Rome*, 1886, p. 416;
CCLXXXVI, 110 and ff. ; Ed. Beaudoin, *La recommendation et la justice
seigneuriale* (1889), p. 110 and XXVIII, 178-194.

on the shoulders of the *inferiores* (313 : Constantine). He obtained at ridiculous prices the concession of the property even of decurions. Finally, there were *potentiores* who, putting aside all pretence, calmly took possession of the good lands of small proprietors, leaving only the bad ones to these poor wretches (398 : constitution of Arcadius and Honorius).

We must stop, as there is no end to the enumeration of the abuses and extortions which the *potentiores* allowed themselves. Some of these fill us with real horror. People dared not lodge a complaint against them.

Even decurions, in order to disarm their hostility, sought as wives the *servulæ* of the powerful and went so far as to sacrifice their honour and private property to them (constitution of Constantine in 313, and of Majorian in 458).

Under the pressure of the landed aristocracy, free men, even belonging to the middle classes, delivered themselves over to the *patronage* of the powerful.

What was this institution which heralded what is called the feudal system, and which under the expiring Empire seems to be making an almost phenomenal progress ?

The *patrocinium potentiorum* was not a new thing.[1] This system was deeply rooted in the past : the recommended person, the *susceptus* of the fourth and fifth centuries was derived from the *cliens* of the republican period. Virgil's commentator Servius is our authority for this (end of the fourth century) *clientes quos nunc susceptos vocamus* (Æneid VI, 609). But with time, the institution underwent a profound change. The clientship of Republican Rome was above all of a political character. It is very difficult to know exactly in what the *obsequium* of the client consisted. What can give us an approximate idea of it is the electoral political clientship of to-day. The difference between the two lay in the fact that the *patrocinium* of the Later Empire bore chiefly an economic character. It placed the protégé or the so-called protégé in a more direct and absolute dependence in relation

---

[1] FUSTEL DE COULANGES, *Le bénéfice et le patronat ;* Fabien THIBAUD, *Le patrocinium vicorum* in *Vierteljahrschrift f. Sozial und Wiertschafts-gesch.*, 1904, and *Nouvelle Revue historique de droit*, 1907, 223 ; G. PLATON, *Démocratie et régime fiscal*, 134-141 ; cf. 103-105 ; ZULUETA, *De Patrocinio vicorum*, in the *Oxford Studies* of Vinogradoff, vol. i. (1909). See also **XXVIII, 15, 160 ; CCLXXXVI, 128, 207 ; DLXXXIII.**

to the *patronus*. Under the Empire, as under the Republic, this system was extra-legal. Under the Republic and the Early Empire the law paid no attention to it, because it did not seem a danger to the State. Under the Later Empire, the Emperors perceived that the patronage system was under-mining their authority. The *potentiores* went so far as to take under their *patrocinium* even whole villages and helped them to defraud the fiscus. Accordingly, Arcadius and Honorius in 395 and 399, and Theodosius II in 415, forbade *vici* to place themselves under a *patrocinium*.

Since 362 Constantine had prohibited in a general way every kind of *patrocinium* (*C. Th.*, XI, 14, 1), a prohibition repeated in 370 (Valentinian, Gratian, and Theodosius), in 399 (Arcadius and Honorius), 415 (Theodosius II). Marcian, Leo and Anthemius (468), later Justinian (531) proceeded against patronage and Tiberius II (578–582) pro-hibited it even to Imperial agents. These prohibitions were vain. The patron had taken precautions ; for in order safely to exercise his authority over his protégé, he had insisted on the latter making over to him first, all his property, of which he left him the usufruct only (Salvian and Zosimus) for a small rent paid by the *susceptus*. Imperial legislation broke against the subtleties of the law of private ownership and the countless snares of its application.

The danger of the *patrocinium* and of the unlimited power of the large landowners appeared so great and the inadequacy of private law showed itself so complete to the Emperors that they were led to introduce into Roman legislation strange novelties which did violence to every principle of jurisdiction. They went so far as to alter the nature of contracts. Accord-ingly, certain portions of this legislation of the Later Empire have been a riddle to students of Roman law who have applied themselves to the Imperial constitutions from the sixteenth to the nineteenth centuries. In France at any rate, their import and spirit have only begun to be grasped since the labours of H. Monier.[1] The following are two or three examples :

1. The *querela non numeratæ pecuniæ* : a receipt is no proof of the payment which it records, if within a certain period (of one, two or five years, as the case may be), the debtor puts

[1] CCCXLVI.

in the *exceptio*. Thus the debtor's denial is enough for the *cautio* or the written document to lose its value as proof. The plaintiff must find other means of proof. This is the reversal of the rule *reus in exceptione actor est*, and a juridical enormity.[1]

The first sign of it appears in two constitutions of Caracalla of 215 and 217 (*Cod. Just.*, IV, 30, 3 and 4).[2] It becomes more and more extended until Justinian. The attempts to interpret all these anomalies by the principles of classical jurisprudence have failed. But everything is clearly explained if we remember the prestige and the abuses of the *potentes*, the δυνατοί and their proceedings in relation to the *humiliores*, or *tenuiores*, the πένητες. Generally, the receipt recording a loan had been extorted and the *potentior* had not paid a single denarius of the sum mentioned in the *cautio*, which did not prevent him from claiming the sum which had not been lent to his so-called debtor. In classical law, it was for the latter to establish the fact that the loan had not taken place. But the morals of the time made this procedure impracticable, since both witnesses and judges stood in fear of the *potentior*.

What did Constantine do ? He shifted the burden of proof ; the judge was forbidden to take into account the written documents, at least within a certain period.

2. Since 285 (Diocletian and Maximian) it was lawful to annul a sale for *læsio ultra dimidium* if the real value of the property sold reached or went beyond double the price.

3. *Jus pœnitendi* in the renting of rural properties : the constitution ἑκατέρῳ ἡ διάταξις ἐπιτρέπει (*Cod. Just.*, IV, 65, 34) is "outside common law": it permits the *locator* and the *conductor* to cancel a contract within the year. It is a law of Zeno, passed between 489–491 in the East, and applicable to Italy. According to H. Monier, it was feared that the *potentior* on pretext of renting, might get possession of the land as tenant in perpetuity.

Many other cases might be quoted, but all the contracts would have to be examined, since everywhere the *potentiores* devised ways of circumventing the law. The impotence of the State was due to manifold causes. That which went

---

[1] M. KROELL, *Du rôle de l'écrit dans la preuve des contrats*, 177 and ff.
[2] The Constitution of Septimius Severus of 197 is an interpolation.

deepest lay doubtless in the fact that if the *potentior* was on the one hand an oppressor, he was on the other hand a protector against the other *potentiores* and against the State itself.   The intervention of public authority on behalf of the weak, was not disinterested ; their help was needed to make work the vast mechanism which the Roman Empire had become.   But what was demanded, in order to enable the Empire to continue to exist, appears henceforth beyond human powers.

CHAPTER VIII

THE DECAY AND END OF ANCIENT ART

IT has been maintained that Christianity put an end to ancient art; to a certain extent this judgment is justifiable. Christianity, and also Islam, in imitation of their parent Judaism, are essentially opposed to that which makes the charm and beauty of ancient art, the plastic element : " thou shalt not make unto thee any graven image, or any likeness of any thing that is in heaven above, or in the earth beneath, or in the water under the earth " (*Exodus*, xx, 4).

The Church Fathers, in attacking idolatry, condemned *eo ipso* the most magnificent creations of art, the representation of the gods and heroes. Not merely statuary, but all representations of mythological scenes, by means of mural painting, of painting on vases, and engraving on precious stones, fell under the blow of an inexorable reprobation. Many of them, even though simply ornamental, bore a licentious character. The nude in art was not permissible for the Christian Church.[1]

But this iconoclastic strain, which moreover is not peculiar to the Church (it is found amongst the Pythagoreans and the Stoics), produced its effects, and that in the East, only in the eighth and ninth centuries, during and after the " Quarrel of the Images," and also after the seventh century, in the regions which fell under the power of the Musulmans.

Christianity accommodated itself to ancient art, by neglecting large parts of it. It even imitated servilely many of its methods, just as it did in literature.[2] Properly speaking, Christianity buried ancient art, rather than killed it.[3]

Art, at the moment of the triumph of Christianity, had already received its death blow and had for a long time been

---

[1] **CDLXII, 716-718; CCL, 406.**
[2] For this reason we shall pass over Christian art almost entirely, contenting ourselves with a reference to the big treatises of KRAUS (**CCLXIX**) and of LECLERCQ (**CCLXXXIII**) and to the books of BRÉHIER (**LV, LVII**).
[3] **CDLXXII, 774; LVIII, 870.**

dragging out a lingering existence. Ancient, that is to say Greek art, had reached its zenith in the fifth and fourth centuries B.C. It maintained itself longer by means of magnificent creations after Alexander. But despoiling Greece and the East and bringing back a whole world of statues and objects of art to Rome, did not make creative artists of the Romans : they became only amateurs and dilettanti. Under the Empire, artists were still Orientals and the studios were not so much in Rome, as in Athens and Alexandria. The rôle of Rome was to give orders so as to maintain production, chiefly the imitation of models, up to Hadrian's time.

I. ARCHITECTURE

There was at least one kind of art in which Romans excelled—*Architecture.* The triumphal arch, baths, and amphitheatres are the creations of the Roman, or at least of the Italic genius.[1] The taste for building did not cease. After the example of Augustus, the Flavians, and later Trajan, Hadrian and lastly Septimius Severus (the Septizonium, on the Palatine, a portico in seven storeys) and Caracalla (Thermæ) erected grandiose buildings. The Emperors of the Later Empire, Diocletian and Constantine, were also great builders. To the first are due, at Rome, huge baths (with sides four hundred metres long), buildings at Nicomedia, the great palace of Salona (*Spalato*) ; the second built baths and basilicas at Rome ; he even made a whole town spring from the ground, Byzantium. This tradition was carried on till quite late : in 374, a great portico was erected at Rome by Gratian, Valentinian and Theodosius. The building of amphitheatres was carried on in Italy (Verona and Pola belong to the third century) and even in Africa, at Thysdrus (El Djem). Similarly with circuses : Maxentius built another one in 309, two miles from Rome : it was more than five hundred metres long. We have not mentioned works of public utility : roads, harbours, light-houses, aqueducts (as late as under Alexander Severus), ramparts and towers, etc.

Unfortunately the above are merely vast buildings, but not works of art. Made of coarse materials swamped in mortar, rather than of fine stones deftly prepared, they were

[1] **LXXXII.**

erected too fast. The buildings of Constantine's reign bear the same hasty character of improvization as the social reforms of that Emperor.

One of the last great pagan works, which seems to us striking rather than beautiful, in the " colossal bombastic " style, is the temple of Baalbek in Syria, dedicated to Jupiter Heliopolitanus : finished by Caracalla, it had been begun previously under Antoninus, that is to say at the end of the good period. It has been said[1], not without some justification, that " After the great architects of the Antonines, there are only masons ".

The plan of the Christian Church, as we know, was derived from the ancient basilica, a large space serving for a tribunal, market, etc. It had a rectangular shape and a timber framework. Many centuries were needed to give the basilica an artistic character. Besides, the first Christian basilicas, erected under Constantine, were so badly built that they fell to ruin.

Speaking generally, after the second century A.D., art lost its qualities of purity and taste extremely rapidly. Even technique underwent a profound change. Art, even imitative art, did not succeed in weathering the storm of the third century. It gave a last feeble gleam under Diocletian and was extinguished under Constantine. In this respect, the Middle Ages began from the fourth century.

II. PLASTIC ART

The irrefutable evidence of these death-throes is provided by *plastic art*.

Statues.—That the representation of the gods should lose all originality was inevitable ; for the accepted types of majesty or grace become very soon fixed in all religions. But the statues raised to the Emperors, magistrates, and even gladiators—they are countless up to the fourth century— lost all representational value, especially the *statuæ loricatæ* (mail-clad) : only the head presents individual features, because it was " let in ", but the gestures and details all resemble each other. The colossal statue claiming to be a

---

[1] **CXXVIII,** vol. vi., 387 ; vol. v., 699.

representation of Constantine is among the most mediocre in execution.

Of a genre which was a favourite with the Romans and was perhaps of Etruscan origin, the *bust*, remarkable specimens have been preserved, characterized by a strong realism, from the beginning of the first century A.D.   From Augustus to Antoninus we possess a splendid series of Imperial busts which are in no way idealized with the exception perhaps of the head of Augustus, and which form excellent portraits.[1] Under Alexander Severus this genre began to deteriorate. In the middle of the third century, interesting though conventional busts are still found, such as those which represent the Emperor Gallienus.   But, from Constantine onwards, there is no longer anything which has any worth : there are only lifeless images in the Oriental frontal style.   Of Constantine himself we do not possess a single reliable portrait.

Bas-reliefs.[2]—These more especially decorate triumphal arches.   Several are works of art ; such are the arch of Titus, commemorating his triumph over the Jews (finished by Domitian in 81) and the arch of Trajan, the conqueror of the Dacians.   But already that of Marcus Aurelius proclaims the setting in of decadence.   Its style is tame.   " Everyone looks good, even the barbarians ; the horses have a melting philanthropic eye.   The Antonine column is a curious work but devoid of fineness in its execution, and far inferior to the temple of Antoninus and Faustina under the preceding reign.[3] The equestrian statue of the Capitol charms us by the sincere idealization of the excellent Emperor which it offers us, but the artist is not justified in treating it as a real portrait."[4]

Coming only thirty years later, the art of Septimius Severus is coarse work : the reliefs are no more than a plan drawn on stone, shapes are reduced to lines and objects to schemata, in the words of a good judge,[5] who refuses to pursue the subject any further.   The triumphal arch of Constantine is a confession of impotence : its decoration is partly formed by pieces taken from the arches of Trajan, Marcus Aurelius, and perhaps Diocletian.   In the original portions, the execution is feeble

[1] XXXII.
[2] XCII.
[3] It is perhaps later than the death of Marcus Aurelius (XCII, 186).
[4] CCCV, 46.
[5] XCII, 191.

and stiff and the human body is drawn in a schematic manner.[1]
Already from the middle of the third century onwards, the
human form was reduced to a decorative function : e.g. on
the sarcophagus on which was represented (in 242) Timositheus,
the father-in-law of Gordian III. The reason was that the function of bas-relief was no longer understood, and the characters
stand out like marionettes, from a flat background. Bas-
relief lived on in Christian sarcophagi, where unfortunately
the abuse of symbolism brought forth conventional and frigid
works.

Ivories.[2]—Sculpture on ivory tusks produces statuettes,
toilet articles of common use (combs), diptychs (tablets) with
a wax interior which was written on with the stylus, and on
the outside the sculptured image of an important personage
(Consul or Emperor). We have some of these belonging to
the fifth century, which seem to be portraits, Christian diptychs
(St. Paul on the ivory of the cathedral of Rouen : fifth to
sixth century), pyxes (boxes containing consecrated wafers),
and book covers. The centres of production were in Egypt,
where the Alexandrine workshops were specially celebrated.
We have further beautiful products of the 6th century, such
as the episcopal throne of Maximian at Ravenna, characterized
by an admirable realism and Oriental inspiration in its treatment of the figures. It marks an artistic event, " but a
triumph with no to-morrow ".[3]

There was however a Latin art of ivory-work : there is the
diptych of the Bargello at Florence of the fifth to sixth
century, representing scenes from the life of Adam and Saint
Paul, of Græco-Roman inspiration : " it is the last monument of Augustan art and as it were its impressive and last
justification at the very moment of its disappearance ".
After this only pierced ivories are found, in the style of stone
carving, of which we shall speak presently.

Glyptics.[4]—The art of engraving on precious stones (γλύπτω :
I engrave) reached its zenith in antiquity. The Renaissance
and modern times have not equalled or at any rate have not

---

[1] P. ALLARD shows, against Frothingham (in the *Revue des questions
historiques* of 1914, p. 325) that the arch of Constantine belongs to the
fourth century. See also CCL, 242 and 398.
[2] CDLXII, 792-793 ; CCLXXXIII, 327, 360.
[3] VIII, vol. i., 165 ; CCLXXXIII, 353.
[4] XI, 186 and ff. ; CCL, 426 ; CCLXXXIII, 363.

surpassed the ancient products which have reached us. The apotheosis of Germanicus (in 19 or 37) and that of Augustus (cameo of Vienna) are unmatched pieces of work. There are two series : the *cameo* or engraving in relief (ἀναγλυφή, *cœlatura*, *scalptura*) and the *intaglio* or incised engraving (διαγλυφή, *cavatores*, *signarii*). Their vogue, which was extra-ordinary, called forth glass paste imitations of remarkable excellence.

It is a strange thing that the art of engraving fell into a profound decline from the middle of the second century. It was not that the taste for it passed away in the least, but after Caracalla's reign, the products of this art no longer possess any artistic value. Sixth century articles even bear witness to a complete technical degeneration. " What a barbarity in the work, what gross inexperience in the handling of the graver and of the drill." The portrait was replaced by the cabalistic riddle, or the beauty of the precious stone itself sufficed.

No less strange is the fact that decadence set in, though a little later, elsewhere outside the Empire. From the third to the fifth century, the Sassanid engraving of Susa and Ctesiphon had rivalled that of the Roman world. After Shapur's reign it lived on as a mere process, that is to say, it was no longer an art but an industry.

III. THE DECORATIVE ARTS

The Goldsmith's art.[1]—Toreutic (high reliefs on patera or repoussé work) produced silver cups (scyphi), vases, basins, goblets, mirrors, etc. It reached its zenith under the successors of Alexander. From the middle of the first century A.D., this art, according to the evidence of Pliny the Elder,[2] was in full process of decay.

The cause doubtless was that taste was making for jewelled goldsmith's work, a combination of precious stones with gold. This was of Oriental origin and always remained Oriental in style.

It should be noted that the recrudescence of the Oriental

---

[1] CDLXXII, 216; CCL, 429, 437; CCLXXXIII, vol. ii., 393, 413-446; CCXCVIII; XII.

[2] *Hist. Nat.*, XXXVI, 157.

influence becomes emphasized from the middle of the third century, not merely in the jewelry and ornaments of the common people, but also in the adornment of the Emperor's person. From the time of Constantine, and perhaps even from that of Marcus Aurelius, the Emperors imitated the Sassanid Kings. After the example of the latter, instead of the laurel, they substituted as their ceremonial head-dress the jewelled crown, which was to become a rigid diadem under Justinian ; on their belts gems sparkled. The monarch's raiment is covered with a constellation of precious stones, in the Persian taste. The chair adorned with goldsmith's work, or the throne, was adopted.

Another foreign conquest was the introduction of cloisonné into the goldsmith's art : the metal disappears under the covering of gems (amongst which the garnet dominates), natural or artificial (glass paste) or mounted in metal settings. The origin of this art, which the Western Goths and Germans spread throughout Europe from the fifth century,[1] seems very ancient. It is an offshoot of Iranian art, planted amongst the Scythians, in the South of modern Russia, and afterwards amongst their successors the Sarmatians.[2]

Enamelling.[3]—The same applies to enamelling, which consists in applying to terra cotta, and especially to metal, a metallic oxide, reduced to a powder or paste : in the baking, the oxide becomes incorporated with the article ; the enamel protects it from air and water, while at the same time adorning it with bright reflections. Known in very ancient times in the East and afterwards in Greece, the art of enamelling had disappeared about the third century B.C., and the Romans were ignorant of it until (about the third century) barbarian artists "from the neighbourhood of the Ocean", having preserved the secret of this process, which was lost in the Hellenistic world, spread some specimens of it.[4]

It is a strange thing that, whether because the taste for it early came to an end, or because its secret became locked up amongst a few initiated, this art suffered a new eclipse from

[1] CCCXII.

[2] Rostowtzew, *Iranians and Greeks in South Russia* (1922), Minns *Scythes and Greeks* (1913) ; viii., vol. i., 1st part, 405-435.

[3] CCLXXXII, vol. ii., 447-461.

[4] According to Emile Molinier (in viii., vol. i., 484-671), enamelling is of Oriental origin.

the sixth to the tenth century.   Enamelling was to have a
true rebirth only in the eleventh century.

Glass-making.[1]—This complex industry must be subdivided.

1.   *Glass paste.*—This was used to imitate precious stones
(the ruby, topaz, beryl, agate, sardonyx) for cameos and
polished uncut stones, but also and chiefly to make vases with
mythological decorations.   It produced magnificent works
at Alexandria and Sidon, and later also in Campania.   The
most celebrated is the so-called Portland vase in the British
Museum, representing Peleus and Thetis, which does not
belong to the third century A.D. but to the age of Augustus.
But in Christian times, the specimens which have been preserved, bear witness to a degenerate art.

2.   *Cut, engraved, and painted glass and fondi d'oro.*—
Unfortunately, the examples are very few (half-a-dozen).
The ornamentation underwent the same vicissitudes as in
the other arts.   Finally the technique altered : the paste,
which was still clear and transparent in the fourth century,
became opaque in the sixth century.   We have, however,
preserved an example representing Galla Placidia, Valentinian
and Honorius (therefore about 425).

Terra cotta.[2]—Greek pottery, whose products have never
been equalled, was imitated in Italy, from the third century
B.C.   In the second century the most renowned centre was
Arezzo in Tuscany, where red clay is found.   Noble families
set up factories ; the artists, who were slaves, signed their
works ;   the Asiatic origin of these works is attested
by the mythological and naturalistic decoration, which is
an imitation of that of the Greeks.   In the first century A.D.,
this art degenerated, perhaps because of the competition of
Pozzuoli in Italy and especially of the provincial factories
at Tarragona, in Gaul (central), even in Germany and Great
Britain.   The forms are rarely elegant and the decoration
remained heavy.

Towards the third century, the process of lustre used in
Roman pottery was lost.   Under the Later Empire, the making of terra cotta figurines ceased to be an art, and pottery
was reduced to the production of common articles.

---

[1] CLXV ; CCCXLIX ; CCL, 437 ; CCLXXXIII, vol. ii., 463-507.
[2] CCCXLIV, vol. xv., 285-324 ;   CCLXXXIII, 517-518 ;   CCL, 440
XXXIX ; CVI.

The ancient lamp, still light and delicate under the Early Empire, altered in the third century from motives of an economic nature : people were no longer willing or no longer able to buy anything but cheap wares, made of yellow or grey clay, shaped in plaster instead of bronze moulds and made ugly by a varnish of paste. However, in Christian times, the decoration of earthen-ware, in default of art, kept up a great variety of subjects.

The dishes of Italy and Africa no longer bore anything but an execrable ornamentation. Pottery, entirely lost as an art in the West, was only continued in the Byzantine Empire, according to written evidence, for no examples have been preserved.

Iron-work (*wrought iron or bronze*).[1]—At Constantinople and in Egypt, the industrial art of bronze and copper was carried on in the making of candelabra, lustres, doors, or furniture (basins, ewers, coppers, vessels) or of liturgical articles (vases, chandeliers, crosses, bells, etc.). The scarcity of articles in precious metals (in the course of the fifth century) maintained the market for them. The style (for instance, that of chandeliers) is ugly.

Wood-work.—Only very rare specimens have been preserved : " sculpture in wood is only the imitation of monumental sculpture ; it presents no originality ".

With it is connected a type of decoration called " ornament in flat relief " of Syrian origin and no artistic value.

Stucco is made of marble dust mixed with lime. Monuments of this material are very rare ; they bear witness to a complete decadence, e.g. in San Vitale at Ravenna.

Stained-glass Windows.—Here we have a case not of decrepitude but of infancy. Referred to in texts, such church windows as existed in the fourth and fifth centuries, appear to be as yet only painted glass, a kind of transparent mosaic.

Coins and Medals.[2]—From the artistic point of view, the finest period for coinage is the Hellenistic. Unfortunately, under the Later Empire, the artists who engraved the dies of the special medals commemorating an event deteriorated. The figures are no longer treated in full relief, but flattened.

---

[1] **VIII,** vol. i., 12, 410 ; **CCLXXXIII,** vol. ii., 555.
[2] Prou in **VIII,** vol. i., 2nd part, 903.

Even the representation of the Emperor's figure is no longer a portrait but a conventional type.

Painting and miniatures.[1]—No examples have remained of the good, that is to say, of the Hellenistic period of ancient painting. The interesting examples at Pompeii and on the Palatine, although some of them possess charm, are nevertheless of the second rank, being imitations of more ancient works which have disappeared. Moreover, ancient painting was far inferior to sculpture and architecture. This inferiority was due partly to shortcomings in technique : only fresco and tempera painting were known. The laws of perspective were scarcely glimpsed and generally even misunderstood. The canon of proportion from which artists dared not free themselves, perpetuated unchangeable postures.

Pliny speaks of painting as a dying art.   In fact, the specimens of Christian painting, which have a direct affinity with those of Pompeii and the Palatine, show not merely an arrest, but a decay. The shading in all is bad, the knowledge of flesh colouring has gone ; the contours of the body and clothes are coarsely outlined with black strokes ; shadows are awkwardly represented by dark bands. The drawing is worse than clumsy, it is flatly incorrect. Even on coming out from the catacombs to be produced in broad daylight, painting was not destined to become renewed. Symbolism was to cause hieratic monotony and stiffness.

The only painting which still had a great future was manuscript painting or miniature. Only a very small number of specimens of the ancient pagan tradition have been preserved : the Vatican Virgil and the Ambrosian Homer (they belong to the fourth century, at the earliest). After this, in the West at least, we have nothing. When painted manuscripts reappear, they are obvious imitations of Byzantine, or even simple copies of Syrian manuscripts. Byzantine miniature presents magnificent specimens. But the influence of Oriental taste (Syrian, Egyptian or Iranian) in them is strongly in evidence.[2]

The Western manuscripts of the seventh, eighth and ninth centuries, show in the ornamentation of the letters the use of ornamental decoration : broken lines, interlacing and plaiting ;

---

[1] **CCLXXXIII,** 556, 631.
[2] **CXV,** 613, 619.

finally, animals and sometimes human figures are treated fancifully.[1] This is servile imitation of Irish and Anglo-Saxon miniature, the ornamentation of which appears to be of Oriental origin ; but it reached the West through the intermediacy of the barbarian peoples of central Europe. We have here a movement parallel to that of the goldsmith's art.

Thus the German invasions, by transplanting in the West seeds brought from the East, helped to destroy the tradition of ancient art.

Mosaic.[2]—The Romans had borrowed this from the Greeks, but, from the time of Sulla, they had developed it to such an extent, that they had made a national art of it, which they carried to the four corners of the globe. For these compositions, sometimes covering a vast area, not only small marble cubes, but also cubes of enamel and glass paste were used. The floors (pavements) and also the walls and domes were decorated with them : the dome of St. George at Salonica, nine hundred metres square, required 36 million cubes.

The decoration of pavements in marble was the first to decline : the artists no longer renewed their models but went on treating the same subjects. Nevertheless, in Africa, they clung to hunting scenes which were picturesque and amusing.

In Christian times, pavements are no longer of interest : perhaps people were afraid to represent religious subjects on parts of the building which were necessarily trodden under foot.

On the other hand, mosaics in enamel, which decorated walls and domes, were able to adapt themselves to the new religion and sentiments and produced remarkable works such as the mosaic in the church of S. Pudenziana at Rome (fourth century), perhaps the masterpiece of ancient mosaic. Nevertheless, even at this time, difficulties were evaded rather than faced; the designers used draperies to hide their ignorance of anatomy. Finally, mosaic " fell from the rank of the arts to that of industry, and gave up the representation of life, to content itself with geometrical decoration ". This decay, clear enough at Rome in the fourth century, became more and more pronounced, and reached the lowest stage of barbarism in the eighth and ninth centuries. It is a relief to see this wretched art come to an end.

---

[1] **VIII,** vol. i., 2, 307 ; **CCCXII.**
[2] **CLXIII; CDXCII; CCLXXXIII,** vol. ii., 193.

Textiles.[1]—Woollen, linen and silk stuffs on which were woven or embroidered fanciful subjects at first pagan and later Christian, saw their manufacture at first limited to the Eastern part of the Empire; but after the iconoclastic quarrel, which drove out the artisans at the end of the eighth century, this art was introduced into the West. Its Oriental origin is undeniable: Carolingian or Capetian copes still represent subjects, such as the tigers affrontés which are familiar to the Sassanid art of Persia.

Tapestries.—The tapestries discovered in Egypt and in the Crimea (fragments belonging to the fourth century A.D.) have been a revelation: there was no example of tapestry previous to the eleventh century A.D. It is a very curious thing, that the texture appears identical with that of our Gobelins. But, from the fourth and fifth centuries, tapestry begins to decline: it becomes incapable of reproducing living models. After the fourth century, only the decorating is tolerable, while every attempt to reproduce life results in monstrous shapelessness.

IV. MUSIC[2]

This is summed up in Greek music, of which the plainsong of the Greek Orthodox and Latin churches can give us some idea. But, to speak accurately, modern music, based on harmony and counterpoint, is a creation of the Middle Ages and of the sixteenth century. The same applies to musical notation[3]. Ancient song music was closely bound to the poetic text. Melody did not succeed in freeing itself and remained recitative. It moved within the narrow interval of one or two octaves. As regards choral singing, the choir knew only unison.

Instrumental music.—String and wood instruments were few and not very powerful. The interpreters of modern music, the violin, violoncello and organ, are a creation of the Middle Ages.

Here there has been not decadence but progress, although only after a very long time.

---

[1] CLXIV; CCLXXXIII, 585, 593.
[2] Theodore REINACH, *La Musique grecque* (1926).
[3] TANNERY in *Revue de synthèse historique*, 1902, 336.

V. CAUSES OF THE RETROGRESSION OF ANCIENT ART

To what was the retrogression of ancient art due ?

Two chief reasons may be discovered, one economic and the other æsthetic.

Economic reason.—The connection between art and wealth is well known. For art to be able to arise, flourish, maintain itself and become widespread in any civilization, the demand for works of art by the public must be abundant and continuous. Art requires a faultless technique, one therefore which is difficult to acquire and to transmit and easy to forget. If the demand becomes weak or scarce, the craft is bound to deteriorate. Through lack of orders the craftsman or artist ceases to obtain recruits ; technique is lost and schools die out one after another. Such is the danger which threatens art in all periods and in all countries. The economic retrogression of the second century and the ruin of the third century certainly played a principal part in the sudden arrest (about 150) and then the rapid decline of ancient art. In the fourth century there are no more artists or even artistic craftsmen. When we read an edict of Constantine (337), granting immunity from public burdens to fifty-eight liberal professions or artistic industries, in order that the *artifices* may improve themselves in their crafts and bring up their children better in them, we realize that the " arts and crafts " were on the way to disappear.

Aesthetic reason.—This is complex. We must place in the forefront the blighting effect of masterpieces.

A work of art brings about imitation and then the imitation of an imitation. This tendency is absurd, since imitation is condemned by its very definition, but nevertheless inevitable. When the Empire was established, the creative period had long since passed away. Great virtuosi, after Sulla's time, ordered works, which were inspired by ancient works : chiefly the style of Praxiteles and Lysippus was imitated.[1] Nevertheless fine works were preserved, saved by technique which remained faultless till the time of Hadrian. Under this Emperor, unfortunately, and partly under his influence[2] an archaising movement arose which brought forth a blighting

[1] CDLXII, 722.
[2] CCL, 396.

academicism. We know the evil effect of the virtuoso with a taste for archaism, one of the worst scourges of art. His breed nearly killed the applied arts in France and Europe in the nineteenth century. Hadrian and the collectors of his age played an equally fatal part.

To this reason must be added the exhaustion due to a too long tradition. Greek art weighed on the Roman world with the burden of a past already heavy with many centuries. Further (there is no reason why this should not be admitted), ancient art is monotonous. In Imperial times, a rooted tradition perpetuated affectation in works of art. In gardens there were stone or marble statues of sleeping Ariadne, or slumbering Ganymede, dancing Satyrs, Sirens, Pan, Herma- phrodites, and Nymphs ; on basins and fountains, Neptune on a dolphin, Narcissus, fishermen, Silenus with his wine-skin, the child with the goose, Nereids astride an animal; in the baths, Venus Anadyomene; in the Palæstrae annexed to the baths, Hermes, Hercules and statues of athletes. For mosaics the subjects are equally fixed. From Syria to Spain, from Great Britain to Africa, the same decoration obtains. Neither sky nor climate seems ever to change. Ancient civilization in Imperial times gives us the impression of a crushing uniformity.

The limits of ancient art are arraigned, though with the discretion of a devotee, in a celebrated page of Renan.[1]

Let us recall the end of the prayer to Athena on the Acropolis : " Ages shall arise in which thy disciples shall be held the disciples of boredom. The world is greater than thou deemest. If thou hadst beheld the polar snows and the mysteries of the Southern sky, thy brow, O goddess everlastingly calm, would not be so serene; thine ampler head would embrace different kinds of beauty ".

We must resign ourselves to the fact: Greek plastic art, the " Greek marvel", after bewitching the world for seven or eight centuries, ended by leaving it indifferent, as indifferent as the gods which it glorified under a faultless shape.

One might have thought that new sentiments would bring a new life to ancient art. It was not so. Mithraism and Christianity imitated servilely its debased products while

[1] *Souvenirs d'enfance et de jeunesse*, p. 71.

Islam proscribed plastic art ; the Christian Orthodox Church did the same in the East. But, in the West, Christianity begins to have its deep and original æsthetic expression only in the eleventh and twelfth century, that is to say in astonishingly recent times, eleven or twelve centuries after the death of its founder!

Nevertheless, in the course of this period, art did not die out entirely. Only its expression became completely changed. Decoration supplants the line and colour dethrones plastic art.

It has been observed[1] that religious feeling cannot alone be held responsible for the ruin of plastic art. The iconoclasts did not specially vent their wrath on statues ; all anthropomorphic representation under whatever form they held objectionable. Why did plastic art alone succumb ?

There seems to be no doubt that this was due to a change, or to speak more correctly, to a revolution in taste. Greek art, after having held undivided sway, came under the influence of the East which returned and made a more and more triumphant attack on the art of the third century.

Oriental art was not ignorant of sculpture but used it to ornament surfaces and not to represent objects in space. Accordingly it scarcely uses anything but bas-relief ; disdaining to model the human body, it sees in it only an element of decoration. It does not understand the ornamentation of a building without panels of enamelled earthenware, without mosaics with gold backgrounds, and even without woven material. Under its influence technique became transformed. The drill replaced the chisel ; stone was hollowed and pierced instead of being modelled. Subjects for sculpture were acanthus leaves, ovoli and ogees which project into the full light on a pierced or trellised background.

The effect produced is that of a wonderful textile, the subjects of which, bathed in light, blaze out of the dimness of the background : the effect of softness is the same as that produced by the finest Persian carpets. The price paid for this is that the human figure becomes monstrously inaccurate.

In architecture, the dome, of Iranian origin probably, comes into constant use and characterizes a new period.

[1] **LVIII; CXV; CCLXXXIII,** vol. ii., 73, 114.

Constantinople focussed and afterwards spread the new art which came from Asia Minor, Syria or from further still, and which has with more or less reason been called Byzantine.[1]

Art therefore did not die. But ancient art perished with plastic art. In the *pars Orientis* the descendants of the Greeks were destined to lose even the feeling for it. In the West, sculpture was destined to be reborn, towards the eleventh century, differing profoundly both in inspiration and style from ancient sculpture.

Thus, in the sphere of art, as in that of religion, a new soul takes the place of the ancient soul.

[1] CDLXXI; III.

CHAPTER IX

THE DECADENCE OF LITERATURE
THE DISAPPEARANCE OF ANCIENT PHILOSOPHY AND SCIENCE

I. PAGAN LETTERS

IF the standard of ancient art was lowered from the second century onwards, the fall of literature was no less rapid, especially in the West.

After Trajan's reign, made brilliant by such names as those of Tacitus, Juvenal and Pliny the Younger, Hadrian's reign has to show only Suetonius, the collector of doubtful anecdotes, and the reign of Marcus Aurelius only Apuleius, an African from Madaura, more interesting as a personality than as a writer. The most celebrated author of this reign, the tutor of the Emperor Marcus Aurelius, who liberally bestows on him marks of a deep respect, Fronto, an African from Cirta, is below the standard of mediocrity ; the discovery of his works (forensic speeches, public harangues, Praises of Smoke and Dust) in the nineteenth century, has dealt a blow to his reputation ; they show him as a superficial, vainglorious and hollow declaimer.

Aulus Gellius, at the end of the second century, shows us the type of writer who was destined to prevail, the compiler. In his Noctes Atticæ he compiles without method or even without any definite end in view. He collects masses of information gathered from every quarter. He himself compares his work to a provision-store : *quasi quoddam litteratum penus*, a shop which is all in disorder, a work with no individual thought, composition or style. After him there is only barrenness. The third century is a literary Sahara.

This was the case in the West at least. In the East it was different. The evolution there, chronologically speaking, was not at all parallel. The period of decadence had begun much earlier. The barren period had been the first century A.D. It has nothing to show except the works of Philo of Alexandria, which moreover we owe not to the Greeks, but to Jews living in Greek lands. They are of interest to ancient philosophy and Jewish history rather than to literature.

Of purely literary works, poems for example, there is nothing to mention, except some epigrams.

But after this long period of weakness, there was a kind of "Renaissance "[1] lasting from Nerva and Trajan to the end of Diocletian's reign and consequently covering about two centuries. Greek thought outgrew the limits of the small Greek cities and even those of the kingdoms which sprang from the dismemberment of the Empire of Alexander, and took on quite a new character of universality and humanity. Nevertheless the different branches of literature were not all characterized by the same fertility. The theatre, which had been dying since the third century B.C., could not be revived. Poetry scarcely counts, since we can point only to didactic poems (two examples belonging to the third century, the Κυνηγετικὰ and Ἁλιευτικὰ on hunting and fishing; also the fables of Babrius). History, which in the West was dead after Tacitus and Suetonius, can cite (at the end of the second and third century) the names of Appian, Dio Cassius, Herodian and Dexippus, who deal with the history of Rome and of their times; these writers take pains with their style, which yet comparatively speaking is not too inflated. Unfortunately they do not resemble either Thucydides or Polybius; they are mediocre minds, entirely devoid of any vigour of thought or personality. Arrian, a contemporary of Marcus Aurelius, has left us a history of Alexander which is an honest piece of work; unfortunately his other historical works, which were very numerous and very important (the successors of Alexander, the History of Bithynia, his native country; the History of the Parthian wars under Trajan; Ἀλανικὴ) have perished. On the whole, historical writing declined.

A new genre began to flourish, the novel: the *Aethiopica* or *Theagenes and Charicleia* by Heliodorus (third century), *Leucippe and Clitophon* by Achilles Tatius (fourth century ?), *Daphnis and Chloe* by Longus (second to fifth century). Artificial, insipid and diffuse, these novels have nevertheless exercised a real influence on the literature of the Middle Ages and even of modern times.

[1] **XCIII,** 718.

Leaving aside the works of rhetoricians, scholars, compilers, grammarians, etc., and the technical treatises, such as those of Galen on medicine and Ptolemy on geography, there remain in the second century great or fair names, those of the moralists: Dio Chrysostom, Plutarch, Epictetus, Lucian(c. 125—c. 192), the latter unrivalled. This Semite, a Syrian of Samosata, who wrote in Greek, by his satirical, witty and fanciful turn of mind, almost passes beyond the limits of Antiquity; his mind shows kinship with many a modern French author, with Voltaire for example. Lucian seems to be the creator of the satirical dialogue, of the pamphlet and of the tale of phantasy.

In the third century, thought, if not literature, counts a great man, the Egyptian Greek Plotinus, born in 204, who taught at Rome from 264 to 270, the date of his death. His teachings were collected by his disciple Porphyry, who published them in nine books (whence the title Enneads), " a strange and obscure work scornful of form ", but the fruit of one of the most powerful metaphysical minds which mankind has ever known. As for Porphyry (born at Tyre in 233, died at Rome towards the beginning of the fourth century), his philosophical writings are far inferior to his teacher's and their literary merit is slight. The proposition may be put forward that between these two there is a qualitative as well as a quantitative difference. The former is the last thinker of pagan Antiquity, while the latter begins the series of commentators similar to those in the Middle Ages.[1]

In the Christian world, another Egyptian Greek, Origen (185–254) is a profound metaphysician and the most prolific author of Antiquity.[2]

To match this fertility and these names, three or four of which are dazzling, what can the Roman literature of the second half of the second century or of the whole of the third century show ? Nothing.[3] Its sole originality must be looked for in the work of the Jurists Gaius, Ulpian and Papinian, whose works however do not really come within the province of literature.

---

[1] **CXXIV; CXXXI.**

[2] See Ch. Bigg, *The Christian Platonists of Alexandria*, 2nd ed., Oxford, 1913.

[3] See a comparative table of dates in which the Greek authors are set out in relation to the Latin authors. The effect is striking in **CCCLXXXIV, 954.**

Hence the prestige of Greek letters and thought remained without a rival. It influenced the Roman Emperors. Hadrian was quite Greek in his tastes, while Marcus Aurelius, who was on the contrary so emphatically Roman, none the less wrote his thoughts in Greek. His young and feeble imitator, Alexander Severus (222–235) expressed himself better in Greek than in Latin. If Constantine was ignorant or had but little knowledge of Greek, there was a revival of Hellenism under Julian. It is true that this was the last revival. After him Hellenism died in the West.

In Latin literature, from Constantine onwards and up to the beginning of the fifth century and after, a kind of renewal took place. The word " Renaissance " has even been applied to it. But this is a gross exaggeration. We must clear the ground of the works of grammarians, commentators and epitomizers who are given a place in manuals but who do not belong to literature.

The *Panegyrics* of the Emperors and the verbiage of the *Scriptores Historiæ Augustæ* scarcely count as history. The panegyrics, those of Eumenes for example, under Constantine and his successors are inflated works devoid of substance. Nearly the same must be said unfortunately of the six real or imaginary writers (Spartianus, Vulcacius Gallicanus, Lampridius, Capitolinus, Trebellius Pollio, Vopiscus), who claimed to write the biographies of the Roman Emperors from Hadrian to Carus, Diocletian's predecessor. These authors, or the forgers who in the fourth to fifth century wrote under these supposititious names, have neither style nor ideas : " Our biographers are the most mediocre and narrow minds imaginable, the completest representatives of this intellectual decadence, this barbarism of the third century."[1] We have merely a collection of frivolous anecdotes, speeches and fictitious letters. If these speeches and letters were at least authentic, we should be able to give the writers of the *Augustan History* the credit of being diligent compilers. But alas ! a ruthless examination has shown their documentation to be entirely fictitious. Even when the author has under his eyes an authentic letter, or the reproduction in shorthand of an Imperial address to the senate, he would think it a disgrace to reproduce it just as it is. This would not be " literary ".

[1] CCLXXXVIII, 406 ; CDXXX, viii., part iv., 56.

He refashions or even fabricates every detail. This is perhaps the most striking example of the evil influence of pseudo-literature. It is exasperating to make use of a work of this kind, in which it is almost impossible to separate the true from the false, or, what is worse, from anachronisms. At every step we run the risk of ascribing to the third and second century an institution of the time of Diocletian or Constantine. The writers of the *Augustan History* are perfect types of the mountebank of literature.

The only historian deserving of the name who has written Roman literature after Tacitus, is Ammianus Marcellinus, who was born at Antioch about 330 and died about 400.[1] He undertook to continue Tacitus from Nerva (96) onwards. Of the thirty books of his history there have been preserved the last seventeen, covering the period from 353 to 378. Fortunately this is the period contemporary with the writer, of which he was an eye-witness and about which he could gather personal information. It is therefore an invaluable document for the history of this quarter of a century. We should like to possess its equivalent for what precedes and follows. The work has rare qualities, those of an enquiring and impartial mind. Moreover, a man of action, an officer and a friend and admirer of the Emperor Julian, the writer took part in several of the campaigns which he describes. Yet in spite of all, Ammianus is not a real writer. His style is laborious and betrays the effort to follow his model Tacitus, whom he never succeeds in approaching. There are too many speeches, too much shoddy rhetoric, and too many reflections which aim at profundity but which are too often only platitudes. Ammianus Marcellinus, in spite of his efforts, is to Tacitus what Constantine's triumphal arch is in art to that of Titus or of Trajan.

The most noteworthy prose writer is Q. Aurelius Symmachus (345–405), who was Prefect of Rome in 384 and was raised to the Consulship in 391. He is the author of panegyrics of the Emperors (Valentinian and Gratian), of speeches in the Senate, and of letters.[2] He was considered in his time a fine man of letters and reverenced by his co-religionists the pagans and even by the Christians. St. Ambrose and Prudentius do not dare to compare themselves to him in eloquence.

[1] CCLXIV. [2] CCXVI.

When we read his works, they give us the impression that the author was a good and worthy man, a friend to belles-lettres, very polished in discussions and a gentleman, but intellectually a distressing nonentity. There is little to be got from his correspondence.

In poetry, two or three names are worth remembering: Ausonius (310–395), Claudian (died about 408), Rutilius (wrote in 416). This comes to little numerically, but it is much if we remember that for more than two centuries, since Juvenal (died in 149), that is to say since the reign of Trajan and Hadrian, Latin literature had not produced a single work in verse which so much as possessed distinction, if we except the *Pervigilium Veneris*, the only flower of lyrical poetry between Horace and Prudentius. Ausonius (D. Magnus Ausonius), born at Bordeaux, professor and tutor of the Emperor Gratian, and wrote a good deal in verse until extreme old age. We will cite only the *Mosella* and the *Ephemeris*. Most of the time he is boring and devoid of originality. "His style, crammed with quotations, plagiarisms and pastiches, is that of an old professor whose head is well stored with classical tags, and who thinks he is paying supreme homage to the authors whom he has for so long been explaining by modelling himself on them in his thought and speech. In his writings he pours forth the mass of heterogeneous information which he has accumulated during the thirty years of his professorship."[1] This "undigested erudition" spoils portions of his work in which we find that which it would be vain to look for amongst the classics, "a certain note of intimacy and homeliness"[2]; he speaks of himself, his life, his family and friends, and of his little native place Bordeaux, with simplicity and grace.

Claudian, of Alexandria, is known by his official poems in honour of the Emperor Honorius, especially of the semibarbarous Patrician Stilicho, whom he does not seem to have survived (408). He is a rhetorician in verse ; his very frigid compositions are spoilt by sycophancy, declamations, invectives against the enemies of his patron, and by the extravagant use of mythology.[3] But his language is pure, his style

---

[1] CCCLXXXIV, 155.
[2] CCLIII, 7.
[3] CCCLXX.

vigorous and his verse has a magnificent ring like that of the poets of the best period. As for Rutilius Claudius Namatianus, if his *Itinerary from Bordeaux to Rome*, composed in elegiacs in 416, is cited, the chief reason is that it includes a striking eulogy of Rome at the very moment when her might was making for an irreparable fall.[1]

The " Renaissance " is summed up in three or four names for a whole century, names of distinction but not brilliance. Except, perhaps, for Symmachus, who is a dolt, not one of these authors is a native of Rome, or even of Italy. Ausonius and Rutilius Namatianus are Gauls of Aquitania, and they are men of the second rank ; Ammianus Marcellinus is a Syrian of Antioch, and Claudian a Greek of Alexandria.

Ammianus certainly spoke Latin fluently, though some have imagined that Græcisms or Semiticisms can be found in his language. But Claudian seems to have learnt Latin by reading the classics, which explains his being steeped in their subject-matter and his writing in a pure style.[2] But is not this fact itself a disquieting symptom ?

Claudian, as well as Ausonius before him, and after him Sidonius Apollinaris and many others, are suspected of having written in a purely artificial language which was meaningless not merely to the vulgar, but also to the average contemporary man, which was accessible only to a few refined educated men whose very limited number was destined to continually diminish. Therein lay a great danger ; literature, which was the pastime of a small circle of initiated persons, had no longer any roots in the soil of life. But it could not be otherwise. As in art, so in literature, the masterpieces exercised a blighting influence, especially in " classical " works which are not like the products of the romantic periods refreshed and inexhaustibly quickened by subjectivism. Being the expression of a pagan society the members of which were becoming fewer and fewer, ancient literature was not able to hold men's minds or warm their hearts. It was even destined to be an abomination to that teaching which was more and more capturing mankind, Christianity.

---

[1] CCCLXXXII.
[2] CCCLX, 648.

II.   CHRISTIAN LITERATURE

The most living parts of Latin if not of Greek literature in the third and fourth centuries, do in fact come under the influence of the Christian spirit.[1] Tertullian of Carthage (about 150–230), Saint Cyprian bishop of the same town (200–253), Minutius Felix, Arnobius of Sicca (a contemporary of Diocletian), Lactantius the tutor of Constantine's son Crispus, Firmicus Maternus (about 347), all of them Africans, bear striking witness to the fact that the third century and the first half of the fourth were barren only in pagan literature. Tertullian was not inferior in vigour of expression to any of the writers of the golden age, whether Cicero or Juvenal, while in power of imagination and in passion he is at least their equal.   The little dialogue *Octavius*, which we owe to Minutius Felix, is as good as Cicero.   Arnobius approaches Tertullian ; Cyprian, with his diffuseness and unction, is a kind of ancient St. François de Sales.   Lactantius was already entitled by St. Jerome, indulgently it is true, " the Christian Cicero ".

In the middle of the fourth century begins the series of the writings of the Fathers of the Church in the West, the doctors —for their predecessors are first and foremost polemical and apologetic writers, fighting against paganism.   Their work consists of controversies directed against dissenters (Arians, Pelagians and Donatists) and of commentaries on the Holy Scriptures.   Wholly encumbered as it is with theology, it cannot present the same literary qualities as that of the apologists of the preceding period.   Nevertheless it would be a mistake to banish entirely from the realm of literature the writings of St. Hilary of Poitiers, a Gaul, of St. Ambrose of Milan, an Italian (died in 397), or of St. Jerome (died in 420) a Dalmatian or Italian.   St. Augustine, an African of Tagaste (died in 430), is not merely the greatest doctor of the Latin church, the man who has left an all-powerful impress on it right up to modern times ; he belongs to universal literature by his *City of God* and his *Confessions*, the only works of those times which are still readable in our days.

The formation of a Christian poetry in the Latin language is also a great literary event.   Towards the middle of the

[1] **CCLXXV, XXI, CCCXLV.**

third century, Commodian, of Gaza in Palestine, had attempted, following the common use, certainly in Africa, a poetry founded less on quantitative prosody than on stress accent ; the distinction between shorts and longs beginning to get blurred, a system formed by the succession of stressed and unstressed syllables was the only one to which the ears of uneducated people were sensitive.

Strictly speaking, Commodian's poetry is a compromise : in hexameters it takes no account of shorts and longs for the first four feet but insists on keeping regular or nearly regular the last two feet, which more particularly hold the attention ; if you add a cæsura after the second foot, you obtain a line which, if one has no accurate knowledge of quantity, produces the illusion of a correct hexameter. Claudian's verse is therefore far more an imitation of classical verse than verse in the language of the people. His work from a literary point of view stood condemned in advance ; also from a political point of view, since in his *Instructiones* and his *Carmen apologeticum* he makes an onslaught with apocalyptic virulence on Jews, pagans and even Rome. This attitude was no longer acceptable when Christianity had become reconciled with the Empire. Of his form, educated Christians were ashamed. A priest from Spain, Juvencus (about 330) went to the opposite extreme ; in his *Evangeliorum libri IV* he dresses up sacred history in Roman garb ; he apes Virgil, with the result that he produces a grotesque travesty, which however does not mean that Juvencus enjoyed no success ; far from it.

It was reserved for two Church Fathers, St. Hilary and especially St. Ambrose (from 386) to compose for the congregation of the faithful hymns characterized by loftiness of thought and correctness of technique, which were yet capable of being understood or nearly understood by the masses and of moving them. Ambrose also composed the music for them. Their success was immediately great and it was lasting. These prayers passed into the liturgy. Christian Latin poetry can even boast a great man, the Spaniard Aurelius Prudentius Clemens (died a little after 405). Author of didactic poems (against heresies) and lyrics, both famous, the latter especially (*Cathemerinon* : hymns for the different hours of the day) περὶ Στεφάνων (a hymn on the martyrs),

Prudentius is the only lyric poet whom literature produced since Horace. In depth of feeling and originality of expression he is greatly his superior. To find again a real artist in verse, the world was destined to wait more than nine centuries, for Dante. Below Prudentius are a few writers of distinction such as the Aquitanian St. Paulinus of Nola (353–431) and Prosper (403–463)[1]. The fifth century produced five or six other names, but of the second rank.

If we turn to the Eastern part of the Empire, that in which the Greek language predominated, we see that here too, in the fourth and fifth centuries, only the expression of Christian thought is of any real interest for literature. The Renaissance of the second and third centuries was not sustained. Not that some writers of merit (historians and philosophers especially) are not still found, the Emperor Julian being the most interesting of them, but Christian literature undeniably predominates. Even apart from the matter the pagans have nothing in literary form to set against the great doctors of the Church. With Athanasius (he wrote chiefly from 356 to 368) Christian eloquence is already in possession of all its power. In the second half of the century it was to add to it sweetness, grace, brilliant finish and charm with the writers who are called the Cappadocians, Basil the Great (born at Cæsarea in Cappadocia about 331) whose letters and homilies show " the nobleness of simplicity "[2], and Gregory Nazianzen in Cappadocia, about 338, friend of the former (wrote encomia, funeral speeches, and theological poems), a very poor poet ; his eloquence possesses more brilliance and less simplicity than that of his friend.[3] Below these is Gregory, bishop of Nyssa in Cappadocia, better as a theologian than as a writer ; for his eloquence is commonplace. John, surnamed Chrysostom (born at Antioch about 345, metropolitan of Constantinople in 397, died in exile in 407), has left treatises, homilies and letters. Less a theologian than a moralist, he is endowed with the gift of oratory to a high degree ; he is a surprising improvisor, one of the greatest doubtless the ancient world ever knew, " the finest genius of the new society grafted on to the ancient

[1] CDXCI.
[2] XCIII, 809.
[3] CLXXXVIII.

world ". He is pre-eminently "the Greek turned Christian ".[1]
But after him, Christian eloquence under the Greek form
suffered an almost entire eclipse.

Apart from the drama, doomed without the possibility of
reprieve, there is no ancient literary genre which Christian
literature did not attempt, and we have just seen that in
eloquence in the East and West, and in poetry in the West
with Prudentius, it had had some brilliant successes. There
remained history. Eusebius of Cæsarea (267–338) undertook
to compose the history of the Church ; but, though his book
is filled with invaluable information, the author is not a real
man of letters. The same verdict must be given about his
continuators of the fifth century. Socrates, Sozomen and
Theodoret. Eusebius' work was to become known in the
West by the Latin translation of Rufinus of Aquileia, made
in 403, and Sozomen's by that of Cassiodorus, about 550.

Far superior is the *Historia sacra* in which an Aquitanian,
Sulpicius Severus, in 403, condensed the Old and New
Testament in a charming style imitated from Sallust. The
work had no success. Dry chronicles in which the facts of
history are strung together from the creation were preferred
to it.

The task of establishing a parallelism between the pagan
history of the Greeks and Romans and that of the chosen
people, the Hebrews, was under Alexander Severus undertaken by S. Julius Africanus, whose χρονογραφίαι came
down to the year 221. This African was the founder of
Christian chronology. A century later, the same Eusebius
of Cæsarea resumed this task and carried up to 324 a chronological series beginning with the creation. Known in the
West through St. Jerome's Latin translation, it is the foundation of the chronology of the Latin Middle Ages.

These works are outside literature proper. On the other
hand the work of a disciple and friend of St. Augustine, the
Spaniard Paulus Orosius, *Adversus paganos historiarum libri
septem* (it goes up to 417) is literary, in intention at least.
It is a universal history written with the pessimistic intention
of proving by means of examples that earthly life has always
been unhappy and filled with calamities. The original idea
runs through this compilation, is that of the design of

[1] CDXCVIII, 207 ; CCCXCIV.

providence; the successive falls of Empires are willed by God; their downfall prepares the way for the Roman Empire, the triumph of which is the necessary condition for the spread of Christianity. These views have had an immense vogue which lasted on into the seventeenth century (Bossuet). From Orosius onwards, all real understanding of the history of Antiquity is lost.

Finally we must draw attention to the rising of a more curious genre possessed of an inexhaustible fertility, *Lives of the Saints*.[1] At first, people confined themselves to recalling the anniversary of the martyr's death, and the glorious deed which was the reason for the feast-day. A small number of the authentic passions preserved in the first three centuries (about 70) possess the beauty of simplicity. With the triumph of Christianity, martyrdom ceased; admiration turned to doctors, pious bishops, and above all anchorites. Christian monasticism, born in the East in the fourth century, won the West during the second half of this century. In the East, the life of St. Antony, typical of the lives of the Fathers of the Desert, is nevertheless not very original. It is a literary genre which existed in pagan antiquity, aretology, in which the life and strange deeds of the philosophers and sages were narrated. A good many Christian commonplaces are found already in Eunapius (*Lives of the Sophists*, about 400), in the *Life of Pythagoras* by Iamblichus (died in 333), and in the *Life of Apollonius of Tyana*, by Philostratus (died about 265). These sages commanded the elements, removed plagues, tamed wild beasts, drove evil spirits out of the bodies of possessed persons, and effected marvellous cures. Even the practices of asceticism were not unknown to the pagan religion; before St. Simeon Stylites, devotees stood on a column of the temple of the Syrian goddess of Hieropolis.[2]

The insincerity of the pagan aretologists seems unfortunately to have been handed on, along with the literary genre, to the Lives of the Christian Saints.[3] At an early date, it is admitted that no blame attaches to a writer, if in recounting the life of a saintly man, he borrows a fact from another life, for the purpose of edification. The study of the lives of saints of

---

[1] DELEHAYE, *Les passions des martyrs et les genres littéraires* (*Revue d'histoire ecclésiastique*, 1922); cf. CIX.
[2] TOUTAIN *in Revue d' histoire des religions* (January, 1912).
[3] XVI, 94-108.

the East and West (there are thousands of them) has in store for us great critical difficulties and also painful literary disappointments. Very few of these *Vitæ* are sincere and have real emotion. The vast majority of them are abominable trash. Hagiography is a low form of literature like the serial novel in our own days.

If Christian inspiration, by renewing ancient Greek and Latin literature which was drying up, quickened certain literary forms, it did not give to them a very long new lease of life. In its turn Christian literature was very quickly exhausted, speaking from an æsthetic point of view ; for the total of the writings in Greek and Latin composed after the end of the Empire, though it forms an enormous mass, is devoid of artistic value.

It is a strange thing that form underwent no change. Pagans and Christians say different things in similar terms. All the works of Græco-Roman literature of Imperial times are washed with the same tint : rhetoric seems to be the uniform distemper over all of them.

In verse as in prose every one declaims.

The deep cause of this evil was the pseudo-humanistic education.[1] Since the end of the republican period, the crowning stage of education was the study of the figures of rhetoric. Grammatical studies, that is to say the apprenticeship in correct speech and the explanation of the poets, were only a preparation for declamation, the apprenticeship of eloquence. This was a strange phenomenon ; eloquence was never so prized as from the moment when it no longer answered any need, all liberty having disappeared. But we must believe the facts, and these show that this verbal gymnastic roused an unparalleled enthusiasm which did not abate.[2] Esteemed as the highest achievement of the human mind, rhetoric led to everything ; it was not rare, in the fourth century, for the Emperor to appoint a professor as Governor or even to raise him to the highest honour, the Consulship. This art finally became identified with Roman nationality

---

[1] **XLIX, LXXXV, CXIX, CXXIV, CXCIX, CCLVIII, CCLXII, CCCXXXIII CCCLXXXII** and **CCCLXXXIV, CDXVII, CDXXXII, CDXXXVIII,** part iv., 546.

[2] Some examples will be found in **CDXVLI,** 191 ; the grief of Thetis over Achilles' body ; against a father who refuses to ransom his son from the pirates and who later asks him for help ; against a man who has set up a statue of Minerva in a place of ill fame. In Greece, the sophist offered to talk indefinitely on anything and to maintain any opinion (CROISET, 757-8).

and with civilization. "A man is lettered and a Roman when he can understand and appreciate the studied elegance, subtleties of expression, ingenious turns, and periods which fill the speeches of the rhetoricians. The very lively pleasure which listening to them gives us, is increased by the secret feeling we have, that by admiring them we are showing ourselves to belong to the civilized world." "If we lose eloquence," Libanius was wont to say, "what then will there be left to distinguish us from the barbarians ? "[1]

It will not surprise us therefore to find Rome carrying her schools of grammar and of rhetoric wherever she carried her arms.

So unrivalled was the prestige of rhetoric that the Christians could not escape from its influence. This education, steeped as it was in idolatry and denounced by Tertullian (De anima, 39) since it was based on the explanation and imitation of the classical and hence pagan authors, the Church had always feared, but for a long time its verdicts of condemnation remained purely academic. The Roman had the poison in his blood. A St. Jerome or a St. Augustine admit that they were secretly repelled by the sacred books which were not strong enough meat for their corrupted taste. In order to make peace with their conscience, and to quicken the scruples of uncompromising purists who condemned the study of the ancient authors, these fathers have recourse to arguments such as the following : St. Augustine authorizes Christians to seek what is theirs among the heathen, following the example of the Israelites who seized the Egyptians' golden vessels to consecrate them to the Lord ; Jerome wrote appeals to Deuteronomy (xxi, 12) where the Hebrew takes to wife the faithless captive woman ; it is true that he makes her shave her head and pare her nails.[2] We should show indulgence to these puerile utterances ; they did after all secure the transmission of ancient literature.

If some educated Christians, such as Commodian, thought it sufficient to address themselves to the vulgar or rather the half-educated, the great majority realized that it was absolutely necessary to win over to Christianity the ruling classes. A

---

[1] XLIX, i., 230.
[2] XLIX, vol. i., 230, 394 ; vol. ii., 50, 176, 497 ; **CLXXXVIII** ; **CDXVII**, 135-140.

right instinct told them that they would get nowhere unless they were a match for the pagan controversialists in correctness and elegance. This, in spite of what has been said of it, was a proof of wisdom. Consequently, the most intelligent of the Christian doctors deliberately set themselves to study the ancient models in order to beat the enemy with his own weapons. They attracted to them young men, by teaching them the beauty of language.

Like their opponents, they were professors of rhetoric. Tertullian, Minutius Felix, Lactantius, Ausonius, Prudentius and Augustine all taught. In the East it was the same: St. Basil is the son of a rhetorician and the disciple of pagan rhetoricians or philosophers, Himerius and Libanius; John Chrysostom also began by applying himself to the study of the sophists and rhetoricians.

The literature of Imperial times, Christian as well as pagan, is thus a literature of professors and pupils, an academic literature. Hence it strikes us as conventional, artificial and senile. It has neither freshness nor spontaneity, nor even any seriousness, except with the Christians. Rhetorical and sophistical recipes, turned into laws and enforced as such, infected the best minds.

The heritage of a great literary past is a heavy burden to bear. In other civilizations, a too long historical continuity has crushed all invention, as in China where classics already existed at a time when our ancestors were still savages.

Further, the classical spirit which characterizes Græco-Roman antiquity was an obstacle ot the renewal both of form and substance. It wished to stereotype language by placing before men the imitation of unsurpassable models. Since it is as impossible to prevent language from evolving as it is to prevent the earth from going round, the Schools made an abyss between thought and expression. In poetry, sounds ceased to be the harmonious translation of thought or feeling. The verse of the fourth, fifth and sixth centuries is only a laboured production or conundrum. Prudentius, addressing Christians and wishing to edify and instruct them, but using a language which they cannot understand without racking their brains, is more absurd than Claudian laden with the spoils of Virgil.

As for the substance, classicism is interested in the universal

only.   It rejects everything which is particular or " singular ".
If the truth be told, it lives on commonplaces.   Inevitably
it became, and that very soon, monotonous, poor and barren.
Death lies in wait for all "objective" classical literature.
It is only since yesterday, since the eighteenth century, that
man has dared to show his fellows that he is not ashamed
of displaying his personal joys and griefs.   Since the triumph
of subjectivism, literature stands assured of an infinite future.

If the schools had a large share in the decadence of
ancient literature, by reason of their very superstitious
devotion to the great models, their services in other respects
are immense.   It is the grammarians and the rhetoricians
who have maintained the commerce between minds.   Their
work was as great and lasting as that of the Imperial armies
and bureaucracy.   Without them, the feeling of the unity of
civilization would soon have faded among men separated by
considerable distances and scattered from the Euphrates to the
Ocean, and from the North Sea to the Sahara.   Life tended
to decomposition, diversity and lack of comprehension.   The
rhetorician struggled tragically against the forces of nature,
as the Emperor did against the economic and racial forces
which made for the end of the Empire.   When there were
no more schools, grammarians and rhetoricians, in the sixth
century, the unity of *Romania* was to disappear for ever.

Grammar and rhetoric made up the whole or nearly the
whole of education under the Empire.   Law was taught
chiefly by practice ;   there were only three schools, at Rome,
Constantinople and Beirut[1].   Philosophy was not taught,
at least in public institutions, except at Rome, Constantinople
and Athens.   Moreover, the ancient schools had been for a
long time decaying.   Through their mutual influence, they
ended in eclecticism.   After Plotinus,[2] Neo-Platonism became
finally lost in mysticism.   Iamblichus, a Syrian, is not so much
a philosopher as a visionary and thaumaturgist ;   his disciples
looked upon him as a supernatural being.   Neo-Platonism
turned to religion.[3]   In the fifth century Proclus (died in 480)
turned it into an arid but powerful scholastic system ;   but
he also was a visionary and his followers regarded him as a

[1] LXXXVII.
[2] CXXIV.
[3] CXXXI, CDXC.

miracle-worker. When Justinian closed (529) the school of Athens, the last school of philosophy to survive, life had already left it.

III. THE DISAPPEARANCE OF THE SCIENTIFIC AND PHILOSOPHIC SPIRIT

Science is a creation of the Greek genius. Apart from and before the Greeks, there were discoveries ; but, since these were not the result of method, they remained barren.

In the Greek countries themselves, not all the sciences flourished with equal splendour. The Greek genius manifested itself chiefly in mathematics, of which it was the real founder.[1] Unfortunately, mathematical speculation, in which the mind forever moves without coming up against the obstacle and the control of facts, presents analogies to metaphysical speculation. Its methods and discoveries throw the mind into an ecstasy which may even become a cerebral disorder. Discovery by the mere force of reasoning leads to the belief that through juggling with formulæ one may penetrate the secrets of nature and so subject them to man's will. Thoughtless admiration for mathematics keeps up or reintroduces the mentality of magic. Already in the middle of the sixth century B.C., Pythagoras had taught the principle of harmony which upholds the Universe by the force of Numbers. In the fourth century A.D., Iamblichus had his brain almost turned by the science of numbers. As for astronomy, in spite of some brilliant discoveries, it only freed itself completely from astrology in the seventeenth century.

There is no doubt that mathematics, left to itself, is powerless to sustain the scientific spirit. It needs the help of the sciences of observation and experiment. But during Antiquity, the natural sciences remained in their infancy.[2] Physics was almost non-existent. Chemistry remained bound up in magic and was only a collection of mysterious recipes.[3]

Greek science also suffered from the misfortune of not succeeding in freeing itself completely from philosophy. The most intelligent man of Antiquity and perhaps of all time, Aristotle, never conceived the necessity of such a distinction. Not that he rejected observation and experiment, the preliminaries

[1] CCCXXXI ; cf. XVII, LXXIV, CCXX.
[2] CIII.　　　　　　　　　　　　[3] XXXIII, vol. i.

of all science. The simplest examination of his works declares
the contrary to have been the fact, since the majority of them
consist of a series of theories based on a vast mass of material
consisting of physical, natural, political and psychological
facts gathered with unparalleled curiosity and zeal. Many
of his writings (for example, *The Constitution of Athens*) are
what we should call proofs and illustrations ; such were
many which have been lost to us ; his friends and pupils
collected more than 150 constitutions for him.[1] His system
appears even eminently adapted to stimulating research.
While Plato attributes reality to the world of ideas and even
declares that it is the only reality, Aristotle maintains that the
ideas exist only in things.   While Plato subordinates the ideas
to the Idea of the Good, or to speak more correctly makes
this Idea, which is the supreme essence, absorb them, Aristotle
maintains the distinction of essences and refuses to allow the
unity of the substance to swallow them up.   In consequence
it is necessary to study these essences in and for themselves,
not in order to discover in them the Idea of the Good, but,
on the contrary, in order to grasp its specific differences.

What is knowledge ? It is that which is concerned with
essence, and the essence of an object is reduced to four elements
which determine it and are its causes : (1) the matter ($\H{v}\lambda\eta$),
that of which it is made ; (2) the form ($\epsilon\hat{\iota}\delta\circ\varsigma$) which the matter
has taken on ; (3) the efficient cause ($\tau\grave{o}\ \kappa\iota\nu\circ\hat{\nu}\nu$) which has
effected this change ; (4) the end ($\tau\grave{o}\ \tau\acute{\epsilon}\lambda\circ\varsigma$) realized thanks
to it.   " It is the concurrence of the four causes which makes
matter pass from potentiality to actuality. We must know
therefore all of them, in order to possess complete knowledge
of the object. Dialectic does not suffice."[2] So little does
it suffice, that the founder of Logic, after imagining that " he
was creating thereby an intellectual aid of the first rank,
an organon of all scientific research,"[3] never has recourse in
his innumerable treatises to the modes and figures of the
syllogism. The Aristotelian logic, the evil influence of which
in the Middle Ages and up to Descartes is well known, is
therefore not enough to account for the scientific barrenness
of the work of the Stagirite.[4]

[1] CLXXVI.
[2] XCIII, 473, 493.
[3] CLXXVI, vol. iii., 50.
[4] CDXXIII.

What was barren were the speculations on Being : " the distinction between matter and form, in particular, was quite unfit for suggesting or promoting truly scientific enquiries capable of contributing in the long run factors which might control or correct the ideas which the understanding can conceive *a priori* about the Universe. The general *a priori* theory of form and quality is barren in comparison with the Cartesian theory of quantity and the Leibnizian theory of force. *It is an error of Greek thought ;* the meaninglessness of the controversies which it has raised everywhere for two thousand years proves this super-abundantly ".[1]

Nevertheless it would be unjust and contradictory to attribute the arrest of ancient science exclusively to Aristotle's influence. Apart from the " *Dialogues* " which made Aristotle's literary reputation and which we no longer have, his works nearly perished, and they had no general circulation until about the middle of the first century B.C., thanks to the edition produced by Andronikos of Rhodes.[2] But at this time, ancient science had long since lost all creative force. Greek science had taken refuge and was concentrated in Alexandria where it displayed no originality whatsoever ; there were still names of scientists but no school.

Aristotle's influence by means of the book, was consequently influence at long range, destined to work in the far future. Moreover, counter-balanced by other competing systems, it did not have the field to itself. The Pyrrhonians did not wait for the eighteenth century to show, against Aristotle and his teacher Plato, that " all knowledge is relative, that absolute truth does not exist, that attempts at logical explanation by causes and invisible things manifesting themselves under the signs of appearances rest only on illusions ".[3] Beside Plato's day-dreams about the Idea, from which Aristotle did not succeed in freeing himself in spite of all his efforts, there was a sane scientific theory about matter, capable of yielding fruitful results, the atomic theory of Democritus.[4]

It would not then be possible to make Aristotle alone bear

---

[1] Ch. V. LANGLOIS, in *Questions d'histoire et d'enseignement,* 80-81; **CLXXVI,** vol. iii., 94-96 : " The concept has not been able to lead to any explanation of the world ".
[2] **CLXXVI,** 33-34; **CCII.**
[3] **CCCXXXI,** 262-263, 255-256.
[4] **CLXXVI,** vol. iii., 88.

the responsibility for the arrest of science in the ancient world, and still less to declare that the narrowly logical tendencies of Greek thought prevented the development of the experimental method, that is to say, the creation of modern science. In order to be set up independently of philosophical or theological speculations, science needed " a passionate attachment on the part of men to truth and reason "[1], a disinterested attachment, we should add. But the exclusive pursuit of science calls for efforts and self-sacrifice which from all time have been repugnant to the immense majority of mankind. It calls also for independence, and for support from public authority and public opinion, and for a sheltered retreat. It has a frail life and its transmission is constantly endangered. Now the Greeks, and still more the Romans, were inclined to see in science its utilitarian side only. Then, as now, the masses were interested only in practical results. The higher branches of science were never the subjects of a regular independent teaching supported by the State. Bound up with the personal life of a very small number of scientists, they were constantly threatened with extinction, were unable to spread, and finally succumbed.

Lastly, science as well as philosophy suffered from the formidable competition of the spirit of mythology, which offers at a smaller cost more attractive solutions of the problems of life and death. Scientific abstraction cannot stir men's hearts or rouse their longings, as does religion which promises happiness here below or in another world to the sentimental egotism of mankind. Science and philosophy, unable to strive against mysticism, which secures for the initiated union with the absolute Being, were submerged in the torrent of religiosity coming from the East, which, especially since the first century A.D., tolerates nothing outside itself. Philosophy was to emerge anew at the end of the eleventh century. But of science all that was to remain was a mass of processes which no systematic explanation would bring to life. From Antiquity the Middle Ages or at least the Christian Middle Ages were to gather nothing but a collection of recipes, and even that a collection which was for a long time very incomplete.

---

[1] CCCXXXI, 270.

CHAPTER X

The Corruption of Public Spirit

WE have finished with the account of the remedies employed by the Roman Emperors, especially by Diocletian and Constantine, to put a stop to the dissolution of the State and of Society. We have seen them completing the transformation of the *imperium* of republican origin into a monarchical power; trying the tetrarchy system and then the division of the Empire into two halves; changing the organization of the army in order both to tame the legions and to adapt them to the new requirements of tactics; and re-moulding the system of imposts with a view to unification and simplification, and also the better to squeeze the taxpayer. We have seen Constantine substituting for the administration by magistrates, the method of the *comitiva* in the central and provincial administration, that is to say, absolute government by the " friends " of the princeps, while at the same time completing the separation between the military and civil functions and giving pre-eminence to the latter. We have spoken of his efforts to improve civil and criminal law as well as procedure. Lastly, we have studied the establishment of a real caste system by means of the institution of a hierarchy of functions and by the obligation imposed on every one of continuing in his occupation to the end of his life and of handing it on to his children. At the same time, impelled by an inspiration of unparalleled boldness, the Emperor, breaking with the most venerable traditions, set about changing the religion of the Empire.

Rarely has society undergone as many upheavals as in the half-century which followed the elevation of Diocletian in 284. The greatness of the task was paralleled by the extent of the evil. By superhuman efforts it was possible to retard the fall of the Empire in the West, and to check decay in the East; but in a general way, the State and ancient civilization continued to decline. What was the cause? This is one of the most vexing questions in history, certainly the one to which the answer is most difficult. The fall of the ancient world "is perhaps the most important and most interesting problem of universal history ".[1] It is " the biggest problem of history ".[2]

We will try, if not to solve, at least to define it.

The explanation has been sought in the personal character of the heads of the State ; this is the simplest method and the one which immediately occurs to the mind. A forcible exposition of it is given in V. Duruy's *Histoire des Romains :* " In States in which the monarch is everything and institutions nothing, decay may quickly follow upon greatness ; for if there are no men sent by providence, there are men who are necessary. Let Trajan, Hadrian or Severus be at the head of government, and a hundred million Romans live in peace and prosperity ; let them be replaced by incapables, and there is disorder in the armies and the barbarians are in the pro- vinces . . Civilization is advanced by superior men and not by crowds ; if nature, then, no longer creates men of this calibre, civilization falls back ".[3]

In the conclusion of his great work he says : " Could this fate (the invasion of the barbarians) have been avoided ? Yes, to a certain extent, if Augustus, Trajan and Hadrian had had heirs instead of unworthy successors. But there is in human affairs a force of circumstances of which clever men make use and which carries everything before it when vulgar men of ambition have taken the place of men of experience."[4]

This idea needs a good many reservations. It forgets that the result is not always in direct proportion to the effort. In order to be impartial, we must reckon up the difficulties which the man of action, the political or military chief has to overcome. A general may display a thousand times greater ability and energy in effecting an honourable retreat with demoralized troops than in winning a brilliant victory with an army well in hand and perfectly equipped over an opponent inferior in number and in arms. Diocletian, who is so little known owing to the lack of contemporary historians, may have given proof of greater genius in putting life once

---

[1] **CCCXXVII**, 160.
[2] Jul. Beloch, *Sybels Histor. Z.*, vol. lxxxiv., 1900.
[3] **CXXVIII**, vol. vi., 392.
[4] **CXXVIII**, vol. vii., 544.

more into the ageing body of the Roman State, than even Augustus in curing a stricken organism which was still full of youth and strength.[1]

But these discussions are very useless, because the assertions of Duruy, and of many others, are erroneous or exaggerated.

The Roman world saw on the throne a succession of sovereigns, to which subsequent history has shown no parallel, and that too precisely after the period of the stagnation and then the decay of the ancient world[2] : Marcus Aurelius, Septimius Severus, Claudius II, Aurelian, Probus, Diocletian, Constantine, Julian, Valentinian, Theodosius. Their unfortunate rivals also were not unworthy of their conquerors. In default of Septimius Severus, his rivals Albinus or Pescennius Niger would have made heads of State of the first rank. What Diocletian did, Carus would no doubt have accomplished. Amongst the thirty tyrants of the third century, several were men of vigour. In the fourth century, Maxentius has been underestimated to the advantage of Constantine, and the " tyrant " Maximus would have been a very worthy legitimate Emperor.

Amongst these men, more than one gave proof of a pitiless cruelty, as did Valentinian, but all showed an incomparable energy. Statesmen, legislators and warriors, they flew from Britain to the Rhine, from the Rhine to the Danube, and from the Danube to the Euphrates to defend the Roman world and civilization against the German or Sarmatian barbarians or against the Parthians and later the Persians. All of them knew their life to be constantly in danger ; the friends of yesterday were the rivals of to-morrow ; they knew that the soldiers who had forced upon them the purple, would cut their throats from a mere whim. Yet they gave themselves up fearlessly to their tragic destiny of super-men. For if ever there have been super-men, they must be sought amongst the Roman Emperors of the second and fourth centuries. Compare them to our medieval kings and you will be astounded by the greatness of these Emperors. How pale and ludicrous, in comparison, do the physiognomies

[1] Ed. MEYER places Diocletian's work above that of Augustus (**CCCXXVIII**).

[2] Already a century ago, NAUDET (**CCCLI**, vol. ii., 286-287) noticed this.

of the Merovingians or of the majority of the Capetians appear to us ![1]

But if the heads of State, apart from their personal morality, were strong and active, their servants present the spectacle of a terrible degradation and corruption.

The reform of the taxation system contained in itself nothing that was not praiseworthy. The old customary methods of the Republic and of the Early Empire benefited Italy and certain provinces at the expense of the rest. Unfortunately the most deplorable abuses arose in its application. The making of the survey and the collection of the land tax were the occasions for horrible scenes : Lactantius (*De mort. persecut.*, c. 23) describes for us the surveyors summoning the people of the town and of the country to the public squares and applying torture, making children give evidence against their parents, wives against their husbands, and servants against their masters ; extorting from them by means of blows exaggerated returns which they then made still higher, placing on the register children and old men.

It must be admitted that the taxpayers were singularly recalcitrant ; the Egyptians made it a point of honour not to pay except after a sound drubbing (according to Ammianus Marcellinus).

The collection of the *chrysargyron* called forth no less terrible scenes.[2] Libanius (*Contr. Florent.*, p. 427) tells us : "Gold and silver tax, intolerable tax which makes everyone shiver when the fifth year approaches. . . While merchants can recoup themselves by speculations, those for whom the work of their hands scarcely furnishes a livelihood are crushed beneath the burden. The lowest cobbler cannot escape from it. I have seen some who raising their hands to heaven and holding up their shoe-knife swore that they would pay nothing more. But their protests did not abate the greed of their cruel oppressors, who pursued them with their threatening shouts and seemed quite ready to devour them. It is the time when slavery is multiplied, when fathers barter away

---

[1] It is no doubt because they felt this greatness of the fate of the Roman Emperors, that our ancestors, from the sixteenth to the eighteenth century, were so fond of the history of these times. It was because of this that they found it so difficult to be interested in the history of the Middle Ages, which seemed to them boring and paltry, in comparison with Roman history even in the Later Empire.

[2] CCCXLIV, vol. x., 297.

the liberty of their children, not in order to enrich themselves with the price of this sale, but in order to hand it over to their persecutors ".

Zosimus also writes : " Constantine imposed a tribute of gold and silver on all who engaged in commerce, even on the pettiest tradesmen in the towns ; wretched courtesans even were not exempt from the tax. On the return of the fourth year, as the fatal time approached, all the towns were seen in tears and grief. When the period had arrived, the scourge and the rack were used against those whose extreme poverty could not support this unjust tax. Mothers sold their children, and fathers prostituted their daughters, obliged to obtain by this sorry trade the money which the collectors of the *chrysargyron* came to snatch from them ".[1]

To the severity of the collection were added the frauds in the making up of the registers and in the apportioning of the *juga*, or quotas. The *tabularii* of the cities, who were entrusted with the survey, reduced the taxes of the rich, to place the burden on the shoulders of the poor. The collector (*exactor*) and the receiver (*susceptor*) refused to hold valid the tax-payer's receipt, though it was in order. They clipped the specie paid to the State. The *curiales* exacted from the country people contributions in kind and excessive or undue labours. Ground down by the Counts and Governors and beaten by the Senators, the *curiales* in their turn oppressed the poor wretches ; *tot curiales, tot tyranni*, Salvian says[2].

It was necessary in 364 to set up *defensores civitatis*, whose principal charge was to prevent the abuses of the fiscal system. Just as the decurions were exempted in 383 from entry on the lands of the *potentiores* for the purpose of levying the land tax, the *defensor* was charged with the *exactio* on the lands of the *minores possessores*.[3]

It is probable that what reached the coffers of the State represented only a portion of the contributions in kind or in money collected from the tax-payers. The collectors made these men their personal prey. We must add to these evils the abuses of the personal,[4] class, or corporate exemptions, which reached such a pitch that Lactantius says, though not

[1] CCCLI, vol. ii., 217.
[2] DI, vol. iii., 284, 531.
[3] CVII, 287, 291 ; CCLXXXVI, 103.
[4] CVII, 83 ; CXXVIII, vol. vii., 185, 211.

without obvious exaggeration : "Those who live on the taxes are more numerous than those who pay them ".

To harshness and dishonesty were added venality and peculation. Everyone stole. In the army, the clerks stole the pay ; the *navicularii* charged with the service of the *annona*, stole from the corn ; they themselves were exploited by those set over the ports. The recruiters accepted for conscripts the refuse of the *coloni*. The postal administration exploited travellers. Public servants (*officiales*) took bribes for judicial audiences : "Back! rapacious hands of public officials, back! I say ; if, after being warned, they do not draw back, let them be cut off " (law of 388). It was fortunate when the all-powerful *judex* (the governor) was not an accomplice.[1]

Another abuse was that of the gratuity or present. "The new arrival in an office (cohort) owed a present " ; the new arrival in the corps of the *domestici* paid fifty gold solidi. Under the pretext of the right of entrance fee or footing, real or honorary *curæ* came to be bought and sold : a sort of tariff (*suffragium*) was set up ; and the abuse was so inveterate, that the Emperors, after vainly trying to extirpate it, confirmed it and took advantage of it. From the time of Constantius, they claimed *auri argentique collationes* from those on whom they conferred favours, and Justinian insisted on the payment of fifty gold solidi "to the most pious Empress ". In the fifth century, Synesius was able to say to a Sovereign : "Everything is bought ".

There was a still more terrible evil, delation.[2] Not that the Emperors did not try to put a stop to it. Constantine writes in 313 : "The greatest scourge of mankind, the detestable race of the delators, must be stopped. We must stifle it in its first efforts and tear out the pernicious tongue of envy. Let not judges receive the calumniating information of the delators ; let them be given up to punishment as soon as any of them appear ". In 335, he repeats his complaints ; denouncing does not cease. The regulations assigning a portion of the spoils of the victims to the informer had fallen into disuse, but the court intrigues of the powerful served instead of the zeal of these scoundrels. Even courtiers who had grown rich were never sated. Constantius in 338

---

[1] **DI,** vol. iii., 285.
[2] **CCCLI,** vol. ii., 237, 241.

rescinded his father's rescripts while at the same time maintaining the prohibition against secret delations.

The result was as follows : " Clear proofs have shown that Constantine was the first to arouse the cupidity of those about him. Constantius fattened them on the blood and marrow of the provinces ". (Ammianus Marcellinus, xvi., 8 ; cf. Julian and Zosimus.) The same Ammianus Marcellinus bears witness to the atrocities to which even the humblest private individuals were subjected on the slightest and even most ridiculous imputation of conspiracy, treason or magic. The evil dated from far back, from Tiberius ; it had never been, and it was destined never to be, possible to extirpate it ; it was connected with the very essence of the Imperial power.

From the " functionaries " and from the Court let us pass to the subjects.

The only part of the population with whom the government really concerned itself, was the plebs of the large towns, because it alone seemed formidable. The " Roman people " had in fact disappeared. Since the end of the Republic Latium had been uninhabited. This result, it must be admitted, was inevitable. Latium was not destined by nature to nourish a large population. When this over-populated district had conquered Italy and then the Mediterranean world, it was unavoidable that the population should abandon this territory of mediocre fertility for more favoured countries. The Romans spread in the second and first centuries B.C. throughout Italy, Spain, Gaul, even the East, and the cradle remained empty. Greece after the Macedonian conquests had already presented the same phenomenon, and Spain was to reproduce it in the sixteenth century.

The population flowed back into the " city ", whose environs were half deserted since the Empire. What was there to do in the city ? There were no big industries. People earned their living by means of humble crafts and small business, and that with great difficulty owing to the competition of slave labour. The plebs lived chiefly on alms, State alms (public largesses) and the *sportulæ* of private individuals, of the rich families inhabiting the 2,500 palaces (*domus*) of Rome. The " Roman people " was debarred from the army since the time of Augustus and Vespasian (except for the Prætorian cohorts) and deprived of political

rights ever since Tiberius, in the year 14, had transferred
to the Senate the right of election. The *comitia* (by tribes)
survived theoretically ; the laws proposed on the Campus
Martius were acclaimed by a few supernumeraries ; then
this farce ceased at some uncertain period.

Without work, or practically without work, this Roman
populace could be dangerous, when worked up by intriguers.
To distract it was a prime political necessity. Hence, along
with the free distributions, the " games " formed one of the
most important public services of the State. The number
of holidays went on increasing continually. From 65 days
under the Republic it went up to 135 under Marcus Aurelius,
then to 175. From this date we may say that the people
spent its life in the theatre, the amphitheatre and the circus.
" The circus is its temple ", says Ammianus Marcellinus
(xxviii., 4) speaking of the populace of Rome. " The rest of
the time they live only on the memory of the last or on the
hope of the next festivals."

In the fifth century, and later still, it was in the circus
and the amphitheatre that the barbarians surprised the
populace (Trèves and Antioch). In order to win its support,
the enemy kings celebrated the games ; they continued at
Rome under the Goths. Totila, recapturing Rome in 549,
gave games ; the Persian King Chosroes attended the games
after the capture of Antioch.

Some Sovereigns (Marcus Aurelius and Julian) thought,
we are told, of abolishing them. The idea was quite impracticable. Every attempt to keep within bounds their number
or importance failed. Gratian restored in Africa the athletic
combats, declaring that " the amusements of the public
must not be checked. The people should on the contrary
be encouraged to show its joy, since it is happy " (*Cod. Theod.*,
xv., 7, 3).—Arcadius restored the May festivals (*Maiuma*)
protesting that he was no enemy to games and shows. " He
does not desire to cast the Empire into gloom by abolishing
them " (*C. Th.*, xv., 6, 2).

The Emperor was obliged to attend them and not to be
fastidious. Otherwise, the populace showed its discontent.[1]

---

[1] Similarly in the seventeenth and eighteenth centuries, in Spain, the
sovereigns attended the bull fights, and the ambassadors were hooted if
their faces betrayed boredom or disgust.

It was to win popularity that Commodus descended into the arena.

It must be said that it was only at the games, especially the circus games, that contact was established between the ruler and the people. There the relations were direct and brutal ; in the nature of praise or of an attack, the dialogue began. The people showed itself exacting and capricious. " In short they were the two masters of the Empire (facing each other), for the peace of one of whom and the pleasure of the other, the rest had been put into slavery."[1] The games, by their multiplication, kept the populace of the towns and even that of the country districts (for the theatres and amphitheatres were for the *pagus* and not merely for the town) in an incurable idleness. But their worst influence came perhaps from their nature. They stimulated and encouraged the taste for cruelty and lust. The exhibitions of exotic animals and peoples were comparatively innocent ; they held the place of our zoological gardens. But the people took delight chiefly in the sanguinary contests not merely of beasts against beasts, but of human beings (gladiators) against other human beings, or against beasts. Condemned criminals or barbarian prisoners were used. In default of criminals, the populace demanded that the Christians should be seized to be given over to the wild beasts and the magistrates tremblingly obeyed. The panegyrists celebrate as a noble deed the fact that Constantine having captured some Frankish chieftains threw them to the wild beasts to amuse the people of Trèves.

Candidates for " honours " sent everywhere for curious or wild beasts and for gladiators and prisoners. In 392, Symmachus, Prefect of Rome, was stricken by a great sorrow. His young son having been designated for the quæstorship, he, like a good father, undertook in his place the care of the festival and the expenses which this honour necessarily entailed. The sensational " item " was to have been a combat of twenty-nine Saxon prisoners ; but on the very day of the festival, these, without caring about the people's disappointment, without reflecting that they were going to wreck the young quæstor's popularity, strangled themselves with their

---

[1] **XLIX**, vol. i., 440 ; see also **CVII**, 124.

own "impious" hands. The father resigned himself "invoking Socrates and philosophy ".[1]

Even at the theatre, the public was not satisfied if in the representation fiction was not replaced by sanguinary reality. It only tolerates the tragedy of *Hercules on Mount Oeta*, if at the end the hero is really burnt. The mime Laureolus is crucified, not in play, but in reality.[2] The sanguinary games were succeeded by obscene pantomimes. To them were joined the orgiastic festivals of the *Maiuma*, in the month of May, which an Emperor in vain tried to suppress.

All writers from Seneca to Libanius and St. Augustine testify to the terrible and almost irresistible attraction exercised by these sanguinary or lustful shows. Very few amongst the Ancients had an insight into the horrible danger which society incurred from these psychological aberrations. Seneca was the only one, or nearly the only one, who realized through having seen it that these games fostered cruelty and at the same time cowardice in the people. It may appear extraordinary that a State should have cultivated throughout many centuries so pernicious a neurosis. But doubtless some day people will be astonished that our civilization should have tolerated alcoholism, not to speak of shows and exhibitions no less deleterious than the games of the Ancients.

The Church had infinite difficulty in at least softening down the games (it was never able to succeed in extirpating them). The gladiatorial combats seem to have disappeared under Theodosius in the East, and under Honorius in the West.[3] The monk Telemachus, hurling himself into the arena to part the gladiators, was stoned by the people ; we are told that the Emperor made use of the scandal to put an end to the evil. Constantine, in 325, had already wished to abolish the fights of criminals with wild beasts, but it is not certain that he was obeyed. In the sixth century, only the chariot races, the exhibitions, and at most the fights of animals against animals, remained. In the West, only the public ruin put an end to them in the second half of the sixth century.

---

[1] **DI**, vol. iii., 423, 544.
[2] **XLIX**, vol. i., 472.
[3] K. Scheider in **CCCXCVII**, vol. iii., supplement, col. 780-784 ; cf. V. Chapot in *Bull. Soc. antiquaires de France*, 1922, 130.

The Imperial government succeeded, in the west at least, in keeping in check and in satisfying the towns. It seems to have accorded with the aspirations of the town-dwellers amongst the lower and middle classes of the Mediterranean world. It gave them as much as and more than any previous government ; it was truly the State acting as Providence. Thanks to it, with very little work or none at all, people lived and amused themselves. If they had no political rights, they could criticize, jeer, and, in the theatre, shout. Familiarity and insolence live happily together with despotism amongst the peoples of the South. For the city plebs, the Roman Empire seems really to have been the golden age. It was in line with the aspirations of the Ancients for whom " the City State was a pooling of interests as well as a moral association ; every man claimed his share of material profits ".[1] Rome never had the power or the wish to break the mould of the " city ".[2]

The other side of the system was the terrible apathy of the populace. The monarchy of the Later Empire was raised on an "inert mass ".[3] The country plebs were systematically reduced to the rank of human chattels. The plebs of the towns, sated and care-free, took no real interest in anything but its pleasures, and later when it became Christian in religious controversies. The greatest political events passed over the heads of the people like black or golden clouds. Later it was to watch even the ruin of the Empire and the coming of the barbarians with indifference. It was a worn-out body whose fibres no longer reacted to any stimulus. If need be, it would let itself be butchered by an army not very numerous and really not at all formidable, without even the start of the animal defending its life.

About the upper classes of society, it is very difficult to form an opinion. For a long time writers declaimed on the corruption of the upper classes, wandering from the point. Then a reaction set in. Moralizing historians asked themselves whether fourth century pagan society was as bad as it was made out to be. Gaston Boissier has no difficulty in pointing out all the vague, declamatory and conventional

---

[1] **CLXXXIX**, 148 ; Alfred Croiset, *Démocratie antique.*
[2] **LI**, 171 ; **CCCXXXII**, vol. i., 257 ; **II**, 24 ; **DIII**, vol. ii., 7.
[3] A phrase of Edward Meyer, **CCCXXVIII** ; cf. **CDXLVII**, vol. ii., 1, 305, n. 2.

matter contained in the imputations of Ammianus Marcellinus, St. Jerome, and later, Salvian ; they are commonplaces which apply to all times and all countries. The few fragments of correspondence we have show us humane noblemen, busy in educating their children and helping their friends ; they seem to be good husbands. The impression is no less favourable than that which is left after reading Pliny the Younger on the Society of the Trajans and the Antonines. Symmachus thinks he is living in a " century friendly to virtue " ; true, he is a fool.

Fustel de Coulanges, studying the aristocratic society of the following century, gives a favourable verdict : " There is nothing that brings before us the picture of a fundamentally corrupt society . . . family life was highly valued. One of the outstanding features of this society was its taste for the labours and pleasures of the mind ; never was literary education more highly esteemed."[1] His proofs, however, are sometimes strangely naïve : " the inscriptions continually attest, in the language of simplicity and candour, the filial piety, the habits of family life, the respect for marriage, the affection of servants for their masters and the solicitude of masters for their servants ". If a city wishes to express a eulogy of one of its members, it recalls in an inscription " his seriousness and the rectitude of his morals ". Fustel de Coulanges, adds, it is true : " This cannot prove that these virtues were always practised, but it proves at least that they were universally esteemed ". That may be so, but malicious critics might retort that we esteem especially the blessings we do not own. The same writer has diagnosed the true cause of the public malady : " It was not the corruption of morals, but the weakening of the will and the unnerving, so to speak, of character. The virtue which was most lacking was strength. While the lower classes lacked energy precisely because of their dependence, the upper class lacked it quite as much in spite of their superiority ".[2] He accuses the indifference of the latter to the public welfare, its want of character, and its distaste for the profession of arms. He seems to throw on it the responsibility for the ruin of the Empire. His reproaches are not free from injustice ; for

[1] CL, 211.
[2] CL, 217, 224.

it was the government itself which closed the army to this social class, and its very real passiveness is actually the effect of despotism.

Turning away from public duties, the aristocracy became more passionately attached than ever to the land, which was henceforth the sole source of wealth. It took refuge on its vast estates, leading there an easy life, as safe as possible from the enticements and also from the threats of authority. In appearance it was as submissive as ever, bowed under the yoke of the monarch. In reality, it drew to itself silently and almost unconsciously, by virtue of its economic power, all the life that was left in society.

SUMMARY AND CONCLUSIONS OF THE FIRST PART

The Roman Empire nearly perished in the great crisis which covers the period from 235 to 268. At last, the barbarians were repelled by the Illyrian Emperors, Claudius II, Aurelian and Probus, and political unity was restored. Nevertheless the situation remained precarious. The necessary changes were effected by two personalities of the highest calibre, Diocletian and Constantine. Some would have them idealists, visionaries and dreamers. This is an amazing misconception ; they were practical minds, the former especially. They began by jettisoning what was necessary to save the ship. It was obvious that one man alone could not govern from the Euphrates to the Atlantic, and from the Sahara to Caledonia, two worlds, the Greek and the Latin, incapable of being welded together. To prevent any revolt on the part of a rival, Diocletian chose one and tried to turn him into both a colleague and a friend. The unity of the Empire, at least in theory, was thus maintained. Constantine made the separation of the two worlds final by changing aggrandized Byzantium into a new Rome (330). Thanks to its position, Byzantium could be saved from invasion ; but for this inspiration of genius, Greek civilization would have disappeared, and like that of Chaldæa, it would be known to us only by some shapeless fragments.

A religious malady, Christianity, was threatening Roman society. Diocletian had not advanced beyond the old idea that the sect could be destroyed by force. Constantine in an apparent or real fit of madness saw in it a power to be utilized in the service of the Roman State. In the East, the Orthodox Church, Greek civilization and the State came to be so well fused that to be received into the bosom of the Church was *eo ipso* to become a Greek-speaking " Roman ", at least for several centuries.

After capturing Christianity, the emperors next turned to the fiscal machinery which they strained to its utmost. To fight the barbarians and also to buy them off, and to keep the magnificent edifice of the Empire standing, great resources were needed.

But the Mediterranean world had suffered from a very serious economic upheaval. It was ruined and completely retrograde at the moment when the needs of the State were more pressing than ever. Fiscal ruthlessness ended by setting up a real caste system. The peasant was henceforth bound to the soil ; this was not the only cause of the serfdom of the soil, the origins of which go back to a remote past, but the extension of this system to free labourers is one of the features of the Later Empire. Obliged to become a member of a *collegium*, the artisan was bound to his craft and the merchant to his calling. What shall we say of the workers in the mines and in the imperial factories who were branded with red-hot iron ? They could not run away and their condition was hereditary. The middle classes were no less " regulated ". The *curiales* formed a *consortium* responsible for the taxes and the putting of the land under cultivation ; every avenue by which they might escape from the *curia* was closed.

The following was the result : the government broke all resistance, but also all independence ; it completely changed the people into a herd of " rayahs ", in the Turkish fashion.

Nevertheless we have not before us a purely selfish despotism, nor a long-matured, scientific and planned system. It was not with any deliberate purpose that the Emperors achieved centralization, unification and uniformity. A blind, unavoidable, irresistible necessity forced them to grind down everything so that the Empire might be able to exist.

These Emperors were busy with humanitarian schemes to

which their legislation bears ample and frequent evidence, too frequent indeed for their decisions to have been effective. They wished to protect the lower and middle classes of the towns and they set up *defensores civitatis*. The *collegia* of tradesmen and artisans enjoyed privileges ; they were allowed to make their own regulations and they were not harassed in their internal arrangements.

The Emperors wished to allow the complaints of their subjects to reach their own ears. They wished to put a check on the absolutism of their functionaries. Hence significant though at bottom fruitless institutions, such as the provincial councils, one of which, that of the Gauls, was to last until the end of the Western Empire. Lastly, individual measures, such as remissions of taxes, and the punishment of men in high places guilty of the betrayal of trust or of oppression, were not rare.

In spite of all, the State failed in its rôle of protector. It was ill served and betrayed by its own agents. The latter, the high functionaries, or, to speak more accurately, the " magistrates " and " judges ", belonged to the class of large landowners. They shared its ideas, customs and interests. This aristocracy was disloyal in its service to the government, while cowering before it. It secretly thwarted it, not so much from hatred as from a spirit of opposition and from selfishness. Debarred from the army, confined to honorary functions, suspected and watched, the ruling class lost all spontaneity and initiative, and in its case also, character fell very low.

The fundamental cause of the decay and later of the breaking up of the Roman Empire appears to us to have been the following :

The Empire had become too vast, too cunning and too complicated a mechanism ; the Mediterranean world, economically retrograde since the third century, could no longer support its weight. It split in two, the *pars Orientis* and *pars Occidentis*, from the end of this century. Even for the exercise of its authority, the State was under the necessity of narrowing its field of action. The same necessity was soon to force the West to break up into half-Roman, half-barbarian States. The latter in their turn would become subdivided, and the territorial splitting up was to go on increasingly without a stop for long centuries, until the twelfth century. This narrowing of political action was accompanied by a narrowing of public spirit, which was destined to go as far as the annihilation of the conception of public interest, and the disappearance of the notion of a State in the period of the barbarians.

Thus, under a still majestic appearance, the Roman Empire, at the end of the fourth century, was no longer anything but a hollow husk. It was powerless to withstand a violent shaking and soon it was to suffer a new and terrible attack from the barbarians. The East was destined to emerge from it as best it could, but the West was to be shivered in pieces.

There is something deeper and more stable than political forms, which are always ephemeral, and that is what is called civilization. In its highest reaches, literature, the arts, philosophy and religion, the changes are no less striking than in the political sphere. The old naïve nature deities, Greek or Latin, gave place to the Oriental "superstitions", Judaism, Christianity, Mithraism, Manicheism, etc., coming from Egypt, Syria and Persia. These foreign arrivals transformed the ethics and altered the psychology of the man of Antiquity. His art and literature felt the consequence of these great mutations. The blighting worship of the great models and certain defects inherent in the classical spirit, made an æsthetic renewal almost impossible. The triumph of Christianity and later of Islam were to detach men's souls from the ancient forms of beauty. Even before being condemned by religion, plastic art was to succumb, a victim to a revolution in taste originating in the East ; line was sacrificed to colour and nobility of style to the fantastic and chimerical. Ancient literature was condemned by the Church. Wholly pagan, it ceased to be understood and to be loved. Unfortunately the twofold Christian literature, Greek and Latin, which sought to replace it, thought it would succeed in this by pouring itself into the same mould. But new thoughts and feelings need a new form. Christian literature, from the point of view of art, was still-born. Science and philosophy succumbed under the competition of Oriental mysticism which brought about a real transformation of values.

This transformation is as phenomenal as if a sleeper on waking should see other stars shining above his head.

PART TWO

THE DOWNFALL

CHAPTER I

Rome and the Barbarians in the Second Half of the
Fourth Century (350 to 395)[1]

THE Roman Empire, in spite of economic retrogression,
the political shortcomings of its constitution and
lastly of the general decay manifesting itself in morals,
literature, the sciences and arts, might have been able to
continue with a diminished life, like many other Empires
which have dragged out their existence through long centuries, if the struggle against the barbarians had not engrossed
the life of the State from the middle of the second century A.D.

After Trajan's reign the period of conquest ceased. Under
the peaceful reigns of Hadrian and Antoninus, aggression
came to a stop. From Marcus Aurelius onwards it was
replaced by an exhausting policy of defence. From that
time, there was a ceaseless struggle against that mysterious
danger which came especially from the North and the East,
the barbarians.

These barbarians belonged to every race ; in Europe,
Germans, Iranians (Sarmatians and Iazyges), Scots and
Picts in the British Isles, and later Slavs ; in Africa, Moors
and Nubians. In Asia, Iran (the Persians) represents
a rival civilization to the Græco-Latin, and not barbarism.

Of all these peoples, those who dealt the fiercest blows
at the Empire and who succeeded it, at least in the West,
were the Germans.

We have seen that the Emperors of the second half of the
third century, Claudius, Aurelian and Probus, had succeeded
as by a miracle in stopping the Germans and even in driving
into the steppes of South-Eastern Europe the most formidable amongst them, the Goths, new arrivals who had come
from Scandinavia towards the end of the second century.

[1] On the sources, **CCLXXXVII.**

These great men rendered to Italy, Gaul and civilization, the same service as Marius and Cæsar. What a deep night would have fallen on the world if barbarism had mastered the West two or three centuries sooner ! Thanks to the barrier which they raised between it and *Romania*, ancient civilization was enabled to grow old slowly, change partially, and hand on some fragments of itself to the new generations and even to the barbarians themselves.

Nevertheless the danger was not exorcized. The waves of barbarism broke constantly against the frail barrier separating it from the Empire. The struggle, which had turned in Rome's favour under Diocletian and Constantine, was bound inevitably to set in again with violence some day or other.

I. THE STRUGGLE AGAINST THE BARBARIANS AFTER CONSTANTINE (350-375)

(a) *In the West.*[1]

The position became serious once more only in consequence of the struggle between Constantius and the usurper Magnentius, which lasted from 350 to 353. The frontiers being unprotected, Franks and Alemans crossed the Rhine and penetrated into Gaul. The former settled on the lower reach of the Rhine, at Cologne and in the island of Betuwe, the latter on the upper and middle reaches of the river. It was against these latter that war had first to be carried on. As soon as he was rid of Magnentius, the Emperor Constantius fought (354-355) against the Alemans near Basle and Lake Constance ; then he handed over the command to the Cæsar Julian. The Alemans were at this moment masters of the whole of North-eastern Gaul, up to Autun. Julian succeeded in clearing it in two campaigns. The most famous episode is the battle of Strassburg, where, with 13,000 men, he beat seven Aleman Kings at the head of 35,000 warriors (summer of 357)[2]. Of the Franks, one body (the Chamavi) was beaten back beyond the Rhine, while another (the Salians) was admitted into Toxandria (North of Brabant), under the authority of the Empire.

---

[1] **CDXLIII** and **CDXLIV ; LXXIII**, vol. i., 183 ; **CCCI ; CCCLXXIX.**
[2] **VI, CLVI.**

The line of the lower Rhine was fortified (at Bingen, Andernach, Bonn, Neuss)[1].

But Julian's departure for the East and his death in Mesopotamia (363) left the field free for the barbarians. For ten years, Valentinian had to defend Gaul, Britain and the Danubian regions against the Alemans, Franks and Saxons, not to speak of Britain against the Scots, Picts and Attacotti. He succeeded partly by hard campaigns in which he advanced as far as the Rhine and beyond, partly by diplomacy, by which he turned some newcomers, the Burgundians, issuing from Scandinavia and recently arrived on the Main, against the Alemans. He left Gaul only in the spring of 375 to fly to the defence of the Danubian provinces against the Sarmatians, an Iranian tribe, and the Quadi (Sueves). He died, it is said, in a fit of passion, on November 17th, 375, while receiving at Bregetio, near Komorn (half-way between Vienna and Budapest) an embassy of the Quadi which had come to tender him their submission.[2] In Africa, the insufficiently Romanized Moors of Mauretania Cæsariensis were tenacious and hard to conquer. Theodosius, the father of the future Emperor of this name, succeeded however in subduing Firmus (374).

(b) *In the East.*

Here all was quiet till 332. In this year a movement arose on the Danube (Sarmatians, Taifali, and Tervingi, the last a branch of the Goths). The Tervingi, having been beaten by Constantine, submitted. They were received as Federates[3] with the task of defending the outlying parts of the Empire. They discharged this duty for thirty-five years and became a little civilized. In this period of peace is placed the introduction of runes, a cryptic writing of Antiquity, which from the Goths was to pass to the Scandinavians. Christianity was preached amongst the Goths and Vandals by Ulfilas, a Goth himself and bishop of the Gothic Christians in 341. He translated the Gospels into Gothic. Unfortunately Ulfilas was an Arian, and this was destined to have serious consequences ; these Christian barbarians

[1] **CCLXXIV.**
[2] **CDX.**
[3] This expression does not appear till later.

were to be separated from the Roman peoples through heresy, and the fusion of races was to be retarded.

Hostilities recommenced in 367. The aggressor this time was the Roman Valens, the brother and colleague of Valentinian ; furious that the Goths should have furnished troops (two years before) to a claimant to the throne, Procopius, a relation of Julian, he crossed the Danube. The Goths withdrew into Transylvania. The same thing happened in 369.

The chief of these Goths, Athanaric, had a hatred for the Empire and for Christianity. Valens succeeded for a moment in defeating and replacing him by Fritigern who was a Christian. Upon the whole, these Eastern Goths, affected as they were by civilization, would by themselves not have been very dangerous, especially if they had been able to settle in the land.

Jovian had bought peace from the Persians, by the humiliating concession of Nisibis and Singara, fortresses in Mesopotamia, of the five provinces beyond the Tigris, and the giving up of Armenia. In 372-373 the war of Valens against Shapur brought about no very decisive result. In any case, at this date, Persia was more threatened than threatening.

When Valentinian was on his death-bed (375), the Empire seemed strongly defended, but at the cost of unremitting and almost superhuman vigilance and activity on the part of its leaders.[1] Now, in the same year, on the Caspian Sea, there appeared the Huns, horsemen belonging to a barbarian race unknown till then. These plunderers were the fore-runners of the catastrophe destined to fall on the Roman world and to shatter it to pieces beyond the possibility of recovery. Before continuing the story, we must stop a moment at the year 375, a year fraught with fate.

II.   THE ARRIVAL OF THE HUNS.
THE SETTLEMENT OF THE GOTHS IN THE EASTERN EMPIRE.
THEODOSIUS (375-395)

Beside the division of the Goths who were in hostile or friendly contact with the Romans of the East, another and

[1] **CLXI,** vol. iii., 232.

no doubt the greater body had established itself, about the third and fourth century, in the South-east of Europe, on the Dnieper (the *Borysthenes*).

These Goths, called Greutungs, were after the fifth century called *Ostrogoths*, that is " bright Goths " (*austr*) (not Eastern Goths), while those of whom we have spoken above were destined to be called *Visigoths*, that is " wise Goths " (not Western Goths).[1] In the middle of the fourth century, we are told, King Ermanarich founded an empire extending over about half of the territory of modern Russia. He had as neighbours the Finns on the North-east, and the Slavs on the North-west ; on the West the boundary was the Dniester (*Tyras*), on the West of which were the *Visigoths*, on the South-east the Heruls of the Palus Mæotis were subject to him. On the East, the boundary seems to have been the Don (*Tanais*), beyond which were the Alans, of Iranian race and ancestors of the present Ossetes. This State, which was very huge but lacking in cohesion, was unable to resist the attack of the newcomers, the Huns.

The origin of these has long been and still is under discussion. It seems to be established that they are of Turkish race and identical with the Hiung-nu, whom the Chinese annals show us on the frontiers of the Chinese Empire, South of the desert of Gobi, bordering on the province of Kan-su, as early as six centuries before the Christian era.[2] It was in order to protect Kan-su, and also the provinces of Chin-si and of Chan-si, that about 214 B.C. the building of the famous " Great Wall " was undertaken.[3] In the second century B.C. the Hiung-nu began their expansion. They destroyed the Empire (perhaps Iranian) of the Yueh-chi, north of Kan-su, and passed into Ferghana. In the first century they stretched in the direction of lake Balkash, of the Tarim, of the Iaxartes and even towards the Ural, at the expense of the Empire of the Aorsi. The centre of the Hun Empire was the Yuepan, North of the Tien-Shan mountains. The powerful Chinese dynasties of the Hans (from 206 B.C. to 200 A.D.) and then that of the Tsins, which restored the unity of China in 265 A.D. and lasted

[1] CDXLIII, 84.

[2] XC, LXXI, CCXXX, CCLXXX, vol. ii., 890 ; CLXXXIII, CLXXXVII, vol. i.

[3] CLVII.

till 419, for a long time kept in check these hordes, which finally streamed towards the West and Europe.

From five to six tents (*Yurta* in Mongolian) related by blood, and consisting of families which averaged from five to six heads, made up a camp (Turkish *aul*, Mongolian *Khotan* or *Khotun*, Roumanian *catun*). The chief of the camp was the elder who owned the greatest number of cattle. Several camps formed a clan (Turkish *tvie*, Mongolian *aïmak*). Several clans constituted a tribe (*uruk*) and several tribes a people (Turkish *il*, Mongolian *uluss*). Disputes between tribes and between peoples were submitted to the arbitration of the assembly of the clan chiefs. Finally, a group of peoples might form a horde commanded by a Khagan or Khan.[1]

As long as these peoples could find the means of subsistence in the steppes, the ties uniting these different groups were slack, in direct proportion to the largeness of the group ; the tribe disintegrated more quickly than the clan, the clan than the camp and the tent, which are the real organic cells of these communities. The chiefs and the assemblies of chiefs did not always succeed in settling the disputes, which were nearly always about the pastures. But given a personality with intelligence and energy, such a one might succeed in uniting camp to camp, clan to clan, tribe to tribe and people to people, with a disconcerting rapidity. This is explained by the nomadic life ; peoples who spend their life roaming on horseback are but feebly attached to the soil. If, whatever the motives or the means, any one succeeds in bringing together some fragments, the latter bring these nomads under them by consent or force, and the mass grows rapidly. The whole, if it maintains itself, bears the name of the chief (Seljuks and Ottomans) and indeed without him this group would never have existed. It is a torrent, or rather several torrents united, the destructive power of which is practically boundless. Settled peoples of whatever race or civilization are invariably crushed. No defence is effective against the nomads. Their unforeseen attack is made *en masse*. In the exceptional case of its not succeeding, the horde falls back with all speed on the steppe, where it is impossible for settled peoples to pursue them, for many

[1] CCCLXXIV, CCCXV.

reasons ; they do not know the tracks ; they are not accustomed to the very rough life which must be led there ; they have not the extraordinary physical endurance of the Turk, the Mongol or the Bedouin, who can support lack of food and of sleep, heat and cold, and can live on horseback for an almost indefinite length of time.

All the Empires based on an agricultural peasantry have regularly and repeatedly been the prey of the nomads : Egypt was subject to the Hyksos and Iran to the Massagetæ, while central Asia was conquered by the Turks in the ninth century A.D.[1] ; India and China have been subjugated many times, India by the Aryans, white nomads, and later by the Mongols and the Turks, yellow nomads ; China ten times by the Tartars, the Mongols and the Manchus. In Africa, in the Sudan and in Arabia the nomads keep the settled peoples in subjection.

It is true that though the Empires founded by the nomads extend over an immense area (the whole of the Roman Empire would have formed only a fraction of the Mongol Empire of Gengiskhan at the end of the twelfth century, or of Tamerlane at the end of the fourteenth), they are unmade as quickly as they are made, their cohesion depending on the personality of the founder himself and not on economic or political necessities.

Towards the middle of the fourth century, one of these ethnic cyclones began to form in the centre of Asia, in the Yue-pan, North and West of the Tien-Shan mountains. The Alans, an Iranian nomad people, whose Empire extended from the Ural to the Aral lake, were subjugated and incorporated into the Hun army. About 370, the Empire of the Goths (the Greutungs or Ostrogoths) was attacked. The old King Ermanarich, we are told, committed suicide in despair. His successor Witimer risked a battle and was slain. Thereupon the Greutungs split into two. One body, submitting to the authority of the Huns, shared their destinies until the dissolution of their Empire ; the other commanded by Alatheus and Safrac made for the West and reached the Dniester. On this river Athanaric, the chief of the Western Goths, also bore down to watch developments. We are in

---

[1] Ed. CHAVANNES, *Documents sur les Tou-Kiue* (*Mémoires de l'Académie de Saint-Petersbourg*, 1903). Cf. PELLIOT in *Toung-Pao*, 1915.

375, the year which saw the death of the Emperor Valentinian.

One part of the Western Goths decided to flee into the
Carpathians. Another, under the command of Fritigern,
turned as suppliants to the Roman Empire and asked to be
settled on Roman territory. An agreement was reached,
although with difficulty. In the spring of 376, a group of
Goths crossed the Danube, towards *Durostorum* (Silistria)
perhaps, and settled on the right bank of the river. It was
followed by the branch of Greutungs which was under
Alatheus and Safrac and by another horde of Western
Goths under Farnobius. The whole of these Goths became
fused into one people which henceforth we shall call the
Visigoths.

The peace with the Romans was very quickly broken. The
Goths complained of being oppressed and exploited. On
the other hand, it was impossible for these hordes to remain
peaceful. In 377 they crossed the Balkans and Moesia
and Macedonia were ablaze. The Emperor Valens, who
was preparing an expedition against the Persians, could not
return from Asia before the end of May, 378. The danger
proved so threatening that his nephew, Gratian, flew to his
help from Gaul by way of Illyria. Gratian, the elder son of
Valentinian I, had succeeded him in the West; he had just
renewed the exploits of Julian, in the same parts; at
Argentaria (Horburg on the Ill, near Colmar)[1], he had
crushed the Aleman invasion and retaken the line of the
Rhine which was to be held for another quarter of a
century, until 406-407.

Valens refused to wait for his nephew's help, whether
because he was jealous of him or because he reckoned the
enemy's forces (10,000 men) unimportant. The Goths
were entrenched behind their chariots in a plain near Hadrianople. The Emperor attacked on the 9th of August; the
Roman army, by which we must understand the barbarians in the service of the Empire, was destroyed with all the
generals and thirty-five tribunes. The Emperor perished
in action. His body could not be found; it is said that
having been wounded, he was carried into a hut to which
the Goths set fire. The account of Ammianus Marcellinus—

[1] CDXLIII, 195.

who ends his work at this point—is not very clear ; it seems that the victory was decided by a flank attack of the Gothic cavalry.[1]

Since Gibbon,[2] there has been a tendency to see in this battle a turning point in history, at least in military history.

Confining his observations to the art of war, C. Oman assigns to the battle of Hadrianople a representative value ; from the day on which the cavalry succeeded in prevailing over the infantry, as was almost the rule from the year 378 onwards, the art of war no longer really exists. It will be born again only in the fourteenth century in the course of the Hundred Years' War, and especially in the fifteenth century with the Swiss infantry. Victor Duruy writes about this date of 378 : " We might stop here ; for of Rome nothing remains ; beliefs, civil institutions, military organization, arts, literature, everything has disappeared and the invasion has begun : Fritigern has come right up to the walls of Constantinople ; in a few years Alaric will take Rome ".[3]

These estimates seem at first sight much exaggerated. However grievous, the event of August 9th, 378, was not without precedent. One hundred and twenty-five years before, the Emperor Decius had also been beaten and slain by the Goths ; a little later, Valerian, beaten and made prisoner by the Persian Shapur in 260, ended his days in an ignominious captivity. Nevertheless, as we have seen, in spite of anarchy certainly no less terrifying than that of the years 377-378, the world had recovered. But at the period which we have reached, the case will no longer be the same. The cohesive forces of the Empire are greatly impaired ; life is leaving the Roman world at the very moment when the pressure from Asia, from the Huns and Alans and later the Avars and Turks is no longer intermittent and becomes even more and more violent. That is why the battle of Hadrianople, in itself a mere episode, appears as an important stage in the development of an incurable decay, and the year 378 as an important turning point.

Gratian's first care was to look for a collaborator. His

[1] CVIII, vol. ii., 280-297 ; CCCLXIII ; especially CDXXV.
[2] CLXVI.
[3] CXXVIII, vol. vii., 436.

choice fell on a Roman from Spain, Theodosius, the son of
the Count of the same name who had distinguished himself
in Britain and Africa and whom he had rewarded by forcing
him to commit suicide. Theodosius was proclaimed
" Augustus " on January 19th, 379, at Sirmium (Mitrovitza,
west of Belgrade), a kind of capital of *Illyricum*. There
followed four years of fighting and negotiating, which ended
with a peace treaty with the Goths (October 3rd, 382). At
this time a rapprochement took place between Goths and
Romans. The old adversary Athanaric was received with
pomp at Constantinople. Dazzled by Roman civilization,
he stayed there until his death ; he was given a magnificent
funeral. Many Goths entered into the service of the Empire
as soldiers and even as functionaries. In the Capital, the
Goths of low birth held a great number of small offices.
Theodosius, moreover, according to Zosimus (iv., 48) had a
liking for this people, just as Constantine had had for the
Franks. It was in order to avenge a Goth officer, Botheric,
that he committed the deed which has remained a stain on
his reign ; he massacred in the circus the population of
Salonica, the town in which he himself had for a long time
lived and where he had received his baptism. We know that
the bishop of Milan, St. Ambrose, forbade the Emperor
entry into the sacred places. Theodosius was only reconciled with the Church at the Christmas of 390, after a long
penance.[1]

What was serious was that Rome did not even attempt
to assimilate the Goths settled on her territory in Moesia.
Under the name of Federates they kept their chiefs, their
customs and their language ; they were not placed under the
laws of the Empire. From this time onwards, the barbarians
disdained to become Romanized. The tie binding them to
the Empire was indeed very slack ; even during Theodosius'
reign, the Goths did not cease to make trouble, and from
this moment it is obvious that partly as members of the
regular army, partly as Federates, they are, or will be in a
short time, masters of the situation.

In the *pars Occidentis*, the foreign soldiery in Rome's
service felt itself moreover indispensable. Further, Gratian
surrounded himself with Alans, whence the disaffection of

[1] **CXXVIII**, vol. vii., 447, 482-486 ; **XXIII**, 73-76.

the Romano-Germanic army in the West; hence, when a usurper, Maximus, commanding the armies in Britain, rose in revolt and penetrated into Gaul, Gratian was deserted and slain (August, 383); the Frank Merobaudes and a Count Wallia shared his fate.

Being so busy in the East, Theodosius had to recognize the usurper, who was a compatriot of his (a Spaniard) and perhaps also a comrade-at-arms, on condition that he would be content with the prefecture of the Gauls (Gaul, Britain and Spain) and leave that of Italy (Italy, Africa and Illyria) to Valentinian II, Gratian's younger brother. Four years later, under the pretext of defending orthodoxy threatened by Justina, the young Emperor's mother, who favoured Arianism, Maximus made himself master of Italy. Theodosius, who had married Galla, the sister of Valentinian II, marched against Maximus at the head of an army of Goths, Alans and Huns commanded by the Franks Richomer and Arbogast. Maximus, beaten at Aquileia, was captured and beheaded (August, 388).

When Theodosius left Italy three years later, the real master in the West was the "master of the militia", the Frank Arbogast, who defended Gaul against the raids of the Franks (392). The relations between him and Valentinian II were already prophetic of those between Honorius and Stilicho, of Valentinian III and Aetius, and even of Ricimer and the last phantom Emperor. The "master of the militia" suspected Valentinian of wishing to have him assassinated; he forestalled him (May, 392) and raised to the throne a puppet Emperor, the grammarian and rhetorician Eugenius, recommended to him by his compatriot the Frank Richomer. This act was premature. Theodosius intervened both as a relative and as the representative of orthodoxy which Arbogast and Eugenius, both of them pagans, were threatening. The battle took place on September 5th, 394, not far from Aquileia on the bank of the Frigidus. Arbogast brought Franks and Alemans, and Theodosius Goths, Alans and Iberians from the Caucasus and even Huns; amongst his generals are found the Goth Gainas, the Vandal Stilicho who was to defend Rome and the Goth Alaric who fifteen years later was to capture it. The first day Arbogast was victorious, but on the second he was betrayed and later he committed suicide. Eugenius having been put to death, Theodosius re-united in his own hands the whole of the Empire, but only for five months ; he died on January 17th, 395.

Theodosius' reign is one of transition.[1] It held back the Roman world from its dizzy descent on the slope down which it was slipping. His importance has been exaggerated by ecclesiastical writers because, contrary to all expectation, it was found possible to extirpate Arianism from the *pars Orientis*, where it had taken deep root, especially in Constantinople. Theodosius placed force at the service of Athanasian orthodoxy and combated Arianism so effectively that after him it was destined to lead a poor and vegetative existence in the Roman world and to maintain itself only among the barbarians.[2]

But in fact, politically and socially the Emperor was not able to do much. The disintegration was already so far advanced, that whatever the ruler's merits and efforts, a great reign was no longer possible. The springs of the polity of Rome were used up. The latter could only maintain herself against the invading barbarism by the help of barbarians, at first of those who had become Romanized, but later of such as differed less and less from their fellow-countrymen who had remained independent.

The real masters of the Empire after Theodosius were the "masters of the militia ", semi-barbarians or even complete barbarians. But the last step at least was never taken. Never did these men, all-powerful though they were through the fact that they had the army in their hands, dare to lift their eyes to the throne.

The two or three examples which are used to prove the contrary are worthless. As early as the third century, the Emperor Maximin (235-238), we are told, was a Goth or Alan by birth. This is a tendencious invention of the end of the fourth century. Though born in Thrace, Maximin was a Roman citizen, on the same ground as Philip, an Emperor of Arab origin.[3]

The second example is that of Magnentius, the chief of the Jovians and Herculians, who was proclaimed Emperor in

[1] CXCIII, XXIII.
[2] CDVIII.
[3] DESSAU in *Hermes*, vol. xxiv., 359 ; cf. XVIII, 91.

January 350 ; amidst scenes of drunkenness the soldiers had acclaimed him Emperor and forced him to accept the diadem under pain of death.

Julian speaks of him as " the wretched dregs of German blood reduced to slavery". According to Aurelius Victor and Zosimus, he was descended from a German family transported into Gaul in the preceding century. Magnentius (*Magnus Magnentius*) was therefore a " *Laetus* " by origin. But born on Roman territory, in Britain perhaps, he was a Roman[1] ; his appointment was a scandal because of his low social standing, but not because of his nationality.

The third example is that of the Frank Sylvanus.[2] He had served with distinction in Pannonia and Gaul, but he had at the Court of Constantius enemies who forged letters which compromised him. Sylvanus, knowing Constantius' suspicious cruelty, thought himself lost. He had himself proclaimed Emperor at Cologne (August 355) ; it sufficed for an envoy from the court to present himself, for Sylvanus to be seized by his own men and be put to death. The incident is without significance. Moreover it is possible that Sylvanus was a Roman citizen ; it is at least interesting to notice that he had assumed a Roman name. His father was a Frank, who had distinguished himself under Constantius (Ammianus Marcellinus, xv., 5, 335).

Officers who were really barbarians never dared to assume the purple. They were satisfied with disposing of the throne and with being Emperor-makers, content with the title of masters of the militia and the dignity of Patricians, that is to say of adoptive fathers of the Emperor, which were accorded them.

We may ask whether this restraint was not of more harm than use to the Empire. In the third and fourth centuries, a discontented or ambitious army chief assumed the purple. If he was beaten, he was put to death, and this restored peace, provisionally at least. If he vanquished, he slew his rival or rivals and immediately mounted guard, instead of them, on the frontiers, against the barbarians. His fate always had a tragic greatness. The Emperor of the third and of the fourth century was the priest of Nemi

---

[1] **XXXVIII,** 312-318.
[2] **CDLVII,** vol. ii., 488 ; **CXXVIII,** vol. vii., 238.

defending the sacred wood against every profaner. The first comer might succeed him by slaying him ; but the murderer was obliged to take his victim's place and to continue his terrible and sublime destiny.

In the fifth century it was no longer the same. Theodosius when he died, left behind him two incapable minors only. People expected to see them put out of the way for the benefit of a stronger hand or brain. Nothing of the kind happened. The reason was the respect preserved for the memory of the great orthodox Emperors, and some clever diplomacy. They were proclaimed Augusti from their infancy, without even passing through the stage of "Cæsar", a title or function which disappears. In short, these two young people were spared and reigned until their death, one, Arcadius, in the East, the other, Honorius, in the West. The Emperor ceased to be the first soldier and the chief of the army, the master of power ; he was a weakling who lived imprisoned in a palace.

The reality of power passed into the hands of Patricians who were half-Roman, half-barbarian, like Stilicho and Aetius, or wholly barbarian, like Ricimer or Odovacar. Patrician and Emperor intrigued against each other. The former did not dare to assume the purple, the latter could not dispense with the former's services but at the same time feared and hated him. During the first part of the century, in the West, when the Emperor found the Patrician too powerful, or when the burden of his gratitude was too heavy, he had him assassinated (408-454). During the second part the patrician took better care of himself, keeping the Emperor under ceaseless supervision and slaying him when he disobeyed orders. Finally, he suppressed the Empire in the West (476).

PLATE II

IVORIES REPRESENTING STILICHO, SERENA AND THEIR SON EUCHER

Basilica at Monza

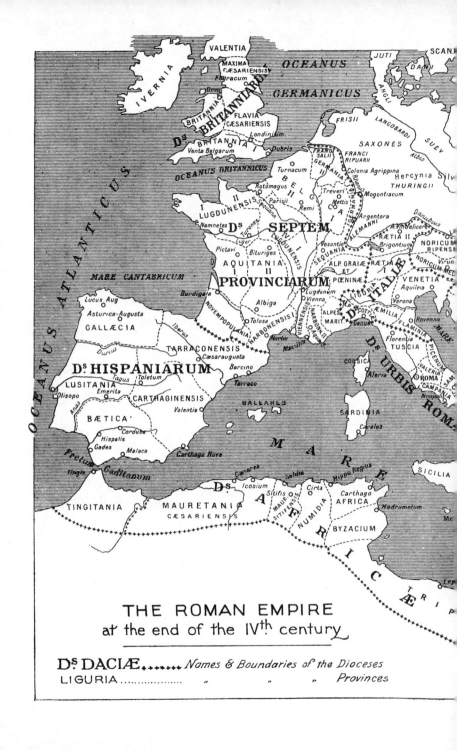

THE ROMAN EMPIRE
at the end of the IVth century

D^s DACIÆ .... *Names & Boundaries of the Dioceses*
LIGURIA .... " " " *Provinces*

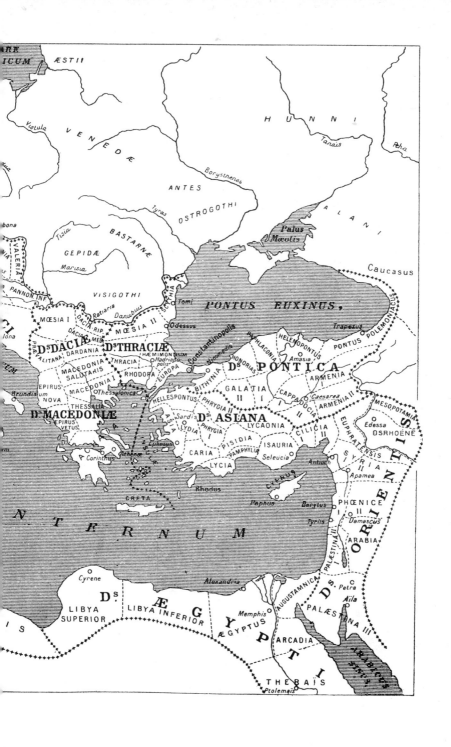

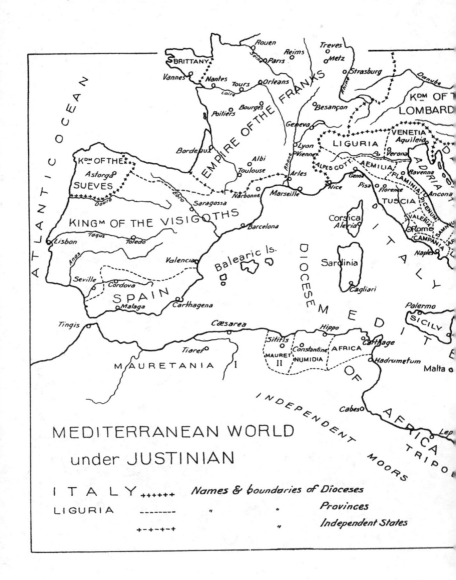

MEDITERRANEAN WORLD
under JUSTINIAN

ITALY ++++++   Names & boundaries of Dioceses

LIGURIA --------   "   "   Provinces

+-+-+-+   "   "   Independent States

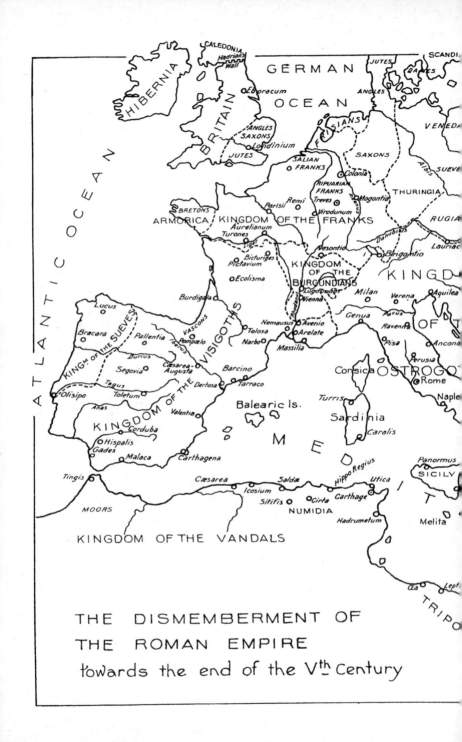

THE DISMEMBERMENT OF
THE ROMAN EMPIRE
towards the end of the Vth Century

PLATE III

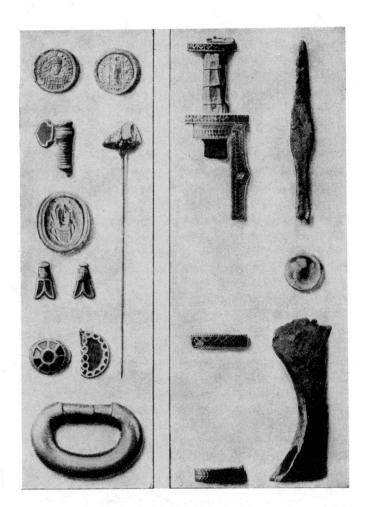

JEWELS FROM THE TOMB OF CHILDERIC

Left: The King's Seal and various glass and gold ornaments
Right: Fragments of sword, Francic battle axe and "framée"

CHAPTER II

The Roman Empire in the West from 395 to 476[1]

I. THE SETTLEMENT OF THE BARBARIANS

AFTER the death of Theodosius, the decay of the Roman Empire became rapidly more marked. The proximate cause of this headlong decline seems to have been the incompetence of the descendants of this ruler. Arcadius, his eldest son (eighteen years old) is described as an under-sized and sorry-looking creature. Morally his weakness of character was extreme; he spoke slowly and looked sleepy. Honorius (aged eleven) was pious; his appears to have been a gentle nature, but he was as incompetent as his brother, with fits of stupid obstinacy which he mistook for energy.

These minors and weaklings were succeeded by other minors who were just as great weaklings. Theodosius II, who in 408 replaced his father Arcadius, was seven years old. He was brought up by his sister Pulcheria with the greatest care. He was well educated, morally pure in the midst of the vices of his century, and comparatively humane. Physically he was better than his father; he was tall and fair, being of German origin, since his mother, Eudoxia, was the daughter of the Frank Bauto. Morally he was a bigot, utterly devoid of character and so lazy that he did not even read the Imperial Constitutions which have made his name immortal. There is not a single act which was due to his personal initiative in a reign lasting forty-two years (408-450). In the end, he drove away his wife, disgraced his sister and came under the power of the eunuchs. He spent his time in copying and illuminating manuscripts. He was surnamed the " Calligrapher ".

The successor of Honorius, who died in 423, was even more worthless. Valentinian III was the son of Galla Placidia, Honorius' sister, and of Constantius, who (with Boniface) was

---

[1] **CXLIV, CXXVIII, vol. vii. ; CCXXXI, vol. i. ; CDXCVII, vol. i. ; CDXIX, CDLXXIV, CXCII, CDLXXX, CDLXXXI, CDLXXXII** and above all **LXVI.**

the last Roman general of the Western Empire. Born in
July, 419, he was four years old at the death of Honorius.
Associated with Theodosius II in 425, he reigned until 455.
As weak in character as his uncle, he was in addition dissolute.
The Emperors who followed were better. Marcian (Pulcheria's
husband) in the East and Majorian in the West were very
superior in character. But they came too late. The bar-
barian Patrician and Army Chief was henceforth the master.

The mode of life of the head of the State changed profoundly. Until Theodosius, the Emperor's life was a constant
chasing from one end of the Empire to the other. The struggle
against the barbarians and his rivals absorbed him to such an
extent that he had not even the time to reside in Rome.
He passed through it post haste. In the West, since Maximian (286), Diocletian's colleague, the Emperor dwelt at the
centre of the army, at Milan, near the frontiers. Theodosius'
successors adopted a sedentary mode of life. They were
never seen at the head of the armies. They lived hidden away
at Constantinople or Ravenna, which were impregnable or
facilitated flight. The Emperor was a recluse ; his was the
existence of the shadow-sovereigns of the Far East. The
Emperor's life, if life it may be called, centred in the palace.
There the Emperor was the plaything of his entourage of
women, eunuchs, bishops, servile officials, and half or wholly
barbarian military chiefs. All these hated and informed
against each other. Perhaps there has never been so much
plotting and spying. There was no security for any one ;
the favourite of yesterday might have a sudden fall, victim of
information lodged against him. The Patrician, the saviour
of the Empire, was always secretly suspected and ended by
being assassinated. Even the bishop was not safe from these
disgraces. The most glaring example is that of St. John
Chrysostom, Arcadius' favourite, who was twice driven from
Constantinople and died in exile (407).[1]

There was a continual going to and fro from the imperial
side to the side of a rebel, Roman or barbarian. The conduct
of the invading barbarians presents surprising oscillations.
At the moment when it seems they are going to destroy
everything, they send deputations to the Emperor to negoti-
ate with him. Traitors swarmed in the entourage of the

<hr>

[1] CCCXCIV ; CDLXXIX.

Patricians and barbarian chiefs as well as at the Emperor's court. The disorder is universal. Nothing seems unlikely. It is impossible for us to reconstruct the psychology of the men in high places who directed affairs in this age and to pass judgment on them. Their contemporaries even are at sea here and their judgments are only the echo of probably absurd reminiscences and personal rancours. Very bold must be the man who will try to reconstruct the real character of a Stilicho, Rufinus, or Aetius. Who shall dare assert that Rufinus was a traitor and Stilicho a devoted servant ? It is in detail that this period should be studied to give some idea of the political and social disintegration shown by the Roman Empire in the last moments of its life. We shall confine ourselves to pointing out some stages in its progress towards the abyss.

It might have seemed that the Western part of the Empire had at least as many chances of lasting as the Eastern. It was in fact governed by Stilicho, Theodosius' trusted man and the most renowned war lord of the time, which renown was, it would seem, justified.[1]

For some years Stilicho seemed to carry on the Emperor's work without his title. Gildo's revolt in Africa was easily put down ; Gaul was defended against the barbarians ; similarly Italy. In 405, Stilicho exterminated near Faesulae loose bands of Alans, Quadi, Vandals and Ostrogoths, who had come from the Danube under the leadership of Radagaïsus. But the following year he was unable to prevent a big army of Vandals, Alans and Sueves (Quadi) from crossing the Rhine (end of December, 406), nor could he stop the usurpation of Constantine III, who crossed into Gaul and Spain. Constantine III led away the last Roman troops from Britain, leaving the island at the mercy of the invasions of the Picts of Caledonia, the Scots of Ireland, and lastly of the Saxons and Angles. Despairing of obtaining the help of Rome, part of the inhabitants fled into Armorica ; the rest submitted to the Saxons between 429 and 441. The island was lost for *Romania*, save for its Western part. Far removed from the centre, the loss of this province was not much felt at Rome.

The nearest and toughest adversary was Alaric with the Visigoths.[2] Encamped in Illyria with the title of *magister*

---

[1] CCLXIII.
[2] CDLXXX.

militum, Alaric, after ravaging the Empire in the East, turned towards the West. From 401 onwards he threatened it constantly. Stilicho was the only one who was able to defend Italy against him, and he defeated him several times. But it seems that at the same time he spared him with the idea of one day making use of him. Stilicho had, in fact, bitter enemies. He was hated because he was of barbarian origin and favoured the Arians and also because he ruled the Emperor and was related to him : his wife Serena was the niece of Theodosius, and Honorius married two of his daughters one after the other (he had no children by them). It seems probable that Stilicho dreamed of the Empire for his own son Eucherius. His enemies having persuaded Honorius that he was a traitor, he was put to death with his family (408).

The position of Honorius at once became very critical. Gaul, Spain and Great Britain, were in the power of the barbarians and the usurpers. In Africa, Stilicho's assassin, Heraclius, proclaimed his independence and stopped the convoys destined for Italy. Italy very soon fell to Alaric. His claims were very moderate ; he asked for permission to settle in depopulated Noricum whence he would have defended the approaches to Italy. Honorius, hidden in inaccessible Ravenna, refused every overture. He was under the influence of the party hostile to Stilicho and to the barbarians. Alaric finally seized Rome (August 24th, 410). He pillaged it, but his occupation was comparatively mild. Alaric was a pious Christian and although an Arian, he respected the churches of Rome. Formerly, in Greece, he had shown his piety by destroying the pagan temples. Alaric was, moreover, not a stranger to the Roman world ; he had been in the service of the State under Theodosius, and he was doubtless a " Roman citizen ".

The capture of Rome conferred no material advantage, apart from pillage. Rome was large and still populated, but it now lived only on what came from Africa. Alaric had reduced it by starvation rather than by force ; though impregnable, thanks to Aurelian's wall, Rome was easily cut off from the sea, while the New Rome derived its strength from its position on the Bosphorus. The Senate, deprived of real authority, had nevertheless retained a shadow of prestige.

Since Stilicho's death, it was with it that Alaric had negotiated for three years. In spite of all, Alaric did not for a moment think of really conquering Italy, still less of seizing the Imperial throne. That a barbarian could be Emperor was an idea which did not occur to anyone. It would have appeared fantastic and ridiculous. Alaric had for a moment set up a rival Emperor, the Prefect of Rome, Attalus. Attalus, who was a fool, took himself seriously, thwarted Alaric and was deposed. A storm frustrated Alaric's design of crossing into Africa, to settle his people there.

This storm changed the history of Western Europe. After Alaric's death (end of 410) his brother-in-law, Athaulf, established himself in Southern Gaul and placed himself at the service of a usurper, Jovinus. He seized Narbonne and married Galla Placidia (414), Honorius' sister, who had been made prisoner in the sack of Rome. The ex-Emperor Attalus sang the epithalamium. Athaulf only asked to enter the Emperor's service. He was assassinated by the party hostile to Rome, Sigerich, whose father Sarus was in the service of Honorius and induced him to oppose all the demands of Alaric. These facts show the confusion of parties. Honorius then had a return of good fortune. Constantius rid him of the usurpers of Gaul and Spain and he obtained Galla Placidia, by whom he had a son Valentinian III. The Visigoths were used to clear Spain of the barbarians who had had a hold there since 409 ; they acquitted themselves very well of this task and exterminated one of the two Vandal tribes, the Silings, encamped in Baetica, which has kept their name under the form of Andalusia. Constantius, fearing they might become too strong in Spain, brought the Visigoths back north of the Pyrenees and settled them in Aquitania Secunda (Bordeaux, Agen, Angoulême, Poitiers) and in the *civitas* of Toulouse (418).

Lavisse has brought out excellently the true nature of the relations of the barbarians to the Empire, especially of the Visigoths :

" Let us imagine France disused to war, tribes of Arabs employed in the defence of our country, honours heaped on their chiefs who are made generals and marshals, their men paid and fed, quite a little nation of foreigners of an independent temper and incapable of discipline, but also incapable of doing anything else but serving, always looking for better quarters, trailing their smalahs from province to province, the chiefs asking for greater honours and the tribe for more generous distributions of victuals and gold ; such were the Visigoths. Often revolting, they always returned to obedience ".[1]

We may also compare the bands of Goths, Alans, Burgundians, Franks, and Alemans who ravaged Gaul, Italy and Spain, during the first fifty years of the fifth century, to the Great Companies of the fourteenth century, the bands of " Ecorcheurs " of the fifteenth and the *condottieri* of the fifteenth and sixteenth centuries. Several of their chiefs founded dynasties, but the majority had one aim only, to hire themselves out to a king. The usurpers of the fifth century, Constantine III, Constans, Gerontius, Sebastian and Jovius, took the barbarians into their service. The Emperor did the same.

Thanks to Constantius, Gaul appeared pacified and Honorius re-organised the provincial councils by the edict of 418.[2] The centre was Arles which, since the first years of the fifth century, had become the residence of the Prætorian Prefect of the Gauls, instead of Trèves, too much threatened by the Franks and Alemans.[3] Until the end of the Empire, the council met at Arles and there were Prætorian Prefects of the Gauls. Persons of standing are even known who continued to bear this honorary title after 476.[4]

The minority of Valentinian III was wholly taken up by the quarrels between Count Boniface, who commanded in Africa, and Aetius, appointed *magister militum*. Constantius, proclaimed " Augustus ", had died before Honorius. Boniface, who commanded in Africa, was a Roman. He had a great reputation for military ability and for piety. Aetius[5] had been born in Little Scythia (Dobrudja), consequently upon Roman territory, but he had lived amongst the Huns and kept up friendly relations with them. A civil war broke out between these two important persons. It ended in a pitched battle in which Boniface perished (432). For twenty

[1] *Revue des Deux Mondes*, of July 15th, 1885, p. 402.
[2] CXC.
[3] DXVI, DCXVII.
[4] Ed. Cuq in *Atti del Congr. intern. di scienze storiche* (Rome, 1903), vol. ix., 339-346.
[5] CCCXXXVII, CCCII.

years Aetius was the most important personage in the West. He could not prevent the loss of Africa. Gaiserich, the King of the Asding Vandals,[1] penetrated it, and in ten years (429-439) made himself master of Mauretania and Africa. It was a very serious loss, for Carthage was the first city in the West after Rome, and Rome lived on the corn sent from Africa. Without a fleet, Aetius could do nothing against the Vandal.

The Empire was just as unable to recover Britain. Aetius had to leave unanswered the appeals for help from the Britons, who from 441 were under the yoke of the Saxons and Angles from Germany, the Picts from Caledonia, and the Scots from Ireland.[2]

The Patrician succeeded at least in keeping Gaul. He defeated in a series of encounters the Franks who were advancing in the valley of the Rhone, the Moselle, the Meuse and the Escaut and were beginning to settle in and to populate these districts. He succeeded also in keeping in check the Visigoths, who were trying to extend their cantonments. Arles they coveted especially.

As for the Burgundians, it was with the agreement of the Emperors or usurpers (Honorius, Constantine III and Jovinus) that they had crossed the Rhine and settled on the right bank (413). The epic of the Nibelungen, in spite of the late date of its editing (thirteenth century) preserves the memory of their stay at Worms.[3] But it has distorted the defeat which they suffered in 435, a defeat which brought about the extermination of the royal line ; the Huns who inflicted this disaster on them were not the subjects of Etzel (Attila) but mercenary Huns in the service of the Empire. Aetius was fond of employing these barbarians and it was with Hun troops that he fought against the Franks and Visigoths. Settled by Aetius in 443 in *Sapaudia* (between Yverdon and Grenoble, with Geneva as centre) the remnants of the Burgundians showed themselves loyal servants of the Empire.

In Gaul Attila's invasion did not have the importance which has been attributed to it.[4] It was a storm which passed over (451). His invasion of Italy was more serious ; it was

[1] CDXLV, CCCXIX.
[2] CCCVII, CCCVIII.
[3] E. TONNELAT, *La Chanson des Nibelungen* (1926).
[4] CLXVII, CDLXXXII.

bought off with money; Valentinian had fled to Rome. The destruction of Aquileia forced the Veneti to take refuge in the islands bordering on the coast between the mouths of the Piave and the Adige. They established their capital successively at Grado, Heraclea, Torcello and Malamocco. At the beginning of the ninth century, their seat was transferred to Rivo-alto (Rialto) which took the name of the people— Venice. Attila's empire did not last more than twenty years and crumbled immediately after his death (453). It was typical of the Mongolian and Turkish dominions—a coalition of tribes of horsemen whose impetus in war is such that no force can withstand it (cf. Temudjin and Timur); but the coalition is held together only by the personality of the chief. As soon as he disappears, everything goes to pieces.

Meanwhile Valentinian III had no son. Aetius thought of having his own son Gaudentius, betrothed to Eudocia the daughter of Valentinian, associated to the Empire. Valentinian in alarm treacherously brought him to his court and assassinated him with his own hands (September 21st, 454). Valentinian III suffered the same fate a few months later; on March 16th, 455, he was slain by two of Aetius' officers. His death marks the end of the Imperial rule in the West. As early as 455, Rome was pillaged by Gaiserich, who gathered in one haul the relations of his enemies (Eudoxia, the widow of Valentinian, her daughters, and lastly Gaudentius, Aetius' son).[1]

Not that the Emperors who came after in the twenty years following were all contemptible.[2] Some of them, like Majorian (457-461), Anthemius (467-472), Julius Nepos (474-475), were far superior to a Honorius or a Valentinian. They resided at Rome, while the Patrician resided at Milan. Majorian seems to have been a remarkable person. Instead of mouldering in the marshes of Ravenna, he was continually on the move. In 458, he stayed in Gaul, where for sixty-six years no (legitimate) emperor had set foot. He got himself recognised not only by the Burgundians but also by the Visigoths (by Theodoric II) who had set up an Emperor, Avitus, at the death of Valentinian III. Then he crossed into Spain (459) to prepare an expedition against the Vandals,

---

[1] LXXVII.
[2] CDLXXXI.

which failed. He perished in 461, a victim to the Patrician Ricimer, the son of a Sueve of royal lineage and of the daughter of Wallia, the successor of the Visigoth Athaulf.

The reason was that, taught by the fate of Stilicho and Aetius, the Patrician kept a close watch over the Emperor and left him only a shadow of authority. In the names of Severus, Anthemius and Olybrius, it was Ricimer who ruled. On the death of the latter (472), Orestes, a Roman from Illyria, who had lived amongst the barbarians as a servant of Attila, assumed the power in the name of his son Romulus Augustulus. He drew upon himself the hatred of the German army in the service of the Empire, composed of Rugi, Scyrians and Heruls, and quartered in Northern Italy, round Milan. The chief of these barbarians, Odovacar, simplified the situation (476). He dispensed with a phantom Emperor in the West and carried on the real government of what remained of the Empire under the nominal authority of the Emperor who reigned at Constantinople.[1]

II. THE EMPIRE IN 476

If we confine ourselves to appearances, the unity of the Empire has been restored. It had never been broken. In virtue of the principle of *unanimitas*, after as before Theodosius, no emperor could be legitimate if he had not the approval of his colleague. As the succession was more rapid in the West, the East since 475 had come to give a kind of investiture to the West. From 476 onwards there was only one Emperor for the Roman world and this Emperor resided at Constantinople. In fact by 476 the Western Empire had long since lost the major part of its territory.

The Danubian Provinces.[2]—These, being the most exposed of all, and having been terribly ravaged for a century, were lost early to the Empire. Pannonia was abandoned to the Huns about 433, then to the Ostrogoths after 454, and lastly after the departure of the Ostrogoths (471) to the Gepids, who got Illyria, Moesia and Macedonia. A Prefect of *Noricum* is still found in 488, but the Roman peoples of this province and also of Vindelicia and Rhaetia were withdrawn

---

[1] CDLXXXI.
[2] CCLVI, CCCLXXXI, CXLII.

into Italy by the order of Odovacar. In their place settled the Marcomanni who came from Bohemia, and who, for this reason, from that time assumed the name of *Baiuwari* (Bavarians). Dalmatia alone still remained Roman.

Great Britain.[1]—Denuded of Roman troops since 411, it had fallen to the power of the Saxons in 441-442. The North, inhabited by the Picts or Caledonians, had remained independent of Rome. The Western Coasts from Alban in the North to Dumnonia (the present Devon and Cornwall) in the South were already under the dominion of the piratical Scots coming from Ireland. The remnants of the Britons, pushed back in the West towards the Severn, the Cumberland and Westmorland hills and the Clyde valley, and losing touch with the continent, forgot the Roman language and institutions.[2]

Africa.[3]—It would be doing injustice to the truth of history to deny that the crossing of the Asding Vandals into Africa, in May, 429, was other than a conquest. Six years afterwards, it is true, the barbarians having failed against Carthage entered into negotiations with the Empire, which they had moreover served in Spain since 411 as Federates. By an agreement dated February 11th, 435, they were established with this title in Proconsular Numidia, and Gaiserich became a kind of military functionary with Hippo as his residence. But this peace did not last long. On October 19th, 439, the "King of the Vandals and the Alans", having captured Carthage by a surprise attack, considered himself independent; he dated public and private documents in his name with this date (439) as the starting point of his rule. Terrified by the Vandal's piratical expeditions, Valentinian III had to acknowledge him in 442 in the possession of Mauretania, of the Proconsular Province, of Byzacena, of Proconsular Numidia, and of " Gaetulia " (South of Byzacena). Soon afterwards (before 458) Gaiserich seized the rest and reigned from Tangier to Tripoli.

His pillaging expedition against Rome in June 455 cannot without difficulty be taken as a mere reprisal for the assassination of Valentinian III, as the barbarian himself wanted it to be considered; for the widow of the late Emperor and her

---

[1] LXXIX, CCCVI, CCCVII, CCCVIII.
[2] According to BURY, Roman rule continued in Great Britain until about 428. On this hypothesis, see *Revue des Etudes anciennes*, January, 1923.
[3] CD, LV, CCCXIX.

daughters Eudocia and Placidia formed part of the booty brought back by the Vandal. If he plays an important part in the affairs of the dying Empire, and has his candidates, such as Olybrius, who was related by marriage to his son Hunerich, can it be concluded from this that he considered himself a member of the Empire ? Attila also had intervened in the internal politics of the Empire. Despairing of being able to subdue him, Zeno, the Emperor of Constantinople, was obliged, in this same year which saw the end of the Western Empire, to recognize the Vandal in the possession of the whole of Northern Africa and, in addition, of the islands of the Western Mediterranean : Sicily, Sardinia, Corsica and the Balearic Islands. In return for this there was between the Vandal Empire and Constantinople a peace which lasted more than half a century, until 530.

Moreover, for a long time Africa had been tending to drop away from the Empire. Since the beginning of the fourth century, she had been a prey to political, religious and social upheavals.[1] The origin was the Donatist schism, which derives its name from Donatus, bishop of Carthage (315). At the beginning it was a rigorist movement directed against the too lukewarm Christians who had weakened under Diocletian's persecution. Having been censured by the Italian and Gaulish bishops, the African rigorists started a schism ; they looked upon the other Christians as corrupt and declared invalid the sacraments administered by non-Donatist bishops. It followed therefore that the value of the sacrament depended on the man who administered it, on his state of grace ; this meant a renewal of the errors of the Anti-Pope Novatian, who had refused pardon to the Christians who had become apostates during the Emperor Decius' persecution in 251-253. The Donatists were very numerous ; they had, it is said, 300 bishops. The schism could not be extirpated, either by Roman authority, or by Gaiserich who, as an Arian, persecuted impartially both Donatists and Catholics.

This religious movement aroused the sect of the *milites Christi* (Circumcellions), which in the country districts assumed the character of a social uprising and was a kind of peasant war.

Lastly, the governors of Africa were not reliable. Firmus

[1] **CCCXVII, CCCXXV, CCLXXXII, CCCXLV,** vol. iv.

about 379 and Gildo in 398 caused the Empire great anxiety. Heraclian, Stilicho's assassin, having been appointed to Africa, immediately revolted. Fore-runners of Gaiserich, these rebellious governors starved Italy ; some of them even planned expeditions against that country. The last of them, Boniface, according to legend, invited the barbarians into Africa.

In the Western extremity of Lesser Africa, the Romans had made but little impression, the rule of Rome scarcely passing south of the present Morocco, beyond Volubilis (North of Meknès)[1]. The Moors of the two Mauretanias appear very independent as early as the fourth century. They must early have forgotten Latin and returned to the use of the Libyan language which was the ancestor of the " Berber " dialects of to-day. If the ruling classes in Numidia, the Proconsular Province and Byzacena were highly Romanized, the populace seems still to have kept for a long time the use of the Punic tongue.

Spain and Aquitania.—In the middle of the fifth century (454) only about half of Spain was left to the Empire, Tarraconensis and Carthaginiensis. The other three provinces (Gallaecia, Lusitania and Baetica) had been in the power of the Sueves for over forty years. The King of the Goths, Theodoric II, the successor of Theodoric I, who perished, killed by the Huns, at the battle of *Campus Mauriacus*[2], undertook an expedition into Spain which secured for him the greater part of the country (456). He too engaged in Emperor-making ; he gave the purple to Avitus who had taught him Latin letters. For a while the Emperor Majorian and the *magister militum* Aegidius kept his ambition in check. But under Euric (466-484), the fratricide who slew and succeeded Theodoric II, the expansion of the Goths became irresistible. About 470 they gained a footing in Provence. On the North they encountered a serious obstacle ; the most important "city" of Aquitania Prima, Auvergne (*civitas Arvernorum*), put up an obstinate resistance, although abandoned to its own resources. This resistance was directed by the son and the son-in-law of the ex-Emperor Avitus, Ecdicius and Sidonius Apollinaris.

---

[1] The *limes* of Tingitana began only 6 kilometres South of Rabat. See ROULAND-MARESCHAL in *Mémoires présentés par divers savants à l'Académie des inscriptions*, vol. xiii., 2nd part, 1924.

[2] CLXVII.

The last Emperors gave up Auvergne to the Goths. Glycerius (473-474), in order to rid himself of a band of Ostrogoths commanded by Widemir, sent them into Gaul. Julius Nepos did better; he yielded Auvergne to the Visigoths in 475. Euric in addition took possession of the region South of the Durance and completed the occupation of Provence.[1] In Spain, Tarraconensis, where the population had attempted a resistance similar to that of the Gallo-Roman aristocracy in Auvergne, was also subjugated. Euric obtained the Emperor Zeno's sanction for his conquests immediately after the fall of the Western Empire, and for a moment was the most powerful of the barbarian chiefs.

South-Eastern Gaul.—The Burgundians[2] settled in *Sapaudia* in 443, kept the *fœdus* with Rome until the death of Aetius and of Valentinian III (455). But from 456, they began to extend beyond their cantonments. The arrival of Majorian, the only " legitimate " Emperor who set foot in Gaul after Valentinian II, was enough to bring them back to obedience. But, after his death (461), their expansion no longer met with any obstacle; Lyons fell into their power, then Vienne, then Die, then Vivarais (from 461 to 470). Nevertheless they could not spread in Provence, being prevented on this side by the Visigoths. They were more successful in the East and in the North where they pushed back the Alemans; the latter had advanced up to Langres and Besançon and held *Vindonissa* (Windisch), at the confluence of the Aar and the Limmat. At the end of the century, the Burgundians extended from the Durance in the South, up to the neighbourhood of Champagne in the North, and from the Cévennes up to the Reuss. Their kings resided at Lyons, Vienne, Geneva and Besançon, but especially at Geneva and Lyons. These kings belonged to a new line, the ancient dynasty having perished, slain by the Huns in 436. Weaker than the Goths whom they feared, these sovereigns took care not to throw away all fiction of an alliance with Rome. Chilperic and Gundioc acted as *magistri militum*. Gundobad, appointed Patrician by the Emperor Olybrius, disposed of the Empire in the course of a visit to Rome and raised to the throne an Italian, Glycerius, the Chief of the Guard of the preceding Emperor. But

[1] DXV.
[2] DXXXIII, CDXXIX.

Constantinople (Leo I) having refused Glycerius the *unanimitas* and *sent* Julius Nepos as Emperor, Gundobad returned to the valley of the Rhone.[1]

Northern Gaul : from the Rhine to the Loire.—After having been ravaged in 407-408 by the Alans, Vandals and Sueves, then delivered through the crossing of the barbarians into Spain (409), it suffered the terrifying but quickly passing storm of Attila's invasion.[2] Far more serious was the continuous pressure of the Franks and Alemans who began to settle on the left bank of the Rhine and to replace the Roman populations by German *coloni*.[3] The Salian Franks had already settled in Toxandria (North of Brabant) as early as 358, as subjects of Rome. Being hampered by the Carbonarian Forest, they extended their tilths along the North Sea, in the former country of the Celtic Menapians. Aetius succeeded in keeping in check these tribes led by Chlodio. But after his death, the Frankish chiefs, following the Roman road from Cologne to Cambrai, took possession of Tournai and Cambrai, and reached the Somme.[4] But in these cities they did not impose their language.

Far deeper ethnographically was the thrust of the Ripuarian Franks, politically inferior to the Salians. Masters of Cologne, which was their capital, they extended West up to the Eifel plateau, without however touching the Ardennes. In the South, they reached Mayence. The valley of the Moselle was repopulated by Ripuarians or Hessian Franks (*Chatti*), as was that of the Main. Trèves, four times captured and re-captured, was lost to Rome about 455.[5]

In the same period the Alemans occupied the left bank of the Rhine from Worms to Basle and even for a moment advanced up to Langres, Besançon and Mandeure. Soon afterwards Rhætia fell into their power. In Germany, the Lech separated them from the Bavarians who came from Bohemia.[6]

The Saxon pirates, not satisfied with conquering Great Britain, settled here and there on the shores of Gaul, in the

---

[1] CDLXXXI, DXXXIII.
[2] CDXLIII, CDXLIV.
[3] CCLXXVI.
[4] CCLXXIV.
[5] CDXLIII.
[6] DCXLVII.

neighbourhood of Boulogne, in Bessin, and on the lower reach of the Loire.[1]

Armorica was occupied by the Britons from Great Britain, fleeing from the rule of the Angles, Jutes and Saxons, and also from that of their Celtic neighbours from Ireland, the Scots, who were settling on the Western shores of Great Britain. These emigrants even tried to spread to the centre of Gaul ; about 470, one of their chiefs, Riothamus, was beaten by the Goths near Déols in Berry.[2]

Against these enemies two men fought valiantly, Count Paul and the *magister militum* Aegidius.[3] The latter succeeded in using the Franks as Federates ; Meroveus and Chilperic, in particular, were in the service of the Empire against the Saxons, Goths and Alans. But Aegidius died suddenly in 464. He had maintained himself by his own forces, hated by Ricimer. It was the same with his son and successor Syagrius, who kept a shadow of independence in the country situated between the Meuse, the Somme and the Loire. Separated from the Empire, he made use of the barbarians. We know that he spoke German as well as a German. Thus, in order to command the last " Roman " armies in Northern Gaul, it was useful to speak German !

In 476, the Empire had in fact lost the greater part of the West, and existed only in Italy, and even there in theory. It is this which explains the fact that " its fall, which had been preparing for a long time, was scarcely felt by the rest of the world ; it fell without a sound ; it was the death of an old man who, deprived of his limbs, dies of decay ".[4]

For a moment it was thought possible to revive it ; in 477 the assembly of the Gauls, reduced to the deputations from Aix, Arles, and Marseilles, asked Zeno to restore Julius Nepos in the West. This attempt to resuscitate a corpse had no sequel. The year 476 really marks the end of the Roman Empire in the West.

---

[1] CCCVI, CCCVIII, CCCIV, 178.
[2] CCCVIII.
[3] CDLXXV.
[4] CCLXXXI, vol. viii. (1764), p. 109.

CHAPTER III

The Roman Empire in the East
from 395 to 518[1]

THE *pars Orientis*, so threatened and tried in the fourth century, carried on a miserable existence in the fifth century, but was not swept away by the storm. Nevertheless Arcadius was a puppet, the plaything of Rufinus, of the eunuch Eutropius and of the Empress Eudoxia, one after the other. Bloody tragedies succeeded each other; Rufinus was slain by his enemy Gainas who, like the whole army in the East, was a Goth. This Gainas, the prop of the Empire, conspired and perished, beaten by Fravitta, who was also a Goth. The favour shown to men of this race, after reaching its zenith under Theodosius, came to an end; they were massacred at Constantinople (400)[2]. From this time onwards there were practically no Germans in the armies of the Eastern Roman Empire. Their place was taken by Caucasians, Alans, Isaurians, etc.

After Rufinus, the power belonged to the eunuch Eutropius, an old man whom his enemies accuse of every vice; he also perished, a victim in his turn to the resentment of the Empress whom he had offended. St. John Chrysostom also drew upon himself Eudoxia's hatred and died in exile. Arcadius did not interfere, and was merely a dazed spectator of these tragic events.

His son, Theodosius II, grew up under the guardianship of Anthemius, the Prætorian Prefect of the East, and of his sister, Pulcheria, who was only two years older than himself and who is considered the most remarkable woman of this period. The most striking events of his reign are his romantic marriage with Athenais (Eudokia), the daughter of a pagan philosopher of Athens, the foundation of the University of Constantinople, the extension of the walls of Constantinople (due to Anthemius), his legislative work (the Code, 429-438)

---

[1] LXVI, CXCII, DLXI.
[2] LXVI, 135.

and especially the Christological controversies which resulted
in the condemnation of Nestorius at the Ecumenical Council
of Ephesus (431).

Nestorius, following the example of Theodore of Mopsuestia,
separated the two natures of Christ ; the man, born of woman,
of Mary, is not Θεοτόκος but Χριστοτόκος. In reaction
against this, Eutyches, an archimandrite of Constantinople,
made the divine nature absorb everything. He was condemned at the Fourth Ecumenical Council, that of Chalcedon
(457) which decreed that we must acknowledge one Lord in
two natures.

These controversies interested passionately the Emperor,
the court, the aristocracy and the crowd ; the certainty of
faith and therefore of salvation was at stake. Hence there
was no subject more important and the anxieties caused by
the barbarians assumed a secondary rôle.

These anxieties were nevertheless very serious. The Goths
(Visigoths) turned away from the ravaged Balkan Peninsula
and sought their fortunes in the West ; after Stilicho's death,
the *pars Orientis* had nothing further to fear from them.
There remained, amongst others, the Persians and the Huns.
The government staved them off as best it could by
means of treaties or money. With the Persians a hundred
years' treaty was concluded in 422. Towards the Huns,
whose empire, including not merely hordes of Tartars, but
also German subjects (Ostrogoths), Alans, Sarmatians and
probably also Slavs, extended right into Hungary and Pannonia, the Empire adopted a policy of submission ; it paid
tribute to Rugila, and later from about 444 to his nephew and
successor Attila. Like the Chinese Empire, the Roman
Empire tried to save its face ; it pretended to look upon the
Huns as Federates and upon the Tartar Khan as a general in
the service of Rome ; Attila was the so-called *Magister militum*.
The chief of the Huns sometimes lent himself to this farce,
but at other times insolently reminded the Emperor of Constantinople that he was his subject and slave, since he paid
him tribute. Moreover, on more than one occasion (441, 443,
447) the Huns invaded and ravaged the territory of the
Empire.

This ignominious but perhaps unavoidable position changed
on the death of Theodosius II (July 28th, 450). His successor

Marcian refused to continue paying the so-called Federates. Marcian, born in Thrace, had risen from the ranks, becoming Tribune, Senator, and the spiritual husband of Pulcheria the sister of Theodosius II. Brave and pious, when he died in 457 (January) at the age of sixty-five, he was considered by the Christian Church in the East, a saint, as was his wife, or rather sister.

His resistance to Attila's demands would have cost him dear if ambition had not induced the Khan to hurl himself on the West. Attila's failure and death brought about the disruption of his empire and the Roman world could breathe once more. The Ostrogoths settled in Illyricum, as Federates, under three brothers of the ancient royal line of the Amalungs.

After Marcian's death, the real master of the Empire was the *domesticus*, Aspar, the son of an Alan warrior Ardaburius who had distinguished himself under the preceding reign. He raised to the throne Leo, called " the Thracian," an ex- " tribune," who had been his bailiff.

The Senate of Constantinople was in a state of agitation because of his obscurity and his subordinate station in relation to the barbarians. To give him some éclat, a new ceremony was devised : the Patriarch of Constantinople, Anatolius, placed the crown on the head of the new *basileus* (February 7th, 457). This is the first example of the crowning of an Emperor by an ecclesiastic. It is big with consequences for the future. At the same moment, in the West, another barbarian, Ricimer, half Sueve, half Goth, disposed of the Empire, making and unmaking half a dozen Emperors.

In the East it was not the same. Leo was perhaps more suspicious and Aspar more lenient. However that may be, the fact was that the barbarian had the worst of it in the war of intrigues and treacheries which constituted the sole politics of this time. Aspar wished to have his son appointed Cæsar, but this son was an Arian and the Senate of Con- stantinople opposed the idea. In 471, Aspar was surprised and assassinated by Leo's order by the palace *excubitores*. With him perished his sons, one of whom, Ardaburius, was *magister militum*. This execution put an end to the predomin- ance of the Alans as that of 400 had done to the domination of the Goths.

It should be said that Leo had the support of his son-in-law,

Zeno, an Isaurian, who placed at the service of the Empire his compatriots of Isauria in Asia Minor, who, wild mountaineers though they were, had been subjects of Rome for centuries. Zeno himself was half barbarian, his real name being Tarasicodissa, son of Rusumbladestus. Zeno took Leo's place from 474 to 491. His successor was the " silentiary " Anastasius from Durazzo, already old (aged sixty-one), who owed his elevation to Zeno's widow, Ariadne, whom he married. He had a long reign, dying on July 9th, 518.

These were very poor reigns. These three men were of obscure origin and mediocre intelligence and courage. Zeno was gross and cruel. Anastasius was better ; he had a certain gentleness of soul and cared for the public welfare. He abolished gladiatorial and wild beast combats (499) ; he suppressed the *chrysargyron* (498) and the corporate responsibility of the *curiales*. He hoarded ; the Treasury was found full at his death. Above all he built " the long walls," 65 kilometres in length, across the Thracian peninsula.[1]

These emperors were the playthings of factions ; they were constantly assailed by revolts of their generals and riots of the populace in big towns. Above all, theological controversies troubled men's hearts deeply. Monophysism, which had been stifled at Constantinople, won Egypt and Syria, where it kindled fires of hatred against Byzantium, a fact destined to have important consequences in the seventh century. The emperors thought it their duty to enforce orthodoxy, that is, their own doxy. But their good intentions thwarted the end they had in view. Zeno, by his *Henoticon* or Letter calling for unity (482), started the schism with Rome, a schism destined to last long (forty years). Anastasius, through wishing to enforce the phrase " who was crucified for us ", introduced by the monk Peter the Fuller into the liturgical formula of the *Trisagion*, provoked the most serious troubles. Being accused of Monophysism and threatened with dethronement, the Emperor had to clear himself in the circus (November, 512).

He was not spared dangers from external quarters. Not only were the Ostrogoths troublesome and threatening guests, but the remnants of the Huns made inroads ; lastly, the Bulgarians appeared ; these were still pure Tartars (Turks),

[1] OBERHAMMER in *Geographisches Jahrbuch*, vol. xxxiv.

and behind them were heralded their kinsmen the Avars, who would soon be followed by the irresistible tide of the Slavs.[1] Nevertheless the Empire was neither broken nor submerged. At the end of the fifth century, the only really alarming enemies were the Ostrogoths, especially since their various branches had become united under the authority of a young prince, Theodoric, of the illustrious line of the Amalungs. He succeeded his father Theodemir in 475 ; he had spent his youth in Constantinople, from the age of eight to eighteen (461-471).

Thanks to its clever diplomacy, the Empire succeeded in ridding itself of this dangerous people and even dreamed of using it for its own advantage. Odovacar had given Zeno cause for complaint and anxiety. In 488, Theodoric with the Goth people, of whom 20,000 were warriors, made for Italy. He bore the title of *magister militum* ; it was as a barbarian chief rather than as a functionary and general in the service of the New Rome that he took possession of Italy after a hard struggle lasting five years.[2] Only in March 493, after the murder of Odovacar, did he receive the royal title from his companions-at-arms. He was thus King of the Goths. But in relation to the Romans of Italy, his legal position remained uncertain. Theodoric was, from the point of view of civil law, a "Roman citizen" and he bore the designation of Flavius, reserved for the Imperial family. Hence, in the West, he was a kind of representative of the Empire, invested with ill defined but in fact absolute constitutional powers. This, in the future, was going to be a cause for rupture between Constantinople and the Ostrogothic Monarchy. For the moment, it was not the part of wisdom to insist on too exact definitions.

Thus, while the *pars Occidentis* had broken up into fragments never to be put together again, the *pars Orientis* succeeded in living on somehow or other. Henceforth it alone constituted *Romania*. Only a favourable opportunity was needed for it to attempt under Justinian to reconstruct the Empire in its past unity and to try to turn back the course of destiny.

---

[1] On the Avars, see **CCCXCVII**, under *Hunni*.
[2] **CDXLIII**, 92-95 ; **CDLXX**, 566 ; **CCXXXI**, vol. i.-ii. ; **DXCV**, vol. i.

The characteristic of the Empire was that it was in fact the power of an absolute monarch, while being in intention merely that of a moderator. The Emperor was the first citizen of the State, in whose hands had been gathered the powers necessary to prevent the citizens from killing each other and to maintain the cohesion of the Roman world. The Empire was a magistracy.

The Emperor, as the supeme arbiter, who was armed with formidable rights, could not leave the provinces a prey to the intensive exploitation of which they were the victims under the Republic, by which must be understood the government of the senatorial aristocracy. The countries conquered by Rome only began to breathe from the date of the establishment of the Empire.

The Roman State was not a real State.[1] Its organs were adapted to the government of an ancient city and not of a great Empire. As soon as she had passed beyond the stage of conquest and of the brutal or hypocritical exploitation of the conquered, Rome did not know exactly what attitude to adopt towards her conquests. The City State was too narrow a crucible for re-fashioning the world. The most ancient method was that of the colony, a miniature Rome established at the heart of the conquered countries. This was still used, but insufficiently. The provinces were either geographical designations or artificial divisions, seldom former States (Egypt). The true organic division of the Mediterranean world was the City. Amongst the conquered cities Rome made distinctions : those which it was in her interest to treat well or whose services she wished to reward, received the honorary titles of federal, allied, friendly and even of free cities, though in one form or another they paid the tax of subjects, the *stipendium*, just like the subject cities. The Roman Empire was thus a federation of cities grouped round the most powerful of them, Rome.

But a federation of this kind, if it had been real, would very soon have broken up. In actual fact, all the cities were subject to the arbitral, that is to say arbitrary, decisions of the

---

[1] Another aspect of the question will be found in M. Homo's *Institutions politiques romaines*, vol. xviii.

ruler, the Emperor. His person was the bond which united the different pieces of the mechanism. Unfortunately, this absolute power was practically without legal organs, without functionaries. The princeps was not a king, and no principle of succession could ever be imposed. The Roman Empire at first had at its disposal only the old organism of the Republic, unfit for the administration of a vast State. It had no institutions proper to it. In the end, everything depended on the will of the ruler, and the latter, appointed in theory by the Senate and the people, was in fact the choice and plaything of the armies.

This radical vice, the absence of institutions, became aggravated from the end of the second century A.D. onwards, under the action of three great phenomena : the economic retrogression, the religious crisis and the recrudescence of the pressure of the barbarians who had long been besetting the Mediterranean world.

Economic crisis : Rome had seized the riches accumulated since Alexander. She had squandered them and did not know how to renew them by work. Her capitalism, if it may be thus called, was only a blighting usury ; the ancient mines, having been intensively exploited, were nearly exhausted.

Religious crisis : this in itself would have been enough to have shaken a more robust organism.

The barbarians : Scandinavia overflowed and the waves, extending to the Germans of the West, broke against the Roman world, against which they were to beat until they swept away its defences.

Then broke loose the storm of the third century in which the Græco-Roman world was nearly destroyed, not so much by external assaults as through the action of its internal maladies. The third century is a pre-medieval age, in which the ancient religion, literature (in the West at least) and art were seriously impaired.

Nevertheless the forces of society were still vital enough to triumph over these diseases, although with difficulty. Aurelian, and especially Diocletian, and later, Constantine succeeded in restoring Roman unity. But the amorphousness of the Early Empire was no longer possible. To prevent disruption, it was necessary to have centralization, to turn the imperial magistracy into a quasi-monarchy, to give it organs, functionaries, and to divide it amongst several heads (first a tetrarchy, then portioning between the sons of emperors).

This work of reconstruction was hindered by the religious crisis and the economic ruin. Diocletian under the influence of Galerius thought to put an end to a sect reputed dangerous, by a systematic and prolonged oppression. His successor Constantine adopted a diametrically opposite method, less from policy than from personal conviction : he granted the Christians liberty, then favours and privileges, and finally proclaimed himself a Christian.

The economic retrogression these great men met with measures which were either successful, like the re-establishment of a sound currency, or inoperative like the edict of maximum prices. Above all, they instituted a sort of caste system which at first bound a man for life to his function or trade and then made it hereditary.

The vices of society the emperors met with a legislation which was either more humane (for the family and slavery) or more severe to the point of cruelty (for crimes against persons and morals). The army was changed. The legions were split up into detachments garrisoned in the fortified towns which were reduced in extent and made more compact. " Pronunciamentos " diminished in violence, without, however, ceasing entirely.

Thanks to all these measures, the Roman world could go on living, keep in check the barbarians, shape itself to Christian life and adapt to it what remained of ancient pagan civilization, and this was to be of great consequence. These were inestimable services. What a deep night, what a retarding of progress there would have been, if the Roman world had disintegrated as early as the third century!

Unfortunately, the Empire was at bottom only a " ruin in repair ", and in spite of all, there was a tragic contrast between the vastness of the effort and its result. The economic decay was scarcely checked and was soon to start again for very long centuries.

The change of religion was from the strictly political point of view a bad bargain ; the Emperor enforced Christianity at the very moment when that religion was undergoing a terrible crisis, Arianism, and the government threw itself headlong into the whirlpool of theological controversies to the great loss of the Church and also of the State.

The inevitable and natural culmination of the imperial magistracy was the monarchy of the Later Empire. But this monarchy was not a real monarchy ; both from its lack of hereditary succession, which it was not able to establish, and by the august and almost mysterious character of its representatives ; etiquette and pomp could create no illusion about the too humble origin of most of the emperors. The Emperor, in spite of his terrifying power, was by no means respected by the populace, which when occasion arose, showered upon him jeers and insults. The only thing which the urban plebs had preserved of its republican past, was its lack of respect, and loyalty was, of all feelings, the most alien to it.

Neither could the monarch count on the devotion of a warrior aristocracy rallying round the throne. The aristocracy had been disarmed by the imperial government. It served the State in civil careers, being at the head of the bureaucracy, to use a rather too modern term, which worked the administrative machine, and thanks to which the Empire still held together. But in these high functions the aristocracy did not aim so much at the general welfare as at its own interests. This aristocracy, though frightened and cringing before the ruler, from the earliest times of the Empire economically possessed a formidable power. The large landed property which had killed or subjugated the small and average property and which, since the ruin of commerce and industry, was the sole source of wealth, was entirely in its hands. Under an apparent submission, the aristocracy was the rival of the monarchical power, and when it became once more military, in the West, it was destined to replace it. The economic if not the legal and political foundations of the medieval feudal system were already established in the Later Empire.

The people, under the two-fold political and economic pressure of the Emperor and of the aristocracy respectively, was reduced to almost absolute insignificance. It was interested only in its material comfort and its amusements. It was Roman only in name. Rome partially succeeded in Romanizing the Mediterranean world, but only the upper classes had the Roman mentality. Even when they had learnt to speak Latin, these Britons, Spaniards, Africans, and Illyrians, still more these Egyptians and Asiatics, were unable to acquire a collective Roman consciousness. Only the religious controversies were sometimes able to rouse this congeries of peoples out of its profound apathy and incurable paralysis of the will.

To maintain the political and " cultural " unity of the Mediterranean world, it had been necessary to break by force all resistance and to establish an absolute power, which power could exist only by suppressing everything. There was no more political life, no more public spirit. The philosophic, scientific, artistic and literary barrenness was due to both economic and psychological causes ; there was no escape from this jail except by the door of mysticism. By an inexorable fatality, the Empire could exist only by means of despotism, and despotism stifled all spontaneity of life, undermined the State, and was destined inevitably to bring about its destruction. The inert mass of the serfs and coloni in the country districts and of the lazzaroni in the towns provided no support or strength for the State. The economic decay was one of the causes of the æsthetic decay ; a poor society is rarely fertile in works of art.

Another cause was the influence of the East, which replaced the ideal of Greek plastic art by its own. The East, Asia, took possession of the West æsthetically, through its art in all its forms (architecture, tapestry, sculpture) as well as ethically through religion : Mithraism, Manicheism, Christianity.

The decay of literature is still deeper, first at Rome, then in the Greek East. Literature could not, like art, be renewed or even at the least be given a new lease of life by any external influence. We have tried to see why Christianity, far from bringing a fresh breath of air to ancient literature, had adapted itself to the most obsolete forms of a literary tradition which had been petrified into conventional forms. Undoubtedly objective literatures, not being founded on personal emotions, are always threatened with exhaustion after a short time. Not only the literatures of antiquity, but modern letters also nearly perished, one hundred and fifty years ago, through desiccation. Rousseau and the Romantics, by introducing subjectivism into modern literature, saved it from death.

The ancient languages were also impaired by the blows of

time. The Ancients did not admit of any writing in forms other than those sanctioned by masterpieces. But as languages change without any force being able to oppose the process, at the end of a few centuries the difference between the written and spoken language becomes so great, that the writing of literature consisted in painful composition in a stereotyped, artificial and dead language.

Philosophy and science had been completely decadent for a long time. This decadence had begun even before the birth of the Roman Empire, even before the hegemony of Rome, as early as the second century B.C. It became rapid afterwards for many reasons : the scientific spirit, not clearly distinguished from the philosophic, had with Aristotelian logic entered a blind alley. The too narrow foundations of ancient science rested on mathematics and certain branches of physics ; the sciences of chemistry and biology were almost non-existent. Above all, there was the competition of religion. Religious feeling, which had lain dormant in the centuries preceding and following the Christian era, recovered with mighty vigour about the third century ; it made a triumphal entry into the human soul and meant to hold there undivided sway.

The enfeeblement of the Empire showed itself in its most striking form in the decay of the army. Rome's military glory, practically still intact in spite of the convulsions of the third century, was suddenly eclipsed after Constantine. As early as the fourth century, it is obvious that if the Roman State in appearance has not yet fallen, its might has gone from it and passed into the hands of the barbarians who are in its service.

How was this astonishing change able to take place ?

The reform of the ancient organization of the army was assuredly inevitable. The advance of the barbarians into Gaul and even into Italy, the sanguinary defeats in which the emperors (Decius and Valerian) had lost their life or liberty, had shown its inefficiency. Bitter experiences had condemned the system of the continuous frontier, the *limes*. The heavy legion, still a marvellous weapon in the hands of a Septimius Severus, perhaps even of an Aurelian, had proved itself inefficient against the onslaught of the Empire's new adversaries, the Goths in Europe and the Sassanid Persians in Asia.

They were unrivalled horsemen, as later were the Vandals amongst the Germans, and the Huns and other Turkish tribes. Tactics, strategy, fortifications, all had to be changed from top to bottom.

The fundamental change, which gave its character to the art of war for twelve or thirteen centuries, was the passing of supremacy from the infantry to the cavalry. It was the latter which was to rule battles until the reappearance of a real infantry with the Swiss bands at the very end of the Middle Ages. From Constantine onwards, by soldier (*miles*) is pre-eminently meant the horseman. The medieval writers always expressed the idea of cavalryman by this Latin word.

In the last third of the third century, in imitation of Persia, horsemen were employed in the Roman army, and these horsemen were always clad in coats of mail from head to foot. The *clibanarii, cataphracti, scutarii* of the imperial guard were cuirassiers.

The weapons of attack were also changed. From their campaigns against the Parthians and later against the Sassanids, the Romans brought back the use of the bow, a powerful arm whose arrows were deadly even at a distance of from 123 to 130 metres, and they armed their horsemen with it. Out of seventeen cavalry corps, the Duke of Syria had four of *sagittarii* and one of *scutarii*. The Duke of Moesia commanded three *cunei* of *scutarii* and two of *armigeri*. The imperial guard had squadrons of cuirassiers armed with bows, like Persian or Turkish horsemen. The " Palatine " infantry also included some corps of *sagittarii*.

The legions, ceasing to be pre-eminently the shock troops, saw a radical change in their armament, tactics and composition. The armament was made lighter ; the enormous semi-cylindrical *scutum* was replaced by a small round buckler ; there was a suggestion to abolish the iron helmet and metal breast-plates. The drill with the *pilum*, the characteristic weapon of the legionary, was henceforth neglected. The phalanx formation eight deep, which was still in favour under Caracalla and Alexander Severus, was abandoned. In the probably rarer and rarer cases when the legion was used for attack, it adopted the " boar's head " formation, after the German fashion.

All these reforms tended to make the legion lighter. They were logical since the rôle of shock troops had passed to the heavy cavalry. The sole function of the infantry, henceforth, was to support the cavalry, to cover its evolutions, and to enable it to re-form after the attack, and this rôle it was to keep right through the Middle Ages. The last and unavoidable consequence was the breaking up of the legion. Each of the ten cohorts composing it tended to become an individual unit and ended by forming an independent corps (*numerus*, ἀριθμὸς), comprising from 300 to 500 men commanded by a " tribune ". What is called a " legion " at the end of the fourth and in the fifth century, was a large cohort of from 800 to 1,200 men.

These detachments were employed in guarding the towns of the interior, after they had been transformed into forttresses. It was realized that it was impossible to defend at every point the " Chinese walls " which the Early Empire had raised between the Rhine and the Danube, in Britain from the North to the Irish Sea, on the Euphrates, etc.

The *limes* (except in Britain) was henceforth an open frontier, a border. It was guarded by troops of *limitanei*, or *riparienses*, or *ripenses*, farmer soldiers rewarded with land, but hereditarily bound to their condition, true military serfs, from the fourth century onwards. As it was foreseen that their resistance in the open country would be short and not very effective, a number of block-houses, called *castella* or by a German word *burgi*, were built for them on the border and in these it was their task to keep guard (*castellani*). At the same time the great military commands on the frontier were kept, their number was multiplied and their depth increased. They were *tractus : tractus Armoricanus, tractus Nervicanus, tractus Moguntiacensis, tractus Argentoratensis* in Gaul. The command of these districts was entrusted to important personages, " friends " of the Emperor, the *comites*; whence the title of Count (*comes*) added to the title of general (*dux*) and itself tending to become a title. Nevertheless people were not deceived. The *limes* or the *tractus* might be able to retard the invasion of the barbarians, but would be powerless to stop it.

In the time of the " thirty tyrants " the organic cell of the Roman world, the *Civitas*, had most often for its centre an entirely undefended town ; in Gaul at least, excepting Nîmes, Autun and Trèves, the towns of the Early Empire which were surrounded with fortifications were very few. Hence they had easily been taken and destroyed by the barbarians. From about the years 260-270, the fortification of the capitals of the *civitates* occupied the government. For many reasons (depopulation, strategic necessities) the towns had to be very much contracted ; they had henceforth only a considerably reduced area, which was just over 40 acres in the case of the most important ones, and often half of this and even less ; they were now only fortresses. Only Rome had its circuit enlarged; Aurelian increased its perimeter to nearly 19 kilometres.

It is more than likely that it was in order to guard the fortified towns that the legions were split up into *numeri* or ἀριθμοί. We need only open the *Notitia dignitatum* (v. 40a) to realize that the innumerable corps mentioned there are in the vast majority only garrisons. If we count up these corps, they reach a number close to one thousand heads, including both the East and the West.

This total must be nearly doubled if we count the contingents of the frontier troops (*limitanei, ripenses*).

The total of the forces of the Empire may have been as high as 523,000 or 533,000 men. It is true that the *Notitia dignitatum* contains lacunæ. But these lacunæ or omissions do not come to much : they merely make it possible to believe that the total may have been as high as 550,000 men. We must add the double imperial guard of the *domestici*, whose exact number is unknown (it was 3,500 in the sixth century for the East) and the *scholæ* (seven in the East, and five in the West) of the two " Masters of the offices."

If this army had been entirely a fighting army, the success of the great invasions could not be explained at all. The barbarians who invaded the Empire had actually only a small number of warriors. The Goths who defeated and slew Valens at the celebrated battle of Hadrianople numbered only 10,000. The Vandals who conquered Africa were only 80,000 all told, men, women and children, that is to say 20,000 combatants at the most. The whole people of the Ostrogoths led by Theodoric was for a short time contained in Pavia, which was still quite a small town at the end of the fifth century. We may also suspect that Attila's "innumerable hordes" were at the time of the battle of the *Campus Mauriacus* reduced to a few thousand horsemen.

To be unable to hold their own against adversaries with such small numbers, the Roman armies must for the greater part have been in the end only a militia without real military training and without any value as a fighting force.

Their numerical weakness is moreover pitiful. From this period onwards, the armies consisted of 15,000 men at the most, while the expeditionary forces consisted of from 5,000 to 6,000 men, or even of less. Thus it would be henceforth right through the Middle Ages ; big battles were encountered in which from 3,000 to 4,000 " knights " and " horse sergeants " and from 8,000 to 10,000 " foot sergeants " opposed each other on either side.

It must be said that the vast extent of the Empire and its defensive policy towards the barbarians, after Trajan's reign, condemned it to weakness at every point, although it kept up a high number of troops. Further, the economic retrogression of the Roman world made it necessary to pay in kind (save for exceptional presents), that is to say, to make the soldier live on the country. The farmer-soldiers of the *limes* and the barbarians (Laeti and Sarmatians) attached to the soil in the interior of the country, soon lost all military value. Legions and *auxilia palatina* even, by dint of keeping garrison indefinitely in the same town, or in the same *castrum*, became unaccustomed to fighting in the open country. The lowering of the fighting value of the so-called " Roman " army, no less than the difficulties of the transport of provisions, increased by the economic decay and perhaps also by the bad upkeep of the roads, explain the fact that it became more and more difficult to raise an expeditionary force. To make up the small army of Mascezel in 398, he had to be given the best troops of the Empire, the Herculian and Jovian legionaries, and cohorts from the North of Gaul. To help Rome when attacked by Alaric, there were drawn from Dalmatia five large legions the effective force of which came to 6,000 men ; it was a select army, and yet it was exterminated by the Goths. Thus each of the great provinces included only a very small number of shock troops. When these left the country for any cause, Gaul, Britain, or Illyria immediately became a prey to the barbarians, in spite of the *limitanei* and urban garrisons.

Rome paid with her life for the negative policy which, under the pretext of peaceful penetration, had prevented her from achieving the conquest of Central Europe, Caledonia and Ireland at the time when (in the first and even in the second century) this was possible. The " wisdom " of a Tiberius or of a Hadrian was bound in the long run to bring about the catastrophe.

There was still worse :

The fundamental phenomenon of the history of the Roman army was the fact that since Constantine, and perhaps even before, it was being emptied of Romans so that very rapidly it came to consist only of barbarians. "Roman army" in the fourth and fifth centuries meant only an army in the service of Rome (later of Byzantium).

From very early on, the non-Romans had been in the service of Rome, forming the *auxilia* (infantry and especially cavalry), but under the Republic, these were Latins or Italians, closely related in race and language and rapidly Romanized. Under the Empire, the barbarians, especially the Germans, entered the personal guard of the Emperor, as early as the Principate of Augustus. It is a phenomenon common to all times and countries, that the ruler likes to surround himself with foreigners, who are more loyal than his fellow-countrymen and safe from political or other influences. During the whole course of the Roman and Byzantine Empire this was the case. This measure is generally not very danger-ous ; for these foreigners do not betray the master who pays them, for the good of the population which hates them. For the Germans of the left bank of the Rhine to serve in the auxiliary corps or even in the legions was natural ; they were Roman citizens (all free men were since Caracalla's edict of 212) and were Romanized.

The barbarians living beyond the frontiers were, as early as the third and even the end of the second century, admitted into the Roman army as auxiliaries. Nevertheless the nerve of the army was always the legion (with an effective force of from 5,000 to 6,000 men) recruited on the spot from the principate of Hadrian onwards. If in certain parts of the Empire this measure yielded poor results only, the Empire had the good fortune to find a reservoir of men and later of generals in *Illyricum*. These Illyrian peoples (of Pannonia, Noricum, Rhaetia, Dalmatia and Prævalitana) which had for a long time remained barbarian, were in the third and at the beginning of the fourth century the army of Rome, just as their descendants the Albanians were that of the Turkish Empire. They were, however, Romanized in language and customs.

Unfortunately, in the course of the fourth and of the following century, these peoples, as well as the Thracian peoples of the Balkan Peninsula, were practically exterminated by the barbarian invasions. In their place, the legions received these very barbarians, Germans and Sarmatians as well as some Gauls and Germans from the North of Gaul, Moors and Caucasians (Iberians and Armenians). As early as the second century, there were scarcely any more provincial Romans ; at the end of the same century there were none at all, the Roman legions counting in their ranks only Western Germans (Alemans, Franks, etc.) or Eastern Germans (Goths, Vandals and Heruls), some Moors, and even people of Oriental race, Alans, Huns, etc. In the middle of the fourth century, soldier, *miles*, was the synonym of *barbarus*. We may here repeat Tacitus' phrase: *Nihil validum in exercitibus nisi quod externum*. We have here something which became serious. An analogy would be found in the French army if it came to be composed only of Algerians, Moroccans, Senegalese and Annamites.

But as long as the officers, the training, the language for commands, the armament, and tactics remained Roman, this was only half an evil. Unfortunately, things did not stop here. As early as the middle of the third century, the suspicious policy of Gallienus debarred from the army Roman Senators ; then the senatorial class of the provinces, then the decurions and finally the *subjecti curiæ* were rigorously forbidden military service. These measures were only too welcome to the desires of the enervated aristocracy and bourgeoisie. Very soon a prejudice was established which looked upon all military service, even in the capacity of an officer, as a disgrace, and the Church emphasized these prejudices. The paradoxical result of these ill-considered measures was to deliver the army and consequently the State into the hands of men of very humble station. This aristocracy, which was so deeply imbued with the principles of birth and wealth and despised people of low station, yielded to them the throne in leaving them the military career. Soldiers of fortune of low birth rose from grade to grade right up to the supreme power ; soldier, protector (centurion), tribune, Cæsar, such was the *cursus honorum* of Constantius Chlorus, Maximian Daïa, Valentinian, Valens, etc. And the Empire was lucky to be, from Claudius II. onwards, in the hands of these rude but energetic Illyrian generals.

After the beginning of the fourth century, this source dried up. The officers like the soldiers had perforce to be taken from amongst the barbarians. Already under the principate of Gallienus, the Herul Naulobatus had received the *ornamenta consularia*, a mere honour, it is true. But from Constantine's reign onwards, the elevation of the German barbarians to the highest posts at Court, and the highest grades in the army, was frequent and almost systematic. The Aleman chief, Eroc (Crocus) had carried Constantine to the throne. Three other Alemans (Latinus, Agilo and Scudilo) formed part of the army of Constantius. One king of this nation, Vadomir, was made Duke of Phœnicia, another king " tribune " of an auxiliary corps. But Constantine's predilection was for the Franks : *Franci quorum multitudo in palatio florebat*, says Ammianus Marcellinus. They continued in favour until the end of the century ; Mellobaudes was Chief of the Guard (*comes domesticorum*) in 378 ; Dagalaïf (366) and Merobaudes (377) obtained the highest distinction, the consulship. The Roman armies were commanded by Franks, Bauto, Arbogast and Richomer ; by Goths, Gainas, Sarus, Fravitta, and even Alaric ; by the son of a Vandal, Stilicho ; by a Sarmatian, Victor ; in the following century, in the East, by Alans, Asper and Ardaburius. A Frank, disguising his origin under a Latin name, Sylvanus, was even seen for a moment aspiring to the Empire.

Nevertheless, it is important to point out that these personages, though of Germanic origin, were " Roman citizens ". The elevation to the consulship and to the patriciate, and the " conubium " leave no doubt on the point. Fravitta married a Roman woman, Stilicho married Serena, niece of Theodosius, and the latter's son Honorius married a daughter of Stilicho. Theodosius II. was by his mother grandson of the Frank Bauto. Many barbarian generals were even born on

territory of the Empire and were its subjects, such as Magnentius and Stilicho.   But was it not, nevertheless, alarming
that all the higher officers belonged to a race which was
foreign to the Roman world ?

But why alarming ?   Did they betray the Empire ?   Never.
The Franks who had remained independent and barbarians
had no more redoubtable opponents than the Franks Sylvanus,
Arbogast and Richomer.   Even after the fall of the Empire,
the Rugians, barbarians of the Danube, were exterminated by
the very man who put an end to the Western Empire,
Odovacar, who was himself a Rugian or Scyrian.   In truth,
every brave man in the fourth and fifth centuries could choose
between two alternatives—barbarism or *Romania*.   If he
adopted the latter he stuck to it.

Where then, it will be asked, was the harm ?   The majority
of the population worked, enjoying peace and civilization,
exempt from military service, while the brute force was recruited
from amongst brutes and these brutes were faithful.   This
was a rational division of labour and all was for the best.

But in reality, by acting in this fashion, the Empire let
power slip from its hands.   The Roman army had been a
powerful Romanizing agent as long as it had included Italians
or even provincials.   In the fourth century this was not the
case.   Composed of Germans and commanded by Germans,
this army was no longer Roman in anything but the name, and
it became, without even wanting to, an agent in Germanizing,
and that from a period when the stability of the Empire seemed
still unshakable.   When we read an account of the campaigns
of Julian and of his successors, it appears that the most valued
troops are not so much the legions as certain auxiliary corps
with picturesque names (*Petulantes, Braccatœ, Ursi,* etc.).

Now, these corps no longer seem to be armed in the Roman
fashion and no longer use Roman tactics.   The ancient
traditions of discipline and military science being lost, it was
better to use barbarian impetuosity in the service of Rome.
The more barbarian the so-called Roman soldier was, the
greater his value.   In fact, Julian's army was entirely German.
It attacked in " boar's head " formation, uttered bellowings
called *barritus*, and raised Julian on the shield, like a
Merovingian King.   Its dress was wholly German.   The
Emperor himself came to be clad in skins of wild beasts and the

Roman costume became a ceremonial dress only, even for the Head of the State.

The command was naturally in Latin. Nevertheless, when, at the end of the fifth century, we find Sidonius Apollinaris complimenting Syagrius on speaking German perfectly, we must conclude from this that it became indispensable to speak German in order to be understood by the last " Roman " soldiers of Gaul !

This Germanization of the Roman world shows itself as early as the middle of the fourth century in nomenclature. If some barbarian generals assumed a Latin name such as Victor, Magnentius, Sylvanus and Sebastianus, the majority preferred to keep their German names : Merobaudes, Dagalaïf, Bauto, Arbogast, Richomer, Gaïnas, Stilicho, Ricimer, etc. Of the Latin writers of the fifth century, Merobaudes and Frigeridus, bear the one a Frankish, the other a Gothic name. Roman men and women born before the fall of the Western Empire already have German names, such as Saints Medard and Gildard, St. Vast (*Vedastus*), St. Genevieve (*Genovefa*). The extraordinary vogue of German names, which was to bring about the complete extermination of the Latin nomenclature in the seventh and eighth centuries, had already begun.

The serious thing was that there never had been confidence between the barbarian generals and the Roman population. As long as the Empire seemed unshakeable, the distrust between them remained latent. After Theodosius it flared up, fed by the jealousy of some generals of really Roman origin, generals whose plaything the Emperor was. The Emperor, who was henceforth a weakling, feared the " Patrician ". Once the danger had passed away, and he thought he need fear the barbarians no longer, he got rid of him by assassination (Stilicho in 408 ; Aetius in 454 ; Aspar in the East in 471). But, in the second half of the fifth century, in the West, the barbarian chief who was the master of the army, took better precautions ; it was he who kept the Emperor under surveillance and held him at his mercy. His origin, because of the ideas of the time, forbade his assuming the purple for himself and this perpetuated a fatal dualism. On two occasions Ricimer, after leaving the throne vacant, restored it. At last Odovacar put an end to the farce by ceasing to put on the throne an Imperial marionette. But he had neither the necessary resources nor the prestige for saving the Empire in the West. The latter was, in fact, reduced to Italy. Britain had been lost for ever; the Danubian provinces, *Illyricum*, had been transformed into a desert scoured by the Hun, Goth, Gepid, Lombard, Herul horsemen, etc. Gaul, Spain and Africa were in the power of the barbarian Federates, Visigoths, Sueves, Vandals, Burgundians and Franks. The *foedus* with the barbarians admitting them on the territory of the Empire, which they undertook to defend, had proved itself at once a disastrous expedient. Keeping their national arms, tactics, customs, language and Kings, the "Federates" were recalcitrant to all Romanization. Without having, at the beginning, intended to destroy the Empire, they nevertheless inflicted terrible blows on it from the year 376 onwards, through their turbulence, lack of discipline and insatiable appetites. If the Germans who composed the regular "Roman" army of the fourth and fifth centuries, never betrayed it, the Federates were in a nearly constant state of revolt. When the Empire was suddenly eclipsed in the West, from the middle of the fifth century, their Kings, who were the heads of the army, naturally seized the supreme power in the provinces in which they were quartered. The Roman population, accustomed to identifying the army with the "barbarians", would scarcely have noticed the change, since the administration on Roman lines went on without any appreciable alteration, if the new masters had not been Arians or pagans.

On the whole, except in Britain and along a line West of the Rhine and South of the Danube, where the Germanic elements entirely replaced *Romania*, the barbarians did not destroy the Roman Empire in the West. The Empire died of an internal malady. During the last two centuries of its existence, it adopted a policy of unyielding conservatism, to fight the economic, social and racial forces which made for its dissolution. Never has a more obstinate struggle been put up against Fate. Nevertheless, since the end of the fourth century, its resistance rapidly ceased. In the fifth century, there was a collapse without hope of recovery, until Rome finally let power drop from her fainting hands.

This tragedy of the ancient world refusing to die, is one of the most poignant spectacles which can present themselves to the eyes of the historian or sociologist.

PART THREE

AFTER THE DOWNFALL

CHAPTER I

Italy after the Disappearance of the Western Empire from 476 to 526

NONE of the great events, such as the invasions of the barbarians (Radagaisus, the Visigoths, Huns, etc.), the disappearance of the " Empire " in 476, the arrival of the Goths and their occupation of the country, affected deeply the social life or even the organization and administrative geography of the country. People imagine, or rather used to imagine, some mysterious revolution in 476 which was not merely political but also social : Odovacar distributing a third of the soil of Italy to his Germanic bands which had revolted against the Empire. Things did not, however, happen in this way. In the fact that the Germans were masters of the army, there was nothing which could surprise the Italians. For nearly two centuries, even in the time when the Empire's brilliance was still undisputed, under Constantine—and perhaps even as early as Diocletian—the army in the service of Rome had been composed chiefly of barbarians, the majority being Germans. This fact was at the time of no consequence, since these troops were faithful.

As early as the fourth century, *barbarus* is the synonym of *miles* or soldier.[1]

A more serious thing was that the leaders of these barbarian armies which were armed and trained in the Roman fashion, but barbarian by race and language, were often themselves also barbarians, from the fourth to fifth century. But they were barbarians who had broken with their fellows and had become officers of the Roman State. A Sylvanus, Dagalaïf or Arbogast in the fourth century, and even an Alaric in the fifth century, was a *civis Romanus*. There is no doubt that it

[1] **CVIII,** vol. ii., 263 ; **DXLV,** vol. i., 39.

was the same with Ricimer who ruled the West after Aetius, and even with Odovacar himself.

The latter, as the sole master of Italy, defended it like a bull-dog. In 487, in mid-winter he fell upon the Rugians threatening Italy. Being taken by surprise in the region of the Danube, the barbarians sustained a crushing defeat and their King was led prisoner to Italy. Two years later there was a new victorious expedition ; the Rugian tribe was reduced to a handful of warriors and soon after disappeared from history.[1]

Odovacar, although his comrades were the remnants of the Scyrian, Herulian, Turcilingian and Rugian nations, in reality commanded the last Roman army, by which is meant an army in the service of Rome. If it rose in 476 against the Patrician Orestes and the phantom emperor Romulus—this is what is called the end of the Western Empire—the reason was, it is said, that a distribution of lands was refused to it. What did this distribution mean ? Was it a social revolution ? " It would have been a social revolution the like of which is not found in the history of the world."[2] No such revolution took place. These mercenary " Roman " soldiers really demanded to have their condition assimilated to that of the Federates.

Let us briefly recall the conditions of the settlement of the Federate barbarians on Roman soil. Their occupation, or the quartering of these barbarians, was called " hospitality " (*hospitalitas*). The barbarian Federate, as guest (*hospes*), lived at the expense of a landed proprietor (*possessor, dominus*). Both shared an estate and the means of working it (*coloni* and slaves, who were real human chattels). The proportion varied. In Gaul the Visigoths and Burgundians received two-thirds ; in Italy Odovacar's and later Theodoric's troops received one-third. But this was of small importance. What was shared was not the whole of the possessions of a landed proprietor, but an estate (shared between ten or twenty) or a fraction of an estate enough for the upkeep of a barbarian soldier, his family and servants. In the countries like Italy, in which he received a third, the barbarian got a third of a larger estate ; that was all.[3]

---

[1] **CDXLIII**, 134-136.
[2] **CVIII**, vol. ii., 342.
[3] **CDXXIX**, 72, 95 ; **CVIII**, vol. ii., 345.

Why did the soldiers of the last Roman army prefer the system of *hospitality* to that of pay in money, or chiefly in kind, which had been used till then for the regular troops ? We do not know exactly. Perhaps because the military stores no longer received from the " provincials " the customary provisions.[1] The only thing that is certain, is that there was no revolution in the social structure of Italy. The only change was the assimilation of the regular soldiers to the Federates, and this was not a great one, Further, this army, of which Odovacar was king, remained cantoned only in the North of Italy round Milan ; for two centuries it had been like this ; the troops defending Italy remained massed near Milan, Verona or Ravenna.

But the administration did not change. The administrative geography remained the same. The provinces remained without any alteration.[2]

The civil and financial administration functioned as before. There was still a Senate, a Prefect of Rome, Consuls (until 541) and *curiæ*. Rome was still the finest city of the West. The sight of it struck strangers and even the barbarians with admiration. It went on, moreover, with its life of idleness ; there was no intermission of the circus and amphitheatre games. It does not, in truth, appear that the Italian populace had to make any real changes in its habits.

Nor was anything changed when Odovacar's government was succeeded by that of Theodoric and the Ostrogoths. After the dissolution of Attila's Empire, the Ostrogoths had made themselves independent of the Huns and had established themselves in Pannonia and Illyria. They were so-called allies or subjects of the Empire. In reality they were turbulent and predatory guests or neighbours. They became dangerous when their bands were united under a single authority, that of Theodoric of the illustrious line of the Amalungs.

The Imperial policy brought off a master stroke ; it managed to get rid of this redoubtable people and at the same time to make use of it. Odovacar, although he had been recognized by Zeno and honoured with the title of " Patrician " had given the Emperor grounds for complaint. In 488, Theodoric, at the head of the whole of his people,—it

---

[1] **DXLV,** vol. i., 74.
[2] **DLXIII,** 134 ; **DCLI,** vol. i., 110.

was not a very numerous body, numbering perhaps no more than 20,000 warriors—marched towards Italy. He bore the quite Roman designation of *magister militum* and the title of *Patrician*. It was less as a barbarian chief than as a general in the service of New Rome, that he made himself master of Italy, after a fierce struggle lasting five years. It was only in March, 493, after the defeat and murder of Odovacar, that he received the royal title from his companions in arms. He was King of the Goths but not of the Romans of Italy. In relation to them his position was ill-defined. From the point of view of civil law, Theodoric, who had spent his youth at Constantinople, was not a foreigner, being a " Roman citizen ". He joined to his name the gentile name *Flavius*, which was supposed to connect him with the imperial family by a vague bond of adoption. He thus governed the people of Italy by what was tacitly at least a kind of delegated power, a *magisterium militum præsentale*, with wide scope.

In theory, he recognized the supremacy of the Empire, or rather he did not even think of explicitly denying it ; for under the hyperbolical expressions of his Chancery, diplomacy lay concealed. Nevertheless not only did he lavish flattering words on the Emperor, but he called himself his son and servant (*ego qui sum servus voster et filius*). In 508, he writes :[1] *Regnum nostrum imitatio vestra est, unici exemplar imperii . . . qui quantum vos sequimur, tantum gentes alias anteimus. Additur etiam veneranda Romanæ urbis affectio a quo segregari nequeunt, quæ se nominis unitate junxerunt. Romani regni unum velle, una semper opinio sit.*

Theodoric did not give himself out to be king of the Romans. The moneys issued at Rome, Ravenna, Milan, etc., were always struck in the emperor's name ; only on the reverse, and that not always, was Theodoric's monogram found. It should be noticed that Ricimer, when the Western Empire still existed, had done the same.[2]

He did not legislate. What is called his political legislation consisted of *Edicts*, that is to say, decisions of the authorities, such as could be issued by the Roman magistrates.[3] Moreover, Theodoric did not live at Rome, like an Emperor. Only

---

[1] **CDIII**, 27.
[2] Friedlaender, *Die Münzen der Vandalen* (1849), 5.
[3] **CDIII**, 30 ; **DXLV**, vol. i., 525 ; **DXCV**, vol. i., 90.

in 500 he made his first appearance in the Eternal City and gave festivals in the circus. His residence was Ravenna, and it is more than probable that the cantonments of the Gothic Federates were chiefly in the North of Italy.

Externally, Theodoric was a *magister militum*, a sort of viceroy. He wrote with deference to the Senate, which, unlike him, was at Rome ; addressing it by the title of *patres conscripti*. He nominated the Consuls in the West, in agreement with the Emperor at Constantinople. Dating went by the Consuls and not by the years of his reign, a practice continued under his successors, as late as 534, which was an obvious sign that the Goths recognised, at least theoretically, the authority of the Emperor at Constantinople.

Although an Arian, Theodoric defended the Church.

His greatest care was perhaps that of provisioning the capital. Fortunately for Rome, he saved Sicily, while Africa, Sardinia, and Corsica had fallen to the power of the Vandals. He repaired the aqueducts. He was anxious not to let intellectual life disappear. He and his successors saw to the upkeep of the State Chairs in Latin grammar and rhetoric.

The administration remained the same as before.[1] The civil posts were reserved for Romans. It is true that we meet with *Comites Gothorum* or " Counts of the Goths ". The latter functioned in places where Goths were numerous and their task was to settle differences amongst these Goths according to their national customs. But they did not replace Roman functionaries in matters which, mostly, interested Romans only. It is true, that in certain provinces or *civitates*, we see the *præses* or the *curia* replaced in the exercise of their functions by a Gothic or Roman Count, furnished with full powers ; thus the Count of Syracuse was both the governor of Sicily and the commander of the military forces of this island. These measures were due to exceptional circumstances. Yet they did not constitute an innovation. As early as the middle of the fifth century, there were already Roman *Counts* of provinces or cities.[2] Marriages between Goths and Romans were forbidden. Should we not see in this a proof of the contempt of the victors towards the

---

[1] **DCLIV**, 378-398 ; **DXCV**, vol. i., 88 ; **DLXX**.
[2] **DLVII**, 32-38.

vanquished ? No. It was due to the imperial constitutions which prohibited *connubium* between Romans and barbarians.

Only the instrument of power, the army, was entirely Gothic. The exclusion of the Goths from civil functions was matched by the exclusion of the Romans from the army. But this was the continuation of the principle of the absolute separation of the civil and military functions, which went back to the third century. From that period, there had not been any Romans from Italy in the Roman army. Comparing barbarians with barbarians, the Ostrogoths were quite as good as the bands of Odovacar or Ricimer or even the so-called Roman armies of Theodosius, Valentinian and even Constantine.

In relation to the regions which had composed the Western Empire, Theodoric appeared as the successor of the emperors. He posed as the protector of the Visigoths and prevented the Franks from pressing home their gains after their victory of Vouillé (507). In Spain he was looked upon as a kind of suzerain. He received the Alemans defeated by Clovis. In Germany even, the kings of the Thuringians and of the Heruls (on the Danube) stood to him in the relations of protégés to protector. On the whole, Theodoric appears nearer to a Stilicho than to a Germanic king such as Clovis.

He made clever use of the policy of marriages ; his sister Amalafrida married Thrasamund, king of the Vandals (500). A daughter was betrothed to the Burgundian Sigismund, while another married the Visigoth Alaric II. He himself had married, in 493, Audofleda, sister of Clovis. Thus in the person of the chief of the Gothic people, established on her soil with the task of defending it, Italy seemed to continue to exercise a kind of hegemony over the West, during the first quarter of the sixth century.[1]

[1] DCLIV, 47, 7.

CHAPTER II

THE PERSISTENCE OF ROMAN POLITICAL INSTITUTIONS IN THE WEST. THE PROBLEM OF THE DISAPPEARANCE OF THE EMPIRE

I. THE PERSISTENCE OF ROMAN POLITICAL INSTITUTIONS IN THE WEST

THE Empire and the Visigoths.—At the moment when the Western Empire was dying " like an old man expiring from decay ", without its death stirring any real feeling on the part of the people, the Visigoths were masters of Spain and of two-thirds of Gaul (from the Pyrenees to the Loire, and from the Atlantic to the Cevennes).

We have seen that they had entered the service of the Empire as Federates, at first in the East in 376, then in the West in 412. The celebrated Alaric, who captured Rome in 410, had been a general in the service of Theodosius ; he was a *magister militum* and a " Roman citizen ". During the first half of the fifth century, it was thanks to the Goths that the Empire was able to clear Spain of the Vandals (a branch of whom, the Silings, was exterminated), the Alans, Sueves, and lastly of the Asding Vandals who preferred to take refuge in Africa in 429. It was thanks to the support of their contingents that it was possible to repel Attila from Gaul in 451.

But the Visigoth King (466-484) seeing the Western Empire leaning towards its fall, undertook to occupy Gaul and Spain *jure suo.* In 469, he expelled the Sueves from Lusitania and thrust them back into Gallæcia. At the beginning of his reign, he was in communication with the Emperor at Constantinople, Leo, but we do not know the details and the nature of these relations.[1]

Between the fall of the Empire and the triumph of Theodoric the Ostrogoth, Euric was the most powerful of the German kings in the West. He protected Gaul from the pirate Saxons and other barbarians. Southern Gaul was the centre of the

---

[1] **DXV,** 11-46 ; **DLIV,** vol. v. and vi.

Visigothic rule. There the king resided, in Toulouse for preference. Even after the catastrophe of 507, the Visigothic kingdom clung to this country ; the young king Amalaric resided in Septimania, at Narbonne, where he died in 531. He lived under the protectorate of the Ostrogoth Theodoric, who ruled his protégé's kingdom by governors appointed by himself.

It was only when the ancient line of the Baltungs had died out in his person, that an Ostrogoth adventurer, Theudis, seized the monarchy and transferred the seat of power into Spain ; and even then it was still in the North, at Barcelona. The Visigothic kingdom did not really exercise any influence on the centre and the South of Spain except from the middle of the sixth century, when Agila established himself at Merida on the Guadiana. Agila himself did not manage to impose his authority on the Hispano-Romans of the South. He was defeated by the inhabitants of Baetica, which district changed its name into Andalusia (because a century before it had been occupied by the Vandals).

What was the attitude of the Visigoths towards the Empire during this period ? Did they consider themselves really independent or were they conscious of being part, theoretically at least, of a whole ?

Our documents do not throw the same light as in the case of the Ostrogoths and Burgundians. Two texts seem to indicate that as early as Euric's reign, the Visigoths broke with Rome: (1) *Euricus ergo crebram mutationem principum Romanorum cernens Gallias suo jure nisus est occupare*[1] ; (2) *Evarix, rex Gothorum, rupto dissolutoque antiquo fœdere.*[2] But Jordanes, who wrote a hundred years after Euric's reign, sums up in one phrase the real policy of the Gothic king, without perhaps our being justified in concluding that the latter repudiated the theoretical sovereignty of the Empire ; and this is the only point in question for the moment. As for Sidonius, he refers perhaps to a passing and not to a permanent rupture.

The thing which would make us believe that the existence, at least in theory, of the Roman Empire, still continued to be recognized in the countries occupied by the Visigoths, is that

[1] JORDANES, *Getica*, 4.
[2] SIDON. APOLLIN., *Epist.*, vii., 6, 109.

the Visigothic coins, one hundred years after Euric's death, bear the Emperor's name.[1] Further, documents of the council are dated in the Roman fashion with the names of the Consuls, to which, in the time of Theodoric's protectorate over the kingdom of the Visigoths, is joined the year of the Ostrogoth's reign, unused in Italy.[2]

The administrative organization could not be maintained strictly as in Italy.[3] It was not possible to keep a Prætorian Prefect, Vicars, etc., who would have hampered the Gothic kings. Besides, even in the East, the administration underwent serious modifications ; the Vicars disappeared, or else this was a new name applied to the " governor " of a province. The " provinces " continued, at least in the fifth and sixth centuries : Aquitania and Narbonensis in Gaul ; Baetica, Tarraconensis, Carthaginiensis, Lusitania, Gallaecia and the Balearic Islands in Spain, although the capitals were changed : Saragossa instead of Tarragona, Toledo instead of Carthagena, etc. These provinces became archbishoprics. But it is doubtful whether " governors " continued to be there for long. Perhaps the " dukes " under another name and with plenary powers were the successors of the *rectores provinciae*.

The *civitas* was chosen as the unit of administration instead of the province and took over the name *provincia*. It was administered by a *count*, who joined in himself the administrative, judicial and police powers. This count was a real governor for a smaller territory. This, moreover, was the development of a practice in vogue during the last days of the Roman Empire.[4]

The Roman financial administration continued with its defects.[5] The *curiæ* were still oppressed. The legislation was entirely Roman.

There was no change in social conditions ; the large proprietors, masters of the soil, dominated society.

The Latin language caused Gothic to disappear early. Latin literature was fairly flourishing ; Gothic Kings wrote in Latin : *Sisebut* is the author of the *Life of St. Didier* in the seventh century.

---

[1] **DC**, 28-29.
[2] **DCLIV**, 378, 477.
[3] **DLIV**, vol. vi., 300, 331 ; **DCXIII**, 281.
[4] **DLVII**, 41.
[5] **DLIV**, vol. vi., 252, 279, 306 ; **DCLI**.

At the end of the sixth century the adoption of Catholicism by the Goths made possible a rapprochement between them and the Hispano-Romans, a rapprochement with which only the question of religion really interfered.

The Burgundians.[1]—Amongst the barbarian peoples which had entered the territory of the Empire, none, undoubtedly, kept up longer the consciousness of its dependence in relation to the Imperial government. This is easily explained. In the fifth century their ancient power was broken. They had been established since about 405 as Federates on the left bank of the Rhine at Mayence and Worms, when the Hun mercenaries in the pay of Aetius inflicted on them a heavy defeat in 436. The remnants of the people were in 442 cantoned still as Federates in the service of Rome, in *Sapaudia*, that is to say in the country extending from the lake of Neuchâtel to Grenoble.[2] They received two-thirds of the soil and a third of the slaves.

In 451 they provided Aetius against Attila with a contingent which was practically annihilated. In 456 they were with the Visigoths in the service of the Gaulish Emperor Avitus. Under the leadership of kings of a new dynasty they made an expedition in Spain against the Sueves. Chilperic and Gundioc were both kings of the Burgundians and *magistri militum*.

From this time they began to covet Lugdunensis where the aristocracy seems to have called them in ; in 461 Lyons was in their hands. They stretched on the West up to the Rhone, on the South up to the Durance, on the North up to the Saône valley and in the East beyond the Jura. As Federates they fought against other Federates, the more turbulent and less faithful Visigoths.

The career of one of their kings, Gundobad, who reigned from 480 to 516, is very typical of this troubled and confused period. Before being King of the Burgundians and ruling over a territory which extended from the plains of Champagne to the Durance, he had been a Roman Patrician. It was on him that the task of seeing to the succession to the Imperial throne one day devolved. The Emperor-maker Ricimer, who had made and unmade five Emperors in the West,

---

[1] **DXXXIII**, and **DCIX**.

[2] In spite of what Mommsen has said, *Ebrodunum* is not Villeneuve at the point where the Rhone flows into Lake Geneva, but Yverdon.

had just died suddenly (473). The Burgundian, appointed Patrician by Olybrius in 472, was at Rome. He appointed Glycerius and then returned to Gaul.[1]

His son, Sigismund (516-523) writes to the Emperor Anastasius in the following terms : " My ancestors have always been devoted to the Empire ; no honour was greater to them than the titles conferred on them by Your Greatness. All my family have solicited the dignities given by the Emperors, holding them in higher esteem than those they had from their fathers ". He thinks himself bound to announce his accession : " At the death of my father, who was very faithful to you, and one of the leading men (*proceres vestri*) at your Court, I sent you one of my Councillors, as was my duty, to place under your patronage the first offers of my service. . . . My people belongs to you. I obey you while commanding it and I have greater pleasure in obeying you than in commanding it. Amongst my subjects I appear a King, but I am only your soldier. Through me you administer countries, the furthest removed from your residence. I await the orders which you shall deign to give me ".[2]

In another letter, Sigismund thanks the Emperor for having granted him *militiae fasces* (the honorary title of *magister militum*), *aulae contubernium* (the title of Patrician ?) and *venerandam Romani nominis participationem* (alliance with the Empire).

On their side the Romans looked upon the Burgundians as the allies of the Roman people, according to Jordanes.[3]

The Vandals.[4]—The successors of the great Gaiserich (died in 477), conscious of their weakness, were torn between the Ostrogothic rule of Theodoric and that of Constantinople. Hilderich (523-530), the son of Hunerich and Eudocia, and consequently the grandson of a Roman Emperor of the West (Valentinian III), seems to recognize, at least in theory, the authority of the Empire, by which is meant of Constantinople. The coins are struck with the effigy of Justin I. It is true that a violent anti-Imperial reaction took place under his successor, Gelimer. But it called forth from Justinian a crushing

---

[1] CL, 452-458 ; CDLXXXI.
[2] Avitus, l. 83 (Peiper's ed., 94).
[3] *Getica*, 45.
[4] CDXLV.

retort : in a single battle, the Vandal Kingdom was over-thrown (532).

Nevertheless, if, save for two or three occasions, the Vandals freed themselves from the fiction of the Emperor's sovereignty, we ought not to conclude from this that they introduced any profound changes into the social or even the political life of Northern Africa. Nothing would be further from the facts. Their acts of violence against persons were perhaps not worse than those of the other barbarians. The " Vandalism " they perpetrated on monuments is imaginary.[1] Their reputation is due to their continuous persecutions of the Catholics, they themselves being convinced Arians. As powerless with the Moors as were the Romans, they did not change anything in the social structure of the civilized parts of Africa. They accepted the machinery of the Roman Government. They took good care not to abolish the financial administration but turned it to their own profit. Never was the collection of Roman taxes more oppressive in Africa than under the Vandal rule. The monetary system was the same. The administrative geography underwent no essential change. The Romans of Africa frequented the palace and filled the civil posts. Municipal life went on as before ; the *curiæ* were still left. The country people was still reduced to the serfdom of the colonate. The urban populace spent its time, as in the past, at the circus or amphitheatre. It is needless to add that Roman law continued to govern the Roman subjects of the Vandal king.

Latin was the language of diplomacy and legislation. If Gaiserich, when he crossed over into Africa, knew it little or badly, there is no doubt that it was a language of everyday use for his successors.

Grammarians and rhetoricians still kept their schools open, and not only Africo-Romans, but also young men of Vandal origin thronged to them. Africa, which since the end of the second century was by far the most fertile part of the world in Latin letters, continued to produce writers of worth con-sidering the times, for example, the poet Dracontius.

In the matter of usages and customs, the Vandals in the sixth century tended to forget their own for those of the Romans, and that to their great detriment.

---

[1] KLEINSCHMIDT (*Progr. Torgau*, 1875).

We see that though Vandal Africa was in fact severed from the Western Empire half a century before the fall of the latter, Roman life in all its forms was not for that reason appreciably altered.

The Empire and the Franks.—It is a well known thing that the relations between the Empire and the Franks were not continuously hostile. Many Franks were on the best of terms with Rome. As early as the fourth century, there were complaints that the Franks crowded the " palace ", that is to say the Court of the Emperors. But these Franks were no longer barbarians. They were adventurers, sometimes of royal blood, who had renounced barbarism. They were not Franks in feeling or nationality and did not hesitate, when occasion demanded, to crush their fellow countrymen who had remained barbarians.

As a people, the Franks did not put up a united opposition against Rome. A body of them obtained permission to settle on territory of the Empire : about 358 Julian authorized them to live in Toxandria (North of the modern Brabant). Too far removed, they did not become Romanized, but were subjects of the Empire.

Even the chiefs who extended their power at the expense of the Empire in the fifth century were not completely independent of it. They were perhaps " Federates". It is more than probable that Childeric, father of Clovis, was in the service of Rome. In 463 he fought under the orders of the *magister militum* Aegidius ; in 469, in co-operation with Count Paul, he beat the Saxons and the Alans.

Was Clovis himself a conqueror ?

That Clovis was a conqueror in relation to other Franks and Germans, such as the Alemans and the Visigoths, cannot be doubted. But his struggle with Syagrius was " a contest of ambition between two chiefs " and not a clash of nationalities.

In relation to the Gallo-Romans Clovis did not pose as a conqueror. To tell the truth, we have very little information about the feelings of the Gallo-Romans north of the Loire or about the way in which Clovis extended his authority up to this river. We know only that many Gallo-Romans living under the rule of the Visigoth kings preferred the Franks. They were induced to go to the help of the Franks by the Catholic bishops who hated the Visigoths not as barbarians but as Arian heretics. After Clovis had conquered at Vouillé the chief of the Goths, Alaric II, the people rallied to his side. His authority over the Gallo-Romans, it seems, won a sort of official sanction immediately afterwards. In theory, Gaul formed part of the Roman Empire, the capital of which was henceforth Constantinople. On his return from his victorious expedition into Aquitania, Clovis found an embassy from the Emperor Anastasius at Tours in 508. We are told that Clovis received from it the insignia of the Consulship. Clad in a purple tunic and a chlamys and with the diadem on his head, the Frankish king rode on horseback over the few hundred metres which separate the basilica of Saint Martin from the Cathedral of Tours, throwing gold and silver to the people. From that day he was called Consul or Augustus.

According to Dubos, to be recognized Consul in the circumstances in which Clovis stood, was really to be in fact Emperor of the Gauls.[1] By presenting the " letter " of the Emperor Anastasius to the people, he was acquiring over them a legal authority, according to Fustel de Coulanges[2] : " Henceforth Clovis appeared in the eyes of the Gallo-Romans as the Emperor's delegate, and consequently as the representative of the ancient order of things, which in the midst of the troubles of those times remained the expression of law. His conquests were in some sort legitimized ".[3]

Nevertheless even those who hold that the Emperor's authority continued in Gaul theoretically at least, admit that things changed in the course of the sixth century. Fustel de Coulanges tries hard to pick out expressions of deference in the formulæ of the letters of the Frankish Kings who succeeded Clovis to the Emperors at Constantinople. But he admits that the subject position of the Merovingians has ceased.[4] He even adopts a date (539) for the disappearance of this state of things, but unfortunately only on the evidence of what he calls a " chronicler ", but which is only an inferior life of a saint of late date (the *Vita Treverii*).

Even in Italy the fiction of the Imperial hegemony was

[1] DLXVIII.
[2] CL.
[3] BAYET in CCLXXIX, vol. ii., 1, 103.
[4] CL, 508-511.

kept up only with difficulty. While showering marks of respect on the Emperor, Theodoric meant to be really master. On a mere suspicion of communicating with Constantinople he put to death Symmachus and Boethius about 524, and cast into prison Pope John, who died there. It should also be mentioned that the Gothic king, who was attached to Arianism, was exasperated by the persecutions of which his coreligionists were victims in the East. After his death (May, 526), his daughter Amalasuntha reigned in the name of her son Athalaric, but the latter died at the age of eighteen (534). His mother wished to keep the power but fell victim to an anti-Catholic and anti-Roman reaction. But then the Emperor—Justinian—intervened. He thought the moment had come to restore the authority of the Empire not merely in Italy, but over the whole of the West. In his mind, as in that of many cultivated men, the Empire had not ceased to exist. Its life went on in spite of appearances.

II. THE PROBLEM OF THE DISAPPEARANCE OF THE WESTERN EMPIRE[1]

Did contemporaries notice that something was coming to an end and that something new was being born in the year 476 ?

The men of this period had the bitter feeling that the Empire was decaying, especially from the time of the reigns of Honorius and Arcadius and of their successors. But they do not seem to have perceived that one of the two halves of the *Respublica Romanorum*, the Empire in the West, had ceased to exist. The year 476 was not for them prophetic. When in this year Odovacar, the barbarian chief of the Germano-Roman army in Italy, decided it was useless to raise to the throne a phantom sovereign, he recognized or pretended to recognize as his sovereign, in agreement with the Roman Senate, the Emperor who reigned at Constantinople. The unity of the Empire was re-established in its majesty.[2] This fiction went on for a long time. We have just said that in the parts of the Empire which had fallen into the power of the barbarian invaders, Visigoths in Gaul and Spain, Ostrogoths in Pannonia and later in Italy, Burgundians in Gaul,

[1] CDIII.
[2] CL, 518.

and perhaps even Vandals in Africa, the chiefs were for a long time considered as exercising a power delegated to them by the Emperor's authority.

Whether this was an understanding or a misconception is proved by the difficulty Justinian had in bringing back Italy under his real authority, after the terrible resistance of the successors of Theodoric the Ostrogoth. Nevertheless, in the middle of the sixth century, when Italy, North-East Africa, Provence in Gaul, and the coasts in Spain were subject to the law of the Roman Emperor residing at Constantinople, minds endowed with a superficial optimism could imagine that after a century's storm the Roman world had been restored, at least in the Mediterranean region. Conceptions of ecclesiastical theorists helped to prolong this theoretical existence of the Empire. Christian eschatology had for a long time imagined that the end of the world was near. Pious Christians in the fourth, fifth and sixth centuries and even much later, awaited the cataclysm in fear and trembling, some of them in ecstasy and with a passionate hope. Already Tertullian draws from a text of St. Paul (2 Thess. ii. 7) the idea that the Roman Empire is to be the last of the Empires and that its existence is retarding the end of the world (*Apol.*, 32).[1] Lactantius does the same.[2]

Christian historians and chronologists divided the life of mankind into a certain number of *ages*, some into four, others into six.

The belief in a division of the history of the world into large epochs or ages, a golden, silver, brass and iron age, goes back very far. It is accompanied, as is known, by a belief in a progressive decay. St. Jerome identifies the Iron Age with the Roman Empire and it is the last which mankind will see. But the most wide-spread conception, at least in the Western world, was that of St. Augustine. He divides history into six ages. The fifth was from the captivity of Babylon to the birth of Christ; the sixth began with the coming of Christ. It was to end with the arrival of the Anti-Christ and the final catastrophe. It began under the Empire, and was that in which those devout and learned Christians lived.

Thus the Roman Empire was the last age of mankind,

[1] **CLXXXVI.**
[2] **XXII, 7.**

and it was impossible that it should be replaced by a different state of things. If it was falling into ruin, and if whole parts were the prey of the barbarians, there was nothing surprising in that. It was because the cup of iniquity was overflowing and the times were at hand. Adopted by Isidore of Seville in Spain in the seventh century, the Venerable Bede in England in the eighth, and after them by the chroniclers and computers until the thirteenth century and later, this system enjoyed an immense vogue.

For these reasons, the idea of the end of the Roman Empire was very slow to establish itself. The Empire had really been dead for a long time in the West, before people took account of this ; or rather the intellectuals of the time refused to notice it. Its theoretical prolongation, its survival, was indispensable to them. The Empire, in the words of Lavisse, appeared " as a necessary mode of being of the world, above the accidents of historical facts ".[1]

Nevertheless these conceptions corresponded so little to reality, even as early as the second half of the sixth century, and especially in the seventh and in the eighth century, that they would have scattered like smoke, if the event of December 25th, 800, the crowning of Charles as Emperor, had not given them fresh strength. We know to-day that this ceremony was a farce practically improvized by a handful of antiquarian ecclesiastics. We know that Charles and the most powerful of his successors drew their strength from social conditions which no longer resembled in anything those of the Early and even of the later Empire. But clerks and scholars, from this time onwards, fancied that the Charleses, the Ottos, the Henrys and the Frederics were really the successors of Justinian, Theodosius, Constantine, and even of Augustus and Trajan.

The constitutions of these German Emperors, in which matters are dealt with never dreamt of by the Roman Emperors, claim to be a continuation of the constitutions of the latter, and the tradition on this point is so strong that till quite recently the law text-books used by our teachers still contained them.

Emperors, historians, and jurists of the Middle Ages and of modern times sincerely believed that the Empire, though

[1] **CCLXXX**, vol. i., 205.

its head was of German nationality, was really the continuation of the Roman Empire in the West. So much was this the case, that from the point of view of constitutional law, if we wish to draw up the death certificate of the Roman Empire, we must come down as late as August 6th, 1806, the day on which Francis II of German nationality gave up his title of Roman Emperor to assume that of Emperor of Austria.[1]

[1] JAMES BRYCE, *The Holy Roman Empire* (4th ed., London, 1873, p. 366).

CHAPTER III

The Return of the Empire. Justinian and the "Reconquista"[1]

ON the day following Theodoric's death (526) the Imperial throne was ascended by Flavius Petrus Sabbatius Justinianus, or Justinian, who was to overthrow his work. The man who dreamt of restoring the Roman Empire in all its extent, of reviving its splendour, was of humble origin. He was born of a family of Illyrian peasants near Uskub, on the confines of Macedonia and Albania, that is, in the part of the "Illyrian" provinces where Latin was spoken.[2] The chances of a military career made his uncle Justin an Emperor. An illiterate old soldier, Justin had reached the important post of chief of the Imperial Guard (comes excubitorum) when the Emperor Anastasius died in 518. The claimants were the deceased's nephew and Vitalian, grandson of the Aspar who had ruled the Empire in the preceding century. Justin disappointed their hopes and took possession of the throne. It is said that he had received a large sum of money from the Grand Chamberlain, the eunuch Amantius, to buy the soldiers' and people's support for one of his creatures, and that Justin used the money to further his own ambition. However that may be, there is nothing extraordinary in Justin's career. Since the third century, the Imperial throne had been almost the regular culmination of a military career; the Imperial power seems to be the highest grade in the army.[3] This was the democratic element in the life of the Roman and Byzantine world. A similar career would have been impossible in the barbarian kingdoms, where the king was considered to be descended from the gods.

Uneducated and old,—he was a septuagenarian—Justin took as his partner his nephew Justinian who had received a careful education at Constantinople. He won the popular favour by an easy means, the games, which consisted in chariot

---

[1] **DLXIII, DCIII.**
[2] The Slav origin of Justinian is a late invention.
[3] C. Jullian, in *Bulletin épigraphique*, vol. iv.

races and wild beast fights, the gladiatorial combats having been abolished a century ago under the influence of Christianity. He tried to bring peace back to the Church. Powerless with the Monophysites, he at any rate stopped the kind of schism with the Western Church which had already lasted a third of a century ; in 484, Pope Felix III had excommunicated the patriarchs of Constantinople and of Antioch, authors of the *Henotikon* by which the Emperor Zeno had thought to be able to put an end to the quarrels between the Monophysites and the Catholics. Unfortunately Justin was a zealot. He persecuted not merely the Manicheans and the Jews, but also the Christian sects, the Monophysites and the Arians. In 523 he ordered the churches of the latter to be given up to the Catholics. It was over this order that the Empire and Theodoric fell out. The Ostrogoth who was tolerant to the Catholics of Italy would not suffer his coreligionists to be deprived of the same favours in the East.

Justinian, when he succeeded his uncle in 527, at the age of forty, inherited his religious opinions. He stood forth as the champion of the orthodox faith which was denied by the barbarian kings in the West, who were nearly all Arians. In his expeditions against the Vandals and the Goths there was already something of the spirit of the crusader. But above all he stood as the heir of the Cæsars. His task here below was to make good his predecessors' mistakes and to restore the Roman world within its ancient boundaries, from one ocean to the other. He writes on a Novel (30, 11, 2)[1] : " God has given us to bring the Persians to conclude peace, to subdue the Vandals, Alans, and Moors and to recover the whole of Africa and Sicily, and we have good hope that the Lord will grant us the rest of the Empire, which the Romans of old extended up to the bounds of the two oceans, and which they lost through indolence ".

It was always a principle at Byzantium never to recognize the territorial losses suffered by the monarchy.[2] They knew well enough that Italy, Africa, Spain and Gaul had fallen away from the Empire. But the German kings governing the West only did so by virtue of a formal or tacit delegation on the part of the Emperor at Constantinople. We have

---

[1] **DLXIII**, 23 ; **CDXLV**, 126, note 1.
[2] **DLXIII**, 129.

said that the German chiefs themselves were not far from sharing these ideas.

In actual fact, the West was detached from the Empire, since it did not furnish the latter with either soldiers or money, at least in the way of regular impost, and since the Imperial constitutions, at any rate those promulgated after about 470, no longer had the force of law.

The prescription would inevitably have become established, if things had continued to remain in this state. But, as no German king intended to relinquish his powers, it was only too evident that force would have to be used to restore the Empire in the West. Wholly Latin though he was in intention, and though his eyes were turned towards the West, Justinian could not overlook the dangers threatening the Eastern part of the Empire, the only part whose existence was real and not fictitious. These dangers consisted in the onslaught of the barbarians upon Europe. There were remnants of the Germans, Lombards, Gepids and Heruls in the valley of the Danube, remnants of Huns, behind whom there already appeared Turkish, Bulgarian and Avar tribes, and finally the innumerable herds of the Slavs; in Asia there was above all the Persian Empire. Here it was not a question of barbarians. It was a rival civilization to that of the Romans. Persia represented along with China and Rome one of the three or four organized civilizations amongst which mankind was divided, and it was exceedingly formidable because of the religious fanaticism inspiring the Persians, who were followers of Mazdaism. Fortunately for Justinian, there were difficulties about the succession of Khobad. Chosroes, being a prey to internal troubles, accepted the peace overtures, the issue of which was the treaty for " perpetual " peace of 532, disadvantageous to the Romans but securing the frontiers for some years. The barbarians were neutralized as far as was possible by means of subsidies and dissensions fomented by the Imperial diplomacy. Hence in 523 Justinian had his hands free. He forthwith began the attack against the German kings of the West.

The weakest at this moment was the Vandal. The State, created by the military and above all diplomatic genius of Gaiserich had never been powerful.[1] The Vandals were

[1] DLXIV, 3; CDXLV.

not at all numerous; when they had crossed the Mediterranean a hundred years before (422), they were only 80,000 all told, including even the remnants of the Alan people. Gaiserich had at once seen that it would have been folly to disperse his people over the vast area of Northern Africa. Having conquered, he had concentrated it in Proconsular Africa (North of modern Tunisia). Slowly but surely the attraction of Latin civilization had worked on the Vandals and enervated them.[1]

A German reaction had however carried a new man, Gelimer, to the throne (May 19th, 530). But in spite of his magnificent dash, he possessed none of the qualities of a statesman. Justinian, under a specious pretext, posed as the avenger of the family of the dethroned King, Hilderich, and attacked the Vandal Kingdom in Africa. The enterprise frightened very much the Emperor's entourage. People remembered the disaster of the previous century; in 468, a Byzantine great Armada, commanded by Basiliscus, had been surprised at the *promontorium Mercurii* (Cape Bon) and annihilated by the Vandal fleet. Justinian's will, however, prevailed over the pusillanimous prudence of his Court.

In June, 533, a fleet of 500 vessels sailed for Africa. It conveyed a small army of 10,000 infantry and 5,000 cavalry, in all 15,000 men, this being all the forces that the Empire could muster. At the head of the " Romans " was Belisarius, the best general of the time, who had already distinguished himself in the struggle against the Persians. The army was able to disembark without meeting any resistance near *Caput Vada* (Ras Kapudia) between Sousse and Sfax, the Vandal fleet and best troops being in Sardinia, engaged in putting down a revolt (September 533). Belisarius marched on Carthage, following the coastline and accompanied by the fleet.

The encounter with Gelimer took place at *Decimum* not far from modern Tunis. It was disastrous for the Vandal, who fled into Numidia. Carthage fell into the hands of Belisarius who made his entry on September 15th, 533. Gelimer made a second attempt; he rallied the remnants of the Vandals in Africa, recalled the troops from Sardinia, hired some Moors, and offered battle at *Tricamarum* (30 kilometres

---

[1] See above, p. 209.

from Carthage) ; one charge of the Byzantine cavalry sufficed to break the Vandal army (the middle of December). This was the end. A few months later, Gelimer had to surrender with his family to the conqueror. He figured in the train of Belisarius, in the Roman triumph which was celebrated with great pomp at Constantinople. The remnants of the Vandals were enrolled in the army of the new Rome. The Vandal Kingdom was destroyed for ever. After this unforeseen and decisive success Justinian's head was turned ; he celebrated it in grandiloquent terms and assumed the titles of Vandalicus and Africanus.

For the moment, the conquest was only partial. Besides Tripolitana, it included Byzacena and Proconsularis or roughly Tunisia, Numidia and Mauretania Sitifensis, that is to say, the province of Constantine in modern Algeria, scattered posts along Africa up to Septem (Ceuta) which was considered impregnable, and lastly Corsica, Sardinia and the Balearic Islands. But the Empire could not recover a footing in the interior of Mauretania Cæsariensis and in Mauretania Tingitana, that is to say the provinces of modern Algiers, Oran and the North of Morocco. We have seen[1] that these last districts had in fact fallen away from Roman rule long before the coming of the Vandals ; as early as the beginning of the fifth century and even in the second half of the fourth century, they were virtually lost to Rome. The Moors there had made themselves independent and were rapidly returning to barbarism. They became " Berbers " as we still call them nowadays.

But even within these reduced boundaries, it was a fine conquest. The sequel however showed that it was not very solid.

Italy[2].—The death of Theodoric the Great in 526 relaxed the strain between the Goths and the Empire. The old king had designated as his successor his grandson Athalaric, aged ten, who until his majority was to be under the authority of his mother Amalasuntha. The Empire accepted and encouraged these arrangements. The regent mother, conscious of the difficulties of her task, was careful in her relations with the Empire and the Roman element in Italy ;

---

[1] See page 246.
[2] DLXIII, LXVI, vol. ii. ; CCX, CCXXXI.

the Senate was treated with deference, the Catholics were in favour, the children of Boethius and of Symmachus were recalled and their possessions restored to them. A Roman, Liberius, was even seen holding, with the title of *Patricius præsentalis*, military functions which allowed him to command the Gothic army.

This Roman reaction went too far and roused the indignation of the Goths. The rumour spread that the regent wanted to deliver Italy to the Emperor. The unforeseen death of Athalaric at the age of eighteen (October 2nd, 534), finally ruined the situation. The regent wished to keep her power by taking as partner her cousin Theodahad whom she married. But he meant to seize the throne. Amalasuntha was imprisoned in the island on Lake Bolsena (North of Viterbo) and there she was found dead soon afterwards (April 30th, 535).

Justinian found the pretext for which he was looking. Amalasuntha had recognized the nominal authority of the Empire and her accession to the throne had been brought about with the consent of the Empire. All relations with the royal assassin were broken off.

Belisarius was charged to take possession of Italy. He had at his disposal only a ridiculously insufficient army (about 10,000 men). These weak forces were enough for him to take Sicily while the *magister militum* Mundo was making himself master of Dalmatia (end of 535).

Theodahad, even more than the Vandal Gelimer, was incapable of putting up a serious resistance to the " Romans " of the East. He was no longer anything of a Goth. Brought up in the Roman fashion in the love of letters, he prided himself on being a Platonist and on despising arms.[1] At the end of 536, Belisarius, landing in Italy, seized Naples and entered Rome, acclaimed by the people, who hated the Goths for being foreigners and above all Arians.

It seemed that the recapture of Italy was now only a question of days and would be as rapid as that of Africa. But this illusion was soon shattered. The Goths showed infinitely more energy and ability than the Vandals. Theodahad had just been overthrown ; on the field of *Regeta* (near Rome), the degenerate Amalung was despoiled of his attributes of royalty by the Gothic army, which raised on the shield an officer

[1] **DLXIII,** 182.

of low birth but full of bravery, Witigis. The retaking of Italy, which had seemed mere child's play, took eighteen years of sanguinary and ruinous wars, in which the Imperial arms suffered such serious reverses that more than once victory seemed to slip from them. Byzantium employed the system of small detachments which the French have too often used in their colonial wars and which protracts the fighting interminably. We will not give the details. They may be read in the *History of the Gothic Wars* of the Syrian Procopius of Cæsarea, the secretary of Belisarius.

The following are only some noteworthy stages in the war : the first siege of Rome in which Belisarius had to take refuge (in March 537) ; with 5,000 men he succeeded in defending the huge town against Witigis for a whole year. In March 538, Witigis had to raise the siege and a Byzantine auxiliary army took possession of Northern Italy. In 540, Witigis, shut in at Ravenna, fell into the power of the Byzantines, thanks to an act of treachery on the part of Belisarius, and was led off to Constantinople ; there he received honourable treatment.

The Goths submitted and Justinian thought the conquest of Italy complete. He added to his titles that of *Gothicus*, appointed a Prætorian Prefect as governor of the province and led back the greater part of the army to the East.

But the Goths recovered. After some unsuccessful attempts, their choice fell on Totila (or rather Badvila) who is undoubtedly the most attractive character of the period. Both generous and humane and a good warrior and statesman, he prevented the massacre of women and children in the assaults of towns and forbade carnage in the country districts. He is the only chivalrous figure in these times of trickery and treachery. He had not made up his mind to be an enemy to the Empire. He was even negotiating for his submission at the moment when he was elected. But as soon as he was chosen by his people he thought only of saving them.

With 5,000 men he defeated a Byzantine army of 12,000 near Faenza and detached Northern Italy ; a second victory at Mugillo (*Mucella*) in Tuscany delivered Central Italy to him. In the spring of 543 he was master of Naples and of the south. Finally he besieged Rome. Belisarius, sent to the help of Rome, disembarked at Porto ; but, owing to insufficient troops, he failed in his move. Rome opened her gates to the Gothic King (December 17th, 546). Totila in his exasperation thought of rasing the city to the ground, but was stopped by the representations of his opponent Belisarius who made him realize the horror of this action. In the years which followed, the Gothic King completed the conquest of Italy to which he added Sicily, Sardinia and Corsica ; he formed a fleet which ravaged the coasts of Dalmatia and Epirus. Established at Rome, Totila seemed more master of Italy than Theodoric had ever been. " All the West was in the hands of the barbarians," says Procopius (*B.G.*, 416). Justinian's plan was now no more than a dream of the past. He himself seemed to forget it ; he appeared overcome by old age and lost in theological controversies.[1]

At last, in 551, the Emperor resolved to make a supreme effort. His apparently quite absurd choice lighted on an aged eunuch, seventy-five years old, Narses, who was filling the post of Grand Chamberlain. Narses possessed unshakeable fidelity and was endowed with an unconquerable energy. Justinian supplied him with the resources which he had grudged Belisarius, 20,000 to 25,000 men.

Narses chose as the base of his operations Dalmatia and resolved to gain a footing in Northern Italy first of all, although hitherto it had been the practice to begin with Southern Italy. Totila, being alarmed, offered to acknowledge the Emperor's supremacy and to pay tribute, but Justinian refused. The decision came quickly in 552. Narses, setting out from Ravenna, marched straight South. Totila, issuing from Rome by the *via Flaminia*, went to encounter him. The engagement took place at *Tadinæ* (not *Taginæ*), the present Gualdo Tadino in the Umbrian Apennines.[2]

The Roman force was a large army, superior to the Gothic and numbering about 20,000 men. The elements composing it illustrate what a " Roman " army consisted of in the sixth century. There were 2,500 Lombards sent from Pannonia by their King Audoin, for a sum of money, of course ; under Narses, 3,000 Heruls and a great number of Huns ; Dagisthæus, a Persian enemy of Chosroes, drawn from his captivity, with his suite ; a Herul, Aruth, with his band ; and Johannes

[1] DLXIII, 196.
[2] CDXLIII, 109.

with his band. It was an army of *condottieri*, not a single soldier of which was Roman, not even the commander Narses being, as is shown by his name, of Armenian or Persian origin. The main body consisted of cavalry, and these horse-men were cuirassiers armed with the sword and bow ; they charged while shooting arrows rather like the cuirassiers of the time of Louis XIV, who charged with pistols in their hands. The vicissitudes of the battle, it is said, present some analogies to those of Crécy.[1] The lines of the Goths were broken and Totila was mortally wounded (the Spring of 552).[2] The Goths, in spite of this, wished to make one last trial of their fortune. At Pavia they elected Teïas who was finally run down by Narses in Campania on *Mons Lactarius* (Monte Lettere) opposite Vesuvius. The Goths put up a desperate resistance ; Teïas, after having fought like a hero, met his death (553).

The following year Frankish and Aleman bands, called in by the Goths, traversed Italy, pillaging enemies and friends indifferently, under the leadership of Leutharis and Buccelin. They were decimated by illness and crushed by the Byzan-tines, near Capua (Autumn of 554). Meanwhile there still remained some Goths who had taken refuge in a fortress amongst the Apennines, Compsæ ; these capitulated to the number of 7,000. Having been enlisted in the service of the Empire, they were led against the Persians in the East (555). The last Gothic garrisons holding Brescia and Verona in the North persevered in their resistance until 563.[3]

The Gothic nation was thus extirpated in Italy. It has no racial or linguistic part in the history of the country.

" *Narses patricius Italiam Romano imperio reddidit urbesque dirutas restauravit totiusque Italiæ populos, expulsis Gothis, ad pristinum reducit gaudium* ", says a chronicler.[4] An inscription in honour of Narses, found on the bridge of the Anio (destroyed by the Neapolitans in 1798), spoke of him as having restored liberty to Rome and the whole of Italy.[5]

The Pragmatic Sanction of 554 reorganized Italy into a Roman province. It was governed by a Viceroy or

---

[1] **CCCLXIII**, 34.
[2] **CVIII**, vol. ii., 367-379.
[3] **CCCLXIII**, 34.
[4] Prosper, *Mon. Germ.*, *Auctores antiq.*, ix., 267, 337.
[5] *Corpus inscript. Lat.*, vi., 1199.

Exarch, residing at Ravenna, and bearing the title of Patrician.

Justinian applied himself to restoring the Roman Government in all its details, as though nothing had happened since 476. The absolute separation of civil from military functions, which he himself tended to abandon for the East, was re-established in all its strictness. This shows an obvious resolve to go back to the past.

Spain.[1]—For a moment it seemed likely that Justinian would be able to reunite Spain also to the Empire. The Visigothic State seemed to be in a sorry position after the defeat of Alaric II (508). Without the all-powerful protection of Theodoric the Great it would have been swept away by the storm. After the great King's death (526), Amalaric once more found himself powerless to resist the Franks. Yet he had married a daughter of Clovis, named Clotilda after her mother ; but he ill-treated her to make her abandon Catholicism for Arianism. The queen complained to her brother, Childebert, the "King of Paris", who led a victorious expedition against his brother-in-law. Having been vanquished near Narbonne, Amalaric took to flight and was assassinated by his own soldiers (531). The Visigothic Kingdom was saved by Theudis, an Ostrogoth who had been Governor of Spain when that country had been under the authority of Theodoric. He repelled the Franks who were taking possession of Septimania and had invested Pampeluna and Saragossa. For a moment he recaptured *Septem* (Ceuta) from the Byzantines. But he was assassinated by a madman at Seville in 548. His successor met with the same fate, in the same town, a year later.

Agila, who assumed the power, was unable to take possession of Baetica, where the population rose against the Goths, not so much for reasons of nationality as from religious motives, since Agila, who was a zealous Arian, persecuted the Catholics.

A great Visigoth, Athanagild, who was perhaps a Catholic in secret, then set up as a claimant to the throne and appealed to Justinian for help. The Emperor sent to him the Patrician Liberius (he had been previously entrusted with the task of recapturing Sicily from Totila) with some troops. The

[1] **DLIV,** vol. v. ; **DXXIII,** vol. i. ; **DXXV,** vol. i.

Roman Patrician met with no serious resistance ; for, although he was an old man and little versed in the art of war, he was able quickly to become master of the Mediterranean coasts of Spain, Valencia, Carthagena, Malaga, and later Murcia and Cordova. King Agila, attacked by Liberius and Athanagild near Seville, was beaten, and soon afterwards slain by his soldiers, who acknowledged Athanagild (554).

Athanagild would have liked very much to get rid of his allies. But the Romans from the East were in possession practically of the old provinces of Baetica and Carthaginiensis. The Visigothic King then transferred his seat of government to the centre of the peninsula, at Toledo ; from there he was more easily able not only to fight against the invaders of the Empire, but also to proceed in the North against the Franks and the Basques who had made themselves independent in the mountains of Cantabria. It was there that he died at the end of 567.

His successor Leovigild announced his accession to the throne to Justin II—Justinian had died two years before—and asked for his approval. Hence it appears that the Visigothic King still acknowledged the theoretical supremacy of the Empire for the part of the Spanish territory over which he reigned. Having vanquished the Sueves in the Northwest, he struck a commemorative medal on the reverse of which still appears the bust of Justin II. Nevertheless, with the exception of the coasts, the interior of the peninsula slipped from the real rule of the Empire.

Gaul.—Against Gaul Justinian attempted nothing.[1] He even abandoned to the Franks (536) Provence, which the Ostrogoths had held as an annex of Italy.[2]

With these reservations, it must be acknowledged that, in the middle of the sixth century, the coasts were almost without a break in the power of the Emperor, and the Mediterranean became once more a " Roman " lake.

At the end of his days, Justinian was able to imagine that he had, after all, nearly realized the plan of his youth and maturity, the recapture of the West by the Empire.

He knew that his legislative work, and his monumental

---

[1] **DLXIII**, 206.
[2] G. DE MANTEYER, *La Province du premier au douzième siècle*, p. 26.

and artistic achievements, the innumerable fortifications scattered from the Atlantic to the Euphrates and from the Danube to the deserts of Africa, the construction of St. Sophia, the world's marvel, would hand down his name to future generations. " To-day two things still remain : the code of Justinian and St. Sophia plead for ever before posterity the cause of the great Emperor."[1] He could consider himself the worthy successor if not of Augustus and Trajan, at least of Diocletian, Constantine and Theodosius.

We shall see that this greatness was artificial and that his work was perishable and even harmful.

---

[1] **DLXIII**, 32, 662-666.

CHAPTER IV

THE FAILURE OF JUSTINIAN'S WORK

I. IN AFRICA[1]

THE victory of Belisarius in 533 was too sudden to be lasting. He had easily vanquished the Vandals. His successors were as powerless with the natives, the Moors (Berbers), as the Vandals, and before them, the Romans in the fourth century had been. The soldiers in the service of the Empire displayed extraordinary cupidity and lack of discipline. From 535 to 548, Africa enjoyed scarcely a moment's rest. The best generals of the Empire, Belisarius, Germanus, the eunuch Solomon and Johannes Troglita exhausted themselves for nearly fifteen years in fruitless attempts to restore peace. When they succeeded, in the middle of the sixth century, the provinces were depopulated and ruined.

We may allow that the work of the Byzantines in Africa is not entirely to be condemned. The Vandals' rule had doubtless been worse ; it had harassed its subjects and even practised religious persecution and had been powerless with the Berbers. But it may be asked if, for the good of the Empire itself, it would not have been better to concentrate instead of scattering its forces. What proves how little solid was its rule in Africa, is the ease of the Moslem conquest in the following century. Cyrenaïca was conquered as early as 660 ; Proconsular Africa was attacked in 670 ; finally Carthage succumbed in 698.

II. IN ITALY

Italy and Rome, which were still flourishing under the Gothic rule, came out exhausted from the interminable wars of the *reconquista*. The Byzantine armies composed of

---

[1] **DLXIV, CCCXXV**, vol. iii.-iv.

barbarians more savage than the Goths, were at least as much
to be feared by the inhabitants as the latter. Franks and
Alemans, towards the end of the wars, fell like wolves upon
this country. In 554, when all was finished, Italy was
ruined, depopulated and at her last gasp, in a worse position
than Germany's after the Thirty Years' War.[1] To crown
her sufferings, she had to taste the *pristinum gaudium* mentioned
by the continuator of Prosper and the inscription of the Anio
bridge.[2] This "joy of yore" presented itself to the people
become once more " Roman " under the form of a crushing
taxation.[3]

Rome, taken and re-taken five times, was only the shadow
of herself. Under Theodoric she still had a population of
several hundred thousand inhabitants and was the finest
town in the West. After the Gothic wars we find her deprived
of nine-tenths of her population. Many buildings had perished in the flames ; not only the temples but the Imperial
palaces on the Palatine were falling in ruins, through want
of upkeep. The aqueducts had been cut and in the neighbourhood of Rome the " Roman Campagna " finally took on
the look of poignant melancholy which it has kept to our own
times.[4]

For a moment Rome was even nearly destroyed. In
December 546, Totila thought of rasing her to the ground.
Procopius attributes to Belisarius an eloquent protest against
the idea of annihilating the finest work which mankind had
ever raised, the wonderful monument of man's greatness.
Totila dtd noi carry out his threats. He did not destroy
Rome and committed no massacres, but he insisted
on the complete evacuation of the town by its inhabitants.
For forty days, Rome presented the spectacle of Nineveh or
Babylon.

Even after the storm had passed, Rome, deeply stricken,
could not recover even a feeble portion of her past splendour.
It had been an artificial splendour for many centuries, the
population being kept by distributions of provisions. These
Justinian abolished. Henceforth, a few thousand inhabitants lived on the pilgrims whom they exploited and on the

---

[1] This at least is the opinion of L.-M. HARTMANN, **DXCV,** vol. i., 353.
[2] See above, p. 263.
[3] **DLXV, DXCVI.**
[4] **DLXXXIX** and **DXC, DCXX, XXII, DCLXXXVII.**

charity of the Pope. The last circus games were given by
Totila himself in 549. The last triumph was that of Narses
in 552. But there was no longer any Consul after 541. The
Senate disappeared in an obscure fashion; the last certain
mention of this body is in 579[1]: it was an embassy to Constantinople, which was at the same time a delegation from
the Pope, a sign of the times.

The " Prefect of the City " continued, but he fell under
the authority of the Pope, who replaced the Emperor for
the purpose of maintaining and feeding the people. " In
the terrible storm of the Gothic war, ancient life had disappeared for ever. In the burnt and deserted town, only
the ruins bore witness to its vanished prosperity. The
Sibyl's prophecy was accomplished. A deep night spread
over the Latin world and in this darkness no light shone any
longer except the tapers of the churches and the solitary
lamp of the monk inside the monasteries ".[2]

The irony of things brought it about that Justinian, who
wanted to reunite Italy to the Empire, dealt that country
a terrible blow. By extirpating the Goths, he took away
from it the only force capable of protecting it against the
barbarians of the Danube, the Lombards and Avars who
threatened it. By subjugating and dominating over the
bishop of Rome, he gradually suggested to him the idea of
detaching himself from Constantinople which oppressed him
and of seeking for support elsewhere. The pontifical theo-
cracy of the Middle Ages and of modern times germinated
amongst the ruins of ancient Rome.

III. IN THE EAST

Even in the East, if Justinian's was a great reign, it was
so only in comparison with his contemporaries. It is
certain that our Frankish and Visigothic sovereigns were
kinglets in comparison. But what shadows there are in the
picture !

To have his hands free in the West, the Emperor had been
obliged to pay the barbarians and Persians tributes disguised
under the name of subsidies. He gained only a precarious

---

[1] **DLXIII,** 662 ; **DXC,** 146.
[2] **DLXXXIX,** vol. i., 453.

security from them. Several times the Balkan peninsula and even Greece were terribly ravaged. The Slavs introduced themselves into the Empire by committing horrible massacres. They seized Hadrianople and reached the Adriatic at Durazzo. In 558, the Emperor was threatened by the Kuturgur Huns, and even in Constantinople he trembled for his safety. A Tartar tribe, the Avars, appeared in 562 and showed itself perhaps no less terrible for the Empire than the Huns in the fifth century.

Plagues, famines, and repeated earthquakes completed the gloom of his reign.[1]

In Asia, the Persians indisputably had the upper hand.

The largest and richest town in the Empire after Constantinople, Antioch, suffered a terrible disaster. Already ruined under Justinian, in 526, by earthquakes of which, it is said, there were 250,000 victims, the town was wiped out by the Persian King Chosroes in 540. The population was massacred or led off into captivity. Not a stone was left standing. So complete was the disaster, that later, when an attempt was made to re-build the town, no trace was found of the streets or squares and a church was the only building which could be identified. Having reached the Mediterranean, the Iranian took possession of it by a symbolic ceremony. Justinian had to buy for gold (545) a five years' truce which was twice renewed. "Sad price for the successes won in the West,"[2] and won with what difficulty, as we have seen !

The internal reforms failed lamentably. At the beginning of his reign, the Emperor had set himself the task of putting an end to the peculation and tyranny of his functionaries ; he wanted to relieve the peoples of the burden of an oppressive and rapacious system of taxation, and at the same time to increase the State's revenues. All was useless. At the end as at the beginning of the reign, fulminations are still hurled against the oppression of a hateful and corrupt administration which sold justice, appropriated the public revenues and did not even ensure security, since brigandage was rife. The finances were in a desperate condition and the straits of the Treasury paralysed the Emperor's undertakings.

[1] DLXIII, 218, 410, 423.
[2] DLXIII, 222.

The evil was too deep to be corrected by means of *Novels*. Its seat was at the Court itself. The Emperor's circle left much to be desired. Trebonian, the Quæstor of the Sacred Palace, that is to say the Grand Chancellor and Minister of Justice, a famous jurist, sold justice ; the Prætorian Prefect, John of Cappadocia, amassed an enormous fortune at the expense of the State. The Empress herself, Theodora, who controlled the government at least as much as Justinian, was not exactly without stain, even if we do not accept the infamies recounted by Procopius who takes his revenge like a dismissed footman in his *Secret History*. Byzantine corruption was incurable.

Justinian would have been very much surprised if he had been told that he was a " Byzantine " Emperor. He looked upon himself as the true successor of the Cæsars, as a Roman Emperor whose task it was to restore the Roman world in its integrity. His ephemeral successes inflated him with a naïve pride : " Never except under our reign has God granted the Romans to achieve such triumphs (*Nov.* I., *præf.*). Inhabitants of the world, give thanks to heaven, which has reserved for our century the accomplishment of so great a work. That of which Antiquity did not seem worthy, in God's judgment, has been realized in our time (Constitution *Tanta*, 19)."[1]

But in reality as early as the reign of Justinian even, the Roman Empire, the old *pars Orientis*, was no longer Roman except in name.[2] It owed to Rome its political organization which it would have been incapable of establishing by its own forces. But its spirit and fortunes were rapidly moving it away from all intercourse with Latinity.

In the first place, in this " Roman " Empire, which until the end of the eighth century was still called the *Respublica Romanorum*, where are the Roman citizens ? The country population, composed of peasants of every race, was reduced to a condition of base subjection to the State and the large landed proprietors. It was a mob from which the fiscus and the aristocracy could demand forced labour and *taille* and which counted for absolutely nothing in the political life of the Empire.

[1] **DLXIII**, 661-666 ; cf. 31.
[2] **DLII**.

The population of the towns was even more heterogeneous racially, consisting of tradesmen of every race and of a miserable and insolent plebs, capable of raising a riot on the slightest pretext, and therefore feared, fed and kept amused, but devoid of all feeling of patriotism and of any high political conception. The forces of the State resided (1) in the army, that is to say, in the barbarian *condottieri;* (2) in the bureaucracy. The latter maintained Rome's traditions of unification and centralization. The landed aristocracy, Roman by origin as regards a small fraction of it (a few senatorial families at Constantinople) was completely severed from the West and Latinity.

The strongest support of a nationality or a civilization is language. Latin was still the " national " language of the Empire in the sixth century. Justinian himself declares it.[1] The real founder of the Empire which was to become the " Byzantine " Empire, Constantine, knew so little Greek that he had to have the Latin speeches which he made before the Councils translated into this language.[2] At Constantinople Latin remained the language of the Court and of the administration. At the beginning of the fifth century, according to the evidence of St. John Chrysostom, it was impossible to make one's way without a knowledge of Latin. The inscriptions even in Batanæa (*Hauran*) populated by Arabs are in Latin. Latin was the language of the army. Even in Syria the soldiers were for a long time obliged to use Latin. In Egypt, on the Statue of Memnon inscriptions are found made by the garrisons, and they are in Latin.

Latin was the language of legislation. The oldest code, a collection of Imperial constitutions, was due to Theodosius II, an Emperor who had never left Constantinople (408-450). The larger collections, compiled by Justinian, the Code and the Pandects, are naturally in Latin. Even the titles and commentaries, which might have been in Greek, are in Latin. Similarly the law manual for students and practising lawyers, the *Institutions*, drawn up by Theophilus and Dorotheus, was also in Latin.

---

[1] *Nov.*, vii., 1 ; cf. *Nov.*, xv., praef., 66, 1. 2.
[2] **CXXVI**, vol. ii., 146 ; **CCCXXII**, vol. ii. ; **CXXXIV**, note 7.

In the two great Law faculties, at Constantinople and especially Beirut (Berytus), there is no doubt that the teaching was in Latin.[1] Moreover, the great Latin lawyers of the West in the third century, Papinian and Ulpian, had already come from this school.

In contradistinction to a Julian, an Alexander Severus, a Marcus Aurelius and even a Hadrian, who felt themselves more Greek than Latin, Justinian wished to be a Latin Roman Emperor.

He was confirmed in these feelings by his horror of Hellenism. A Roman Emperor, Justinian was also a Christian Emperor. He considered himself the pillar of the Christian orthodox faith. The Hellenic spirit is profoundly pagan and Justinian abominated it. For him, as for his contemporaries and successors, Hellene was synonymous with pagan and to call anyone by this term was to insult him. The Greek peoples themselves assumed the name ' Ῥωμαῖοι (Romans). Even to-day *Romios* is still used by the common people. Hellene is an artificial term revived in the nineteenth century. The capital of the Empire is called *Roum* by the Arab and Turkish peoples of Asia.

But, in reality, the language and consequently the thought was no longer Latin in any degree. The only part of the Empire where the *lingua Romana* was still spoken was the fragment of *Illyricum* which had been left to the *pars Orientis*. It was of this part of the Empire that Justinian (born near Uskub) was a native, and to this circumstance must be attributed the artificial prolongation of the Latinity of the Empire.

Further, Latin Illyria, thirty years after Justinian's death, was submerged by the Slavs, and the fragments of the Illyrian populations who still spoke the *lingua Romana*, whence sprang *Vlak*, the Roumanian-Macedonian language, were reduced to wandering shepherds or else pushed back towards the coast. The coast towns, Durazzo, Spalato-Salona and Ragusa, up to the fifteenth century, kept the use of a language sprung from Latin and later from Venetian.[2]

Not far from Uskub began the undisputed predominance

---

[1] However Greek replaced Latin as early as the end of the fourth century, according to COLLINET, LXXXVII, 222. This date seems to us too early.

[2] CCXLIX, DCCXIV. Cf. HAMMANT in *Revue Historique*, March, 1917, 287-304.

of Greek. The boundary between the two languages[1] and the two civilizations ran between *Remesiana* (nowadays Bela-Palanka, about 50 kilometres east of Nish in Serbia) which was Latin-speaking, and *Turres* (now Pirot) which was Greek-speaking. Not only in Thrace, Moesia and Asia Minor but even in Syria and Egypt the everyday and official language was Greek. Even in the capital of the Empire, the New Rome, the preponderance of Greek was marked in spite of all. In the first half of the fifth century, Latin and Greek seem nearly to balance each other. Under Theodosius, at the University of Constantinople, we find ten Chairs of Grammar for Latin and ten for Greek ; but only three Chairs of Rhetoric for Latin against five for Greek ; on the other hand if the Chair of Philosophy, as was certainly the case, taught in Greek, the two Chairs of Law as certainly taught in Latin.

The inscriptions of the town were sometimes in Latin, sometimes in Greek. But it is to be noted that under Theodosius I, the Governor of the town, Cyrus of Panoplia, published his orders in Greek. If we are told that Pulcheria, the sister of Theodosius II, spoke and wrote Latin, the reason is that this fact, no doubt, appeared unusual enough to be noticed.

In the course of the fifth and of the following century, the retreat of Latin was rapid. It became headlong even under the reign of Justinian. The commentaries on his collections of laws are in Greek and the authors of these commentaries are partly men like Theophilus and Dorotheus, who were employed to write the manual called the *Institutions*. It is obvious that for the everyday practice of law, it was necessary to use the spoken language, Greek. It was at Byzantium as in England, where the law commentaries even in the seventeenth century were still in French, although French was unknown to the large majority of the people ; the jurists nevertheless thought themselves bound to write their treatises in French, though a very curious French.

There was more and worse : the Emperor himself, after the great compilations of the *Code* and the *Digest*, which form the basis of law but represent the past, had to issue new constitutions, *Novels*, for the needs of the present. We possess 154 of these, from 534 to 565 ; the great majority

[1] CCXXXIII, 320.

are written in the Greek language and Justinian tells us the reason : " We have not written this law in the *national* language (Latin), but in the common tongue, which is Greek, *in order that it may be known by all*, because of the ease with which it will be understood ".[1]   A confession significant in its unconsciousness.

Nov., vii., 1.

CHAPTER V

VISIGOTHIC SPAIN[1]

WHILE Italy, and especially Gaul and the East, had had to suffer without any respite from barbarians who had been constantly pressing against the frontiers since the third century, Spain had enjoyed an almost uninterrupted peace, politically at least; for the severe measures against the Christians continued longer in Spain than in Gaul. Gaul was in effect governed by Constantius Chlorus, the Cæsar, while Spain was governed directly by Maximian Herculius, the Augustus. But in 305, Constantius Cæsar took Spain, and the persecution ceased. In 332, the political and administrative geography of the country underwent an alteration. The number of provinces was increased from three to five by the parcelling out of Tarraconensis.[2] There were henceforth five provinces: Baetica, with its capital *Hispalis* (Seville), Tarraconensis proper (capital Tarragona, later Cæsarea Augusta or Saragossa); Lusitania, with its capital Merida (*Emerita Augusta*); Gallaecia with its capital Astorga or *Braccara* (Braga); and Carthaginiensis with its capital Carthagena. There were two annexes: the Balearic Islands with Palma as the capital and Mauretania Tingitana with the capital *Tingis* (Tangier). Together these formed the diocese of the Spains, governed by a Vicar who resided at *Hispalis* and was under the Prætor of the Gauls, residing at Trèves, later at Arles. The ecclesiastical was modelled on the administrative organization: a metropolitan was established in every capital of a province; but Toledo was substituted for Carthagena, and this was to bring about political consequences in the far future. In 409 this calm was suddenly troubled by the arrival of the barbarians who had been devastating Gaul for two years: Alans, Sueves, Asding Vandals and Siling Vandals. For two years Spain was sacked,

---

[1] **DXXIII**, vol. i.; **DXXV**, vol. ii.; **DLIV**, vol. v. and vi.
[2] ALBERTINI, *Les divisions administratives de l'Espagne romaine* (1923).

especially in the West where there were no longer any Roman troops. The towns however seem to have escaped, except Carthagena, which was ruined, though not till later (425). In 411, a treaty with the Empire intervened. The brigands were cantoned as Federates : the Sueves and Asding Vandals in Gallaecia ; the Siling Vandals in Baetica ; the Alans, who were probably the most numerous, in Lusitania and Carthaginiensis. There remained Tarraconensis. But from the following year Honorius abandoned it, along with Narbonensis in Gaul, to Athaulf and the Visigoths. Athaulf's successor Wallia undertook to clear Spain of the barbarians in the name of the Emperor ; the Siling Vandals were exterminated and their King (Fredbal) was sent to Italy as a prisoner ; the Alans found themselves so weakened that they joined the Asding Vandals and acknowledged their King who henceforth took the title of *rex Vandalorum et Alanorum*. But the Visigoths were led back into Gaul in 418 and settled from Bordeaux to Toulouse. The Asding Vandals were then the masters of Spain. They pushed the Sueves back into the mountains of the North (Cantabria) and defeated a Roman army led by Castinus (421-422). They did not however stay there. A new king, Gaiserich, led all his people (Asding Vandals and Alans) into Africa. The embarkation took place in May 429. The whole of the barbarian people numbered only 80,000 souls.[1]

There remained now in Spain only the Sueves, the least numerous of the invaders, weakened moreover by a sanguinary defeat near Merida, sustained at the hands of Gaiserich before his embarkation. Hence it would seem that nothing could have been easier than to re-establish the authority of the Empire in Spain. But it was not so. The Suevian Kings defeated the Roman troops (439) and succeeded in taking Merida and Seville, which made them masters of Lusitania and Bætica. Rome suffered a new defeat in 446. The treaty of 454 now only left to the Empire Tarraconensis and Carthaginiensis.

The only force which could be opposed to the Sueves were the Visigoths. As early as 456, Theodosius II crossed the Pyrenees, beat the Sueves, captured their King Rechiar, who was put to death, and set up a governor (a Varnian,

[1] **CDXLV.**

Agiwulf) over the conquered people. In spite of their further raids, the power of the Sueves was broken. Theodoric pretended to act in the name of the Emperor Avitus, who was his creature and was deposed in this very year.

The year 459 saw for the last time a Roman Emperor in Gaul, Majorian, who came there to prepare an expedition against the Vandals, which failed.

It was with Euric[1] that the Goths took possession of the whole of Spain. In 469 he expelled the Sueves from Lusitania and thrust them back into Gallæcia, where they were henceforth confined, undergoing the influence of the Goths, who made them pass from Catholicism to Arianism. At the fall of the Western Empire, only Tarraconensis was left to the Empire. Zeno yielded it to Euric (477). The whole of Spain henceforth belonged to the Visigoths. Yet their kings did not live there. They prefered Gaul where they extended their rule as far as the Loire.

The Gothic power was nearly wrecked after the defeat and death of Alaric II at Vouillé in 507. The Visigothic Monarchy was saved by Theodoric, King of the Goths in Italy, who prevented the Franks from taking possession of Provence and Septimania, and posed as the guardian of Amalaric, the son of Amalaric II and of his own daughter Thiudigotha, Amalaric being a minor. Until 536 Gaulish Gothia, from the Alps to the Pyrenees, as well as Spain, was under the influence of Theodoric. Amalaric continued to reign in Gaul at Narbonne. It was there that he died (in 531) after being beaten by the Franks. The line of the Baltungs came to an end in his person.

The disappearance of this sacred family had serious consequences for the stability of the kingdom in Spain. Amalaric's successor was his governor Theudis, who transferred his seat to Barcelona in Spain. He succeeded in fighting against the Franks ; in 532, Theodebert and Guntrum advanced as far as Béziers ; in 542 Childebert and Clotar took Pampeluna and besieged Saragossa.

Until then the Hispano-Roman peoples had submitted to everything for nearly a century and a half. We hear of only one attempt at resistance by the aristocracy of Tarraconensis in 476, similar to the one in Auvergne in the same

[1] DXV.

period. But it was not of any great importance; some nobles, large landowners, armed their clients and slaves.

Spain like Gaul knew the "Bagaudæ": they are mentioned in 435, 436, 449; Tarragona was then taken by Basil, the leader of the rebels. In 453, the Bagaudæ were exterminated close to Tarragona by Frederic, the brother of Theodoric II. We have no reliable information about this movement. It seems really to have been a social revolution, a kind of peasants' revolt, directed against all the rich, Romans as well as barbarians, and not a national movement against foreigners.

In the mountains of Cantabria, the imperfectly Romanized inhabitants became once more barbarians; they lost the use of Latin and spoke only the Iberian language, Basque. They took the offensive and began to spread over the plains. Later they were a source of serious anxiety to the Gothic and Frankish Kings; they advanced as far as the Adour; in the seventh century under the name of Vascons or Gascons they took possession of the country between the Pyrenees and the Garonne.[1]

Apart from this exception, all was quiet. But the Goths were pious and fanatical Arians. They persecuted the Catholics and left the bishoprics vacant; whence the hatred against them of the Catholic bishops of Spain, the only persons who had an ascendancy over the peoples since the disappearance of Roman authority.

The second successor of Theudis, Agila, who reigned from 549 to 554, transferred his seat from Barcelona to Merida on the Guadiana. His action was thus more direct on the South of Spain (Lusitania and Bætica) which till then had been neglected. When he tried to make his authority real, he came up against a rising of the Catholic peoples and was completely defeated under the walls of Cordova. We have seen that Justinian then intervened; the Patrician Liberius then seized the ports of Carthagena, Malaga and Cadiz and Bætica became for a time once more a Roman province. But the Emperor had too much business on his hands to go on with the *reconquista*, which was nevertheless not very difficult, and he stopped at that. Athanagild secured the neutrality of the Franks by marrying his daughters, Galswintha to

[1] **CCCIV**, 330.

Chilperic, and Brunhild to Sigebert, and transferred the capital
to Toledo. He died there in 567.

The Gothic monarchy was restored by Leovigild in the
second half of the sixth century. He retook Cordova and
Malaga from the Romans of the East, kept the Basques in
check (he founded Vittoria), annexed the kingdom of the
Sueves and repelled the Franks who had invaded Narbonensis.
Yet Leovigild dressed in the Byzantine fashion, had a throne,
and struck gold coins. His reign would have been a great
one but for the revival, at the end, of the hostilities between
Arians and Catholics. One of the King's sons, Hermenegild,
who was born of a Greek and Catholic mother and was the
husband of Ingundis the daughter of Brunhild and Sigebert,
was converted to Catholicism by Leander the metropolitan
of Seville. He revolted against his father and found support
in the towns of Merida, Seville and Cordova, which were still
opposed to Arianism. Having been defeated after a struggle
of several years, Hermenegild was put to death. Leovigild
died the following year (586).

His other son, Recared, immediately became converted to
Catholicism (589) and caused Arianism to disappear.[1] From
that time there was no longer any obstacle to the rapprochement if not to the immediate fusion of the Goths and the
Hispano-Romans. The Court adopted more and more
Byzantine ways ; Gothic disappeared before vulgar Latin ;
it goes without saying that official documents were always
written in classical Latin. The Gothic Kings of the seventh
century write in an inflated Latin. The prohibition against
marriage between Goths and Romans in conformity with
Roman law, doubtless a mere fiction in practice, had already
been removed by Leovigild.

Finally came the unity of law. Recared wished his edicts
to have the force of law for all the peoples living under his
authority, Goths, Sueves and Romans.[2] At last, in 654,
King Receswinth promulgated a code[3] the use of which he
imposed on the Romans as well as on the Goths, the *Lex
Romana Recessvindiana*, and forbade the use of the *Lex
Romana Visigothorum*, also called Alaric's Breviary, which

---

[1] **DCXXVII.**
[2] **DXLV,** vol. i., 489, 491, 514.
[3] His father Chindaswinth (642-653) had had the idea of this undertaking,
but had not been able to carry it out.

had been promulgated for the Romans by Alaric II at Toulouse in 506. Alaric's Breviary was henceforth used only in Septimania and Southern Gaul. The code of 654, in imitation of the Roman codes, is divided into twelve books and repeats the previous legislation, which is wholly steeped in Roman law. The legislative activity of the Visigothic King continued without any intermission, from Euric's reign to the fall of the kingdom. We have still Novels of Egica (died in 702) and of Witiza (died in 710). But this legislation of the seventh and eighth centuries, wholly ecclesiastical in inspiration and style, is only a mass of verbiage with no juridical force.[1]

It is a curious thing that apparently, in practice, Gothic law thrust forth deeper roots than the wholly Roman legislation of the Visigoth Kings would lead us to suppose. The Spanish *fueros* present striking resemblances to Norwegian-Icelandic law, according to Ficker, d'Amira, and K. Maurer.

In the seventh century, the lay and even the ecclesiastic Hispano-Roman aristocracy began to feel itself Gothic. Compare for example, the Chronicle of John of Biclar and that of Isidore of Seville, both of them dating from the reign of the Emperors ; the first is a Goth, but has resided at Constantinople, the second a Roman, the brother of the Leander of Cordova who brought about the conversion of the Kingdom to Catholicism. They are practically contemporaries (Isidore died in 636, John, it seems, twenty years before). The history of the second is of completely Gothic inspiration.[2] He applauds the recapture by Sisebut and Swinthila (in 624) of the towns which they took from the *Romana militia*, that is to say from the Byzantine Empire.

The descendants of the Hispano-Roman aristocracy gloried in their descent from the Goths.[3] The fusion of races was more advanced in Spain than elsewhere ; the country enjoyed a long rest and was less harassed than Gaul, Italy, and Africa. Nevertheless we see a deep and incurable decay of the State in the seventh century, in spite of the personal energy of the majority of the sovereigns.

[1] **DXLV**, vol. i., 493-494.
[2] See his *Laus Spaniae* and his *Dedicatio ad Sisenandum regem* (Mommsen's ed. *Chron. minora*, vol. ii., 26, 304, 479).
[3] *Hidalgo*, however, should not be taken as "son of a Goth". The meaning is *hi* (son) *d'algo* (of some property).

The Monarchy amongst the Visigoths in Spain was in principle all-powerful.[1] As amongst the Vandals and the Franks
it was the whole State. The Gothic despot imitated, as
much as he could, the Emperor of the Romans. In the
middle of the seventh century, Recesswinth re-organized the
hierarchy of his Court after the model of Byzantium. He
put on the Byzantine costume, although up to about 630 the
Gothic Kings had worn their hair long in the barbarian fashion.
He imitated Byzantium also in committing atrocities against
rivals and rebels. But under its appearance of absolutism,
the Visigothic monarchy was as unstable as the Empire.
The royal line of the Baltungs had died out in 531 in the
person of Amalaric, the son of Alaric II. The men who
took possession of the throne, the Ostrogoth Teudis, then
Agila (549-554), then, after the glorious interlude of Athanagild (died in 567), Leovigild (died in 587), Recared and Sisebut,
who had been raised to power by force, were not able to
impose themselves on their rivals, the members of the Gothic
aristocracy. The crown could not remain for more than
two generations in the same family. Finally, in the seventh
century, the monarchy became elective.

The principle of election was laid down at the Council
of Toledo under Sisenand (631-636). It was in virtue of this
principle that Swinthila was elected in 636. The monarchy
naturally tried to break free of it. Chindaswinth, a noble
elected by his peers in May 642, tried to crush the aristocracy ;
he put to death or reduced to slavery 700 nobles ;   many
others fled in dismay into Africa. These savage measures
did not achieve their end. The elective character of the
monarchy was confirmed at the eighth Council of Toledo in
653 ; the king had to make pledges to the aristocracy and
the high clergy, including one by which he bound himself
to punish the Jews.

The fundamental " institution " of the Visigothic State
became the Council of Toledo at which the affairs of the State
and of the Church were treated indiscriminately.[2] Against
the aristocracy, the monarchy invoked the support of the
Church, and the latter made it pay dear without always
being faithful. If Wamba was dethroned by the aristocracy

[1] **DLIV**, vol. vi., 305.
[2] **DLIV**, vol. vi. ; **DCXXVII**, 333.

in 680, the conspiracy against Egica was fomented by Sisebut, the metropolitan of Toledo. It was after the abdication of the brother of the old king Wamba that the decay of the Visigothic Monarchy became rapid. Wamba had advanced as far as Nîmes to seize a rival, Paul. He had rebuilt Toledo and its walls. As people were becoming more and more careless about the fulfilment of military service, Wamba made it obligatory on all, in cases of an invasion of the country, without distinction of birth or position, even on the clergy ; he even wished to force the large landowners, including ecclesiastics, to feed the army with their serfs. These ordinances, which were so characteristic and alarming, were revoked by his successors. All that the latter could do, was to increase the atrocity of the measures against the Jews. This enfeebled monarchy was nevertheless feared by the aristocracy. After Witiza (701-708), the aristocracy refused the throne to his children and gave it to an obscure person, Rodrick (Ruderico), who was the last Gothic King.

Intellectually, Visigothic Spain presents the spectacle of an irresistible decay. Isidore of Seville (died in 636) is only a compiler ; his *Etymologies* are only " a lumber-room in which he has put away the cast-off clothes of Antiquity " :[1] but at least he possessed a good library. At the end of the century under St. Julian, the library of the metropolis, Toledo, contained only one profane author, a Cicero. The decadence of classical Latin, although less rapid than in Gaul, was already marked.

The kings however do not present the sorry spectacle of the Merovingians. Several of them, Leovigild, Chindaswinth and Wamba, showed themselves men of energy. But the Monarchy came up against social forces which were too strong for it, or rather it was swallowed up in a general apathy. Only the question of religion had been able to draw the people from their torpor. After the triumph of Catholicism, they fell back into their listlessness and remained indifferent to public concerns.

Thus, wherever we turn, we see the decrepitude of the ancient world becoming more marked. The barbarian dynasties in Italy and Spain and still more in Africa did not succeed in arresting its decay any more than did the Roman

[1] **DCXXVII, 319.**

pseudo-Empire which continued at Constantinople. The peculiarity in Spain is that the Romano-Gothic organization, instead of dragging on as in the East, or being regenerated as in Gaul, received its finishing stroke suddenly.

One army of 12,000 Berbers and a single battle, near the locality afterwards called Medina Sidonia, sufficed to put an end to the Visigothic Monarchy (July 19th, 711). In two or three years of expeditions or rather of military saunters, Tarik and Musa took possession of Spain up to the Pyrenees without encountering any serious resistance. The Visigothic State appears as worm-eaten as the Vandal State two centuries before.

CHAPTER VI

The Lombard State[1]

SCARCELY had the last Gothic troops which were garrisoned in the North of Italy surrendered to Narses, scarcely had Justinian been lowered into his grave (565), when Italy saw the arrival of the Lombards, who conquered it and exercised a deep influence on its political fortunes, its public and even its private law. This time it had to do not with Federates united to the Empire by more or less real ties of dependence, but with real conquerors.

The Lombards scarcely appeared to be destined some day to play an important part in the history of Europe. Renowned as early as the first century for their valour and ferocity, but few in numbers and not very powerful,[2] they occupied on the lower reach of the Elbe only the small territory which kept their name, *Bardengau* (*Longo-bardengau*), round what is now Lüneburg. After the great invasions, we find them in the centre of Europe, in Pannonia. They fought fiercely against other neighbouring Germanic peoples, the Heruls (East of Bohemia) and the Gepids. They finally exterminated them (567), but only by allying themselves with a Turkish people, the Avars, who succeeded the Huns. They did not seem dangerous to the Empire, which they supplied with mercenaries ; the army of Narses which won Italy from the Ostrogoths was, as we have seen, largely composed of Lombards.

The Lombards suddenly became formidable when their bands became united under the direction of a single king and when the pressure of the Avars, driving them out from Central Europe, thrust them towards Italy. In the Spring of 568, under the leadership of Alboin, the Lombard people, increased by Saxon and even by Bulgarian contingents, crossed the Eastern Alps and by way of Istria penetrated into Italy.

---

[1] **CDXIX, CDXCVII, CDXCV, CDXCVI; DLXV; CCXXXI**, vol. vii ; **DLIV,** vol. xii. ; **DXCV,** vol. ii. ; **DCLI.**

[2] TACITUS, *Germania*, 40.

They took Verona and entered Milan as early as September, 569. Only Pavia stood a regular siege. With this exception, neither the populations nor even the troops in the service of Byzantium had offered any serious resistance.

But if the ravages of the Lombard bands were numerous and savage—they spread as far as the South of the peninsula and in Gaul as far as the Rhone Valley—the Lombard State, if so grandiose a term may be used, had no cohesion. It was held together only by the person of the King. But the conqueror Alboin was assassinated by his own wife, Rosamund, we are told, in 572 ; his successor Cleph met with the same fate eighteen months later. The Monarchy was then abolished (574) and the bands were divided amongst thirty-five dukes, who established themselves each in one of the *cities* of Northern Italy and, naturally, quarrelled and fought with each other. The Saxon auxiliaries re-crossed the Alps.

It seemed a favourable opportunity for the Empire, which had been stunned by the sudden attack of the barbarians, to recover.

It is certain that a little energy would have sufficed to overthrow the Lombard dukes and their small bands. But the Empire was henceforth incapable of the necessary effort. After Justinian, Byzantium was at her last gasp. His successor, Justin II, had to abandon the old-fashioned " world " policy of his illustrious predecessor. The resources left to the Empire were only just sufficient to enable it to struggle against the Avars and the Slavs in Europe, and against the Persians, and later Islam, in Asia.

The Empire looked towards the East, and the West could only take a secondary place in its thoughts. This was an unavoidable necessity which existed already in the sixth century, and it was the condemnation of Justinian's policy ; by overthrowing the Goths of Italy, Justinian took away from that country the only force which might have been able to save it from the barbarians and he himself was unable to replace it by another.

Reduced to their own resources, the Lombards were so weak that the Austrasian Franks, urged on by the Empire, thought of trying to wrest Italy from them. From 584 to 590 they sent five expeditions into the country. But already the

Merovingian Frankish State was beginning slowly to decline. There was no continuity in these undertakings ; nevertheless they were sufficiently threatening for the Lombards to acknowledge the supremacy of the Franks and to pay them tribute.[1]

The Lombards realized their danger. Ten years after the abolition of the Monarchy, the dukes restored it for Authari (584). The latter joined to his title of *rex gentis Longobardorum* the epithet *Flavius* and the title of *vir excellentissimus*. This is significant. The Gothic Kings had acted in this way to connect themselves by a fictitious relationship with the Empire whose representatives were so-called descendants of the second Flavian dynasty.[2] There seems to be no doubt that, by acting in this way, the new King tried to gain the goodwill of his Roman as well as of his Lombard subjects.

Towards the Empire he adopted an attitude of prudence ; he preferred to consolidate his possession and to abstain from attacking in return for the payment of a tribute of 500 gold pounds. For half a century, the expansion of the Lombards in Italy, without ever coming to a full stop, went on slowly. Let us quickly review what remained to the Empire, that is to say, to Byzantium, in the seventh century.

In the North-East of Istria only the coasts were left : Trieste and Grado which replaced Aquileia. The populations of *Venetia* had taken refuge amongst the lagoons, at Heraclea, Malamocco, etc. ; only in the ninth century was the capital of this " duchy " established at *Rivo Alto* (Rialto), to which was attached the name of the duchy *Venetia*, Venice, and in which the duke (doge) resided. The interior of Istria, Friuli (*Forum Julii*) belonged to the Lombards and formed a powerful March against the Avars who seriously threatened Italy (seventh century), and also against the Slavs who had replaced the Germans in the Eastern Alps.

South of the Po, Byzantium had Ravenna, the capital of Italy since the beginning of the fifth century, where resided the Exarch, a kind of Viceroy, whence the name of *Exarchate* given to the surrounding country. The Byzantines also annexed Bologna. Further South, along the Adriatic, Pentapolis formed a Byzantine duchy (Rimini, Ancona, and in the interior, Urbino and Gubbio).

---

[1] Cf. below, p. 329.
[2] **DXCV**, vol. ii., 2, 30.

The Southern part of the peninusula also, Bruttium, Apulia and Calabria were still left to the Byzantines.

The coasts of Campania formed the duchy of Naples.

The remnants of the Roman Campagna and of Sabina, and the South of Tuscany, formed the duchy of Rome. Finally, in the North, until 640, the Empire kept Genoa and the coast of Liguria.

All the rest, that is to say the interior of the country, was in the power of the Lombards. By the setting up of the principality of Spoleto the road between Rome and Ravenna was cut. Hence there was no easy communication between the different Byzantine regions; henceforth they tended to lead an independent life.

The real authority of the Lombard King extended only over the plain of the Po which afterwards bore the name of *Lombardy*. The principalities of Beneventum and of Salerno in the South of Italy, of Spoleto in the centre, and of Friuli in the North-east, were practically independent; even the Lombard duke of Tuscany was not bound to the King of Pavia by any strong ties.

The contacts between the Romans of the countries subject to the Lombards and the Romans who were subjects of Byzantium were close and permanent. At the beginning, the Lombards behaved like savages, pillaging and butchering for the pleasure of it. It is generally estimated that in the first period of their inroads, the Lombards reduced to an inferior position all those belonging to the upper classes whom they had not put to death. But, strictly speaking, on this important point we have only one statement, that of Paul the Deacon : *His diebus multi nobilium Romanorum ob cupiditatem interfecti sunt. Reliqui vero per hospites divisi, ut partum suarum frugum Longobardis persolverent, tributarii efficiuntur* (II, 32). This statement is thus very late and perhaps questionable. However that may be, once masters of the country, the Lombard Monarchy and aristocracy took good care to profit from the advantages of the Roman social organization. They made no change in the mode of the exploitation of the land, in the agrarian economy. The Roman *colonus* (*massarius*) or the German one (*aldio*) paid the Lombard master (*dominus*) what he had paid the Roman ; for him nothing was changed.

An important thing was that urban life went on, although
diminished ; there were no more *curiæ*, it seems ; but from
the seventh century these disappeared even in the parts of
Italy left to the Empire. Yet Italy remained a country of
towns,[1] and the class consisting of Lombard freemen, that of
the *arimanni*, settled in these towns and led an urban life ;
this was a great difference from the Frankish or Visigothic
aristocracy, not to speak of the Germanic countries (Germany
and England). In these thoroughly Roman surroundings
marriages became frequent. The Lombards learned the
lingua Romana, and of all the invading people, it was this,
it seems, which was to abandon most quickly its native language in order to adopt the language of the vanquished.[2] The
division into clans (*fara*), and *sippe* disappeared.

Finally, Catholicism developed early and without any very
serious obstacles. In Pannonia already, the majority of the
Lombards, if not all, had been converted to Christianity,
though to the Arian form, it is true, which meant that they
were not recognized as brothers by the Italians, who were
all Catholics. Two things however favoured the introduction and later the triumph of Catholicism : (1) the weakness
of the Lombard Arian clergy who were neither numerous nor
cultivated ; (2) the influence of the Court, as amongst the
Salian Franks a century before. The wife of Authari, in whose
person the Monarchy was re-established, Theodelinda, daughter
of Garibald, Duke of Bavaria, was a Catholic. She even
brought up in Catholicism Adaloald, the son she had by
Agilulf, the Duke of Turin, who succeeded Authari. She
reigned in her son's name (616-626) and he allowed himself
to be won over by the Catholic and even by the political
influence of Byzantíum so that a reaction broke out and he
was dethroned and perhaps poisoned.

The reigns of Arioald, Duke of Turin (626-636), and of
Rothari (636-652) Duke of Brescia, mark a nationalist and
Arian reaction. Rothari took up once more the forward
march. He captured the coasts of Liguria with Genoa (640)
and in his work of conquest renewed the savage methods
of the preceding century. He wished to make real the royal
power over the dukes and he was ambitious to be a legislator.

[1] **DXCV**, vol. ii., 2, 11, 18.
[2] **DXLIV**, 13 ; **DCLI**, vol. i., 24 ; **DXCV**, vol. ii., 2, 16.

Under the name of *Edict* he had a Lombard code drawn up
which was promulgated by the people, that is to say the
army, at Pavia, November 22nd, 643.

Nevertheless, under his successors, Catholicism became
established and gained the mastery even at Pavia. After the
death of Rothari, the power was not kept in his family ; the
Duke of Benevento, Grimoald (died 671) is the first among
the Lombards whom we hear of as having reigned for a few
years from the North to the South of Italy, except for the
coasts.

The greatest of the Lombard Kings is Liutprand (712-744).
He succeeded in making almost real the royal power over
the dukes of the north. He was a zealous Catholic, generous
and a great founder of monasteries. He had no definitely
anti-Roman policy ; but he had firmly resolved to unite under
the authority of the Lombard Monarchy the whole of Italy.
With this end in view, he did not hesitate to enter on a struggle
with the Lombard rulers of the Centre, of the South, with
the Exarch and Constantinople, and even to attack the territory
administered by the Papacy. His policy seemed to be successful ; the Lombard rulers in the South were subdued and the
Respublica was hard pressed. After the short interregnum
of the Duke of Friuli, Ratchis, who was "imperialist" and
devoted to the Holy See, the policy of Liutprand was resumed
and carried on with vigour by Aistulf (Ratchis' brother)
who was raised on the shield at Milan in June, 749. Two
years later, in July, 751, Ravenna capitulated. In the North
only Venetia was left to Constantinople. In Central and
Southern Italy there was only the duchy of Rome, administered ostensibly in the name of the Empire by the Bishop or
Pope. This duchy, the last refuge of the *Respublica Romanorum*, once taken away, there would be left for Byzantium
no serious support, and the unification of Italy, under the
sceptre of the King of Pavia, would be complete. Everything seemed to foretell that this was the turn which things
would take. Italy, under the rule of a monarchy descended
from German conquerors who had become Romanized in
customs and language, was going to recover the unity which
the Gothic Monarchy of Theodoric had nearly realized. But
the Lombard Monarchy, though all-powerful in appearance,
was destined to break itself against the Papacy served by

the Franks. Before setting forth this great conflict let us halt and try to draw a picture of the Lombard State at its zenith.

It was the same with the Lombard State as with all the Germanic States founded on Roman territory, Vandal, Visigoth, Burgundian and Frankish. The State was confused with the Monarchy. The ancient Germanic constitutions, aristocratic or other, had been knocked to atoms during the migrations. The assembly of the people was not an independent power ; it met only by the King's orders. Amidst these ruins only one institution remained, the Monarchy[1] ; but at the beginning it was very insecure and even intermittent (it was abolished from 574 to 584). Amongst the Lombards the old royal families claiming descent from the gods died out with Alboin and were replaced by new men. The king was only a duke chosen by the other dukes. Hence came the insuperable difficulties in imposing his authority. Further, as no strong and lasting dynasties could be established, the Monarchy became, in fact if not in law, elective as amongst the Visigoths in the seventh century. The King was raised on the shield by the people, that is to say by the army assembled on a plain under the walls of Pavia or Milan.

The establishment of absolute Monarchy met with difficulties incalculably greater than in Africa, Spain, Gaul, or Germany. The *duchies*, which elsewhere, as in Gaul for example, were temporary and entrusted to men who in the sixth and seven centuries were functionaries, stood opposed to the Monarchy right from the beginning of the Lombard State. The reason was that they were contemporaneous with and even older than the Monarchy, since the latter was abolished and re-established only with the dukes' consent. We are not speaking of the duchies of Southern and of Central Italy, founded by adventurers independent of the King as early as the end of the sixth century.

What exactly was the King's power inside each of these thirty or forty duchies of the North, which together really formed the Lombard State ? Is it not to be expected that in each of these duchies, although in theory the duke is appointed by the King, a small dynasty will be established, and that as early as the seventh century, the king will find

[1] **DCLI,** vol. ii., 162 ; **DCXCIII.**

himself nearly in the position of the King of France in the
tenth century and of the Sovereign of Germany in the twelfth
or thirteenth ?   In practice such was nearly the case, the
duke being appointed for life and his son always succeeding him.[1] The Monarchy was not however inoperative.
At the time of its re-establishment, every duke gave up half
of his ducal " domain " in the *civitas*, and this domain was
administered by a royal steward, the *gastaldus*.   The latter
corresponded pretty closely to the Frankish *domesticus*.
In relation to the *arimanni* corresponding to the class of the
Frankish freemen from the seventh to the ninth century,
the *gastaldus* fulfilled roughly the function of the Frankish
count.   He was not hereditary nor for life, as was the duke ;
he was thus a kind of functionary.[2] The Lombard State,
in comparison with the Frankish, is one in which the authority
in each *pagus* is represented by the *domesticus* and not by
the count, and in which the armed contingent of each *civitas*
marches under the leadership of an irremovable duke.

The legislative and judicial powers were in principle reserved
for the King.   It was the Monarchy which, with Rothari,
conceived the idea of putting into writing the Lombard
customs.   His *Edictum*, published in Latin, is by far the
best of barbarian laws.   Though its editor in the preface
draws his inspiration from a Novel of Justinian, and certainly
knows the Visigothic *Lex Antiqua* revised by Leovigild,
the Edict is an original work.[3] It represents a purely Germanic
law, less akin to Frankish and Gothic than to Anglo-Saxon
law, proving the faithfulness with which the Lombards preserved their customs, which dated from the period when they
inhabited *Bardengau*.   Its ordinances are intended only for
the Lombard subjects of the King.

His Roman subjects came under Roman laws, especially
those which were previous to Justinian, the latter's legislation not having had time to establish itself in Northern Italy.
The " Roman " who was a Lombard subject did not come
under the *Edictum* except in cases of conflict between Roman
and Lombard law[4], and that, moreover, only in questions of
public law.

---

[1] **DXCV**, ii., 2, 33-35 ; **DCXCIII**, 210.
[2] **DXCV**, vol. ii., 2, 37-39 ; **DCXCIII**, 760.
[3] **DXLV**, 530, 536, 538.
[4] *Contra*, **DXLIII**, vol. i., 102, note 3.

The legislative ordinances of the Lombard Sovereigns, Grimoald, Liutprand, Ratchis and Aistulf, claim to be additions to the Edict, or Novels. But it is always specified that the King made them only in the presence of the judges and of the assembly of the people, which was held regularly on the 1st of March. It is true that in the eighth century it consisted only of the dukes, functionaries, and palatines. Liutprand's legislation even presents itself as a series of fifteen *volumina* (713 to 725), each passed in an assembly. The ordinancès in favour of the Catholic Church naturally appear here (the right of asylum, and Christian marriage). We may also discern some traces of the influence of Roman law. Even after the Frankish conquest, Lombard legislative activity went on in Southern Italy, in the principality of Benevento.[1]

The influence of Lombard law continued very late in Northern Italy. Not only at Pavia and Milan but even at Bologna, the town of the renaissance of Roman law in the eleventh century, Lombard law, the *Lombarda,* was edited and commented on even in the thirteenth century and later.

The Monarchy's resources.[2]—In the storm, the land tax disappeared. It was not possible to subject the Lombard to it, still less to the *capitation*, which was considered as a sign of servitude. The *chrysargyron* on the trading classes also disappeared.

The conquerors kept up indirect imposts and various taxes : (1) taxes on communications and tolls (*tractatica, pulveratica, pedatica, rotatica, pontatica, ripatica*) ; (2) customs (*telonea*) and taxes on merchandise (*foratica*), on commerce (*laudatica, salutatica*) ; (3) dues of all kinds : the rights of lodging and procuration (*paratæ, mansiones, albergariæ*), providing of horses (*paraveredi*) and of fodder (*fodra*), a remnant of the ancient *annona militaris* ; (4) personal labour (*angariæ*); lastly, the profits of minting.

But the yield of these taxes, there is reason to believe, remained chiefly in the hands of the dukes and the *gastaldi* and only a very small portion must have reached the coffers of the King.

---

[1] Poupardin, *Institutions des principautés lombardes de l'Italie du sud,* 1907.
[2] **DXCV,** vol. ii., 2, 42 ; **DCLI,** vol. i., 308 ; **DCXCIII,** 21.

The King lived chiefly on the produce of his domain. In every *ducatus*, it was held by tradition that the duke had given up to the crown on the re-establishment of the Monarchy in 584, half of the taxable lands. The King, as we have seen, managed them by means of his *gastaldi*. Hence his resources were principally those of a large landed proprietor.

Consequently, the Lombard State also was a State without finances. Its loose and rudimentary structure made it possible for it to exist in this way. There were no public services, public works (roads, bridges) being carried out indifferently by those who were interested ; there were no theatres or amphitheatres any longer. Charity and help were left to the Church, also education. Justice and administration cost nothing, the judges getting their payment from court fines (part of which even reached the King). The army also cost nothing, every freeman (*arimannus*) owing military service at his own expense. The King had the right to have his fortresses defended.

The Court also, the *sacrum palatium* (in imitation of Byzantium) was not a complicated affair. It consisted of some high personages, who fulfilled functions of a German or Roman origin : the Marshal (*marpahis*), the Majordomus (*stolesaz*), the Treasurer (*vesterarius*), the Sword-bearer (*spatharius*), the Chancellor (*referendarius*), with a small number of clerks (*notarii*) under their orders.

Actually, the King had no direct hold on the mass of his free subjects. The practice of the *commendatio*,[1] derived both from the German *comitatus* and the Roman system of patronage, partially supplied the deficiency of the weak State. There was a class of subjects which had close, personal relations with the King, the class of the *gasindi* (" domestics ", *Gesinde*). They had a superior wergeld, and amongst them were distinguished *gasendi* of the first rank, or *optimates*. There is no doubt that, to be effective, the action of the Monarchy had to lean on the fidelity of these people.

Unfortunately this " fidelity " had to be fed and kept warm by means of presents. In this economically retrograde State, the sole wealth was land ; the King distributed (in full ownership) parts of the fiscal lands to his faithful supporters, and however great the royal domain was, it is certain that it was constantly diminished by these largesses which had become obligatory. The power of the Monarchy, even under a Liutprand or an Aistulf, was far more apparent than real. But the Monarchy was the State. Once it fell, nothing was left but a sand-heap of local interests.

It is in fact doubtful whether there existed a Lombard national feeling, a political unity resulting from the fusion of the invaders and the ruling classes, as with the Visigoths in Spain in the second half of the seventh century. The respective position of the Lombards and the Romans of the Lombard territory is a very disputed question. In the seventh century personal law still existed : thus, a Lombard woman became Roman by marrying a Roman subject of the Lombard King, and as long as such personal law exists, there is no real nationality.

It is true that some think they see a great change in the course of this century. Military legislation underwent important alterations : military service was established according to property qualifications. A law of 750, due to Aistulf, imposed it on whoever possessed at least seven *casæ massariæ* and the owner of 40 *jugera* owed service on horseback, with lance, shield and coat of mail.[1] Perhaps we ought to conclude from this that the Roman landowner owed service as well as the Lombard. Consequently he was placed on the same footing as the latter, becoming an *ariman*, and a member of the Lombard political State.[2] But it is equally possible that no Roman landowners were left and that all those possessing land were Lombards.[3]

Thus it does not appear in any certain way that, even in the middle of the eighth century, the Lombard State succeeded in welding together the different political elements which constituted it.

The Lombards of the aristocracy, the only class which counted here as elsewhere, forgot their language ; the mixture of blood through mixed marriages probably did not make it possible to distinguish by physique the lord of Germanic origin from the Italian natives ; the names (Lombard) and

[1] **DXCV**, vol. ii., 2, 50, 63 ; **DCXCIII**, 49, 285.
[2] **DCLI**, vol. i., 2-5, 28, 46-48, 414.
[3] **DXCV**, vol. ii., 2, 4, 50.

costume even did not suffice to differentiate them.[1] But juridically there existed a Lombard law and nationality which still raised a barrier between these descendants of the conquerors, though they had become Romanized in blood and language, and several million *Romans* who were their subjects.

It is possible that, joined to the absence of solid means for the Monarchy, this duality of race and institutions and this degeneracy of the Lombard aristocracy are the causes which explain the fact that the Lombard State crumbled to dust at the mere touch of the Carolingian Franks.

---

[1] HARTMANN (**DXCV,** vol. ii., 2, 21-22) thinks that in the eighth century the Lombards were no longer distinguished from the other inhabitants of Italy by their appearance and costume. PAUL THE DEACON (iv., 22), wishing to describe the external appearance and the costume of his fellow countrymen in the past, is obliged to have recourse to the paintings in the palace of Monza, done under Queen Theodelinda. For the contrary, see the texts quoted by Ernst MAYER, **DCLI,** vol. i., 46-48 and note 85. Cf. DUCHESNE, **DLXIX,** 10-12.

CHAPTER VII

THE PAPACY AND ITALY FROM THE MIDDLE OF THE SIXTH TO THE MIDDLE OF THE EIGHTH CENTURY (554-753)

THE recapture of Italy by the Roman Empire under Justinian at first contributed little to the authority, either spiritual or secular, of the Papacy. The personal position of the Pope seemed actually to be deteriorating. It is true that under the dominion of the Goths as well as in the days of the Western Empire, the nomination of each new Pope was subject to the approval of the Sovereign. But the Bishops of Rome never had to submit to such a despotic and brutal régime as after the recapture of Rome by the Empire.

Scarcely had Belisarius arrived in Rome when, by command of the Emperor and of Theodora, Silverius was deposed and exiled. Vigilius was removed to Constantinople, where he remained for several years, submitting at first to the theological decrees of Justinian and condemning (548) the three Chapters (1, Theodore of Mopsuestia ; 2, Theodoret ; 3, Letter from Ibas to Maris) on the ground that they were tainted with Nestorianism. In spite of his docility and his concessions, Vigilius was considered contumacious, and was exiled, his name being struck off the diptychs by Justinian. The Emperor of Constantinople, following the example of his predecessors, takes upon himself to decide questions of faith, and this system of Cæsaro-Papism is to be imitated later by his successors. In 653, Martin I is sent by order of Constans II to the Tauric peninsula and dies there. In 692, Sergius I, threatened with a similar fate by Justinian II, owes his escape to a rising of the populations of Italy. During the Pontificate of John VII (705-707) and of Constantine (708-715) imperial commissioners come to Rome with the object of taking away the Pope's councillors and of endeavouring to work on him by means of threats, flattery and bribes.

DCXXXVIII, vol. i., 66; DCLXXXVII, 53-55, 134, 141.

The attitude of the Pope towards the Emperor is deferential and very humble.   The flattery which a man like Gregory the Great lavishes upon such a coarse brute as the Emperor Phocas is beyond all measure.   In the seventh century the Popes are Greek ;   from 685, for thirty years, the chair of Saint Peter is filled by a succession of seven Greek Popes.

The people of Italy showed no open hostility towards Byzantium in the sixth and seventh centuries.[1]   In the fifth century ancient Rome had no love for the new Rome. She was jealous of her splendour and envious of her security.   In the sixth and eighth centuries, all idea of competing with Constantinople was abandoned.   Rome had become aware of her own decadence and had resigned herself to it, politically at all events ;   usurpers had no success in Italy.

The position of the Pope seemed to be equally weakened from the point of view of outward honour and even in matters concerning the faith, by the re-establishment of the Imperial authority.   The Bishops of Constantinople, strengthened by the fact that they inhabited the capital of the Empire, and frequented the Court where they played a prominent part, were anxious to carry into the domain of things spiritual the political supremacy of Constantinople.

The second Ecumenical Council of Constantinople in 381 decreed that the Bishop of that town should have precedence after the Bishop of Rome " because Constantinople is the New Rome (Canon 3)."   But this council was ecumenical in name only ;   it was heard of but little and contemporaries scarcely mention it.   It does not appear to have been regarded seriously.[2]   On the contrary, Valentinian III in 445 proclaimed the doctrinal and juridical authority of the Pope. In 451 at the Council of Chalcedon, the Legate of Leo I deposed Dioscorus, the Patriarch of Alexandria.   It was a Pyrrhic victory[3], for, from this date onward, Egypt and Syria detached themselves from Rome in order to draw near to Constantinople, and later, to adopt the Monophysite heresy until the Arab conquest.

---

[1] **DCLXXXVII,** 118-130.
[2] **CXXV,** 177 ;   **XXIII,** 134.
[3] **CXXV,** 193 ;   **XXIII,** 582-589.

In 484 and 536 it was Acacius and Anthemius, the Patriarchs of Constantinople themselves, who were deposed, the latter by Pope Agapitus in person.

However, the pretensions of Constantinople come forward once again. In the second half of the sixth century, the Patriarchs call themselves ecumenical. The East wishes to teach Rome its lesson. The Council of 692, *in Trullo* (Quinisextine) condemns a number of ecclesiastical practices and peculiar forms of discipline in the churches of Africa and Rome. The aim is to extend Byzantine practices over the whole of the Church. The Roman legates, under the pressure of Justinian II, are obliged to accept and to subscribe.

A yet more serious fact is that the sixth Ecumenical Council (Constantinople, 681), aimed at Monotheletism, while condemning the doctrine of Sergius, one of the Patriarchs of Constantinople (610-638), also includes in a retrospective anathema Pope Honorius (625-628), who had expressed approval of Sergius in a letter to him.

Hence, Rome is fallible. It is true that Honorius was not speaking *ex cathedra*, which in the eyes of modern Catholics saves the principle of infallibility. But did this distinction hold in an age when the attempt was being made to establish orthodoxy by means of every kind of text, of epistles, visions, etc. ? The pastor of the church which, according to the saying of Saint Ignatius (end of the first century) " has never led any astray and has instructed others, whose teaching is undisputed "[1] could therefore err.

Rome, at this moment, seemed to have fallen fairly low, at least in the eyes of the East. It might have been thought that, in the political sphere as well as in that of discipline or even of the faith, she would resign herself voluntarily or involuntarily to following the lead of Constantinople.

There was a sudden change in the aspect of affairs in 726. Leo III the Isaurian had just issued his decree forbidding the worship of images. This measure appeared to be animated by a truly Christian spirit. Christianity was becoming paganized ; the worship of relics was becoming a substitute for Paganism.[2] Some scholars have even held that very often Christian saints are nothing but pagan gods under

---

[1] **CXXV**, 128.
[2] **DCIV**.

slightly different names : Saint Pelagia, it is said, is Aphrodite Pelagia, Saint Demetrius the god worshipped at Thessalonica, Saint Lucian, whose day is October 15th and whose
body was brought back by a dolphin, is Dionysus (Apollo)
who was drawn by dolphins and whose festival is October
15th. Thus paganism is supposed to have survived, thinly
disguised by a veneer of Christianity.

This theory seems an exaggeration.[1]   However, whether
the worship of saints comes by direct succession from the
ancient cults, whether it is the morbid eruption of a virus
with which moribund paganism infected Christianity, or
whether it merely represents a psychological need of the
masses, a constantly recurring form of hero-worship, one
fact is certain, namely, that the Christian populations were
tending more and more to manifest their piety under forms
reminiscent of idolatry.

The edict was issued in a real spirit of sincere piety and
apparent wisdom. The Emperor had with him the majority
of the educated classes and of the clergy. Yet iconoclasm
did not succeed; in 787 and 842 it became necessary to withdraw the iconoclastic edicts.[2] Christian paganism survived, and
the art of the Middle Ages was saved for posterity. If iconoclasm had triumphed, painting and above all sculpture
would have suffered the same fate as they have in Moslem
countries ;   and a clean proof of this is that the triumph of
the upholders of tradition was only partial in the East. Painting was tolerated, albeit conventional, stiff and lifeless, but
representation by means of statues was forbidden. The
renascence of statuary was not possible in the Byzantine
world. The descendants of the Hellenes, or at least the
inheritors of Greek culture, lost the feeling for plastic beauty
and have never succeeded in recovering it.

In the East, the reform came up against popular feeling
and the opposition of the monks. In the West, it was combated by the Papacy immediately and violently, under the
influence of the spirit of tradition, and also of self-interest ;
Rome lives on the worship of relics, and without her tombs
would be deserted. The Pope at that time was Gregory II,
a Roman for the first time for thirty years. He appealed

---

[1] CCCIX, CCCLXXVIII.
[2] CIX.

to the Emperor, and as the Imperial officers threatened him, popular risings took place at Rome and at Ravenna. The fact must also be mentioned that the Emperor with singular want of diplomacy had augmented the tax in 726. The Lombards made common cause with the natives. Had the Pope desired it, Italy would have been lost to the Empire from this moment (in 732 there was a fruitless expedition). Yet there was no separatism. The insurgents were merely aiming at a change of emperors. The intervention of the Lombards seems to have been an embarrassment and an anxiety to Pope Gregory II and his successor Gregory III, rather than to have been solicited by them. There was nevertheless a serious cause for complaint : in 732 the Emperor Leo III transferred from the jurisdiction of Rome to that of Constantinople the ancient eastern *Illyricum* (Thessalonica, Nicopolis, Athens, Patras, Crete) and in Italy, Reggio, Sicily, and Sardinia. He also tried to attach Naples to Constantinople. It was useless ; the Pope made an attempt to succour the fleeing Exarch (Ravenna was temporarily seized, from 732 to 735), fought against the usurpers, and allowed the appointment of a Byzantine *dux et patricius* in Rome. Whence did the Pope acquire this new power which enabled him to resist the Emperor, and why did he use it with such moderation ? In order to attempt a solution of this double and contradictory question, we must recall the political geography of Italy.

The Lombard conquest (568), which received a temporary check after the establishment of the barbarians in the plain of the Po, began again in the course of the seventh century, until the whole of the interior of the Peninsula fell into their hands. The Imperial territory was pushed back towards the coast : Venetia, the Exarchate (Ravenna), Ferrara, Pentapolis, the Duchy of Rome, the Duchy of Naples. The South (Bruttium and Calabria) came under the " theme " of Sicily which was still wholly Greek.

Constantly threatened as it was by the Lombards, the organization restored by Justinian on the model of the Later Empire (a Præfectus Prætorio, two Vicarii, provinces ruled by governors) could not survive. The civil offices were absorbed into the military offices. The general in chief, the Exarch, governed the whole of Roman Italy.[1] The

---

[1] DLXV, DXCVI.

dukes took the place of the civil governors. The towns became places of refuge from the barbarians, for the country people. The *tribunus* in command of the detachment (*numerus*) in garrison, became, with the bishop, the master of the city.

The old municipal organization (*curiœ*, *defensores*) disappeared in the seventh century in Italy, as it did in Gaul.[1] It was only kept for the recording of the *acta ;* the *curiales* were no longer anything more than scriveners (at Naples for example).

The Empire, occupied with wars against the Bulgarians, the Persians, and finally the Arabs, had no more troops to send into Italy. In order to supply these, it had to fall back on local recruiting. The inhabitants would have to defend the towns and strongholds. The militia, powerless to resist the barbarians in open country, could stand firm behind ramparts. In fact, the Lombard invasion was no longer able to advance more than a step at a time ; the country districts were overrun but the towns resisted.[2]

A change took place in the psychology of the Italians. They no longer took a passive part in events. A new aristocracy arose, consisting of the local heads of these *numeri* or bands, the *judices de militia*. They were the ancestors of that Italian nobility of the Middle Ages that was so turbulent and so bloodthirsty. When the Empire was going through the troublous times that followed on the death of Heraclius in 642, it was inevitable that the activity of this militia, recruited in Italy, should increase. In the eighth century, these armies elected their leaders and their dukes, without troubling themselves further about the Exarch. Then the Pope found that he had in these Italian forces an unsolicited support, in case of a dispute, against Byzantine despotism.

His prestige, albeit lessened in the East, was in no way affected in the West. In Italy the Pope was venerated. The first rising of the *exercitus*, the militia, against Constantinople was in order to save Sergius I in 692. In Spain, the Episcopate and the Pope were in frequent relationship. In Gaul, striking testimony was to be given, under the Carolingians, of a deep reverence for the see of Saint Peter.

[1] **DXCV,** vol. ii., 364 ; **DCLXXXVII,** vol. i., 71.
[2] **DLXV,** 308-312 ; **DXCV,** vol. i., 124 ; **DXCVI,** 54, 151-165 ; **DCLXXXVII,** vol. i., 119.

The loss of Syria, Egypt and Africa, which fell into the hands of Islam, actually served to better the position of the Papacy in the eyes of the West. Since Justinian's day, the idea had taken root, even in the Latin world, that the Church was directed by five patriarchs,[1] and St. Gregory the Great gave notice of his accession to the patriarchs of Constantinople, Alexandria, Antioch and Jerusalem. The Arab invasion caused three of the five patriarchates to lie in Moslem territory, namely : Antioch, Jerusalem, Alexandria. The last-named was the most dangerous of all for the Papacy. In the fifth century, the patriarch of Alexandria had been within an ace of becoming the head of the Church in the East ; he had deposed the Patriarch of Constantinople three times, Chrysostom in 403, Nestorius in 431, Flavian in 449.[2] As for Carthage, its position was quite unique, by reason of the wide autonomy enjoyed by the Church in Africa ; the Bishop of Carthage did not receive the *pallium* like the other metropolitans.[3]

There was left to confront Rome only Constantinople, whose origin did not date from the time of the Apostles. In the East, thanks to the support of the Empire and to the scorn of the Byzantine peoples for the Latins and the Barbarians of the West, Constantinople was able to equal Rome and finally to triumph over her. In the West, this was impossible. Thus the indirect result of the triumph of Islam was to exalt Rome upon the ruins of the great towns of the East which was the cradle of Christianity.

In the West, Christianity suffered a cruel blow in the loss of Spain. The Moslems did not suppress Christianity violently there, but its existence was weakened. In the South, at Seville and at Cordova, the most living part of Spain, conversions to Islam were numerous.

But this loss was counter-balanced by the acquisition of Great Britain. British and Irish Christians lived a life apart, separated from their co-religionists on the continent by differences of ritual (the date of the Easter festival, the shape of the tonsure) which seemed matters of grave import to the people of that time. The British hated the Angles and

---

[1] **CXXV**, 167.
[2] **CXXXV**, 192.
[3] **CXXV**, 236.

Saxons. The effort to evangelize the Scots from Ireland bore fruit especially in the North of the main island, inhabited by the wild Picts. Gregory the Great[1] continued, for England, the work that Celestine had done for Ireland in the previous century, when Palladius had been sent from Rome to convert the Scots (431).[2] He despatched forty monks, under the leadership of Augustine, to Ethelbert, King of Kent, whose wife, daughter of the Merovingian Chariberht, was a Christian. The bishopric of Canterbury was founded in 597. The conversion of the North, of Northumbria, took place in 627. In spite of the resistance of the pagan party, by 673 the little kingdoms of Kent, Essex, Wessex, East Anglia, Mercia, Northumbria and Sussex, inhabited by Saxons, Angles and Jutes, were converted to Christianity. In 735, York became the metropolitan See of the North.

Rome kept a firm hand on Christianity in England.[3] The British and Scotch missionaries were kept at arm's length, and Roman discipline and ritual were enforced. The coming of Christianity brought a reflection of ancient civilization to the island, which had fallen back into barbarism since the German conquest in 441. At the beginning of the eighth century the Venerable Bede (died in 735) was both the last representative of ancient literature and the forefather of the medieval writers.[4]

The Anglo-Saxons knew nothing of the Eastern churches, and nothing of the Emperor. They only knew Rome, and their piety led them in crowds to the Eternal City. More than one of their kings chose to die there : Ceadwalla of Wessex in 684, Conrad of Mercia and Offa of Essex in 709. The Papacy was to find in them allies who were more submissive, more ingenuous, and more enthusiastic than the clergy of Italy, or even of Gaul. It made use of them later to Christianize Germany, to reform the clergy in Gaul, and to induce it, by means of monasticism, to recognize Roman supremacy.[5]

Monasticism took root in the West in the fourth century,

[1] DLXX, DCLXXIII.
[2] DLXXXVII; DCCXLI.
[3] DXLVIII; LXXIII, 496-541.
[4] CDXVII, DCLXXXVI.
[5] DCXXVI.

in spite of the " secular " clergy's repugnance to it.   It put off the individualistic and contemplative character of Eastern monasticism.   The most famous of the Western monks was Benedict of Norcia (died about 543) whose rule was finally adopted everywhere.[2]   It prescribed a claustral life, a strict discipline, an asceticism which was rigorous without being excessive, manual work, and also a certain amount of intellectual occupation.   The monks took up their abode in the country, far from the towns, or else in the *suburbium*, close   to   the   towns.   Saint   Benedict   founded   Monte Cassino, on a lonely mountain half-way between Rome and Naples.

Frowned upon by the episcopate, monasticism looked to the Papacy for support.   From the seventh century the request began to be made first in Italy, then in Gaul, that the monks should be placed under the direct authority of the Holy See, and be independent of the " ordinary ".   The monks of the Middle Ages, less preoccupied with the world, and well disciplined, were to be the best agents for Papal politics.   Without them, it is doubtful whether the Papacy could have exercised its authority so widely or made its activity so deeply felt.

The secret of the temporal power of the Pope must be sought in the economic resources of the Holy See, in its patrimony, in the huge donations to Saint Peter.   The Pope was the greatest land-owner in Italy.   The vast domains of the Holy See, the *massæ*, spread over the whole of Italy, into Sicily, Illyria and the East.[3]   The correspondence of Gregory the Great throws much light on the economic activity of the Papacy (590-604).   He is the first in date of the Popes of the Middle Ages,[4] the first monk-pope.   He detests ancient culture and art ;   he knows no Greek, although he lived some years at Constantinople.   His writings are full of allegories and superstitions, and had a strong influence on the minds of medieval authors.

The absence of any civil authority in permanent residence at Rome was also extremely advantageous to the Papacy. For some centuries Rome had been abandoned by the Emperor.

[1] **XXXI, XXXV** and **XXXVI, DXXI** ; cf. **XIV** and **XVI.**
[2] **DXLVII.**
[3] **DLXXVII** *bis* and **DCCVII** *bis.*
[4] **DLXX, DCLXXIII.**

The only occasion on which it received a visit from the sovereign, between 476 and 800, was on April 5th, 663, when Constans II made his entry there ; but he only stayed twelve days. The Pope felt no restraint put upon him by anything in his surroundings. And in the eyes of the barbarians who made pilgrimages to the Holy City, he was the master of it ; they were not necessarily aware of the indignities to which he was subjected by the Emperor and the Exarch.

During the first half of the eighth century, the Pope, Master of Rome and of the Ducatus, went so far as to identify the Papacy and the patrimony of St. Peter with the territory that still belonged to the Empire in Italy, to the *Respublica*. The fact is that he had become the sole force that the Empire could use against the Lombards, and for this reason the Emperors Leo III and Constantine V did not dare to thwart him seriously.

The period of the Lombard conquests begins again with Liutprand (712-744). The Empire had practically no forces with which to oppose him. The militia of Ravenna was too weak to struggle by itself against the Lombard king. It was by means of negotiations that Gregory II, just when his theological fight with Leo III was at its hottest, obtained the support of the " Venetians ", who recaptured Ravenna, which had been momentarily snatched from the Empire.

With the independent Lombard Dukes of Spoleto and Benevento the Pope alone was in a position to make terms: the former was particularly dangerous, since he had the power to cut the communications between Ravenna and Rome. In many cases, under Gregory III (731-741), Zacharias (741-751) and Stephen II (752-757) an embassy from the Pope or a personal application made by him to the Lombard King at Pavia, was the sole means at the disposal of the Empire of inducing the barbarians to stop their forward march or to restore certain places.[1] Pope Zacharias used his influence to establish a truce of twenty years with Ratchis, Liutprand's successor, and Ratchis even entered a monastery. Only, when Zacharias obtained from Lombard Tuscany the restoration of four places, it followed almost inevitably that these places that were given back to the Holy See and

[1] **DCIV,** 34, 36 ; **DCLXXXVII,** vol. i., 147-160.

administered by it, were confused with the " patrimony " of St. Peter.

After the Gothic war had piled up ruins on every side, Rome, depopulated and brought low, depended for her existence on the Papacy alone. Without the Christian memories connected with the latter, without the tombs of the apostles, without the trade in relics, her decadence would have been so marked that she would no doubt have become a dead city. Her idle population, without industry or commerce, was incapable of providing for her needs. She depended for her livelihood on the alms of the Holy See, just as she had on those of the Emperor. Soon the Holy See became her sole defence ; it repaired the town walls. The Prefect of Rome, who was also chief of the police and judge in the criminal court, continued to function as a pontifical official. Twelve regiments (*numeri*) were organized for the defence of Rome with their *patroni*. As they received little or no pay from Byzantium, they fell quite naturally under the influence of the Pope ; they acclaimed him at the time of his election and gave him military support.

Even the Duke, introduced late to Rome, ended by falling under Papal authority. He was destined to disappear when the Frankish King was called in as " patrician ".

In civil life, the seven judges (*primicerius, secundicerius, arcarius, sacellarius*, etc.) became officials of the pontifical palace. The corporations (*collegia*) and their heads (*patroni*), called consuls after the tenth century, were in too close an economic dependence upon the pontifical court, not to be politically subject to it.[1]

Rome presents, on a grander scale, the spectacle of what is taking place in every town. The bishop rules everywhere. In the East, he benefited by the " Pragmatic " of 554 : the bishop took part in the choice of the municipal governors and magistrates (*judices provinciarum*). He was present at trials and brought to the Emperor's notice any abuses committed in the exercise of justice.

Ratchis, who had retired into monastic life, was replaced by his brother, Aistulf. The latter carried the conquest further and captured Ravenna in 751. The Exarch

---

[1] L. HALPHEN, *Étude sur l'administration de Rome au moyen âge*, 757-1282 (Paris, 1907), pp. 11-15, 20, 40.

disappeared. There was no longer any Byzantine official in Italy (except in the theme of Sicily). The sole representative of the Empire was the Pope.

Thereupon, having become master of Ravenna and of the Exarchate, Aistulf made up his mind to lay hands on the whole of Italy. He gave out that he was about to exact tribute from Rome. The Lombard dukes of Spoleto, Benevento and Naples had not been able to withstand him. Venice and Sicily alone were able to escape from him.

The new Pope, Stephen II, was in consternation, and yet to become Lombard was not so terrible a fate. Certainly at the beginning the Lombards had committed atrocities, but later they had grown less violent. The harshness of their rule has perhaps been exaggerated. In any case, there were no rebellions in the Italian districts attached to the Lombard State.

From the middle of the seventh century, the Lombards had renounced Arianism ; their Kings were extremely pious and lavished gifts upon the Holy See. Why should the popes in the eighth century find a situation intolerable which had been accepted with resignation in the sixth century by their predecessors under Gothic rule ? Why did they submit to the many affronts from Constantinople and consent to defend the Emperor ? They may have feared lest the Lombard King should come and take up his residence in Rome, with the result that their spiritual authority would be restricted. It was an unlikely contingency. The King would have continued to live at Pavia. Upon the whole, whether as Pope or as Bishop of Rome, or as head of the Church, the Pope would not have lost much by passing, together with all his supporters, from Byzantine to Lombard rule.[1]

But the Pope had identified himself with the *Respublica*, and the Italian population identified him with it. The temporal power of the Pope was born of the Romans' repugnance to becoming Lombard.[2] This repugnance, which was sentimental, was increased by a material consideration. There were estates belonging to St. Peter everywhere, and everywhere they were menaced by the Lombard Kings. The only practical method of retaining these lands was to

---

[1] **DLXIX**, ii.
[2] **DLXIX**, 12-13, 115, 219 ; **DCLXXXVII**, 162.

be political master of the regions in which they were situated.

On October 14th, 753, Stephen II left Rome for Pavia, charged by the ambassadors of the Emperor Constantine V with the task of negotiating for the restitution of the Exarchate and of Pentapolis. He obtained nothing from King Aistulf. A month later, on November 15th, he left Pavia, but instead of returning to Rome, he turned northward and crossed the Alps, to go into France. He carried with him the destiny of Italy. It was fated that that country should no longer be attached to the Byzantine Empire, nor be unified under the authority of a barbarian king as in the case of Gaul and of Spain, but should for innumerable centuries bend beneath the authority of sovereigns who came from north of the Alps.

CHAPTER VIII

THE SEIZURE OF GAUL BY THE FRANKS

CLOVIS[1]

WE have seen that the Romano-Germanic States, born of the disintegration of the Roman world in the West, had shown themselves short-lived. Neither the Vandal State in Africa, nor the Ostrogothic State in Italy could defend themselves against the operations of the Roman Empire in the West, although these were carried on with very mediocre resources. In Spain the Visigothic State was able finally to get free of Byzantium, but it dragged out a wretched and uneasy existence which came to an abrupt end in 711, owing to the catastrophe of the Moslem invasion.

The new Rome herself was not able to maintain the territory she had recovered from the barbarians in the West. Italy had scarcely been reconquered when it escaped again, and the subjugation of Africa was hardly more than nominal. In the East, although she had succeeded, at the cost of exhausting efforts, in driving out of Syria and Egypt the rival civilization of Iran, she succumbed immediately after to the attack of a new force—Islam. Moreover, she was Roman in name alone after Justinian's reign. With the second half of the sixth century, contact with the West was lost and her memories of her Latin past finally faded altogether. From now onwards, this Empire deserves to be given the traditional epithet of " Byzantine." It is still a powerful organism, beneficent in certain respects, a stronghold of the Christian spirit amalgamated with Hellenism, against the barbarians of Central and Eastern Europe, and against the Moslems of Asia and Africa ; but it is no longer anything but a fiction to call it a Roman State.

North of the Alps and between the Adriatic and the Danube,

---

[1] **CCLXXIX**, vol. ii., 1 ; **LI** and **DLXXXII, DCXXVIII, DCXV, DCXVI** and **CCLXXIV, DCXXXV, DCLXX, DLXVIII, DLXXVIII, DXLIII, CDXLIII** and **CDXLIV, DCXCVII, DCCV, DCCXVI.**

Latinity finally dies out in the seventh century. Rhaetia, Vindelicia and Noricum are Germanized, becoming on the one hand Aleman, on the other Bavarian. Illyria is repopulated by the Slavs in the valleys of the Save, the Drave and the Morava. Pannonia is in the hands of the Avars, a Turkish tribe. It is only with difficulty that the " Romans " are able to maintain their existence on the shores of the Adriatic, in certain ports and on the islands, and even there not for very long.[1] Central Europe is a nameless chaos, and the invaders, no matter what their race may be, are utterly incapable of founding anything stable and great.

Great Britain, an outlying part of the Roman world from the fifth century, sees the constant advance of invading Angles, Saxons and Jutes, who, as they push their conquests further, wipe out all trace of Latinity. Their adversaries, the Britons in the little kingdoms of Dumnonia (Devonshire and Cornwall), Wales, Elmet, Cumberland and Strathclyde manage to survive, it is true, and hold their own against the odds of fortune, until about the end of the seventh century. But although they consider themselves " Romans "[2] until the middle of the sixth century, these Britons have already forgotten the language and the law of Rome. Their struggle is really that of Celts against Germans. Divided as it is into twelve or fifteen British or " Saxon " States, Great Britain naturally plays no " world part ".

The Lombards, a Germanic people with a reputation for extreme ferocity, seemed capable, for one short moment, of founding on Italian soil a stable State of a new character. Without hampering itself by any pretence of a " fœdus ", it chose the method of violent conquest, and imposed its political law on the vanquished. It seemed as if it were going to play the same part in the peninsula as the Franks in Gaul. But although it left a deep mark on the laws of the Middle Ages, and enriched the popular Romance language in Italy with a number of new terms, the Lombard people saw its career come to almost as sudden an end as that of the Visigothic State. An attempt has been made above to sketch the reasons which may explain why the Lombard State was unable to withstand the onset of the Franks.

---

[1] See above, p. 273.
[2] See J. LOTH, *Les mots latins dans les langues britanniques* (1892), p. 9.

The name we have just quoted is that of the Germanic people for whom the highest destiny was in store after the disintegration of the ancient world. For them was reserved the happy fortune of creating a new type of State, which dominated Eastern Europe for four centuries, from the end of the fifth to the end of the ninth. The political centre of history, after Theodoric's death in 526, was to be no longer Rome, nor Ravenna, nor Milan, nor Pavia, still less Arles and Toulouse. It was to be removed to the far north of Gaul, to the Seine Valley, and later to the Valley of the Meuse. Even when the Frankish State perished finally in 888, its foundations proved deep and solid enough to serve as supports for the Germano-Roman Holy Empire on the one hand, and for the Capetian Monarchy on the other. And from the sixth to the twelfth century, the region between the Loire and the Rhine was to be the most important in Western Europe from the point of view of civilization.

Nevertheless the Franks seemed in no way predestined to play this great part. No doubt in the third and again in the fourth century, this remnant of the ancient amphictyony of the Istævones had ranked among the most fearless raiders on Roman soil, but actually they were no more formidable than the Saxons, the Alemans, or the Heruls. Julian and Gratian had partially conquered them and had settled them on Imperial territory, in Betuwe (between the Lek and the Waal) and in Toxandria (Brabant) as subjects, and as farmer-soldiers. Individuals among them made a brilliant career, as we have seen,[1] as Roman officers and magistrates.

In the reign of Honorius the Frankish tribes began to cross the Rhine and settle themselves, by consent or by force, on the left bank. Cologne fell early into the hands of the Bructeri, known later as the Ripuarians. Coblenz and the Valley of the Moselle, then Mainz, and Worms after the departure of the Burgundians for Sapaudia, were occupied by the "Ripuarian" or perhaps the "Hessian" Franks. But these groups seem to have lost some of their lust for battle in the second half of the fifth century, and to have contented themselves with repopulating the left bank of the Rhine and the valley of the Moselle which was just becoming Germanized.

[1] See Part II, Ch. III.

Fewer in number perhaps, but more aggressive, were the Salians. The Salians, an offshoot of the great Chamari tribe,[1] after confining themselves for a long while to the small tract of country round the Yssel, one of the branches of the lower Rhine, crossed the river as early as the beginning of the fifth century, and spread over Belgium, carrying all before them. About the year 431, Aetius and Majorian (the future Emperor) beat the Franks at Helesme (North),[2] half-way between Tournai and Cambrai. However, their chief Chloio (the Clodion of French historical tradition) finally established himself in these two cities, and extended his territories as far as the Somme. The process of Germanization did not take place, however, along the great Roman road from Tongres to Bavay, which the Salians followed in their invasions. The Carbonarian Forest and the Ardenne presented a difficult obstacle for them to overcome. The process of " Frankization ", already begun in Brabant during the Roman period, took place between the Carbonarian Forest and the North Sea.[3]

It seems that a sort of " modus vivendi " was then established between them and the Roman government. The Salian Franks, as well as the Ripuarians (whose name first occurs at that time) sided with Rome in the battle of the *Campi Mauriaci*, fought by the patrician Aetius against Attila in 451. They were probably " Federates "—that is to say, considered, more or less by a legal fiction, to be in the service of the Empire. The *fœdus* even survived Aetius (assassinated in 454) whose patronage had been solicited by some of the petty Frankish Kings. It was with the help of Frankish auxiliaries that Aegidius,[4] the *magister militum*, triumphed over the Visigoths near Orleans in 463. Legends, recorded by Gregory of Tours and Fredegar,[5] tell us that this personage reigned eight years over the Franks (by which we must understand that he temporarily re-established Roman authority in Belgica). The Prologue to the *Lex Salica*, written towards the

[1] A theory of Ludwig Schmidt, which has much to recommend it. **CDXLIV,** vol. v., p. 423.

[2] Longnon, **CCCIII.**

[3] See G. des MAREZ, *Le Problème de la colonisation franque* . . . *dans la Basse Belgique* (Brussels, 1926).

[4] **CDLXXV.**

[5] **DCX, DCXVII,DCLXXIX.**

middle of the sixth century, calls to memory the " hard yoke of the Romans ".

It was again as ally of Aegidius that the Salian leader Childeric fought the Saxons who were attempting to establish themselves on the lower reaches of the Loire. After the death of Aegidius (464) Childeric, in conjunction with Count Paul, recovered from these pirates the town of Angers, then by himself conquered the Alans who were infesting the Loire on their way back from Italy. He was buried near Tournai and the coins found in his tomb in 1653 show that he died soon after 476.[1]

The death-throes of the Western Empire had just ended. In Gaul the last troops in the service of Rome were concentrated at Soissons, under the command of Syagrius, son of Aegidius. But this handful of men, cut off from Constantinople, henceforth to be the only seat of the "Roman Empire", could do no more than prolong an obviously hopeless resistance to the advance of the barbarians.

Trèves also presented an obstacle to the Franks. It was under the command of Arbogast, grand-son of Theodosius' enemy, who, in the Moselle basin, was the last leader in the service of Rome.[2] His ultimate destiny is not known, but this much is certain, that, before the end of the Empire, Trèves was taken from *Romania* and Germanized.

It would however be a great mistake to imagine that in 476 the Franks already appear as the chosen people, destined by force of circumstance to hold sway over Gaul and Germany. In the first place they are not united. The Ripuarians inhabit the Rhine Valley and the lower reaches of the Moselle, but they are no longer aggressive. The more bellicose Salians are divided among several petty kings. The " kingdom " of Tournai under Childeric has rivals at Cambrai and elsewhere in Belgium, and even in the department of Marne.

Another German people, no less famous and no less dangerous to the Roman world, the Alemans, also appear as extremely formidable rivals.

As early at least as the second half of the fifth century, these Swabians repeated the manœuvre of Ariovistus in the

---

[1] E. BABELON, **XII.**

[2] In spite of the view expressed by D. BRANDES (*Des Auspicius von Tout rythmischer Epistel an Arbogastes*, Wolfenbuttel, 1905), pp. 21-23.

first century B.C., and established themselves in Alsace, in Rhaetia.

They quarrel with the Franks over Worms and even Mainz. Further west they seize the capital of the Sequani, Besançon, and their tribes (the *Varasci* and the *Scotingi*) begin to settle in the territory of the future Franche-Comté.[1] They even advance for a moment as far as Langres, from which point they threaten both Champagne in the north, and the Valley of the Saône in the south. It is true that the Burgundians established at Geneva, Lyons and Chalon-sur-Saône, recaptured from them the advanced positions of Langres and Besançon (about 480). The Alemans, thrown back from the Rhine, are all the greater menace to the Franks.

The Burgundians, who occupied henceforth a very extensive territory from the plains of Champagne to the Durance, were established in the Valleys of the Saône and the Rhône, and beyond the Jura, in the eastern part of the *Maxima Sequanorum* of ancient times. Nevertheless it was clear to everyone that their power was weak and that they would have difficulty in maintaining their position. They themselves felt it so much that they tried to attach themselves again, almost in desperation to the Empire and Constantinople which was all too far away.

The chosen people are the Visigoths. One year after the extinction of the Western Empire, they had just made the Emperor of the East realize the fact of their dominion over Auvergne. From that time Euric, their King, reigned over half Gaul, from the Pyrenees to the Loire. As he was already master of Spain, and as the Ostrogoths were to settle in Italy a few years later, it seemed as though the Roman world in the West were going to continue its career under the protectorate of the most civilized of the Germanic nations, the great people of the Goths.

Gaul seems to have been assigned to them by fate, if not in entirety, at least for the greater part. Indeed it was quite clear that Euric's successor, Alaric II, who succeeded him in 485, was not going to stop at the Loire, but would attempt to push as far as the Seine, and would also like to

---

[1] Longnon, **CCCIV**, 198, attributes to the Burgundians place-names which are Aleman.

take the Rhone Valley from the Burgundians. As for the country between the Seine, the Marne and the Rhine, the *Belgium* of ancient times, contended for by the Franks and the Alemans, its future appeared to be settled ; it was destined to fall once more into barbarian hands and to become Germanized. It was necessary to jettison it. But the rest of Gaul was to become a Romano-Gothic State, governed by the dynasty of the Baltungs.

Such probably is the forecast that would have been made immediately after the fall of the Western Empire by minds endowed with foresight. No doubt it actually was made by many. The accession in 481 of a young Frankish *regulus* of some fifteen years of age, Childeric's son, whom we call Clovis, was to overthrow this forecast and change the course of the destinies, first of Gaul, and afterwards of the West.

The ambition of the little king of Tournai knew no bounds. It was served by an audacity and a skill that were exceptional. Success came rapidly. Soon after his accession (five years after, according to Gregory of Tours), Clovis attacked Syagrius, who appeared to the Franks as a " King of the Romans." The little army of the Roman, consisting naturally of barbarians, and more than probably of Franks, was conquered, and its remains were incorporated in the troops of Clovis (486). This victory immediately brought such prestige to the Frankish King that Alaric II dared not shelter the fugitive Syagrius ; he handed him over to Clovis who had him put to death.

The last vestige of Roman authority having disappeared, how was the conquest of the country between the Meuse and the Seine, and between the Seine and the Loire, achieved ? We have no information on this subject that deserves the slightest credence. It is obvious that Clovis, before seizing that vast territory, which represents a third of Gaul, must have gathered together all the forces of the Salians. The tortuous proceedings by means of which he succeeded in suppressing the little Frankish (Salian) kingdoms belonging to his relations and rivals must be placed after his victory over Syagrius. Towards the year 492 the prestige of Clovis was already so great that the mighty Theodoric married his sister Audefleda. The submission of the Thuringians at this same period remains an enigma; it is doubtful whether Clovis was yet in a position to lead an expedition into the heart of Germany.

The war against the Alemans[1] is a turning-point in the history of the rivalry between this people and the Franks. The Swabians, at the end of the fifth century, disputed with the Ripuarians for the possession of the middle, and even of the lower Rhine ; in a battle fought at Zülpich, in the neighbourhood of Cologne, Sigeburt the King had been wounded. Clovis showed that he had some political sense by hurrying to the aid of the Ripuarians. After a fierce fight, during which success hung long in the balance, between the Alemans and the united forces of the Salians and the Ripuarians, the Franks gained the upper hand. The victory was decisive. The vanquished Alemans had to implore the help of the King of the Ostrogoths, in order to escape destruction. Henceforth they were a subject people of their ancient rivals (496 or 497).

The baptism of Clovis, in spite of what tradition may say, has no connection with the King's victory over the Alemans. Clovis, a pagan, was urged to accept Christianity. But would he be Arian, like the other barbarian kings, or Catholic ? Conflicting influences were at work in his own family. The exhortations of the Burgundian Queen, Clotilda, niece of Gundobad, were able to move the heart of Clovis, but his conversion seems to have been effected by the sight of " miracles " performed at the tomb of St. Martin of Tours, on November 11th, some time between 496 and 499. Nevertheless there is no reason to doubt that Clovis was baptized at Rheims by Bishop Rémy.[2]

It is impossible to overestimate the significance of this event. It was the decisive moment in the history of the reign, and even of the Frankish hegemony. Clovis found himself, at the end of the fifth century, the only catholic head of a state in the whole of the West. The " Roman " clergy realized to the full the importance of an event for which they had done their best to pave the way and they saw in the erstwhile pagan a second Constantine. Baptism into the Catholic Church won for the cruel and cunning barbarian the sympathy and the adoration of the episcopate, not merely

---

[1] DCXIII.
[2] DCXXX, DCXXXV, DCLXXI, DCLXXXIII.

in his own kingdom, but in those parts of Gaul that were in the power of the Goths and the Burgundians. Through the bishops, the King of the Franks secured the submission of the Gallo-Roman peoples. In the midst of the general confusion and the breaking-up of the political and administrative institutions of the Roman world, the episcopate was the sole moral force, and, thanks to its wealth of territory, the sole economic resource that remained for the peoples. Was Clovis fully alive to the consequences of his gesture when he bowed his head before St. Rémy ? After all, it matters little ; it is enough that these consequences were beyond calculation.[1]

Baptism left the character of the neophyte unchanged. He remained the man he had been—strong, clever, unscrupulous, ready to seize every opportunity of extending his power and his reputation. In the year 500, Clovis still had two rivals in Gaul, the Burgundian State and the Visigothic State. The latter was powerful, or was thought to be. Clovis dealt first with the Burgundians. The quarrels of two of their kings provided an excuse for interference. Clovis supported Godigisel, Clotilda's former guardian, and put Gundobad to flight, in a battle near Dijon. The vanquished king fell back on Avignon ; the Frankish ruler came to besiege him there, but was unable to capture the town. The campaign was thus only partially successful, and after the retreat of the Franks Gundobad was able to seize his brother and put him to death (501). Clovis did not interfere.

Another and a vaster project occupied the mind of the Frankish King, and the support of the Burgundians (which he had been unable to exterminate), served his purpose. His intention was no less than to destroy the Visigoth power, at any rate in Gaul. Such a project appears extremely foolhardy. The Frankish King had to get into touch with the Episcopate of ancient Aquitania. Alaric II took precautions which the Catholics of that time described as persecutions; he removed certain bishops. Perhaps it was also with a view to conciliating the Roman population that he promulgated at Toulouse, on February 2nd, 506, the code of Roman laws known thenceforth by the name of the *Breviarium Alarici*. It was too late. The storm was about to break over the Kingdom of Toulouse and to destroy it. Clovis, worked upon

[1] DCXVII, DCXXXVIII, DCXCVI, DCCIV.

by the Emperor Anastasius, who desired to weaken the Gothic States in Italy and Gaul, made a sudden attack. He had made certain of the support of the Ripuarian Franks and the Burgundians. While the latter proceeded by way of the Central Plateau, the Franks set out from Tours and met the Goths at Vouillé, four leagues to the north-west of Poitiers. Alaric II is said to have perished at the hands of Clovis himself and only the Arvernian nobility put up any resistance. The rest of the campaign was nothing but a route march. Toulouse, the Visigothic capital, was taken and burnt by the Franks and Burgundians and Clovis laid hands on the famous treasure of the Gothic Kings. The son of Alaric II, the five-year old Amalaric, had been removed to Spain. Gisalic, a bastard, attempted to rally the Goths of Septimania, but in vain ; Gundobad and his Burgundians took possession of Narbonne and obliged him to flee into Spain (507-508).[1]

Thus a single campaign was sufficient to crush, in the North of the Pyrenees, the power of those formidable Visigoths who for a century past had dominated South-western Gaul and Spain, made the Empire tremble and triumphantly resisted Attila. Probably their Empire had spread too widely and too quickly. The Visigoths were not sufficiently numerous to effect a stable occupation of the territory stretching from the columns of Hercules to the Loire. In Gaul they have not left a single word of their language ; the place-names that recall their stay in that country are exceedingly rare and their ethnical contribution was insignificant. The Kingdom of Toulouse only existed in the person of its sovereign ; if he met with a cleverer or more powerful rival, it would be bound to crumble without even leaving ruins to recall the fact that it had once been.

In Italy, Theodoric had discovered the machinations of the Emperor and tried to form a league of West-Germanic kings—Burgundians, Thuringians, Heruls and Warnians, in opposition to Clovis. He himself had held out threats which were rendered vain by the necessity of his own struggle against Constantinople. All that the King of the Ostrogoths could do was to prevent the Franks from taking possession of Provence, the district between the lower Rhône and the

[1] DCXV, DLXXXV.

Pyrenees, known as Septimania, which was held by the Visigoths of Spain (509).[1]

It was none the less evident that from this moment the whole of Gaul was destined to fall into the hands of the Franks. Clovis secured the hegemony of his people by taking possession of the kingdom of Cologne, thus uniting Salians and Ripuarians. Legend has it that he accomplished this by means of treason. With surprising insight he established himself in Paris after the destruction of the Visigothic State. He only lived a short time there, for he died in 511, at the age of 45, in the prime of life.

The attempt has been made to rehabilitate the " private individual ",[2] but such an undertaking is fantastic, indeed almost ridiculous ; the psychology of Clovis is and always will be unknown. His work alone is of importance to the historian,[3] and it would be impossible to exaggerate its interest. Clovis was the founder of a new type of State. The " Conquest of Gaul ", to use a current expression, was not a conquest of the sort effected by the Anglo-Saxons in Great Britain, in which they substituted for the inhabitants whom they slew, a new population, language and culture. Nor was it any more similar to the conquest effected by the Vandals in Africa or the Lombards in Italy, in which a small band of invaders subjugated the bulk of the population and imposed on them its public law without troubling to alter the private law, the language or the culture of the conquered peoples.

Nor did the Frankish rule pass through the phase of the *fœdus*, as in the case of the Visigoth, Burgundian and Ostrogoth rule, or rather, it very quickly left this stage behind. The barbarian people (Goths, Burgundians, etc.) established on Roman soil, was at first only an army of mercenaries whose leader was a kind of official. The Roman organism, political, administrative and financial, remained intact or almost so. It was only gradually, in the second half of the fifth century, that the leader of the army, the barbarian king, laid his hand upon this mechanism and manipulated it to his own advantage.

It was not so with the Franks. Except in one region

---

[1] **DCXV.**
[2] Kurth, **DCXV.**
[3] On the whole, Kurth's opinion is that " his greatness is entirely in his work ; the man himself is largely unknown to us " (vol. ii., 220, 230).

(Belgica Secunda) and for a very short period (under Childeric) when it may be supposed that they ruled as Federates, they established their supremacy rapidly, and almost without any transition, and yet the Gallo-Romans were neither massacred nor reduced to a state of slavery nor even degraded socially. The invincible Salians have no political nor social privileges whatsoever in the State founded by their leader. If their *wergeld* is 200 *solidi* while that of a Roman is only 100, the reason is that the composition is divisible into three parts, namely,[1] that of the victim's heirs, amounting to 66⅓ *solidi* ; (2) that of the relatives who were under the obligation of exacting vengeance, and (3) that of the king, which was half of the preceding total. Since the second category did not exist in the case of a Roman, he was estimated at 66⅔ *solidi*, plus half for the king, making 100 *solidi*.[1]

The Frankish peasants continued, like their ancestors, to cultivate the land in Brabant and Flanders, but there is no indication that a victorious aristocracy despoiled the " Romans " and appropriated their lands, even partially, as the German Federates had done in the preceding century.

The truth is that there was no " conquest of Gaul ", at least as regards the Gallo-Romans. Northern Gaul, after 476, was really *res nullius*. Clovis laid hands on it, it appears, without coming up against any other obstacle than the rivalry of Syagrius, the Roman leader of barbarian troops. When the king had been converted, whatever hostility there may have been finally disappeared and his rule met with no resistance at all on the part of the native population.

It has been thought that a legal basis[2] could be found for the sway of Clovis over the Gallo-Romans. The foundation for this belief is the ceremony which took place on his return from the victorious campaign against the Visigoths. At Tours, where he celebrated his triumph, " Clovis received from the Emperor Anastasius the diploma of the consul. In the basilica of St. Martin he donned the purple robe and chlamys, and placed on his head a diadem, after which he rode on horseback from the door of the *atrium* of the basilica to the church of the town, scattering gold and silver coins to the people as he went. From that day he was called Consul and *Augustus* ".

---

[1] This, at any rate, is H. BRUNNER's explanation. **DXLV, DXLVI.**
[2] **DLXVIII, LI,** 499.

This account of Gregory of Tours, written long after the event, contains glaring inaccuracies ; it is impossible that Anastasius should have granted to a barbarian chief the imperial insignia, the diadem and the title of *Augustus*. Clovis obtained the honorary consulship, as other barbarian leaders had done before him, and in consequence gave the usual largesse. It has been said that " henceforth Clovis appeared to the Gallo-Romans as the delegate of the Emperor, and in consequence, as the representative of that ancient order of things which, in the midst of these troublous times, still remained the expression of law : his conquests were in a certain manner legitimatized ".[1] This reads too much into the text. It may be that the astute policy of Constantinople, while it honoured a useful ally, yet wished to put him in the position of a subject, but there is nothing to prove that Clovis in any way recognized such claims. He accepted the insignia of the consulship as one of those foreign decorations with which kings, even until quite recently, loved to adorn themselves, and nothing more. Nor did his successors, any more than himself, ever recognize formally the hegemony of the " Roman " Empire ; the laws of Justinian were never accepted in Gaul, at least as an official document.

As for the Gallo-Roman subjects of the Frankish kings, they at once accepted the *de facto* conditions : the Empire, henceforth fixed at Constantinople, could not affect them seriously. The clergy had been won over beforehand. The Council held at Orleans by the conqueror shortly before his death brought together bishops from every part of Gaul— the " alliance of altar and throne " was already sealed there.[2] The lay aristocracy rallied at once to the Merovingian dynasty.

As for the bulk of the population, composed mainly of *coloni*, that is of peasants who were legally free but socially outcast, it had no say in anything, nor had the inhabitants of the poverty-stricken little towns, which did not make themselves heard until six or seven centuries later.

The conquest, or rather the seizure, of Gaul by Clovis gave birth to a State more original in form and more vigorous in structure than the other barbarian kingdoms that arose out of the disintegration of the Roman world. Does this imply

---

[1] BAYET in **CCLXXIX** (II, 1, 103).
[2] **DCCXXXVIII, DXCVII, DCXXXVIII.**

that Clovis foresaw all the results which we distinguish in his work today ? Most certainly not. " He certainly did not have the idea of a kingdom of France, for nobody at that time was capable of imagining such a thing. Clovis saw nothing of what we see, and for that reason it is not right to make him a founder of the French Monarchy. All that existed of the France that was to come were the plains and mountains, the rivers and woods, and the human material that would become a nation only after long centuries. The real claim of Clovis to an important place in history is the fact that he united the Frankish populations in one people. . . . From being simply a Frankish King, he became King of the Franks. . . . It was not a nation that he created but a historic force ".[1]

---

[1] LAVISSE, in *La Revue des Deux Mondes*, Jan. 15th, 1885, p. 417.

CHAPTER IX

The Descendants of Clovis[1]

CLOVIS had not had the time, nor perhaps had the idea occurred to him, to create a political organization for the future in those countries of which he had taken possession. Being primarily king of the Salian Franks, he had only concerned himself with putting into writing (between 507 and 511) some points of Germanic law and a table of monetary "compositions" known as the "Salic Law". After his death, no lofty idea nor even common sense determined his succession. The founder of the new State left four sons, three of whom were by Clotilda ; the lands belonging to him were divided into four portions, exactly as though it were a question of a private inheritance. From the outset there appears the organic vice which is to weigh heavily on the French monarchy during the whole of the Middle Ages and up to the middle of the seventeenth century ; the monarchy is not a magistracy like the "Empire" but a patrimony subject to the rules of private ownership. From the start the Germanic spirit, which was still in the stage of childhood, prevailed and militated against the idea of the common interest.

At first the illusion prevailed that a plurality of kings would not destroy the unity of the *regnum Francorum*. The four capitals, if so modern a term is permissible, Paris (Childebert's), Orleans (Chlodomir's), Soissons (Chlotar's) and Rheims (Theodoric's) were brought closer together, in order that the kings and their armies might come swiftly to one another's aid and defy the attacks of the enemies of the Frankish people. It is remarkable that these kings should immediately have followed their father's example in abandoning the purely Germanic parts of Gaul. The son, to whom was assigned the East, might, later on, prefer Metz to Rheims, but he did not fix his residence at Trèves or Mayence or Cologne, in those districts of his kingdom that were already Germanized.

[1] Cf. for Bibliography, p. 310.

However, if the first partition did not imperil the *regnum*, the fact is that the rivals of the Franks, the Goths of Spain and Italy, were not in a position to pursue an aggressive policy. In Gaul, the Bretons from Great Britain, who had been established in Armorica for nearly a century, were turbulent but not dangerous, and the weakness of the Burgundians was patent. The warlike spirit of the Franks had not been broken nor had their appetite for booty and for conquest been satisfied by the death of the great man who had united them. The sons of Clotilda, revengeful and ambitious, completed the destruction of the kingdom of Burgundy in two campaigns (523 and 534).

Theodoric (Thierry or Theuderich), the eldest son of a former wife of Clovis, planned for his part to secure the protection of Gaul on the German side and to crush the rival peoples. The Alemans were no longer to be feared, nor were the Bavarians who recognized (under Chlotar I) the Frankish hegemony.

The most dangerous of the Germanic nations were, for the time being, the Thuringians, who were no other than the ancient Hermunduri.[1]

The main part of this people had advanced in the middle of the fifth century from the Elbe towards the upper Danube. In about 480 the Thuringians threatened Passau and Lorsch. Thrown back in the north by the Bavarians, they nevertheless constituted in the sixth century a powerful State between the Thuringian forest and the Elbe, and were dangerous for the Ripuarian Franks. Although he was the most warlike of the sons of Clovis, Theodoric did not consider himself strong enough ; he summoned Chlotar to his aid. On the banks of the Unstrut, the Salians and the Ripuarians, who were joined unadvisedly by the Saxons, made an onslaught upon the Thuringians.[2] Their King, Hermanfrid, was conquered and later assassinated (531). His widow, Amalaberga, fled into Italy with her children and took refuge with her brother Theodobat, the Ostrogoth. His son, Amalafrid, had an uncommon fate. Brought up at Ravenna, he was made prisoner in 540 with Witiges ; he was sent off to Constantinople where he took service and ended his days in the

East, as an official of the "Roman Empire". Among the spoils of the Franks was a daughter of another Thuringian King, Berthari. Chlotar took her and married her; she was Saint Radegund, patroness of Fortunatus, foundress of the convent of Ste. Croix at Poitiers, and the most touching female character in the whole of the Merovingian epoch.

The destruction of Hermanfrid's kingdom wrought a great change in the aspect of ancient Germany. Henceforth Thuringia was governed by Frankish dukes. The region between the Main and the Thuringian forest was colonized by the Franks, who left it their name, Franconia. In the north, the Saxons took possession of the Harz, but were tributary to the Franks. In the east the Wends, that is to say the Slavs, crossed the Elbe and occupied the country as far as the Saal. The hegemony of the Franks over this reduced Germany is unquestionable from the middle of the sixth century.

Theodoric was to be surpassed in ambition by his son Theudebert (Thibert). The latter was engaged in fighting against the Goths in Septimania, and was besieging Arles, after Béziers, when he received news of his father's death (534). While his uncles Childebert and Chlotar were directing operations in Spain against Theudis, King of the Visigoths, devastating Tarragona and besieging Saragossa (542), Theudebert was inciting the Franks in the East and their subject peoples to follow him on adventurous expeditions into Italy. The power of the Ostrogoths declined rapidly after the death of Theodoric the Great in 526. In 535 Justinian decided to recapture Italy from the barbarians.[1] Theudebert put himself in his pay. At the beginning of the year 536 the Burgundians and Alemans, subject peoples of the Franks, penetrated into upper Italy. Witiges thought he could purchase neutrality by surrendering Provence and Gothic Alemannia; Theudebert retained the latter and abandoned the other to his uncles. The Frank, with complete faithlessness, had merely the one aim of deceiving the Ostrogoths and the Byzantines. After several expeditions, the whole plain of the Po, as far as Venetia, fell into his hands. Ruling as he did Alemans, Bavarians and Thuringians, he was master of Germany. The only entirely independent

[1] Cf. Chap. III.

German peoples were, in Pannonia, the Gepids and the Lombards. Theudebert formed an alliance with the latter by marrying the daughter of their king, Wacho. He is supposed to have contemplated marching on Constantinople with their help. He was the first of the Frankish Kings to set himself up as a rival of the Emperor and to efface the name of Justinian on his coins, substituting his own for it.[1] Internally he used the Church as a support. Gregory of Tours, who says little about his expeditions far afield, praises his cleverness and piety. Theudebert made an attempt to increase the resources of the crown by levying taxes on the Franks ; but this plan failed. Theudebert is undoubtedly, together with Clovis, the most remarkable of the Merovingian Kings.[2] He died in 548 in the prime of life.

His policy was continued by his son, Theudebald. The latter was too much of a weakling physically to bear arms, and the conduct of expeditions was entrusted to the Aleman dukes (552-553). But the army of the first, Leutharis, in Venetia, was decimated by sickness, and that of the second, Bucelin, joined near Capua by the Byzantines of Narses, was exterminated. Shortly after this, Upper Italy was lost to the Franks. This territory was destined to fall once more into Lombard hands (568), and on the whole the reverse was lucky for the Franks, who would have exhausted their forces in an over-ambitious and premature effort to expand.

Theudebald died in 555. Soon after, Chlotar, the only remaining Merovingian, united the whole of the Franks under his authority. It was not too soon. The Saxons, allies until then, were adopting a threatening attitude. Three expeditions sent out against them did not result in a decisive victory. All that Chlotar could do was to drive them back into their own territory. It was left to Charlemagne to complete the conquest of Germany. Nevertheless it was under the principate of Chlotar that the *Regnum Francorum* attained its widest limits. Clovis had extended his kingdom over Burgundy, Provence, and the Alpine Valleys of Upper Italy ; the dukes of the Alemans, the Bavarians and the Thuringians, as well as the kings or counts of the Bretons in Armorica,

---

[1] **DCLXXVIII, p. xxxi. ; DLXXV,** vol. i., 58.
[2] **DCXCVII,** 122.

were his subjects. Chlotar reigned only three years over the whole of these lands, and died in 561.

Before proceeding further, it is well to dwell for a moment on the sons of Clovis. Christianity had no moral influence on them whatsoever. Treachery, cruelty, lust are the characteristics of their dynasty. Their duplicity equals and even surpasses that of the Byzantines themselves. Their history is nothing but a series of murders and horrible scenes which are recounted by Gregory of Tours with a cold-bloodedness that is at times disconcerting.

The thirty years that elapse between the death of Chlotar (561) and that of King Guntram (593) are the best known in the Merovingian period. It is not that they are of greater interest than the years preceding or following—far from it. But Gregory of Tours, an eye-witness, provides us with information on this third of a century which is abundant, albeit of unequal value.

The partition made in 561 between the sons of Chlotar resembles in every detail that of the year 511 ; the co-inheritors are again four in number, their capitals are the same, but the share of each is augmented owing to the conquests of Burgundy and Provence. Paris remains the centre of the State, and for several years is a neutral city.

The period is characterized by a relentless struggle, not between Neustria and Austrasia which do not as yet exist, but between the two Kings, Sigebert and Chilperic, or rather between their respective wives, Brunhild, daughter of Athanagild, King of the Visigoths, and Fredegund. Sigebert, in a position of inferiority, twice summoned to his aid the "peoples beyond the Rhine", who had been excluded until then from intestine warfare, as they were considered too uncivilized. These barbarians perpetrated numberless atrocities in the region of Paris, and their leader did not dare to check their excesses. At the moment when he was being raised on the shield at Vitry-en-Artois by the Salian Franks themselves, he was assassinated at the instigation of Fredegund (575). For the next ten years Chilperic, although not all-powerful, became a personage of the first importance. He met his death in the forest of Chelles, assassinated by an unknown hand (584). Gregory of Tours paints him in hideous colours, calling him the Nero and the Herod of the century.

Chilperic seems to have been the most intelligent of the successors of Clovis.[1] He had a very lofty conception of the prerogatives of royalty, interested himself in theology, had a knowledge of Latin letters, prided himself on writing poems and tried to reform the very deficient Latin orthography. He even held circus games at Paris and at Soissons in imitation of the emperors, as Theudebert had already done at Arles.

By his death Guntram, until then confined to Burgundy, became master of the *Regnum*. This personage, whose piety and generosity are constantly extolled by Gregory of Tours, who even attributes to him the power of working miracles, was a sort of Géronte ; by turns good-natured and cruel, rash and cowardly, he seems to have been unbalanced in his moral as well as his political life.

Having lost his children, he posed as the protector both of Chlotar II, the infant son of Fredegund, and of Childebert II, Sigebert's son. These heirs of the two enemy brothers were spared for fear of the total extinction of the Merovingian dynasty.

The aged Guntram and the youthful Childebert were drawn together by common dangers. First came the campaign of Gundobald. He was a natural son of Chlotar I. Hated by his father, he fled into Italy and thence to Constantinople. At the death of Chilperic, he set himself up as claimant. It is not known whether he was the instrument of the Eastern Court, which was anxious to make a final effort to attach Gaul to the Empire through the mediation of a king who was its creature.[2] On the other hand it is quite certain that a powerful party, not only in Southern and Central Gaul, but also in the East, looked with favour on Gundobald's attempt. Guntram only got the better of him by alienating the nobility by means of promises and having him put to death, contrary to his sworn oath (585).

The aristocracy, which played an increasingly large part since the death of Sigebert, constituted a far greater danger. The two kings felt this and united closely at Andelot, between Langres and Toul, on the borders of Burgundy and the district which was beginning to be known as Austrasia

---

[1] **DCXCI; CCLXXIX**, vol. ii., 1, 138 ; **DCXCVII**, 160.
[2] **DLXXXV.**

(November 28th, 587).   The sovereigns reciprocally indemnified one another and their followers, and undertook not to try to corrupt their " faithful followers " ;   finally they bequeathed their respective states to the survivor.

This last clause was eminently favourable to Childebert II who stepped into Guntram's succession at the death of the latter (April 28th, 593).   Sigebert's son appears to have been the replica of Theodoric I or Theudebert, and it is significant that he gave his sons the names of these two kings, to whom he was not directly related.   The Austrasian aristocracy had made itself all-powerful.   It openly threatened the young king and his mother Brunhild.   Duke Childebert II had difficulty in bringing to their senses Rauching, Guntram-Boso, Ursio, and Bertefried, a veritable menagery of wild beasts. In Germany he struggled against the Warnians, and subdued the Thuringians once again.   In Italy he continued the policy of his predecessors, selling his support at one time to the Byzantines, at another to the Lombards, and betraying both with calm effrontery.[1]   From 581 to 590 he led at least half a dozen expeditions into Upper Italy.   Finally the Franks concluded peace with the Lombards in 591, keeping only the passage of the Alps from Gaul into Italy, by Susa and Aosta. Childebert II died prematurely in 596, at the age of about 26.

The period following is obscure.   We have nothing to guide us, from 591 to 642, but the anonymous Burgundian chronicle attributed to someone of the name of Fredegar.

The sons of Childebert II, Theodebert and Theodoric, received respectively Austrasia and Burgundy.   Fredegund and her son Chlotar endeavoured to profit by the situation. They took possession of the cities in the neighbourhood of Paris. The Franks in the East marched against them.   Chlotar, after a successful first encounter at Lafaux (Aisne, in the canton of Vailby) was entirely overwhelmed in a second at Dormelles (Seine-et-Marne, in the canton of Moret) and his possessions were reduced to an insignificant territory between the Seine and the Oise (597).   The sons of Childebert II were very young.   Their mother Brunhild was to occupy the centre of the stage.   In about 601 she was driven from Austrasia by the nobles, with the connivance of her own son Theodebert, for whom she conceived a hatred from that moment.

[1] DCLXXXII.

She went to Burgundy, where she governed in Theodoric's name. She endeavoured to get the upper hand over the nobility, both secular and ecclesiastic, by appointing as " Mayors of the Palace " and patricians people of Gallo-Roman origin, such as Protadius, Claudius, Wulf, and Richomer, who came to a disastrous end, being assassinated by the nobles.

The decline of the Merovingians begins with the two sons of Childebert, one of whom was under his mother's sway, the other the plaything of the Austrasian aristocracy. When scarcely more than children, they lived in debauchery, repudiating their wives and surrounding themselves with concubines. The little martial valour that was left in them was wasted in fratricidal quarrels, for they hated one another. Theodoric beat his elder brother under the walls of Toul. Theodebert then appealed to the Thuringians and Saxons, but Austrasians and Germans from beyond the Rhine were beaten at Zülpich, near Cologne, by Theodoric's Franco-Burgundian army. Theodebert was taken prisoner and put to death at Chalon-sur-Saône, as was also his little son, Merovech (612). Theodoric meant to be the only King of the Franks ; he was gathering together an army of Austrasians to march against Chlotar II, when he died unexpectedly at Metz (613). Brunhild then tried to get Sigebert II, the eldest of the sons whom the various wives of Theodoric had borne him, acknowledged as king. But she was feared and hated in Austrasia. The most eminent individuals in this region, Arnulf and Pepin, the two ancestors of the Carolingians, called in Chlotar.

It was Brunhild's turn to seek the help of the trans-Rhenane peoples. But at the moment when the fight was about to begin on the Aisne, Sigebert's army dispersed ; Garnier (Warnachar), Mayor of the Palace, and the " farons " of Burgundy had made common cause with Chlotar. Sigebert fled but was captured on the banks of the Saône and put to death, and his brothers were either massacred or hid themselves and were never seen again. Brunhild, left to Chlotar, was tortured with the utmost refinement of savage cruelty.

The most varied judgments have been passed on her. She is only known to us through her enemies. Through a reaction

against the hostile attitude of the old historians, the attempt
has been made to rehabilitate her by attributing to her the
most lofty political conceptions. All that can be said is that
she was determined to reign, no matter by what means, and
that she was wrecked by the insubordination of the nobles
and also of the higher clergy.[1]

King Chlotar, second of the name, " governed happily
for sixteen years the entire kingdom of the Franks, just as
the first Chlotar had done. He was at peace with the neighbouring nations. He was patient, lettered, God-fearing,
very generous toward the churches and the bishops, a great
almsgiver, benevolent to all and abounding in piety." Fredegar
the chronicler has no fault to find in him except that he was
very fond of the chase and was too ready to listen to women.

In actual fact, Chlotar II was the prisoner of the aristocracy. In 614 he was obliged to issue an edict making important concessions to the Church and the nobles.[2] Garnier,
whose treachery had made Chlotar's fortune, had extorted
from the latter a promise on oath to allow him to keep his
Mayoralty of the Palace of Burgundy for life. Perhaps
Rado in Austrasia and Landry in Neustria obtained the same
guarantee. However, in 626, at the death of Garnier, Chlotar
managed to recover the Mayoralty of the Palace, ostensibly
at the request of the Burgundian nobles.

On the other hand, at about the same time, Chlotar was
obliged to give in to the autonomist feeling in Austrasia
which was growing stronger and stronger, by granting to
this district a king of its own in the person of his eldest son,
Dagobert. Fredegund's son died October 18th, 629 and was
buried, like his grandfather, near Paris, in the Monastery of
St. Vincent, known later as Saint Germain des Près.

Under the rule of Dagobert (629-639) the Merovingian
monarchy shone for the last time, but with a false splendour.

A danger menaced the unity of the Kingdom—Dagobert
had a brother, Charibert, and he had to give up to him,
in Aquitaine, almost the whole of the former Visigothic
Kingdom.

This Charibert died, and so did his son. But Dagobert,
in this quarter, came into conflict with a new people who were

[1] DCXVI, vol. i., 265-356.
[2] DLXXVIII, 323 ; DCXXVIII ; DLXXXII, 612.

to prove extremely troublesome to his successors—namely, the Basques or Gascons. Descended from the ancient Cantabrians, they had been little influenced by Roman civilization, but had kept their customs and their Iberian language which distinguished them from the other European peoples. They alone among the populations of Spain had resisted the rule of the Sueves and Visigoths. Towards the end of the sixth century they crossed the Pyrenees in the West, and began to pillage Novempopulonia, between the Garonne and the Pyrenees, which was destined some day to take their name— Gascony.[1] They established themselves between the mountains and the Adour in such dense masses that even to-day in that district their language still survives. Expeditions sent against them in 581 and 587 by the two kings, Chilperic and Guntram, failed ignominiously. In 602 however, Theodoric and Theodebert succeeded in imposing upon them a tax and a duke. But this was only a temporary submission. Dagobert had to bring against them a large army recruited in the Kingdom of Burgundy. At its head was the referendary Chadoind ; it was commanded by ten dukes, eight of whom were Franks, one a " Roman " (Aquitanian ?) and one a Burgundian. The Basques, driven into the Pyrenees, offered to surrender, but when the Franks started on their journey homeward, the Basques surprised in the Valley of the Soul the contingent of one of the dukes and cut it to pieces (637). It was a tragic preliminary to the celebrated expedition of Charlemagne in 778, when Roland the " paladin " perished.

Dagobert intervened even beyond the Pyrenees. On the death of Sisebert he sent two armies who went as far as Saragossa to establish Sisenand, who paid 200,000 *solidi* for this support. In Italy he took under his protection Queen Gundeberga, one of the Merovingians, and forced Chrotgar, the Lombard duke, to release her from prison. With the " Empire " he kept on friendly terms : a " perpetual " peace was concluded in 631.

In Gaul, in the peninsula of Armorica, the Bretons, who had theoretically been subjects of the Franks since the beginning of the sixth century, had in actual fact remained independent. Expeditions directed against them in 580 and 593 had on the

[1] **DCXXXIX, DXXXIV and DXXXV.**

whole come to nothing. Dagobert was fortunate enough to see one of their kings, Judicaël, no doubt a King of Domnonia (a region lying between the bay of Mont Saint Michel and the Harbour of Brest), come to Clichy to offer his submission. It is true that he was exceedingly pious and was anxious to retire from the world ; the monastery of Gaël was called after him—Saint Juquel.

But Dagobert had little success with Germany. It should be mentioned that the storm had been gathering for some time. Central Europe was overwhelmed by a racial upheaval. Fleeing from the Western Turks, a tribe of the same race known as the Avars (erronously, for the real Avars are different) came from the shores of the Caspian sea and established themselves in ancient Pannonia where they formed the centre of a vast empire.[1]

These nomads were related to the Huns and had the same characteristics of valour and ferocity. They wielded the bow, but also the lance, and when occasion required, formed a strong, mail-clad cavalry. Their first encounter with the Franks dates from 562. Chlotar I was just dead. The Avars hurled themselves on Thuringia. The King of the Eastern Franks hurried to the help of his subjects and met the invaders in an indecisive battle. In 566 there was a fresh encounter, and this time Sigebert was conquered and imprisoned and he had to buy his ransom with gold. Fortunately the Avars soon afterwards turned in another direction. The Emperor Justin II made use of them against the Gepids, who were wiped out. It was in order to escape from their yoke that the Lombards invaded Italy in 568. Central Europe was at this time, from the Carpathians to the Danube and the Eastern Alps, a desert which the Avar horsemen scoured in all directions. Certain historians place in this period the conventional date marking the end of the ancient world.[2]

In 597, these barbarians appeared again in Thuringia. Childebert II was just dead ; Brunhild was obliged to pay them to withdraw. As can be seen, the attitude of the Franks towards the Avars was not very glorious. Charlemagne

---

[1] Kiessling, in **CCCXCVII**, vol. viii., col. 2599, 2607.
[2] Gutschmidt, *Kleinere Schriften*, vol. v., 393, 417. Neumann, in **CLXI**, vol. iii., 413. Peisker, in **LXXIII**, vol. ii., 436.

alone was able later to overthrow the Tartar Empire, established in the heart of Europe.

Behind the Avars, the Slavs, their subjects, had crept in. Samo, who figured in legend as a Frankish merchant, freed them from the yoke of the Asiatics.[1] He founded an Empire the centre of which was Bohemia and which extended from the river Havel to the Styrian Alps. In about 632, war broke out with the Franks. So great was the power of the Slav that Dagobert, in order to combat him, was obliged to ally himself with the Lombards. The latter were victorious, like the Alemans, but Dagobert, who was leading the Austrasians, was cut in pieces at Wogatisburg (perhaps in Bohemia). The Sorbs, between the Oder and the Saale, shook off the suzerainty of the Franks and recognized that of Samo. The Wends actually took the offensive and flung themselves on Thuringia. Dagobert advanced as far as Mainz. He had raised an Austrasian army but, having little confidence in it, he had a Neustrian and Burgundian guard. He dared not cross the Rhine. The Saxons offered to keep the enemy in check in return for the restoration of the tribute money that they had been paying the Franks since the time of Chlotar I. They did not give proper protection to Austrasia and this country demanded autonomy. As for Thuringia, it had its own dukes.

Thus Dagobert met with nothing but failure in the East.

The so-called Fredegar[2] is never tired of praising the benevolence of the King and his justice which struck terror into the hearts of the wicked when he made a tour through Burgundy. But when Dagobert established himself in Paris, things went badly. The King grew rapacious and debauched. The chronicler, who is a partisan of Pepin and the Austrasian aristocracy, is grieved to see the King abandon Austrasia and disgrace Pepin. He admits however that Dagobert was a generous almsgiver. He was also a great builder of churches. Saint Denis, which he enriched[3], was to be, under the succeeding dynasty, the rival of Saint Martin of Tours, until then the most venerated shrine in Gaul. The clergy in the king's circle, such as Audoenus (Saint Ouen) and Eligius

---

[1] PEISKER, in **LXXIII**, vol. ii., 451.
[2] **DCXLII.**
[3] He was not, however, the founder of Saint-Denis. See LEVILLAIN, in the *Bibl. de l'Ecole de Chartes*, vols. **LXXXII** and **LXXXVI** (1921 and 1925).

(Saint Eloi) rank among the greatest names in the Gaulish Church in this age. One catches glimpses through the encomiums or the invectives of Fredegar of a person who, though a sensualist and a lover of pomp, could on occasion be energetic, and who endeavoured to save what remained of the financial system, and to restore something of order and justice. But the glory of his reign is an empty show and the monarchy is sapped by the germs of decay.

CHAPTER X

The Decay and End of the Merovingians[1]

AFTER Dagobert's death in 639, Merovingian history is no longer the history of kings, but of grand viziers, the Mayors of the Palace of the three parts of the *Regnum*, Neustria, Austrasia, Burgundy.

The Mayors of the Palace, themselves leaders of the aristocracy, control it for a long while. The chronicler paints in the most glowing colours the Mayors of the Palace who govern the *Regnum* under the nominal rule of the sons of Dagobert, Clovis II and Sigebert III. Aega, in Neustria, was prudent, mild, eloquent and god-fearing ; he restored to the churches the property taken from them by the " *fiscus*." Erkinoald his successor (641) is mild, kindly, full of deference towards the bishops ; he does not amass riches for himself, and is beloved by all. In Austrasia, Pepin is full of prudence and gentleness and governs " benevolently ". Such praises from a partisan of the aristocracy show that these Mayors were entirely complaisant.

In Austrasia however, one of them, Grimoald, son of Pepin, had illusions and attempted in 656 to secure for his family the succession to the throne.

A violent usurpation was impossible, in view of the almost legendary prestige that still surrounded the line of Merovech. Grimoald got rid of a son of Sigebert (not daring to put him to death, he sent him secretly to the distant country of Ireland) and put on the throne under the name of Childebert III, his own son, who had been adopted by Sigebert. But the pseudo-Merovingian and his father died after a reign of seven years and the attempt made by the Pepin family was not followed up.[2]

In Neustria, on the death of Clovis II in 657, one only of the three sons he left, the eldest, was proclaimed king under

---

[1] For bibliography, see above, p. 310.
[2] **DCXIV,** and especially **DCXXXII.**

the name of Chlotar III. The widow of the deceased king,
the regent Bathildis, who was an Anglo-Saxon of servile origin,
had neither prestige nor authority. The head of the State
was the Mayor of the Palace, Ebroin. One king implied one
Mayor only, but Ebroin was a Neustrian, and came up against
the particularism of the Austrasians and the Burgundians.
In 663 he had to concede to the former a king, Childeric II,
brother of Chlotar III, with a Mayor of the Palace, by name
Wulfoald, who was, it is true, his creature. In Burgundy,
Ebroin encountered the hostility of the bishops of that region.
In the second half of the seventh century, the bishops no
longer had the submissive attitude of their predecessors in
the preceding century. Arnulf, Bishop of Metz, was the real
master of Austrasia. The instigator of the conspiracy by
which Queen Bathildis was banished to the Nunnery of Chelles
which she had founded and where she died in the odour of
sanctity, was Sigebrand, Bishop of Paris. The resistance of
the Burgundians was roused and kept up by Léger (Leodegar),
Bishop of Autun.[1]

In 673, Chlotar III having died, Ebroin, on his own authority,
placed on the throne the youngest son of Clovis II, Theodoric
(Thierry) III. Burgundy and Austrasia rose in revolt.
Ebroin's creature had his locks shorn and was imprisoned in
the Abbey of Saint Denis ; as for the Mayor, although his
life was spared, he was made a cleric and banished to the
Monastery of Luxeuil. The Neustrian aristocracy called in
Childeric II and his Mayor. It was the same procedure as in
614, but in the opposite direction ; then the Austrasians
and Burgundians had gone over to the Neustrian, Chlotar II.
As in 614, the aristocracy demanded pledges : " Upon this,
everyone asked King Childeric to issue decrees in the three
kingdoms he had obtained, to the effect that the judges
should preserve, as in former days, the laws and customs of
each country and that the rectors (Mayors of the Palace)
should not go from one province into another, and that no
one should assume the tyranny, after the example of Ebroin,
nor abase his colleagues (*contubernales*) as he had done ; but
that on the contrary, since each man knew he would come to
the top in his turn, he should not dare to put himself before
others. He gladly acceded to their requests ".

[1] **DLXXII.**

According to this testimony, found in the most ancient " Life of Saint Leger ",[1] it appears that the aristocracy was growing uneasy about the power of the Mayoralty of the Palace, and wished to make it a temporary office. Moreover, particularism had become so inveterate that each of the three big districts wanted its mayor, even when ruled by a single king. But Childeric II took himself seriously and determined to reign. He failed to keep his promises : " Depraved by the counsels of fools who were almost pagan, he suddenly revoked, with the lightness of youth, the ordinances which he had just confirmed with wisdom ".

Bishop Leodegar made himself unbearable. Childeric sent him to join his old adversary Ebroin at Luxeuil. The opposition of the Franks grew stronger. The young king ordered anyone who resisted him to be beaten. A revolt broke out and a certain Bodilon, whom he had had whipped, assassinated him in the forest of Lognes (6 kilometres from Chelles), together with his wife who was pregnant. Audoenus (Saint Ouen), Bishop of Rouen, gave the victims pious burial at Saint Vincent (Saint Germain des Prés) where the Benedictines discovered their bones behind the choir in 1656.[2] Childeric II perished at the age of 25. He was the last Merovingian who attempted to reign (in the autumn of 675). The precarious unity of the *Regnum* was once more shattered.

While Wulfoald was making his escape with great difficulty into Austrasia, Ebroin and Leodegar were escaping from Luxeuil. The Bishop of Autun re-established Theodoric III and chose as Mayor of the Palace of Neustria and Burgundy Leudesius, son of the Mayor Erkinoald, who had made a good impression on the nobility. But Ebroin succeeded in laying hands on the young king and—what was more important— on the " treasure ". Leudesius surrendered and was put to death, contrary to a sworn oath. As for Leodegar, who was besieged at Autun, he was obliged to capitulate. He was made to undergo the Byzantine torture of having his eyes put out ; later a Council met at Villeroy (Yonne) and, under intimidation, declared him to be an accomplice in the assassination of Childeric II. Leodegar was tortured and put to death on October 2nd, 678. The indignation of the Church

---

[1] KRUSCH, *Scriptores rerum Merovingicarum*, vol. v., 289.
[2] DCCXIII.

and the sympathy of the populace transformed into a great saint a person who was certainly nothing more than a meddlesome and excitable aristocrat. A hundred villages in France and Belgium still bear his name to-day, and hundreds of churches have been dedicated to his memory.

Ebroin was master, and absolute master, of Neustria and Burgundy. Guérin, Leodegar's brother, had been massacred and his partisans had fled. It was inevitable that the conflict should begin with the Austrasians. The latter were in a state of complete anarchy. Dagobert II, Grimoald's former victim, who had been exiled in Ireland and recalled by the Austrasians (676), had made himself thoroughly hated. The country was ruled by a certain Martin and by Pepin II, grandson of Pepin I on his mother Begga's side, and son of Ansegis (*Ansegisus*). After twenty years of eclipse, the ambitious descendant of Saint Arnulf of Metz once more appears on the scene. The office of Mayor of the Palace seems to have disappeared momentarily in Austrasia ; at least Martin and Pepin II are only styled " dukes ". Both of them attack Ebroin and his phantom king, Theodoric III, with a large army of Austrasians. The encounter took place at Bois-du-Fay (the Ardennes department, canton of Chateau-Porcien), not far from the Roman road stretching fromTongres to Rheims through the Ardennes. The Austrasians were completely vanquished (679). Pepin managed to escape while Martin fled for refuge to Laon. Ebroin, who was waiting at Ecry (the Asfeld of to-day, in the Ardennes) ; lured him with false promises and had him put to death ; his emissaries are said to have taken an oath on a shrine from which the relics had been removed. At about the same time, Dagobert II was assassinated in the forest of Stenay, " treacherously by the machinations of the dukes and with the consent of the bishops ". He too was considered a martyr and his tomb at Stenay became a centre for pilgrimages (December 23rd, 679).[1]

Ebroin, henceforth the only master, " cruelly oppresses the Franks ", by which are meant the Neustrians. He was assassinated by one of them, Hermanfred, who fled to Austrasia to Pepin II, who was the sole authority remaining in

---

[1] E. TARDIF, *Les Chartes merovingiennes de l'Abbaye de Noirmontier*. p. 55 (offprint from *Nouv. Revue hist. de droit*, vol. xxii.).

that country (681). The most diverse judgments have been passed on this person, as likewise on Brunhild. Like that queen, he is known to us only through his enemies. By reaction, the attempt has been made to turn him into a great statesman. His designs, if he had any beyond his personal ambition, are unknown to us. All that can be said, is that he was a man of exceptional energy and ferocity, and that with him Neustria, which hated him, lost its hegemony.

Indeed, neither Waratton nor his son Gislemarus, who succeeded Ebroin as mayors, were worthy to replace him. The former made peace with Pepin II who acknowledged Theodoric III as king. Henceforth there was to be one sovereign only for the whole of the *Regnum Francorum*. As the king no longer possessed a shadow of power it is useless to trouble ourselves with several puppets. The situation was upset by Gislemarus, who quarrelled with his father and made war on Pepin. As usual, the Austrasians were beaten (about 683) ; but Gislemarus died soon afterwards, as did his father Waratton later (686).

Division arose among the Neustrians. They could not make up their minds whom to choose as Mayor. At the instigation doubtless of Warraton's widow, they decided on his son-in-law, Berthar (Bertharius). He, it seems, was incompetent. Pepin seized the opportunity and fell on him with an Austrasian army. The encounter took place at Tertry (Somme), half-way between Péronne and Saint Quentin, not far from the Roman road going from Cambrai to Soissons, which the armies of Clodio, Childeric and Clovis had marched over so many times two centuries before. Berthar was beaten, took to flight, and a little later was slain, at the instigation of his own mother-in-law (687). A single battle, fought under favourable circumstances, secured the pre-eminence of Austrasia, which had been constantly beaten for more than a century (from the end of Sigebert I in 575).

The triumph of Austrasia was due before all to the cleverness of Pepin II, to the chance which made the line of the successors of St. Arnulf of Metz endure, while in Neustria no dynasty of Mayors of the Palace could establish itself, and lastly to the insubordination of the Neustrians ; on several decisive occasions they could come to no understanding

about the choice of a mayor or refused to obey him and preferred the Austrasian.   Hence the victory of Tertry was not
the victory of one race or of one policy over another.   It
was the victory of a powerful, clever and saintly family of
the East over the Mayors of the Palace of Neustria.[1]   Nevertheless, Tertry is of considerable importance and has a lasting
significance.   Pepin II, called Pepin of Heristal, did not
leave the East to settle in the Parisian district as Dagobert I
had done.   He lived in the country in which the fortune
of his house had been established, to which ties bound him
and from which he drew his strength, the lower valley of the
Meuse.   It was a half-Roman, half-Germanic country.   The
domains of the " Pippinidae " in Roman-speaking (Walloon)
territory were perhaps no less numerous than those situated
in German territory.   Nevertheless the Carolingians' ancestors
were German in speech and customs.

As Aquitania became detached, at the end of the seventh
century, from the *Regnum*, the German character of the
Austrasian State became more marked.   The Carolingians,
although they were polyglots and came under " Salic " law,
remained people of the East.   By tradition they could get
themselves crowned at Soissons and Noyon, and buried at
Saint Denis out of piety; almost to the end they were Austrasians.   Paris, which since Clovis was tending to become,
if not a capital, at least a rallying place for the Frankish
nationality, was abandoned.   But in the East, no real capital
could be founded, an incontrovertible proof of the economically
backward character of Austrasia.

Having vanquished, Pepin seized the " treasure " and won
back Austrasia.   He did not deign to dethrone Theodoric III
but was satisfied with having him supervised by one of his
own creatures, Norbert.   On the latter's death, Pepin replaced
him by his own son, Grimoald (Mayor of Neustria under
the fictitious Kings Clovis III (690-694) and Childebert III
(694-711)), while another of his children, Drogo, was given the
" duchy " of Champagne.

Anarchy, which had been endemic ever since the death
of Dagobert I, had been fatal to the hegemony of the Franks.
Aquitania had slipped from them.[2]   It was in the power of

---

[1] DLXXXIV, 177.
[2] DXXXVIII, DCLXXVII.

a dynasty of dukes who were Frankish in origin but who turned to their own profit the valour of the Gascons ; Aquitania was tending to become *Wasconia*, not only up to the Garonne, but also up to the Loire. In Germany, the Saxons no longer paid tribute since the reign of Dagobert I. Thuringia had recovered its independence ever since Duke Rudolf had beaten Sigebert III, who had been badly supported by the Austrasians. The Bavarians and even the Alemans were trying to do the same. But Pepin compelled them to take their dukes from him. At this time an old people made its appearance, wielding power after long centuries of obscurity, the Frisians. Settled at the mouth of the Ems, and like their kindred the Ampsivarii (men of the Ems), subjects of Rome in the first century, they had made themselves independent in the third century. In the fifth century, when the Franks were advancing in the West up to the Meuse and the Escaut, they themselves spread towards the East, at the expense of the Chauci (Saxons).[1] At the end of the seventh century, they occupied on the coasts of the North Sea the mouths of all the rivers, the Weser, Ems, Rhine, Meuse and Escaut. Their duke, Radbod, made them formidable. Pepin tried to win him over to his side. He asked the hand of his daughter for his son Grimoald ; at the same time he tried to convert these hardened pagans ; the Anglo-Saxon Willibrord, under his protection, founded the church of Utrecht.

In the mist through which we catch a glimpse of him as we do of all the men of his time, Pepin seems energetic, statesman-like and also pious, founding amongst others, the monasteries of Echternach and Susteren in Austrasia. He encouraged the Irish missionaries who completed the Evangelisation of Alemannia and Bavaria.

In spite of all, when he died, at Jupilles on the Meuse, December 16th, 714, it seemed that his work would fall to pieces, and that it would be with his house as with those of his rivals, the Mayors of the Palace of Neustria. His two sons had gone down to the grave before him. Drogo had died in 707 and was buried near Metz, in the Church of the Holy Apostles, which began to take the name of the great ancestor of the house, St. Arnulf. Grimoald, " pious, modest, gentle and just, was assassinated by a Frisian in the Church of

[1] CDXLIII, 157.

St. Lambert of Liège (April, 714). The dynasty was represented by three children, Arnulf and Hugo born to Drogo and Theudoaldus (Thiaud), the illegitimate son of Grimoald.

The Neustrians thereupon tried to put into operation again for their own advantage the plan which had been so successful with Pepin twenty-eight years before. The antagonism between Neustria and Austrasia had become so bitter that the Neustrians did not shrink from an alliance with the Frisians, who were pagans and the enemies of the Franks, against their brothers of the East. They put to flight the child Theudoaldus in the forest of Guise (Compiègne) and chose as their Mayor of the Palace a certain (Rainfroi) Ragenfridus. The latter passed beyond the Carbonarian Forest and devastated Austrasia up to the Meuse (715). The house of Pepin was completely routed. His widow, Plectrude, who fought with courage, had a new enemy on her hands, Charles, a son born to her husband by Alpaidis (Aupaïs).

It seemed that the *Regnum Francorum*, the work of Clovis, would, like its ancient rival the Visigothic State, end up in bankruptcy. Three years before Pepin's death, Arabs and Berbers crossed into Spain from Africa, and in one battle put an end to the Monarchy of the Goths (711). The same fate threatened the Frankish State. The Duke of Aquitania was unable to hold out for long, and if the Neustrians and Austrasians continued to rend each other, it was certain that Gaul, like Spain, would be the prey of Islam. Religion, language, law and civilization would all be changed.

Salvation was to come from Pepin's illegitimate son. Charles escaped from the prison in which he had been placed by Plectrude, and with his supporters he tried to thrust back the Neustrians and Frisians. At first he was unsuccessful, being beaten by Radbod the Duke of the Frisians, while Ragenfridus, with the nominal King Chilperic II, reached Cologne where Plectrude bought his withdrawal. But, on his return, Ragenfridus was surprised by Charles at Amblève, near Malmédy. The following year, a new encounter took place on the border between Neustria and Austrasia, at *Vinciacus* (a sluice of the Canal of Saint Quentin, 9 kilometres south of Cambrai, keeps this name in the form of Vinchy). Ragenfridus and his King were beaten (March 21st, 717). Then Charles turned upon his step-mother and at Cologne Plectrude had to give up to him Pepin's "treasure". Pepin's legitimate posterity was set aside; the destinies of this house and of Austrasia were henceforth in the hands of Charles.

After thrusting the Saxons back as far as the Weser, Charles resumed the fight against Neustria. Ragenfridus and his King had asked for help from Eudes, the *de facto* ruler in Aquitania, promising to acknowledge his reign *de jure*. But the confederates were beaten under Soissons and pursued as far as Orléans (719). The following year, Eudes gave up to Charles King Chilperic and the "treasure", both having been taken by him to Aquitania. The puppet dying soon afterwards, a son of Dagobert III was brought out of a monastery and given the name of Theodoric IV (721). The last Mayor of the Palace of Neustria, Ragenfridus, had disappeared. The unity of the *Regnum Francorum* was restored to the advantage of Austrasia and the descendants of St. Arnulf of Metz.

A superstitious habit was able to keep on the throne for another thirty years a phantom entitled "most glorious king" whose nominal reign served to date the charters; but the Merovingian epoch was at an end. In the person of the new Clovis, Charles "Martel", the Carolingian period had really begun.

CHAPTER XI

THE MEROVINGIAN MONARCHY. INSTITUTIONS[1]

DAGOBERT, who died at the age of thirty-five, at Epinay-sur-Seine, January 19th, 639, is properly speaking the last Merovingian King. After him the power ceased to be really exercised by the sovereign. It passed into the hands of the *major domus*, or the Mayor of the Palace, as he is usually called. It is well to make a halt here and to study the Monarchy and the Institutions of this period.

I. THE MONARCHY

What is the mainspring of the society which we call "Merovingian"?

It is not the patriotism known to the ancients, which subordinated everything to the life and prosperity of the City. It is not, at least until the end of the sixth century, the aristocracy. It is not a bureaucracy led by the army, as was the Later Empire. It is not the patriarchal monarchy of the Middle Ages, subject to the authority of custom. It is not the régime of the clan. Nor again is it the feudal government, the "benefice" being still very far from the fief and the holding of land in full ownership (in "*alleu*") being still the rule.

Properly speaking, there are no institutions, or rather the sole institution, and the sole living force, is the Monarchy. The *regnum* is an estate, the owner of which is called King, and he disposes of it according to the rules of private ownership. On his death, his sons divide it amongst themselves, without any regard for geography, ethnography or the desires or convenience of the peoples. The Regnum Francorum is not a State, or else it is a State which is confused with the personality of the King. On March 3rd, 1766, Louis XV,

---

[1] CCLXXIX, vol. ii., 1, 170; DXLV, vol. i.; DLIX, 90; DLXXVIII, DLXXXII and DLXXXIV, DXCIV, DXCIII, DCXXVIII, DCLXXXIX and DCXC, DCCV, DCCVII, DCCVIII, DCCXXXIV, vol. i. and above all DCCXXXVI, vol. i., 1.

answering the Paris Parliament, defined the nature of the French
Monarchy as follows : " Sovereignty resides in me alone
. . . the legislative power belongs to me alone uncondi-
tionally and undividedly. The public order emanates entirely
from me, and I am its supreme guardian. My people is one
with me. The rights and the interests of the Nation, which
some dare to make into a body separate from the monarch,
are necessarily united with mine, and rest only in my hands "[1].
Louis XV spoke as would have done a Merovingian King,
if he had been capable of reflecting on the nature of the power
which he exercised. But the Merovingian would have spoken
the truth, whereas the Bourbon was deceiving himself, other
social forces outside the Monarchy having arisen, and his
theory being obsolete—no longer applying. A further change
was that even Louis XV recognized that he owed certain
duties to his subjects, while such an idea was totally alien to
his remote ancestor. The end of Merovingian government
was the Monarch's personal satisfaction.[2] The Kingdom
he had acquired was for him only a soil for exploitation. If
he made war, it was to increase his own possessions. His
expeditions to Spain, Germany and Italy had no other end
but pillage and the imposition of a tribute. They were not
crusades to win new peoples for Christianity, though at the
price of atrocities. Still less can the Merovingian's attitude
be likened to that of the Roman Emperor in whose hands
rested the security and welfare of the ancient world. The
ceaseless struggle against barbarism lent a tragic greatness
even to the worst emperors. They knew very well that they
would end their lives under the blows of the enemy, their
rivals or their own soldiers, but yet they carried on a desperate
fight. Personalities like that of a Marcus Aurelius, or a Julian,
are among the highest of which mankind can boast. Beneath
them, Septimius Severus, Claudius II, Probus, Aurelian, and
even Valentinian and Theodosius are soldiers and statesmen
of rare virtue. A Diocletian and a Constantine carried out
successfully a superhuman task, the restoration of the ruin
which the Roman world was at the end of the third century.
To place the Merovingian Kinglets beside these great men, would
be to set up an outrageous comparison and to defy history.

---

[1] *Arrêts du Conseil*, Paris 1766, vol. I, 4.
[2] **DLXXVIII**, 154.

To build his house, the Merovingian King picked up materials from everywhere. It is useless to draw attention to some particular part of the building or to some particular ornament, and then decide that the whole is Roman or German, because a particular stone comes from Rome or Germany. The materials are composite, but the plan and structure are adapted to the needs and tastes of the new owner of Gaul.

The taking possession of the latter country was a private project of Clovis which succeeded. The King used the Franks because they were the only force he had at his disposal. He had in view his own interest and not that of his people. The conquest of Gaul, moreover, had as a result a complete change in the respective position of the King and his people. From his German past, the Merovingian inherited no very extensive prerogatives ; apart from times of war his power was checked by the nobility and the assembly of the tribe. The conquest gave the monarchy so superior a position, that the rights of the people vanished. The assembly ceased to meet and the nobility, apart from the reigning dynasty, had already disappeared.

The King continued to surround himself with Franks and to bear the title of " King of the Franks," but ceased to live in Frankish territory. Clovis established himself in Paris ; his sons and grandsons settled in Paris, Orleans, Soissons, Rheims, Metz, Chalon-sur-Saône. None of these towns was German-speaking. It has been observed that in the divisions, the part sacrificed was that which included the former district of the Salians.[1] Finally, since the army was recruited amongst free men with no distinction of race, the *exercitus Francorum* soon consisted of a majority of Gallo-Romans, except in the East. Thus the conquest brought about a break with the past, detaching the King from the *populus Francorum*, and placing him so far apart and above that henceforth every trace of election disappeared and the monarchy became hereditary and absolute.

If there no longer was a Frankish nobility, the Gallo-Roman aristocracy of the " senators " still survived, but only as a social class. Only the King's favour conferred a superior legal status in the State. There were only his servants, functionaries, guard (the " antrustions "), his "commended",

[1] DLVII.

who enjoyed a three-fold "wergeld", literally "a man's price". The sixth century aristocracy was thus not a true aristocracy, that is to say a class which enjoyed hereditary prerogatives. Or, if it was a nobility, it was a temporary one of functions, at the sovereign's mercy.

The sovereign's power was unlimited and his subjects had no protection against arbitrariness. Even the bishops, the only persons placed by their sacred character above the herd, were not always safe from the master's wrath, and the Councils trembled before the Court.

Like every government, the Merovingian government claimed services from its subjects and demanded money from them. But it gave nothing in return. There were no longer any expenses in the public interest and the very notion of public interest disappeared. The King withdrew from circulation all metal specie and heaped it up in his coffers or "treasure". Thus taxation soon took on the character of an extortion, abuse, or sin with which the King burdened his soul.

II. THE ADMINISTRATION

It would be better to call this "exploitation of the State by the King". What we call central administration was not distinguished from personal service to the King. The high functionaries, as we call them, were personal servants, whether they were of Roman origin, such as the constable (*comes stabuli*), the referendaries, chamberlains (*cubicularii*) and the *camerarii* or keepers of the treasure (*camera*), or of German origin such as the seneschal or senior footman (*sinischalk*) and the marshals over the stable (*marischalk*), etc. Amongst these persons there was no clear-cut division of labour; without regard to the nature of their functions, a referendary or an usher (*ostiarius*) could, during the Frankish period, be employed for diplomatic or military work.

Cases in which persons belonging to the Court and functionaries were involved, were tried at the *Palace*. By the term *Court*, is meant the central administration. The King was its supreme judge; in practice he left the presidency of this tribunal to the "Count of the Palace".

Local administration presents a very simple aspect. The

" province " of imperial times, an artificial administrative division, was not able to survive the changes of the end of the fifth century, and disappeared entirely. Only the city (*civitas*) was left, that is to say the small State of Gallic origin, the organic cell which Rome had preserved while restraining its powers. In each of them the King set up a Count (*comes*) a real viceroy in whose hands were united the full powers of administration, jurisdiction, finance and the army. In the German parts of the *Regnum*, or when the city was too large, there was a count for each *pagus*.

This organisation is also found in the Visigothic State. Its Roman origin appears more than probable, for in the last period of the Western Empire, it had been necessary to set up, not merely in the provinces but in the *civitates* also, a friend of the Monarch, or a *comes* armed with full powers. What little autonomy was able to exist in the " city " finally disappeared. The " curiales " still continued in Gaul to the end of the seventh century, but these were now only a record office for private contracts. Perhaps they passed into the deputation of freemen or "good men" (*boni homines*; rachimburgs) with whom the Count (*judex*) was required by German law to collaborate at the holding of the assizes (the *mallum*).

Though all-powerful over the subjects they ruled, the counts were only the king's creatures. He appointed or recalled them at his pleasure ; on the slightest suspicion, he turned them out, ill-treated them, or put them to death; in short, he treated them like slaves ; and in fact, more than one was of servile origin. The Count paid for the patent appointing him and received no remuneration. He lived on the product of those estates of the treasury which came under his administration and a third of the judicial fines which went to the King (the *fredum*).

In the second half of the sixth century, the dukes (*duces*), specially entrusted with the leadership of the armies, made their appearance in increasing numbers.[1] In this we may perhaps see the influence of the Byzantine organization.

The public property, which was completely identified with the private property of the King, had a special administration. Each of its districts (*fisci*) was managed by a steward,

[1] **DLXXVIII,** 200.

the "domestic" (*domesticus*), with rank equal to that of a count.[1] The head steward, the *major palatii* or Mayor of the Palace assumed a growing importance towards the end of the sixth century. It is a significant fact that the central steward or manager of the economic life of the court or "palace" became the head of the State in the seventh century.

Taxation.[2]—The Frankish kings, like the other barbarians, took good care not to destroy the imperial fiscal machinery. All the imposts were kept on, the land tax, the personal tax, indirect taxes or the *telonea* which included customs, tolls and taxes on articles sold at fairs or markets. Also the contributions in kind, the furnishing of horses (*paravereda*) for the royal post, the dues of lodging and procuration for the sovereign and his men, etc.

But very soon the machinery began to work badly and then was thrown completely out of gear. The land tax, which is by far the most productive of all in agricultural civilizations, requires a numerous and expert administrative staff for its proper working. But the Merovingians were quite incapable of reorganizing a complicated financial system. The census was not renewed, nor were the registers kept up to date. The collection of the taxes, as we may well imagine, came up against countless difficulties, and we have reason to believe that the payments were irregular and negligible in spite of severe measures which were at least as cruel as in the days of the Empire.

The personal tax, the Franks, we are assured, always refused to pay, looking upon it as a mark of social degradation. The Kings' attempts to make their fellow countrymen submit to it brought about terrible uprisings.

In a general fashion, direct taxation was universally disapproved of. We have already said that, the King having ceased to support any public service, the quit-rent could now appear only in the light of extortion. The only moral authority of the time, the episcopate, openly condemned it, and used any fit of piety or grief on the part of the King, when he was bereaved of a child for instance, to induce him to spare the life of his subjects and to save his soul by burning

[1] DXLIX.
[2] DLVI.

the treasury books. The clergy had moreover taken precautions. The churches, at first the most famous ones (those of Tours and Lyons), then the others, and lastly the monasteries, obtained diplomas of " immunity " relieving them of the land tax and even of the indirect taxes.[1]

In the middle of the seventh century, the taxpayers evaded the tax. The Merovingian King, like the Sultan of Morocco recently, only collected the land tax by armed force ; after Dagobert, when it was desired to get rid of a high official, he was sent to collect the " quit-rent ", there being a chance of never seeing him again. Nevertheless, here and there, the land tax or " quit rent" and the capitation tax continued until the ninth century; but in a weakened form, reduced to the level of " customary " dues paid to the sovereign.

On the other hand, the indirect taxes (*telonea*), which were easy to collect, it being necessary for this only to close a road or bridge, not only remained but multiplied. Their names are countless : *portoria* (tolls), *foratica* (market dues), *laudatica* or *salutatica* (fees for plying a trade), *saumatica* (on beasts of burden), *pulveratica*, *rotatica*, *timonatica* (on transport vehicles), *cespitatica* and *ripatica* (on towing paths), *portatica* (on river ports), *pontatica* (on the crossing of bridges), etc. In 614, a complaint was made that for the last thirty years these tolls had gone on multiplying. The taxes on the conveyance and sale of wares seem to be the compensation for the failure of the land tax. Already the nobles tended to appropriate them.

To these revenues must be added : (1) the judicial fines, the king having a right to a third of the " composition " money by which, in German law, the vengeance of a family aggrieved by an offence or crime against one of its members was satisfied ; (2) the presents of the nobles and the " recommended " on the occasion of an event such as the marriage of a princess royal ; these free gifts naturally become obligatory and chargeable on the occasion of the meeting of the *populus Francorum*, that is to say, of the army, in the month of March ; (3) lastly war booty and the tribute of the subject peoples, of some importance until Dagobert's reign.

All these revenues, which were still considerable in the sixth century, were swallowed up fruitlessly in the "treasure".

[1] **DXII, DLXXXIII, 336-425.**

The Army.[1]—The army, which is the great source of expense to States, cost the Merovingian nothing. Every Frank, in theory, owed military service at his own expense, and those who were refractory or negligent payed a heavy fine, the ban of 60 gold solidi. The sons of Clovis extended the obligation of military service to all their subjects, Romans, Burgundians, Alemans, Saxons of Neustria, etc. The poor of free condition were not exempt from it, at least in theory. Hence the armies called " Frankish " were a collection of natives,[2] without military training or real fighting value, more formidable to their fellow citizens than to the enemy. The command was exercised by the King in person or entrusted to counts or dukes (in the second half of the sixth century), chiefly Frankish, but often also Roman, Burgundian or Provençal. A general levy was rare. Most often only the contingents of the *pagi* near to the objective of the expedition were called up. Thus for a war against the Bretons, Chilperic summoned the "Tourangeaux, Poitevins, Baiocassins, Manceaux and Angevins". Against Carcassonne there marched the Berrichons, Saintongeois, Périgourdins and Angoumoisins. Against the Wascons, it was in Burgundy, that is to say in the Rhone valley, that several army corps were raised. One wonders how these confused, undisciplined and badly armed mobs (defensive arms were a rarity), so difficult to transport (horsemen were still in a minority) were able to win victories. The reason probably was that their opponents, Goths of Spain and Italy, Alemans, Thuringians and Bretons were even worse organized and in addition less numerous, so that the Frankish armies crushed them by the force of numbers. But as soon as the Franks had to do, as for instance in the case of the Avars, with well-armed horsemen and consummate warriors, the immediate result was defeat.[3]

Nevertheless in Austrasia, the only place where the ancient March field military training was kept up, there was effected, under the obvious influence of the Pippinidæ, an obscure replacement of the infantry by the cavalry, an evolution of tactics which was to give Charles Martel the instrument

---

[1] DLXXVIII, 54; DLXXXII, 408; DCCXXXVI, vol. II, 2, 205.
[2] CVIII, vol. II, 412.
[3] DCLXXXVIII; DXCII, 97.

enabling him to save the Kingdom of the Franks from its enemies without.[1]

III. THE DECAY OF THE MONARCHY AND THE RISE OF THE ARISTOCRACY

Since the whole State rested ultimately on the king, the Frankish Monarchy was essentially a personal government. This means that, once the ruler's force weakens from some cause or other, the whole machine is out of order. An absolute government can exist only if it wins forgiveness for its harshness by services to the public, or else if, after the example of Byzantium, it succeeds in organizing a stable bureaucracy to bolster it up in its moments of weakness. But the Merovingian performed no services, unless we call the pillaging expeditions services. Of organizing anything he was utterly incapable, very inferior in this to the Gothic kings.

Being a suspicious, cruel, capricious and selfish despot, the Merovingian Monarch could not be loved. No current of sympathy could arise between him and his peoples. But there can be no lasting government without some appeal to the emotions. The Frankish monarchy realized so thoroughly that it was only served from fear or interest, that it multiplied both its punishments and rewards. Though utterly indifferent to the public welfare, it was prodigal in largesses to the king's men, those who, by an unintentional antiphrasis, were termed the " faithful ", the *leudes*. Dukes and Counts ate up the royal estate. The leudes were gorged with gold, and brothers fought each other, not so much with weapons as by the use of bribery. The last word in politics was to bribe a rival's " faithful " followers. From this point of view, the "treasure" was the true *instrumentum regni*.

A perversion of public spirit took place. It was natural that grants of money or of lands should be called " benefices " (*beneficia*). But soon exemptions from taxes, exemptions from or grants of tolls, and even public posts, were to be regarded as benefices or *beneficia*.[2]

[1] DLXXVIII, 194 ; DLXXXIV, 16-111; DCXXVIII ; DCCXXXIV, vol. I, 749 ; DCCXXXVI, vol. II, 2, 363.

[2] DLXXXIII : DCLXXXIX, and DCXC ; DXLV, vol. II, ; DCCXXXIV, vol. I, to be supplemented with two remarkable accounts ; L. CLOTET, Le bénéfice sous les deux premières races ; in Compte rendu du Congrès scientifique international des catholiques, tenu à Paris du 1er au 6 Avril, 1891 ; E. LESNÉ, Les diverses acceptions du terme "beneficium", 1924 (offprint from Revue hist. de droit, 1924).

To obtain a " benefice ", it was necessary to attach oneself to the sovereign by a close bond, that of the *Commendatio*. Thus one became the King's man. The official finally disappeared behind the protégé or servant. The notion became deeply fixed in men's minds that service to the State was the correlate of a "benefice ". No function was performed, no obedience even was given, except for reward. Whence followed the logical deduction, that when no benefices had been received from the King, one was justified in not obeying and in not serving the State.

The " benefice " procured the so-called benefactor only a fleeting gratitude. The beneficiary knew too well that the King acted more from necessity than kindness. Besides, the beneficiary never had more than a precarious enjoyment of the benefice granted to him. Not that the benefice granted for a time or for life, the fief, as yet existed ; on the contrary, it should be noted that the king's gifts of land were, in the Merovingian period, in full ownership and hereditary. But, on the slightest suspicion of disloyalty, the sovereign did not hesitate to take back his word, revoke his gift and annex the land once more to the treasury. Under these conditions, the monarchy was not loved even by those who profited from its abssolutism and there was an irresistible tendency amongst the great men to strengthen their position. There being no political life, and no guarantee of security, the bulk of the freemen had no legal means of making their grievances known and of obtaining justice. They could have recourse only to revolt.

There was however one occasion on which the Merovingian's free subjects of all nationalities could raise their voice and take up a threatening attitude. This was the time of the " field of March " when a general review of the troops took place preceding a military expedition. When they had weapons in their hands, the subjects thought they could do anything, and often enforced their will or caprice. The Merovingian King practically ceased to be absolute when he mustered this heterogeneous collection of Salian Franks, Ripuarian Franks, Hessian Franks, Burgundians, Gallo-Romans from the North and Aquitania, Provençals, and even Alemans, which was called by the title of *populus Francorum*.

With no real institutions to back it, the Frankish Monarchy was at the mercy of chance. Its decay was hastened on by the civil wars which arose from the German method of dividing an inheritance and later by a series of minorities. What calls for astonishment is that it should have been able to figure as a great power for more than a century after the death of Clovis.

Behind the façade of a despotic monarchy, a social force was rising, during the second half of the sixth century, which was to supplant the Merovingian Monarchy, and this force was the Aristocracy.

We have seen that amongst the Franks, the nobility, which maintained itself amongst the Saxons, Frisians and other Germanic peoples, had disappeared; there no longer was a noble family beside the Merovingians. Amongst the Gallo-Romans, on the other hand, there existed a real noble class, that of the "senatorial" families.[1] But it was decidedly small and on the way to extinction; it has been remarked that Gregory of Tours, who belonged to this class and was not a little proud of it, cites many men of senatorial family in the part of his *Ecclesiastical History of the Franks* which relates to the first half of the century, but very few for the second half, that of his contemporaries.[2] As it was from this class that the most distinguished members of the episcopate were recruited, its disappearance was inevitable, even if no biological law existed making for the extinction of old rich families.

Besides, the privileges of this class were not of a legal but of an economic and moral character ; the only privilege which raised a man above the common ruck was the service of the King. Only, as we have said, in this economically retrograde society, grants of land were the regular form of remuneration for services, and no one consented to serve without the grant of a " benefice " of this kind.

On the other hand, the "functionaries", to make use of a too modern term, tended to be taken from amongst the large landed proprietors. Alongside of the Gallo-Romans, the Franks acquired large stretches of land, not only in the parts of Gaul which they colonized (Flanders, Brabant, the left

---

[1] See above, p. 126.
[2] A remark by FAHLBECK, **DLXXVIII**.

bank of the Rhine, the lower valley of the Moselle) but also in the districts in which the " Romans " were in a numerical majority. Thousands of villages or hamlets still bear witness to-day to the fact that Franks owned them and even gave them their own manes. All the places in which the terms *ville* and *court* form part of the name, have as another part of their name that of a Frank ; for example : Regnierville (*Reginhari villa*), Villeaugeard (*villa Adalgardis*), Courtomer (*curtis Audomari*), Cortambert (*curtis Ansberti*). In some places even families and not merely individuals settled. The four places in Champagne with the name " La Fère " prove the existence of a *fara* (clan). In Lorraine, Franche-Comté, and Romance Switzerland, the villages with names terminating in *-age* and *-ans* are beyond count, a phenomenon which is easily explained, since these were limitrophic districts of the Germanized parts of Gaul, and Frankish and also Aleman influence was therefore natural. Even in the Seine Valley, Houdans or Hodencs and Dourdans are found, the old forms of which (Hosdinc, Dordinc) also bear witness to the German suffix *-ing*, which indicates the settlement of a family. These and other formations, however, are met with in considerable numbers only in the region from the Meuse to the Loire, especially between the Meuse and the Seine and in the North of " Burgundy ". In Aquitania, practically none are found ; obviously, if the Franks occupied it politically, they did not establish themselves strongly there. From this point of view also, the *regnum Francorum* did not effectively go beyond the Loire.[1]

Only service to the king gave privileges, the triple *wergeld* (*vira-gilda*, " a man's price "), for example. Hence the man who served the King, or was even simply " commended " to him, was in fact an " aristocrat " or noble. This nobility was not in law hereditary. But it was impossible for it not to become so, and that very soon. The spirit of the times was profoundly aristocratic. Amongst the Romans it had become exaggerated to such a pitch that it resulted in the setting up of a kind of caste, the " senatorial family ".[2] It was inevitable that the same thing should take place amongst the Franks, who had become large landed proprietors.

---

[1] Longnon, **CCCIV.**
[2] See above, p. 126.

Normally, the son of the great landlord who was a functionary, entered in his turn the king's service and claimed his " benefices ".   After several generations the practice was established and the king's service with the prerogatives it entailed became hereditary.   The Merovingian Monarchy thus restored the aristocracy which was to destroy it.

Finally a rapprochement took place between great " Romans " and great " barbarians ".   Mixed marriages were frequent at an early date.   Doubtless personal law continued ; but even admitting that it was always strictly observed, which is doubtful, we must not exaggerate to ourselves its importance.   The solidarity of economic interests and class privileges worked in a quite different direction and brought the two races together.   The fusion of the two aristocracies was doubtless completed in the course of the seventh century.

For a long time the Gallo-Frankish aristocracy remained unorganized.   Its opposition took the form of betraying the King or of passing from the service of one king to another.   But at the beginning of the seventh century, the disappearance of the young kings of Austrasia and Burgundy, and the tyranny of a hated woman, Brunhild, made it possible for the aristocracy to impose its conditions on the only adult Merovingian, Chlotar II.   Weak, and for a long time confined to a corner of Gaul, where he reigned with great difficulty, the son of Chilperic and Fredegund easily yielded to the wishes of the bishops and of the great men of Burgundy and Austrasia, who agreed to betray in his favour the descendants of Childebert II.   In Neustria even, the Council of Paris raised bitter complaints against the despotism of the court.   Chlotar by a celebrated edict of October 18th, 614, delivered at Paris, pacified these complaints of the ecclesiastical and lay aristocracy.[1]

To the Church, the sovereign grants that in the case of a vacancy of an episcopal see, he will allow the man elected (being appointed according to the canon laws) to be consecrated, if he is worthy of this position.   If the bishop is chosen in the " palace ", account will be taken of merit and knowledge.   Clerics appointed to any ecclesiastical post are forbidden to come to court in order to intrigue against their bishop.   The abduction of nuns and women consecrated to the service of

[1] See above, p. 332.

God, by obtaining the authorization of a royal diploma, is prohibited. He will have bequests to the churches carried out. He extends the sphere of ecclesiastical jurisdiction.

To the nobles, he confirms the possession of lands granted to them by himself or his predecessors and restores to them those they have lost in the course of the last wars. He gives assurance that no accused man shall be condemned without a hearing. In the general interest he abolishes the land tax and the tolls established since the reigns of Guntram, Chilperic and Sigebert.

An important concession is made to particularist feeling : the King will not appoint as " judge " any person foreign to the province or district which he has to administer, and the same ordinance is extended to the subordinates of the bishops and counts. Henceforth the recruiting of all the government's agents, including the most important of all, the Mayor of the Palace, becomes strictly local.

Finally, the Sovereign, obviously in order to reassure the assembly of the bishops and nobles about the future, determines that the " palace ", that is to say the central administration, shall not deliver " precepts " (diplomas) contrary to previous precepts.

Ever since the eighteenth century, historians and jurists have been struck by this deed. They speak of this event as " a revolution in law "[1], and as " a constitutional charter ". This is obviously using language which does not apply. In reaction to this, Fustel de Coulanges has interpreted the edict as a deed meant to repress the abuses committed by the nobles, an obviously untenable paradox.[2] The edict of 614 was not the charter of 1215,[3] but it marks none the less the Merovingian monarchy's recognition that its arbitrary will is subject to serious limitations.[4]

Further, two years later, Chlotar II, assembled the Mayor

---

[1] MOREAU, *Principes de morale publique ou discours de l'histoire de France* (Paris, 1777 and foll.), vol. II, 2-19 ; vol. III, 13.

[2] DLXXXII, 612-630.   In DLXXXIV, 70, 80, 84, 101, FUSTEL softens his statement with some modifications.

[3] Thus, LEHUEROU, DCXXVIII, 485, 491 ; WAITZ, DCCXXXVII, vol. 2, 389-398 ; LOENING, DCXXXVIII, vol. II, 526-532 ; FAHLBECK, DLXXVIII, 218-225, 323-337 ; BRUNNER, DXLV, vol. I, 446, 541 ; SCHULTZE, DCXCVII, 174 ; VIOLLET, DCCXXXIV, vol. I, 394-8, etc.

[4] DIGOT, DLXVII, vol. III, 157, 161 ; PFISTER in CCLXXIX, vol. II, 1, 156.

Warnahar, with the bishops and the nobles of Burgundy, at Bonneuil, near Paris, and there " agreeing to all their just demands, he confirmed them by precepts " (Fredegar, c. 44). Sixty years after the famous Edict, Childeric II had to repeat its most particularist ordinances.[1]

If the aristocracy was winning, the reason was that recently it had acquired a head, the Mayor of the Palace.[2] Not the least paradox of the Merovingian period is the fact that the head of the officials became the leader of the aristocratic opposition against the King's absolutism. That the *major domus* should have risen to the top of the hierarchy which we call the " central administration " is in itself already surprising. It would be intelligible if the chief of the referendaries, the King's secretary, or the " Count of the Palace ", the president of the tribunal of the Palace, both of whom were sometimes entrusted with military commands, had, when occasion arose, taken in hand the government of the State. The functions of the *major domus* were of great economic importance, since he looked after the public property, that is to say the private property of the Sovereign. It was his duty to see that the treasury lands were not misappropriated ; the stewards (*domestici*) of the large estates were under him. Originally, as his name indicates, he had even the duty of looking after the provisioning of the King and of the Court. In a society which had returned to the State of " natural " economy, these duties were of primary importance. Nevertheless there is an element of mystery in the rise of the " Mayor of the Palace ". The other barbarian States were acquainted with the *major domus*, but he remained in the shade. There is reason to admit with Fahlbeck[3] that the elevation of the " Mayor of the Palace " was due to personal relations in the course of the regencies of Brunhild and Fredegund; " the post was raised with the holder, who was the first to know how to make for himself a place by the side of the King ; once this place was taken, the institution became permanent ". The power of precedent is, in fact, tremendous in a society without any principles, in which the specialization of functions is rudimentary. It should further be noted that even under

---

[1] Cf. above, pp. 338-9.
[2] **DCCXXXVI**, vol. II, 2, 83-100 ; **DLXXXII**, 166-182.
[3] **DLXXVIII**, 151.

Sigebert I, the Mayors of the Palace, Gogo and Lupus, described for us by Fortunatus, already appear as Grand Viziers.

We must add that the "mayor" exploited for his own profit the practice of "commendation". As his authority increased, an ever greater number of men sought his protection. Finally, even the King's clients fell under his authority. When the Sovereign received under his protection or *patrocinium* (*mundeburdis* in German), "under his word" (*sub sermone tuitionis*), an individual or an ecclesiastical foundation, he was not going to trouble himself personally with the ways and means of carrying his patronage into effect. The task of following the business of the protégé was entrusted to the "mayor". A time was bound to come when, owing to the fact that the exercise of the *defensio* devolved upon the *major domus*, the King would be only the nominal *senior*. Thanks to this practice, the Mayor of the Palace was to succeed to the patronage, as well as to the power of the King.[1]

It is to the intimate union between large landed property and the public service that we must attribute the at first puzzling fact that the head of the officials, " the first minister or rather the only minister of this absolute monarchy " (according to the true description of Fustel de Coulanges), should have become the aristocracy's mouthpiece against the royal despotism. Repeated minorities and the reigns of two women, Brunhild and Fredegund, who were tyrannical and vindictive but unable to hold their position without masculine support, allowed the aristocratic party to lift up its head once more and even to enforce its conditions.

The chief of these conditions was the appointment of the Mayor of the Palace, by all the nobles both lay and ecclesiastic, or, to speak more correctly, by all the nobles of each of the three large districts into which the *Regnum Francorum* was henceforth divided.

At the beginning of the seventh century we notice in fact that three " nationalities "—we use this term through want of another—had arisen in some obscure fashion. That which shows itself foremost, although it gained its name only later (Gregory of Tours does not yet name it) is Austrasia.[2] What a strange nationality! Austrasia included not only the regions

---

[1] **DLXXXIV**, 161.
[2] **DLXVII.**

of the Rhine and the Moselle, but also Northern Champagne, Auvergne with its annexes, Poitou and Touraine. The King of Austrasia resided at Reims and Metz, but almost never on the Rhine, which remained a frontier as in antiquity. A distinction was even still made between the other Franks and the Franks beyond the Rhine who had remained completely barbarian ; it was only many centuries later that the Rhine was to become an artery which fed the economic life of the country, and a political division.   Austrasia was in the main the portion of Theodoric, the elder son of Clovis. Theodoric's successors, like himself, had each only one son ; the result was that for a whole century this portion was not divided.   This circumstance favoured the rising of a feeling of autonomy.   In the seventh century, even when the kingdom was re-united in the hands of a single king, the Austrasians demanded a Sovereign of their own, who was most often a young child, which fact enabled the great men to make themselves independent.   It was thus that Chlotar II had to set up Dagobert in Austrasia in 623, and Dagobert in his turn his son Sigebert III in 634 ; Childeric II, the brother of Chlotar III, was King of Austrasia from 663.

Merovingian Austrasia already foreshadows the States of the Middle Ages, aggregates of countries without any geographical, racial, or linguistic unity.   History however shows that these organisms, though they appear to us monstrous, were possessed of a robust vitality.   The community of interests and customs which arose from obedience to one and the same dynasty was able to make these States last for several centuries, and sometimes even to create a " nationality ".   Austrasia was not to become " Germanic ", and then only half so (for it still included many " Romans ") till the end of the seventh century, when Aquitania was separated from it.

Burgundy, even after its conquest by the Franks, kept up a particularist feeling.   For many centuries this name stands for a large district without any natural unity, stretching from Champagne to Provence.

Starting almost from the suburbs of Paris, at Montereau, it included the upper courses of the Seine, the Yonne and the Marne, with Sens, Troyes, Langres, the Valleys of the Saône and the Doubs and that of the Rhone.   Passing the Jura, it embraced more than half of present Switzerland, up to the Reuss.[1] This country owed its name to the Burgundians ; but it owed them practically nothing else. Being very few in numbers, the Burgundians must very rapidly have become fused with the native population. They did not leave it a single word of their Scandinavian language. The place-names in -ans and -ange, found in fairly large numbers in the departments of the Doubs and the Ain and in Romance Switzerland, are of Aleman origin.[2] Six or seven pagi of the Duchy and of the Comté of Burgundy, as they were later to be called, bear German names, but these are foreign to the Burgundians. In the Comté, the names Varais (pagus Varascorum) and Escuens (pagus Scotingorum) are due, the first certainly and the second probably, to settlements of Alemans. In the Duchy, the Amous and the " Atuyer " recalled for a long time the memory of the Chamavian Franks (pagus Chamavorum, Hamavorum, Amavorum) and of the Hattuarii Franks, another branch of whom was North of Cologne. These barbarians, the Franks at least, had been transported by force in the fourth century to re-people the devastated Civitas Lingonum. It is significant that the physical type of the inhabitants of Burgundy and Franche-Comté is so far removed from that of the Germanic race (except for traces in the Doubs department). They rank amongst the most brachycephalic peoples in Europe.[3] Of the Burgundians, very tall and dolichocephalic Scandinavians, there remained only the German code which was drawn up by the order of King Gundobad (about the year 500) and which kept his name : " la loi Gombette ". It was still operative in the ninth century, but its use appeared obsolete and inconvenient ; we know that the archbishop of Lyons, Agobard, begged Louis the Pious to abolish it. Thus the " Burgundians " of the Early Middle Ages were Gallo-Romans, who adopted that name in order to mark themselves off from the Franks and Romans of Northern Gaul and from the Aquitanians.

Neustria, from the Loire to Champagne approximately,

---

[1] DCXLVII.

[2] See above, p. 357.

[3] J. DENIKER, Les races de l'Europe : I, L'indice céphalique ; II, La taille, Paris (Offprint from Association française pour l'avancement des sciences, Congrès de Saint Étienne, 1897 ; Congrès de Lyon, 1906). Cf. RIPLEY, The Races of Europe (London), and PITTARD, vol. v.

was the country of the Franks par excellence, of the Salians as distinct from the Ripuarians and the Aquitanians of what is called the Kingdom of " Austrasia " and from the " Burgundians " of the South-east. Paris formed their natural centre. The term " Franks " in the seventh century was most often understood of the Neustrians.[1] For a long time, until the battle of Tertry, Neustria held sway over both Burgundy and Austrasia. It was doubtless through seeing the aristocracy of Austrasia and that of Burgundy each demanding its " Mayor of the Palace " that the Neustrians also claimed an elective " mayor".

It is a significant fact that as soon as the Mayors of the Palace come into the full light, they are proposed to the Sovereign by the great men of the three great States of the Regnum. It is obvious that this was an infallible way of getting hold of the power. It was, *mutatis mutandis*, a method analogous to that employed later by the nobles of England in 1215 and 1258 and by those of France in 1316, when they wished to place the Monarchy under tutelage ; they asked to appoint the members of the " King's Council ", which was the mainspring of the machine of government. From 614 to 751 the mainspring was the *major domus*, " the sole minister of this absolute monarchy."[2] It was quite natural that the aristocracy which henceforth dominated the Frankish State should demand that he should be at its disposal. In 641, the widow of Dagobert, Nanthilda, guardian of Clovis II, by negotiations succeeded in making the " bishops and the dukes of Burgundy " accept as their mayor Flaochat, although he was a Frank ; but he had to promise in writing and on oath given to them to guard for them their " grade of honour (their public posts), their dignity and an everlasting friendship ".

Henceforth there was a covenant not only between the Monarchy and the aristocracy, but also between the latter and the Mayor of the Palace. And already the public posts tended to remain fixed in the same noble families.

---

[1] **DCXVI**, vol. i., 76-77.
[2] Fustel, **DLXXXII**, 176.

CHAPTER XII

Economic Life

THE economic life, in Gaul as elsewhere, was a continuation of that of the Later Empire, without any very appreciable change.[1] The upheaval of the fifth century, the settlement of the barbarians on the soil of the Empire, did not modify its essential features. They merely hastened the return to " natural economy " which characterized the Mediterranean world from the third century onwards. The land was wealth *par excellence*, almost the only wealth. The consequence was that, more than ever, services, whether private or public, came to be paid by temporary or permanent grants of land and this practice was to have political and social reactions of prime importance.

I. AGRICULTURE.[2] THE RURAL CLASSES

The exploitation of the land was carried on by the same means as under the Later Empire. Large landed property was still supreme, but it did not involve as a consequence exploitation on a large scale. If the owner or master (*dominus*) reserved for himself the woods and pastures, he farmed directly a fraction only and that the smallest (a third or a quarter) of the arable lands, meadows and vineyards. The greater part of the arable land was cultivated by hereditary farmers, the *coloni*. They received for themselves and their family a tenure called *mansus*. The latter was never continuous ; it consisted of pieces of land and of meadows situated in the different portions of the estate (*villa*, *fundus*), which fact allowed of the triennial rotation of crops. The *coloni* had rights of user to the forest where they picked dead wood and sent their pigs to graze. In return for these concessions they were obliged to pay certain dues in money or more often

---

[1] Cf. Book I, chap. iv.
[2] **CLI ; DCCII.**

in kind, and especially to perform certain services. The *coloni* owed base service and labour on the demesne of the landlord (*mansus indominicatus*) ; the slaves whose number was very diminished would indeed not have sufficed to work the " seignorial mansus ". Lastly the *coloni* did carting, went on errands on foot or on horse-back, etc.

The institution of the " colonate " proved profitable both to the peasant and the landlord. To the first it secured, if not the ownership, the possession for his life, and, in practice, for the life of his children, of a farm of an average area of from 12 to 15 hectares ; custom did not allow the rent or the services incumbent upon him to be increased. To the second it secured, if not large rents, considerable services and unpaid labour. The institution was considered so profitable that it was extended to slaves (*mancipia, servi*). It is to be noted however that in the Roman districts the tenures of *coloni* continued to preponderate vastly numerically. In the German districts on the other hand, the tenures of serfs and of " *lidi* " were in a larger proportion. The servile tenure owed more frequent services, half the week (three out of six working days) being devoted to the master's land.

The *colonus* continued to be considered in the eyes of the law as a free man, and his tenure was for a long time entitled " *ingenuilis* ". But this was only a fiction which deceived no one. It was a strange kind of free man who could not dispose of his *prœdium*, nor leave it, or even take a wife outside the estate to which he was chained for ever ! Hence this class on which the whole of society rested was treated with profound contempt ; it played no part in the State and was not admitted to the honour of bearing arms ; instead it had to pay the *hostilitium* in kind or money.

It does not appear that agricultural methods had profited from the slightest improvement except in one important point, the water-mill. This had been known from the end of the Roman Republic, but more as a curiosity, it seems. Its use does not seem to have become wide-spread before the fourth or fifth century A.D.[1] In Merovingian times it was in common use ; no charter but mentions the *farinaria* ; and this was an unquestionable advance.

---

[1] **XLV,** vol. ii., 83 ; **CCCXLIV,** vol. xv., 45 ; **DIII,** vol. ii., 85.

II. COMMERCE AND INDUSTRY. THE TOWN[1]

The establishment of the barbarians had no deep influence, after the period of the settlement, on commerce and industry.[2] Communications with England were especially by way of Quentovic, which is now Etaples, on the mouth of the Canche. Nantes traded with Ireland.[3] But the Mediterranean remained the great thoroughfare which joined West and East. In Gaul, Narbonne, Arles and especially Marseilles kept up relations with Egypt, Syria and Constantinople. The *reconquista* of Africa, Italy and Southern Spain by Justinian must have encouraged the resumption of business. But from the middle or the end of the seventh century, the advance of the Moslems dealt a fatal blow to the commerce of the Romano-Germanic States in the West. After the taking of Carthage (698), and the invasion of Spain (711), the relations between Christians and the East were reduced to very little, while on the other hand the unity of religion, language and civilization encouraged vigorous commercial progress in the world of Islam.

The way of the Danube had not been completely closed by the racial upheavals of the fifth century. But after the establishment of the Tartar Empire of the Avars in the heart of Europe, relations between Gaul and Germany on the one hand, and Salonica and Constantinople on the other, must have stopped almost entirely.

Commerce was carried on as in Roman times, by *negotiatores* grouped in corporations. But the Gallo-Franks, like the Gallo-Romans, do not seem to have had much aptitude for business. Many merchants were Syrians and Jews, not only in the South, but also in Central Gaul (at Clermont) and Northern Gaul, at Orléans and Paris.[4] The predominance of Orientals in business went far back, as early as the first or second century.

Our information on industry is very poor. The only industry which seems to have prospered is that of precious articles, the craft of the goldsmith and of enamelling, if we

---

[1] **CCXCV,** vol. i. ; **CDXXXIX.**

[2] PIRENNE in *Revue belge de philologie et d'histoire,* vol. i., 77-86 ; vol. ii., 223-235.

[3] **DXX.**

[4] BRÉHIER, *Les colonies d'Orientaux en Occident au commencement du moyen âge,* in *Byzantin. Zeitschrift,* xii., 1903, 1-39.

leave aside that of the armourer. The workmen probably still formed professional and religious guilds. The industry of the country interfered with the development of that of the town. Every country estate had to be self-sufficient. Naturally bread was baked there, wine was made, and in the North a light beer ; but there were also workshops for carpenters, wheelwrights, saddlers, smiths, etc. Linen and woollen garments were woven by the women, chiefly serfs or *lidœ*, collected in work-rooms or women's quarters. Under these conditions the markets of the " cities " and of the free villages or " vics " (*vici*) could not have many customers. Nevertheless there were renowned fairs, amongst others that of Lendit, between Paris and Saint-Denis. As early as the 7th to 8th century it attracted merchants even from abroad, from Saxony, Lombardy and Spain ; but the only articles of trade mentioned are wine, honey and madder, and no industrial products.

An infallible sign of the economic unimportance of the life of the early Middle Ages, is the small size of the town and its stagnation. We have seen[1] that the barbarian inroads had forced the towns in the second half of the third century to concentrate into a small corner of their former area. The town of the Later Empire was a stronghold with an insignificant area (10 to 20 hectares) and a very much diminished population of 3,000 or 6,000 inhabitants at the most. In these straitened quarters there was just room for the palace of the *praeses*, later of the Count, for the cathedral church which replaced the temple, and for the houses of the clergy and of the bishop's servants. The rest was occupied by the houses of the merchants and those of the " curiales," men of birth ; for a handful of nobles still lived in these dreary gaols which were called " cities " when they were sees, and " chateaux " (*castra*) when they were fortified but had no bishops residing in them.

Such a wretchedly small area was enough for the feeble urban life of the times. We have no proofs that these towns, which were so small, had any suburbs. The *suburbium* was a rural outskirt of the city and an indispensable adjunct for its material life. Here were founded the monasteries, which could not be contained within the old Roman walls. This " city " was not only diminutive, but itself also presented a

[1] See p. 229.

rural appearance ; it was full of small gardens, and animals walked about freely in it.

Neither the area nor the number of the Roman towns increased, but rather the contrary was the case. No new town was founded, an incontrovertible proof of economic stagnation.

Besides the fortified towns, Merovingian Gaul also counted a number of free villages, the *vici ;* the names of nearly a thousand have been noted from coins.[1] But in the course of this period their number went on decreasing and in the Carolingian period the *vici*, which were supposed to be under the protection of the nobles lay and ecclesiastic, became their property ; they fell to the rank of *villæ*, or private estates. These *villæ* were not yet villages. The village, as a personality, did not yet exist, seeing that the " parish " was scarcely beginning to be formed in the country districts.[2]

III. THE COINAGE

The Frankish Sovereigns, like the other barbarians, confined themselves to imitating Roman coins.[3] It could not be otherwise, since the Roman coinage alone had world currency. This explains why the Franks, and also the Visigoths, kept for so long the names and effigies of the emperors on their coins, counterfeiting as it were the coinage of the Empire which was henceforth confined to Byzantium. Theodebert was the first who dared to strike gold coins with his own effigy ; even then, some mints such as Marseilles went on striking in the name of the Byzantine Emperor in the middle of the seventh century.

Thus the Frankish monetary system was a servile copy of the Roman system which Constantine restored. For the gold coinage, it seems that in Gaul the issue was continued of 84 sous (*solidi, aurei*) to the Roman pound of 327½ grammes, while in Italy the issue was only in the proportion of 72 to the pound. Thus the *solidus gallicus* weighed only 3.79 grammes instead of 4.55, which means that its intrinsic value was 13.39 francs instead of 15.67. In practice half sous (*semisis*) or thirds of a sou (*tremissis* or *triens*) were chiefly struck.

---

[1] See BARTHÉLEMY in *Revue archéologique*, 1865,1.
[2] DCV.
[3] XIII ; XXXIX, vol. i., 238 ; **DCLXXVIII** and in *Moyen Age*, 1910, 132.

For the silver coinage in Gaul, under the old name of " denarius " a piece was struck equal in value to the Romano-Byzantine half-*siliqua* which weighed 1.30 grammes.

But the standard of the gold *triens* or the silver *denarius* was not very high and their weight was irregular ; whence came the practice of weighing coins or of melting them down into bullion for important deals.

In the seventh century, the right of coinage, the royal prerogative *par excellence,* passed over to the episcopal or monastic churches or to private persons ; the treasury perhaps still collected part of the profits of coining. Mints multiplied in the cities, " châteaux " (*castra*), *vici,* and even mere villas. The history of the coinage shows in a striking fashion the disintegration of the royal power.

After the end of the seventh century, the issue of gold coins slowed down and then completely disappeared, to re-appear in France only under the reign of St. Louis, an undeniable sign that relations with the gold-producing countries had ceased and also that Gaul, if it still perhaps bought something from the East, no longer sold it anything. In the eighth century even silver money tended to pass out of currency, at least in the Rhine districts, payments being made in grain, cattle, horses, etc., rather than in metal specie.[1]

These are unequivocal signs of the retrograde trend of the economic system to more primitive forms.

[1] DCLXXVIII, p. xiv., xxx.-xxxiii.

CHAPTER XIII

Intellectual and Artistic Life
Education[1]

"THE cult of literature declined, or rather disappeared, in the towns of Gaul. In the midst of actions both good and bad, whilst the ferocity of nations and the fury of kings was breaking loose, when the Church was being attacked by heretics and defended by the faithful, and the Christian faith, burning in many hearts, died down in others, when religious establishments endowed by godly folk were despoiled by the impious, there was no grammarian, skilled in dialectic, to be found who could retrace these events either in prose or in verse. Hence many lamented saying : " Woe to our times, because the study of letters is dying out among us and no man is capable of preserving in writing the doings of the present ".[2] And a century after Gregory of Tours, the chronicler whom it has been agreed to call Fredegar takes up the same lament : " Behold how the world grows old and the blade of wisdom becomes blunt ; no man of this time is equal to the orators of past times, nor dare he claim to be ".[3]

Contemporaries gain an impression of decadence, a decadence which is incurable. And they are not mistaken. The deterioration of classical Latin literature had begun with the Antonines. The barrenness of the third century is disconcerting.[4] At the end of the fourth and the beginning of the fifth century, Ausonius and Claudian certainly write in an excellent style, the reason being that their work is a collection of centos borrowed from Virgil, Lucan, Ovid and Martial. In the fifth century, a prose writer such as Sidonius Apollinaris writes with intolerably bad taste. The so-called renascence of letters at the end of the Empire is a mask concealing decay. It seems that the men of this period are incapable

---

[1] XXI, XXVI, CCLXXV, CDXVII, DLXXIII, DCXLV.
[2] Preface by Gregory of Tours to his *Historia Francorum*.
[3] Prologue to Book IV.
[4] See above, p. 152.

of producing anything whatsoever out of themselves, and that they have nothing to say.

Moreover, after the conversion of the Empire to Christianity, pagan literature would have been condemned, even if its representatives had been superior men, which was by no means the case. Let us not forget that poetry was intimately bound up with mythology and the theatre with religion. For the Christians of those times the gods of the poems were not, as they are for us, harmless abstractions. Either they believed in their reality and feared and dreaded them, or they considered them contemptible and hateful figments of the imagination. Gregory of Tours warns his readers from the outset : " I shall not concern myself with the fall of Saturn, nor with the anger of Juno, nor the adulteries of Jupiter. I scorn all these things which crumble into dust. I shall turn my attention to divine things, to the miracles of the Gospel ".

The Fathers of the Church were on the whole hostile to classical letters and this disapproving attitude continued throughout the whole of the Middle Ages. There are numerous examples, at this time, which show the best representatives of the Church fearing and condemning classical literature.[1] Saint Cæsarius of Arles had studied under the rhetorician Pomerius. He had a dream in which he saw a dragon devouring his arm which rested on a pagan book ; from that moment he renounced the study of letters. The lives of the saints are full of traits of this kind ; thus the *Life of Saint Eloi*, attributed to Saint Ouen and dating from the beginning of the eighth century, denounces the " rascally " poets, Homer and Virgil, and asserts that the writings of the " gentiles " are worthless to Christians. In Italy, Gregory the Great pronounces a similar condemnation. In Spain, Isidore of Seville, the last of the Latin writers, hates ancient culture.[2]

It may be wondered why the Christians did not destroy this pagan literature instead of studying and preserving it. But under the Empire letters enjoyed an unparalleled prestige amongst the educated ruling classes. To have scorned the resources of " rhetoric " in the feud against the pagans and the heretics who were thorough masters of it would have meant sacrificing an indispensable weapon and running the risk of

[1] **XLIX**, vol. ii. ; **CDXVII**, 156.
[2] **CDXVII**, 195-201 ; **DXL**.

being neither read nor understood. Besides, in the fourth and early fifth centuries, the most eminent Christians were attached to Rome, in spite of everything. They too felt that the maintenance of the national spirit was bound up with a certain form of culture.[1]

Finally it must not be forgotten that, in default of didactic treatises, men acquired their notions of history, philosophy, physical and natural science, etc., from classical commentaries, and these notions were indispensable for the interpretation of the sacred books ; hence the hesitation on the part of the Fathers of the Church in pronouncing final sentence against profane letters. Saint Jerome and Saint Augustine, who enjoy them without frankly admitting it, condemn them in theory but do not forbid the study of them. An attempt was even made to appropriate their form on the authority of the Bible. The Hebrews on their departure from Egypt carried away the gold and silver vessels of the enemy ; Saint Paul in the Epistle to Titus quotes Menander. Legends grow up ; Plato is supposed to have known the Scriptures (according to Saint Ambrose and Saint Augustine), and Virgil is said to have foretold Christianity.

Nevertheless, while a Christian literature is taking shape, the form of which is inspired, alas, to only too great a degree, by profane literature, the latter is taking a secondary place. Instead of the great models we have the writings of the Fathers—Tertullian, Lactantius, Hilary, Ambrose, Jerome, Augustine, poems by authors like Commodian, Juvencus, Sedulius, Dracontius, Arator, and lastly Prudentius, the only one whose reputation has survived. In the episcopal and monastic schools, they might occasionally copy a Virgil or an Ovid ; but less and less use was made of parchment to transcribe pagan works. And everywhere it was the same. In Spain the *Etymologiæ* of Isidore of Seville, who died in 636, bears witness to the wealth of his library. At the end of the same century, the episcopal library of the Visigothic capital, Toledo, no longer contains more than one classical author, Cicero.[2] At the same time the losses were appalling.[3] If Ireland had not been converted in the fifth century and become

[1] Cf. above, pp. 166-7.
[2] DCXXVII, 319, 324.
[3] CCCLXXIII, CDXXXII, CDXVII, CDLXXVII, DCLVIII, DCCIII.

a refuge for the culture of the ancient world in its last days, the losses would have been even greater.[1]

As for Greek culture, it disappeared in the West just as Latin letters did in the East. From the end of the fourth century, the knowledge of Greek rapidly died out in the West : even men of letters and teachers, like Ausonius or Saint Augustine, knew it badly or not at all.[2]

From the fourth century, the teaching of philosophy was neglected amongst the Latin peoples. As Hellenism retreated and was finally wiped out in the West, philosophy and science suffered irreparable injury. There were Latin translations of Greek authors. The translation known by Saint Augustine of the works of the Neo-Platonists by Victorinus was lost at an early date. Philosophy was to be familiar to the Latin Middle Ages only by the summaries of Boetius (who died in 526).[3] This epitome could not possibly stimulate thought. The Carolingian Renaissance itself was destined in its philosophy to lack metaphysical originality. With the possible exception of Joannes Scotus of Ireland, no philosophic spirit was to be found until Saint Anselm.[4]

Theologia,[5] so closely bound up with philosophy in the Middle Ages that it is scarcely possible to separate one from the other, had no better fate. From the fifth to the eighth centuries it was in the East that dogma was given a complete form. The West confined itself to listening in silence. No new heresy arose during this period, which was a proof of intellectual stagnation or religious indifference. Theologically the Carolingian period was to be almost as barren as it was philosophically : it reiterated perpetually the old arguments. There was really no fresh stir until about the middle of the eleventh century.

Science.[6]—Science made no progress at all. It would be truer to say that it went back, in the West. Euclid's geometry, and the arithmetic of Nicomachus, translated into Latin about the sixth century, only survived in the form of propositions, enlivened by demonstrations. Latins and Latinized Barbarians,

[1] **CCXVIII, CCCXXIX, DXV, DXVI, DCXCVIII, DCCXLI.**
[2] See above, p. 155.
[3] **DXXXII.**
[4] J. DE GHELLINCK, *Le Mouvement théologique du XII° Siècle* (1914).
[5] **CCIII**, vol. iii. ; **CDLXXXIII**, vol. iii.
[6] **XVII ; LXXIV**, vol. i., 573-590 ; **CDLXXVI.**

as well as Byzantines, confined themselves to epitomizing, and compiled a typical work in the *Etymologiæ*, " a vast, lumber room in which were stowed away all the cast-off clothes of Antiquity—arts, science, grammar, logic, rhetoric, arithmetic, geometry, astronomy, medicine, agriculture, navigation, etc., all of it demonstrated and explained by going back to the etymology of the words signifying the various objects ".[1] With Isidore of Seville, who died in 636, it is usual to conclude the history of ancient Latin literature.

In the domain of physical and natural science, some useful recipes succeeded in getting transmitted, and their number was possibly added to, but these were mere tricks, not inspired by the scientific spirit.[2]

Mysticism and allegory.—The scientific spirit, born by a kind of miracle amongst the Hellenes, never succeeded in taking root amongst the Romans. It was too tender a plant. Even in Greece it faded rapidly, at any rate from the first century, under the scorching breath of mysticism. Neo-Platonism, Gnosticism, Christianity, later Islam, not to mention the religions and systems which had a less brilliant career, were fatal to it in the East, and even more so in the West.[3] The religious spirit crushed observation and experiment, that is to say, the scientific method. It put in its place the interpretation of texts.

The study of texts is the basis of criticism, and the latter has proved, in modern times, to possess formidable power. But criticism bears no sort of resemblance to the " interpretation " current in the last days of Antiquity and in the Middle Ages.

The Alexandrian School considered that every written text is capable of several interpretations which agree with, complete and reciprocally explain one another. Origen in the third century applied the system to the Christian books, which could be interpreted in three different senses —the literal, the moral and the mystic. In the fourth century, Saint Hilary and Saint Ambrose spread this method in the West, where it immediately had an extraordinary success. Saint Augustine himself, while protesting against

[1] **DCXXVII**, 309.
[2] **XXXIII, CIII.**
[3] Cf. above, pp. 169-70.

the dangerous neglect into which the literal significance of the Holy Scriptures had fallen, is thoroughly imbued with the method. For example, here is the analysis of his sermon on David and Goliath, preached at Hippo :—" David pre-figures Christ, and Goliath the Devil. David takes five stones from the brook and puts them in the vessel used for milking his sheep ; then, armed, he marches against the enemy. The five stones are an image of the five books of the law of Moses. The Law, in its turn, contains ten precepts ; that is why David fights with five stones and sings to an instrument of ten strings. Observe that he does not sling five stones but only one, which is the Unity that fulfils the Law, namely Charity. Observe likewise that he takes the five stones from the bed of the stream. What else can the stream represent save that frivolous and unstable people, whom the violence of their passions drags down into the waters of oblivion—the Jewish people ? They had received the Law, but they passed over it as the stream passes over the stones, and therefore the Lord took the Law and raised it up to Grace, just as David took the stones from the bed of the stream. He put them in a milk-bowl. What could be more apt as a figure of Grace than the abundant sweetness of milk ? "[1]

Countless examples may be found elsewhere, equally entertaining or equally melancholy, as you will, of this danger-ous folly. A mind accustomed from childhood to interpret texts in this fashion becomes, in our opinion, radically incap-able of understanding them in any way whatever. This kind of spiritual expression has grown so foreign to us that the difference between these minds and our own may be said to be not merely quantitative, but qualitative.[2] Yet the mania for *Allegory*, which was a *science* for the men of this period of mankind, dominated the whole of the output of the Middle Ages, not only of ecclesiastical literature but of letters in the vulgar tongue.[3]

Language.—Ancient literature is neglected in Gaul and in the West, not merely because it does not any longer correspond to the intellectual and moral needs of the men of this age,

---

[1] Sermon, **XXXIII.** Cf. MALE, *L'Art religieux, xiiiᵉ siècle,* 167.
[2] **DLXXIV, CCXVIII, CDXXIII.**
[3] See ERNEST LANGLOIS, *Origines et sources du Roman de la Rose.*

but because it becomes almost impossible to understand it
without a wearisome initiation. Christian literature whose
form is modelled on that of profane literature is within an
ace of being swallowed up in ruin. What happened was that
the gap between the written and the spoken language gradually
widened and the contact between them was broken.[1]

In *vocabulary*, the losses were enormous; the popular
language, simplified to excess, got rid of synonyms, and
replaced by popular terms numbers of words employed by
good authors. *Morphology* was in ruins: no more neuter
genders, comparatives, adverbs (replaced by the feminine
adjective combined with the word *mente*); no more deponents,
no more passives even (replaced by the participle with the
verb " to be "), no more cases, no more futures (instead, the
infinitive combined with the verb " to have "). The pre-
positions *de* and *ad* take the place of the case endings. *Syntax*
was seriously affected by the ruin of declensions as well as
by that of the conjugations. Notice the substitution of
the subordinate clause with conjunction for the infinitive
clause : *scies quod ego sum salvator mundi.* The demonstrative
becomes the article. In *word-formation* we see the development of new suffixes. Finally and perhaps worst of all,
phonology is affected. It matters little, relatively, that the
consonant-system should suffer—for example that in many
places *b* and *v* should be confused; but the vowel-system
is turned upside down. Classical Latin had five short and
five long vowels, plus the three diphthongs: *æ, œ, au.* Vulgar
Latin reduced these thirteen sounds to seven, by the complete
confusion of *ō* and *ŭ*, *ē* and *ĭ*, *ā* and *ă*, and by the suppression
of the diphthongs (except *au* which survived only in South
Gaul). Close and open vowels replaced short and long.
Immediately the whole of Latin poetry, Christian as well as
pagan, became incomprehensible to the bulk of the Romance
population. Henceforth the only intelligible poetry will be
based on the succession of high and low syllables, and
thus on a rhythm of intensity, whereas the ancient rhythm
was constituted by the musical alternation of long and short
syllables.

A problem arises with regard to this subject. Did the
literary language, the language of good society, still exist

[1] CLXXVIII.

in the living condition of a spoken language, in the sixth or even the fifth century ?

It seems certain that, even before the fall of the Western Empire, the number of families who made fluent use of correct language was not large, comparatively at least. The fate of Latin letters was bound up with the existence of an aristocratic class with a taste for culture. Such a class existed, without a doubt, in Gaul in the fifth century, although it was not large ; Sidonius Apollinaris is its most typical representative. In the sixth century it was even more restricted in numbers : we saw[1] in fact that the "senatorial" class declined in the second half of that century.

Usage was no longer sufficient to maintain even the approximate purity of the language ; it is impossible that the cultivated families, who were growing more and more rare, should, when in daily contact with the untutored masses, preserve the correct usage indefinitely. From the sixth century Gregory of Tours, who was related to the most noble families of Gaul, no longer dared write in verse, and spoke with reason of the rusticity of his style in prose.[2] His contemporary, Fortunatus,[3] is not without merit in his poems, in which, however, he does not venture on any lyrical form with the exception of the elegiac distich. Moreover he makes mistakes in quantity. But Fortunatus is Italian and with him Latin poetry comes to an end ; after him no one, even in Italy, composes any poems worthy of preservation. For the same reason rhythmic prose, which became fashionable in the third and fourth centuries in the language of the Chancellery, in correspondence, etc., dropped out of use in the sixth century.

In the seventh century Desiderius, Bishop of Cahors, is the only person in Gaul who has a smattering of ancient letters. Fredegar the chronicler makes desperate efforts to write in Latin. His language, and that of the diplomas, charters, formularies and lives of saints (when they have not been re-written in the Carolingian period) are comic in their barbarism. It is not in the least because Merovingian Latin is influenced by the vulgar language, but, on the contrary, because the people who write wish at all costs to use Latin

---

[1] See pp. 126, 127, etc.
[2] DXXXIX.
[3] DCXI. Cf. Ch. NISARD, *Le poète Fortunat.* (1890.)

correctly, to decline and conjugate at a time when no one any longer uses either genitive or dative, deponent, passive or future, to distinguish between vowel-sounds which every ear confuses, etc. They employ ablative and genitive, deponents and futures, here, there and everywhere, relying on vague reminiscences, and by the irony of chance, too frequently out of place. The less classical Latin is known, the more it is reverenced. The enigmatic Virgil the grammarian comes to regard it as a hermetic language, or rather as a series of mysterious languages, for he distinguishes twelve kinds of Latinities. He is, however, an ignoramus who has no real knowledge of profane literature nor of the rules of prosody. In the eighth century the chain is broken and when Charlemagne wishes to revive the knowledge of letters north of the Alps, he has to call upon foreigners, drawn from Italy, Spain, England and Ireland.[1]

After that, and very rapidly, written Latin again becomes correct. Indeed there is talk of a " Carolingian Renaissance." Since the oral transmission of the classical language has long ceased, Latin is learnt artificially, at school, by methods which are in the main analogous to ours. Latin has again become correct because now it is a dead language.

The Schools.[2]—Education was unable to keep tradition alive for long. In the fifth century there still existed schools of rhetoric subsidized by the imperial government. In Italy the Ostrogothic kings preserved them and Justinian restored them. It was only the Lombard invasion that dealt them their death blow. In Gaul the Merovingian kings did not trouble themselves with subsidizing educational institutions, although several of them were educated in sacred and profane letters. The so-called " school of the palace " is a myth, born of a misconception : the *scholares* are not scholars or students, but recommended young men of good family who go to court to serve their apprenticeship in the art of war and of administration.

The monasteries and bishops' palaces are in future the only places where letters find a refuge, but the education given there naturally takes on a specifically ecclesiastical character. Already it is a very unusual fact if from time to time a pagan

[1] DCXXXIII.
[2] DCCXXVII, CCLXI.

author is copied. The curriculum of Quintilian in the first century and of Ausonius in the fourth is already reduced in the fifth, in Martianus Capella's work which had an extraordinary vogue for ten centuries, *De Nuptiis Philologiæ et Mercurii*. This composition divides human knowledge into seven *arts*, subdivided into two groups : (1) The *Trivium*, comprising Grammar, Rhetoric, Dialectic ; (2) the *Quadrivium*, which claims to cover the Sciences and includes Arithmetic, Geometry, Astronomy, Music.[1] This inadequate curriculum, which neglects philosophy proper, appears ambitious from the sixth century—Gregory of Tours regards it as the highest degree of human wisdom and dares not flatter himself with the hope of attaining to such an ideal. After him, the curriculum in ecclesiastical schools confines itself usually to Grammar in the Trivium, and the Quadrivium is reduced, in practice, to notions concerning reckoning and singing for the purpose of determining the dates of the sacred festivals, and of celebrating the religious offices.

The confiscation of church property by Charles Martel, the installation by force of rough, rapacious, uncivilized warriors in the bishoprics and monasteries extinguished the last faint gleams of ancient culture. In the eighth century night descended upon Gaul.

Literature in the Vulgar tongue.—Latin letters, whether sacred or profane, classical or barbarian in form, are the appanage of the higher ranks of society, and later, at the end of the Merovingian period, of a small number of clerics only. As to the bulk of the population, not only the peasants attached to the soil, but the ordinary freemen of no education, had they no æsthetic needs, and were they able to satisfy them ? No people exists, however savage it may be, that does not have its songs of love and of mourning, and does not take delight in telling tales and histories. How can it be believed that the Gallo-Romans had nothing of the sort ? There must have been an oral literature in the vulgar *lingua romana*.[2] But the clerics would not condescend to collect the smallest portion of it, and the origins of French lyric and epic poetry lie hidden in the deepest obscurity. Only in the eleventh century do any texts emerge.

[1] IX ; CDXVII, 127.
[2] GASTON PARIS, *La littérature Française au moyen âge*. 3rd. ed., 191.

The Germans had epic chants from the most ancient times. There is abundant evidence on this subject. Charlemagne had transcribed " in order that their memory might be preserved," the most ancient barbarian poems in which were sung the exploits and the wars of the old kings. Unfortunately nothing has survived. It has been thought possible to reconstruct some of these compositions by utilizing the *Historia Gothorum* of Jordanes, the *Historia Ecclesiastica Francorum* of Gregory of Tours, the *Historia Langobardorum* of Paul the Deacon ; tempting but dangerous experiments, for every legendary account does not of necessity represent an epic.

The semi-mythical cycle of Siegfried, the Niebelung, specifically Frankish and Rheno-Frankish, is familiar to us chiefly in the thirteenth century High German poem—" The Niebelungen ", where it has undergone fundamental alterations ; similarly in the case of the historical compositions dedicated to Theodoric, son of Clovis, " the Huga " (the Frank) and his son Theodebert ; the poems of *Hug-Dietrich* and *Wolf-Dietrich* are of a late period and completely transformed.[1]

The German epic of the early Middle Ages is attested by the Anglo-Saxon poems *Widsidh* and *Beowulf*, the form of which is eighth century, while the matter may date from the period when the Angles and Saxons were still living on the continent, north of the Elbe, in the Cymbric peninsula; and also by a short fragment preserved in a MS. of the eighth century, the Combat of Hildebrand and Hadubrand ; it is a portion of a vast cycle of which Theodoric the Ostrogoth is the central figure. Nothing remains of it but remodelled versions of the thirteenth century, such as *Dietrichsflucht* and *Rabensschlacht*.[2] Such remnants, however, are sufficient to give a highly favourable impression of the German epic ; it was a rude and virile poetry, inspired by the true epic spirit. Its almost complete disappearance is all the more regrettable.

Art.—There is scarcely anything to be said of Merovingian any more than of Visigothic art.[3] It lacks originality. It is a poor continuation of ancient art which was in full decadence

[1] G. Paris, *op. cit.*, 21 ; **DCXVII, DCLXXIX.**
[2] **DCCXVII.**
[3] **VIII,** vol. 1, 1 ; **DLXXVI ; DCLXXVII, 247.**

as early as the fourth century. Of religious architecture, nothing remains in Gaul save three crypts and two baptisteries. Contemporaries boast of the churches, both cathedral and monastic, built in the fifth and sixth centuries. But we know that they were very mediocre in dimensions, even the famous basilica of Saint Martin of Tours,[1] and there is no doubt that they were weak imitations of the cold though grandiose edifices still found in Italy, such as the two basilicas of Saint Apollinaris at Ravenna, and Santa Maria Maggiore and Santo Paolo-fuori-le-Mura at Rome. Several cathedrals were simply built of wood. We know scarcely anything of their decoration—painting, mosaics, marble veneer ; there is no comparison, as far as the mosaics are concerned, with Italian art, which was still interesting, at any rate until the seventh century.[2]

Not a single secular building has been preserved. The native aristocracy, while it did not absolutely abandon the gloomy towns of the Later Empire, lived mainly in the country, in very spacious " villas " in the portico style, continuing the Roman tradition. These dwellings were not fortified, or only very weakly. The *castellum* constructed by Nicetius, Bishop of Treves, to serve as a refuge to his peasants, and which Fortunatus describes, is an exception. Not until the tenth century does the appearance of France change, to bristle for many centuries with castles, fences, strongholds, " plessis ", etc.

It is best to say nothing about sculpture.[3] Even in Italy, statuary was forgotten from the fourth century. Fine bas-reliefs are still to be met with on the *sarcophagi*, but the tradition of high relief is lost in the fifth century. Even at Ravenna the sculpture of the *sarcophagi* is in low relief and entirely Eastern in inspiration and it dies out in the seventh century. After this, for many a long year no one in the West knows how to represent the human face, at least in marble or in stone, for the goldsmiths continue to manufacture sacred effigies in gold and silver.

As sculpture on ivory and glyptics had also disappeared, at any rate in Gaul, and even ceramics had sunk into

---

[1] DCXXIII.
[2] DLXXVI., vol. i., 103-150.
[3] DL.

insignificance æsthetically, the goldsmith was the only genuine artist of the Merovingian era.[1]

This was not merely because jewellery is the last form of art to appeal to the decadent, as it is the first to appeal to barbarians, but also because the art of jewellery was revived by the barbarian invasions. The Goths brought back from their long sojourn in South Russia the knowledge of " cloisonné ", a process consisting of setting precious stones, or failing these, coloured stones, in sockets or on pierced plaques. From the Goths the new art passed to the other Germans and from them to the peoples on whose territory they established themselves. Here again the barbarians were certainly not inventors : the process, form and ornamentation of jewels, arms, sacred vessels, etc., point to the imitation of Sarmatian art, a branch of Iranian art.[2] Again, there is no doubt that the specimens of this art that are preserved in the West are inferior, in spite of the beauty of several of them, to the marvellous treasures discovered in South Russia, and even in the Caucasus. Nevertheless, in propagating a new style, the Barbarians revived the exhausted imagination of the East. The popularity of this style and the extraordinary success of the artists who made use of it—a success which is symbolized by the appointment of Saint Eloi to the episcopacy—are therefore justified.

Another importation from the West, enamel work, appeared at the same time and through the same channels ; however, this art was destined to lie dormant among us for a long time before bursting forth in all its glory.[3]

Again it was from the East, the Iranian and perhaps also the Egyptian East, that the new ornamentation came which wrought a fundamental change in the aspect of books.[4] In Gaul the manuscript decorated with paintings had not disappeared, but there only remained a small number of representatives of this form of art, in which the imitation of the antique was mediocre to the last degree. On the other hand the ornamentation of letters displays an entirely new trick of the imagination. Figures of animals, birds, fishes, serpents, lions, dragons are intertwined in whimsical combinations with the geometric design to form initials. The whole is drawn

[1] **CCCXXXV, DXXVI.**
[2] See above, pp. 140, 141.
[3] See above, p. 142.
[4] **CXV**, 214, 555.

with the pen with inimitable delicacy and firmness of touch ; and the design, after being drawn, is coloured by brush in uniform tints ; the effect is startling yet harmonious. It is thought that the penmen of Gaul display less originality than their rivals in Italy, Spain, and above all, Ireland and England ; the audacious productions of the latter bear witness to a real artistic temperament.[1]

As for handwriting, it is purely and simply a continuation of Latin writing, at least as regards the capital, the uncial and the semi-uncial, the latter being used especially for sacred texts. But the cursive handwriting, which already has a very unattractive appearance during the Empire, loses its form and becomes the horrible " Merovingian " used for writing treatises of all kinds and also the royal diplomas.[2]

---

[1] **VIII**, vol. i., 1, 303, 321, 435. See also, Aug. MOLLINIER, *Les Manuscrits et les Miniatures* (1892), and E. H. ZIMMERMANN, *Vorkarolingische Miniaturen* (Berlin, 1916).

[2] PROU, *Manuel de paléographie*, 4th ed., by A. de BOÜARD.

CHAPTER XIV

Religious Life[1]

IN the collapse of the Roman Empire, the Catholic Church alone remained standing. It was towards her that the peoples directed their hopes.

In Gaul her organization remained intact save, for one moment, on the frontiers stormed by the Barbarians. Ecclesiastical geography survives; not only the city and the the diocese but even the province, the see of the metropolitan, though it disappears in the civil organization. Thanks to the conversion of Clovis, the Catholic Church succeeds even in routing Arianism, and attempts the conversion of the Germans to Christianity.

The Church in the sixth century is primarily the Episcopate. In his diocese (*parochia*) the bishop is a kind of sovereign. He dominates his parishioners : (1) by his superiority of birth, which is always noble ; in the sixth century as in the fifth he is recruited from the " senatorial " nobility, in the seventh from the Gallo-Frankish aristocracy. (2) By his knowledge : he combines the knowledge of the Holy Scriptures with a certain smattering of ancient scholarship. (3) By the purity of his life : though often married when he is raised to the episcopate, he separates from his wife and lives in continence. Moreover the clergy and the people keep a jealous watch over his conduct, for the prosperity of the country is bound up with the sanctity of the pastor's life and the flock is afraid of the effects of the Divine wrath. Between it and the shepherd there reigns a close solidarity ; the *parochia* is a big family. (4) By his wealth, thanks to the economic and social influence which it brings with it. The possessions of the churches in Gaul had increased considerably.[2] The bishop administered in conjunction with the archdeacon. Having at his disposal considerable sums of money, he played

[1] **CCLXXIX**, vol. ii., 1, 216 ; **DCXXV, DLXXXII ; DXCVII**, vols. i. and ii. ; **DCXXXVIII**, vol. vi. ; **DCCIV, DCCXXXVIII, DCCXXVIII** and **IX, DCCXXX, DCCXXXIX, CXXVI**.
[2] **CCXCIV**.

the part of Providence to the clergy as well as to the laity. Indeed the State ceased to interest itself in the public services ; the organs of the " cities ", the *curiæ*, had neither money nor authority. The bishop replaced them. Not content with practising charity towards the poor "matriculated" (*immatricularii*), he ransomed captives, and relieved and fed prisoners. Hospices, hospitals, orphanages, even inns, were annexes of the churches and monasteries. Sometimes the bishop undertook public works at his own expense. Felix of Nantes constructed embankments against the flooding of the Loire ; a bishop of Mainz dammed in the Rhine ; Didier of Cahors restored the fortifications of the town.

Thanks to the right of sanctuary, every sacred building was an oasis for those in distress, but also, over-frequently, for criminals.

The bishop defended his flock against the *fiscus :* from an early date (Lyons from the fifth, Clermont and Tours in the sixth century) he obtained exemption from taxation for the cathedral city, and later for the country regions of the bishopric. In the seventh century *immunity* was no longer merely exoneration from taxes ; it meant that the "judges" were debarred from access to the lands of the immune person, for the purpose of holding legal assizes there, seizing sureties or arresting accused persons.[1]

Very soon the whole of the land on which the city and its suburbs stood became the property of the bishop. The life of the capital of the *civitas* depended, from Merovingian times, on the bishop ; its material as well as its spiritual existence was concentrated in his hands. This, moreover, was a general phenomenon. The preponderance of the episcopacy existed everywhere, in Italy, in Egypt, in the East.[2]

The Merovingians took no offence at this state of affairs ; on the contrary, the bishop was even invited to assist the count in the exercise of his functions, that is to say, to supervise him. Better still, episcopal jurisdiction was strongly developed (614). In criminal law, priests and deacons could not be judged by the secular powers without a previous examination conducted by the bishop. In civil law, though

---

[1] **DLXXXIII, DCXII.**
[2] **CDIX.** Cf. VAN CAUWENBERGH, in *Mélanges Ch. Moeller* (Louvain, 1914), 234.

the secular tribunals had authority in cases referring to real estate or to persons even in matters concerning clerics, the bishop alone had authority in civil cases proper, such as admitted of a monetary composition.[1]

If we add that, besides contentious jurisdiction, the bishop had authority in voluntary jurisdiction, acted as guardian to orphans and the disabled, and protected widows, we shall have some idea of the extent of his social activities.

Finally, the person of the bishop was inviolable. Only by a Council could he be legally condemned.

Should these privileges be looked upon as a sort of abdication on the part of a Frankish monarchy incapable of administering affairs and feeling the weight of government too heavy for it ? That would be going too far. In the Roman Empire of the East, the same prerogatives were granted to the Episcopacy. The truth is that our idea of the separation of spiritual and temporal power, at bottom a very artificial one, did not yet exist. The Church was one of the organs of the State, even the only one which was fairly reliable. There was every advantage, therefore, in developing its privileges and its field of action. But, if he favoured the episcopacy, the king intended that it should be to his advantage. He was anxious to keep a firm control over his bishops as well as his counts. For that purpose, the safest procedure was to appoint the bishop directly. The election of the prelate by the clergy and by the " people " was a mere fiction. The king selected the bishop.[2] The choice was often unfortunate. Gregory of Tours already describes to us his colleagues of Embrun, Gap, Rheims and Le Mans as veritable pirates. What will they be in the following century ? The higher clergy long submitted with docility to the royal despotism. In order that the bishop might dare to cross the whims of the king, questions of dogma had to come into play, upon which it was impossible to compromise. The Catholic Church in Gaul rallied to the side of the Merovingian monarchy which had put down Arianism. It was in a certain sense " Gallican ". Not that the doctrinal supremacy of the Pope was in any way attacked. But the spiritual relations between Gaul and Rome were so infrequent at this time that the pontifical pre-eminence remained

---

[1] DCCLXXVIII. Cf. above, p. 13.
[2] DLI.

more theoretical than actual. Moreover communications between the Roman Court and the Gallo-Frankish clergy could only take place through the medium of the Frankish King.[1]

In the seventh century, a great change took place. The episcopate ceased to obey slavishly, and more than once put itself at the head of the opposition to the monarchy or to the Mayoralty of the Palace. At the end of the Merovingian period, we even see bishops such as Savary of Auxerre or Eucher of Orléans carving out principalities for themselves. It was to take all the energy of Charles Martel to put down these "tyrants" who were the forerunners of the future bishop-counts of the Capetian period.

The clergy of Gaul often met in Council. The first "Gallican" Council was convoked by Clovis at Orléans in 511, the very year of his death. In the course of the sixth century, no fewer than forty Synodic assemblies were held. Since the suppression of Pelagianism in the fifth century, and of Arianism in the sixth century, no important speculations about dogma had disturbed the clergy of Gaul. It was in the East that Catholic dogma finally took shape from the fifth to the end of the seventh century. The West confined itself to registering the decisions of the great Ecumenical Councils held on territory of the "Roman" Empire.

The thoughts of the clergy of Gaul were preoccupied with discipline and problems of practical life. The bishops wished to enforce a regular life upon the clergy, and upon the faithful the strict observance of the rites and festivals of Christianity. They endeavoured to prevent the interference of the King's officers with the affairs of the clergy.

But as time went on, the number of the Councils decreased and the assemblies were held at longer intervals. In the seventh century, there are scarcely forty Councils to be found, and the last one, that of Auxerre in 695, was held after an interval of fifteen years. There was nothing more after that until 742.

The life of the country clergy during this period is unknown to us; but Gregory of Tours repeatedly speaks of priests and deacons residing in the towns. Too often they present a most unedifying spectacle. They are grasping, ambitious,

[1] **CCXXVI**, vol. ii., 516 ; vol. iii., 700 ; **DCXCVII**, 509 ; **DCCXXXIX**.

quarrelsome, always ready to spy on their bishop and to denounce him to the king on the slightest pretext, and what is more, they were as violent and bloodthirsty as the laity. Moreover the separation between the two worlds was not sufficiently well defined. It was usual to confer holy orders, even the episcopate, upon old or undesirable officials as a pension or compensation. Religious life withdrew from the secular clergy. It took refuge in the monasteries.[1] Oriental monasticism, which had met with real hostility in the West when it established itself there in the fourth century, triumphed in the sixth century. Monastic foundations were no longer confined to the South of Gaul. They travelled Northward, and kings set the example. Clovis founded the abbey of SS. Peter and Paul (Sainte Geneviève) in Paris, Sigismund the Burgundian King built Saint Maurice d'Agaune in the Valais, Childebert Saint Vincent (Saint Germain-des-Prés) at the gates of Paris ; in the seventh century Dagobert was the benefactor of Saint Denis. We must also mention Saint Calais at "*Anisola* in the department of Maine, *Fontinella* (Saint Wandrille) and Jumièges on the lower reach of the Seine, *Centule* (Saint Riquier) in the Somme Valley, in the North *Sithier* (Saint Bertin), etc. The queens took their share. Radigund founded Sainte Croix at Poitiers, Bathildis Chelles and Corbie. Nothing could stop the movement. From the seventh century there was not a single nobleman or bishop who did not wish to ensure the salvation of his soul by a foundation of this kind.

In principle, the monks were neither priests nor even clerics. The rules determining their association were those of the monasteries of the East (Egypt, Syria) adapted to Western life by Cassian and Cæsarius. At the end of the sixth century the Irishman Columbanus reinforced them in the direction of greater austerity. In the eighth century, his rule was replaced by that of the Italian Benedict of Norcia, the founder of the Monte Cassino monastery, who died in the middle of the sixth century. The monks did not spend their time in dreaming but in toiling and praying. They lived in the country. The lack of room in the cities would have precluded the building of monasteries in them even if the monks had not shunned crowds of set purpose. The Irish cenobites even

---

[1] **XIV and XVI, XXXI, XXXV and XXXVI, DXXI, DXLVII.**

sought out solitude deliberately.[1] They fled into the most out of the way islands, the Shetland Islands, the Orkneys and even Iceland. On the continent they sought the forests and steep mountains, as is shown by their foundations in Gaul: Luxeuil in the Vosges, *Condastico* (Saint Claude) in the Jura and Stavelot and Malmédy in the Ardenne; in Rhaetia, Saint Gall in the Appenzell; in Italy, Bobbio on the Apennines.

Even at a distance, these foundations roused popular piety and called forth a flood of gifts. Abbeys like Saint Germain-des-Prés, Saint Wandrille and many others had never been so rich as at the end of the Merovingian period.

The favour of the kings meant privileges of immunity for them. On their side, the bishops, under whose authority were placed the monks and nuns, began in the seventh century to grant privileges of exemption, which slackened the bonds between the cathedral and the monastery, so that religious foundations came to form almost independent miniature sovereignties.

The spread of Christianity. There was a great task for the secular as well as for the regular clergy, the spreading of Christianity amongst the Gallo-Romans as much as amongst the barbarians. In the fifth century, the evangelization of Gaul was very superficial.[2] Outside the capitals of the *civitates* where the bishop dwelt, no domiciled clergy is found except in the " châteaux " (*castra*), that is to say, the fortified towns and the *vici* or free villages. The religious needs of the majority of the country dwellers, of the peasants or pagans (*pagani*), were not permanently provided for.

These peasants, *coloni*, and serfs attached to the soil, had neither freedom of movement nor means. It was for their seigniors, the large landowners whose estates or villas they cultivated, to see about building for them " oratories " or " chapels ", regularly served. Bishops and abbots were the first to set the example. But the Merovingian period only began the great work which was to be completed only in the Carolingian period. Then only was the rural parish, the ancestor of the modern village, established and it could be said that the Christian religion was really practised by the mass of the country population.[3]

[1] DLXXXVII.
[2] XVI.
[3] DCV.

More practised doubtless than understood; for we cannot
but ask what there was that believers or even the clergy,
whether Gallo-Romans or Germans, could understand in the
sacred rites celebrated in an obsolete language, Latin, which
the populace understood but imperfectly even before the fall
of the Roman Empire.

At the same time the fight against paganism went on without respite. The religions and systems which competed with
Christianity, Mithraism, Manicheism, Gnostic sects had all
disappeared or were hiding underground. The old Græco-
Roman mythology was now only a memory. Only some
superstitions remained, but these were tenacious; honours
paid to fountains or trees, here and there the worship of
statues, and animal sacrifices on feast days. All this was not
very dangerous, being only local rites and mechanical traditions, little understood or not at all.

The only districts in Gaul where the clergy had some difficulty in destroying " idolatry " were those occupied by the
Franks either *en masse* or in groups. This explains why the
most famous missionaries worked in these places, Saint Amand
and Saint Bavon in the Valley of the Escaut, Saint Lambert in
that of the Meuse, Saint Valéry in that of the Bresle and Saints
Romain, Ouen and Wandrille in the Caux district. The
double diocese of Cambrai and Arras had to be evangelized
anew by Saint Géry and that of Noyon and Tournai by Saint
Éloi. The Irishman Gall destroyed a *fanum* near Cologne,
Vulfilaïc a colossal statue of Diana at Ivois in the diocese
of Trèves, etc. Upon the whole, the work was crowned with
success, for after the end of the seventh century, there was
left in Gaul no pagan worship, Roman or German; at least
no organized worship.[1]

But, it must be definitely admitted that outside the territories subject to the authority of the kings, the propaganda
of the Gallo-Frankish Church proved powerless. It was
unable to bring over to Christ independent Germany, the
Frisians and the Saxons. Even in Southern Germany, in
the valley of the Main, Christianization was only on the
surface. In the eighth century, Scots, that is to say Irishmen,
and especially Anglo-Saxons, Willibrord, Winfrid (Saint Boniface) and Lull had to be called in. The clergy of Gaul had

[1] **DCCXXVIII.**

become too incompetent or too corrupt to be entrusted with a missionary task bristling with difficulties.[1]

The form of Christianity which triumphed in the West was of neither a high nor a pure quality. Even the best bishops were superstitious, believing in omens and haunted by fear of the Devil. Their notion of the deity was too often that of a jealous vindictive god who favoured his devotees without troubling about their morality. What are we to say of the bulk of believers ? Certain practices contributed to the degradation of Christian feeling, such as the use of " penitentials ", coming apparently from Ireland ; these were tariffs of prices for the redemption of sins.

From this period, the worship of God gave way to the worship of the Saints. The admiration and reverence for the martyrs, and later for the confessors of the Church, quickly changed into a veritable worship.[2] From the saint was expected not only intercession with God, but also material benefits. His body was supposed to protect the country in which it was buried ; even its fragments or relics were talismans which cured infirmities and maladies. He was thus a miracle-worker, curing the evils of the soul and of the body. Gradually differentiations between the saints were set up which specialized the effects of their intervention, so that the healing saints replaced the gods and heroes of Antiquity. Not that the saints were under new names ancient Greek, Latin, Semitic, Egyptian, Syrian, or German gods ; this has been proved only for a small number of minor saints.[3] But mankind, unable to be satisfied with a good and righteous god, since it is itself neither good nor righteous, turned to more easily accessible powers which it considered more favourable to its needs, that is, more indulgent to its vices. Left to itself the human mind fell back wholly into paganism.

The hope and gratitude of believers showed themselves by plentiful gifts, especially to the monasteries, that is to say to the saints of whom the abbot and the monks were only the mandatories. The clergy's excessive landed wealth created a danger for it. When the State no longer had anything to distribute, because it no longer possessed anything

[1] **DCXXV** and **DCXXVI.**
[2] **DXXXI, DCXLVI.**
[3] *Cf.* above, p. 51.

itself, it cast a glance of envy on the lands of the Church. The Mayor of the Palace, the head of the government, was obliged to reward the fidelity of his supporters. Not daring or not wishing to have recourse to evictions by force, he turned to his own advantage a practice of the Church, borrowed from Roman usages, that of the *precarium*. The *precarium* (or one of its forms) was a grant, for a long time extra-legal, which was essentially revocable. The holder of a *precarium*, though in the position of possessor as regards third persons, had no rights in relation to the owner making the grant, who was free to take back his property when he chose, without any reason. In practice the holder enjoyed a right of usufruct and this right was considered dangerous enough for him to be required to send every five years an *epistola precatoria* in which he set forth, purposely in very humble terms, his request for the grant, and recognized that he was not the owner ; or else he was obliged to pay an annual though very small rent, which served as a legal proof that he was merely a tenant. Being obliged by the canons not to alienate its lands, the Church made use of this practice, which enabled it, while respecting the letter of the canons, to reward services or adherents, and to attach clients to itself.[1]

In the second half of the seventh century, the Mayor of the Palace, by this shift, obtained for his supporters Church lands, such as the estate of Taverny granted by Saint Denis to a *fidelis* of Ebroin. Needless to say, the request of the chief was a command. Charles Martel only applied this measure on a large scale. To reward the Austrasian warriors who had supported him, he resorted to vast confiscations. His successors were not in a position to make restitution, and in fact confined themselves to confirming the spoliation by giving it a legal colouring. The old churches and monasteries were never able to recover from the blow which was dealt them at the moment when the Merovingian period came to an end.[2]

---

[1] CCXCIV, 314.
[2] CCXCIV, 314, vol. ii.

CHAPTER XV

LAY SOCIETY

TO attempt a comprehensive picture[1] of the lay society of this period would be fantastic. Thanks to Gregory of Tours, we catch lightning glimpses of the court, and the vision presented is a horrible one, perpetual plotting of brother against brother, of nephews against their uncles and of sons against their fathers. Delation thrived as in the Later Empire, and the King's wrath struck at random without any discrimination or pity. Morality was at its lowest level; the king wallowed in debauchery and his courtiers imitated him. In the second half of the seventh and in the eighth century it was even worse; the sovereign was literally a vicious degenerate who died young, a victim to his excesses.

At the end of the sixth and in the seventh century, the aristocracy of officials, which was also the land-owning class, showed a coarseness and corruption which pass all bounds. At the same time a great lowering took place in its intellectual level and education. Fortunatus kept up a modest literary correspondence not only with ecclesiastics, but also with some laymen of high rank, such as Gogo and Lupus, Mayors of the Palace of Sigebert, Magnulfus brother of Lupus, Jovinus the Patrician of Provence, Mummolenus, perhaps the Mayor of the Palace of Chilperic, the *domesticus* Conda, the Referendary Boso, etc. But it should be noticed that even if these important men were able to take pleasure in the laborious futilities of the Latin poetaster, or to pretend to do so, they were unable to reply to him.

The type of the lettered nobleman presented by Sidonius Apollinaris and his correspondents in the fifth century,[2] began to die out in the course of the following century, and then completely disappeared. The service of the Merovingian did not require any great literary cultivation, although some kings (Chilperic, Caribert) knew classical Latin, and contact

---

[1] The attempt has been made by A. MARIGNAN, **DCXLVI.**
[2] **VII.** Cf. above, p. 348.

with the Franks was not calculated to make for elegance of manners and of style. On the contrary, the Gallo-Roman aristocracy very soon felt the attraction of the rude warrior life of the barbarians. Being in constant contact at court, in the army, in the towns and in the country, "Romans" and Franks could not long remain strangers to each other. Mixed marriages certainly became frequent, and if personal law remained, in practice it doubtless interfered very little and was not strictly observed. In the course of the seventh century the fusion between the Gallo-Roman and the Frankish families was completed. Then was formed the "French" aristocracy, a turbulent, pugnacious and ignorant class, scornful of things of the mind, incapable of rising to any serious political notion and fundamentally selfish and unruly. It was this social class which was to dominate France, and sometimes Europe, for ten centuries.

In the constitution of Gallo-Frankish society, from the seventh and eighth centuries onwards, the German contribution was considerable, and in many points prevailed.

Doubtless Clovis and his Franks were not conquerors after the Turkish or Mongolian fashion.[1] Doubtless they did not despoil the natives, at least not systematically ; nor did they look upon them as an inferior race. They tried to assimilate whatever suited them in the Roman organization and civilization of Gaul, taking care not to despise anything. It is true also that the kings at once ceased to reside on purely Frankish territory. None the less the fact remained that the prestige of the Franks was and for four centuries remained without any rival. The nomenclature provides unquestionable evidence for this fact. The further we go in the sixth century, the more we find "Romans" abandoning their Latin names to adopt Frankish ones. In the seventh century practically German names only are left.[2] This was a fashion only, but a fashion is indicative of a state of mind. We have no information about the dress and arms of the Romans of Gaul ; but we may be quite sure that they made haste to copy those of the Franks in order not to be different from them in anything. Only the clergy imposed on the barbarians its Roman dress which had become ritual.

[1] Cf. above, p. 322.
[2] Albert DAUZAT, *Les noms de personne* (1925), 37.

The influence of the barbarians on the language of the Romans of Gaul is undeniable. Not that the Germanic languages spread very much beyond the territories they occupied at the time of the disappearance of the Empire or that they modified in any respect the grammatical structure of Vulgar Latin, but a stream of words poured from the Frankish language into the Romance vocabulary, and these were words in common use[1] : terms connected with war : guerre (war), escrime (fencing), épier (to spy), guetter (to watch), blesser (to wound) ; with arms : heaume (helmet), haubert (hauberk), éperon (spur), étrier (stirrup) ; with clothing and ornament : robe (robe), guimpe (wimple) ; with law : ban (ban), gage (pledge), saisir (seize), garantir (guarantee), nantir (to give security), déguerpir (to relinquish possession), alleu (allodium), fief (fief) ; with habitation and furniture : bourg (burg), hameau (hamlet), beffroi (belfry), fauteuil (arm-chair), banc (bench) ; with food : gâteau (cake), gaufre (waffle), rôti (roast) ; with amusement : danse (dance), harpe (harp). The vocabulary used for the world and nature was enriched by the names of the four points of the compass : nord (North), sud (South), est (East), ouest (West) ; by words such as : forêt (forest), bois (wood), jardin (garden), gazon (turf), haie (hedge), gerbe (sheaf) ; by names of animals : épervier (sparrow-hawk), héron (heron), gerfaut (gerfalcon), mésange (pinnock), esturgeon (sturgeon), écrevisse (cray-fish), hareng (herring) ; by names of plants : hêtre (beech), houx (holly), if (yew), mousse (moss), roseau (reed) ; by the names of the parts of the body : hanche (hip), échine (chine), téton (teat), quenotte (tooth). There are even words which indicate a subtler and deeper influence, names of colours : blanc (white), bleu (blue), blond (fair), brun (brown), gris (grey), blême (pale) ; psychological terms : adjectives such as frais (fresh), gai (gay), gaillard (merry), morne (gloomy), joli (pretty), laid (ugly); nouns : honte (shame), orgueil (pride), and lastly verbs : haïr (to hate), effrayer (to frighten), gagner (to gain), choisir (to perceive), honnir (to disgrace), épargner (to spare), hâter (to hasten), fournir (to furnish), etc.

If we observe that these words belong to the language of everyday use, that they are numerous and were still more so

---

[1] Ferdinand Brunot, *Histoire de la langue française*, vol. i., Nyrop, *Grammaire historique de la langue française*, vol. i., (1904).

in the Middle Ages, we shall realize the importance of the German element in the vocabulary of Romance. A number of these words which are expressive and charming have become organic to the French language and will endure with it.

German law has left a deep and lasting mark on the whole of Northern Gaul and even on part of Aquitaine up to the central plateau. Not that the Franks made any systematic attempt to extend their national customs. They scarcely troubled themselves about this, and, like the other barbarians, they thought it right and natural that the " Romans " should be judged by Roman law. Their law spread, in spite of them as it were, through the practice of the assizes (the *mall*), in which the " goodmen " of every nationality " declared the law ". In every *pagus*, even in the districts in which they were not settled in large groups, the Franks were considerable enough in numbers for mixed law-suits between them and Romans or Burgundians to be frequent. Frankish law, which, from daily practice even the Romans learnt to handle, profited from the prestige enjoyed by the Frankish nation amongst the peoples. Hence the ambition of every free man was to bear a Frankish name, to dress like a barbarian, and to follow the barbarians' customs. From the Rhine to the Loire, and even further still, German law gained ground so much that in the ninth century no one is found in the Orléans district with any knowledge of Roman law.

Moreover, condensed in the Breviary of Alaric, and petrified ever since the imperial constitutions of Rome and later of Constantinople had ceased to come to quicken it, Roman law in Gaul declined to the level of a custom. From the middle or the end of the Merovingian period, German law proved irresistible. Marculf's collection of the formulæ shows that the Parisian district used it in the middle of the seventh century. The collections of formulæ of Angers, Tours, and even Auvergne do not entirely escape its influence.

It cannot be said that this influence was good. German law, as it appears in the Salic law and the Ripuarian law and in their derivatives, the laws of the Alemans and of the Bavarians (eighth century), is an archaic law.[1]

In the family, the power of the father remained excessive.

---

[1] **DCXCIX, DCCXXXIII,** Heusler, *Institutionen des deutschen Privatrechts,* vol. i.

His *mundium* gave him full authority over his wife and children ; it went so far as to confer on him the right of selling them. All the more could the father marry his daughters as he wished. Marriage did not set free even the sons from the paternal authority. The German woman's position in law, as compared to that of the Roman woman, was very low ; she was a minor for life under the *mundium* of her father, husband, or even her son. The minor and his property were practically at the discretion of his *mainbur*. Further, custom by no means tempered the strictness of the law.

Marriage laws, which are indications of the level of morality reached by any society, scarcely existed. Divorce by mutual agreement or the putting away by the husband of his wife with no other motive than caprice, was common. The kings and the nobles openly practised polygamy. So inveterate was the evil, that in the Merovingian period, we do not find the bishops combating it, as though they were disheartened by the immensity of the public corruption.

German law is rich in formalism, a sure sign of a backward civilization. Naturally, the conception of contracts by mutual agreement, which the Roman law had reached, remained completely alien to it, and covenants were subjected to a symbolic form. Obligations were of so narrowly personal a character that a chose in action, for example, could not be assigned to a third party. Needless to say, good faith or error was not taken into consideration in estimating the value of a contract.

The chapter on inheritance is no less imperfect. A male privilege excluded women from inheriting real estate. Ascendants never came in as heirs. The transmission of property was so strictly regulated that no account was taken of the wishes of the deceased, and the will proper was unknown.

The narrow, implacable spirit of German law, which sacrificed everything to formalism, is shown even more clearly in procedure.[1] The slightest mistake in a word or gesture entailed the loss of the case. Procedure remained an essentially private affair, the serving of the summons being carried out by the plaintiff, who also effected the seizure.

The rules of evidence[2], unsatisfactory enough even in Roman law, were quite primitive. The oath supported by the oaths

---

[1] DCCXII, DCCXX.
[2] DLVIII.

of others and the ordeal (trials by fire or water) were given precedence over proof by witness, and still more over written proof. The burden of proof devolved upon the defendant and not upon the accuser. What was at first a secondary proof, the trial by combat or "the judgment of God", which results in the very negation of justice, took on an extraordinary development to the detriment of the others.

Jurisprudence was not able to correct the shortcomings of the law. When the experts, the "good men" (*boni homines*, *rachimburgs*) had "declared the law", the "judge", that is to say the count, was bound, as were also those doing suit, the "people", whose tacit or expressed assent completed the sentence. It remained finally to make the losing party, who might refuse to do so,[1] accept the sentence.

The contrast between the rigid and savage formalism of German law and the Roman legislation of the Later Empire, which was permeated throughout by a liberal spirit and was more careful about equity than about form, leaves a painful impression. We are astonished that the Franks, and in Italy the Lombards, though in daily contact with the Romans, should have been able to spread their customs, which were so backward. The retreat of Roman law before German law in the districts where the Romans formed by far the majority of the population, is one of the surest signs of the barbarism of these times. It is also possible that the striking nature of German symbolism was one of the causes of the success of this law amongst the Romance peoples of Northern Gaul, who were less civilized than those in Narbonensis and Aquitania.

The best known feature of the German penal law is the *composition*, which allowed compensation in money for blows, wounds and even murder. This procedure was soon accepted by the Romans and was encouraged by the Church, which saw in it a means of avoiding bloodshed, and by the State which was practically incapable of ensuring public order. In many cases, the law's standard of severity or indulgence in the matter of the indemnity owed by the guilty person is baffling ; to squeeze a woman's arm above the elbow entails a fine of 35 solidi, five more than for wounds which have broken the skull or ripped open the belly of the victim. The reason is that the composition was not at bottom either a fine or an

[1] CLXIX.

indemnity in the modern sense, but a means of escaping vengeance or the *faida*. The factors which entered into the composition were not only the wrong suffered and the resentment felt, but the respective social position of the offender and the victim, or more correctly of their " families ". For indeed the duty of vengeance devolved upon the kinsmen in the widest possible sense. The ransom was heavy in proportion as the kinsmen were powerful.

This also explains the fact that the composition was owed even when the offending intention had not been followed by any effect, when consequently there was no damage incurred ; the reason was that the resentment of the person attacked was feared. Also, if the murderer paid less to the child of the murdered man than to the father of the murdered child, this was because the guilty person had less to fear from a child than from a grown-up man.

Hence the composition answered to no generous thought. It did not at all aim at protecting the weak. It troubled itself as little as possible about what we call to-day the sacred rights of the individual. It was simply the payment of a premium to insure against the exercise of the right of vengeance.[1] The security it bought, was itself very precarious ; for, in spite of the efforts of the king, powerful men and men of violence did not refrain from the practice of the vendetta. Gregory of Tours shows us the latter rife from the sixth century, and not only amongst the Franks. Henceforth vengeance did not stay its course. From the barbarians it passed to the Romans, from the upper classes of society to the people, and a wide trail of blood runs through the centuries.[2] The spirit of German law is certainly responsible for a great part of the constant, unrestrainable, frenzied violence which characterizes the manners of the Middle Ages.

It was also responsible for the insecurity of property. The confused notion of *seizin*, which distinguished imperfectly between ownership, possession, and detention, afforded only precarious guarantees.[3] The conception of donation was not clear either ; a gift could be revoked on a worthless pretext.[4]

---

[1] **DCCXXV.**

[2] FRAUENSTAEDT, *Blutrache im deutschen Mittelalter* (1881); P. DUBOIS, *Les assurements . . . recherches sur le droit de vengeance* (1900).

[3] E. CHAMPEAUX, *Essai sur la vestitura au saisine* (1899).

[4] **DXLV**, vol. i., 294, 308.

Thus the introduction into Western Europe of an archaic law, suitable only for a society little developed economically and politically, had the effect of thrusting the nations back into barbarism. From this point of view the invasions mark a setback for mankind.[1]

Thus the Frankish monarchy, the most vigorous as well as the most original of the States born of the disintegration of the Roman world in the West, also foundered in bankruptcy. In every sphere the Merovingian age marks a fall from the preceding age. It is truly an accursed period of history.

It must have seemed intolerable to those fine and pure spirits who had the misfortune to live in those times. On what could they feed their intellectual and moral life ? Patriotism after the ancient fashion was dead, devotion to the monarchy was weakening, disheartened by the worthlessness of the Merovingians, and feudal loyalty was as yet only a domestic and almost servile sentiment. Philosophy and science were as good as dead. Literature, little accessible in languages which had become practically incomprehensible, was without savour or life and no contemporary original production came to re-quicken it. Of art, which can transfigure the darkest periods, the West caught only a very feeble gleam coming from the East.

One way only remained open, religion. But the secular Church was stained with the passions and vices of the laity ; the spiritual life of the bishops even was of the sorriest. The only place in which men and women who feared the contact of a perverse world could find a refuge was the cloister. The monastery realized on earth the city of God. Outside was the kingdom of violence and sin, the " world ".

---

[1] The conclusion of **DCLXXVII** is on the contrary optimistic.

CONCLUSION

WHEN Roman unity had broken up in the West, two policies were possible, if the desire was to save the world from being shipwrecked in the sea of barbarism. These were the restoration of the Empire, and the establishment of a *modus vivendi* between the Romans and the Germans who had settled amongst them.

Justinian thought himself strong enough to re-build Roman unity. He was able to recover Africa and with difficulty Italy, and then some parts of Spain. Gaul was beyond his reach, and without it no reconstruction was practicable in the West. The *reconquista* answered to no desire of the Romans in the West. The peoples did not call in the Romans of the East, who in mind, manners and language were already foreigners to them. The position of Constantinople was too far from the centre to enable it to dominate the whole Mediterranean. On the whole, Justinian's work shows itself as out-of-date, artificial and harmful; for it resulted in leaving Italy defenceless against the Germans from the Danube and in delivering Africa to the half-savage Berbers.

Another way was marked out by events themselves. Since the years 378 and 407 it was evident that Rome would not be able to keep away from her frontiers the barbarian world, nor any longer to assimilate and Romanize the hordes settling upon her soil. Nevertheless harmony was not impossible with the Germans, especially with the Goths. These peoples had no thought of destroying the Roman world, but wished to place themselves in its service, or rather to live at its expense. In fact, in spite of countless sufferings of individuals, no social revolution, or fatal blow to ancient civilization, resulted from the settlement of the Ostrogoths in Illyria and later in Italy, of the Visigoths in Gaul and Spain, of the Burgundians in the Rhone Valley and even of the Vandals in Northern Africa.

The Roman world had been able to endure only by means of a ruthless compression, and this compression by breaking every spring in the life of the peoples had made the Empire the prey of the barbarians, who by themselves were neither numerous nor very dangerous. When the bonds uniting peoples which were Romanized, but separated from each other by geography and differences of race, customs and aspirations, had been broken, would it not have been possible to turn to advantage this *fait accompli* ? By putting an end to a decaying political form, the Empire, could not the barbarians have freed the peoples, and thus, without knowing or wishing it, have been indirectly beneficial to them ?

Italy, Gaul, Great Britain and Northern Africa are geographical units. Each of these regions could and ought to have been the seat of an independent civilization. For a moment it had seemed that the great third-century crisis, by breaking the Roman world into fragments, might set up nationalities based on later civilization. But the peoples had lost all national and even particularist feeling. They were only fragments whose ambition was to be re-united and form once more the imposing whole of the Empire. Two centuries later the peoples formed only an amorphous mass without any initiative and fundamentally incapable of ruling their own destinies. By crystallizing round a barbarian dynasty what latent forces had been able to survive amongst the natives, it would have been possible to give back to these countries, which had been crushed under Roman uniformity, an individual character and original life.

This is in fact what took place in Spain, even in spite of the obstacle constituted by the Arianism of the ruling race. At the end of the seventh century, the fusion between Goths and Hispano-Romans was very far advanced, and, from every point of view, Spain was making for unity. This is what undoubtedly would have happened in Lesser Africa and in Italy with the Vandals and the Ostrogoths but for the thoughtless venture of Justinian, and in Gaul with the Visigoths but for the accident of Clovis.

Unfortunately these Romano-German States very soon proved to be frail. Roman civilization was not good for the barbarians. They aped without succeeding in assimilating it. The Southern climate certainly weakened them. They were not numerous and their armies remained very poor numerically, where, as in Africa and Italy, they continued to keep apart. The Visigoths in Gaul and Spain, who incorporated the natives, were undoubtedly swamped by the superior numbers of the latter. Lastly, these uprooted peoples brought no political institution apart from the monarchy. Their cohesion was due solely to the ascendancy of an illustrious chieftain or the prestige of a dynasty. When the old divine families of the Amalungs and the Baltungs amongst the Goths had disappeared, the throne was henceforth a prey to the continual strife of competitors. The Vandal State in Africa, the Gothic State of Toulouse, and the Gothic State of Toledo, fell in a single battle. If the Ostrogoths put up a long and glorious resistance, this was largely due to the fact that Justinian could bring against them only insignificant forces.

The States founded by the Franks and the Lombards did not, at the beginning at least, possess the mixed, amphibious character of the Gothic States. The Lombards were rude and ruthless conquerors, but the monarchy was amongst them almost immediately checkmated by the aristocracy. The kings failed to unite Italy under their authority not only because of the opposition of Byzantium and of the Papacy, but because their State scarcely included more than the Po Valley and part of Tuscany, the Lombard principalities of Central and Southern Italy being in reality independent. The Lombard nation had never been numerically a large people, either in Germany or Pannonia. When transported in its entirety to Italy, it must have been very soon swallowed up by the native population. In the eighth century, a Lombard was a man living under the authority of a king of barbarian origin and in conformity to German law, but in language and blood he was probably already an Italian. Two battles sufficed to put an end to the Kingdom of Pavia.

We have seen the peculiar nature of the Frankish State. It was founded by the ambition of one man. The Gallo-Roman population at once accepted the domination, or more correctly, the superior position of the Franks. The centre of power was very soon transferred to Roman territory. Nevertheless, it had behind it, what the Lombard State lacked, strong German reserves, on the Escaut, the lower Meuse, the Moselle and the Rhine. The Franks kept their individual character in the midst of the natives. They even imposed themselves on these by their prestige. From the beginning of the sixth century they formed the most formidable power in Western Europe, and they were destined to rule Gaul, almost the whole of Germany, and for a moment Northern Italy. But with them also the only institution was the Monarchy. The latter began to decay at the end of the sixth century. The Aristocracy prevailed in the seventh century. Only the institution of the Mayor of the Palace, a real Viceroy, prevented the breaking up of the State. A clever and ambitious family of Austrasia even succeeded in restoring the unity of the *Regnum Francorum* by removing its rivals in Neustria and Burgundy, and then by reigning under the name of the degenerate Merovingian. But at the beginning of the eighth century, it seemed that this house would, in its turn, also disappear. Failing the appearance of a new Clovis or Charles Martel, the Frankish State was being destroyed by the blows of the heathen Germans on one side and of the Moslems of Spain on the other.

In the eighth century, the bankruptcy was thus general. The more German States of the Franks and of the Lombards seemed to be crumbling as much as the Romano-German States of the Goths.

Hence the entry of the barbarians into the Roman world, under whatever form it took place, did not succeed in regenerating the ancient world or in replacing it by better political forms.

The regeneration by the barbarians is *à priori* a tempting thesis to maintain. But after we have had a glimpse, in our texts, of the terrible corruption of these times, it is impossible to see in it more than a theme for declamation. The Frankish, Visigothic, Ostrogothic and Lombard monarchies were only so many German Byzantiums, a combination of senility and barbarism. Such States, devoid of freshness and purifying virtue, could not live or could only drag on a miserable life. No vital force animated them, after the fighting days during which they took shape. The Catholic Church showed itself powerless to improve these new societies, howsoever little. Here too there was bankruptcy.

On the borders of these States, the Germans founded others, which were purely barbarian, on territories which had once been Roman, between the upper course of the Danube and the

Alps and in Great Britain. We need not linger over them. The duchies of Alemannia and Bavaria came under the influence of the Franks and were an adjunct to their *Regnum*. In Great Britain, Angles, Jutes and Saxons carried out the most ruthless of conquests and wiped out, as far as they could, all memory of Rome. The history of their petty kingdoms and their feuds contains nothing which deserves to detain us. The wholly German States do not, any more than the mixed Romano-German States, mark any appreciable progress in the march of humanity, in this period of history.

Meanwhile new forces had been or were being born, and it was for these that the future was reserved : Islam, whose prodigious success was of the nature of a miracle, the Papacy, which was about to seize the reins of the Church and to try to dominate civil society, and lastly Vassalage, the germ of the feudal system, in which was to be embodied the life of Western Europe for very many centuries.

With these forces, the Middle Ages really begin.

NOTES ON THE BIBLIOGRAPHY

P. 411. Bury's work has been reprinted, New York, 1958.

P. 414. *For* Geffecken *read* Geffcken.

P. 423. The *Realencyclopädie der classischen Altertumswissenschaft* has continued publication and now (1960) comprises 31 volumes with 8 supplements.

P. 425. Schanz's *Römische Literaturgeschichte* has reached the third and fourth editions of some sections, edited by Carl Hosius and Gustav Krüger, 1922-1935.

P. 426. Henry Osborn Taylor's *The Classical Heritage of the Middle Ages* is now available in the Harper Torchbook series with a foreword and bibliography by Kenneth M. Setton, 1958.

P. 431. Heyd's work has been reprinted, Leipzig, 1936.

P. 479. Haarhoff's work has been reprinted, Johannesburg, 1958.

BIBLIOGRAPHY*

FIRST AND SECOND PARTS

AEBERG (Nils) *Die Franken und Westgoten in der Völkerwanderung*, Upsala-Paris, 1922 — I

ALBERT-PETIT (A.) *Comment meurt une civilisation*, in *Revue de Paris*, 15 June, 1922, p. 841-52 — II

ALLARD (Paul) *Le Christianisme et l'empire romain de Néron à Théodose*, Paris, 7th edit., 1908 — III

—— *Les Dernières persécutions du III⁰ siècle*, Paris, 1887 — IV

—— *La Persécution de Dioclétien*, Paris, 1890, 2 vols — V

—— *Julien l'Apostat*, Paris, 1900-03, 3 vols — VI

—— *Saint Sidoine Apollinaire*, Paris, 1909 — VII

ANDRÉ-MICHEL. *Histoire de l'art depuis les premiers temps chrétiens jusqu'à nos jours*, Paris (vol. I) — VIII

APPUHN (A.) *Das Trivium und Quadrivium, I. Das Trivium*, Erlangen, 1900 — IX

ARBOIS DE JUBAINVILLE (H. d') and DOTTIN (G.) *Recherches sur l'origine de la propriété foncière et des noms de lieux habités en France*, Paris, 1890 — X

BABELON (Ernest) *La Gravure en pierres fines, camées et intailles*, Paris, 1894 — XI

—— *Le Tombeau du roi Childéric et les origines de l'orfèvrerie cloisonnée*, Paris, 1923 (Extr. from *Mémoires de la Soc. des Antiquaires de France*) — XII

—— *Traité des monnaies grecques et romaines*, Paris, 1901 — XIII

BABUT (E.-A.) *Priscillien et le Priscillianisme*, Paris, 1909 (*Bibliothèque de École des Hautes ètudes*, 169th fasc.) — XIV

—— *Recherches sur la garde impériale et sur le corps d'officiers de l'armée romaine aux IV⁰ et V⁰ siècles*, Paris, 1914 (Extr. from *Revue Historique*, vols. CXIV and CXVI, 1913 and 1914) — XV

—— *Saint Martin de Tours*, Paris, n.d. — XVI

BAILEY, see *The Legacy of Rome*

BALL (W. R.) *A Short Account of the History of Mathematics*, London, 4th ed., 1908 — XVII

BANG (Martin) *Die Germanen im römischen Dienste bis zur Regierung Constantins*, Berlin, 1906 — XVIII

BARBAGALLO (Corrado) *Contributo alla storia economica dell' Antichità*, Rome, 1907 — XIX

—— *L'Oriente et l'Occidente nel mondo romano*, in *Nuova Rivista storica*, vol. VI, 1922, 141-67 — XX

BARDENHEWER (Otto) *Geschichte der altkirchlichen Literatur*, 2nd ed., Freiburg, 1913 ; Fch. tr., *s.t. Les Pères de l'Eglise*, by Godet et Verschaffel, Paris, 1899, 3 vols. — XXI

BATIFFOL (Pierre) *La Paix Constantinienne et le catholicisme*, Paris, 1914 — XXII

—— *Le Siège apostolique (359-451)*, Paris, 1924 — XXIII

—— *Les Eglises gallo-romaines et le siège apostolique*, in the *Revue d'histoire de l'Église de France*, vol. VIII, 1922, p. 145-69 — XXIV

—— *Le Catholicisme de saint Augustin*, Paris, 1920, 2 vols. — XXV

* As the author frequently refers to pages in books given in this bibliography, it has been thought advisable to give the editions quoted by him. In many cases later editions have been published and English translations exist.

BAUMGARTNER (A.) *Geschichte der Weltliteratur :* IV, *Die lateinische Literatur der christlichen Völker*, Freiburg-i.-B., 1905   XXVI

BAVIERA (Giovanni) *Concetto e limiti dell' influenza del cristianesimo sul diritto romano* (*Mélanges offerts à P. Frédéric Girard*, vol. 1, 1912, p. 67-121)   XXVII

BEAUDOUIN (Edouard) *Les grands domaines dans l'Empire romain*, Paris, 1909 (Extr. from *Nouvelle Revue historique de droit français et étranger*, 1897 and 1898)   XXVIII

BELOCH (Julius) *Die Bevölkerung der griechisch-römischen Welt*, Leipzig, 1886   XXIX

——— *Die Bevölkerung Italiens im Altertum*, in *Klio*, vol. III, 1903, p. 471-490   XXX

——— *Der Verfall der antiken Kultur*, in *Histor. Zeitschrift*, vol. LXXXIV, 1900, p. 1-38   XXX*bis*

BERLIÈRE (Dom Ursmer) *L'Ordre monastique des origines au XIIIᵉ siècle*, Maredsous, 1912 ; 2nd ed., 1921   XXXI

BERNOUILLI (J.-J.) *Römische Ikonographie*, Stuttgart, 1882-94, 3 vols. in 4   XXXII

BERTHELOT (Marcellin) *Essai sur la transmission de la science antique au moyen âge* (vol. I of *Histoire des sciences : La Chimie au moyen âge*, 1893, 3 vols.)   XXXIII

BESNIER (Maurice) *Le Commerce du plomb à l'époque romaine d'après les lingots estampillés*, in *Revue archéologique*, 1920 and 1921   XXXIV

BESSE (Dom. J.-M.) *Les moines d'Orient antérieurs au concile de Chalcédoine* (451), Paris, 1900   XXXV

——— *Les moines de l'ancienne France : période gallo-romaine et mérovingienne*, Paris, 1906   XXXVI

BEUGNOT (A.) *Histoire de la destruction du paganisme en Occident*, Paris, 1835   XXXVII

BIDEZ (J.) *Amiens ville natale de l'empereur Magnence*, in *Revue des études anciennes*, 1925, pp. 311-18   XXXVIII

BLANCHET (Adrien) *Étude sur les figurines en terre cuite de la Gaule romaine* (*Mémoires de la Société des antiquaires de France*, année 1891)   XXXIX

——— *Les Enceintes romaines de la Gaule*, Paris, 1907   XL

——— *Les Trésors de monnaie romaine et les invasions germaniques en Gaule*, Paris, 1900   XLI

BLOCH (Gustave) *L'Empire romain*, Paris, 1922   XLII

——— *La Gaule indépendante et la Gaule romaine*, Paris, 1900 (*Histoire de France* by Ernest Lavisse, I, vol. 2)   XLII*bis*

BLUEMNER (Hugo) *Die Gewerbliche Thätigkeit der Völker des klassischen Alterthums*, Leipzig, 1869   XLIII

——— *Die Römischen Privataltertümer*, Munich, 1911 (*Handbuch* by Iwan von Muller, 3rd ed., IV. II, 2)   XLIV

——— *Technologie und Terminologie der Gerwerbe und Künste bei Griechen und Römern*, Leipzig, 1875-87, 4 vols., 2nd ed. of vol I, 1912   XLV

——— *Der Maximaltarif des Diocletian erläutert*, Berlin, 1893   XLVI

BOAK (Arthur) *The Master of the Offices in the Later Roman and Byzantine Empires*, New York, 1919   XLVII

—— and DUNLOP (James) *Two Studies in Later Roman and Byzantine Administration*, New York, 1924   XLVIII

BOISSIER (Gaston) *La Fin du Paganisme : étude sur les dernières luttes religieuses en Occident au IVᵉ siècle*, Paris, 1891, 2 vols.   XLIX

BOTSFORD (George W.) *Roman Imperialism* in *American Historical Review*, vol. XXIII, 772-8   L

BOUCHÉ-LECLERCQ (A.) *L'Intolérance*, Paris, 1911 LI
―――― *Leçons d'histoire romaine*, Paris, 1909 LII
―――― *Manuel des institutions romaines*, Paris, 1886 LIII
BOUCHIER (E. S.) *Spain under the Roman Empire*, Oxford, 1914 LIV
BRÉHIER (Louis) *L'Art chrétien : son développement iconographique des origines à nos jours*, Paris, 1918 LV
―――― *Constantin et la fondation de Constantinople (Revue Historique*, vol. CXIX, 1915, II, pp. 241-72) LVI
―――― *Etudes sur l'histoire de la sculpture byzantine*, Paris, 1911 (*Archives des Missions Scientifiques*) LVII
―――― *Les Origines de la sculpture romane (Revue des Deux Mondes*, 15 August, 1912, pp. 870-901) LVIII
BREMER (Otto) *Ethnographie der germanischen Stämme* in the *Grundriss der germanischen Philologie* by Hermann Paul, 2nd ed., Strasbourg, 1900, vol. III, pp. 735-950 LIX
BROGLIE (Albert de) *L'Église et l'Empire Romain au IVᵉ siècle*, Paris, 1856-66, 6 vols. LX
BRY. *L'Édit de Caracalla de 212 d'après le papyrus de Giessen* (in *Etudes Juridiques . . . Paul F. Girard*, vol. I, p. 1) LXI
BUCHSENSCHÜTZ (B.) *Die Hauptstätten des Gewerbefleisses im klassischen Alterthum*, 1869 [*Schriften der Fürstlich-Jablonowskischen Gesellschaft zu Leipzig*, 14] LXIII
BUECHER (Karl) *Études d'histoire et d'economie politique*, French transl. by Alfred Hansay, Bruxelles, 1901 LXII
BUEHLMANN (J.) and WAGNER (A.) *Das Alte Rom mit dem Triumphzuge Kaiser Constantins in Jahre 312 nach Christ*, Munich, 1913 LXIV
BURCKHARDT (Jakob) *Die Zeit Constantin's des Grossen*, 2nd edit., Leipzig, 1880 LXV
BURY (J. B.) *History of the Later Roman Empire, from the Death of Theodosius I to the Death of Justinian* (395-565), 2nd edit., London, 1923, 2 vols. LXVI
BUTLER (E. Cuthbert) *The Lausiac History of Palladius* (*Texts and Studies*), Cambridge, 1898-1904 LXVII
CAGNAT (René) *L'armée romaine d'Afrique et l'occupation militaire de l'Afrique sous les empereurs*, Paris, 1892 ; 2nd edit., 1912 LXVIII
―――― *L'Annone d'Afrique (Mémoires de l'Acad. des Inscriptions*, vol. XL) LXIX
―――― and CHAPOT (V.) *Manuel d'archéologie romaine*, Paris, 1916-17, 2 vols. LXX
CAHUN (Léon) *Introduction à l'histoire de l'Asie : Turcs et Mogols des origines à 1405*, Paris, 1896 LXXI
CALZA *La statistica delle abitazioni ed il calcolo della popolazione in Roma Imperiale*, in *Rendiconti della reale Accademia dei Lincei*, vol. XXVI, series V, fasc. 2, 1920 LXXII
Cambridge Medieval History, vol. I : *The Christian Empire and the Foundation of the Teutonic Kingdoms*, Cambridge, 1911 LXXIII
CANTOR (Mor.) *Vorlesungen über Geschichte der Mathematik*, Leipzig, 3rd edit., 1907, 4 vols. (vol. I) LXXIV
CAUSSE (A.) *Essai sur le conflit du christianisme primitif et de la civilisation*, in *Revue d'Histoire des Religions*, March-April, 1919 LXXV
CAVAIGNAC (Eug.) *Population et capitalisme dans le monde méditerranéen antique*, Strasbourg, 1923 LXXVI

CESSI (R.) *La crisi imperiale degli anni 454-455 e l'incursione vandalica a Roma*, in *Archivio della R. Societa romana di storia patria*, vol. XL, 1917, pp. 161-204   LXXVII

CHABOT (J.-B.) *Choix d'inscriptions de Palmyre traduites et commentées*, Paris, 1912   LXXVIII

CHADWICK (H. Munro) *The Origin of the English Nation*, Cambridge, 1907   LXXIX

CHARLESWORTH (M. P.) *Trade Routes and Commerce of the Roman Empire*, Cambridge, 1924   LXXX

CHÉNON (Emile) *Conséquences juridiques de l'édit de Milan* (*Nouvelle Revue Historique de Droit*, 1914, pp. 255-63)   LXXXI

CHOISY (Auguste) *Histoire de l'architecture*, Paris, 1904, 2 vols.   LXXXII

CHRISTENSEN (Arthur) *L'Empire des Sassanides. Le peuple, l'État, la loi*, Copenhagen, 1907   LXXXIII

CICOTTI (E.) *Le déclin de l'esclavage antique*, French transl. by G. Platon, Paris, 1910   LXXXIV

COLE (P.-R.) *Later Roman Education in Ausonius, Capella and the Theodosian Code*, New York, 1909   LXXXV

COLEMAN (Christopher Bush) *Constantine the Great and Christianity*, New York, 1914 (*Columbia University Studies in History*, LX, 1)   LXXXVI

COLLINET (Paul) *Histoire de l'école de droit de Beyrouth*, Paris, 1925   LXXXVII

COMBARIEU (J.) *La Musique au moyen âge*, in *Revue de Synthèse Historique*, vol. I, 1900   LXXXVIII

—— *Histoire de la musique, des origines à la mort de Beethoven*, Paris, 1913   LXXXIX

CORDIER (Henri) *Histoire générale de la Chine*, Paris, 1920, 4 vols   XC

COULANGE (Louis) *Le Christ Dieu* (*Revue de l'Histoire des Religions*, May-June, 1914)   XCI

COURBAUD (Edmond) *Le Bas-relief romain à représentations historiques*, Paris, 1899   XCII

CROISET (Alfred and Maurice) *Histoire de la littérature grecque*, 2nd edit., Paris, 1896-99, 5 vols.   XCIII

—— *Manuel d'histoire de la littérature grecque*, Paris, 4th edit., 1904   XCIII *bis*

CUMONT (Franz) *Pourquoi le latin fut-il la seule langue littéraire de l'Occident* (in *Mélanges Paul Frédéricq*, Bruxelles, 1904)   XCIV

—— *Les Religions orientales dans le paganisme romain*, Paris, 2nd edit., 1909   XCV

—— *Les Mystères de Mithra*, 3rd edit., Bruxelles, 1913   XCVI

CUQ (Édouard) *La Cité punique . . .* (*C. R. Académie des inscriptions*, 1920)   XCVII

—— *Le Colonat partiaire dans l'Afrique romaine* (*Mémoires présentés par divers savants à l'Académie des inscriptions* 1st series, vol. XI, part I, 1897, pp. 83-146   XCVIII

—— *Le Consilium principis d'Auguste à Dioclétien* (*Ibid.*, 1st series, vol. XI, part II, 1884, pp. 311-504)   XCIX

—— *Les Contrats . . . première dynastie babylonienne* (*Nouvelle Revue Hist. du Droit*, 1910)   C

—— *Les Institutions juridiques des Romains ;* vol. II : *Le droit classique et le droit du Bas-Empire*, Paris, 1902   CI

—— *Une statistique des locaux affectés à l'habitation dans la Rome impériale* (*Mémoires de l'Académie des inscriptions*, vol. XL, 1915)   CII

DANNEMANN (E.) *Die Naturwissenschaften*, vol. I, Leipzig, 1912   CIII

DATTARI (G.) *Nuova teoria sopra il sistemo monetario della riforma di Diocleziano e de l'epoca Constantinia,* in *Rivista italiana di Numismatica,* 1906   **CIV**

DÉCHELETTE (Joseph) *Manuel d'archéologie préhistorique, celtique et gallo-romaine,* Paris, 1908-1914, 2 vols. in 4   **CV**

—— *Les Vases céramiques ornés de la Gaule romaine,* Paris, 1904, 2 vols.   **CVI**

DECLAREUIL (J.) *Quelques problèmes d'histoire des institutions municipales au temps de l'empire romain,* Paris, 1911 (Extr. from the *Nouvelle Revue Hist. du Droit*)   **CVII**

DELBRUECK (Hans) *Geschichte der Kriegskunst im Rahmen der politischen Geschichte,* Berlin, 1907, 3 vols.   **CVIII**

DELEHAYE (Hippol.) *Les Légendes hagiographiques,* Bruxelles, 2nd edit., 1906   **CIX**

DEL MAR (Al.) *Les Systèmes monétaires anciens et modernes,* French transl. by Chaly, Paris, 1899 (Engl. original, London, 1895)   **CX**

DELOUME (Antonin), *Les Manieurs d'argent à Rome,* 2nd edit., Paris, 1892   **CXI**

—— *La Passion de l'argent dans les institutions les lois et les mœurs des Romains,* Paris, 1907   **CXII**

DESJARDINS (Ernest) *Géographie historique et administrative de la Gaule romaine,* Paris, 1878-93, 4 vols.   **CXIII**

DESROCHES (J.-P.) *Le Labarum,* Paris, 1894   **CXIV**

DIEHL (Charles) *Manuel d'art Byzantin,* Paris, 1910, 2nd edit., 1925, 2 vols.   **CXV**

Dictionnaire des antiquités grecques et latines, pub. under the editorship of Saglio, Paris, 1878-1916, 5 vols. in 10   **CXVI**

DIETERICH (Albrecht) *Der Untergang der antiken Religion,* in *Kleine Schriften,* Leipzig, 1911, pp. 449-539   **CXVII**

DIEUDONNÉ (Ad.) *Les Monnaies françaises,* Paris, 1923   **CXVIII**

DILL (Samuel) *Roman Society in the Last Century of the Western Empire,* 2nd edit, London, 1899   **CXIX**

DOELGER (F. Jos.) *Konstantin der Grosse und seine Zeit* (in *Festgabe zur Konstantin Jubiläum,* 1913, pp. 377-477)   **CXX**

DOMASZEWSKI (A. von) *Die Rangordnung des römischen Heeres,* Berlin, 1908 (*Bonner Jahrbücher,* fasc. 117)   **CXXI**

—— *Der Truppensold der Kaiserzeit,* in *Neue Keidelberger Jahrbücher,* vol. X, 1900, pp. 218-241   **CXXII**

DOPSCH (Alfons) *Wirtschaftliche und soziale Grundlagen der Europäischen Kulturentwicklung aus der Zeit von Caesar bis auf Karl den Grossen,* part I, 2nd edit., Vienna, 1923   **CXXIII**

DREWS (Arthur) *Plotin und der Untergang der antiken Weltanschauung,* Jena, 1907   **CXXIV**

DUCHESNE (Louis) *Autonomies ecclésiastiques, Églises séparées,* Paris, 1905   **CXXV**

—— *Histoire ancienne de l'Église,* Paris, 1906-25, 4 vols.   **CXXVI**

DUREAU DE LA MALLE *Economie politique des Romains,* Paris, 1840, 2 vols.   **CXXVII**

DURUY (Victor) *Histoire des Romains,* illus. edit., Paris, 1879-85, 7 vols. (vols. VI and VII), [Engl. tr., 6 vols. London, 1883-6]   **CXXVIII**

EBERSOLT (Jean) *Les Arts somptuaires de Byzance, étude sur l'art impérial à Constantinople,* Paris, 1925   **CXXIX**

EFFERTZ (Otto) *Antagonismes économiques,* Paris, 1906   **CXXX**

ELSEE (C.) *Neoplatonism in relation to Christianity,* Cambridge, 1908   **CXXXI**

EMMEREAU (C.) *Notes sur les origines de Constantimople ; les grands centres historiques,* in *Revue Archéologique,* 1925, I, pp. 1-25, map   **CXXXII**

FADDA (Carlo) *Il diritto commerciale dei Romani*, Naples,
   1904   **CXXXIII**
FERRERO (Guglielmo) *Grandeur et décadence de Rome*, trad.
   Mengin, Paris, 1914-18, 6 vols. [Engl. tr., 5 vols.,
   London, 1907-9]   **CXXXIV**
—————— *La ruine de la civilisation antique*, Paris, 1921   **CXXXV**
FIGGIO (J.-N.) *The Political Aspects of St. Augustin's City
   of God*, London, 1921   **CXXXVI**
FIRTH (John-B.) *Constantine the Great, the Reorganisation
   of the Empire and the Triumph of the Church*, London,
   1923   **CXXXVII**
FLACH (Jacques) *La Table de bronze d'Ajustrel*, Paris, 1879   **CXXXVIII**
FRANCOTTE *L'Industrie dans la Grèce antique*, Bruxelles,
   1900, 2 vols.   **CXXXIX**
—————— *La Polis grecque* (*Studien zur Geschichte und Kul-
   tur des Altertums*, 1907, p. 252.)   **CXL**
FRANK (Tenney) *An Economic History of Rome to the End
   of the Republic*, Baltimore, 1920   **CXLI**
FRANZISZ (Franz) *Bayern zur Römerzeit*, Regensburg, 1905   **CXLII**
FRÉDÉRICQ (Paul) *Conséquences de l'évangélisation sur le
   développement de la langue nationale des peuples convertis*,
   in *Bulletin de l'Académie Royale de Belgique*, 1903   **CXLIII**
FREEMAN (E. A.) *Western Europe in the Fifth Century*,
   London, 1904   **CXLIV**
FRIEDLAENDER (Ludwig) *Darstellunger aus der Sitten-
   geschichte Roms in der Zeit von August bis Ausgang der
   Antonine*, 8th edit., Leipzig, 1910, 3 vols. in 4;
   —Engl. tr., 4 vols., London, 1908-13—Free trans. of
   the 2nd ed. by Ch. Vogel, with the title : *Mœurs
   romaines du règne d'Auguste à la fin des Antonins*, Paris,
   1865-74, 4 vols.   **CXLV**
—————— *Ueber den Kornpreis und den Sachwerth des Geldes
   in der Zeit von Nero bis Trajan*, in *Jahrbücher für
   Nationalœkonomie*, vol. XII   **CXLVI**
FROTHINGHAM (Arthur L.) *Roman Cities in Northern Italy
   and Dalmatia*, London, 1910   **CXLVII**
—————— *The Monuments of Christian Rome, from Constantine
   to the Renaissance*, New York, 1908   **CXLVIII**
FUSTEL DE COULANGES *La Gaule romaine*, Paris, 1891   **CXLIX**
—————— *L'Invasion germanique et la fin de l'Empire*, Paris,
   1891   **CL**
—————— *L'Alleu et le domaine rural*, Paris, 1889   **CLI**
—————— *Le Colonat romain*, in *Recherches sur quelques
   problèmes d'histoire* (pp. 3-186), Paris, 1885   **CLII**
GARSONNET (E.) *Histoire des locations perpétuelles et des baux
   à longue durée*, Paris, 1879   **CLIII**
GASQUET (Am.) *De l'autorité impériale en matière religieuse à
   Byzance*, Paris, 1879   **CLIV**
GAUPP (E. Th.) *Die Germanische Ansiedlungen in den
   Provinzen des römischen Reiches*, Breslau, 1884   **CLV**
GEFFECKEN (Joh.) *Kaiser Julian*, Leipzig, 1914 (*Das Erbe
   der Alten*, fasc. VIII)   **CLVI**
GEIL (William Edgar) *The Great Wall of China*, London,
   1909   **CLVII**
GELZER (H.) *Das Verhältniss von Staat und Kirche in Byzanz*
   in *Ausgewählte kleine Schriften* (pp. 57-141), Leipzig,
   1907   **CLVIII**
—————— *Das Römertum als Kulturmacht*, in *Histor.Zeitschrift*,
   vol. CXXVI, 1922, pp. 189-206   **CLIX**
—————— *Studien zur byzantin. Verwaltung Aegyptens*, Leipzig,
   1909   **CLX**

GERCKE and NORDEN *Einleitung in die Altertumswissen-*
schaft, Leipzig, 1912, 3 vols.   **CLXI**
GEROSA (Pietro) *Sant' Agostino e la decadenza del imperio*
romano, Turin, 1916   **CLXII**
GERSPACH *La Mosaïque*, Paris, 1881   **CLXIII**
—— *La Tapisserie*, Paris, n.d.   **CLXIV**
—— *L'Art de la verrerie*, Paris, 1885   **CLXV**
GIBBON (Edward) *The History of the Decline and Fall of the*
Roman Empire, 1776-81 ; ed. by J. B. Bury, 1896,
7 vols. Fr. trans. by F. Guizot, Paris, 1812, 13 vols.   **CLXVI**
GIRARD *Le Campus Mauriacus*, in *Revue Historique*, vol.
XXVIII, 1885   **CLXVII**
GIRARD (P. Frédéric) *Histoire de l'organisation judiciaire chez*
les Romains, I, Paris, 1901   **CLXVIII**
GLOTZ (Gustave) *Le Travail dans le Grèce antique*, Paris,
1920 [Engl. tr., London, 1926]   **CLXIX**
GLOVER (T. R.) *Life and letters in the Fourth Century*, Cam-
bridge, 1901   **CLXX**
GOELZER (H.) *Etude lexicographique et grammaticale sur le*
latin de saint Jérôme, Paris, 1884   **CLXXI**
—— *Le Latin de saint Avit, évêque de Vienne* (450-526),
Paris, 1909   **CLXXII**
GOLDSCHMIDT (L.) *Handelsgeschichte*, 3rd edit., Stuttgart,
1891   **CLXXIII**
GOLDSTAUB (M.) *Der* Philologus, in *Philologus*, Suppl. vol.
VIII, Leipzig, 1901   **CLXXIV**
GOLDZIHER (I.) *Le Dogme et la loi de l'Islam*, Paris, 1921   **CLXXV**
GOMPERZ (Theodor) *Griechische Denker : eine Geschichte der*
antiken Philosophie, Leipzig, 1896, 2 vols. ; —Engl.
tr. by L. Magnus, 4 vols., London, 1901-12—Fr. trans.
by Raymond : *Les Penseurs de la Grèce, histoire de la*
philosophie antique, Lausanne, Paris, 1904-05, 2 vols.   **CLXXVI**
GOYAU (Georges) *La Tétrarchie*, in *Etudes d'histoire juridique*
offertes à Paul-Frédéric Girard, vol. I, 1913, pp. 65-83   **CLXXVII**
GRANDGENT (C. H.) *An Introduction to Vulgar Latin*, Boston,
1907   **CLXXVIII**
GRINDLE (G. E. A.) *The Destruction of Paganism in the*
Roman Empire, Oxford, 1892   **CLXXIX**
GROSSE (Robert) *Rangordnung der römischen Armee der*
4-6 Jahrhunderten, in *Klio*, vol. XV, 1917, pp. 122-61   **CLXXX**
—— *Römische Militärgeschichte von Gallienus bis zum*
Beginn der byzantinischen Themenverfassung, Berlin,
1920   **CLXXXI**
GROTHE (H.) *Die Geschichte d. Wolle und Wollen-manufaktur*
im Altertum, in *Deutsche Vierteljahrschrift*, 1866,
pp. 259-304   **CLXXXII**
GROUSSET (René) *Histoire de l'Asie*, Paris, 1922, 3 vols.   **CLXXXIII**
GRUPP (Georg) *Kulturgeschichte der römischen Kaiserzeit*,
Munich, 1904, 2 vols.   **CLXXXIV**
GUIGNEBERT (Ch.) *Le Christianisme antique*, Paris, 1921   **CLXXXV**
—— *Tertullien, étude sur ses sentiments à l'égard de*
l'Empire et de la société civile, Paris, 1901   **CLXXXVI**
GUIGNES (J. de) *Histoire générale des Huns, Turcs, Mogols et*
des autres peuples tartares occidentaux, Paris, 1756-8,
5 vols.   **CLXXXVII**
GUIGNET *Saint Grégoire de Nazianze et la rhétorique*, Paris,
1911   **CLXXXVIII**
GUIRAUD (Paul) *Etudes économiques sur l'antiquité*, Paris, 1905 **CLXXXIX**
—— *Les assemblées provinciales de l'Empire romain*,
Paris, 1887   **CXC**
—— *La propriété foncière en Grèce*, Paris, 1893   **CXCI**

GULDENPENNING (A.) *Geschichte des Oströmischen Reichs unter den Kaisern Arcadius und Theodosius II*, Halle, 1885 — CXCII

—— and IFFLAND *Der Kaiser Theodosius der Grosse*, Halle, 1878 — CXCIII

GUMMERUS (Herman) *Der römische Gutsbetrieb als wirtschaftlicher Organismus, nach den Werken des Cato, Varro und Columelle*, Leipzig, 1906 (Extr. from *Klio*, Suppl. issue V) — CXCIV

—— *Römische Industrie*, in *Klio*, vol. XV, 1918, pp. 256-302 — CXCV

GUNTER (H.) *Legenden Studien*, Köln, 1906 — CXCVI

GWATKIN (H.-M.) *Studies of Arianism*, 2nd edit., Cambridge, 1900 — CXCVII

—— *The Knowledge of God*, Edinburgh, 1906, 2 vols. — CXCVIII

HAARHOFF (Theodor) *Schools of Gaul, a Study of Pagan and Christian Education in the Last Century of the Western Empire*, Oxford, 1920 — CXCIX

HAHN (Ludwig) *Das Kaisertum*, Leipzig, 1913 (*Das Erbe der Alten*, fasc. VI) — CC

—— *Zum Gebrauch der lateinischen Sprache in Konstantinopel,* in *Festschrift für Martin von Schanz*, Würzburg, 1912, (pp. 173-83) — CCI

HAMELIN (O.) *Le système d'Aristote*, Paris, 1920 — CCII

HARNACK (Adolph von) *Lehrbuch der Dogmengeschichte*, Freiburg, 1894-97, 3 vols. — CCIII

—— *Précis de l'histoire des dogmes*, tr. by Choisy, Paris, 1893 — CCIV

—— *Geschichte der altchristlichen Literatur bis Eusebius*, Leipzig, 1893-94, 2 vols. — CCV

—— *Mission und Ausbreitung des Christentums in den ersten drei Jahrhunderten*, 2nd edit., 1906, 2 vols. — CCVI

—— *Militia Christi*, 1906 — CCVII

—— *Das Mönchtum, seine Ideale und seine Geschichte*, 6th edit., 1903 — CCVIII

HARRISON (F.) *The Meaning of History*, New York, 1908 — CCIX

HARTMANN (Ludo-Moritz) *Ueber die Ursache des Untergangs des römischen Reichs*, in *Archiv für sozial. Gesetzgebung und Statistik*, vol. II — CCX

—— *Weltgeschichte in gemeindverstandlicher Darstellung*, Gotha, 1921-24, 7 vols. — CCXI

HATZFELD (Jean) *Les Trafiquants italiens dans l'Orient hellénique*, Paris, 1919 — CCXII

HAVERFIELD (F.) *Ancient Rome and Ireland*, in *English Historical Review*, vol. XXVIII, 1913, pp. 1-12 — CCXIII

—— *The Romanisation of Roman Britain*, Oxford, 1905 — CCXIV

HAVET (Julien) *Du partage entre les Romains et les Barbares chez les Burgondes et les Wisigoths*, in *Œuvres*, vol. II, 1896 — CCXV

—— *La Prose métrique de Symmaque et les origines métriques du cursus*, Paris, 1892 — CCXVI

HAYES (Carlton H.) *An Introduction to the Sources relating to the Germanic Invasions*, New York, 1909 (*Columbia University Studies in Political Science*, vol. XXXIII, 3) — CCXVII

HEALY (J.) *Insula Scotorum et Doctorum, or Ireland's Ancient Schools and Scholars*, 5th edit., Dublin, 1908 — CCXVIII

HEDLAM *The Emperor Constantin and the Edict of Milan*, in *Church Quarterly Review*, vol. LXXII, Jan., 1914 — CCXIX

HEIBERG (J. L.) *Geschichte der Mathematik und Naturwissenschaft im Altertum*, Munich, 1925 (*Handbuch*. Iwan von Müller, vol. I, 1, 2) — CCXX

HEISENBERG (Aug.) *Grundzügen der byzantinischen Kultur,* in *Neue Jahrbücher für Philologie,* 1909, p. 196 — CCXXI

HEITLAND (W. E.) *Agricola, a Study of Agriculture and Rural Life in the Grœco-Roman World,* Cambridge, 1921 — CCXXII
—— *The Roman Fate: an Essay of Interpretation,* Cambridge, 1922 — CCXXIII

HINNEBERG (P.) *Die Griechische und Lateinische Literatur und Sprache,* Berlin, 1905 (*Die Kultur der Gegenwart,* part I, sec. 8) — CCXXIV
—— *Die Romanischen Literaturen und Sprachen, mit Einschluss der Keltischen,* Berlin, 1909 (*Die Kultur der Gegenwart,* part I, sec. 11) — CCXXV

HINSCHIUS (Paul) *System des Katholischen Kirchenrechts,* Berlin, 1869-95, 5 vols in 6 — CCXXVI

HIRSCHFELD (Otto) *Die Kaiserliche Verwaltungsbeamten,* 2nd edit., Berlin, 1905 — CCXXVII
—— *Die Rangordnung der römischen Kaiserzeit,* in *Sitzungsberichte* of the Berlin Academy, 1901, pp. 579-610 — CCXXVIII
—— *Kleine Schriften,* Berlin, 1913 — CCXXIX

HIRTH (F.) *Ancient History of China,* New York, 1908 — CCXXX

HODGKIN (T.) *Italy and her Invaders,* Oxford, 1880-99, 8 vols.; 2nd edit. of vols. I-VI, 1916 — CCXXXI

HOLMES (Rice) *The Roman Republic and the Founder of the Empire,* London, 1923, 3 vols. — CCXXXII

HOMO (Léon) *Essai sur le règne de l'empereur Aurélien,* Paris, 1904 — CCXXXIII
—— *La grande crise de l'an 238 après J. C. et le problème* de l'Histoire Auguste (*Revue Historique,* 1919, II, 209-64) — CCXXXIV
—— *L'Empereur Gallien et la crise de l'Empire romain au IIIᵉ siècle* (*Revue Historique,* 1913, II, p. 248) — CCXXXV
—— *Les privilèges administratifs du Sénat romain et leur disparition graduelle au cours du IIIᵉ siècle* (*Revue Historique,* 1921, II, pp. 161-203) — CCXXXVI
—— *L'Empire romain,* Paris, 1925 — CCXXXVII

HOUDOY (Armand) *Le Droit municipal.* Part I : *De la condition et de l'administration des villes chez les Romains,* Paris, 1876 — CCXXXVIII

HUART (Clément) *Ancient Persia and Iranian Civilization,* trans. by M. R. Dobie, London, 1927 (*The History of Civilization*) — CCXXXIX

HUELSEN (F.) *Formae urbis Romae antiquae,* Berlin, 1912 — CCXL

HUET *Histoire du commerce et de la navigation des Anciens,* Lyon, 1763 — CCXLI

HUMBERT (Gustave) *Essai sur les finances et la comptabilité publique chez les Romains,* Paris, 1887, 2 vols. — CCXLII

HUMPHREY (Edward Frank) *Politics and Religion in the Days of Augustine* (395-430), New York, 1912 (Columbia Univ. Thesis) — CCXLIII

HUNZINGER (Aug. Wilh.) *Die Diokletianische Staatsreform* (Rostock Dissertation, 1898-99) — CCXLIV

HUTTMANN (Maude A.) *The Establishment of Christianity and the Proscription of Paganism,* New York, 1914 (*Columbia University Studies*) — CCXLV

HUVELIN *Mercatura* in *Dictionnaire des Antiquités grecques et romaines* — CCXLVI

IORGA (Nicholas) *Essai de synthèse de l'histoire de l'humanité.* vol. I : *l'Antiquité,* Paris, 1926 — CCXLVII

JAMES (H. R.) *Our Hellenic Heritage,* London, 1921-24, 2 vols. — CCXLVIII

JIRECEK (J.-C.) *Die Romanen in der Städten Dalmatiens während des Mittelalters*, in *Denkschriften* of the Vienna Academy, hist.-philol. section, vol. XLVIII, 1902   CCXLIX

JONES (H. Stuart) *Companion to Roman History*, Oxford, 1912   CCL

―――― *The Roman Empire :* B.C. 29-A.D. 476, London, 1908   CCL *bis*

JOUGUET (Pierre) *La Vie municipale dans l'Égypte romaine*, Paris, 1911   CCLI

―――― *En quelle année finit la guerre entre Constantin et Licinius* (*Comptes rendus des séances de l'Académie des inscriptions*, 1906)   CCLII

JULLIAN (Camille) *Ausone et Bordeaux, études sur les derniers temps de la Gaule romaine*, Paris, 1893   CCLIII

―――― *Histoire de la Gaule*, Paris, 1910-26, 6 vols.   CCLIV

―――― *Notes sur l'armée romaine au IV* siécle, in *Annales de la Faculté des lettres de Bordeaux*, 1884, pp. 59-85   CCLV

JUNG (Julius) *Die Romanischen Landschaften des Römischen Reiches*, 1881

―――― *Römer und Romanen in der Donauländern*, 2nd edit., 1887   CCLVI

―――― *Orbis romanus* in Iwan von Muller's *Handbuch der Klassischen Altertumswissenschaft*, vol. III, part 3, 1897, pp. 1-178   CCLVII

―――― *De Scolis romanis in Gallia comata*, 1885   CCLVIII

KAERST (Julius) *Geschichte des Hellenistischen Zeitalters*, Leipzig, 1901   CCLIX

KARLOWA (Otto) *Römische Rechtsgeschichte*, I : *Staatsrecht und Rechtsquellen*, Leipzig, 1885   CCLX

KAUFMANN (G.) *Rhetorenschulen und Klosterschulen oder heidnische und christliche Cultur in Gallien während des 5 und 6 Jahrhunderts*, Leipzig, 1869, (*Historisches Taschenbuch*)   CCLXI

―――― *Ueber das Föderatverhältniss des Tolosanischen Reiches zu Rom*, in *Forschungen zur deutschen Geschichte*, vol. VI, 1866, pp. 435-76   CCLXII

KELLER (R.) *Stilicho oder die Geschichte des Weströmischen Reichs von 395-408*, Berlin, 1884   CCLXIII

KLEIN (Walter) *Studien zu Ammianus Marcellinus* (*Klio*, supplement 13), 1914   CCLXIV

Konstantin und seine Zeit, Festgabe zum Konstantinjubiläum, ed. by Franz-Joseph Doelger, Fribourg, 1913 (*Römische Quartalschrift* (Supplement 19)   CCLXV

KORNEMANN (Ernst) *Die Organisation der Afrikanischen pagi*, in *Philologus*, vol. LX, 1900   CCLXVI

―――― *Die römische Kaiserzeit*, in Gercke and Norden, *Einleitung*, vol. III, pp. 210-306   CCLXVII

―――― *Zur Stadtentstehung in den ehemals keltischen und germanischen Gebieten des Römerreichs* (Giessen Diss, 1898-99)   CCLXVIII

KRAUS (Franz-Xav.) *Geschichte der Christlichen Kunst*, Fribourg, 1896-1903, 2 vols. in 3   CCLXIX

KREBS (Eug.) *Die Religionen im Römerzeit zu Beginn des IV. Jahrhunderts*, in *Konstantin . . . Festgabe*, pp. 1-39   CCLXX

KUHN (Emil) *Beiträge zur Verfassung des römischen Reichs, mit besonderen Rücksicht auf die Periode von Constantin bis auf Justinian*, 1849   CCLXXI

―――― *Die Städtische und bürgerliche Verfassung des römischen Reiches bis auf den Zeiten Justinians*, Leipzig, 1864-65, 2 vols.   CCLXXII

―――― *Ueber die Entstehung der Städte der Alten*, Leipzig, 1878   CCLXXIII

KURTH (Godefroid) *La Frontière linguistique en Belgique et dans le Nord de la France*, Bruxelles, 1896-98, 2 vols.   CCLXXIV

LABRIOLLE (Pierre de) *Histoire de la littérature latine chrétienne*, Paris, 1920   CCLXXV

LAMPRECHT (Karl) *Fränkische Ansiedlungen und Wanderungen im Rheinland*, in *Westdeutsche Zeitschrift*, vol. I, 1882   CCLXXVI

LANGEN (Jos.) *Geschichte der römischen Kirche bis zum Pontifikat Leos I.* vol. II : *Von Leo I bis Nicolaus I*, Gotha, 1885   CCLXXVII

LARDÉ (G.) *Le Tribunal du clerc dans l'Empire romain et la Gaule franque*, Moulins, 1920   CCLXXVIII

LAVISSE (Ernest) *Histoire de France*, Paris, 1900-03, vols. I and II in 4   CCLXXIX

——— and RAMBAUD *Histoire générale du IV siècle à nos jours*, vol. I : *Les origines* (395-1905), 2nd edit., Paris, 1905   CCLXXX

LEBEAU (C.) *Histoire du Bas-Empire*, Paris, 1757-1817, 28 vols. (I to X)   CCLXXXI

LECLERCQ (Dom H.) *L'Afrique chrétienne*, Paris, 1904   CCLXXXII

——— *Manuel d'archéologie chrétienne depuis les origines jusqu'au VIIIᵉ siècle*, Paris, 1907, 2 vols.   CCLXXXIII

——— *Les Martyrs*, Paris 1906-1909, 4 vols.   CCLXXXIV

——— *Cénobitisme*, in *Dictionnaire d'archéologie chrétienne et de liturgie*, edited by Dom Cabrol, vol. II, 2, pp. 3047-3248   CCLXXXV

LÉCRIVAIN (Ch.) *Le Sénat romain depuis Dioclétien, à Rome et à Constantinople*, Paris, 1888   CCLXXXVI

——— *De Agris publicis imperatoriisque ab Augusti tempore usque ad finem imperii romani*, Paris, 1887   CCLXXXVII

——— *Études sur l'Histoire Auguste*, Paris, 1904   CCLXXXVIII

The Legacy of Rome ; Essays, edited by Ch. Bailey, Oxford, 1923   CCLXXXIX

LEGGE (F.) *Forerunners and Rivals of Christianity*, London, 1915   CCXC

LEJAY (P.) *Ancienne philologie chrétienne, monachisme oriental*, in *Revue d'Histoire et de Littérature Religieuse*, 1916   CCXCI

LENAIN DE TILLEMONT (Séb.) *Histoire des empereurs qui ont régné pendant les six premiers siécles de l'Eglise*, Paris, 1692-1738, 6 vols.   CCXCII

——— *Mémoires pour servir à l'histoire ecclésiastique des six premiers siècles*, Bruxelles, 1693-1707, 15 vols. ; 2nd edit., Paris, 1701-1712, 16 vols.   CCXCIII

LESNE (E.) *La Propriété ecclésiastique en France aux époques romaine et mérovingienne*, Lille, 1910-26, 3 vols.   CCXCIV

LEVASSEUR (E.) *Histoire des classes ouvrières et de l'industrie en France*, vol. I, 2nd edit., Paris, 1900   CCXCV

LIEBENAM (W.) *Geschichte des römischen Vereinwesens*, Leipzig, 1890   CCXCVI

——— *Städteverwaltung in römischen Kaiserreiche*, Leipzig, 1900   CCXCVII

LINAS (Ch. de) *Les Origines de l'orfèvrerie cloisonnée*, Paris, 1877-87, 3 vols.   CCXCVIII

LINDNER (Theodor) *Weltgeschichte seit der Völkerwanderung*, Stuttgart, 1901-1917, 8 vols. (vols. I-III)   CCXCIX

LINSENMAYER (A.) *Die Bekämpfung des Christentums durch den römischen Staat bis zum Tode des Kaisers Julian* (363), Munich, 1905   CCC

LITTRÉ (Emile) *Rome et les Barbares*, Paris, 1867   CCCI

LIZERAND (Georges) *Aetius*, Paris, 1910 (Thesis)   CCCII

LONGNON (Auguste) *Atlas historique de la France*, Paris, 1885-1907 CCCIII
―――― *Les noms de lieu de la France, leur origine, leur signification, leurs transformations*, Marichal and Mirot, Paris, 1920-23, 3 fasc. CCCIV
LOT (Ferdinand) *De l'étendue et de la valeur du caput fiscal sous le Bas-Empire*, in *Revue Historique du Droit*, 1925, pp. 5-60, 177-92 CCCV
―――― *Les migrations saxonnes en Gaule et en Grande-Bretagne du IIIᵉ au Vᵉ siècle*, in *Revue Historique*, vol. CXIX, 1915 CCCVI
―――― *Hengist, Hors, Vortigern : la conquête de la Grande-Bretagne par les Saxons*, in *Mélanges d'histoire offerts à M. Charles Bémont*, Paris, 1913 CCCVII
LOTH (Joseph) *L'Émigration bretonne en Armorique du Vᵉ au VIIᵉ siècle de notre ère*, Rennes, 1883 CCCVIII
LUCIUS (Ernest) *Les Origines du culte des saints dans l'Église chrétienne*, Paris, 1908 CCCIX
MACDONALD (George) *The Roman Wall in Scotland*, Glasgow, 1911 CCCX
MADVIG (J.-N.) *Verfassung und Verwaltung des römischen Staates*, 1881-82, 2 vols. Fr. trans. by Ch. Morel, 1889, 3 vols. CCCXI
MALE (Emile) *L'Art allemand et l'art française du moyen âge* Paris, 1917 CCCXII
MANARESI (Alfonso) *L'Imperio romano e il Christianesimo*, Turin, 1914 CCCXIII
MANRION (J.) *Les Origines du christianisme chez les Gots*, in *Analecta Bollandiana*, vol. XXXIII, 1914 CCCXIV
MARQUART (J.) *Osteuropäische und Ostasiatische Streifzüge*, Leipzig, 1903 CCCXV
―――― see *Mommsen*
MARSH (Frank Burr) *The Founding of the Roman Empire*, Oxford, 1922 CCCXVI
MARTROYE (F.) *La Répression du donatisme et la politique religieuse de Constantin*, Nogent-le-Rotrou, 1914 (Extr. from *Mémoires de la Soc. des antiquaires de France*, vol. LXXIII) CCCXVII
―――― *L'Édit de Milan*, in *Bulletin d'ancienne littérature et d'archéologie chrétienne*, 1914 CCCXVIII
―――― *Genséric : la conquête vandale et la destruction de l'Empire d'Occident*, Paris, 1907 CCCXIX
MARX (Karl) *Das Kapital*, ed. Engels, Hamburg, 1890-4, 3 vols. in 4 (vols. I-II) ;―Fr. trans. by Molitor, Paris, 1924, 3 vols. ;―Engl. tr. by Eden and Cedar Paul, London .. CCCXX
MAURICE (Jules) *Constantin*, Paris, 1924 CCCXXI
―――― *Numismatique Constantinienne*, Paris, 1911, 3 vols. CCCXXII
―――― *Les Origines de Constantinople*, in *Mémoires publiés á l'occasion du Centenaire de la Société des antiquaires de France*, 1904 CCCXXIII
MERCIER (E.) *La Population indigène de l'Afrique sous la domination romaine, vandale et byzantine*, in *Rec. de la Société archéol. de Constantine*, 1895-96 CCCXXIV
MESNAGE (le P. J.) *Le Christianisme en Afrique*, Paris, 1914-15, 4 vols. CCCXXV
MEYER (Eduard) *Bevölkerungswesen*, in *Handwörterbuch d. Staatswissenschaft* CCCXXVI
―――― *Kleinere Schriften*, Halle, 1910-24, 2 vols. CCCXXVII
―――― *Die wirthschaftliche Entwicklung des Altertums*, Iéna, 1895 (Extr. from *Jahrbücher für Nationaloekonomie*) .. CCCXXVIII

MEYER (Kuno) *Learning in Ireland in the Fifth Century and the Transmission of Letters*, Dublin, 1912   CCCXXIX

MISCHAUT (Gustave) *Le Génie latin*, Paris, 1898   CCCXXX

MICHEL (André) see *André-Michel*.

MILHAUD (G.) *Etude sur la pensée scientifique grecque*, Paris, 1906   CCCXXXI

MISPOULET (J.-B.) *Institutions politiques des Romains*, Paris, 1883, 2 vols.   CCCXXXII

MITTEIS (Ludwig) *Reichsrecht und Volksrecht in den östlichen Provinzen des römischen Kaiserrechs*, Leipzig, 1891   CCCXXXIII
—— *Zur Geschichte der Erbpacht im Altertum*, Leipzig, 1901   CCCXXXIV

MOLINIER (Emile) *Histoire générale des arts appliqués à l'industrie du Vᵉ à la fin du XVIIIᵉ siècle*, Paris, 1896-1902, 4 vols.   CCCXXXV

MOMMSEN (Theodor) *Histoire romaine*, trans. by Cagnat and Toutain, 1872-89, 11 vols.   CCCXXXVI
—— *Aetius*, in *Gesamm. Schriften*, vol. V, p. 438   CCCXXXVII
—— *Apollinaris Sidonius und seine Zeit*, in *Reden und Aufsätze*, Berlin, 1905   CCCXXXVIII
—— *Boden und Geldwirtschaft der römischen Kaiserzeit*, in *Gesamm. Schriften*, vol. V, pp. 558-617   CCCXXXIX
—— *Die Erblichkeit des Decurionats*, in *Festschrift Hirschfeld*, 1903, pp. 1-7   CCCXL
—— *Militärwesen seit Diocletian*, in *Hermès*, vol. XXIV   CCCXLI
—— *Die römischen Lagerstädte*, in *Gesamm. Schriften*, vol. VI, 1910, pp. 176-203   CCCXLII
—— *Stilicho und Alarich* in *Gesamm. Schriften*, vol. IV, 516-30   CCCXLII
—— and MARQUARDT (J.) *Manuel des Antiquités romaines*, tr. under the direction of Gustave Humbert; vols. I-VIII, *Droit public*, by MOMMSEN, trans. P.-Fréd. Girard; vols. IX-X, *Organisation de l'Empire*, by J. MARQUARDT, trans. A. Weiss and P. Lucas; vols. XII-XIII, *Le culte*, by J. MARQUARDT, trans. Brissaud; vols. XIV-XV, *La vie privée*, trans. V. Henry; vol. XVI, *Histoire des sources du droit*, by P. KRUGER, trans. Brissaud; vols. XVII-XIX, *Le droit pénal*, by MOMMSEN, trans. A. Duquesne, Paris, 1889-1907, 19 vols.   CCCXLIV

MONCEAUX (Paul) *Histoire littéraire de l'Afrique chrétienne depuis les origines jusqu'à l'invasion arabe*, Paris, 1901-23, 7 vols.   CCCXLV

MONNIER (Henry) *Études de droit byzantin : I, De l'ἐπιβολή; II, Méditation sur la constitution ἑκατέρω et le jus poenitendi*, Paris, 1895-1900 (Extr. from *Nouvelle Revue Historique de Droit*)   CCCXLVI

MONTESQUIEU (Bar. de) *Considérations sur les causes de la grandeur et de la décadence des Romains*, 1734   CCCXLVII

MOREAU DE JONNÈS *Statistique des peuples de l'antiquité*, Paris, 1851   CCCXLVIII

MORIN-JEAN *La Verrerie en Gaule sous l'Empire romain*, Paris, 1913   CCCXLIX

MUELLENHOFF (Karl) *Deutsche Altertumskunde*, Berlin, 1870-1900, 5 vols. Vols. I, II, V, new edit. 1891, 1906, 1908   CCCL

NAUDET (J.) *Des changements opérés dans toutes les parties de l'administration de l'Empire romain sous les règnes de Dioclétien, de Constantin et de leurs successeurs jusqu'à Julien*, Paris, 1817, 2 vols.   CCCLI

NEUMANN (Karl Johannes) *Römische Staatsaltertümer*, in GERCKE and NORDEN, *Einleitung*, vol. III, p. 408   CCCLII
—— *Der römische Staat und die allgemeine Kirche bis auf Diocletian*, Leipzig, 1890   CCCLIII
—— *Entwicklung und Aufgaben der Alten Geschichte*, Strasbourg, 1910   CCCLIV
NEURATH (O.) *Antike Wirthschaftsgeschichte* 1909, in *Aus Natur und Geisteswelt*, vol. 258   CCCLV
—— *Zur Anschauung der Antike über Handel, Gewerbe und Landschaft*, in *Jahrbücher für Nationaloekonomie*, vol. XXXIII, 1907   CCCLVl
NIESE (Benedictus) *Grundriss der römischen Geschichte, nebst Quellenkunde*, 2nd edit., Munich, 1897   CCCLVII
NISSEN (Henrich) *Italische Landeskunde*, Berlin, 1883-1902, 3 vols.   CCCLVIII
—— *Der Verkehr zwischen China und dem Römischen Reiche*, in *Bonner Jahrbücher*, vol. XCV, 1894, pp. 1-28   CCCLIX
NORDEN (Eduard) *Die antike Kunstprosa von VI Jahrhundert vor Christus bis in die Zeit der Renaissance*, 2nd edit., Leipzig, 1909, 2 vols.   CCCLX
—— *Die lateinische Literatur im Uebergang vom Altertum zum Mittelalter*, in Hinnebert, *Die Kultur der Gegenwart*, part I, sec. 8, 3rd edit., 1912, pp. 483-522   CCCLXI
OBERZINER (Lodovico) *Le Guerre germaniche di Flavio Claudio Giuliano*, Rome, 1896   CCCLXII
OMAN (Ch.) *History of the Art of War*, London, 1898   CCCLXIII
OTTO (Walter) *Kulturgeschichte des Altertums*, Munich, 1925   CCCLXIV
OVERBECK (J.) *Geschichte der griechischen Plastik*, 4th edit., Leipzig, 1892-94, 2 vols.   CCCLXV
OZANAM (A. F.) *La Civilisation au V* siècle*, Paris, 1855, 2 vols.   CCCLXVI
—— *Etudes germaniques*, 6th edit., Paris, 1893-94, 2 vols.   CCCLXVII
PAIS (Ettore) *Storia della colonizzacione di Roma antica, Prolegomeni*, Rome, 1923   CCCLXVIII
PARIS (Gaston) *Romania, Romani*, in *Romania*, vol. I, 1872, p. 22   CCCLXIX
PARRAVICINI (Achille) *Studio di retorica sulle opere di Claudiano*, Milan, 1905   CCCLXX
PARVAN (Vasile) *Die Nationalität der Kaufleute im römischen Kaiserzeit* (Diss. Breslau, 1909)   CCCLXXI
—— *La Pénétration hellénique et hellénistique dans la vallée du Danube*, in *Bulletin de la section historique de l'Académie roumaine*, vol. X, 1923   CCCLXXII
PECK (Harry Thurston) *A History of Classical Philology from the Seventh Century B.C. to Twentieth Century*, New York, 1911   CCCLXXIII
PEISKER (T.) *The Asiatic Background*, in *Cambridge Medieval History*, vol. I, pp. 323-59   CCCLXXIV
PÉRATÉ (André) *L'Archéologie chrétienne*, Paris, 1892   CCCLXXV
PERSON (Alex. W.) *Staat und Manufaktur im römischen Reiche*, Lund, 1923   CCCLXXVI
PETER (Hermann) *Die geschichtliche Litteratur über die römische Kaiserzeit bis Theodosius*, Leipzig, 1897, 2 vols.   CCCLXXVII
PETIT (Albert) see ALBERT-PETIT.
PFISTER (Christian) see LAVISSE, *Histoire de France*, vol. II, part I.
PFISTER (F.) *Der Reliquienkult im Altertum*, Giessen, 1909   CCCLXXVIII

PFLUGK-HARTTUNG (Julius von) *Römer und Germanen im 3 und 4 Jahrhundert. Die Grenzwehr von* 268-375, in *Zeitschrift für allgemeine Geschichte,* vol. II, 1885, pp. 321-39   **CCCLXXIX**
―――― *Weltgeschichte,* Berlin, n.d.   **CCCLXXX**

PICHLER (Fritz) *Austria Romana, geographisches Lexikon,* Leipzig, 1902 (*Quellen und Forschungen zur alten Geschichte und Geographie,* edit. W. Seiglin, fas. 2)   **CCCLXXXI**

PICHON (René) *Études sur l'histoire de la littérature latine dans les Gaules. Les derniers écrivains profanes : les panégyristes, Ausone, le Querolus, Rutilius Namatianus,* Paris, 1906   **CCCLXXXII**
―――― *Lactance, étude sur le mouvement philosophique et religieux sous Constantin,* Paris, 1901   **CCCLXXXIII**
―――― *Histoire de la littérature latine,* Paris, 1903   **CCCLXXXIV**

PIRENNE (Henri) *The Stages of the Social History of Capitalism,* in *American Historical Review,* April, 1914, pp. 494-515   **CCCLXXXV**
―――― *Les périodes de l'histoire sociale du capitalisme,* in *Bulletin de l'Académie royale de Belgique,* 1914   **CCCLXXXVI**

PLANCK (M.) *Der Verfall des römischen Kriegswesens am Ende des IV Jahrhunderts,* Stuttgart, 1877 (*Festschrift Gymn. Württenberg zur 4 Säcularfest Univ. Tübingen*)   **CCCLXXXVII**

POHLMANN (Robert von) *Aus Altertum und Gegenwart, Gesammelte Abhandlungen,* 1911, 2 vols.   **CCCLXXXVIII**
―――― *Geschichte des antiken Kommunismus und Sozialismus,* 1893   **CCCLXXXIX**
―――― *Römische Kaizerzeit und Untergang der alten Welt,* in Pflug-Harttung, *Weltgeschichte*   **CCCXC**
―――― *Die Uebervölkerung der antiken Grossstädte,* Leipzig, 1884   **CCCXCI**

PREUSS (Theodor) *Kaiser Diocletian und seine Zeit,* Leipzig, 1869   **CCCXCII**
―――― *Die Franken und ihre Verhältniss zu Rom in letzten Jahrh. des Reiches,* Tilsit, 1889   **CCCXCIII**

PUECH (A.) *Saint Jean Chrysostome et les mœurs de son temps,* Paris, 1891   **CCCXCIV**

RAUSCHEN (G.) *Das griechisch-römische Schulwesen zur Zeit des ausgehenden Heidentums,* Bonn, 1901   **CCCXCV**

RAWLINSON (H. G.) *Intercourse between India and the Western World, from the Earliest Times to the Fall of Rome,* Cambridge, 1916   **CCCXCVI**

Realencyclopædie der classischen Altertumwissenschaft, directed by Pauly ; new edition edited by Wissowa, 1894-1924, 12 vols. with 25 suppl. vols.   **CCCXCVII**

REICHE (Freidrich) *Ueber die Teilung der Zivil und Militär-gewalt im 3 Jahrhundert,* Breslau, 1900   **CCCXCVIII**
―――― *Der Untergang der antiken Welt, Zusammenfassende kritische Betrachtung,* in *Festscrift zur Feier des 50-jährigen Bestehens der Gymnasiums su Schrimme,* 1908   **CCCXCIX**

REID (J. Smith) *Roman Municipalities of the Roman Empire,* Cambridge, 1913   **CD**

REINACH (Salomon) *L'origine et les caractères de l'art gallo-romain,* in *Description raisonnée du musée de Saint-Germain,* 1894   **CDI**

REINHARDT (Ludwig) *Helvetien unter den Römern,* Berlin, 1924   **CDII**

REITTERER (Nikolaus) *Der Glaube an die Fortdauer des römischen Reiches im Abendlande,* Münster, 1899-1900   **CDIII**

Religion in Geschichte und Gegenwart, edit. by Schiele et
  Zscharnack, Tübingen, vol. IV, 1914 — **CDIV**
RENAN (Ernest) *Marc Aurèle et la fin du monde antique*,
  Paris, 1882 — **CDV**
RÉVILLE (Albert) *Histoire du dogme de la divinité de Jésus-
  Christ*, 4th edit, Paris, 1904 — **CDVI**
RÉVILLE (Jean) *La religion à Rome sous les Sévères*, Paris,
  1886 — **CDVII**
RÉVILLOUT (Ch.) *De l'Arianisme des peuples germaniques
  qui ont envahi l'Empire romain*, Paris, 1850 (Thesis) — **CDVIII**
RÉVILLOUT (Eug.) *Les Ostraka*, in *C. R. des séances de
  l'Académie des inscriptions*, 1870, p. 321 — **CDIX**
RICHTER (H.) *Das Weströmische Reich, besonders unter den
  Kaisern Gratian, Valentinian II und Maximus*, Berlin,
  1865 — **CDX**
RICHTER (Otto) *Topographie von Rom*, in Iwan von Müller's
  Handbuch der klass. Philologie, vol. III, part 3 — **CDXII**
RIEGL (Aloïs) *Spätrömische Kunstindustrie nach den Funden
  im Œsterreich-Ungarn*. I, Vienne, 1901-23, 2 vols. — **CDXIII**
RITTERLING (E.) *Zum römischen Heerwesen des ausgehenden
  dritten Jahrhunderts*, in *Festschrift für Otto Hirschfeld*,
  1903 — **CDXIV**
RODBERTUS (J. C.) *Untersuchungen auf dem Gebiete der Nat-
  ionaloekonomie des klassischen Altertums*, in Hilde-
  brand's *Jahrbücher für Nationaloekonomie*, vols. II, IV,
  V, VIII, 1864-67 — **CDXV**
ROGALA (Sig.) *Die Anfänge des arianischen Streits*, Pader-
  born, 1907 — **CDXVI**
ROGER (H.) *L'Enseignement des lettres classiques d'Ausone à
  Alcuin*, Paris, 1905 — **CDXVII**
ROMAN (J.) *Notes sur l'organisation municipale de l'Afrique
  romaine*, I : *Les Curies*, in *Annales de la Faculté de droit
  d'Aix*, vols. IV, 1911, pp. 85-123 — **CDXVIII**
ROMANO (G.) *Le Dominazioni barbariche in Italia* (395-1024),
  Milan, 1909 (*Storia politica d'Italia*, scritta da una società
  di professori) — **CDXIX**
ROSCHER (W.) *Ueber das Verhältniss der Nationaloekonomie
  zum klass. Alterthum*, in *Berichte* of the Saxon Academy,
  1849 — **CDXX**
ROSTOWTZEW (Michel) *Hellenistisch-römische Architektur-
  landschaft*, in *Römische Mitteilungen*, 1911 — **CDXXI**
——— *Studien zur Geschichte des römischen Kolonats*,
  Leipzig, 1910 — **CDXXII**
——— *Social and Economic History of the Roman Empire*,
  Oxford, 1926 — **CDXXII** *bis*
ROUGIER (Louis) *La Mentalité scolastique*, in *Revue Philoso-
  phique*, March-April, 1924 — **CDXXIII**
RUGGIERO (Ettore de) *La Patria nel diritto publico romano*,
  Rome, 1921 — **CDXXIV**
RUNKEL (F.) *Die Schlacht bei Adrianopol*, Rostock, 1903 — **CDXXV**
Du Sage antique au citoyen moderne, edit. by Bouglé, Bréhier,
  Delacroix, Parodi, Paris, 1921 — **CDXXVI**
SAGLIO, see *Dictionnaire*.
SAINT-YVES (P.) *Les Saints successeurs des dieux*, Paris,
  1907 — **CDXXVII**
SALEILLES (Raymond) *L'Organisation juridique des premières
  communautés chrétiennes*, in *Mélanges P.-Fréd. Girard*,
  vol. II, 1912, pp. 469-509 — **CDXXVIII**
——— *De l'établissement des Burgondes sur les domaines
  des Gallo-Romains*, in *Revue bourguignonne de l'enseigne-
  ment supérieur*, vol. I, pp. 43-103 — **CDXXIX**

SALVIOLI (G.) *Le capitalisme dans le monde antique*, trans. by
Alfred Bonnet, Paris, 1906 — **CDXXX**
SANDYS (Sir John) *A Companion to Latin Studies*, 3rd edit.,
Cambridge, 1913 — **CDXXXI**
―――― *A History of Classical Scholarship*, Cambridge,
1906-1908, 3 vols. ; vol. I : *From the Sixth Century* B.C.
to the End of the Middle Ages — **CDXXXII**
―――― *A Short History of Classical Scholarship*, Cam-
bridge, 1915 — **CDXXXIV**
SARWEY *Der Abgrenzung des Römerreiches*, 1894 — **CDXXXV**
―――― and HETTNER, *Der Obergermanisch-rätische* Limes,
Heidelberg, 1894-1913, 39 parts — **CDXXXVI**
SAVIGNY (Carl. von) *Vermischte Schriften*, Berlin, 1850,
2 vols. — **CDXXXVII**
SCHANZ (Martin von) *Römische Literaturgeschichte*, 2nd
edit., Munich, 1898-1914, 4 parts (Iwan von Müller's
Handbuch) — **CDXXXVIII**
SCHAUBE *Handelsgeschichte der romanischen Völker des
Mittelmeergebiets bis zum Ende der Kreuzzüge*, Munich,
1906 — **CDXXXIX**
SCHILLER (Hermann) *Geschichte der römischen Kaiserzeit*,
Gotha, 1883, 2 vols. — **CDXL**
―――― and VOIGT (Moritz) *Die römischen Staats-Kriegs
und Privataltertümer*, 2nd edit., Munich, 1893 — **CDXLI**
SCHLOSSER (J. von) *Zur Genesis der mittelalterlichen Kunstan-
schauung*, in *Mittheilungen des Instituts für Oesterreich.
Geschichtsforschung*, 6th suppl. vol., 1901, pp. 760-91 — **CDXLII**
SCHMIDT (Ludwig) *Allgemeine Geschichte der germanischen
Völker bis zur Mitte des sechsten Jahrhunderts*, Munich,
1909 — **CDXLIII**
―――― *Geschichte der deutschen Stämme bis zum Ausgang
der Völkerwunderung*, Berlin, 1904-1918, 2 vols.
(*Quellen und Forschungen*, edit. by W. Sieglin) — **CDXLIV**
―――― *Geschichte der Vandalen*, Leipzig, 1901 — **CDXLV**
―――― *Die Ursachen der Völkerwanderung*, in *Neue Jahr-
bücher für das klassisches Altertum*, vol. XI, 1903 — **CDXLVI**
SCHMIDT (Richard) *Allgemeine Staatslehre*, Leipzig, 1901-03,
2 vols. — **CDXLVII**
SCHMOLLER (Gustav) *Die geschichtliche Entwicklung der
Unternehmung*, XI : *Die Handelsgeschichte des Alter-
tums*, in *Jahrbuch für Gesetzgebung*, vol. XVI, 1892 — **CDXLVIII**
SCHRIJNEN (J.) *Konstantin de Groote en het edikt van Milaen*,
Utrecht, 1913 — **CDXLIX**
SCHULTHEISS (J.-G.) *Die Germanen im Dienste der römischen
Reichsidee*, in *Zeitschrift für allgemeine Geschichte*,
vol. II, 1885, pp. 801-07 — **CDL**
SCHULTZE (Victor) *Altchristliche Städte und Landschaften*,
I : *Konstantinopol (324-450)*, Leipzig, 1913 — **CDLI**
―――― *Geschichte des Untergangs des griechisch-römischen
Heidentums*, Jena, 1887-92, 2 vols. — **CDLII**
―――― *Konstantin*, in *Realenzyklopaedie für protestant.
Theologie und Kirche*, 3rd edit., vol. X, p. 769 — **CDLIII**
SCHWARTE *Die Technik des Kriegswesen*, 1913, in *Die Kultur
der Gegenwart*, vol. IV, part 12 — **CDLIV**
SCHWARTZ (Ed.) *Kaiser Constantin und die christliche Kirche*,
Leipzig, 1913 — **CDLV**
―――― *Die Konzilien der 4 u. 5. Jahrhunderten*, in *Histor.
Zeitschrift*, vol. CIV, 1910 — **CDLVI**
SEECK (Otto) *Geschichte des Untergangs der antiken Welt*,
Berlin, 1895-1921, 6 vols. ; vol. I, 3rd edit., Berlin, 1910 — **CDLVII**

SEGRE (Arturo) *Storia del commercio*, 2nd edit., Turin, 1923, 2 vols.   CDLVIII

SERRIGNY (D.) *Droit public et administratif romain*, Paris, 1862, 2 vols.   CDLIX

SESAN (Valerian) *Kirche und Staat im römisch-byzantinischen Reiche*, Czernowitz, 1911   CDLX

SIGWART *Kapitalismus*, in PAULY-WISSOWA, *Realencyclopaedie*, vol. III, part 2, col. 1900-1909   CDLXI

SITTL (Karl) *Archäologie der Kunst*, Munich, 1895 (Iwan von Müller's *Handbuch*, vol. VI)   CDLXII

SOMBART (Werner) *Das Moderne Kapitalismus*, 1916-17, 2 vols.   CDLXIII

SOREL (Georges) *La Ruine du monde antique*, new edit., Paris, 1925   CDLXIV

SPECK (E.) *Handelsgeschichte des Alterthums*, 1906, 4 vols.   CDLXV

STEIN (Ernst) *Untersuchungen über das Officium der praetorianer Praefektur seit Diokletian*, Vienna, 1922   CDLXVI

STEINACKER (H.) *Die römische Kirche und die griechische Sprachkenntnisse des Frühmittelalters*, in *Festschrift Th. Gomperz*, Vienna, 1901, pp. 234-41   CDLXVII

STEMPLINGER (Eduard) *Das Plagiat in der griech. Literatur*, Leipzig, 1912   CDLXVIII

STŒCKLE *Spätrömisch und byzantin. Zünfte*, in *Klio*, 9th suppl. vol., 1911   CDLXIX

STREHL (W.) and SOLTAU (W.) *Grundriss der alten Geschichte und Quellenkunde*, vol. II : *Römische Geschichte*, Breslau, 1914   CDLXX

STRZYGOWSKI (Josef.) *Die Bedeutung der Gründung Konstantinopels für die Entwicklung der christlichen Kunst*, in *Konstantin der Grosse*, pp. 363-76   CDLXXI

—— *Orient oder Rom : Beiträge zur Geschichte der späteren und frühchristlichen Kunst*, 1901   CDLXXII

—— *Kleinasien, ein Neuland der Kunstgeschichte*, 1903   CDLXXIII

SUNDWALL (J.) *Weströmische Studien*, Berlin, 1915   CDLXXIV

TAMASSIA (Giovanni) *Egidio e Siagrio*, in *Rivista storica italiana*, vol. III, 1886, pp. 193-234   CDLXXV

TANNERY (Paul) *Mémoires scientifiques*, Paris, 1880-1925, 7 vols.   CDLXXVI

—— *Pour l'histoire de la science hellénique*, Paris, 1887   CDLXXVI *bis*

TAYLOR (Henry Osborn) *The Classical Heritage of the Middle Ages*, 3rd edit., London, 1911   CDLXXVII

TEUFFEL (W.-S.) *Geschichte der römischen Litteratur*, edit. by Kroll et Skutsch, 1910-16, 3 vols. ; French trans. by Bonnard et Pierson, Paris, 1879   CDLXXVIII

THIERRY (Amédée) *Saint Jean Chrysostome et l'impératrice Eudoxie*, Paris   CDLXXIX

—— *Alaric, l'agonie de l'Empire*, 2nd edit., Paris, 1880   CDLXXX

—— *Derniers temps de l'Empire d'Occident, la mort de l'Empire*, 6th edit., Paris, 1883   CDLXXXI

—— *Histoire d'Attila*, Paris, 1864, 2 vols.   CDLXXXII

TILLEMONT see LENAIN DE T.

TIXERONT (J.) *Histoire des dogmes*, Paris, 1912-15, 3 vols.   CDLXXXIII

TOUTAIN (J.) *Les Cultes païens dans l'Empire romain*, Paris, 1905-20, 3 vols. (*Bibl. École Hautes Études, Sc. relig.*, fas. 20, 25, 31)   CDLXXXIV

TREDE (Th.) *Das Heidentum in der römischen Kirche*, Gotha, 1889-91, 4 vols.   CDLXXXV

TROELTSCH (E.) *Augustin : die christliche Antike und das Mittelalter in Anschluss an die Schrift* De civitate Dei, Munich, 1915 (*Histor. Bibliothek*, 36)   CDLXXXVI

TROPLONG *De l'influence du christianisme sur le droit civil des Romains*, Paris, 1843 ; 3rd edit., 1868 — **CDLXXXVII**

UEBERWEG (Fried.) *Grundriss der Geschichte der Philosophie, Das Altertum*, 11th edit. by K. Praechter, Berlin, 1920 ; *Mittelalt-oder d. patrist. und Scholast.*, 10th edit. by M. Baumgartner, 1915 — **CDLXXXVIII**

VACANDARD (E.) *Études de critique et d'histoire religieuse*, Paris, 1905-23, 4 series — **CDLXXXIX**

VACHEROT (Et.) *Histoire critique de l'école d'Alexandrie*, Paris, 1846, 2 vols. — **CDXC**

VALENTIN (Abbé) *Saint Prosper d'Aquitaine, étude sur la littérature latine au V* siècle en Gaule*, Paris, 1900 — **CDXCI**

VAN BERCHEM (Max) and CLOUZOT (Et.) *Mosaïques chrétiennes de l'Italie*, Genève, 1914 — **CDXCII**

VAN CAUWENBERGH (Paul) *Coutumes ecclésiastiques d'après les ostracas coptes*, in *Mélanges Ch. Moeller*, Louvain, 1914 — **CDXCIII**

VAN MILLINGEN (A.) *Byzantine Constantinople. The Walls of the City and Adjoining Historical Sites*, London, 1899 — **CDXCIV**

VASILIEV (N. A.) *The Fall of the Roman Empire and the Disappearance of Ancient Culture and Law*, Kazan, 1921 (in Russian) — **CDXCV**

VENTURI (A.) *Storia del arte italiana*, Milan, 1901 sq. — **CDXCVI**

VILLARI (Pasquale) *Le Invasioni barbariche in Italia*, Milan, 1901 ; English edit. in 2 vols., London, 1902 — **CDXVCII**

VILLEMAIN *Tableau de l'éloquence chrétienne au IVe siècle*, Paris, 1850 — **CDXCVIII**

VOETTER (O.) *Erste christliche Zeichen auf römischen Münzen*, in *Numismatische Zeitschrift*, 1892 — **CDXCIX**

WADDINGTON, (H. W.) *Edit de Dioclétien établissant le maximum dans l'Empire romain*, Paris, 1864 — **D**

WALLON (Henri) *Histoire de l'esclavage dans l'antiquité*, Paris, 1847, 3 vols. — **DI**

WALTZ (Pierre) *Les artisans et leur vie en Grèce*, in *Revue Historique*, vols. CXLI-CXLVII, 1923-24 — **DII**

WALTZING (J. P.) *Etude historique sur le corporations professionnelles des Romains*, Louvain, 1895-1900, 4 vols. — **DIII**

WEBER (Max) *Agrargeschichte des Altertums*, 2nd edit., 1898 — **DIV**

———— *Die socialen Gründen des Untergangs der antiken Kultur*, in *Die Wahrheit*, 1896, VI, 3 — **DV**

WENDLAND (Paul) *Die hellenistisch-römische Kultur in ihren Beziehungen zu Judentum und Christentum*, Tubingen, 1912 — **DVI**

WESTERMANN (W. L.) *The Economic Basis of the Decline of Ancient Culture*, in *American Historical Review*, vol. XX, 1914-15 (pp. 723-43) — **DVII**

WIETERSHEIM (Eduard von) *Geschichte der Völkerwanderung*, Leipzig, 1859-64, 4 vols. — **DVIII**

WILCKEN (Ulrich) *Griechische Ostraka aus Aegypten*, Leipzig, 1899 — **DIX**

WILLEMS (P.) *Le Droit public romain*, 7th edit., Louvain, 1910 — **DX**

WISKEMANN (H.) *Die Antike Landwirthschaft und das Von-Thünensche Gesetz, aus den alten Schriftstellern dargelegt*, 1859 (*Schriften der Fürstlich-Jablonowskischen Gesellschaft zu Leipzig*, 7) — **DXI**

WITTE (Fritz) *Die Kolossalstatue Konstantins des Grossen*, in *Konstantin der Grosse* (pp. 259-268) — **DXII**

XENOPOL (A. D.) *Histoire des Roumains*, Paris, 1896, 2 vols.   **DXIII**

YATES (James) *Textrinum antiquorum*, I, London, 1843   **DXIV**

YVER (Georges) *Euric roi des Wisigoths (466-485)*, in *Études d'histoire du moyen âge dédiées à Gabriel Monod*, Paris, 1896 (pp. 11-46)   **DXV**

ZELLER (Joseph) *Die Zeit der Verlegung der praefectura Galliarum von Trier nach Arles*, in *Historische Zeitschrift*, vol. XXIII (1904), pp. 91-102   **DXVI**

—————— *Das Concilium der Septem Provinciae in Arelate* (*Ibid.*, vol. XXIV, 1905, pp. 1-19)   **DXVII**

ZIMMER (Heinrich) *Celtic Church in Britain and Ireland*, translated by Alice Meyer, London, 1902   **DXVIII**

—————— *Ueber die Bedeutung des irischen Elements für die Mittelalterliche Cultur*, in *Preussische Jahrbücher*, vol. LIX, 1887 ; trans. by J.-L. Edmonds, *The Irish Element in Mediaeval Culture*, 2nd edit., London, 1913   **DXIX**

—————— *Ueber direkte Handelsverbindung West-Galliens mit Ireland in Altertum und früh-Mittelalter*, in *Sitzungsberichte* of the Berlin Academy, 1909   **DXX**

ZŒCKLER (O.) *Askese und Mönchthum*, Frankfort, 1897, 2 vols.   **DXXI**

THIRD PART

AEBERG (Nils) *Die Goten und Langobarden in Italien*, Upsala, 1923   **DXXII**

—————— *Die Franken*, see part I.

ALTAMIRA (Rafael) *Historia de España*, Barcelona, 1906-11, 4 vols. and in *Cambridge Medieval History*, vol. II   **DXXIII**

AMPÈRE (J.-J.) *Histoire littéraire de la France avant le XII⁰ siècle*, Paris, 1839-41, 3 vols.   **DXXIV**

ANDRÉ-MICHEL see part I.

BALLESTEROS y BERETTA (Antonio) *Historia de España y su influencia en la historia universal*, Barcelona, 1919-28, 3 vols.   **DXXV**

BARRIÈRE-FLAVY (C.) *Les Arts industriels des peuples barbares de la Gaule du VI⁰ au VIII⁰ siècle*, Toulouse, 1901, 3 vols.   **DXXVI**

BAYET see LAVISSE, vol. II, 2.

BEAUCHET (Ludovic) *Histoire de l'organisation judiciaire en France : époque franque*, Paris, 1886   **DXXVII**

BEAUDOUIN (Ed.) *La Participation des hommes libres au jugement dans le droit franc*, Paris, 1888 (Extr. from the *Nouvelle Revue Hist. de Droit*)   **DXXVIII**

BERNHEIM (Ernst) *Mittelalterliche Zeitanschauungen in ihrer Einfluss auf Politik und Geschichtsschreibung*, Tübingen, 1918   **DXXIX**

—————— *Politische Begriffe des Mittelatters im Lichte der Anschauungen Augustins*, in *Deutsche Z. f. Geschichtswissenschaft*, 1896-97   **DXXX**

BERNOUILLI (C. A.) *Die Heiligen der Merowinger*, Tübingen, 1900   **DXXXI**

BESSE (Dom), see part I.

BIDEZ (J.) *Boèce et Porphyre*, in *Revue belge de philologie et d'histoire*, vol. II, 1923, 189-201   **DXXXII**

BINDING (C.) *Das Burgundisch-romanische Königreich, von 443 bis 532*, Leipzig, 1868   **DXXXIII**

BLADÉ (J. B.) *Les Vascons avant leur établissement en Novem-
  populanie*, Agen, 1891   **DXXXIV**
—— *La Vasconie cispyrénéenne jusqu'à la mort de
  Dagobert*, I, Le Puy, 1891   **DXXXV**
—— *L'Aquitaine et la Vasconie cispyrénéenne depuis la
  mort de Dagobert jusqu'à l'époque du duc Eudes*, 1891   **DXXXVI**
BLANCHET (Adrien) and DIEUDONNE (A.) *Manuel de numis-
  matique française*, Paris, 1900   **DXXXVII**
BONNELL (H. E.) *Die Anfänge des Karolingischen Hauses*,
  Berlin, 1886   **DXXXVIII**
BONNET (Max) *Le Latin de Grégoire de Tours*, Paris, 1890   **DXXXIX**
BREHAUT (E.) *An Encyclopaedist of the Dark Ages : Isidore
  of Seville*, New York, 1912   **DXL**
BRÉHIER (Louis) *Les Colonies d'Orientaux en Occident au
  commencement du moyen âge*, in *Byzantinische Zeitschrift*,
  vol. XII, 1903, pp. 1-39   **DXLI**
BREYSIG (T.) *Jahrbücher des fränkischen Reichs* (714-741),
  Leipzig, 1869   **DXLII**
BRISSAUD (J.) *Cours d'histoire générale du droit française
  public et privé*, Paris, 1904, 2 vols.   **DXLIII**
BRUCKNER (W.) *Die Sprache der Langobarden*, Strasbourg,
  1895   **DXLIV**
BRUNNER (Heinrich) *Deutsche Rechtsgeschichte*, Leipzig,
  2 vols. ; vol. I, 2nd edit., 1906   **DXLV**
—— *Sippe und Wergeld*, in *Zeitschrift der Savigny,
  Stiftung, Germ. Abteil.*, XVI, 1882 (p. 14)   **DXLVI**
BUTLER (Dom Cuthbert) *Benedictine Monachism*, 2nd edit.,
  London, 1924   **DXLVII**
CABROL (Dom F.) *L'Angleterre chrétienne avant les Normands*,
  Paris, 1907   **DXLVIII**
CAHUN (Léon) see part I.
Cambridge Medieval History, see part I.
CARLOT (Armand) *Etude sur le* Domesticus *franc*, Liége, 1903
  (*Bibl. de la Faculté des lettres de Liege*, fas. 13)   **DXLIX**
CLEMEN (Paul) *Merowingische und Karolingische Plastik*,
  Bonn, 1892, in *Jahrbuch. d. Vereins, j. Altert. im Rhein-
  lande*, fas. 92)   **DL**
CLOCHÉ (Paul) *Les Elections épiscopoles sous les Mérovingiens*,
  in *Le Moyen âge*, Sept.-Dec., 1924-25 (pp. 203-54)   **DLI**
COLLINET (Paul) *Le Caractère oriental de l'œuvre législative de
  Justinien et les destinées des institutions classiques en
  Occident*, Paris, 1912   **DLII**
COURAJOD (Louis) *Leçons professées à l'École du Louvre*,
  Paris, 1899-1906 (vol. I)   **DLIII**
DAHN (Felix von) *Die Könige der Germanen, Das Wesen des
  ältesten Königtums der germanischen Stämme und seine
  Geschichte bis auf die Feudalzeit*, Munich, Wurzburg,
  Leipzig, 1861-1909, 12 vols.   **DLIV**
—— *Urgeschichte der german. und roman. Völker*
  [up to 814], 1889, 4 vols.   **DLV**
—— *Zur Merovingischen Finanzen*, in *Germanistische
  Abhandlungen . . Konrad von Maurer*, Goettingen,
  1893, pp. 335-73   **DLVI**
DECLAREUIL (J.) *Des Comtes de cité à la fin du Vᵉ siècle*,
  in *Nouv. Revue Hist. de Droit*, Nov.-Dec., 1910   **DLVII**
—— *Les Preuves judiciaires dans le droit franc du Vᵉ au
  VIIIᵉ siècle*, Paris, 1899 (Extr. from *Nouv. Revue Hist.
  de Droit*)   **DLVIII**
—— *Cours d'histoire du droit français*, Paris, 1925   **DLIX**
DELOCHE (Max) *La Trustis et l'antrustion royal sous les deux
  premières races*, Paris, 1873   **DLX**

DIEHL (Charles) *Histoire de l'Empire byzantin*, Paris, 1919 — DLXI
——— *Byzance, grandeur et décadence*, Paris, 1919 — DLXII
——— *Justinien et la civilisation byzantine au VIe siècle*, Paris, 1901 — DLXIII
——— *L'Afrique byzantine (533-709)*, Paris, 1896 — DLXIV
——— *Etudes sur l'administration byzantine dans l'Exarchat de Ravenne*, Paris, 1888 — DLXV
——— *Manuel d'art byzantin*, see part I.
DIERKS (S.) *Geschichte Spaniens von den frühesten Zeiten bis auf die Gegenwart*, Berlin, 1895-96, 2 vols. — DLXVI
DIGOT (A.) *Histoire des rois d'Austrasie*, Nancy, 1863, 4 vols. — DLXVII
DUBOS (Abbé) *Histoire critique de l'établissement de la Monarchie française dans les Gaules*, Paris, 1734; new edit., 1742, 4 vols. — DLXVIII
DUCHESNE (Louis) *Les premiers temps de l'Etat pontifical*, Paris, 1898, 2nd edit., 1904 — DLXIX
——— *Histoire de l'Église*, see part I.
DUDDEN (F. H.) *Gregory the Great, his Place in History and Thought*, London, 1905, 2 vols. — DLXX
DUMOULIN (Maurice) *Le Gouvernement de Théodoric*, in *Revue Historique*, 1902, I and II — DLXXI
DU MOULIN-ECKHART *Leudegar Bischof von Autun*, Breslau, 1890 — DLXXII
EBERT (Adolph) *Allgemeine Geschichte der Literatur des Mittelalters im Abendland*, Leipzig, 1874-87, 3 vols.; 2nd edit., 1889; French trans. by Aymeric and Condamin, Paris, 1883, 3 vols. — DLXXIII
EICKEN (H. von) *Geschichte und System der Mittelalterlichen Weltanschauung*, Stuttgart, 1887 — DLXXIV
ENGEL and SERRURE *Traité de Numismatique du moyen âge*, vol. I, 1892 — DLXXV
ENLART (Camille) *Manuel d'archéologie française depuis les temps mérovingiens jusqu'à la Renaissance*, Paris, 1902-16, 3 vols. — DLXXVI
ESMEIN (Adhémar) *Cours élémentaire d'histoire du droit français*, 11th edit., Paris, 1912 — DLXXVII
FABRE (Paul) *De patrimonio Ecclesiae usque ad aetatem Carolinorum*, Lille, 1892 — DLXXVII *bis*
FAHLBECK (Pontus) *La Royauté et le droit royal francs durant la première période de l'existence du royaume (486-614)*, Lund, 1883 — DLXXVIII
FLACH (Jacques) *Les Origines de l'ancienne France*, Paris, 1886-1917, 4 vols. (vols. I-II) — DLXXIX
FLETCHER (C. R. L.) *The Making of Western Europe, being an Attempt to trace the Fortune of the Children of the Roman Empire*, London, 1914, 2 vols. — DLXXX
FRIEDLAENDER (L.) *Das Nachleben der Antike im Mittelalter*, in *Errinnerungen . . .*, Strasbourg, 1905, vol. I, pp. 272-391 — DLXXXI
FUSTEL DE COULANGES *La Monarchie franque*, Paris, 1888 — DLXXXII
——— *Les Origines du système féodal : le Bénéfice et le Patronat pendant l'époque mérovingienne*, Paris, 1890 — DLXXXIII
——— *Les Transformations de la royauté pendant l'époque carolingienne*, Paris, 1892 — DLXXXIV
GASQUET (Am.) *L'Empire byzantin et la Monarchie franque*, Paris, 1888 — DLXXXV
GAUDENZI (A.) *Sui rapporti tra l'Italia e l'imperio d'Oriente fra gli anni 476-554*, Bologne, 1888 — DLXXXVI
GOUGAUD (Dom Louis) *Les Chrétientés celtiques*, Paris, 1911 — DLXXXVII

GRAFF (A.) *Roma nella memoria e nelle immaginazioni del Medio evo*, Turin, 1882-83, 2 vols.   DLXXXVIII

GREGOROVIUS (Ferdinand) *Geschichte der Stadt Rom im Mittelalter*, Stuttgart, 1859-72, 8 vols. ;—Eng. tr., 8 vols., London, 1894-1902 ; illus. Ital. edit., *Storia della Citta di Roma nel medio evo*, Rome, 1900-01, 4 vols.   DLXXXIX

GRISAR (Hartmann) *Roma alla fine del mondo antico*, Rome, 1899   DXC

——— *Geschichte Roms und der Päpste im Mittelalter*, Freiburg-im-Brisgau, 1898 ; —Eng. tr., vols. I-II, London, 1911-12 ; French trans. by G. Ledos, Paris, 1906, etc.   DXCI

GUILHIERMOZ (Paul) *Essai sur l'origine de la noblesse en France au moyen âge*, Paris, 1902   DXCII

GUIZOT (F.) *Histoire de la civilisation en France*, Paris, 1829-38, 5 vols.   DXCIII

HALBAN (Alfred von) *Das römische Recht in den germanischen Volkstaeten*, Breslau, 1899-1907, 3 vols. (Gierke's *Untersuchungen*, fas. 56, 64, 89)   DXCIV

HARTMANN (Ludo Moritz) *Geschichte Italiens im Mittelalter*, Leipzig, 1897, 3 vols. in 4 ; 2nd edit. of vol. I, Stuttgart, 1923   DXCV

——— *Untersuchungen zur Geschichte der byzantinischen Verwaltung in Italien* (540-750), Leipzig, 1889   DXCXVI

HAUCK (Ad.) *Kirchengeschichte Deutschlands*, Leipzig, 1887-1911, 5 vols. ; vols. I-III, 3rd edit., 1906-1911   DXCVII

HASKINS (Charles H.) *Studies in the History of Mediœval Sciences*, Cambridge, (Mass.), 1924   DXCVIII

HELLMANN (S.) *Gregor von Tours*, in *Histor. Zeitschrift*, vol. CVII, 1911, pp. 1-43   DXCIX

HESS (Aloïs) *Description générale des monnaies des rois wisigoths d'Espagne*, Paris, 1872   DC

HEYD (W.) *Histoire du commerce du Levant au moyen âge*, French trans. by Furcy Reynaud, Leipzig, 1886, 2 vols.   DCI

HODGKIN (Thomas) *Theodoric the Goth, the Barbarian Champion of Civilisation*, New York, 1891   DCII

——— *Italy*, see part I

HOLMES (W. G.) *The Age of Justinian and Theodora, History of the Sixth Century*, London, 1905-07, 2 vols.   DCIII

HUBERT (H.) *Etude sur la formation des Etats de l'Eglise*, in *Revue Historique*, vol. LXIX, 1899   DCIV

IMBART DE LA TOUR (Pierre) *Les paroisses rurales*, Paris, 1900   DCV

——— *Des immunités commerciales accordées à l'Église du VII⁰ au IX⁰ siècle*, in *Études . . .G. Monod*, 1896   DCVI

IORGA (N.) *Histoire des Roumains*, Bucarest, 1915-16, 2 vols.   DCVII

——— *Histoire des Etats balcaniques jusqu'à 1924*, Paris, 1925   DCVIII

JAHN (A.) *Geschichte der Burgundionen und Burgundiens bis zum Ende der I Dynastie*, Halle, 1874, 2 vols.   DCIX

JIRECEK *Die Romanen*, see part I.

JUNGHANS (W.) *Histoire critique des règnes de Childeric et de Clodowech*, trans. by G. Monod, 1879 (*Bibl. Ecole Hautes Études*, fas. 37)   DCX

KAUFMANN (G.) *Rhetorenschulen*, see part I.

KOEBNER (Richard) *Venantius Fortunatus*, Leipzig, 1915 (*Beiträge zur Kulturgeschichte*, fas. 22)   DCXI

KROELL (Maurice) *L'Immunité franque*, Paris, 1910   DCXII

432   BIBLIOGRAPHY

KRUSCH (Bruno) *Chlodowechs Sieg über die Alamannen*, in
Neues Archiv für ältere deutsche Geschichtskunde, vol.
XII (1886), p. 289   **DCXIII**
———— *Das Staatsreich des fränkischen Hausmeiers Grimoald
I*, in *Histor. Aufsätze Karl Zeumer . . .*, Weimar, 1910
(pp. 411-38)   **DCXIV**
KURTH (Godefroid) *Clovis*, 2nd edit., Paris, 1901, 2 vols.   **DCXV**
———— *Études franques*, Paris, 1919, 2 vols.   **DCXVI**
———— *Histoire poétique des Mérovingiens*, Bruxelles, 1893   **DCXVII**
LAMPRECHT (K.) *Deutsche Wirthschaftsgeschichte im Mittel-
alter*, Leipzig, 1885-86, 4 vols.   **DCXVIII**
———— *Études sur l'état économique de la France pendant la
première partie du moyen âge*, French trans. by Marignan,
Paris, 1889   **DCXIX**
LANCIANI (R.) *Destruction of Ancient Rome : a Sketch of
the History of the Monuments*, New York, 1899   **DCXX**
———— *Pagan and Christian Rome*, Boston (Mass.), 1893   **DCXXI**
———— *Wanderings in the Roman Campagna*, New York,
1909   **DCXXII**
LASTEYRIE (Robert de) *L'Église de saint Martin de Tours*, in
Mémoires de l'Académie des inscriptions, vol. XXXIV,
I, 1892, pp. 1-52   **DCXXIII**
LAVISSE (Ernest) *La Décadence mérovingienne*, in *Revue des
Deux Mondes*, Dec. 15th, 1885   **DCXXIV**
———— *La Foi et la morale des Francs*, *Ibid.*, March 15th,
1886   **DCXXV**
———— *La Conquête de la Germanie par l'Eglise romaine*,
Ibid., April 15th, 1887   **DCXXVI**
LECLERC (Dom H.) *L'Espagne chrétienne*, Paris, 1910   **DCXXVII**
LEHUEROU (J.-M.) *Histoire des institutions mérovingiennes
et du gouvernement des Mérovingiens jusqu'à l'édit de
615*, Paris, 1842   **DCXXVIII**
LE PRIEUR see ANDRÉ-MICHEL.
LESNE (E.) *Propriété ecclésiastique*, see part I.   **DCXXIX**
LEVILLAIN (Léon) *Le Baptême de Clovis*, in *Bibliothèque de
l'École des Chartes*, 1906   **DCXXX**
———— *Le Formulaire de Marculf*, *Ibid.*, 1923   **DCXXXI**
———— *La Succession d'Austrasie au VIIᵉ siècle*, in *Revue
Historique*, vol. CXII, 1913   **DCXXXII**
LEVISON (Wilhelm) *Die Iren und die fränkische Kirche*, in
Histor. Zeitschrift, vol. CIX, 1912, pp. 1-22   **DCXXXIII**
———— *Das Nekrologium von Dom Racine und die Chrono-
logie der Merowinger*, in *Neues Archiv*, vol. XXXV, 1909   **DCXXXIV**
———— *Zur Geschichte des Frankenkönigs Chlodowech*, in
Bonner Jahrbücher, vol. CIII, 1898, pp. 42-86   **DCXXXV**
LINDENSCHMIDT (L.) *Handbuch der deutschen Altertumskunde
I : Merowingische Zeit*, Brunswick, 1880-89   **DCXXXVI**
LINDNER (Theodor) *Weltgeschichte*, see part I.
LOEBELL (J. W.) *Gregor von Tours und seine Zeit.*, 2nd edit.
1869   **DCXXXVII**
LOENING (Edgar) *Geschichte des Deutschen Kirchenrechts*,
Strasbourg, 1878, 2 vols.   **DCXXXVIII**
LONGNON (Auguste) *Géographie de la Gaule au VIᵉ siècle*,
Paris, 1878   **DCXXXIX**
———— *Atlas historique de la France*, Paris, 1885-1907   **DCXL**
———— *Les noms de lieu de la France*, 2 and 3 fas., Paris,
1922-23   **DCXLI**
LOT (Ferdinand) *Encore la chronique du Pseudo-Frédégaire*,
in *Revue Historique*, vol. CXV, 1914   **DCXLII**
———— *La Nomination du comte à l'époque mérovingienne
. . .*, in *Revue Hist. du Droit*, 1924   **DCXLIII**

LOT (Ferdinand) *De le valeur historique du* De excidio . . .
Britanniæ *de Gildas*, in *Mélanges* . . . *Gertrude
Schoepperle*, 1926 — DCXLIV

MANITIUS (Max) *Gundriss der lateinischen Literatur des
Mittelalters*, I : *Von Justinian bis zum Mitte der zehnten
Jahrhunderts*, 1911 (Iwan von Müller's *Handbuch*,
X, 2, 1) — DCXLV

MARIGNAN (A.) *Etudes sur la civilisation française*, vol. I :
La Société mérovingienne ; vol. II : *Le culte des saints
sous les Mérovingiens*, Paris, 1899, 2 vols. — DCXLVI

MARTIN (Paul-Edmond) *Etudes critiques sur la Suisse à
l'époque mérovingienne*, Genève, 1910 — DCXLVII

MARTROYE (F.) *L'Occident à l'époque byzantine : Goths et
Vandales*, Paris, 1904 — DCXLVIII

MAURER (G.-L. von) *Geschichte de Fronhöfe, Bauernhöfe und
Hofverfassung in Deutschland*, Erlangen, 1862, 2 vols. — DCXLIX

MAYER (Ernest) *Italiensiche Verfassungsgeschichte*, Leipzig,
1909, 2 vols. — DCL

MAYER (Ernesto) *Historia de las instituciones sociales y
politicas de España y Portugal durante los siglos V à
XIV*, vol. I, Madrid, 1925 — DCLI

MEITZEN (Aug.) *Siedelungs und Agrarwesen der West-Germa-
nen und Ostgothen, der Kelten, Römer, Finnen und
Slawen*, Berlin, 1895, 5 vols. and atlas — DCLII

MIGNET *Comment l'ancienne Germanie est entrée dans la
société civilisée de l'Europe occidentale et lui a servi de
barrière contre les invasions du Nord*, in *Notices et
Mémoires Historiques*, Paris, 1843, 2 vols. — DCLIII

MILLET (G.) see ANDRÉ-MICHEL. (Part I)

MOMMSEN (Th.) *Ostgotische Studien*, in *Neues Archiv*,
vol. XIV, 1889, and in *Werke*, vol. VI — DCLIV

MONOD (Gabriel) *Études critiques sur les sources de l'histoire
mérovingienne*, part I : *Grégoire de Tours, Marius
d'Avenches*, Paris, 1872 (*Bibliothèque de l'École des
Hautes Études*, fas. 8) — DCLV

MUNRO (D. C.) *The Attitude of the Western Church towards the
Study of the Latin Classics in the Early Middle Ages*
(vol. VIII of *American Society of Church History*,
1897) — DCLVI

NIEDERLE (Labor) *Manuel de l'antiquité slave*, vol. I :
l'Histoire, Paris, 1923 — DCLVII

NORDEN (W.) *Das Papsthum und Byzanz*, Berlin, 1903 — DCLVIII

OGLE (B.) *Classical Literary Traditions in Early German and
Romance Literature*, in *Modern Language Notes*,
vol. XXVII, 1912 — DCLIX

OMAN (Ch.) *The Dark Ages* (470-918), 2nd edit., London,
1908 — DCLX

———— *England before the Norman Conquest*, vol. I,
London, 1910 — DCLXI

———— *Art of War*, see part I.

OZANAM, *Civilisation chez les Francs*, see part I.

PAETOW (Louis John) *Guide to the Study of Medieval History*,
Berkeley (Cal.), 1917 — DCLXII

PALACKY *Samo*, in *Jahrbücher des bœhmischen Museum* — DCLXIII

PEISKER (J.) *Die älteren Beziehungen der Slawen und Turko-
tataren und Germanen*, in *Vierteljahrschrift für Social-
und-wirtschafts-Geschichte*, vol. III, 1905 — DCLXIV

PELLIOT (P.) *L'origine des Tou Kiue (Turcs)*, in *T'oung Pao*,
1915 — DCLXV

PEREZ-PUJOL (E.) *Historia de las instituciones sociales de la
España goda*, Valencia, 1896, 4 vols. — DCLXVI

PERROUD (Ch.) *Les Origines du premier duché d'Aquitaine*, Paris, 1883   DCLXVII

PERTILE (A.) *Storia del diritto italiano*, Padua, 1873-87, 6 vols. ; 2nd edit., Turin, 1891-1903   DCLXVIII

PÉTRAU-GAY (Jean) *La Notion de* lex *dans la coutume salienne et ses transformations dans les capitulaire*, Grenoble, 1920 (Thesis)   DCLXIX

PFEILSCHIFTER *Die Germanen im römischen Reich : Theodorich der Grosse*, Mainz, 1911   DCLXX

PFISTER (Christian) *Le Baptême de Clovis*, in *Revue Hebdomaire*, Oct. 21st, 1916   DCLXXI

―――― see LAVISSE, part I.

PHILIPP (H.) *Die Historisch-geographischen Quellen in den Etymologiae des Isidores von Sevilla*, Berlin, 1912-13 (*Quellen und Forschungen zur älteren Geschichte und Geographie*, edit by Sieglin, fas. 25, 26)   DCLXXII

PINGAUD (Léonce) *La Politique de saint Grégoire le Grand*, Paris, 1872   DCLXXIII

PIRENNE (Henri) *Histoire de Belgique*, Bruxelles, 1900-21, (vol. I)   DCLXXIV

PIRSON *Le Latin des formules mérovingiennes et carolingiennes* in *Romanische Forschungen*, vol. XXVI, 1909 (pp. 837-944)   DCLXXV

PRESLAND (J.) *Belisarius, General of the East*, London, 1913   DCLXXVI

PROU (Maurice) *La Gaule mérovingienne*, Paris, 1897   DCLXXVII

―――― *Introduction au Catalogue des monnaies mérovingiennes de la Bibliothèque nationale*, Paris, 1892   DCLXXVIII

RAJNA (Pio) *Le Origini dell'epopea francese*, Florence, 1884   DCLXXIX

RAMSAY (Sir James) *The Foundation of England*, London, 1898   DCLXXX

REINAUD (M.) *Invasions des Sarrasins en France*, Paris, 1836   DCLXXXI

REVERDY (Georges) *Les Relations de Childebert II et de Byzance*, in *Revue Historique*, vol. CXIV, 1913 (pp. 61-86)   DCLXXXII

―――― *Note sur l'interprétation d'un passage d'Avitus*, in *Le Moyen age*, 1913   DCLXXXIII

RICHTER (Gustav) *Annalen des fränkischen Reiches im Zeitalter der Merowinger*, Halle, 1873   DCLXXXIV

RODOCANACHI (E.) *Les Monuments de Rome après la chute de l'Empire*, Paris, 1914   DCLXXXV

ROESLER (Margarete) *Erziehung in England vor der normann. Eroberung*, in *Englische Studien*, vol. XLVIII, 1914 (pp. 1-114)   DCLXXXVI

RŒSSLER (Oskar) *Grundriss einer Geschichte Roms in Mittelalter*, vol. I, Berlin, 1909   DCLXXXVII

ROGER *Enseignement*, see part I.

ROLOFF (G.) *Die Umwandlung des fränkischen Heeres von Chlodowig bis Karl dem Grossen*, in *Neue Jahrbücher für das klassische Altertum*, vol. IX, 1902   DCLXXXVIII

ROMANO see part I.

ROTH (Paul) *Geschichte des Beneficialwesens*, Erlangen, 1850   DCLXXXIX

―――― *Feudalität und Unterthanverband*, Weimar, 1863   DCXC

ROUGIER see part I.

ROUSSEL (E.) *Le roi Chilpéric*, in *Annales de l'Est*, 1897   DCXCI

RUEBEL (Karl) *Die Franken, ihr Eroberungs und Siedelungssystem in deutschen Volkskunde*, Leipzig, 1904   DCXCII

SALVIOLI (G.) *Trattato di storia di diritto italiano*, 6th edit., 1908   DCXCIII

SANDYS see part I.

SCHANZ *Ibid.*

SCHAUBE *Ibid.*

SCHLOSSER (Julius von) *Quellenbuch zur Kunstgeschichte des Abendländischen Mittelalters*, Vienna, 1896   DCXCIV

SCHMIDT (Ludwig) see part I.

SCHMIDT (Richard) *Ibid.*

SCHUBERT (Hans von) *Geschichte der christlichen Kirche im Frühmittelalter*, Tübingen, 1917-21, 2 vols.   DCXCV

———— *Staat und Kirche in den arianischen Königreichen und im Reiche Chlodowigs*, Munich, 1912 (*Histor. Bibliothek*, fas. 26)   DCXCVI

SCHULTZE (Walter) *Das Merowingische Frankenreich*, Stuttgart, 1896 (Zwiedeneck-Südenhorst's *Bibliothek deutschen Geschichte II*)   DCXCVII

———— *Die Bedeutung der Irischottischen Mönche für die Erhaltung und Fortdauer der Mittelalterlichen Wissenschaft*, in *Centralblatt. für Bibliothekswesen*, vol. VI, 1884   DCXCVIII

SCHUPPER (Francesco) *Manuale di storia del diritto italiano*, Cittá di Castello, 4th edit., 1908   DCXCIX

———— *Il Diritto privato dei popoli germanici*, Cittá di Castello, 1907-09, 4 vols.   DCC

SCHWARZLOSE (K.) *Die Patrimonien der römischen Kirche bis zur Gründung des Kirchen-Staates*, Berlin, 1887   DCC *bis*

———— *Die Verwaltung und die finanzielle Bedeutung der Patrimoine der römischen Kirche*, in *Zeitschrift für Kirchengeschichte*, vol. I, 1890   DCCI

SÉE (Henri) *Les Classes rurales et le régime domanial en France au moyen âge*, Paris, 1901   DCCII

SEMPER (H.) *Das Fortleben der Antike in der Kunst des Abendlandes*, Essling, 1908   DCCIII

SERESIA (Alfred) *L'Église et l'État sous les rois francs au VIᵉ siècle*, Gand, 1888   DCCIV

SICKEL (Wilhelm) *Die Entstehung der fränkischen Monarchie*, in *Westdeutsche Zeitschrift*, vol. IV   DCCV

———— *Die Reiche der Völkerwanderung, Ibid.*, 1890   DCCVI

———— *Die Merowingische Völksversammlung, Ibid.*, Suppl. vol. II, 1888   DCCVII

———— *Zum Ursprung des mittelalterlichen Staates*, in *Mittheilungen d. Instituts f. Œsterr. Geschichte*, Suppl. vol. II, 1886   DCCVIII

———— *Zum Organisation der Grafschaften im fränkischen Reiche, Ibid.*, Suppl. vol. III   DCCIX

———— *Zum German Verfassungsgeschichte, Ibid.*   DCCX

SOHM (Rudolf) *Fränkische Reichs-und Gerichtsverfassung*, 1873   DCCXI

———— *La Procédure de la Lex Salica*, trans. by Thévenin, Paris, 1873 (*Bibl. École des Hautes Études*, fas. 13)   DCCXII

STEIN (Henri) *La Mort de Childéric II*, in *Le Moyen Age*, 1908   DCCXIII

STRAKOSCH-GRASSMANN (Gustav) *Geschichte der Deutschen in Oesterrich-Ungarn*, Vienna, 1895   DCCXIV

STRUNTZ (F.) *Geschichte der Naturwissenschaft im Mittelalter*, Stuttgart, 1910   DCCXV

SYBEL (Heinrich von) *Die Entstehung des deutschen Königtums*, 3rd edit., 1884   DCCXVI

SYMONS (B.) *Heldensage*, in *Grundriss der german. Philologie* 2nd edit., Strasbourg, 1900, vol. III, pp. 606-734   DCCXVII

436 BIBLIOGRAPHY

TAYLOR (H. Osborn) *The Mediæval Mind, a History of the Development of Thought and Emotion in the Middle Ages*, London, 1911, 2 vols.   DCCXVIII
———— *The Classical Heritage*, see part I   DCCXIX
THONISSEN (J.-J.) *L'Organisation judiciaire, le droit pénal et la procédure pénale de la loi salique*, Bruxelles, 1881   DCCXX
TIERENTEYN (Louis) *Les Comtes francs depuis Clovis jusqu'au traité de Verdun*, Gand, 1893   DCCXXI
TOMASETTI *La Campagna romana antica, mediœvale e moderna*, Rome, 1910-13, 3 vols.   DCCXXII
TOURNEUR-AUMONT (J.-M.) *L'Alsace et l'Alemanie*, Nancy, 1919   DCCXXIII
TRAUBE (Ludwig) *Perrona Scottorum, ein Beitrag zur Ueberlieferungsgechichte und zur Palaeographie des Mittelalters*, in *Sitzungsberichte* of the Munich Academy, 1900   DCCXXIV
TREICH (L.) *Les Tarifs de la loi salique*, in *Revue Historique*, vol. CIV, 1910   DCCXXV
URENA y SMENJAUD (de) *La Legislacion gotico-hispana*, Madrid, 1905   DCCXXVI
VACANDARD (E.) *La scola du palais mérovingien*, in *Revue des Questions Historiques*, vols. LXI, LXII, LXXVI, 1897, 1904   DCCXXVII
———— *L'Idôlatrie en Gaule au VIᵉ et au VIIᵉ siècle*, ibid., vol. LXV, 1899   DCCXXVIII
———— *Vie de sainte Ouen, évêque de Rouen*, Paris, 1902   DCCXXIX
VAES (M.) *La Papauté et l'Église franque à l'époque de Grégoire le Grand*, in *Revue d'Histoire de l'Eglise*, July, 1905   DCCXXX
VAN DER ESSEN (L.) *Etude critique et littéraire sur les Vitae des saints mérovingiens de l'ancienne Belgique*, Louvain, 1907 (*Recueil des travaux de l'Université de Louvain*, fas. 17)   DCCXXXI
VAN WETTER *Le Droit romain et le droit germanique dans la monarchie franque*, Gand, 1899-1900, 2 fas. (in *Rapports sur la situation de l'Université de Gand*)   DCCXXXIII
VILLARI (G.) *Invasioni*, see part I.
VIOLLET (Paul) *Histoire des institutions politiques et administratives de la France*, Paris, 1890-1912 (vols. I and II)   DCCXXXIV
———— *Histoire du droit civil français*, 3rd edit., Paris, 1905   DCCXXXV
WAIZ (Georg) *Deutsche Verfassungsgeschichte*, 3rd edit., Kiel, 1880-1885, 4 vols. in 5   DCCXXXVI
WALTERHAUSEN (A.) *Die Germanisierung der Rätoromanen in der Schweiz*, Stuttgart, 1900   DCCXXXVII
WERMINGHOFF (A.) *Geschichte der Kirchenverfassung Deutschlands im Mittelalter*, Leipzig, 1905   DCCXXXVIII
WEYL (Richard) *Das fränkische Staatskirchliche Recht zur Zeit der Merowinger*, 1888 (Gierke's *Untersuchungen*, fas. 27)   DCCXXXIX
ZEUMER (Karl) *Geschichte der westgothischen Gesetzgebung*, in *Neues Archiv*, vols. XXIII, XXIV, XXVI, 1898-1901   DCCXL
ZIMMER (Heinrich) *Ueber die Bedeutung des Irischen Elements für die mittelalterliche Cultur*, in *Preussiche Jahrbücher*, vol. LIX, 1887   DCCXLI
ZOTENBERG (M.-H.) *Les Invasions des Visigoths et des Arabes en France*, Toulouse, 1876 (Extr. from *l'Histoire de Languedoc*)   DCCXLII

SELECTED ADDITIONAL BIBLIOGRAPHY

Ferdinand Lot supplied an extensive bibliography for his work. An attempt to match this with a full bibliography of the recent publications on all the subjects represented in Lot's original list would pass beyond the bounds appropriate to the present volume. The list offered here is intended only to provide a survey of some of the principal recent publications on the subjects of main interest in Lot's study. Other items are mentioned above, in the Foreword and the Additional Notes, and for reasons of economy of space these are not repeated in the present list.

BIBLIOGRAPHIES

Among works which provide bibliographies of special usefulness may be mentioned:

Cambridge Ancient History, XII (1939).

Cambridge Economic History of Europe, I-II (1941-1952).

Bury, J. B., *History of the Later Roman Empire*, London 1923 (reprinted, New York, 1958).

Hatch, Edwin, *The Influence of Greek Ideas on Christianity*, with Foreword, new Notes and Bibliography by F. C. Grant (Harper Torchbook, 1957).

Piganiol, André, *L'Empire chrétien, 325-395* (Paris, 1947).

Stein, Ernst, *Histoire du Bas-Empire* (Paris, 1949-1959).

Taylor, Henry Osborn, *The Emergence of Christian Culture in the West*, with Foreword and Bibliography by K. M. Setton (Harper Torchbook, 1958).

*   *   *   *   *

Albertini, E., *L'Empire romain*, Paris, 1929.

——— *Tablettes Albertini; actes privés de l'époque vandale, fin du Ve siècle*, Paris, 1952.

Alföldi, A., *A Conflict of Ideas in the Late Roman Empire; the Clash between the Senate and Valentinian I*, transl. by H. Mattingly, Oxford, 1952.

——— *Insignien und Tracht der römischen Kaiser* (*Mitteilungen d. Deutschen Archäologischen Instituts, Röm. Abteilung*, L, 1935).

Altheim, F., and R. Stiehl, *Finanzgeschichte der Spätantike* (Frankfurt, 1957).

Artz, F. B., *The Mind of the Middle Ages, A.D. 200-1500: An Historical Survey* (New York, 1953).

Balon, J., *Les fondements du régime foncier au Moyen Âge depuis la chute de l'Empire romain en Occident* (Louvain, 1954).

Barker, Ernest, *From Alexander to Constantine; Passages and Documents Illustrating the History of Social and Political Ideas, 336 B.C.—A.D. 337; Translated with Introductions, Notes and Essays* (Oxford, 1956).

Beck, H. G. J., *The Pastoral Care of Souls in South-East France During the Sixth Century* (Rome, 1950. Analecta Gregoriana, LI).

Barrett, H. M., *Boethius: Some Aspects of His Time and Work* (Cambridge, Eng., 1940).

Besnier, M., *L'Empire romain, de l'avènement des Sévères au Concile de Nicée* (Paris, 1937).

Boehner, K., "Die Frage der Kontinuität zwischen Altertum und Mittelalter im Spiegel der fränkischen Funde des Rheinlandes," *Trierer Zeitschrift*, XIX, 1950, pp. 82-106.

Burns, C. D., *The First Europe. A Study of the Establishment of Medieval Christendom, 400-800* (London, 1947).

Calmette, J., *Le monde féodal*, 2d ed. (Paris, 1951).

Chapot, V., *Le monde romain* (Paris, 1927).

Charanis, P., *Church and State in the Later Roman Empire* (Madison, Wisc., 1939).

——— "On the Social Structure of the Later Roman Empire," *Byzantion*, XVII, 1944-1945, pp. 39-57.

Chastagnol, A., "Le ravitaillement de Rome en viande au Ve siècle," *Revue Historique*, CCX, 1953, pp. 13-22.

Crombie, A. C., *Augustine to Galileo: The History of Science A.D. 400-1650* (Cambridge, Mass., 1953).

Dannenbauer, H., *Die Entstehung Europas von der Spätantike zum Mittelalter, I: Der Niedergang der Alten Welt im Westen*, (Stuttgart, 1959).

Dawson, C. H., *The Making of Europe, an Introduction to the History of European Unity* (London, 1936).

——— *Medieval Essays* (New York, 1954).

——— *Religion and the Rise of Western Culture* (London, 1950) (Gifford Lectures, 1948-1949).

Deanesley, Margaret, *A History of Early Mediaeval Europe, 476-911* (New York, 1956).

Duckett, Eleanor S., *The Gateway to the Middle Ages* (New York, 1938).

——— *Latin Writers of the Fifth Century* (New York, 1930).

Elliott-Binns, L. F., *The Beginnings of Western Christendom* (London, 1948).

Ensslin, W., "Beweise der Romverbundenheit in Theoderichs des Grossen Aussen- und Innenpolitik," *Settimane di studio del Centro italiano di studi sull'alto medioevo*, III (Spoleto, 1955), pp. 509-536.

——— *Theoderich der Grosse* (Munich, 1947).

Folz, R., *L'idée d'empire en Occident du Ve au XIVe siècle* (Paris, 1953).

Frend, W. H. C., *The Donatist Church: A Movement of Protest in Roman North Africa* (Oxford, 1952).

Ganshof, F.-L., *Le Moyen Âge (Histoire des relations internationales*, I) (Paris, 1953).

Gaudemet, J., *L'Église dans l'Empire romain, IVe—Ve siècles (Histoire du droit et des institutions de l'église en Occident*, III) (Paris, 1958).

——— "Les fondations en Occident au Bas-Empire," *Revue Internationale des Droits de l'Antiquité*, 3d ser., II, 1955, pp. 275-286.

Geffcken, J., *Der Ausgang des griechisch-römischen Heidentums*, Heidelberg, 1929.

Grand, R., *L'agriculture au Moyen Âge, de la fin de l'Empire romain au XVIᵉ siècle* (*L'agriculture à travers les âges*, III) (Paris, 1950).

Greenslade, S. L., *Church and State from Constantine to Theodosius* (London, 1954).

Griffe, E., *La Gaule chrétienne à l'époque romaine* (Paris, 1947-1957).

Homo, L., *Le Haut-Empire* (*Histoire générale*, ed. G. Glotz, III) (Paris, 1925).

—— *Les empereurs romains et le christianisme* (Paris, 1931).

—— *De la Rome païenne à la Rome chrétienne* (Paris, 1950).

Hoyt, Robert S., *Europe in the Middle Ages* (New York, 1957).

Johnson, A. C., *Egypt and the Roman Empire* (Ann Arbor, 1951).

Johnson, A. C., and L. C. West, *Byzantine Egypt: Economic Studies* (Princeton, 1949).

Jones, A. H. M., "Census Records of the Later Roman Empire," *Journal of Roman Studies*, XLIII, 1953, pp. 49-64.

—— —— "The Date and Value of the Verona List," *Journal of Roman Studies*, XLIV, 1954, pp. 21-29.

Jorga, N., *Essai de synthèse de l'histoire de l'humanité*, II: *Le Moyen Âge* (Paris, 1927).

Katz, Solomon, *The Decline of Rome and the Rise of Mediaeval Europe* (Ithaca, 1955).

Kelly, J. N. D., *Early Christian Doctrines* (London, 1958; Second edition, 1960).

Laistner, M. L. W., *Christianity and Pagan Culture in the Later Roman Empire* (Ithaca, 1951).

—— *The Intellectual Heritage of the Early Middle Ages, Selected Essays*, ed. by C. G. Starr (Ithaca, 1957).

—— *Thought and Letters in Western Europe, A.D. 500 to A.D. 900*, 2d ed. (Ithaca, 1957).

La Monte, J. L., *The World of the Middle Ages. A Reorientation of Medieval History* (New York, 1949).

Latouche, R., *Les origines de l'économie occidentale, IVᵉ—XIᵉ siècle* (*L'Évolution de l'humanité*, XLIII) (Paris, 1956).

Lemerle, P., "Invasions et migrations dans les Balkans depuis la fin de l'époque romaine jusqu'au VIIIᵉ siècle," *Revue Historique*, CCXI, 1954, pp. 265-308.

Lewis, A. R., *Naval Power and Trade in the Mediterranean, A.D. 500-1100* (Princeton, 1951).

Lietzmann, H., *From Constantine to Julian*, transl. by B. L. Woolf (*A History of the Early Church*, III), 2d ed. (New York, 1953).

—— *The Era of the Church Fathers*, transl. by B. L. Woolf (*A History of the Early Church*, IV), 2d ed. (New York, 1953).

Lopez, R. S., "An Aristocracy of Money in the Early Middle Ages," *Speculum*, XXVIII, 1953, pp. 1-43.

Mazzarino, S., *Stilicone: La crisi imperiale dopo Teodosio* (Rome, 1942).

Mommsen, T. E., *Medieval and Renaissance Studies*, ed. by E. F. Rice, Jr. (Ithaca, 1959).

Monks, G. R., "The Church of Alexandria and the City's Economic Life in the Sixth Century," *Speculum*, XXVIII, 1953, pp. 349-362.

Moss, H. St. L. B., *The Birth of the Middle Ages, 395-814* (Oxford, 1935).

Ostrogorsky, G., *History of the Byzantine State*, transl. by Joan M. Hussey (New Brunswick, 1957).

Paetow, L. J., *A Guide to the Study of Medieval History*, rev. ed., edited by D. C. Munro and G. C. Boyce (New York, 1931, reprinted New York, 1959). A continuation, *The Literature of Medieval History, 1930-1960,* is planned by G. C. Boyce.

Palanque, J.-R. and E. Delaruelle, "Le rôle temporel de L'Église du IVᵉ au VIIᵉ siècle," *Inspiration religieuse et structures temporelles* (Paris, 1948), pp. 77-106.

Pallasse, M., *Orient et Occident: À propos du colonat romain au Bas-Empire* (Paris, 1950).

Paribeni, R., *Da Diocleziano alla caduta dell'Impero d'Occidente* (Istituto di studi romani, *Storia di Roma,* VIII), Bologna, 1941.

——— *L'Italia imperiale da Ottaviano à Teodosio* (Milan, 1938).

Parker, H. M. D., *A History of the Roman World from A.D. 138 to 337* (London, 1935).

Salin, E., *La civilisation mérovingienne d'après les sépultures, les textes et le laboratoire* (Paris, 1949-1959).

Salmon, E. T. "The Roman Army and the Disintegration of the Roman Empire," *Transactions of the Royal Society of Canada,* 3d ser., LII, sect. 2 (1958), pp. 43-57.

Simon, M., *Verus Israel. Étude sur les relations entre chrétiens et juifs dans l'Empire romain, 135-425* (Paris, 1948).

Sinnigan, W. G., *The officium of the Urban Prefecture during the Later Roman Empire* (Papers and Monographs of the American Academy in Rome, XVII, 1957).

Smalley, Beryl, *The Study of the Bible in the Middle Ages* (2d ed., Oxford, 1952).

Solari, A., *La crisi dell'Impero romano* (Milan, 1933-1937).

Starr, C. G., "The History of the Roman Empire 1911-1960," *Journal of Roman Studies,* L, 1960, pp. 149-160. A critical survey of the literature.

Stevens, C. E., *Sidonius Apollinaris and his Age* (Oxford, 1933).

Stevenson, J., *A New Eusebius: Documents Illustrative of the History of the Church to A.D. 337* (London, 1957).

Strayer, J. R., and D. C. Munro, *The Middle Ages, 395-1500* (New York, 1942).

Stroheker, K. F., "Zur Rolle der Heermeister fränkischer Abstammung im späten vierten Jahrhundert," *Historia,* IV, 1955, pp. 314-330.

Sullivan, R. E., "The Papacy and Missionary Activity in the Early Middle Ages," *Mediaeval Studies,* XVII, 1955, pp. 46-106.

——— *Heirs of the Roman Empire* (Ithaca, 1960).

Taeger, F., "Zur Geschichte der spätkaiserzeitlichen Herrscherauffassung," *Saeculum,* VII, 1956, pp. 182-195.

Thompson, E. A., *The Historical Work of Ammianus Marcellinus* (Cambridge, Eng., 1947).

——— "The Settlement of the Barbarians in Southern Gaul," *Journal of Roman Studies,* XLVI, 1956, pp. 65-75.

Thompson, J. W., *The Middle Ages* (New York, 1931).

Vaccari, P., "Dall'unità romana al mondo barbarico," *Miscellanea G. Galbiati* (Milan, 1951), pp. 135-156.

Vasiliev, A. A., *History of the Byzantine Empire* (Madison, Wisc., 1952).

Wallace-Hadrill, J. M., *The Barbarian West, 400-1000* (London, 1952, Hutchinson's University Library).

West, L. C., *Gold and Silver Coin Standards in the Roman Empire* (New York, 1941) (Numismatic Notes and Monographs, 94).

West, L. C., and A. C. Johnson, *Currency in Roman and Byzantine Egypt* (Princeton, 1944).

Westermann, W. L., *The Slave Systems of Greek and Roman Antiquity* (Philadelphia, 1955) (Memoirs of the American Philosophical Society, XL).

Ziegler, A. K., *Church and State in Visigothic Spain* (Washington, 1930).

INDEX

Revised January, 1970

ḣarper ♯ ꜩorchbooks

American Studies: General

HENRY ADAMS Degradation of the Democratic Dogma. ‡ *Introduction by Charles Hirschfeld.* TB/1450

LOUIS D. BRANDEIS: Other People's Money, *and How the Bankers Use It. Ed. with Intro. by Richard M. Abrams* TB/3081

HENRY STEELE COMMAGER, Ed.: The Struggle for Racial Equality TB/1300

CARL N. DEGLER: Out of Our Past: *The Forces that Shaped Modern America* CN/2

CARL N. DEGLER, Ed.: Pivotal Interpretations of American History
Vol. I TB/1240; Vol. II TB/1241

LAWRENCE H. FUCHS, Ed.: American Ethnic Politics TB/1368

ROBERT L. HEILBRONER: The Limits of American Capitalism TB/1305

JOHN HIGHAM, Ed.: The Reconstruction of American History TB/1068

ROBERT H. JACKSON: The Supreme Court in the American System of Government TB/1106

JOHN F. KENNEDY: A Nation of Immigrants. *Illus. Revised and Enlarged. Introduction by Robert F. Kennedy* TB/1118

RICHARD B. MORRIS: Fair Trial: *Fourteen Who Stood Accused, from Anne Hutchinson to Alger Hiss* TB/1335

GUNNAR MYRDAL: An American Dilemma: *The Negro Problem and Modern Democracy. Introduction by the Author.*
Vol. I TB/1443; Vol. II TB/1444

GILBERT OSOFSKY, Ed.: The Burden of Race: *A Documentary History of Negro-White Relations in America* TB/1405

ARNOLD ROSE: The Negro in America: *The Condensed Version of Gunnar Myrdal's* An American Dilemma. *Second Edition* TB/3048

JOHN E. SMITH: Themes in American Philosophy: *Purpose, Experience and Community* TB/1466

WILLIAM R. TAYLOR: Cavalier and Yankee: *The Old South and American National Character* TB/1474

American Studies: Colonial

BERNARD BAILYN: The New England Merchants in the Seventeenth Century TB/1149

ROBERT E. BROWN: Middle-Class Democracy and Revolution in Massachusetts, 1691–1780. *New Introduction by Author* TB/1413

JOSEPH CHARLES: The Origins of the American Party System TB/1049

WESLEY FRANK CRAVEN: The Colonies in Transition: 1660-1712† TB/3084

CHARLES GIBSON: Spain in America † TB/3077

CHARLES GIBSON, Ed.: The Spanish Tradition in America + HR/1351

LAWRENCE HENRY GIPSON: The Coming of the Revolution: 1763-1775. † *Illus.* TB/3007

JACK P. GREENE, Ed.: Great Britain and the American Colonies: 1606-1763. + *Introduction by the Author* HR/1477

AUBREY C. LAND, Ed.: Bases of the Plantation Society + HR/1429

PERRY MILLER: Errand Into the Wilderness TB/1139

PERRY MILLER & T. H. JOHNSON, Ed.: The Puritans: *A Sourcebook of Their Writings*
. Vol. I TB/1093; Vol. II TB/1094

EDMUND S. MORGAN: The Puritan Family: *Religion and Domestic Relations in Seventeenth Century New England* TB/1227

WALLACE NOTESTEIN: The English People on the Eve of Colonization: 1603-1630. † *Illus.* TB/3006

LOUIS B. WRIGHT: The Cultural Life of the American Colonies: 1607-1763. † *Illus.* TB/3005

YVES F. ZOLTVANY, Ed.: The French Tradition in America + HR/1425

American Studies: The Revolution to 1860

JOHN R. ALDEN: The American Revolution: 1775-1783. † *Illus.* TB/3011

RAY A. BILLINGTON: The Far Western Frontier: 1830-1860. † *Illus.* TB/3012

STUART BRUCHEY: The Roots of American Economic Growth, 1607-1861: *An Essay in Social Causation. New Introduction by the Author.* TB/1350

NOBLE E. CUNNINGHAM, JR., Ed.: The Early Republic, 1789-1828 + HR/1394

GEORGE DANGERFIELD: The Awakening of American Nationalism, 1815-1828. † *Illus.* TB/3061

---

† The New American Nation Series, edited by Henry Steele Commager and Richard B. Morris.
‡ American Perspectives series, edited by Bernard Wishy and William E. Leuchtenburg.
α History of Europe series, edited by J. H. Plumb.
§ The Library of Religion and Culture, edited by Benjamin Nelson.
‖ Researches in the Social, Cultural, and Behavioral Sciences, edited by Benjamin Nelson.
Σ Harper Modern Science Series, edited by James A. Newman.
° Not for sale in Canada.
+ Documentary History of the United States series, edited by Richard B. Morris.
# Documentary History of Western Civilization series, edited by Eugene C. Black and Leonard W. Levy.
Λ The Economic History of the United States series, edited by Henry David et al.
¶ European Perspectives series, edited by Eugene C. Black.
** Contemporary Essays series, edited by Leonard W. Levy.
* The Stratum Series, edited by John Hale.

CLEMENT EATON: The Freedom-of-Thought Struggle in the Old South. *Revised and Enlarged. Illus.* TB/1150

CLEMENT EATON: The Growth of Southern Civilization, 1790-1860. † *Illus.* TB/3040

ROBERT H. FERRELL, Ed.: Foundations of American Diplomacy, 1775-1872 + HR/1393

LOUIS FILLER: The Crusade against Slavery: 1830-1860. † *Illus.* TB/3029

WILLIM W. FREEHLING: Prelude to Civil War: *The Nullification Controversy in South Carolina, 1816-1836* TB/1359

PAUL W. GATES: The Farmer's Age: *Agriculture, 1815-1860* △ TB/1398

THOMAS JEFFERSON: Notes on the State of Virginia. ‡ *Edited by Thomas P. Abernethy* TB/3052

FORREST MCDONALD, Ed.: Confederation and Constitution, 1781-1789 + HR/1396

JOHN C. MILLER: The Federalist Era: 1789-1801. † *Illus.* TB/3027

RICHARD B. MORRIS: The American Revolution Reconsidered TB/1363

CURTIS P. NETTELS: The Emergence of a National Economy, 1775-1815 △ TB/1438

DOUGLASS C. NORTH & ROBERT PAUL THOMAS, Eds.: *The Growth of the American Economy to 1860* + HR/1352

R. B. NYE: The Cultural Life of the New Nation: 1776-1830. † *Illus.* TB/3026

GILBERT OSOFSKY, Ed.: Puttin' On Ole Massa: *The Slave Narratives of Henry Bibb, William Wells Brown, and Solomon Northup* ‡ TB/1432

JAMES PARTON: The Presidency of Andrew Jackson. *From Volume III of the Life of Andrew Jackson. Ed. with Intro. by Robert V. Remini* TB/3080

FRANCIS S. PHILBRICK: The Rise of the West, 1754-1830. † *Illus.* TB/3067

MARSHALL SMELSER: The Democratic Republic, 1801-1815 † TB/1406

JACK M. SOSIN, Ed.: The Opening of the West + HR/1424

GEORGE ROGERS TAYLOR: The Transportation Revolution, 1815-1860 △ TB/1347

A. F. TYLER: Freedom's Ferment: *Phases of American Social History from the Revolution to the Outbreak of the Civil War. Illus.* TB/1074

GLYNDON G. VAN DEUSEN: The Jacksonian Era: 1828-1848. † *Illus.* TB/3028

LOUIS B. WRIGHT: Culture on the Moving Frontier TB/1053

American Studies: The Civil War to 1900

W. R. BROCK: An American Crisis: *Congress and Reconstruction, 1865-67* ° TB/1283

T. C. COCHRAN & WILLIAM MILLER: The Age of Enterprise: *A Social History of Industrial America* TB/1054

W. A. DUNNING: Reconstruction, Political and Economic: 1865-1877 TB/1073

HAROLD U. FAULKNER: Politics, Reform and Expansion: 1890-1900. † *Illus.* TB/3020

GEORGE M. FREDRICKSON: The Inner Civil War: *Northern Intellectuals and the Crisis of the Union* TB/1358

JOHN A. GARRATY: The New Commonwealth, 1877-1890 † TB/1410

JOHN A. GARRATY, Ed.: The Transformation of American Society, 1870-1890 + HR/1395

HELEN HUNT JACKSON: A Century of Dishonor: *The Early Crusade for Indian Reform.* † *Edited by Andrew F. Rolle* TB/3063

WILLIAM G. MCLOUGHLIN, Ed.: The American Evangelicals, 1800-1900: An Anthology ‡ TB/1382

JAMES S. PIKE: The Prostrate State: *South Carolina under Negro Government.* ‡ *Intro. by Robert F. Durden* TB/3085

FRED A. SHANNON: The Farmer's Last Frontier: *Agriculture, 1860-1897* TB/1348

VERNON LANE WHARTON: The Negro in Mississippi, 1865-1890 TB/1178

American Studies: The Twentieth Century

RICHARD M. ABRAMS, Ed.: The Issues of the Populist and Progressive Eras, 1892-1912 + HR/1428

RAY STANNARD BAKER: Following the Color Line: *American Negro Citizenship in Progressive Era.* ‡ *Edited by Dewey W. Grantham, Jr. Illus.* TB/3053

RANDOLPH S. BOURNE: War and the Intellectuals: *Collected Essays, 1915-1919.* ‡ *Edited by Carl Resek* TB/3043

A. RUSSELL BUCHANAN: The United States and World War II. † *Illus.*
Vol. I TB/3044; Vol. II TB/3045

THOMAS C. COCHRAN: The American Business System: *A Historical Perspective, 1900-1955* TB/1080

FOSTER RHEA DULLES: America's Rise to World Power: 1898-1954. † *Illus.* TB/3021

HAROLD U. FAULKNER: The Decline of Laissez Faire, 1897-1917 TB/1397

JOHN D. HICKS: Republican Ascendancy: 1921-1933. † *Illus.* TB/3041

WILLIAM E. LEUCHTENBURG: Franklin D. Roosevelt and the New Deal: 1932-1940. † *Illus.* TB/3025

WILLIAM E. LEUCHTENBURG, Ed.: The New Deal: *A Documentary History* + HR/1354

ARTHUR S. LINK: Woodrow Wilson and the Progressive Era: 1910-1917. † *Illus.* TB/3023

BROADUS MITCHELL: Depression Decade: *From New Era through New Deal, 1929-1941* △ TB/1439

GEORGE E. MOWRY: The Era of Theodore Roosevelt and the Birth of Modern America: 1900-1912. † *Illus.* TB/3022

GEORGE SOULE: Prosperity Decade: *From War to Depression, 1917-1929* △ TB/1349

TWELVE SOUTHERNERS: I'll Take My Stand: *The South and the Agrarian Tradition. Intro. by Louis D. Rubin, Jr.; Biographical Essays by Virginia Rock* TB/1072

Art, Art History, Aesthetics

ERWIN PANOFSKY: Renaissance and Renascences in Western Art. *Illus.* TB/1447

ERWIN PANOFSKY: Studies in Iconology: *Humanistic Themes in the Art of the Renaissance. 180 illus.* TB/1077

OTTO VON SIMSON: The Gothic Cathedral: *Origins of Gothic Architecture and the Medieval Concept of Order. 58 illus.* TB/2018

HEINRICH ZIMMER: Myths and Symbols in Indian Art and Civilization. *70 illus.* TB/2005

Asian Studies

WOLFGANG FRANKE: China and the West: *The Cultural Encounter, 13th to 20th Centuries. Trans. by R. A. Wilson* TB/1326

L. CARRINGTON GOODRICH: A Short History of the Chinese People. *Illus.* TB/3015

Economics & Economic History

C. E. BLACK: The Dynamics of Modernization: *A Study in Comparative History* TB/1321
GILBERT BURCK & EDITOR OF *Fortune:* The Computer Age: *And its Potential for Management* TB/1179
SHEPARD B. CLOUGH, THOMAS MOODIE & CAROL MOODIE, Eds.: Economic History of Europe: *Twentieth Century #* HR/1388
THOMAS C. COCHRAN: The American Business System: *A Historical Perspective, 1900-1955* TB/1180
HAROLD U. FAULKNER: The Decline of Laissez Faire, 1897-1917 △ TB/1397
PAUL W. GATES: The Farmer's Age: *Agriculture, 1815-1860* △ TB/1398
WILLIAM GREENLEAF, Ed.: American Economic Development Since 1860 + HR/1353
ROBERT L. HEILBRONER: The Future as History: *The Historic Currents of Our Time and the Direction in Which They Are Taking America* TB/1386
ROBERT L. HEILBRONER: The Great Ascent: *The Struggle for Economic Development in Our Time* TB/3030
DAVID S. LANDES: Bankers and Pashas: *International Finance and Economic Imperialism in Egypt. New Preface by the Author* TB/1412
ROBERT LATOUCHE: The Birth of Western Economy: *Economic Aspects of the Dark Ages* TB/1290
W. ARTHUR LEWIS: The Principles of Economic Planning. *New Introduction by the Author°* TB/1436
ROBERT GREEN MC CLOSKEY: American Conservatism in the Age of Enterprise TB/1137
WILLIAM MILLER, Ed.: Men in Business: *Essays on the Historical Role of the Entrepreneur* TB/1081
HERBERT A. SIMON: The Shape of Automation: *For Men and Management* TB/1245

Historiography and History of Ideas

J. BRONOWSKI & BRUCE MAZLISH: The Western Intellectual Tradition: *From Leonardo to Hegel* TB/3001
WILHELM DILTHEY: Pattern and Meaning in History: *Thoughts on History and Society.° Edited with an Intro. by H. P. Rickman* TB/1075
J. H. HEXTER: More's Utopia: *The Biography of an Idea. Epilogue by the Author* TB/1195
H. STUART HUGHES: History as Art and as Science: *Twin Vistas on the Past* TB/1207
ARTHUR O. LOVEJOY: The Great Chain of Being: *A Study of the History of an Idea* TB/1009
RICHARD H. POPKIN: The History of Scenticism from Erasmus to Descartes. *Revised Edition* TB/1391
MASSIMO SALVADORI, Ed.: Modern Socialism # HR/1374
BRUNO SNELL: The Discovery of the Mind: *The Greek Origins of European Thought* TB/1018

History: General

HANS KOHN: The Age of Nationalism: *The First Era of Global History* TB/1380
BERNARD LEWIS: The Arabs in History TB/1029
BERNARD LEWIS: The Middle East and the West ° TB/1274

History: Ancient

A. ANDREWS: The Greek Tyrants TB/1103

THEODOR H. GASTER: Thespis: *Ritual Myth and Drama in the Ancient Near East* TB/1281
MICHAEL GRANT: Ancient History ° TB/1190

History: Medieval

NORMAN COHN: The Pursuit of the Millennium: *Revolutionary Messianism in Medieval and Reformation Europe* TB/1037
F. L. GANSHOF: Feudalism TB/1058
F. L. GANSHOF: The Middle Ages: *A History of International Relations. Translated by Rémy Hall* TB/1411
ROBERT LATOUCHE: The Birth of Western Economy: *Economic Aspects of the Dark Ages* ° TB/1290
HENRY CHARLES LEA: The Inquisition of the Middle Ages. || *Introduction by Walter Ullmann* TB/1456

History: Renaissance & Reformation

JACOB BURCKHARDT: The Civilization of the Renaissance in Italy. *Introduction by Benjamin Nelson and Charles Trinkaus. Illus.* Vol. I TB/40; Vol. II TB/41
JOHN CALVIN & JACOPO SADOLETO: A Reformation Debate. *Edited by John C. Olin* TB/1239
FEDERICO CHABOD: Machiavelli and the Renaissance TB/1193
THOMAS CROMWELL: Thomas Cromwell: *Selected Letters on Church and Commonwealth, 1523-1540.* ¶ *Ed. with an Intro. by Arthur J. Slavin* TB/1462
FRANCESCO GUICCIARDINI: History of Florence. *Translated with an Introduction and Notes by Mario Domandi* TB/1470
WERNER L. GUNDERSHEIMER, Ed.: French Humanism, 1470-1600. * *Illus.* TB/1473
HANS J. HILLERBRAND, Ed., The Protestant Reformation # HR/1342
JOHAN HUIZINGA: Erasmus and the Age of Reformation. *Illus.* TB/19
JOEL HURSTFIELD: The Elizabethan Nation TB/1312
JOEL HURSTFIELD, Ed.: The Reformation Crisis TB/1267
PAUL OSKAR KRISTELLER: Renaissance Thought: *The Classic, Scholastic, and Humanist Strains* TB/1048
PAUL OSKAR KRISTELLER: Renaissance Thought II: *Papers on Humanism and the Arts* TB/1163
PAUL O. KRISTELLER & PHILIP P. WIENER, Eds.: Renaissance Essays TB/1392
DAVID LITTLE: Religion, Order and Law: *A Study in Pre-Revolutionary England.* § *Preface by R. Bellah* TB/1418
NICCOLO MACHIAVELLI: History of Florence and of the Affairs of Italy: *From the Earliest Times to the Death of Lorenzo the Magnificent. Introduction by Felix Gilbert* TB/1027
ALFRED VON MARTIN: Sociology of the Renaissance. ° *Introduction by W. K. Ferguson* TB/1099
GARRETT MATTINGLY et al.: Renaissance Profiles. *Edited by J. H. Plumb* TB/1162
J. H. PARRY: The Establishment of the European Hegemony: 1415-1715: *Trade and Exploration in the Age of the Renaissance* TB/1045
PAOLO ROSSI: Philosophy, Technology, and the Arts, in the Early Modern Era 1400-1700. || *Edited by Benjamin Nelson. Translated by Salvator Attanasio* TB/1458
R. H. TAWNEY: The Agrarian Problem in the Sixteenth Century. *Intro. by Lawrence Stone* TB/1315

H. R. TREVOR-ROPER: The European Witch-craze of the Sixteenth and Seventeenth Centuries and Other Essays °   TB/1416
VESPASIANO: Rennaissance Princes, Popes, and XVth Century: The Vespasiano Memoirs. Introduction by Myron P. Gilmore. Illus.
                                                         TB/1111

History: Modern European

MAX BELOFF: The Age of Absolutism, 1660-1815
                                                         TB/1062
D. W. BROGAN: The Development of Modern France ° Vol. I: From the Fall of the Empire to the Dreyfus Affair   TB/1184
Vol. II: The Shadow of War, World War I, Between the Two Wars   TB/1185
ALAN BULLOCK: Hitler, A Study in Tyranny. ° Revised Edition. Illus.   TB/1123
JOHANN GOTTLIEB FICHTE: Addresses to the German Nation. Ed. with Intro. by George A. Kelly ¶   TB/1366
ALBERT GOODWIN: The French Revolution
                                                         TB/1064
H. STUART HUGHES: The Obstructed Path: French Social Thought in the Years of Desperation   TB/1451
JOHAN HUIZINGA: Dutch Civilization in the 17th Century and Other Essays   TB/1453
JOHN MCMANNERS: European History, 1789-1914: Men, Machines and Freedom TB/1419
FRANZ NEUMANN: Behemoth: The Structure and Practice of National Socialism, 1933-1944
                                                         TB/1289
DAVID OGG: Europe of the Ancien Régime, 1715-1783 ° α   TB/1271
ALBERT SOREL: Europe Under the Old Regime. Translated by Francis H. Herrick TB/1121
A. J. P. TAYLOR: From Napoleon to Lenin: Historical Essays °   TB/1268
A. J. P. TAYLOR: The Habsburg Monarchy, 1809-1918: A History of the Austrian Empire and Austria-Hungary °   TB/1187
J. M. THOMPSON: European History, 1494-1789
                                                         TB/1431
H. R. TREVOR-ROPER: Historical Essays TB/1269

Literature & Literary Criticism

JACQUES BARZUN: The House of Intellect
                                                         TB/1051
W. J. BATE: From Classic to Romantic: Premises of Taste in Eighteenth Century England
                                                         TB/1036
VAN WYCK BROOKS: Van Wyck Brooks: The Early Years: A Selection from his Works, 1908-1921 Ed. with Intro. by Claire Sprague
                                                         TB/3082
RICHMOND LATTIMORE, Translator: The Odyssey of Homer   TB/1389

Philosophy

HENRI BERGSON: Time and Free Will: An Essay on the Immediate Data of Consciousness °
                                                         TB/1021
H. J. BLACKHAM: Six Existentialist Thinkers: Kierkegaard, Nietzsche, Jaspers, Marcel, Heidegger, Sartre °   TB/1002
J. M. BOCHENSKI: The Methods of Contemporary Thought. Trans by Peter Caws TB/1377
CRANE BRINTON: Nietzsche. Preface, Bibliography, and Epilogue by the Author TB/1197
ERNST CASSIRER: Rousseau, Kant and Goethe. Intro by Peter Gay
WILFRID DESAN: The Tragic Finale: An Essay on the Philosophy of Jean-Paul Sartre TB/1030

MARVIN FARBER: The Aims of Phenomenology: The Motives, Methods, and Impact of Husserl's Thought   TB/1291
PAUL FRIEDLANDER: Plato: An Introduction
                                                         TB/2017
MICHAEL GELVEN: A Commentary on Heidegger's "Being and Time"   TB/1464
G. W. F. HEGEL: On Art, Religion Philosophy: Introductory Lectures to the Realm of Absolute Spirit. || Edited with an Introduction by J. Glenn Gray   TB/1463
G. W. F. HEGEL: Phenomenology of Mind. ° || Introduction by eGorge Lichtheim TB/1303
MARTIN HEIDEGGER: Discourse on Thinking. Translated with a Preface by John M. Anderson and E. Hans Freund. Introduction by John M. Anderson   TB/1459
F. H. HEINEMANN: Existentialism and the Modern Predicament   TB/28
WERER HEISENBERG: Physics and Philosophy: The Revolution in Modern Science. Intro. by F. S. C. Northrop   TB/549
EDMUND HUSSERL: Phenomenology and the Crisis of Philosophy. § Translated with an Introduction by Quentin Lauer   TB/1170
IMMANUEL KANT: Groundwork of the Metaphysic of Morals. Translated and Analyzed by H. J. Paton   TB/1159
IMMANUEL KANT: Lectures on Ethics. § Introduction by Lewis White Beck   TB/105
QUENTIN LAUER: Phenomenology: Its Genesis and Prospect. Preface by Aron Gurwitsch
                                                         TB/1169
GEORGE A. MORGAN: What Nietzsche Means
                                                         TB/1198
H. J. PATON: The Categorical Imperative: A Study in Kant's Moral Philosophy TB/1325
MICHAEL POLANYI: Personal Knowledge: Towards a Post-Critical Philosophy TB/1158
WILLARD VAN ORMAN QUINE: Elementary Logic Revised Edition   TB/577
JOHN E. SMITH: Themes in American Philosophy: Purpose, Experience and Community
                                                         TB/1466
MORTON WHITE: Foundations of Historical Knowledge   TB/1440
WILHELM WINDELBAND: A History of Philosophy Vol. I: Greek, Roman, Medieval TB/38
Vol. II: Renaissance, Enlightenment, Modern
                                                         TB/39
LUDWIG WITTGENSTEIN: The Blue and Brown Books °   TB/1211
LUDWIG WITTGENSTEIN: Notebooks, 1914-1916
                                                         TB/1441

Political Science & Government

C. E. BLACK: The Dynamics of Modernization: A Study in Comparative History TB/1321
KENNETH E. BOULDING: Conflict and Defense: A General Theory of Action   TB/3024
DENIS W. BROGAN: Politics in America. New Introduction by the Author   TB/1469
LEWIS COSER, Ed.: Political Sociology TB/1293
ROBERT A. DAHL & CHARLES E. LINDBLOM: Politics, Economics, and Welfare: Planning and Politico-Economic Systems Resolved into Basic Social Processes   TB/3037
ROY C. MACRIDIS, Ed.: Political Parties: Contemporary Trends and Ideas **   TB/1322
ROBERT GREEN MC CLOSKEY: American Conservatism in the Age of Enterprise, 1865-1910
                                                         TB/1137
JOHN B. MORRALL: Political Thought in Medieval Times   TB/1076

5

EDWARD CONZE et al, Editors: Buddhist Texts through the Ages TB/113
H. G. CREEL: Confucius and the Chinese Way TB/63
FRANKLIN EDGERTON, Trans. & Ed.: The Bhagavad Gita TB/115
SWAMI NIKHILANANDA, Trans. & Ed.: The Upanishads TB/114

Religion: Philosophy, Culture, and Society

NICOLAS BERDYAEV: The Destiny of Man TB/61
RUDOLF BULTMANN: History and Eschatology: The Presence of Eternity ° TB/91
LUDWIG FEUERBACH: The Essence of Christianity. § Introduction by Karl Barth. Foreword by H. Richard Niebuhr TB/11
ADOLF HARNACK: What Is Christianity? § Introduction by Rudolf Bultmann TB/17
KYLE HASELDEN: The Racial Problem in Christian Perspective TB/116
IMMANUEL KANT: Religion Within the Limits of Reason Alone. § Introduction by Theodore M. Greene and John Silber TB/67
H. RICHARD NIERUHR: Christ and Culture TB/3
H. RICHARD NIEBUHR: The Kingdom of God in America TB/49

Science and Mathematics

W. E. LE GROS CLARK: The Antecedents of Man: An Introduction to the Evolution of the Primates. ° Illus. TB/559
ROBERT E. COKER: Streams, Lakes, Ponds. Illus. TB/586
ROBERT E. COKER: This Great and Wide Sea: An Introduction to Oceanography and Marine Biology. Illus. TB/551
F. K. HARE: The Restless Atmosphere TB/560
WILLARD VAN ORMAN QUINE: Mathematical Logic TB/558

Science: Philosophy

J. M. BOCHENSKI: The Methods of Contemporary Thought. Tr. by Peter Caws TB/1377
J. BRONOWSKI: Science and Human Values. Revised and Enlarged. Illus. TB/505
WERNER HEISENBERG: Physics and Philosophy: The Revolution in Modern Science. Introduction by F. S. C. Northrop TB/549
KARL R. POPPER: Conjectures and Refutations: The Growth of Scientific Knowledge TB/1376
KARL R. POPPER: The Logic of Scientific Discovery TB/576

Sociology and Anthropology

REINHARD BENDIX: Work and Authority in Industry: Ideologies of Management in the Course of Industrialization TB/3035
BERNARD BERELSON, Ed., The Behavioral Sciences Today TB/1127
KENNETH B. CLARK: Dark Ghetto: Dilemmas of Social Power. Foreword by Gunnar Myrdal TB/1317

KENNETH CLARK & JEANNETTE HOPKINS: A Relevant War Against Poverty: A Study of Community Action Programs and Observable Social Change TB/1480
LEWIS COSER, Ed.: Political Sociology TB/1293
ALLISON DAVIS & JOHN DOLLARD: Children of Bondage: The Personality Development of Negro Youih in the Urban South || TB/3049
ST. CLAIR DRAKE & HORACE R. CAYTON: Black Metropolis: A Study of Negro Life in a Northern City. Introduction by Everett C. Hughes. Tables, maps, charts, and graphs Vol. I TB/1086; Vol. II TB/1087
PETER F. DRUCKER: The New Society: The Anatomy of Industrial Order TB/1082
CHARLES Y. GLOCK & RODNEY STARK: Christian Beliefs and Anti-Semitism. Introduction by the Authors TB/1454
ALVIN W. GOULDNER: The Hellenic World TB/1479
R. M. MACIVER: Social Causation TB/1153
GARY T. MARX: Protest and Prejudice: A Study of Belief in the Black Community TB/1435
ROBERT K. MERTON, LEONARD BROOM, LEONARD S. COTTRELL, JR., Editors: Sociology Today: Problems and Prospects || Vol. I TB/1173; Vol. II TB/1174
GILBERT OSOFSKY, Ed.: The Burden of Race: A Documentary History of Negro-White Relations in America TB/1405
GILBERT OSOFSKY: Harlem: The Making of a Ghetto: Negro New York 1890-1930 TB/1381
TALCOTT PARSONS & EDWARD A. SHILS, Editors: Toward a General Theory of Action: Theoretical Foundations for the Social Sciences TB/1083
PHILIP RIEFF: The Triumph of the Therapeutic: Uses of Faith After Freud TB/1360
JOHN H. ROHRER & MUNRO S. EDMONSON, Eds.: The Eighth Generation Grows Up: Cultures and Personalities of New Orleans Negroes || TB/3050
ARNOLD ROSE: The Negro in America: The Condensed Version of Gunnar Myrdal's An American Dilemma. Second Edition TB/3048
GEORGE ROSEN: Madness in Society: Chapters in the Historical Sociology of Mental Illness. || Preface by Benjamin Nelson TB/1337
PHILIP SELZNICK: TVA and the Grass Roots: A Study in the Sociology of Formal Organization TB/1230
PITIRIM A. SOROKIN: Contemporary Sociological Theories: Through the First Quarter of the Twentieth Century TB/3046
MAURICE R. STEIN: The Eclipse of Community: An Interpretation of American Studies TB/1128
FERDINAND TONNIES: Community and Society: Gemeinschaft und Gesellschaft. Translated and Edited by Charles P. Loomis TB/1116
W. LLOYD WARNER and Associates: Democracy in Jonesville: A Study in Quality and Inequality || TB/1129
W. LLOYD WARNER: Social Class in America: The Evaluation of Status TB/1013
FLORIAN ZNANIECKI: The Social Role of the Man of Knowledge. Introduction by Lewis A. Coser TB/1372